BOOK 1. INTRODUCTION: VIEW OF THE AZTEC CIVILISATION

THE country of the ancient Mexicans, or Aztecs as they were called, formed but a very small part of the extensive territories comprehended in the modern republic of Mexico. Its boundaries cannot be defined with certainty. They were much enlarged in the latter days of the empire, when they may be considered as reaching from about the eighteenth degree north to the twenty-first on the Atlantic; and from the fourteenth to the nineteenth, including a very narrow strip, on the Pacific. In its greatest breadth, it could not exceed five degrees and a half, dwindling, as it approached its south-eastern limits, to less than two. It covered, probably, less than sixteen thousand square leagues. Yet, such is the remarkable formation of this country, that though not more than twice as large as New England, it presented every variety of climate, and was capable of yielding nearly every fruit found between the equator and. the Arctic circle.

All along the Atlantic the country is bordered by a broad tract, called the tierra caliente, or hot region, which has the usual high temperature of equinoctial lands. Parched and sandy plains are intermingled with others of exuberant fertility, almost impervious from thickets of aromatic shrubs and wild flowers, in the midst of which tower up trees of that magnificent growth which is found only within the tropics. In this wilderness of sweets lurks the fatal malaria, engendered, probably, by the decomposition of rank vegetable substances in a hot and humid soil. The season of the bilious fever — vomito, as it is called — which scourges these coasts, continues from the spring to the autumnal equinox, when it is checked by the cold winds that descend from Hudson's Bay. These winds in the winter season frequently freshen into tempests, and, sweeping down the Atlantic coast and the winding Gulf of Mexico, burst with the fury of a hurricane on its unprotected shores, and on the neighbouring West India islands. Such are the mighty spells with which Nature has surrounded this land of enchantment, as if to guard the golden treasures locked up within its bosom. The genius and enterprise of man have proved more potent than her spells.

After passing some twenty leagues across this burning region, the traveller finds himself rising into a purer atmosphere. His limbs recover their elasticity. He breathes more freely, for his senses are not now oppressed by the sultry heats and intoxicating perfumes of the valley. The aspect of nature, too, has changed, and his eye no longer revels among the gay variety of colours with which the landscape was painted there. The vanilla, the indigo, and the flowering cocoa-groves disappear as he advances. The sugar-cane and the glossy-leaved banana still accompany him; and, when he has ascended about four thousand feet, he sees in the unchanging verdure, and the rich foliage of the liquid-amber tree, that he has reached the height where clouds and mists settle, in their passage from the Mexican Gulf. This is the region of perpetual humidity; but he welcomes it with pleasure, as announcing his escape from the influence of the deadly vomito. He has entered the tierra templada, or temperate region, whose character resembles that of the temperate zone of the globe. The features of the scenery become grand, and even terrible. His road sweeps along the base of mighty mountains, once gleaming with volcanic fires, and still resplendent in their mantles of snow, which serve as beacons to the mariner, for many a league at sea. All around he beholds traces of their ancient combustion, as his road passes along vast tracts of lava, bristling in the innumerable fantastic forms into which the fiery torrent has been thrown by the obstacles in its career. Perhaps, at the same moment, as he casts his eye down some steep slope, or almost unfathomable ravine, on the margin of the road, he sees their depths glowing with the rich blooms and enamelled vegetation of the tropics. Such are the singular contrasts presented, at the same time, to the senses, in this picturesque region!

Still pressing upwards, the traveller mounts into other climates favourable to other kinds of cultivation. The yellow maize, or Indian corn, as we usually call it, has continued to follow him up from the lowest level; but he now first sees fields of wheat, and the other European grains, brought into the country by the conquerors. Mingled with them he views the plantations of the aloe or maguey (agave Americana), applied to such various and important uses by the Aztecs. The oaks now acquire a sturdier growth, and the dark forests of pine announce that he has entered the tierra fria, or cold region, the third and last of the great natural terraces into which the country is divided. When he has climbed to the height of between seven and eight thousand feet, the weary traveller sets his foot on the summit of the Cordillera of the Andes — the colossal range that, after traversing South America and the Isthmus of Darien, spreads out, as it enters Mexico, into that vast sheet of tableland which maintains an elevation of more than six thousand feet, for the distance of nearly two hundred leagues, until it gradually declines in the higher latitudes of the north.

Across this mountain rampart a chain of volcanic hills stretches, in a westerly direction, of still more stupendous dimensions, forming, indeed, some of the highest land on the globe. Their peaks, entering the limits of perpetual snow, diffuse a grateful coolness over the elevated plateaus below; for these last, though termed "cold," enjoy a climate, the mean temperature of which is not lower than that of the central parts of Italy. The air is exceedingly dry; the soil, though naturally good, is rarely clothed with the luxuriant vegetation of the lower regions. It frequently, indeed, has a parched and barren aspect, owing partly to the greater evaporation which takes place on these lofty plains, through the diminished pressure of the atmosphere; and partly, no doubt, to the want of trees to shelter the soil from the fierce influence of the summer sun. In the time of the Aztecs, the tableland was thickly covered with larch, oak, cypress, and other forest trees, the extraordinary dimensions of some of which, remaining to the present day, show that the curse of barrenness in later times is chargeable more on man than on nature. Indeed the early Spaniards made as indiscriminate war on the forests as did our Puritan ancestors, though with much less reason. After once conquering the country, they had no lurking ambush to fear from the submissive semi-civilised Indian, and were not, like our forefathers, obliged to keep watch and ward for a century. This spoliation of the ground, however, is said to have been pleasing to their imaginations, as it reminded them of the plains of their own Castile — the tableland of Europe; where the nakedness of the landscape forms the burden of every traveller's lament, who visits that country.

Midway across the continent, somewhat nearer the Pacific than the Atlantic ocean, at an elevation of nearly seven thousand five hundred feet, is the celebrated Valley of Mexico. It is of an oval form, about sixty-seven leagues in circumference, and is encompassed by a towering rampart of porphyritic rock, which nature seems to have provided, though ineffectually, to protect it from invasion.

The soil, once carpeted with a beautiful verdure and thickly sprinkled with stately trees, is often bare, and, in many places, white with the incrustation of salts, caused by the draining of the waters. Five lakes are spread over the Valley, occupying one tenth of its surface. On the opposite borders of the largest of these basins, much shrunk in its dimensions since the days of the Aztecs, stood the cities of Mexico and Tezcuco, the capitals of the two most potent and flourishing states of Anahuac, whose history, with that of the mysterious races that preceded them in the country, exhibits some of the nearest approaches to civilisation to be met with anciently on the North American continent.

Of these races the most conspicuous were the Toltecs. Advancing from a northerly direction, but from what region is uncertain, they entered the territory of Anahuac, probably before the close of the seventh century. Of course, little can be gleaned, with certainty, respecting a people whose written records have perished, and who are known to us only through the traditionary legends of the nations that succeeded them. By the general agreement of these, however, the Toltecs were well instructed in agriculture, and many of the most useful mechanic arts; were nice workers of metals; invented the complex arrangement of time adopted by the Aztecs; and, in short, were the true fountains of the civilisation which distinguished this part of the continent in later times. They established their capital at Tula, north of the Mexican Valley, and the remains of extensive buildings were to be discerned there at the time of the Conquest. The noble ruins of religious and other edifices, still to be seen in various parts of New Spain, are referred to this people, whose name, Toltec, has passed into a synonym for architect. Their shadowy history reminds us of those primitive races, who preceded the ancient Egyptians in the march of civilisation; fragments of whose monuments, as they are seen at this day, incorporated with the buildings of the Egyptians themselves, give to these latter the appearance of almost modern constructions.

After a period of four centuries, the Toltecs, who had extended their sway over the remotest borders of Anahuac, having been greatly reduced, it is said, by famine, pestilence, and unsuccessful wars, disappeared from the land as silently and mysteriously as they had entered it. A few of them still lingered behind, but much the greater number, probably, spread over the region of Central America and the neighbouring isles; and the traveller now speculates on the majestic ruins of Mitla and Palenque as possibly the work of this extraordinary people.

After the lapse of another hundred years, a numerous and rude tribe, called the Chichemecs, entered the deserted country from the regions of the far North-west. They were speedily followed by other races, of higher civilisation, perhaps of the same family with the Toltecs, whose language they appear to have spoken. The most noted of these were the Aztecs, or Mexicans, and the Acolhuans. The latter, better known in later times by the name of Tezcucans, from their capital, Tezcuco, on the eastern border of the Mexican lake, were peculiarly fitted, by their comparatively mild religion and manners, for receiving the tincture of civilisation which could be derived from the few Toltecs that still remained in the country. This, in their turn, they communicated to the barbarous Chichemees, a large portion of whom became amalgamated with the new settlers as one nation.

Availing themselves of the strength derived, not only from the increase of numbers, but from their own superior refinement, the Acolhuans gradually stretched their empire over the ruder tribes in the north; while their capital was filled with a numerous population, busily employed in many of the more useful and even elegant arts of a civilised community. In this palmy state, they were suddenly assaulted by a warlike neighbour, the Tepanecs, their own kindred, and inhabitants of the same valley as themselves. Their provinces were overrun, their armies beaten, their king assassinated, and the flourishing city of Tezcuco became the prize of the victor. From this abject condition the uncommon abilities of the young prince Nezahualcoyotl, the rightful heir to the crown, backed by the efficient aid of his Mexican allies, at length redeemed the state, and opened to it a new career of prosperity, even more brilliant than the former.

The Mexicans, with whom our history is principally concerned, came also, as we have seen, from the remote regions of the north — the populous hive of nations in the New World, as it has been in the Old. They arrived on the borders of Anahuac towards the beginning of the thirteenth century, some time after the occupation of the land by the kindred races. For a long time they did not establish themselves in any permanent residence; but continued shifting their quarters to different parts of the Mexican Valley, enduring all the casualties and hardships of a migratory life. On one occasion, they were enslaved by a more powerful tribe; but their ferocity soon made them formidable to their masters. After a series of wanderings and adventures, which need not shrink from comparison with the most extravagant legends of the heroic ages of antiquity, they at length halted on the south-western borders of the principal lake, in the year 1325. They there beheld, perched on the stem of a prickly pear, which shot out from the crevice of a rock that was washed by the waves, a royal eagle of extraordinary size and beauty, with a serpent in his talons, and his broad wings open to the rising sun. They hailed the auspicious omen, announced by an oracle as indicating the site of their future city, and laid its foundations by sinking piles into the shallows; for the low marshes were half buried under water. On these they erected their light fabrics of reeds and rushes; and sought a precarious subsistence from fishing, and from the wild fowl which frequented the waters, as well as from the cultivation of such simple vegetables as they could raise on their floating gardens. The place was called Tenochtitlan, though only known to Europeans by its other name of Mexico, derived from their war-god, Mexitli. The legend of its foundation is still further commemorated by the device of the eagle and the cactus, which form the arms of the modern Mexican republic. Such were the humble beginnings of the Venice of the Western World.

The forlorn condition of the new settlers was made still worse by domestic feuds. A part of the citizens seceded from the main body, and formed a separate community on the neighbouring marshes. Thus divided, it was long before they could aspire to the acquisition of territory on the main land. They gradually increased, however, in numbers, and strengthened themselves yet more by various improvements in their polity and military discipline, while they established a reputation for courage as well as cruelty in war, which made their name terrible throughout the Valley. In the early part of the fifteenth century, nearly a hundred years from the foundation of the city, an event took place which created an entire revolution in the circumstances, and, to some extent, in the character of the Aztecs. This was the subversion of the Tezcucan monarchy by the Tepanecs, already noticed. When the oppressive conduct of the victors had at length aroused a spirit of resistance, its prince, Nezahualcoyotl, succeeded, after incredible perils and escapes, in mustering such a force, as, with the aid of the Mexicans, placed him on a level with his enemies. In two successive battles these were defeated with great slaughter, their chief slain, and their territory, by one of those sudden reverses which characterise the wars of petty states, passed into the hands of the conquerors. It was awarded to Mexico, in return for its important services.

Then was formed that remarkable league, which, indeed, has no parallel in history. It was agreed between the states of Mexico, Tezcuco, and the neighbouring little kingdom of Tlacopan, that they should mutually support each other in their wars, offensive and defensive, and that, in the distribution of the spoil, one fifth should be assigned to Tlacopan, and the remainder be divided, in what proportions is uncertain, between the other powers. The Tezcucan writers claim an equal share for their nation with the Aztecs. But this does not seem to be warranted by the immense increase of territory subsequently appropriated by the latter. And we may account for any advantage conceded to them by the treaty, on the supposition, that however inferior they may have been originally, they were, at the time of making it, in a more prosperous condition than their allies, broken and dispirited by long oppression. What is more extraordinary than the treaty itself, however, is the fidelity with which it was maintained. During a century of uninterrupted warfare that ensued, no instance occurred where the parties quarrelled over the division of the spoil, which so often makes shipwreck of similar confederacies among civilised states.

The allies for some time found sufficient occupation for their arms in their own valley; but they soon overleaped its rocky ramparts, and by the middle of the fifteenth century, under the first Montezuma, had spread down the sides of the tableland to the borders of the Gulf of Mexico. Tenochtitlan, the Aztec capital, gave evidence of the public prosperity. Its frail tenements were supplanted by solid structures of stone and lime. Its population rapidly increased. Its old feuds were healed. The citizens who had seceded were again brought under a common government with the body, and the quarter they occupied was permanently connected with the parent city; the dimensions of which, covering the same ground, were much larger than those of the modern capital.

Fortunately, the throne was filled by a succession of able princes, who knew how to profit by their enlarged resources and by the martial enthusiasm of the nation. Year after year saw them return, loaded with the spoils of conquered cities, and with throngs of devoted captives, to their capital. No state was able long to resist the accumulated strength of the confederates. At the beginning of the sixteenth century, just before the arrival of the Spaniard, the Aztec dominion reached across the continent from the Atlantic to the Pacific; and, under the bold and bloody Ahuitzotl, its arms had been carried far over the limits already noticed as defining its permanent territory, into the farthest corners of Guatemala and Nicaragua. This extent of empire, however limited in comparison with that of many other states, is truly wonderful, considering it as the acquisition of a people whose whole population and resources had so recently been comprised within the walls of their own petty city; and considering, moreover, that the conquered territory was thickly settled by various races, bred to arms like the Mexicans, and little inferior to them in social organisation. The history of the Aztecs suggests some strong points of resemblance to that of the ancient Romans, not only in their military successes, but in the policy which led to them.

THE form of government differed in the different states of Anahuac. With the Aztecs and Tezcucans it was monarchical and nearly absolute. I shall direct my inquiries to the Mexican polity, borrowing an illustration occasionally from that of the rival kingdom.

The government was an elective monarchy. Four of the principal nobles, who had been chosen by their own body in the preceding reign, filled the office of electors, to whom were added, with merely an honorary rank, however, the two royal allies of Tezcuco and Tlacopan. The sovereign was selected from the brothers of the deceased prince, or, in default of them, from his nephews. Thus the election was always restricted to the same family. The candidate preferred must have distinguished himself in war, though, as in the case of the last Montezuma, he were a member of the priesthood. This singular mode of supplying the throne had some advantages. The candidates received an education which fitted them for the royal dignity, while the age at which they were chosen not only secured the nation against the evils of minority, but afforded ample means for estimating their qualifications for the office. The result, at all events, was favourable; since the throne, as already noticed, was filled by a succession of able princes, well qualified to rule over a warlike and ambitious people. The scheme of election, however defective, argues a more refined and calculating policy than was to have been expected from a barbarous nation.

The new monarch was installed in his regal dignity with much parade of religious ceremony; but not until, by a victorious campaign, he had obtained a sufficient number of captives to grace his triumphal entry into the capital, and to furnish victims for the dark and bloody rites which stained the Aztec superstition. Amidst this pomp of human sacrifice he was crowned. The crown, resembling a mitre in its form, and curiously ornamented with gold, gems, and feathers, was placed on his head by the lord of Tezcuco, the most powerful of his royal allies. The title of King, by which the earlier Aztec princes are distinguished by Spanish writers, is supplanted by that of Emperor in the later reigns, intimating, perhaps, his superiority over the monarchies of Tlacopan and Tezcuco.

The Aztec princes, especially towards the close of the dynasty, lived in a barbaric pomp, truly Oriental. Their spacious palaces were provided with halls for the different councils, who aided the monarch in the transaction of business. The chief of these was a sort of privy council, composed in part, probably, of the four electors chosen by the nobles after the accession, whose places, when made vacant by death, were immediately supplied as before. It was the business of this body, so far as can be gathered from the very loose accounts given of it, to advise the king in respect to the government of the provinces, the administration of the revenues, and, indeed, on all great matters of public interest.

In the royal buildings were accommodations, also, for a numerous body-guard of the sovereign, made up of the chief nobility. It is not easy to determine with precision, in these barbarian governments, the limits of the several orders. It is certain there was a distinct class of nobles, with large landed possessions, who held the most important offices near the person of the prince, and engrossed the administration of the provinces and cities. Many of these could trace their descent from the founders of the Aztec monarchy. According to some writers of authority, there were thirty great caciques, who had their residence, at least a part of the year, in the capital, and who could muster a hundred thousand vassals each on their estates. Without relying on such wild statements, it is clear, from the testimony of the conquerors, that the country was occupied by numerous powerful chieftains, who lived like independent princes on their domains. It it be true that the kings encouraged, or indeed exacted, the residence of these nobles in the capital, and required hostages in their absence, it is evident that their power must have been very formidable.

Their estates appear to have been held by various tenures, and to have been subject to different restrictions. Some of them, earned by their own good swords or received as the recompense of public services, were held without any limitation, except that the possessors

6

could not dispose of them to a plebeian. Others were entailed on the eldest male issue, and, in default of such, reverted to the crown. Most of them seem to have been burdened with the obligation of military service. The principal chiefs of Tezcuco, according to its chronicler, were expressly obliged to support their prince with their armed vassals, to attend his court, and aid him in the counsel. Some, instead of these services, were to provide for the repairs of his buildings, and to keep the royal demesnes in order, with an annual offering, by way of homage, of fruits and flowers. It was usual for a new king, on his accession, to confirm the investiture of estates derived from the crown.

It cannot be denied that we recognise in all this several features of the feudal system, which, no doubt, lose nothing of their effect, under the hands of the Spanish writers, who are fond of tracing analogies to European institutions. But such analogies lead sometimes to very erroneous conclusions. The obligation of military service, for instance, the most essential principle of a fief, seems to be naturally demanded by every government from its subjects. As to minor points of resemblance, they fall far short of that harmonious system of reciprocal service and protection which embraced, in nice gradation, every order of a feudal monarchy. The kingdoms of Anahuac were, in their nature, despotic, attended, indeed, with many mitigating circumstances unknown to the despotisms of the East; but it is chimerical to look for much in common — beyond a few accidental forms and ceremonies — with those aristocratic institutions of the Middle Ages, which made the court of every petty baron the precise image in miniature of that of his sovereign.

The legislative power, both in Mexico and Tezcuco, resided wholly with the monarch. This feature of despotism, however, was in some measure counteracted by the constitution of the judicial tribunals — of more importance, among a rude people, than the legislative, since it is easier to make good laws for such a community than to enforce them, and the best laws, badly administered, are but a mockery. Over each of the principal cities, with its dependent territories, was placed a supreme judge, appointed by the crown, with original and final jurisdiction in both civil and criminal cases. There was no appeal from his sentence to any other tribunal, nor even to the king. He held his office during life; and any one who usurped his ensigns was punished with death.

Below this magistrate was a court, established in each province, and consisting of three members. It held concurrent jurisdiction with the supreme judge in civil suits, but in criminal an appeal lay to his tribunal. Besides these courts, there was a body of inferior magistrates distributed through the country, chosen by the people themselves in their several districts. Their authority was limited to smaller causes, while the more important were carried up to the higher courts. There was still another class of subordinate officers, appointed also by the people, each of whom was to watch over the conduct of a certain number of families, and report any disorder or breach of the laws to the higher authorities.

In Tezcuco the judicial arrangements were of a more refined character; and a gradation of tribunals finally terminated in a general meeting or parliament, consisting of all the judges, great and petty, throughout the kingdom, held every eighty days in the capital, over which the king presided in person. This body determined all suits, which, from their importance, or difficulty, had been reserved for its consideration by the lower tribunals. It served, moreover, as a council of state, to assist the monarch in the transaction of public business.

Such are the vague and imperfect notices that can be gleaned respecting the Aztec tribunals, from the hieroglyphical paintings still preserved, and from the most accredited Spanish writers. These, being usually ecclesiastics, have taken much less interest in this subject than in matters connected with religion. They find some apology, certainly, in the early destruction of most of the Indian paintings, from which their information was, in part, to be gathered.

On the whole, however, it must be inferred, that the Aztecs were sufficiently civilised to envince a solicitude for the rights both of property and of persons. The law, authorising an appeal to the highest judicature in criminal matters only, shows an attention to personal security, rendered the more obligatory by the extreme severity of their penal code, which would naturally have made them more cautious of a wrong conviction. The existence of a number of co-ordinate tribunals, without a central one of supreme authority to control the whole, must have given rise to very discordant interpretations of the law in different districts, an evil which they shared in common with most of the nations of Europe.

The provision for making the superior judges wholly independent of the crown was worthy of an enlightened people. It presented the strongest barrier, that a mere constitution could afford, against tyranny. It is not, indeed, to be supposed that, in a government otherwise so despotic, means could not be found for influencing the magistrate. But it was a great step to fence round his authority with the sanction of the law; and no one of the Aztec monarch, as far as I know, is accused of an attempt to violate it.

To receive presents or a bribe, to be guilty of collusion in any way with a suitor, was punished, in a judge, with death. Who, or what tribunal, decided as to his guilt, does not appear. In Tezcuco this was done by the rest of the court. But the king presided over that body. The Tezcucan prince, Nezahualpilli, who rarely tempered justice with mercy, put one judge to death for taking a bribe, and another for determining suits in his own house — a capital offence, also, by law.

The judges of the higher tribunals were maintained from the produce of a part of the crown lands, reserved for this purpose. They, as well as the supreme judge, held their offices for life. The proceedings in the courts were conducted with decency and order. The judges wore an appropriate dress, and attended to business both parts of the day, dining always, for the sake of despatch, in an apartment of the same building where they held their session; a method of proceeding much commended by the Spanish chroniclers, to whom despatch was not very familiar in their own tribunals. Officers attended to preserve order, and others summoned the parties, and produced them in court. No counsel was employed; the parties stated their own case, and supported it by their witnesses. The oath of the accused was also admitted in evidence. The statement of the case, the testimony, and the proceedings of the trial, were all set forth by a clerk, in hieroglyphical paintings, and handed over to the court. The paintings were executed with so much accuracy, that, in all suits respecting real property, they were allowed to be produced as good authority in the Spanish tribunals, very long after the Conquest.

A capital sentence was indicated by a line traced with an arrow across the portrait of the accused. In Tezcuco, where the king presided in the court, this, according to the national chronicler, was done with extraordinary parade. His description, which is of rather a poetical cast, I give in his own words: "In the royal palace of Tezcuco was a courtyard, on the opposite sides of which were two halls of justice. In the principal one, called the 'tribunal of God,' was a throne of pure gold inlaid with turquoises and other precious stones. On a stool in front, was placed a human skull, crowned with an immense emerald, of a pyramidal form, and surmounted by an aigrette of brilliant plumes and precious stones. The skull was laid on a heap of military weapons, shields, quivers, bows, and arrows. The walls were hung with tapestry, made of the hair of different wild animals, of rich and various colours, festooned by gold rings, and embroidered with figures of birds and flowers. Above the throne was a canopy of variegated plumage, from the centre of which shot forth resplendent rays of gold and jewels. The other tribunal, called 'the king's,' was also surmounted by a gorgeous canopy of feathers, on which were emblazoned the royal arms. Here the sovereign gave public audience, and communicated his despatches. But, when he decided important causes, or confirmed a capital sentence, he passed to 'the tribunal of God,' attended by the fourteen great lords of the realm, marshalled according to their rank. Then, putting on his mitred crown, incrusted with precious stones, and holding a golden arrow, by way of sceptre, in his left hand, he laid his right upon the skull, and pronounced judgment." All this looks rather fine for a court of justice, it must be owned. But it is certain, that the Tezcucans, as we shall see hereafter, possessed both the materials and the skill requisite to work them up in this manner. Had they been a little further advanced in refinement, one might well doubt their having the bad taste to do so.

The laws of the Aztecs were registered, and exhibited to the people in their hieroglyphical paintings. Much the larger part of them, as in every nation imperfectly civilised, relates rather to the security of persons than of property. The great crimes against society were all made capital. Even the murder of a slave was punished with death. Adulterers, as among the Jews, were stoned to death. Thieving, according to the degree of the offence, was punished by slavery or death. Yet the Mexicans could have been under no great apprehension of this crime, since the entrances to their dwellings were not secured by bolts, or fastenings of any kind. It was a capital offence to remove the boundaries of another's lands; to alter the established measures; and for a guardian not to be able to give a good account of his ward's property. These regulations evince a regard for equity in dealings, and for private rights, which argues a considerable progress in civilisation. Prodigals, who squandered their patrimony, were punished in like manner; a severe sentence, since the crime brought its adequate punishment along with it. Intemperance, which was the burden, moreover, of their religious homilies, was visited with the severest penalties; as if they had foreseen in it the consuming canker of their own, as well as of the other Indian races in later times. It was punished in the young with death, and in older persons with loss of rank and confiscation of property. Yet a decent conviviality was not meant to be proscribed at their festivals, and they possessed the means of indulging it, in a mild fermented liquor, called pulque.

The rites of marriage were celebrated with as much formality as in any Christian country; and the institution was held in such reverence, that a tribunal was instituted for the sole purpose of determining questions relating to it. Divorces could not be obtained, until authorised by a sentence of this court, after a patient hearing of the parties.

But the most remarkable part of the Aztec code was that relating to slavery. There were several descriptions of slaves: prisoners taken in war, who were almost always reserved for the dreadful doom of sacrifice; criminals, public debtors, persons who, from extreme poverty, voluntarily resigned their freedom, and children who were sold by their own parents. In the last instance, usually occasioned also by poverty, it was common for the parents, with the master's consent, to substitute others of their children successively, as they grew up: thus distributing the burden, as equally as possible, among the different members of the family. The willingness of freemen to incur the penalties of this condition is explained by the mild form in which it existed. The contract of sale was executed in the presence of at least four witnesses. The services to be exacted were limited with great precision. The slave was allowed to have his own family, to hold property, and even other slaves. His children were free. No one could be born to slavery in Mexico, an honourable distinction, not known, I believe, in any civilised community where slavery has been sanctioned. Slaves were not sold by their masters, unless when these were driven to it by poverty. They were often liberated by them at their death, and sometimes, as there was no natural repugnance founded on difference of blood and race, were married to them. Yet a refractory or vicious slave might be led into the market, with a collar round his neck, which intimated his bad character, and there be publicly sold, and, on a second sale, reserved for sacrifice.

The royal revenues were derived from various sources. The crown lands, which appear to have been extensive, made their returns in kind. The places in the neighbourhood of the capital were bound to supply workmen and materials for building the king's palaces, and keeping them in repair. They were also to furnish fuel, provisions, and whatever was necessary for his ordinary domestic expenditure, which was certainly on no stinted scale. The principal cities, which had numerous villages and a large territory dependent on them, were distributed into districts, with each a share of the lands allotted to it, for its support. The inhabitants paid a stipulated part of the produce to the crown. The vassals of the great chiefs, also, paid a portion of their earnings into the public treasury; an arrangement not at all in the spirit of the feudal institutions.

In addition to this tax on all the agricultural produce of the kingdom, there was another on its manufactures. The nature and the variety of the tributes will be best shown by an enumeration of some of the principal articles. These were cotton dresses, and mantles of feather-work, exquisitely made; ornamented armour; vases and plates of gold; gold-dust, bands and bracelets; crystal, gilt, and varnished jars and goblets; bells, arms, and utensils of copper; reams of paper; grain, fruits, copal, amber, cochineal, cocoa, wild animals and birds, timber, lime, mats, etc. In this curious medley of the most homely commodities, and the elegant superfluities of luxury, it is singular that no mention should be made of silver, the great staple of the country in later times, and the use of which was certainly known to the Aztecs.

Garrisons were established in the larger cities — probably those at a distance, and recently conquered — to keep down revolt, and to enforce the payment of the tribute. Tax-gatherers were also distributed throughout the kingdom, who were recognised by their official badges, and dreaded from the merciless rigour of their exactions. By a stern law, every defaulter was liable to be taken and sold as a slave. In the capital were spacious granaries and warehouses for the reception of the tributes. A receiver-general was quartered in the palace, who rendered in an exact account of the various contributions, and watched over the conduct of the inferior agents, in whom the least malversation was summarily punished. This functionary was furnished with a map of the whole empire, with a minute specification of the imposts assessed on every part of it. These imposts, moderate under the reigns of the early princes, became so burdensome under those of the close of the dynasty, being rendered still more oppressive by the manner of collection, that they bred disaffection throughout the land, and prepared the way for its conquest by the Spaniards.

Communication was maintained with the remotest parts of the country by means of couriers. Post-houses were established on the great roads, about two leagues distant from each other. The courier, bearing his despatches in the form of a hieroglyphical painting, ran with them to the first station, where they were taken by another messenger, and carried forward to the next, and so on till they reached the capital. These couriers, trained from childhood, travelled with incredible swiftness; not four or five leagues an hour, as an old chronicler would make us believe, but with such speed that despatches were carried from one to two hundred miles a day. Fresh fish was frequently served at Montezuma's table in twenty-four hours from the time it had been taken in the Gulf of Mexico, two hundred miles from the capital. In this way intelligence of the movements of the royal armies was rapidly brought to court; and the dress of the courier, denoting by its colour that of his tidings, spread joy or consternation in the towns through which he passed.

But the great aim of the Aztec institutions to which private discipline and public honours were alike directed, was the profession of arms. In Mexico, as in Egypt, the soldier shared with the priest the highest consideration. The king, as we have seen, must be an experienced warrior. The tutelary deity of the Aztecs was the god of war. A great object of their military expeditions was, to gather hecatombs of captives for his altars. The soldier, who fell in battle, was transported at once to the region of ineffable bliss in the bright mansions of the Sun. Every war, therefore, became a crusade; and the warrior, animated by a religious enthusiasm, like that of the early Saracen, or the Christian crusader, was not only raised to a contempt of danger, but courted it, for the imperishable crown of martyrdom. Thus we find the same impulse acting in the most opposite quarters of the globe, and the Asiatic, the European, and the American, each earnestly invoking the holy name of religion in the perpetration of human butchery.

The question of war was discussed in a council of the king and his chief nobles. Ambassadors were sent, previously to its declaration, to require the hostile state to receive the Mexican gods, and to pay the customary tribute. The persons of ambassadors were held sacred throughout Anahuac. They were lodged and entertained in the great towns at the public charge, and were everywhere received with courtesy, so long as they did not deviate from the high-roads on their route. When they did, they forfeited their privileges. If the embassy proved unsuccessful, a defiance, or open declaration of war, was sent; quotas were drawn from the conquered provinces, which Were always subjected to military service, as well as the payment of taxes; and the royal army, usually with the monarch at its head, began its march.

The Aztec princes made use of the incentive employed by European monarchs to excite the ambition of their followers. They established various military orders, each having its privileges and peculiar insignia. There seems, also, to have existed a sort of knighthood, of inferior degree. It was the cheapest reward of martial prowess, and whoever had not reached it was excluded from using ornaments on his arms or his person, and obliged to wear a coarse white stuff, made from the threads of the aloe, called nequen. Even the members of the royal family were not excepted from this law, which reminds one of the occasional practice of Christian knights, to wear plain armour, or shields without device, till they had achieved some doughty feat of chivalry. Although the military orders were thrown open to all, it is probable that they were chiefly filled with persons of rank, who, by their previous training and connections, were able to come into the field under peculiar advantages.

The dress of the higher warriors was picturesque, and often magnificent. Their bodies were covered with a close vest of quilted cotton, so thick as to be impenetrable to the light missiles of Indian warfare. This garment was so light and serviceable that it was adopted by the Spaniards. The wealthier chiefs sometimes wore, instead of this cotton mail, a cuirass made of thin plates of gold, or silver. Over it was thrown a surcoat of the gorgeous feather-work in which they excelled. Their helmets were sometimes of wood, fashioned like the heads of wild animals, and sometimes of silver, on the top of which waved a panache of variegated feathers, sprinkled with precious stones and ornaments of gold. They wore also collars, bracelets, and earrings, of the same rich materials.

Their armies were divided into bodies of eight thousand men; and these, again, into companies of three or four hundred, each with its own commander. The national standard, which has been compared to the ancient Roman, displayed, in its embroidery of gold and feather-work, the armorial ensigns of the state. These were significant of its name, which, as the names of both persons and places were borrowed from some material object, was easily expressed by hieroglyphical symbols. The companies and the great chiefs had also their appropriate banners and devices, and the gaudy hues of their many-coloured plumes gave a dazzling splendour to the spectacle.

Their tactics were such as belong to a nation with whom war, though a trade, is not elevated to the rank of a science. They advanced singing, and shouting their war-cries, briskly charging the enemy, as rapidly retreating, and making use of ambuscades, sudden surprises, and the light skirmish of guerilla warfare. Yet their discipline was such as to draw forth the encomiums of the Spanish conquerors. "A beautiful sight it was," says one of them, "to see them set out on their march, all moving forward so gaily, and in so admirable order!" In battle, they did not seek to kill their enemies, so much as to take them prisoners; and they never scalped, like other North American tribes. The valour of a warrior was estimated by the number of his prisoners; and no ransom was large enough to save the devoted captive.

Their military code bore the same stern features as their other laws. Disobedience of orders was punished with death. It was death, also, for a soldier to leave his colours to attack the enemy before the signal was given, or to plunder another's booty or prisoners. One of the last Tezcucan princes, in the spirit of an ancient Roman, put two sons to death — after having cured their wounds — for violating the last-mentioned law.

I must not omit to notice here an institution, the introduction of which, in the Old World, is ranked among the beneficent fruits of Christianity. Hospitals were established in the principal cities for the cure of the sick, and the permanent refuge of the disabled soldier; and surgeons were placed over them, "who were so far better than those in Europe," says an old chronicler, "that they did not protract the cure, in order to increase the pay."

Such is the brief outline of the civil and military polity of the ancient Mexicans; less perfect than could be desired, in regard to the former, from the imperfection of the sources whence it is drawn. Whoever has had occasion to explore the early history of modern Europe has found how vague and unsatisfactory is the political information which can be gleaned from the gossip of monkish annalists. How much is the difficulty increased in the present instance, where this information, first recorded in the dubious language of hieroglyphics, was interpreted in another language, with which the Spanish chroniclers were imperfectly acquainted, while it related to institutions of which their past experience enabled them to form no adequate conception! Amidst such uncertain lights, it is in vain to expect nice accuracy of detail. All that can be done is, to attempt an outline of the more prominent features, that a correct impression, so far as it goes, may be produced on the mind of the reader.

Enough has been said, however, to show that the Aztec and Tezcucan races were advanced in civilisation very far beyond the wandering tribes of North America. The degree of civilisation which they had reached, as inferred by their political institutions, may be considered, perhaps, not much short of that enjoyed by our Saxon ancestors, under Alfred. In respect to the nature of it, they may be better compared with the Egyptians; and the examination of their social relations and culture may suggest still stronger points of resemblance to that ancient people.

THE CIVIL polity of the Aztecs is so closely blended with their religion, that, without understanding the latter, it is impossible to form correct ideas of their government or their social institutions. I shall pass over, for the present, some remarkable traditions, bearing a singular resemblance to those found in the Scriptures, and endeavour to give a brief sketch of their mythology, and their careful provisions for maintaining a national worship.

In contemplating the religious system of the Aztecs, one is struck with its apparent incongruity, as if some portion of it had emanated from a comparatively refined people, open to gentle influences, while the rest breathes a spirit of unmitigated ferocity. It naturally suggests the idea of two distinct sources, and authorises the belief that the Aztecs had inherited from their predecessors a milder faith, on which was afterwards engrafted their own mythology. The latter soon became dominant, and gave its dark colouring to the creeds of the conquered nations — which the Mexicans, like the ancient Romans, seem willingly to have incorporated into their own — until the same funereal superstition settled over the farthest borders of Anahuac.

The Aztecs recognised the existence of a supreme Creator and Lord of the universe. They addressed him, in their prayers, as "the God by whom we live," "omnipresent, that knoweth all thoughts, and giveth all gifts," "without whom man is as nothing," "invisible, incorporeal, one God, of perfect perfection and purity," "under whose wings we find repose and a sure defence." These sublime attributes infer no inadequate conception of the true God. But the idea of unity — of a being, with whom volition is action, who has no need of inferior ministers to execute his purposes — was too simple, or too vast, for their understandings; and they sought relief, as usual, in the plurality of deities, who presided over the elements, the changes of the seasons, and the various occupations of man. Of these, there were thirteen principal deities, and more than two hundred inferior; to each of whom some special day, or appropriate festival, was consecrated.

At the head of all stood the terrible Huitzilopochtli, the Mexican Mars; although it is doing injustice to the heroic war-god of antiquity to identify him with this sanguinary monster. This was the patron deity of the nation. His fantastic image was loaded with costly ornaments. His temples were the most stately and august of the public edifices; and his altars reeked with the blood of human hecatombs in every city of the empire. Disastrous, indeed, must have been the influence of such a superstition on the character of the people.

A far more interesting personage in their mythology, was Quetzalcoatl, god of the air, a divinity who, during his residence on earth, instructed the natives in the use of metals, in agriculture, and in the arts of government. He was one of those benefactors of their species, doubtless, who have been deified, by the gratitude of posterity. Under him, the earth teemed with fruits and flowers, without the pains of culture. An ear of Indian corn was as much as a single man could carry. The cotton, as it grew, took, of its own accord, the rich dyes of human art. The air was filled with intoxicating perfumes and the sweet melody of birds. In short, these were the halcyon days, which find a place in the mythic systems of so many nations in the Old World. It was the golden age of Anahuac.

From some cause, not explained, Quetzalcoatl incurred the wrath of one of the principal gods, and was compelled to abandon the country. On his way, he stopped at the city of Cholula, where a temple was dedicated to his worship, the massy ruins of which still form one of the most interesting relics of antiquity in Mexico. When he reached the shores of the Mexican Gulf, he took leave of his followers, promising that he and his descendants would revisit them hereafter, and then entering his wizard skill, made of serpents' skins, embarked on the great ocean for the fabled land of Tlapallan. He was said to have been tall in stature, with a white skin, long, dark hair, and a flowing beard. The Mexicans looked confidently to the return of the benevolent deity; and this remarkable tradition, deeply cherished in their hearts, prepared the way, as we shall see hereafter, for the future success of the Spaniards.

13

We have not space for further details respecting the Mexican divinities, the attributes of many of whom were carefully defined, as they descended in regular gradation, to the penates or household gods, whose little images were to be found in the humblest dwelling.

The Aztecs felt the curiosity, common to man in almost every stage of civilisation, to lift the veil which covers the mysterious past, and the more awful future. They sought relief, like the nations of the Old Continent, from the oppressive idea of eternity, by breaking it up into distinct cycles, or periods of time, each of several thousand years' duration. There were four of these cycles, and at the end of each, by the agency of one of the elements, the human family was swept from the earth, and the sun blotted out from the heavens, to be again rekindled.

They imagined three separate states of existence in the future life. The wicked, comprehending the great part of mankind, were to expiate their sins in a place of everlasting darkness. Another class, with no other merit than that of having died of certain diseases, capriciously selected, were to enjoy a negative existence of indolent contentment. The highest place was reserved, as in most warlike nations, for the heroes who fell in battle, or in sacrifice. They passed, at once, into the presence of the Sun, whom they accompanied with songs and choral dances, in his bright progress through the heavens; and, after some years, their spirits went to animate the clouds and singing birds of beautiful plumage, and to revel amidst the rich blossoms and odours of the gardens of paradise. Such was the heaven of the Aztecs; more refined in its character than that of the more polished pagan, whose elysium reflected only the martial sports, or sensual gratifications, of this life. In the destiny they assigned to the wicked, we discern similar traces of refinement; since the absence of all physical torture forms a striking contrast to the schemes of suffering so ingeniously devised by the fancies of the most enlightened nations. In all this, so contrary to the natural suggestions of the ferocious Aztec, we see the evidences of a higher civilisation, inherited from their predecessors in the land.

Our limits will allow only a brief allusion to one or two of their most interesting ceremonies. On the death of a person, his corpse was dressed in the peculiar habiliments of his tutelar deity. It was strewed with pieces of paper, which operated as charms, against the dangers of the dark road he was to travel. A throng of slaves, if he were rich, was sacrificed at his obsequies. His body was burned, and the ashes, collected in a vase, were preserved in one of the apartments of his house. Here we have successively the usages of the Roman Catholic, the Mussulman, the Tartar, and the ancient Greek and Roman, curious coincidences, which may show how cautious we should be in adopting conclusions founded on analogy.

A more extraordinary coincidence may be traced with Christian rites, in the ceremony of naming their children. The lips and bosom of the infant were sprinkled with water, and "the Lord was implored to permit the holy drops to wash away the sin that was given to it before the foundation of the world; so that the child might be born anew." We are reminded of Christian morals, in more than one of their prayers, in which they use regular forms. "Wilt thou blot us out, O Lord, for ever? Is this punishment intended, not for our reformation, but for our destruction?" Again, "Impart to us, out of thy great mercy, thy gifts which we are not worthy to receive through our own merits." "Keep peace with all," says another petition; "bear injuries with humility; God, who sees, will avenge you." But the most striking parallel with Scripture is in the remarkable declaration, that "he who looks too curiously on a woman, commits adultery with his eyes." These pure and elevated maxims, it is true, are mixed up with others of a puerile, and even brutal character, arguing that confusion of the moral perceptions, which is natural in the twilight of civilisation. One would not expect, however, to meet, in such a state of society, with doctrines as sublime as any inculcated by the enlightened codes of ancient philosophy.

But, although the Aztec mythology gathered nothing from the beautiful inventions of the poet, nor from the refinements of philosophy, it was much indebted, as I have noticed, to the priests, who endeavoured to dazzle the imagination of the people by the most formal and pompous ceremonial. The influence of the priesthood must be greatest in an imperfect state of civilisation, where it engrosses all the scanty science of the time in its own body. This is particularly the case, when the science is of that spurious kind which is less occupied with the real phenomena of nature, than with the fanciful chimeras of human superstition. Such are the sciences of astrology and divination, in which the Aztec priests were well initiated; and while they seemed to hold the keys of the future in their own hands, they impressed the ignorant people with sentiments of superstitious awe, beyond that which has probably existed in any other country — even in Ancient Egypt.

The sacerdotal order was very numerous; as may be inferred from the statement that five thousand priests were, in some way or other, attached to the principal temple in the capital. The various ranks and functions of this multitudinous body were discriminated with great exactness. Those best instructed in music took the management of the choirs. Others arranged the festivals conformably to the calendar. Some superintended the education of youth, and others had charge of the hieroglyphical paintings and oral traditions; while the dismal rites of sacrifice were reserved for the chief dignitaries of the order. At the head of the whole establishment were two high-priests, elected from the order, as it would seem, by the king and principal nobles, without reference to birth, but solely for their qualifications, as shown by their previous conduct in a subordinate station. They were equal in dignity, and inferior only to the sovereign, who rarely acted without their advice in weighty matters of public concern.

The priests were each devoted to the service of some particular deity, and had quarters provided within the spacious precincts of their temple; at least, while engaged in immediate attendance there — for they were allowed to marry and have families of their own. In this monastic residence they lived in all the stern severity of conventual discipline. Thrice during the day, and once at night, they were called to prayers. They were frequent in their ablutions and vigils, and mortified the flesh by fasting and cruel penance — drawing blood from their bodies by flagellation, or by piercing them with the thorns of the aloe.

The great cities were divided into districts, placed under the charge of a sort of parochial clergy, who regulated every act of religion within their precincts. It is remarkable that they administered the rites of confession and absolution. The secrets of the confessional were held inviolable, and penances were imposed of much the same kind as those enjoined in the Roman Catholic Church. There were two remarkable peculiarities in the Aztec ceremony. The first was, that, as the repetition of an offence, once atoned for, was deemed inexpiable, confession was made but once in a man's life, and was usually deferred to a late period of it, the penitent unburdened his conscience, and settled, at once, the long arrears of iniquity. Another peculiarity was, that priestly absolution was received in Place of the legal punishment of offences, and authorised an acquittal in case of arrest. Long after the Conquest, the simple natives, when they came under the arm of the law, sought to escape by producing the certificate of their confession.

One of the most important duties of the priesthood was that of education, to which certain buildings were appropriated within the enclosure of the principal temple. Here the youth of both sexes, of the higher and middling orders, were placed at a very tender age. The girls were intrusted to the care of priestesses; for women were allowed to exercise sacerdotal functions, except those of sacrifice. In these institutions the boys were drilled in the routine of monastic discipline; they decorated the shrines of the gods with flowers, fed the sacred fires, and took part in the religious chants and festivals. Those in the higher school — the Calmecac, as it was called — were initiated in their traditionary lore, the mysteries of hieroglyphics, the principles of government, and such branches of astronomical and natural science as were within the compass of the priesthood. The girls learned various feminine employments, especially to weave and embroider rich coverings for the altars of the gods. Great attention was paid to the moral discipline of both sexes. The most perfect decorum prevailed; and offences were punished with extreme rigour, in some instances with death itself. Terror, not love, was the spring of education with the Aztecs.

At a suitable age for marrying, or for entering into the world, the pupils were dismissed, with much ceremony, from the convent, and the recommendation of the principal often introduced those most competent to responsible situations in public life. Such was the crafty policy of the Mexican priests, who, by reserving to themselves the business of instruction, were enabled to mould the young and plastic mind according to their own wills, and to train it early to implicit reverence for religion and its ministers; a reverence which still maintained its hold on the iron nature of the warrior, long after every other vestige of education had been effaced by the rough trade to which he was devoted.

To each of the principal temples lands were annexed for the maintenance of the priests. These estates were augmented by the policy of devotion of successive princes, until, under the last Montezuma, they had swollen to an enormous extent, and covered every district of the empire. The priests took the management of their property into their own hands; and they seem to have treated their tenants with the liberality and indulgence characteristic of monastic corporations. Besides the large supplies drawn from this source, the religious order was enriched with the first-fruits, and such other offerings as piety or superstition dictated. The surplus beyond what was required for the support of the national worship was distributed in alms among the poor; a duty strenuously prescribed by their moral code. Thus we find the same religion inculcating lessons of pure philanthropy, on the one hand, and of merciless extermination, as we shall soon see, on the other.

The Mexican temples — teocallis, "houses of God," as they were called — were very numerous. There were several hundreds in each of the principal cities, many of them, doubtless, very humble edifices. They were solid masses of earth, cased with brick or stone, and in their form somewhat resembled the pyramidal structures of ancient Egypt. The bases of many of them were more than a hundred feet square, and they towered to a still greater height. They were distributed into four or five stories, each of smaller dimensions than that below. The ascent was by a flight of steps, at an angle of the pyramid, on the outside. This led to a sort of terrace or gallery, at the base of the second story, which passed quite round the building to another flight of stairs, commencing also at the same angle as the preceding and directly over it, and leading to a similar terrace; so that one had to make the circuit of the temple several times, before reaching the summit. In some instances the stairway led directly up the centre of the western face of the building. The top was a broad area, on which were erected one or two towers, forty or fifty feet high, the sanctuaries in which stood the sacred images of the presiding deities. Before these towers stood the dreadful stone of sacrifice, and two lofty altars, on which fires were kept, as inextinguishable as those in the temple of Vesta. There were said to be six hundred of these altars on smaller buildings within the inclosure of the great temple of Mexico, which, with those on the sacred edifices in other parts of the city, shed a brilliant illumination over its streets, through the darkest night.

From the construction of their temples, all religious services were public. The long processions of priests, winding round their massive sides, as they rose higher and higher towards the summit, and the dismal rites of sacrifice performed there, were all visible from the remotest corners of the capital, impressing on the spectator's mind a superstitious veneration for the mysteries of his religion, and for the dread ministers by whom they were interpreted.

This impression was kept in full force by their numerous festivals. Every month was consecrated to some protecting deity; and every week — nay, almost every day, was set down in their calendar for some appropriate celebration; so that it is difficult to understand how the ordinary business of life could have been compatible with the exactions of religion. Many of their ceremonies were of a light and cheerful complexion, consisting of the national songs and dances, in which both sexes joined. Processions were made of women and children crowned with garlands and bearing offerings of fruits, the ripened maize, or the sweet incense of copal and other odoriferous gums, while the altars of the deity were stained with no blood save that of animals. These were the peaceful rites derived from their Toltec predecessors, on which the fierce Aztecs engrafted a superstition too loathsome to be exhibited in all its nakedness, and one over which I would gladly draw a veil altogether, but that it would leave the reader in ignorance of their most striking institution, and one that had the greatest influence in forming the national character.

Human sacrifices were adopted by the Aztecs early in the fourteenth century, about two hundred years before the Conquest. Rare at first, they became more frequent with the wider extent of their empire; till, at length, almost every festival was closed with this cruel abomination. These religious ceremonials were generally arranged in such a manner as to afford a type of the most prominent circumstances in the character or history of the deity who was the object of them. A single example will suffice.

One of their most important festivals was that in honour of the god Tezcatlipoca, whose rank was inferior only to that of the Supreme Being. He was called "the soul of the world," and supposed to have been its creator. He was depicted as a handsome man, endowed with perpetual youth. A year before the intended sacrifice, a captive, distinguished for his personal beauty, and without a blemish on his body, was selected to represent this deity. Certain tutors took charge of him, and instructed him how to perform his new part with becoming grace and dignity. He was arrayed in a splendid dress, regaled with incense, and with a profusion of sweet-scented flowers, of which the ancient Mexicans were as fond as their descendants of the present day. When he went abroad, he was attended by a train of the royal pages, and, as he halted in the streets to play some favourite melody, the crowd prostrated themselves before him, and did him homage as the representative of their good deity. In this way he led an easy, luxurious life, till within a month of his sacrifice. Four beautiful girls, bearing the names of the principal goddesses, were then selected to share the honours of his bed; and with them he continued to live in idle dalliance feasted at the banquets of the principal nobles, who paid him all the honours of a divinity.

At length the fatal day of sacrifice arrived. The term of his short-lived glories was at an end. He was stripped of his gaudy apparel, and bade adieu to the fair partners of his revelries. One of the royal barges transported him across the lake to a temple which rose on its margin, about a league from the city. Hither the inhabitants of the capital flocked, to witness the consummation of the ceremony. As the sad procession wound up the sides of the pyramid, the unhappy victim threw away his gay chaplet of flowers, and broke in pieces the musical instruments with which he had solaced the hours of captivity. On the summit he was received by six priests, whose long and matted locks flowed disorderly over their sable robes, covered with hieroglyphic scrolls of mystic import. They led him to the sacrificial stone, a huge block of jasper, with its upper surface somewhat convex. On this the prisoner was stretched. Five priests secured his head and his limbs; while the sixth, clad in a scarlet mantle, emblematic of his bloody office, dexterously opened the breast of the wretched victim with a sharp razor of itztli — a volcanic substance hard as flint — and, inserting his hand in the wound, tore out the palpitating heart. The minister of death, first holding this up towards the sun, an object of worship throughout Anahuac, cast it at the feet of the deity to whom the temple was devoted, while the multitudes below prostrated themselves in humble adoration. The tragic story of this prisoner was expounded by the priests as the type of human destiny, which, brilliant in its commencement, too often closes in sorrow and disaster.

Such was the form of human sacrifice usually practised by the Aztecs. It was the same that often met the indignant eyes of the Europeans, in their progress through the country, and from the dreadful doom of which they themselves were not exempted. There were, indeed, some occasions when preliminary tortures, of the most exquisite kind — with which it is unnecessary to shock the reader — were inflicted, but they always terminated with the bloody ceremony above described. It should be remarked, however, that such tortures were not the spontaneous suggestions of cruelty, as with the North American Indians; but were all rigorously prescribed in the Aztec ritual, and doubtless, were often inflicted with the same compunctious visitings which a devout familiar of the Holy Office might at times experience in executing its stern decrees. Women, as well as the other sex, were sometimes reserved for sacrifice. On some occasions, particularly in seasons of drought, at the festival of the insatiable Tlaloc, the god of rain, children, for the most part infants, were offered up. As they were borne along in open litters, dressed in their festal robes, and decked with the fresh blossoms of spring, they moved the hardest heart to pity, though their cries were drowned in the wild chant of the priests, who read in their tears a favourable augury for their petition. These innocent victims were generally bought by the priests of parents who were poor, but who stifled the voice of nature, probably less at the suggestions of poverty than of a wretched superstition.

The most loathsome part of the story, the manner in which the body of the sacrificed captive was disposed of, remains yet to be told. It was delivered to the warrior who had taken him in battle, and by him, after being dressed, was served up in an entertainment to his friends. This was not the coarse repast of famished cannibals, but a banquet teeming with delicious beverages and delicate viands, prepared with art, and attended by both sexes, who, as we shall see hereafter, conducted themselves with all the decorum of civilised life. Surely, never were refinement and the extreme of barbarism brought so closely in contact with each other!

Human sacrifices have been practised by many nations, not excepting the most polished nations of antiquity; but never by any, on a scale to be compared with those in Anahuac. The amount of victims immolated on its accursed altars would stagger the faith of the least scrupulous believer. Scarcely any author pretends to estimate the yearly sacrifices throughout the empire at less than twenty thousand, and some carry the number as high as fifty!

On great occasions, as the coronation of a king, or the consecration of a temple, the number becomes still more appalling. At the dedication of the great temple of Huitzilopochtli, in 1486, the prisoners, who for some years had been reserved for the purpose, were drawn from all quarters to the capital. They were ranged in files, forming a procession nearly two miles long. The ceremony consumed several days, and seventy thousand captives are said to have perished at the shrine of this terrible deity! But who can believe that so numerous a body would have suffered themselves to be led, unresistingly, like sheep to the slaughter? Or how could their remains, too great for consumption in the ordinary way, be disposed of, without breeding a pestilence in the capital? Yet the event was of recent date, and is unequivocally attested by the best informed historians. One fact may be considered certain. It was customary to preserve the skulls of the sacrificed, in buildings appropriated to the purpose. The companions of Cortes counted one hundred and thirty-six thousand in one of these edifices! Without attempting a precise calculation, therefore, it is safe to conclude that thousands were yearly offered up, in the different cities of Anahuac, on the bloody altars of the Mexican divinities.

Indeed, the great object of war with the Aztecs was quite as much to gather victims for their sacrifices, as to extend their empire. Hence it was, that an enemy was never slain in battle, if there was a chance of taking him alive. To this circumstance the Spaniards repeatedly owed their preservation. When Montezuma was asked, "why he had suffered the republic of Tlascala to maintain her independence on his borders," he replied, "That she might furnish him with victims for his gods!" As the supply began to fail, the priests, the Dominicans of the New World, bellowed aloud for more, and urged on their superstitious sovereign by the denunciations of celestial wrath. Like the militant churchmen of Christendom in the Middle Ages, they mingled themselves in the ranks, and were conspicuous in the thickest of the fight, by their hideous aspects and frantic gestures. Strange, that in every country the most fiendish passions of the human heart have been those kindled in the name of religion!

The influence of these practices on the Aztec character was as disastrous as might have been expected. Familiarity with the bloody rites of sacrifice steeled the heart against human sympathy, and begat a thirst for carnage, like that excited in the Romans by the exhibitions of the circus. The perpetual recurrence of ceremonies, in which the people took part, associated religion with their most intimate concerns, and spread the gloom of superstition over the domestic hearth, until the character of the nation wore a grave and even melancholy aspect, which belongs to their descendants at the present day. The influence of the priesthood, of course, became unbounded. The sovereign thought himself honoured by being permitted to assist in the services of the temple. Far from limiting the authority of the priests to spiritual matters, he often surrendered his opinion to theirs, where they were least competent to give it. It was their opposition that prevented the final capitulation which would have saved the capital. The whole nation, from the peasant to the prince, bowed their necks to the worst kind of tyranny — that of a blind fanaticism.

Human sacrifice, however cruel, has nothing in it degrading to its victim. It may be rather said to ennoble him, by devoting him to the gods. Although so terrible with the Aztecs, it was sometimes voluntarily embraced by them, as the most glorious death, and one that opened a sure passage into paradise. The Inquisition, on the other hand, branded its victims with infamy in this world, and consigned them to everlasting perdition in the next.

One detestable feature of the Aztec superstition, however, sunk it far below the Christian. This was its cannibalism; though, in truth, the Mexicans were not cannibals, in the coarsest acceptation of the term. They did not feed on human flesh merely to gratify a brutish appetite, but in obedience to their religion. Their repasts were made of the victims whose blood had been poured out on the altar of sacrifice. This is a distinction worthy of notice. Still, cannibalism, under any form, or whatever sanction, cannot but have a fatal influence on the nation addicted to it. It suggests ideas so loathsome, so degrading to man, to his spiritual and immortal nature, that it is impossible the people who practise it should make any great progress in moral or intellectual culture. The Mexicans furnish no exception to this remark. The civilisation which they possessed descended from the Toltecs, a race who never stained their altars, still less their banquets, with the blood of man. All that deserved the name of science in Mexico came from this source; and the crumbling ruins of edifices, attributed to them, still extant in various parts of New Spain, show a decided superiority in their architecture over that of the later races of Anahuac. It is true, the Mexicans made great proficiency in many of the social and mechanic arts, in that material culture — if I may so call it — the natural growth of increasing opulence, which ministers to the gratification of the senses. In purely intellectual progress, they were behind the Tezcucans, whose wise sovereigns came into the abominable rites of their neighbours with reluctance, and practised them on a much more moderate scale.

IT is a relief to turn from the gloomy pages of the preceding chapter to a brighter side of the picture, and to contemplate the same nation in its generous struggle to raise itself from a state of barbarism, and to take a positive rank in the scale of civilisation. It is not the less interesting, that these efforts were made on an entirely new theatre of action, apart from those influences that operate in the Old World; the inhabitants of which, forming one great brotherhood of nations, are knit together by sympathies, that make the faintest spark of knowledge struck out in one quarter, spread gradually wider and wider, until it has diffused a cheering light over the remotest. It is curious to observe the human mind, in this new position, conforming to the same laws as on the ancient continent, and taking a similar direction in its first inquiries after truth — so similar, indeed, as, although not warranting, perhaps, the idea of imitation, to suggest, at least, that of a common origin.

In the eastern hemisphere, we find some nations, as the Greeks, for instance, early smitten with such a love of the beautiful as to be unwilling to dispense with it, even in the graver productions of science; and other nations, again, proposing a severer end to themselves, to which even imagination and elegant art were made subservient. The productions of such a people must be criticised, not by the ordinary rules of taste, but by their adaptation to the peculiar end for which they were designed. Such were the Egyptians in the Old World, and the Mexicans in the New. We have already had occasion to notice the resemblance borne by the latter nation to the former in their religious economy. We shall be more struck with it in their scientific culture, especially their hieroglyphical writing and their astronomy.

To describe actions and events by delineating visible objects, seems to be a natural suggestion, and is practised, after a certain fashion, by the rudest savages. The North American Indian carves an arrow on the bark of trees to show his followers the direction of his march, and some other sign to show the success of his expeditions. But to paint intelligibly a consecutive series of these actions — forming what Warburton has happily called picture-writing — requires a combination of ideas, that amounts to a positively intellectual effort. Yet further, when the object of the painter, instead of being limited to the present, is to penetrate the past, and to gather from its dark recesses lessons of instruction for coming generations, we see the dawnings of a literary culture, and recognise the proof of a decided civilisation in the attempt itself, however imperfectly it may be executed. The literal imitation of objects will not answer for this more complex and extended plan. It would occupy too much space, as well as time, in the execution. It then becomes necessary to abridge the pictures, to confine the drawing to outlines, or to such prominent parts of the bodies delineated, as may readily suggest the whole. This is the representative or figurative writing, which forms the lowest stage of hieroglyphics.

But there are things which have no type in the material world; abstract ideas, which can only be represented by visible objects supposed to have some quality analogous to the idea intended. This constitutes symbolical writing, the most difficult of all to the interpreter, since the analogy between the material and immaterial object is often purely fanciful, or local in its application. Who, for instance, could suspect the association which made a beetle represent the universe, as with the Egyptians, or a serpent typify time, as with the Aztecs?

The third and last division is the phonetic, in which signs are made to represent sounds, either entire words, or parts of them. This is the nearest approach of the hieroglyphical series to that beautiful invention, the alphabet, by which language is resolved into its elementary sounds, and an apparatus supplied for easily and accurately expressing the most delicate shades of thought.

The Egyptians were well skilled in all three kinds of hieroglyphics. But, although their public monuments display the first class, in their ordinary intercourse and written records, it is now certain that they almost wholly relied on the phonetic character. Strange, that having thus broken down the thin partition which divided them from an alphabet, their latest monuments should exhibit no nearer approach to it than their earliest. The Aztecs, also, were acquainted with the several varieties of hieroglyphics. But they relied on the figurative infinitely more than on the others. The Egyptians were at the top of the scale, the Aztecs at the bottom.

In casting the eye over a Mexican manuscript, or map, as it is called, one is struck with the grotesque caricatures it exhibits of the human figure; monstrous, overgrown heads, on puny misshapen bodies, which are themselves hard and angular in their outlines, and without the least skill in composition. On closer inspection, however, it is obvious that it is not so much a rude attempt to delineate nature, as a conventional symbol, to express the idea in the most clear and forcible manner; in the same way as the pieces of similar value on a chess-board, while they correspond with one another in form, bear little resemblance, usually, to the objects they represent. Those parts of the figure are most distinctly traced, which are the most important. So, also the colouring, instead of the delicate gradations of nature, exhibits only gaudy and violent contrasts, such as may produce the most vivid impression. "For even colours," as Gama observes, "speak in the Aztec hieroglyphics."

But in the execution of all this the Mexicans were much inferior to the Egyptians. The drawings of the latter, indeed, are exceedingly defective when criticised by the rules of art; for they were as ignorant of perspective as the Chinese, and only exhibited the head in profile, with the eye in the centre, and with total absence of expression. But they handled the pencil more gracefully than the Aztecs, were more true to the natural forms of objects, and, above all, showed great superiority in abridging the original figure by giving only the outlines, or some characteristic. or essential feature. This simplified the process, and facilitated the communication of thought. An Egyptian text has almost the appearance of alphabetical writing in its regular lines of minute figures. A Mexican text looks usually like a collection of pictures, each one forming the subject of a separate study. This is particularly the case with the delineations of mythology; in which the story is told by a conglomeration of symbols, that may remind one more of the mysterious anaglyphs sculptured on the temples of the Egyptians, than of their written records.

The Aztecs had various emblems for expressing such things as, from their nature, could not be directly represented by the painter; as, for example, the years, months, days, the seasons, the elements, the heavens, and the like. A "tongue" denoted speaking; a "footprint," travelling; "a man sitting on the ground," an earthquake. These symbols were often very arbitrary, varying with the caprice of the writer; and it requires a nice discrimination to interpret them, as a slight change in the form or position of the figure intimated a very different meaning. An ingenious writer asserts, that the priests devised secret symbolic characters for the record of their religious mysteries. It is possible. But the researches of Champollion lead to the conclusion, that the similar opinion, formerly entertained respecting the Egyptian hieroglyphics, is without foundation.

Lastly, they employed, as above stated, phonetic signs, though these were chiefly confined to the names of persons and places; which, being derived from some circumstance, or characteristic quality, were accommodated to the hieroglyphical system. Thus the town Cimatlan was compounded of cimatl, a "root," which grew near it, and tlan, signifying "near"; Tlaxcallan meant "the place of bread," from its rich fields of corn; Huexotzinco, "a place surrounded by willows." The names of persons were often significant of their adventures and achievements. That of the great Tezcucan prince, Nezahualcoyotl, signified "hungry fox," intimating his sagacity, and his distresses in early life. The emblems of such names were no sooner seen, than they suggested to every Mexican the person and place intended; and, when painted on their shields, or embroidered on their banners, became the armorial bearings by which city and chieftain were distinguished, as in Europe, in the age of chivalry.

But, although the Aztecs were instructed in all the varieties of hieroglyphical painting, they chiefly resorted to the clumsy method of direct representation. Had their empire lasted, like the Egyptian, several thousand, instead of the brief space of two hundred, years, they would, doubtless, like them, have advanced to the more frequent use of the phonetic writing. But, before they could be made acquainted with the capabilities of their own system, the Spanish Conquest, by introducing the European alphabet, supplied their scholars with a more perfect contrivance for expressing thought, which soon supplanted the ancient pictorial character.

Clumsy as it was, however, the Aztec picture-writing seems to have been adequate to the demands of the nation, in their imperfect state of civilisation. By means of it were recorded all their laws, and even their regulations for domestic economy; their tribute-rolls, specifying the imposts of the various towns; their mythology, calendars, and rituals; their political annals, carried back to a period long before the foundation of the city. They digested a complete system of chronology, and could specify with accuracy the dates of the most important events in their history; the year being inscribed on the margin, against the particular circumstance recorded. It is true, history, thus executed, must necessarily be vague and fragmentary. Only a few leading incidents could be presented. But in this it did not differ much from the monkish chronicles of the dark ages, which often dispose of years in a few brief sentences; quite long enough for the annals of barbarians.

In order to estimate aright the picture-writing of the Aztecs, one must regard it in connection with oral tradition, to which it was auxiliary. In the colleges of the priests the youth were instructed in astronomy, history, mythology, etc.; and those who were to follow the profession of hieroglyphical painting were taught the application of the characters appropriated to each of these branches. In an historical work, one had charge of the chronology, another of the events. Every part of the labour was thus mechanically distributed. The pupils, instructed in all that was before known in their several departments, were prepared to extend still further the boundaries of their imperfect science. The hieroglyphics served as a sort of stenography, a collection of notes, suggesting to the initiated much more than could be conveyed by a literal interpretation. This combination of the written and the oral comprehended what may be called the literature of the Aztecs.

Their manuscripts were made of different materials — of cotton cloth, or skins nicely prepared; of a composition of silk and gum; but, for the most part, of a fine fabric from the leaves of the aloe, agave Americana, called by the natives, maguey, which grows luxuriantly over the tablelands of Mexico. A sort of paper was made from it, resembling somewhat the Egyptian papyrus, which, when properly dressed and polished, is said to have been more soft and beautiful than parchment. Some of the specimens, still existing, exhibit their original freshness, and the paintings on them retain their brilliancy of colours. They were sometimes done up into rolls, but more frequently into volumes of moderate size, in which the paper was shut up, like a folding-screen, with a leaf or tablet of wood at each extremity, that gave the whole, when closed, the appearance of a book. The length of the strips was determined only by convenience. As the pages might be read and referred to separately, this form had obvious advantages over the rolls of the ancients.

At the time of the arrival of the Spaniards, great quantities of these manuscripts were treasured up in the country. Numerous persons were employed in painting, and the dexterity of their operations excited the astonishment of the conquerors. Unfortunately, this was mingled with other, and unworthy feelings. The strange, unknown characters inscribed on them excited suspicion. They were looked on as magic scrolls; and were regarded in the same light with the idols and temples, as the symbols of a pestilent superstition that must be extirpated. The first archbishop of Mexico, Don Juan de Zumarraga — a name that should be as immortal as that of Omar — collected these paintings from every quarter, especially from Tezcuco, the most cultivated capital in Anahuac, and the great depository of the national archives. He then caused them to be piled up in a "mountain-heap,"— as it is called by the Spanish writers themselves — and reduced them all to ashes! His greater countryman, Archbishop Ximenes, had celebrated a similar auto-dafe of Arabic manuscripts, in Granada, some twenty years before. Never did fanaticism achieve two more signal triumphs, than by the annihilation of so many curious monuments of human ingenuity and learning!

The unlettered soldiers were not slow in imitating the example of their prelate. Every chart and volume which fell into their hands was wantonly destroyed; so that, when the scholars of a later and more enlightened age anxiously sought to recover some of these memorials of civilisation, nearly all had perished, and the few surviving were jealously hidden by the natives. Through the indefatigable labours of a private individual, however, a considerable collection was eventually deposited in the archives of Mexico; but was so little heeded there, that some were plundered, others decayed piecemeal from the damps and mildews, and others, again, were used up as waste-paper! We contemplate with indignation the cruelties inflicted by the early conquerors. But indignation is qualified with contempt, when we see them thus ruthlessly trampling out the spark of knowledge, the common boon and property of all mankind. We may well doubt, which has the strongest claims to civilisation, the victor or the vanquished.

A few of the Mexican manuscripts have found their way, from time to time, to Europe, and are carefully preserved in the public libraries of its capitals. They are brought together in the magnificent work of Lord Kingsborough; but not one is there from Spain. The most important of them, for the light in throws on the Aztec institutions, is the Mendoza Codex; which, after its mysterious disappearance for more than a century, has at length re-appeared in the Bodleian library at Oxford. It has been several times engraved. The most brilliant in colouring, probably, is the Borgian collection, in Rome. The most curious, however, is the Dresden Codex, which has excited less attention than it deserves. Although usually classed among Mexican manuscripts, it bears little resemblance to them in its execution; the figures of objects are more delicately drawn, and the characters, unlike the Mexican, appear to be purely arbitrary, and are possibly phonetic. Their regular arrangement is quite equal to the Egyptian. The whole infers a much higher civilisation than the Aztec, and offers abundant food for curious speculation.

Some few of these maps have interpretations annexed to them, which were obtained from the natives after the Conquest. The greater part are without any, and cannot now be unriddled. Had the Mexicans made free use of a phonetic alphabet, it might have been originally easy, by mastering the comparatively few signs employed in this kind of communication, to have got a permanent key to the whole. A brief inscription has furnished a clue to the vast labyrinth of Egyptian hieroglyphics. But the Aztec characters, representing individuals, or at most, species, require to be made out separately; a hopeless task, for which little aid is to be expected from the vague and general tenor of the few interpretations now existing. In less than a hundred years after the Conquest, the knowledge of the hieroglyphics had so far declined, that a diligent Tezcucan writer complains he could find in the country only two persons, both very aged, at all competent to interpret them.

It is not probable, therefore, that the art of reading these picture-writings will ever be recovered; a circumstance certainly to be regretted. Not that the records of a semi-civilised people would be likely to contain any new truth or discovery important to human comfort or progress; but they could scarcely fail to throw some additional light on the previous history of the nation, and that of the more polished people who before occupied the country. This would be still more probable, if any literary relics of their Toltec predecessors were preserved; and, if report be true, an important compilation from this source was extant at the time of the invasion, and may have perhaps contributed to swell the holocaust of Zumarraga. It is no great stretch of fancy, to suppose that such records might reveal the successive links in the mighty chain of migration of the primitive races, and, by carrying us back to the seat of their possessions in the Old World, have solved the mystery which has so long perplexed the learned, in regard to the settlement and civilisation of the New.

Besides the hieroglyphical maps, the traditions of the country were embodied in the songs and hymns, which, as already mentioned, were carefully taught in the public schools. These were various, embracing the mythic legends of a heroic age, the warlike achievements of their own, or the softer tales of love and pleasure. Many of them were composed by scholars and persons of rank, and are cited as affording the most authentic record of events. The Mexican dialect was rich and expressive, though inferior to the Tezcucan, the most polished of the idioms of Anahuac. None of the Aztec compositions have survived, but we can form some estimate of the general state of poetic culture from the odes which have come down to us from the royal house of Tezcuco. Sahagun has furnished us with translations of their more elaborate prose, consisting of prayers and public discourses, which give a favourable idea of their eloquence, and show that they paid much attention to rhetorical effect. They are said to have had, also, something like theatrical exhibitions, of a pantomimic sort, in which the faces of the performers were covered with masks, and the figures of birds or animals were frequently represented; an imitation to which they may have been led by the familiar delineation of such objects in their hieroglyphics. In all this we see the dawning of a literary culture, surpassed, however, by their attainments in the severer walks of mathematical science.

They devised a system of notation in their arithmetic, sufficiently simple. The first twenty numbers were expressed by a corresponding number of dots. The first five had specific names; after which they were represented by combining the fifth with one of the four preceding: as five and one for six, five and two for seven, and so on. Ten and fifteen had each a separate name, which was also combined with the first four, to express a higher quantity. These four, therefore, were the radical characters of their oral arithmetic, in the same manner as they were of the written with the ancient Romans; a more simple arrangement, probably, than any existing among Europeans. Twenty was expressed by a separate hieroglyphic — a flag. Larger sums were reckoned by twenties, and, in writing, by repeating the number of flags. The square of twenty, four hundred, had a separate sign, that of a plume, and so had the cube of twenty, or eight thousand, which was denoted by a purse, or sack. This was the whole arithmetical apparatus of the Mexicans, by the combination of which they were enabled to indicate any quantity. For greater expedition, they used to denote fractions of the larger sums by drawing only a part of the object. Thus, half or three-fourths of a plume, or of a purse, represented that proportion of their respective sums, and so on. With all this, the machinery will appear very awkward to us, who perform our operations with so much ease by means of the Arabic, or rather, Indian ciphers. It is not much more awkward, however, than the system pursued by the great mathematicians of antiquity unacquainted with the brilliant invention which has given a new aspect to mathematical science, of determining the value, in a great measure, by the relative position of the figures.

In the measurement of time, the Aztecs adjusted their civil year by the solar. They divided it into eighteen months of twenty days each. Both months and days were expressed by peculiar hieroglyphics — those of the former often intimating the season of the year, like the French months, at the period of the Revolution. Five complementary days, as in Egypt, were added, to make up the full number of three hundred and sixty-five. They belonged to no month, and were regarded as peculiarly unlucky. A month was divided into four weeks, of five days each, on the last of which was the public fair or market day. This arrangement, different from that of the nations of the Old Continent, whether of Europe or Asia, has the advantage of giving an equal number of days to each month, and of comprehending entire weeks, without a fraction, both in the months and in the year.

As the year is composed of nearly six hours more than three hundred and sixty-five days, there still remained an excess, which, like other nations who have framed a calendar, they provided for by intercalation; not, indeed, every fourth year, as the Europeans, but at longer intervals, like some of the Asiatics. They waited till the expiration of fifty-two vague years, when they interposed thirteen days, or rather twelve and a half, this being the number which had fallen in arrear. Had they inserted thirteen, it would have been too much, since the annual excess over three hundred and sixty-five is about eleven minutes less than six hours. But, as their calendar, at the time of the Conquest, was found to correspond with the European (making allowance for the subsequent Gregorian reform), they would seem to have adopted the shorter period of twelve days and a half, which brought them, within an almost inappreciable fraction, to the exact length of the tropical year, as established by the most accurate observations. Indeed, the intercalation of twenty-five days, in every hundred and four years, shows a nicer adjustment of civil to solar time than is presented by any European calendar; since more than five centuries must elapse, before the loss of an entire day. Such was the astonishing precision displayed by the Aztecs, or, perhaps, by their more polished Toltec predecessors, in these computations, so difficult as to have baffled, till a comparatively recent period, the most enlightened nations of Christendom!

The chronological system of the Mexicans, by which they determined the date of any particular event, was also very remarkable. The epoch, from which they reckoned, corresponded with the year 1091, of the Christian era. It was the period of the reform of their calendar, soon after their migration from Aztlan. They threw the years, as already noticed, into great cycles, of fifty-two each, which they called "sheafs," or "bundles," and represented by a quantity of reeds bound together by a string. As often as this hieroglyphic occurs in their maps, it shows the number of half centuries. To enable them to specify any particular year, they divided the great cycle into four smaller cycles, or indictions, of thirteen years each. They then adopted two periodical series of signs, one consisting of their numerical dots up to thirteen, the other, of four hieroglyphics of the years. These latter they repeated in regular succession, setting against each one a number of the corresponding series of dots, continued also in regular succession up to thirteen. The same system was pursued through the four indictions, which thus, it will be observed, began always with a different hieroglyphic of the year from the preceding; and in this way, each of the hieroglyphics was made to combine successively with each of the numerical signs, but never twice with the same; since four, and thirteen, the factors of fifty-two — the number of years in the cycle — must admit of just as many combinations as are equal to their product. Thus every year had its appropriate symbol, by which it was, at once, recognised. And this symbol, preceded by the proper number of "bundles," indicating the half centuries, showed the precise time which had elapsed since the national epoch of 1091. The ingenious contrivance of a periodical series, in place of the cumbrous system of hieroglyphical notation, is not peculiar to the Aztecs, and is to be found among various people on the Asiatic continent — the same in principle, though varying materially in arrangement.

The solar calendar, above described, might have answered all the purposes of the nation; but the priests chose to construct another for themselves. This was called a "lunar reckoning," though nowise accommodated to the revolutions of the moon. It was formed, also, of two periodical series; one of them consisting of thirteen numerical signs, or dots, the other of the twenty hieroglyphics of the days. But, as the product of these combinations would only be 260, and, as some confusion might arise from the repetition of the same terms for the remaining 105 days of the year, they invented a third series, consisting of nine additional hieroglyphics, which, alternating with the two preceding series, rendered it impossible that the three should coincide twice in the same year, or indeed in less than 2340 days; since $20 \times 13 \times 9 = 2340$. Thirteen was a mystic number, of frequent use in their tables. Why they resorted to that of nine, on this occasion, is not so clear.

This second calendar rouses a holy indignation in the early Spanish missionaries, and Father Sahagun loudly condemns it as "most unhallowed, since it is founded neither on natural reason nor on the influence of the planets, nor on the true course of the year; but is plainly the work of necromancy, and the fruit of a compact with the Devil!" One may doubt, whether the superstition of those who invented the scheme was greater than that of those who impugned it. At all events, we may, without having recourse to supernatural agency, find in the human heart a sufficient explanation of its origin; in that love of power, that has led the priesthood of many a faith to affect a mystery, the key to which was in their own keeping.

Year of the Cycle.			Year of the Cycle.		
1.	.		14.	.	
2.	. .		15.	. .	
3.	. . . .		16.	. . .	
4.	. . . .		17.	. . . . .	
5.	. . . . . .		18.	. . . . . .	
6.	. . . .		19.	. . . .	
7.	. . . . . .		20.	. . . . . .	
8.	. . . .		21.	. . . .	
9.	. . . .		22.	. . . .	
10.	. . . .		23.	. . . .	
11.	. . . .		24.	. . . .	
12.	. . . .		25.	. . . .	
13.	. . . .		26.	. . . .	

By means of this calendar the Aztec priests kept their own records, regulated the festivals and seasons of sacrifice, and made all their astrological calculations. The astrological scheme of the Aztecs was founded less on the planetary influences than on those of the arbitrary signs they had adopted for the months and days. The character of the leading sign, in each lunar

26

cycle of thirteen days, gave a complexion to the whole; though this was qualified, in some degree, by the signs of the succeeding days, as well as by those of the hours. It was in adjusting these conflicting forces that the great art of the diviner was shown. In no country, not even in ancient Egypt, were the dreams of the astrologer more implicitly deferred to. On the birth of a child, he was instantly summoned. The time of the event was accurately ascertained; and the family hung in trembling suspense, as the minister of Heaven cast the horoscope of the infant, and unrolled the dark volume of destiny. The influence of the priest was confessed by the Mexican, in the very first breath which he inhaled.

We know little further of the astronomical attainments of the Aztecs. That they were acquainted with the cause of eclipses is evident from the representation on their maps, of the disk of the moon projected on that of the sun. Whether they had arranged a system of constellations, is uncertain; though, that they recognised some of the most obvious, as the Pleiades for example, is evident from the fact that they regulated their festivals by them. We know of no astronomical instruments used by them, except the dial. An immense circular block of carved stone, disinterred in 1790, in the great square of Mexico, has supplied an acute and learned scholar with the means of establishing some interesting facts in regard to Mexican science. This colossal fragment, on which the calendar is engraved, shows that they had the means of settling the hours of the day with precision, the periods of the solstices and of the equinoxes, and that of the transit of the sun across the zenith of Mexico.

We cannot contemplate the astronomical science of the Mexicans, so disproportioned to their progress in other walks of civilisation, without astonishment. An acquaintance with some of the more obvious principles of astronomy is within the reach of the rudest people. With a little care, they may learn to connect the regular. changes of the seasons with those of the place of the sun at his rising and setting. They may follow the march of the great luminary through the heavens, by watching the stars that first brighten on his evening track, or fade in his morning beams. They may measure a revolution of the moon by marking her phases, and may even form a general idea of the number of such revolutions in a solar year. But that they should be capable of accurately adjusting their festivals by the movements of the heavenly bodies, and should fix the true length of the tropical year, with a precision unknown to the great philosophers of antiquity, could be the result only of a long series of nice and patient observations, evincing no slight progress in civilisation. But whence could the rude inhabitants of these mountain regions have derived this curious erudition? Not from the barbarous hordes who roamed over the higher latitudes of the north; nor from the more polished races on the southern continent, with whom it is apparent they had no intercourse. If we are driven, in our embarrassment, like the greatest astronomer of our age, to seek the solution among the civilised communities of Asia, we shall still be perplexed by finding, amidst general resemblance of outline, sufficient discrepancy in the details, to vindicate, in the judgments Of many, the Aztec claim to originality.

I shall conclude the account of Mexican science with that of a remarkable festival, celebrated by the natives at the termination of the great cycle of fifty-two years. We have seen, in the preceding chapter, their traditions of the destruction of the world at four successive epochs. They looked forward confidently to another such catastrophe, to take place like the preceding, at the close of a cycle, when the sun was to be effaced from the heavens, the human race from the earth, and when the darkness of chaos was to settle on the habitable globe. The cycle would end in the latter part of December, and, as the dreary season of the winter solstice approached, and the diminished light of day gave melancholy presage of its speedy extinction, their apprehensions increased; and, on the arrival of the five "unlucky" days which closed the year, they abandoned themselves to despair. They broke in pieces the little images of their household gods, in whom they no longer trusted. The holy fires were suffered to go out in the temples, and none were lighted in their own dwellings. Their furniture and domestic utensils were destroyed; their garments torn in pieces; and everything was thrown into disorder, for the coming of the evil genii who were to descend on the desolate earth.

On the evening of the last day, a procession of priests, assuming the dress and ornaments of their gods, moved from the capital towards a lofty mountain about two leagues distant. They carried with them a noble victim, the flower of their captives, and an apparatus for kindling the new fire, the success of which was an augury of the renewal of the cycle. On reaching the summit of the mountain, the procession paused till midnight; when, as the constellation of the Pleiades approached the zenith, the new fire was kindled by the friction of the sticks placed on the wounded breast of the victim. The flame was soon communicated to a funeral pile, on which the body of the slaughtered captive was thrown. As the light streamed up towards heaven, shouts of joy and triumph burst forth from the countless multitudes who covered the hills, the terraces of the temples, and the house-tops, with eyes anxiously bent on the mount of sacrifice. Couriers, with torches lighted at the blazing beacon, rapidly bore them over every part of the country; and the cheering element was seen brightening on altar and hearthstone, for the circuit of many a league, long before the Sun, rising on his accustomed track, gave assurance that a new cycle had commenced its march, and that the laws of nature were not to be reversed.

The following thirteen days were given up to festivity. The houses were cleansed and whitened. The broken vessels were replaced by new ones. The people, dressed in their gayest apparel, and crowned with garlands and chaplets of flowers, thronged in joyous procession, to offer up their oblations and thanksgiving in the temples. Dances and games were instituted, emblematical of the regeneration of the world. It was the carnival of the Aztecs; or rather the national jubilee, the great secular festival, like that of the Romans, or ancient Etruscans, which few alive had witnessed before — or could expect to see again.

AGRICULTURE in Mexico was in the same advanced state as the other arts of social life. In few countries, indeed, has it been more respected. It was closely interwoven with the civil and religious institutions of the nation. There were peculiar deities to preside over it; the names of the months and of the religious festivals had more or less reference to it. The public taxes, as we have seen, were often paid in agricultural produce. All, except the soldiers and great nobles, even the inhabitants of the cities, cultivated the soil. The work was chiefly done by the men; the women scattering the seed, husking the corn, and taking part only in the lighter labours of the field.

There was no want of judgment in the management of their ground. When somewhat exhausted, it was permitted to recover by lying fallow. Its extreme dryness was relieved by canals, with which the land was partially irrigated; and the same end was promoted by severe penalties against the destruction of the woods, with which the country, as already noticed, was well covered before the Conquest. Lastly, they provided for their harvests ample granaries, which were admitted by the conquerors to be of admirable construction. In this provision we see the forecast of civilised man.

Amongst the most important articles of husbandry, we may notice the banana, whose facility of cultivation and exuberant returns are so fatal to habits of systematic and hardy industry. Another celebrated plant was the cacao, the fruit of which furnished the chocolate — from the Mexican chocolatl — now so common a beverage throughout Europe. The vanilla, confined to a small district of the sea-coast, was used for the same purposes, of flavouring their food and drink, as with us. The great staple of the country, as, indeed, of the American continent, was maize, or Indian corn, which grew freely along the valleys, and up the steep sides of the Cordilleras to the high level of the talbleland. The Aztecs were as curious in its preparation, and as well instructed in its manifold uses, as the most expert New England housewife. Its gigantic stalks, in these equinoctial regions, afford a saccharine matter, not found to the same extent in northern latitudes, and supplied the natives with sugar little inferior to that of the cane itself, which was not introduced among them till after the Conquest. But the miracle of nature was the great Mexican aloe, or maguey, whose clustering pyramid of flowers, towering above their dark coronals of leaves, were seen sprinkled over many a broad acre of the tableland. As we have already noticed, its bruised leaves afforded a paste from which paper was manufactured; its juice was fermented into an intoxicating beverage, pulque, of which the natives, to this day, are excessively fond; its leaves further supplied an impenetrable thatch for the more humble dwellings; thread, of which coarse stuffs were made, and strong cords, were drawn from its tough and twisted fibres; pins and needles were made of the thorns at the extremity of its leaves; and the root, when properly cooked, was converted into a palatable and nutritious food. The agave, in short, was meat, drink, clothing, and writing materials for the Aztec! Surely, never did Nature enclose in so compact a form so many of the elements of human comfort and civilisation!

It would be obviously out of place to enumerate in these pages all the varieties of Plants, many of them of medicinal virtue, which have been introduced from Mexico into Europe. Still less can I attempt a catalogue of its flowers, which, with their variegated and gaudy colours, form the greatest attraction of our greenhouses. The opposite climates embraced within the narrow latitudes of New Spain have given to it, probably, the richest and most diversified Flora to be found in any country on the globe. These different products were systematically arranged by the Aztecs, who understood their properties, and collected them into nurseries, more extensive than any then existing in the Old World. It is not improbable that they suggested the idea of those "gardens of plants" which were introduced into Europe not many years after the Conquest.

The Mexicans were as well acquainted with the mineral, as with the vegetable treasures of their kingdom. Silver, lead, and, tin they drew from the mines of Tasco; copper from the mountains of Zacotollan. These were taken, not only from the crude masses on the surface, but from veins wrought in the solid rock, into which they opened extensive galleries. In fact, the traces of their labours furnished the best indications for the early Spanish miners. Gold, found on the surface, or gleaned from the beds of rivers, was cast into bars, or, in the form of dust, made part of the regular tribute of the southern provinces of the empire. The use of iron, with which the soil was impregnated, was unknown to them. Notwithstanding its abundance, it demands so many processes to prepare it for use, that it has commonly been one of the last metals pressed into the service of man. The age of iron has followed that of brass, in fact as well as in fiction.

They found a substitute in an alloy of tin and copper; and, with tools made of this bronze, could cut not only metals, but, with the aid of a siliceous dust, the hardest substances, as basalt, porphyry, amethysts, and emeralds. They fashioned these last, which were found very large, into many curious and fantastic forms. They cast, also, vessels of gold and silver, carving them with their metallic chisels in a very delicate manner. Some of the silver vases were so large, that a man could not encircle them with his arms. They imitated very nicely the figures of animals, and, what was extraordinary, could mix the metals in such a manner, that the feathers of a bird, or the scales of a fish, should be alternately of gold and silver. The Spanish goldsmiths admitted their superiority over themselves in these ingenious works.

They employed another tool, made of itztli, or obsidian, a dark transparent mineral, exceedingly hard, found in abundance in their hills. They made it into knives, razors, and their serrated swords. It took a keen edge, though soon blunted. With this they wrought the various stones and alabasters employed in the construction of their public works and principal dwellings. I shall defer a more particular account of these to the body of the narrative, and will only add here, that the entrances and angles of the buildings were profusely ornamented with images, sometimes of their fantastic deities, and frequently of animals. The latter were executed with great accuracy. "The former," according to Torquemada, "were the hideous reflection of their own souls. And it was not till after they had been converted to Christianity, that they could model the true figure of a man." The old chronicler's facts are well founded, whatever we may think of his reasons. The allegorical phantasms of his religion, no doubt, gave a direction to the Aztec artist, in his delineation of the human figure; supplying him with an imaginary beauty in the personification of divinity, itself. As these superstitions lost their hold on his mind, it opened to the influences of a purer taste; and, after the Conquest, the Mexicans furnished many examples of correct, and some of beautiful portraiture.

Sculptured images were so numerous, that the foundations of the cathedral in the Plaza Mayor, the great square of Mexico, are said to be entirely composed of them. This spot may, indeed, be regarded as the Aztec forum — the great depository of the treasures of ancient sculpture, which now he hid in its bosom. Such monuments are spread all over the capital, however, and a new cellar can hardly be dug, or foundation laid, without turning up some of the mouldering relics of barbaric art. But they are little heeded, and, if not wantonly broken in pieces at once, are usually worked into the rising wall, or supports of the new edifice! Two celebrated bas-reliefs of the last Montezuma and his father, cut in the solid rock in the beautiful groves of Chapoltepec, were deliberately destroyed, as late as the last century, by order of the government! The monuments of the barbarian meet with as little respect from civilised man, as those of the civilised man from the barbarian.

The most remarkable piece of sculpture yet disinterred is the great calendar stone, noticed in the preceding chapter. It consists of dark porphyry, and in its original dimensions, as taken from the quarry, is computed to have weighed nearly fifty tons. It was transported from the mountains beyond Lake Chalco, a distance of many leagues, over a broken country intersected by water-courses and canals. In crossing a bridge which traversed one of these latter, in the capital, the supports gave way, and the huge mass was precipitated into the water, whence it was with difficulty recovered. The fact, that so enormous a fragment of porphyry could be thus safely carried for leagues, in the face of such obstacles, and without the aid of cattle — for the Aztecs had no animals of draught — suggests to us no mean ideas of their mechanical skill, and of their machinery; and implies a degree of cultivation little inferior to that demanded for the geometrical and astronomical science displayed in the inscriptions on this very stone.

The ancient Mexicans made utensils of earthenware for the ordinary purposes of domestic life, numerous specimens of which still exist. They made cups and vases of a lackered or painted wood, impervious to wet, and gaudily coloured. Their dyes were obtained from both mineral and vegetable substances. Among them was the rich crimson of the cochineal, the modern rival of the famed Tyrian purple. It was introduced into Europe from Mexico, where the curious little insect was nourished with great care on plantations of cactus, since fallen into neglect. The natives were thus enabled to give a brilliant colouring to the webs, which were manufactured of every degree of fineness from the cotton raised in abundance throughout the warmer regions of the country. They had the art, also, of interweaving with these the delicate hair of rabbits and other animals, which made a cloth of great warmth as well as beauty, of a kind altogether original; and on this they often laid a rich embroidery of birds, flowers, or some other fanciful device.

But the art in which they most delighted was their plumaje, or feather-work. With this they could produce all the effect of a beautiful mosaic. The gorgeous plumage of the tropical birds, especially of the parrot tribe, afforded every variety of colour; and the fine down of the humming-bird, which revelled in swarms among the honeysuckle bowers of Mexico, supplied them with soft aerial tints that gave an exquisite finish to the picture. The feathers, pasted on a fine cotton web, were wrought into dresses for the wealthy, hangings for apartments, and ornaments for the temples. No one of the American fabries excited such admiration in Europe, whither numerous specimens were sent by the Conquerors. It is to be regretted that so graceful an art should have been suffered to fall into decay.

There were no shops in Mexico, but the various manufactures and agricultural products were brought together for sale in the great market-places of the principal cities. Fairs were held there every fifth day, and were thronged by a numerous concourse of persons, who came to buy or sell from all the neighbouring country. A particular quarter was allotted to each kind of article. The numerous transactions were conducted without confusion, and with entire regard to justice, under the inspection of magistrates appointed for the purpose. The traffic was carried on partly by barter, and partly by means of a regulated currency, of different values. This consisted of transparent quills of gold dust; of bits of tin, cut in the form of a T; and of bags of cacao, containing a specified number of grains. "Blessed money," exclaims Peter Martyr, "which exempts its possessors from avarice, since it cannot be long hoarded, nor hidden under ground!"

There did not exist in Mexico that distinction of castes found among the Egyptian and Asiatic nations. It was usual, however, for the son to follow the occupation of his father. The different trades were arranged into something like guilds; having each a particular district of the city appropriated to it, with its own chief, its own tutelar deity, its peculiar festivals, and the like. Trade was held in avowed estimation by the Aztecs. "Apply thyself, my son," was the advice of an aged chief, "to agriculture, or to feather-work, or some other honourable calling. Thus did your ancestors before you. Else, how would they have provided for themselves and their families? Never was it heard, that nobility alone was able to maintain its possessor." Shrewd maxims, that must have sounded somewhat strange in the ear of a Spanish hidalgo!

But the occupation peculiarly respected was that of the merchant. It formed so important and singular a feature of their social economy, as to merit a much more particular notice than it has received from historians. The Aztec merchant was a sort of itinerant trader, who made his journeys to the remotest borders of Anahuac, and to the countries beyond, carrying with him merchandise of rich stuffs, jewelry, slaves, and other valuable commodities. The slaves were obtained at the great market of Azcapotzalco, not many leagues from the capital, where fairs were regularly held for the sale of these unfortunate beings. They were brought thither by their masters, dressed in their gayest apparel, and instructed to sing, dance, and display their little stock of personal accomplishments, so as to recommend themselves to the purchaser. Slave-dealing was an honourable calling among the Aztecs.

With this rich freight, the merchant visited the different provinces, always bearing some present of value from his own sovereign to their chiefs, and usually receiving others in return, with a permission to trade. Should this be denied him, or should he meet with indignity or violence, he had the means of resistance in his power. He performed his journeys with a number of companions of his own rank, and a large body of inferior attendants who were employed to transport the goods. Fifty or sixty pounds were the usual load for a man. The whole caravan went armed, and so well provided against sudden hostilities, that they could make good their defence, if necessary, till reinforced from home. In one instance, a body of these militant traders stood a siege of four years in the town of Ayotlan, which they finally took from the enemy. Their own government, however, was always prompt to embark in a war on this ground, finding it a very convenient pretext for extending the Mexican empire. It was not unusual to allow the merchants to raise levies themselves, which were placed under their command. It was, moreover, very common for the prince to employ the merchants as a sort of spies, to furnish him information of the state of the countries through which they passed, and the dispositions of the inhabitants towards himself.

Thus their sphere of action was much enlarged beyond that of a humble trader, and they acquired a high consideration in the body politic. They were allowed to assume insignia and devices of their own. Some of their number composed what is called by the Spanish writers a council of finance; at least, this was the case in Tezcuco. They were much consulted by the monarch, who had some of them constantly near his person; addressing them by the title of "uncle," which may remind one of that primo, or "cousin," by which a grandee of Spain is saluted by his sovereign. They were allowed to have their own courts, in which civil and criminal cases, not excepting capital, were determined; so that they formed an independent community, as it were, of themselves. And, as their various traffic supplied them with abundant stores of wealth, they enjoyed many of the most essential advantages of an hereditary aristocracy.

That trade should prove the path to eminent political preferment in a nation but partially civilised, where the names of soldier and priest are usually the only titles to respect, is certainly an anomaly in history. It forms some contrast to the standard of the more polished monarchies of the Old World, in which rank is supposed to be less dishonoured by a life of idle ease or frivolous pleasure, than by those active pursuits which promote equally the prosperity of the state and of the individual. If civilisation corrects many prejudices, it must be allowed that it creates others.

We shall be able to form a better idea of the actual refinement of the natives, by penetrating into their domestic life, and observing the intercourse between the sexes. We have fortunately the means of doing this. We shall there find the ferocious Aztec frequently displaying all the sensibility of a cultivated nature; consoling his friends under affliction, or congratulating them on their good fortune, as on occasion of a marriage, or of the birth or the baptism of a child, when he was punctilious in his visits, bringing presents of costly dresses and ornaments, or the more simple offering of flowers, equally indicative of his sympathy. The visits, at these times, though regulated with all the precision of Oriental courtesy, were accompanied by expressions of the most cordial and affectionate regard.

The discipline of children, especially at the public schools, as stated in a previous chapter, was exceedingly severe. But after she had come to a mature age, the Aztec maiden was treated by her parents with a tenderness from which all reserve seemed banished. In the counsels to a daughter about to enter into life, they conjured her to preserve simplicity in her manners and conversation, uniform neatness in her attire, with strict attention to personal cleanliness. They inculcated modesty as the great ornament of a woman, and implicit reverence for her husband; softening their admonitions by such endearing epithets, as showed the fulness of a parent's love.

Polygamy was permitted among the Mexicans, though chiefly confined, probably, to the wealthiest classes. And the obligations of the marriage vow, which was made with all the formality of a religious ceremony, were fully recognised, and impressed on both parties. The women are described by the Spaniards as pretty, unlike their unfortunate descendants of the present day, though with the same serious and rather melancholy cast of countenance. Their long black hair, covered, in some parts of the country, by a veil made of the fine web of the pita, might generally be seen wreathed with flowers, or among the richer people, with strings of precious stones, and pearls from the Gulf of California. They appear to have been treated with much consideration by their husbands; and passed their time in indolent tranquillity, or in such feminine occupations as spinning, embroidery and the like; while their maidens beguiled the hours by the rehearsal of traditionary tales and ballads.

The woman partook equally with the men of social festivities and entertainments. These were often conducted on a large scale, both as regards the number of guests and the costliness of the preparations. Numerous attendants, of both sexes, waited at the banquet. The halls were scented with perfumes, and the courts strewed with odoriferous herb and flowers, which were distributed in profusion among the guests, as they arrived. Cotton napkins and ewers of water were placed before them, as they took their seats at the board; for the venerable ceremony of ablution, before and after eating, was punctiliously observed by the Aztecs. Tobacco was then offered to the company, in pipes, mixed up with aromatic substances, or in the form of cigars, inserted in tubes of tortoise-shell or silver. They compressed the nostrils with the fingers, while they inhaled the smoke, which they frequently swallowed. Whether the women, who sat apart from the men at table, were allowed the indulgence of the fragrant weed as in the most polished circles of modern Mexico, is not told us. It is a curious fact, that the Aztecs also took the dried leaf in the pulverised form of snuff.

The table was well provided with substantial meats, especially game; among which the most conspicuous was the turkey, erroneously supposed, as its name imports, to have come originally from the East. These more solid dishes were flanked by others of vegetables and fruits, of every delicious variety found on the North American continent. The different viands were prepared in various ways, with delicate sauces and seasoning, of which the Mexicans were very fond. Their palate was still further regaled by confections and pastry, for which their maize-flour and sugar supplied ample materials. One other dish, of a disgusting nature, was sometimes added to the feast, especially when the celebration partook of a religious character. On such occasions a slave was sacrificed, and his flesh elaborately dressed, formed one of the chief ornaments of the banquet. Cannibalism, in the guise of an Epicurean science, becomes even the more revolting.

The meats were kept warm by chafing-dishes. The table was ornamented with vases of silver, and sometimes gold, of delicate workmanship. The drinking-cups and spoons were of the same costly materials, and likewise of tortoise-shell. The favourite beverage was the chocolatl, flavoured with vanilla and different spices. They had a way of preparing the froth of it, so as to make it almost solid enough to be eaten, and took it cold. The fermented juice of the maguey, with a mixture of sweets and acids, supplied also various agreeable drinks of different degrees of strength, and formed the chief beverage of the elder part of the company.

As soon as they had finished their repast, the young people rose from the table, to close the festivities of the day with dancing. They danced gracefully, to the sound of various instruments, accompanying their movements with chants of a pleasing, though somewhat plaintive character. The older guests continued at table, sipping pulque, and gossiping about other times, till the virtues of the exhilarating beverage put them in good humour with their own. Intoxication was not rare in this part of the company, and, what is singular, was excused in them, though severely punished in the younger.

The Aztec character was perfectly original and unique. It was made up of incongruities apparently irreconcilable. It blended into one the marked peculiarities of different nations, not only of the same place of civilisation, but as far removed from each other as the extremes of barbarism and refinement. It may find a fitting parallel in their own wonderful climate, capable of producing, on a few square leagues of surface, the boundless variety of vegetable forms which belong to the frozen regions of the North, the temperate zone of Europe, and the burning skies of Arabia and Hindostan!

THE reader would gather but an imperfect notion of the civilisation of Anahuac, without some account of the Acolhuans, or Tezcucans, as they are usually cared; a nation of the same great family with the Aztecs, whom they rivalled in power, and surpassed in intellectual culture and the arts of social refinement. Fortunately, we have ample materials for this in the records left by Ixtlilxochitl, a lineal descendant of the royal line of Tezcuco, who flourished in the century of the Conquest. With every opportunity for information he combined much industry and talent, and, if his narrative bears the high colouring of one who would revive the faded glories of an ancient, but dilapidated house, he has been uniformly commended for his fairness and integrity, and has been followed without misgiving by such Spanish writers as could have access to his manuscripts. I shall confine myself to the prominent features of the two reigns which may be said to embrace the golden age of Tezcuco; without attempting to weigh the probability of the details, which I will leave to be settled by the reader, according to the measure of his faith.

The Acolhuans came into the Valley, as we have seen, about the close of the twelfth century, and built their capital of Tezcuco on the eastern borders of the lake, opposite to Mexico. From this point they gradually spread themselves over the northern portion of Anahuac, when their career was cheeked by an invasion of a kindred race, the Tepanecs, who, after a desperate struggle, succeeded in taking their city, slaying their monarch, and entirely subjugating his kingdom. This event took place about 1418; and the young prince, Nezahualcoyotl, the heir to the crown, then fifteen years old, saw his father butchered before his eyes, while he himself lay concealed among the friendly branches of a tree, which overshadowed the spot. His subsequent history is full of romantic daring and perilous escapes.

Not long after his flight from the field of his father's blood, the Tezcucan prince fell into the hands of his enemy, was borne off in triumph to his city, and was thrown into a dungeon. He effected his escape, however, through the connivance of the governor of the fortress, an old servant of his family, who took the place of the royal fugitive, and paid for his loyalty with his life. He was at length permitted, through the intercession of the reigning family in Mexico, which was allied to him, to retire to that capital, and subsequently to his own, where he found a shelter in his ancestral palace. Here he remained unmolested for eight years, pursuing his studies under an old preceptor, who had had the care of his early youth, and who instructed him in the various duties befitting his princely station.

At the end of this period the Tepanec usurper died, bequeathing his empire to his son, Maxtla, a man of fierce and suspicious temper. Nezahualcoyotl hastened to pay his obeisance to him, on his accession. But the tyrant refused to receive the little present of flowers which he laid at his feet, and turned his back on him in presence of his chieftains. One of his attendants, friendly to the young prince, admonished him to provide for his own safety, by withdrawing, as speedily as possible, from the palace, where his life was in danger. He lost no time, consequently, in retreating from the inhospitable court, and returned to Tezcuco. Maxtla, however, was bent on his destruction. He saw with jealous eye the opening talents and popular manners of his rival, and the favour he was daily winning from his ancient subjects.

He accordingly laid a plan for making away with him at an evening entertainment. It was defeated by the vigilance of the prince's tutor, who contrived to mislead the assassins, and to substitute another victim in the place of his pupil. The baffled tyrant now threw off all disguise, and sent a strong party of soldiers to Tezcuco, with orders to enter the palace, seize the person of Nezahualcoyotl, and slay him on the spot. The prince, who became acquainted with the plot through the watchfulness of his preceptor, instead of flying, as he was counselled, resolved to await his enemy. They found him playing at ball, when they arrived, in the court of his palace. He received them courteously and invited them in, to take some refreshments after their journey. While they were occupied in this way, he passed into an adjoining saloon, which excited no suspicion, as he was still visible through the open doors by which the apartments communicated with each other. A burning censer stood in the passage, and, as it was fed by the attendants, threw up such clouds of incense as obscured his movements from the soldiers. Under this friendly veil he succeeded in making his escape by a secret passage, which communicated with a large earthen pipe formerly used to bring water to the palace. Here he remained till nightfall, when, taking advantage of the obscurity, he found his way into the suburbs, and sought a shelter in the cottage of one of his father's vassals.

The Tepanec monarch, enraged at this repeated disappointment, ordered instant pursuit. A price was set on the head of the royal fugitive. Whoever should take him, dead or alive, was promised, however humble his degree, the hand of a noble lady, and an ample domain along with it. Troops of armed men were ordered to scour the country in every direction. In the course of the search, the cottage in which the prince had taken refuge was entered. But he fortunately escaped detection by being hid under a heap of maguey fibres used for manufacturing cloth. As this was no longer a proper place for concealment, he sought a retreat in the mountainous and woody district lying between the borders of his own state and Tlascala.

Here he led a wretched wandering life, exposed to all the inclemencies of the weather, hiding himself in deep thickets and caverns, and stealing out at night to satisfy the cravings of appetite; while he was kept in constant alarm by the activity of his pursuers, always hovering on his track. On one occasion he sought refuge from them among a small party of soldiers, who proved friendly to him, and concealed him in a large drum around which they were dancing. At another time, he was just able to turn the crest of a hill, as his enemies were climbing it on the other side, when he fell in with a girl who was reaping chian — a Mexican plant, the seed of which was much used in the drinks of the country. He persuaded her to cover him up with the stalks she had been cutting. When his pursuers came up, and inquired if she had seen the fugitive, the girl coolly answered that she had, and pointed out a path as the one he had taken. Notwithstanding the high rewards offered, Nezahualcoyotl seems to have incurred no danger from treachery, such was the general attachment felt to himself and his house. "Would you not deliver up the prince, if he came in your way?" he inquired of a young peasant who was unacquainted with his person. "Not I," replied the other. "What, not for a fair lady's hand, and a rich dowry beside?" rejoined the prince. At which the other only shook his head and laughed. On more than one occasion, his faithful people submitted to torture, and even to lose their lives, rather than disclose the place of his retreat.

However gratifying such proofs of loyalty might be to his feelings, the situation of the prince in these mountain solitudes became every day more distressing. It gave a still keener edge to his own sufferings to witness those of the faithful followers who chose to accompany him in his wanderings. "Leave me," he would say to them, "to my fate! Why should you throw away your own lives for one whom fortune is never weary of persecuting?" Most of the great Tezcucan chiefs had consulted their interests by a timely adhesion to the usurper. But some still clung to their prince, preferring proscription, and death itself, rather than desert him in his extremity.

In the meantime, his friends at a distance were active in measures for his relief. The oppressions of Maxtla, and his growing empire, had caused general alarm in the surrounding states, who recalled the mild rule of the Tezcucan princes. A coalition was formed, a plan of operations concerted, and, on the day appointed for a general rising, Nezahualcoyotl found himself at the head of a force sufficiently strong to face his Tepanec adversaries. An engagement came on, in which the latter were totally discomfited; and the victorious prince, receiving everywhere on his route the homage of his joyful subjects, entered his capital, not like a proscribed outcast, but as the rightful heir, and saw himself once more enthroned in the halls of his fathers.

Soon after, he united his forces with the Mexicans, long disgusted with the arbitrary conduct of Maxtla. The allied powers, after a series of bloody engagements with the usurper, routed him under the walls of his own capital. He fled to the baths, whence he was dragged out, and sacrificed with the usual cruel ceremonies of the Aztecs; the royal city of Azcapotzalco was razed to the ground, and the wasted territory was henceforth reserved as the great slavemarket for the nations of Anahuac. These events were succeeded by the remarkable league among the three powers of Tezcuco, Mexico, and Tlacopan, of which some account has been given in a previous chapter.

The first measure of Nezahualcoyotl, on returning to his dominions, was a general amnesty. It was his maxim, "that a monarch might punish, but revenge was unworthy of him." In the present instance, he was averse even to punish, and not only freely pardoned his rebel nobles, but conferred on some, who had most deeply offended, posts of honour and confidence. Such conduct was doubtless politic, especially as their alienation was owing, probably, much more to fear of the usurper, than to any disaffection towards himself. But there are some acts of policy which a magnanimous spirit only can execute.

The restored monarch next set about repairing the damages sustained under the late misrule, and reviving, or rather remodelling the various departments of government. He framed a concise, but comprehensive, code of laws, so well suited, it was thought, to the exigencies of the times, that it was adopted as their own by the two other members of triple alliance.

He divided the burden of government among a number of departments, as the council of war, the council of finance, the council of justice. This last was a court of supreme authority, both in civil and criminal matters, receiving appeals from the lower tribunals of the provinces, which were obliged to make a full report, every four months, or eighty days, of their own proceedings to this higher judicature. In all these bodies, a certain number of citizens were allowed to have seats with the nobles and professional dignitaries. There was, however, another body, a council of state, for aiding the king in the despatch of business, and advising him in matters of importance, which was drawn altogether from the highest order of chiefs. It consisted of fourteen members; and they had seats provided for them at the royal table.

Lastly, there was an extraordinary tribunal, called the council of music, but which, differing from the import of its name, was devoted to the encouragement of science and art. Works on astronomy, chronology, history, or any other science, were required to be submitted to its judgment before they could be made public. This censorial power was of some moment, at least with regard to the historical department, where the wilful perversion of truth was made a capital offence by the bloody code of Nezahualcoyotl. Yet a Tezcucan author must have been a bungler, who could not elude a conviction under the cloudy veil of hieroglyphics. This body, which was drawn from the best instructed persons in the kingdom, with little regard to rank, had supervision of all the productions of art, and of the nicer fabrics. It decided on the qualifications of the professors in the various branches of science, on the fidelity of their instructions to their pupils, the deficiency of which was severely punished, and it instituted examinations of these latter. In short it was a general board of education for the country. On stated days, historical compositions, and poems treating of moral or traditional topics, were recited before it by their authors. Seats were provided for the three crowned heads of the empire, who deliberated with the other members on the respective merits of the pieces, and distributed prizes of value to the successful competitors.

The influence of this academy must have been most propitious to the capital, which became the nursery not only of such sciences as could be compassed by the scholarship of the period, but of various useful and ornamental arts. Its historians, orators, and poets were celebrated throughout the country. Its archives, for which accommodations were provided in the royal palace, were stored with the records of primitive ages. Its idiom, more polished than the Mexican, was indeed the purest of all the Nahuatlac dialects; and continued, long after the Conquest, to be that in which the best productions of the native races were composed. Tezcuco claimed the glory of being the Athens of the Western World.

Among the most illustrious of her bards was the emperor himself — for the Tezcucan writers claim this title for their chief, as head of the imperial alliance. He, doubtless, appeared as a competitor before that very academy where he so often sat as a critic. But the hours of the Tezcucan monarch were not all passed in idle dalliance with the Muse, nor in the sober contemplations of philosophy, as at a later period. In the freshness of youth and early manhood, he led the allied armies in their annual expeditions, which were certain to result in a wider extent of territory to the empire. In the intervals of peace he fostered those productive arts which are the surest sources of public prosperity. He encouraged agriculture above all; and there was scarcely a spot so rude, or a steep so inaccessible, as not to confess the power of cultivation. The land was covered with a busy population, and towns and cities sprung up in places since deserted, or dwindled into miserable villages.

From resources thus enlarged by conquest and domestic industry, the monarch drew the means for the large consumption of his own numerous household, and for the costly works which he executed for the convenience and embellishment of the capital. He fined it with stately edifices for his nobles, whose constant attendance he was anxious to secure at his court. He erected a magnificent pile of buildings which might serve both for a royal residence and for the public offices. It extended, from east to west, twelve hundred and thirty-four yards; and from north to south, nine hundred and seventy-eight. It was encompassed by a wall of unburnt bricks and cement, six feet wide and nine high for one half of the circumference, and fifteen feet high for the other half. Within this enclosure were two courts. The outer one was used as the great marketplace of the city; and continued to be so until long after the Conquest. The interior court was surrounded by the council chambers and halls of justice. There were also accommodations there. for the foreign ambassadors; and a spacious saloon, with apartments: opening into it, for men of science and poets, who pursued their studies in this retreat, or met together to hold converse under its marble porticos. In this quarter, also, were kept the public archives; which fared better under the Indian dynasty than they have since under their European successors.

Adjoining this court were the apartments of the king, including those for the royal harem, as liberally supplied with beauties as that of an eastern sultan. Their walls were incrusted with alabasters, and richly tinted stucco, or hung with gorgeous tapestries of variegated feather-work. They led through long arcades, and through intricate labyrinths of shrubbery, into gardens, where baths and sparkling fountains were overshadowed by tall groves of cedar and cypress. The basins of water were well stocked with fish of various kinds, and the aviaries with birds glowing in all the gaudy plumage of the tropics. Many birds and animals, which could not be obtained alive, were represented in gold and silver so skillfully as to have furnished the great naturalist Hernandez with models.

Accommodations on a princely scale were provided for the sovereigns of Mexico and Tlacopan, when they visited the court. The whole of this lordly pile contained three hundred apartments, some of them fifty yards square. The height of the building is not mentioned. It was probably not great; but supplied the requisite room by the immense extent of ground which it covered. The interior was doubtless constructed of fight materials, especially of the rich woods, which, in that country, are remarkable, when polished, for the brilliancy and variety of their colours. That the more solid materials of stone and stucco were also liberally employed, is proved by the remains at the present day; remains which have furnished an inexhaustible quarry for the churches and other edifices since erected by the Spaniards on the site of the ancient city.

We are not informed of the time occupied in building this palace; but two hundred thousand workmen, it is said, were employed on it! However this may be, it is certain that the Tezcucan monarchs, like those of Asia, and ancient Egypt, had the control of immense masses of men, and would sometimes turn the whole population of a conquered city, including the women, into the public works. — The most gigantic monuments of architecture which the world has witnessed would never have been reared by the hands of freemen.

Adjoining the palace were buildings for the king's children, who, by his various wives, amounted to no less than sixty sons and fifty daughters. Here they were instructed in all the exercises and accomplishments suited to their station; comprehending, what would scarcely find a place in a royal education on the other side of the Atlantic — the arts of working in metals, jewelry, and feather-mosaic. Once in every four months, the whole household, not excepting the youngest, and including all the officers and attendants on the king's person, assembled in a grand saloon of the palace, to listen to a discourse from an orator, probably one of the priesthood. The princes, on this occasion, were all dressed in nequen, the coarsest manufacture of the country. The preacher began by enlarging on the obligations of morality, and of respect for the gods, especially important in persons whose rank gave such additional weight to example. He occasionally seasoned his homily with a pertinent application to his audience, if any member of it had been guilty of a notorious delinquency. from this wholesome admonition the monarch himself was not exempted, and the orator boldly reminded him of his paramount duty to show respect for his own laws. The king, so far from taking umbrage, received the lesson with humility: and the audience, we are assured, were often melted into tears by the eloquence of the preacher.

Nezahualcoyotl's fondness for magnificence was shown in his numerous villas, which were embellished with all that could make a rural retreat delightful. His favourite residence was at Tezcotzinco; a conical hill about two leagues from the capital. It was laid out in terraces, or hanging gardens, having a flight of steps five hundred and twenty in number, many of them hewn in the natural porphyry. In the garden on the summit was a reservoir of water, fed by an aqueduct that was carried over hill and valley, for several miles, on huge buttresses of masonry. A large rock stood in the midst of this basin, sculptured with the hieroglyphics representing the years of Nezahualcoyotl's reign and his principal achievements in each. On a lower level were three other reservoirs, in each of which stood a marble statue of a woman, emblematic of the three states of the empire. Another tank contained a winged lion, cut out of the solid rock, bearing in his mouth the portrait of the emperor. His likeness had been executed in gold, wood, feather-work, and stone, but this was the only one which pleased him.

From these copious basins the water was distributed in numerous channels through the gardens, or was made to tumble over the rocks in cascades, shedding refreshing dews on the flowers and odoriferous shrubs below. In the depths of this fragrant wilderness, marble porticos and pavilions were erected, and baths excavated in the solid porphyry. The visitor descended by steps cut in the living stone, and polished so bright as to reflect like mirrors. Towards the base of the hill, in the midst of cedar groves, whose gigantic branches threw a refreshing coolness over the verdure in the sultriest seasons of the year, rose the royal villa, with its light arcades and airy halls, drinking in the sweet perfumes of the gardens. Here the monarch often retired, to throw off the burden of state, and refresh his wearied spirits in the society of his favourite wives, reposing during the noontide heats in the embowering shades of his paradise, or mingling, in the cool of the evening, in their festive sports and dances. Here he entertained his imperial brothers of Mexico and Tlacopan, and followed the hardier pleasures of the chase in the noble woods that stretched for miles around his villa, flourishing in all their primeval majesty. Here, too, he often repaired in the latter days of his life, when age had tempered ambition and cooled the ardour of his blood, to pursue in solitude the studies of philosophy and gather wisdom from meditation.

It was not his passion to hoard. He dispensed his revenues munificently, seeking out poor, but meritorious objects, on whom to bestow them. He was particularly mindful of disabled soldiers, and those who had in any way sustained loss in the public service; and, in case of their death, extended assistance to their surviving families. Open mendicity was a thing he would never tolerate, but chastised it with exemplary rigour.

It would be incredible, that a man of the enlarged mind and endowments of Nezahualcoyotl should acquiesce in the sordid superstitions of his countrymen, and still more in the sanguinary rites borrowed by them from the Aztecs. In truth, his humane temper shrunk from these cruel ceremonies, and he strenuously endeavoured to recall his people to the more pure and simple worship of the ancient Toltecs. A circumstance produced a temporary change in his conduct. He had been married some years, but was not blessed with issue. The priests represented that it was owing to his neglect of the gods of his country, and that his only remedy was to propitiate them by human sacrifice. The king reluctantly consented, and the altars once more smoked with the blood of slaughtered captives. But it was all in vain; and he indignantly exclaimed, "These idols of wood and stone can neither hear nor feel; much less could they make the heavens and the earth, and man, the lord of it. These must be the work of the all-powerful, unknown God, Creator of the universe, on whom alone I must rely for consolation and support."

He then withdrew to his rural palace of Tezcotzinco, where he remained forty days, fasting and praying at stated hours, and offering up no other sacrifice than the sweet incense of copal, and aromatic herbs and gums. At the expiration of this time, he is said to have been comforted by a vision assuring him of the success of his petition. At all events, such proved to be the fact;

and this was followed by the cheering intelligence of the triumph of his arms in a quarter where he had lately experienced some humiliating reverses.

Greatly strengthened in his former religious convictions, he now openly professed his faith, and was more earnest to wean his subjects from their degrading superstitions, and to substitute nobler and more spiritual conceptions of the Deity. He built a temple in the usual pyramidal form, and on the summit a tower nine stories high, to represent the nine heavens; a tenth was surmounted by a roof painted black, and profusely gilded with stars on the outside, and incrusted with metals and precious stones within. He dedicated this to "the unknown God, the Cause of causes." It seems probable, from the emblem on the tower, as well as from the complexion of his verses, as we shall see, that he mingled with his reverence for the Supreme the astral worship which existed among the Toltecs. Various musical instruments were placed on the top of the tower, and the sound of them, accompanied by the ringing of a sonorous metal struck by a mallet, summoned the worshippers to prayers at regular seasons. No image was allowed in the edifice, as unsuited to the "invisible God"; and the people were expressly prohibited from profaning the altars with blood, or any other sacrifice than that of the perfume of flowers and sweet-scented gums.

The remainder of his days was chiefly spent in his delicious solitudes of Tezcotzinco, where he devoted himself to astronomical and, probably, astrological studies, and to meditation on his immortal destiny — giving utterance to his feelings in songs, or rather hymns, of much solemnity and pathos. At length, about the year 1470, Nezahualcoyotl, full of years and honours, felt himself drawing near his end. Almost half a century had elapsed since he mounted the throne of Tezcuco. He had found his kingdom dismembered by faction, and bowed to the dust beneath the yoke of a foreign tyrant. He had broken that yoke; and breathed new life into the nation, renewed its ancient institutions, extended wide its domain; had seen it flourishing in all the activity of trade and agriculture, gathering strength from its enlarged resources, and daily advancing higher and higher in the great march of civilisation All this he had seen, and might fairly attribute no small portion of it to his own wise and beneficent rule. His long and glorious day was now drawing to its close; and he contemplated the event with the same serenity which he had shown under the clouds of its morning and in its meridian splendour.

A short time before his death, he gathered around him those of his children in whom he most confided, his chief counsellors, the ambassadors of Mexico and Tlacopan, and his little son, the heir to the crown, his only offspring by the queen. He was then not eight years old; but had already given, as far as so tender a blossom might, the rich promise of future excellence.

After tenderly embracing the child, the dying monarch threw over him the robes of sovereignty. He then gave audience to the ambassadors, and when they had retired, made the boy repeat the substance of the conversation. He followed this by such counsels as were suited to his comprehension, and which when remembered through the long vista of after years, would serve as lights to guide him in his government of the kingdom. He besought him not to neglect the worship of "the unknown God," regretting that he himself had been unworthy to know him, and intimating his conviction that the time would come when he should be known and worshipped throughout the land.

MEXICAN PEONS

He next addressed himself to that one of his sons in whom he Placed the greatest trust, and whom he had selected as the guardian of the realm. "From this hour," he said to him, "you will fill the place that I have filled, of father to this child; you will teach him to live as he ought; and by your counsels he will rule over the empire. Stand in his place, and be his guide, till he shall be of age to govern for himself." Then, turning to his other children, he admonished them to live united with one another, and to show all loyalty to their prince, who, though a child, already manifested a discretion far above his years. "Be true to him," he added, "and he will maintain you in your rights and dignities."

Feeling his end approaching, he exclaimed, "Do not bewail me with idle lamentations. But sing the song of gladness, and show a courageous spirit, that the nations I have subdued may not believe you disheartened, but may feel that each one of you is strong enough to keep them in obedience!" The undaunted spirit of the monarch shone forth even in the agonies of death. That stout heart, however, melted as he took leave of his children and friends, weeping tenderly over them, while he bade each a last adieu. When they had withdrawn, he ordered the officers of the palace to allow no one to enter it again. Soon after he expired, in the seventy-second year of his age, and the forty-third of his reign.

Thus died the greatest monarch and, perhaps, the best who ever sat upon an Indian throne. His character is delineated with tolerable impartiality by his kinsman, the Tezcucan chronicler. "He was wise, valiant, liberal; and, when we consider the magnanimity of his soul, the grandeur and success of his enterprises, his deep policy, as well as daring, we must admit him to have far surpassed every other prince and captain of this New World. He had few failings himself, and rigorously punished those of others. He preferred the public to his private interest; was most charitable in his nature, often buying articles at double their worth of poor and honest persons, and giving them away again to the sick and infirm. In seasons of scarcity he was particularly bountiful, remitting the taxes of his vassals, and supplying their wants from the royal granaries. He put no faith in the idolatrous worship of the country. He was well instructed in moral science, and sought, above all things, to obtain light for knowing the true God. He believed in one God only, the Creator of heaven and earth, by whom we have our being, who never revealed himself to us in human form, nor in any other; with whom the souls of the virtuous are to dwell after death, while the wicked will suffer pains unspeakable. He invoked the Most High, as Him by whom we live, and 'Who has all things in himself.' He recognised the Sun for his father, and the Earth for his mother. He taught his children not to confide in idols, and only to conform to the outward worship of them from deference to public opinion. If he could not entirely abolish human sacrifices, derived from the Aztecs, he, at least, restricted them to slaves and captives."

I have occupied so much space with this illustrious prince that but little remains for his son and successor, Nezahualpilli. I have thought better, in our narrow limits, to present a complete view of a single epoch, the most interesting in the Tezcucan annals, than to spread the inquiries over a broader, but comparatively barren field. Yet Nezahualpilli, the heir to the crown, was a remarkable person, and his reign contains many incidents, which I regret to be obliged to pass over in silence.

Nezahualpilli resembled his father in his passion for astronomical studies, and is said to have had an observatory on one of his palaces. He was devoted to war in his youth, but, as he advanced in years, resigned himself to a more indolent way of life, and sought his chief amusement in the pursuit of his favourite science, or in the soft pleasures of the sequestered gardens of Tezcotzinco. This quiet life was ill suited to the turbulent temper of the times, and of his Mexican rival, Montezuma. The distant provinces fell off from their allegiance; the army relaxed its discipline; disaffection crept into its ranks; and the wily Montezuma, partly by violence, and partly by stratagems unworthy of a king, succeeded in plundering his brother monarch of some of his most valuable domains. Then it was that he arrogated to himself the title and supremacy of emperor, hitherto borne by the Tezcucan princes, as head of the alliance. Such is the account given by the historians of that nation, who in this way, explain the acknowledged superiority of the Aztec sovereign, both in territory and consideration, on the landing of the Spaniards.

These misfortunes pressed heavily on the spirits of Nezahualpilli. Their effect was increased by certain gloomy prognostics of a near calamity which was to overwhelm the country. He withdrew to his retreat, to brood in secret over his sorrows. His health rapidly declined; and in the year 1515, at the age of fifty-two, he sunk into the grave; happy, at least, that, by his timely death, he escaped witnessing the fulfilment of his own predictions, in the ruin of his country, and the extinction of the Indian dynasties, for ever.

In reviewing the brief sketch here presented of the Tezcucan monarchy, we are strongly impressed with the conviction of its superiority, in all the great features of civilisation, over the rest of Anahuac. The Mexicans showed a similar proficiency, no doubt, in the mechanic arts, and even in mathematical science. But in the science of government, in legislation, in the speculative doctrines of a religious nature, in the more elegant pursuits of poetry, eloquence, and whatever depended on refinement of taste and a polished idiom, they confessed themselves inferior, by resorting to their rivals for instruction, and citing their works as the masterpieces of their tongue. The best histories, the best poems, the best code of laws, the purest dialect, were all allowed to be Tezcucan.

What was the actual amount of the Tezcucan civilisation, it is not easy to determine, with the imperfect light afforded us. It was certainly far below anything which the word conveys, measured by a European standard. In some of the arts, and in any walk of science, they could only have made, as it were, a beginning. But they had begun in the right way, and already showed a refinement in sentiment and manners, a capacity for receiving instruction, which, under good auspices, might have led them on to indefinite improvement. Unhappily, they were fast falling under the dominion of the warlike Aztecs. And that people repaid the benefits received from their more polished neighbours by imparting to them their own ferocious superstition, which, falling like a mildew on the land, would soon have blighted its rich blossoms of promise, and turned even its fruits to dust and ashes.

BOOK 2. DISCOVERY OF MEXICO

IN the beginning of the sixteenth century, Spain occupied perhaps the most prominent position on the theatre of Europe. The numerous states, into which she had been so long divided, were consolidated into one monarchy. The Moslem crescent, after reigning there for eight centuries, was no longer seen on her borders. The authority of the crown did not, as in later times, overshadow the inferior orders of the state. The people enjoyed the inestimable privilege of political representation, and exercised it with manly independence. The nation at large could boast as great a degree of constitutional freedom as any other, at that time, in Christendom. Under a system of salutary laws and an equitable administration, domestic tranquillity was secured, public credit established, trade, manufactures, and even the more elegant arts, began to flourish; while a higher education called forth the first blossoms of that literature, which was to ripen into so rich a harvest, before the close of the century. Arms abroad kept pace with arts at home. Spain found her empire suddenly enlarged, by important acquisitions, both in Europe and Africa, while a New World beyond the waters poured into her lap treasures of countless wealth, and opened an unbounded field for honourable enterprise.

Such was the condition of the kingdom at the close of the long and glorious reign of Ferdinand and Isabella, when on the 23rd of January, 1516, the sceptre passed into the hands of their daughter Joanna, or rather their grandson, Charles the Fifth, who alone ruled the monarchy during the long and imbecile existence of his unfortunate mother. During the two years following Ferdinand's death, the regency, in the absence of Charles, was held by Cardinal Ximenes, a man whose intrepidity, extraordinary talents, and capacity for great enterprises, were accompanied by a haughty spirit, which made him too indifferent as to the means of their execution. His administration, therefore, notwithstanding the uprightness of his intentions, was, from his total disregard of forms, unfavourable to constitutional liberty; for respect for forms is an essential element of freedom. With all his faults, however, Ximenes was a Spaniard; and the object he had at heart was the good of his country.

It was otherwise on the arrival of Charles, who, after a long absence, came as a foreigner into the land of his fathers. (November, 1517.) His manners, sympathies, even his language, were foreign, for he spoke the Castilian with difficulty. He knew little of his native country, of the character of the people or their institutions. He seemed to care still less for them; while his natural reserve precluded that freedom of communication which might have counteracted, to some extent at least, the errors of education. In everything, in short, he was a foreigner; and resigned himself to the direction of his Flemish counsellors with a docility that gave little augury of his future greatness.

On his entrance into Castile, the young monarch was accompanied by a swarm of courtly sycophants, who settled, like locusts, on every place of profit and honour throughout the kingdom. A Fleming was made grand chancellor of Castile; another Fleming was placed in the archiepiscopal see of Toledo. They even ventured to profane the sanctity of the cortes by intruding themselves on its deliberations. Yet that body did not tamely submit to these usurpations, but gave vent to its indignation in tones becoming the representatives of a free people.

The same pestilent foreign influence was felt, though much less sensibly, in the Colonial administration. This had been placed, in the preceding reign, under the immediate charge of the two great tribunals, the Council of the Indies, and the Casa de Contratacion, or India House at Seville. It was their business to further the progress of discovery, watch over the infant settlements, and adjust the disputes, which grew up in them. But the licences granted to private adventurers did more for the cause of discovery than the patronage of the crown or its officers. The long peace, enjoyed with slight interruption by Spain in the early part of the sixteenth century, was most auspicious for this; and the restless cavalier, who could no longer win laurels on the fields of Africa and Europe, turned with eagerness to the brilliant career opened to him beyond the ocean.

It is difficult for those of our time, as familiar from childhood with the most remote places on the globe as with those in their own neighbourhood, to picture to themselves the feelings of the men who lived in the sixteenth century. The dread mystery, which had so long hung over the great deep, had indeed been removed. It was no longer beset with the same undefined horrors as when Columbus launched his bold bark on its dark and unknown waters. A new and glorious world had been thrown open. But as to the precise spot where that world lay, its extent, its history, whether it were island or continent — of all this, they had very vague and confused conceptions. Many, in their ignorance, blindly adopted the erroneous conclusion into which the great Admiral had been led by his superior science — that the new countries were a part of Asia; and, as the mariner wandered among the Bahamas, or steered his caravel across the Caribbean seas, he fancied he was inhaling the rich odours of the spice-islands in the Indian Ocean. Thus every fresh discovery, interpreted by his previous delusion, served to confirm him in his error, or, at least, to fill his mind with new perplexities.

The career thus thrown open had all the fascinations of a desperate hazard, on which the adventurer staked all his hopes of fortune, fame, and life itself. It was not often, indeed, that he won the rich prize which he most coveted; but then he was sure to win the meed of glory, scarcely less dear to his chivalrous spirit; and, if he survived to return to his home, he had wonderful stories to recount, of perilous chances among the strange people he had visited, and the burning climes, whose rank fertility and magnificence of vegetation so far surpassed anything he had witnessed in his own. These reports added fresh fuel to imaginations already warmed by the study of those tales of chivalry which formed the favourite reading of the Spaniards at that period. Thus romance and reality acted on each other, and the soul of the Spaniard was exalted to that pitch of enthusiasm, which enabled him to encounter the terrible trials that lay in the path of the discoverer. Indeed, the life of the cavalier of that day was romance put into action. The story of his adventures in the New World forms one of the most remarkable pages in the history of man.

Under this chivalrous spirit of enterprise, the progress of discovery had extended, by the beginning of Charles the Fifth's reign, from the Bay of Honduras, along the winding shores of Darien, and the South American continent, to the Rio de la Plata. The mighty barrier of the Isthmus had been climbed, and the Pacific descried, by Nunez de Balboa, second only to Columbus in this valiant band of "ocean chivalry." The Bahamas and Caribbee Islands had been explored, as well as the Peninsula of Florida on the northern continent. To this latter point Sebastian Cabot had arrived in his descent along the coast from Labrador, in 1497. So that before 1518, the period when our narrative begins, the eastern borders of both the great continents had been surveyed through nearly their whole extent. The shores of the great Mexican Gulf, however, sweeping with a wide circuit far into the interior, remained still concealed, with the rich realms that lay beyond, from the eye of the navigator. The time had now come for their discovery.

The business of colonisation had kept pace with that of discovery. In several of the islands, and in various parts of Terra Firma, and in Darien, settlements had been established, under the control of governors who affected the state and authority of viceroys. Grants of land were assigned to the colonists, on which they raised the natural products of the soil, but gave still more attention to the suggar-cane, imported from the Canaries. Sugar, indeed, together with the beautiful dye-woods of the country and the precious metals, formed almost the only articles of export in the infancy of the colonies, which had not yet introduced those other staples of the West Indian commerce, which, in our day, constitute its principal wealth. Yet the precious metals, painfully gleaned from a few scanty sources, would have made poor returns, but for the gratuitous labour of the Indians.

The cruel system of repartimientos, or distribution of the Indians as slaves among the conquerors, had been suppressed by Isabella. Although subsequently countenanced by the government, it was under the most careful limitations. But it is impossible to license crime by halves — to authorise injustice at all, and hope to regulate the measure of it. The eloquent remonstrances of the Dominicans — who devoted themselves to the good work of conversion in the New World with the same zeal that they showed for persecution in the Old — but, above all, those of Las Casas, induced the regent Ximenes to send out a commission with full powers to inquire into the alleged grievances, and to redress them. It had authority, moreover, to investigate the conduct of the civil officers, and to reform any abuses in their administration. This extraordinary commission consisted of three Hieronymite friars and an eminent jurist, all men of learning and unblemished piety.

They conducted the inquiry in a very dispassionate manner; but, after long deliberation, came to a conclusion most unfavourable to the demands of Las Casas, who insisted on the entire freedom of the natives. This conclusion they justified on the grounds that the Indians would not labour without compulsion, and that, unless they laboured, they could not be brought into communication with the whites, nor be converted to Christianity. Whatever we may think of this argument, it was doubtless urged with sincerity by its advocates, whose conduct through their whole administration places their motives above suspicion. They accompanied it with many careful provisions for the protection of the natives — but in vain. The simple people, accustomed all their days to a life of indolence and ease, sunk under the oppressions of their masters, and the population wasted away with even more frightful rapidity than did the aborigines in our own country, under the operation of other causes. It is not necessary to pursue these details further, into which I have been led by the desire to put the reader in possession of the general policy and state of affairs in the New World, at the period when the present narrative begins.

Of the islands, Cuba was the second discovered; but no attempt had been made to plant a colony there during the lifetime of Columbus; who, indeed, after skirting the whole extent of its southern coast, died in the conviction that it was part of the continent. At length, in 1511, Diego, the son and successor of the "Admiral," who still maintained the seat of government in Hispaniola, finding the mines much exhausted there, proposed to occupy the neighbouring island of Cuba, or Fernandina, as it was called, in compliment to the Spanish monarch. He prepared a small force for the conquest, which he placed under the command of Don Diego Velasquez; a man described by a contemporary, as "possessed of considerable experience in military affairs, having served seventeen years in the European wars; as honest, illustrious by his lineage and reputation, covetous of glory, and somewhat more covetous of wealth." The portrait was sketched by no unfriendly hand.

Velasquez, or rather his lieutenant Narvaez, who took the office on himself of scouring the country, met with no serious opposition from the inhabitants, who were of the same family with the effeminate natives of Hispaniola. The conquest, through the merciful interposition of Las Casas, "the protector of the Indians," who accompanied the army in its march, was effected without much bloodshed. One chief, indeed, named Hatuey, having fled originally from St. Domingo to escape the oppression of its invaders, made a desperate resistance, for which he was condemned by Velasquez to be burned alive. It was he who made that memorable reply, more eloquent than a volume of invective. When urged at the stake to embrace Christianity, that his soul might find admission into heaven, he inquired if the white men would go there. On being answered in the affirmative, he exclaimed, "Then I will not be a Christian; for I would not go again to a place where I must find men so cruel!" The story is told by Las Casas in his appalling record of the cruelties of his countrymen in the New World.

After the conquest, Velasquez, now appointed governor, diligently occupied himself with measures for promoting the prosperity of the island. He formed a number of settlements, bearing the same names with the modern towns, and made St. Jago, on the south-east corner, the seat of government. He invited settlers by liberal grants of land and slaves. He encouraged them to cultivate the soil, and gave particular attention to the sugar-cane, so profitable an article of commerce in later times. He was, above all, intent on working the gold mines, which promised better returns than those in Hispaniola. The affairs of his government did not prevent him, meanwhile, from casting many a wistful glance at the discoveries going forward on the continent, and he longed for an opportunity to embark in these golden adventures himself. Fortune gave him the occasion he desired.

An hidalgo of Cuba, named Hernandez de Cordova, sailed with three vessels on an expedition to one of the neighbouring Bahama Islands, in quest of Indian slaves. (February 8, 1517.) He encountered a succession of heavy gales which drove him far out of his course, and at the end of three weeks he found himself on a strange but unknown coast. On landing and asking the name of the country, he was answered by the natives, "Tectetan," meaning, "I do not understand you,"— but which the Spaniards, misinterpreting into the name of the place, easily corrupted into Yucatan. Some writers give a different etymology. Such mistakes, however, were not uncommon with the early discoverers, and have been the origin of many a name on the American continent.

Cordova had landed on the north-eastern end of the peninsula, at Cape Catoche. He was astonished at the size and solid material of the buildings constructed of stone and lime, so different from the frail tenements of reeds and rushes which formed the habitations of the islanders. He was struck, also, with the higher cultivation of the soil, and with the delicate texture of the cotton garments and gold ornaments of the natives. Everything indicated a civilisation far superior to anything he had before witnessed in the New World. He saw the evidence of a different race, moreover, in the warlike spirit of the people. Rumours of the Spaniards had, perhaps, preceded them, as they were repeatedly asked if they came from the east; and wherever they landed, they were met with the most deadly hostility. Cordova himself, in one of his skirmishes with the Indians, received more than a dozen wounds, and one only of his party escaped unhurt. At length, when he had coasted the peninsula as far as Campeachy, he returned to Cuba, which he reached after an absence of several months, having suffered all the extremities of ill, which these pioneers of the ocean were sometimes called to endure, and which none but the most courageous spirit could have survived. As it was, half the original number, consisting of one hundred and ten men, perished, including their brave commander, who died soon after his return. The reports he had brought back of the country, and still more, the specimens of curiously wrought gold, convinced Velasquez of the importance of this discovery, and he prepared with all despatch to avail himself of it.

He accordingly fitted out a little squadron of four vessels for the newly discovered lands, and placed it under the command of his nephew, Juan de Grijalva, a man on whose probity, prudence, and attachment to himself he knew he could rely. The fleet left the port of St. Jago de Cuba, May 1, 1518. It took the course pursued by Cordova, but was driven somewhat to the south, the first land that it made being the island of Cozumel. From this quarter Grijalva soon passed over to the continent and coasted the peninsula, touching at the same places as his predecessor. Everywhere he was struck, like him, with the evidences of a higher civilisation, especially in the architecture. He was astonished, also, at the sight of large stone crosses, evidently objects of worship, which he met with in various places. Reminded by these circumstances of his own country, he gave the peninsula the name "New Spain," a name since appropriated to a much wider extent of territory.

Wherever Grijalva landed, he experienced the same unfriendly reception as Cordova, though he suffered less, being better prepared to meet it. In the Rio de Tabasco or Grijalva, as it is often called after him, he held an amicable conference with a chief, who gave him a number of gold plates fashioned into a sort of armour. As he wound round the Mexican coast, one of his captains, Pedro de Alvarado, afterwards famous in the Conquest, entered a river, to which he also left his own name. In a neighbouring stream, called the Rio de Vanderas, or "River of Banners," from the ensigns displayed by the natives on its borders, Grijalva had the first communication with the Mexicans themselves.

The cacique who ruled over this province had received notice of the approach of the Europeans, and of their extraordinary appearance. He was anxious to collect all the information he could respecting them, and the motives of their visit, that he might transmit them to his master, the Aztec emperor. A friendly conference took place between the parties on shore, where Grijalva landed with all his force, so as to make a suitable impression on the mind of the barbaric chief. The interview lasted some hours, though, as there was no one on either side to interpret the language of the other, they could communicate only by signs. They, however, interchanged presents, and the Spaniards had the satisfaction of receiving, for a few worthless toys and trinkets, a rich treasure of jewels, gold ornaments and vessels, of the most fantastic forms and workmanship.

Grijalva now thought that in this successful traffic — successful beyond his most sanguine expectations — he had accomplished the chief object of his mission. He steadily refused the solicitations of his followers to plant a colony on the spot — a work of no little difficulty in so populous and powerful a country as this appeared to be. To this, indeed, he was inclined, but deemed it contrary to his instructions, which limited him to barter with the natives. He therefore despatched Alvarado in one of the caravels back to Cuba, with the treasure and such intelligence as he had gleaned of the great empire in the interior, and then pursued his voyage along the coast.

He touched at St. Juan de Ulua, and at the Isla de los Sacrificios, so called by him from the bloody remains of human victims found in one of the temples. He then held on his course as far as the province of Panuco, where finding some difficulty in doubling a boisterous headland, he returned on his track, and after an absence of nearly six months, reached Cuba in safety. Grijalva has the glory of being the first navigator who set foot on the Mexican soil, and opened an intercourse with the Aztecs.

On reaching the island, he was surprised to learn that another and more formidable armament had been fitted out to follow up his own discoveries, and to find orders at the same time from the governor, couched in no very courteous language, to repair at once to St. Jago. He was received by that personage, not merely with coldness, but with reproaches for having neglected so fair an opportunity of establishing a colony in the country he had visited. Velasquez was one of those captious spirits, who, when things do not go exactly to their minds, are sure to shift the responsibility of the failure from their own shoulders, where it should lie, to those of others. He had an ungenerous nature, says an old writer, credulous, and easily moved to suspicion. In the present instance it was most unmerited. Grijalva, naturally a modest, unassuming person, had acted in obedience to the instructions of his commander, given before sailing; and had done this in opposition to his own judgment and the importunities of his followers. His conduct merited anything but censure from his employer.

When Alvarado had returned to Cuba with his golden freight, and the accounts of the rich empire of Mexico which he had gathered from the natives, the heart of the governor swelled with rapture as he saw his dreams of avarice and ambition so likely to be realised. Impatient of the long absence of Grijalva, he despatched a vessel in search of him under the command of Olid, a cavalier who took an important part afterwards in the Conquest. Finally he resolved to fit out another armament on a sufficient scale to insure the subjugation of the country.

He previously solicited authority for this from the Hieronymite commission in St. Domingo. He then despatched his, chaplain to Spain with the royal share of the gold brought from Mexico, and a full account of the intelligence gleaned there. He set forth his own manifold services, and solicited from the country full powers to go on with the conquest and colonisation of the newly discovered regions. Before receiving an answer, he began his preparations for the armament, and, first of all, endeavoured to find a suitable person to share the expense of it, and to take the command. Such a person he found, after some difficulty and delay, in Hernando Cortes; the man of all others best calculated to achieve this great enterprise — the last man to whom Velasquez, could he have foreseen the results, would have confided it.

HERNANDO CORTES was born at Medellin, a town in the south-east corner of
Estremadura, in 1485. He came of an ancient and respectable family; and historians have
gratified the national vanity by tracing it up to the Lombard kings, whose descendants crossed
the Pyrenees, and established themselves in Aragon under the Gothic monarchy. This royal
genealogy was not found out till Cortes had acquired a name which would confer distinction
on any descent, however noble. His father, Martin Cortes de Monroy, was a captain of
infantry, in moderate circumstances, but a man of unblemished honour; and both he and his
wife, Dona Catalina Pizarro Altamirano, appear to have been much regarded for their excellent
qualities.

In his infancy Cortes is said to have had a feeble constitution, which strengthened as he grew
older. At fourteen, he was sent to Salamanca, as his father, who conceived great hopes from
his quick and showy parts, proposed to educate him for the law, a profession which held out
better inducements to the young aspirant than any other. The son, however, did not conform to
these views. He showed little fondness for books, and after loitering away two years at college,
returned home, to the great chagrin of his parents. Yet his time had not been wholly misspent,
since he had laid up a little store of Latin, and learned to write good prose, and even verses "of
some estimation, considering"— as an old writer quaintly remarks —"Cortes as the author."
He now passed his days in the idle, unprofitable manner of one who, too wilful to be guided by
others, proposes no object to himself. His buoyant spirits were continually breaking out in
troublesome frolics and capricious humours, quite at variance with the orderly habits of his
father's. household. He showed a particular inclination for the military profession, or rather for
the life of adventure to which in those days it was sure to lead. And when, at the age of
seventeen, he proposed to enrol himself under the banners of the Great Captain, his parents,
probably thinking a life of hardship and hazard abroad preferable to one of idleness at home,
made no objection.

The youthful cavalier, however, hesitated whether to seek his fortunes under that victorious
chief, or in the New World, where gold as well as glory was to be won, and where the very
dangers had a mystery and romance in them inexpressibly fascinating to a youthful fancy. It
was in this direction, accordingly, that the hot spirits of that day found a vent, especially from
that part of the country where Cortes lived, the neighbourhood of Seville and Cadiz, the focus
of nautical enterprise. He decided on this latter course, and an opportunity offered in the
splendid armament fitted out under Don Nicolas de Ovando, successor to Columbus. An
unlucky accident defeated the purpose of Cortes.

As he was scaling a high wall, one night, which gave him access to the apartment of a lady
with whom he was engaged in an intrigue, the stones gave way, and he was thrown down with
much violence and buried under the ruins. A severe contusion, though attended with no other
serious consequences, confined him to his bed till after the departure of the fleet.

Two years longer he remained at home, profiting little, as it would seem, from the lesson he
had received. At length he availed himself of another opportunity presented by the departure of
a small squadron of vessels bound to the Indian islands. He was nineteen years of age when he
bade adieu to his native shores in 1504 — the same year in which Spain lost the best and
greatest in her long line of princes, Isabella the Catholic.

Immediately on landing, Cortes repaired to the house of the governor, to whom he had been
personally known in Spain. Ovando was absent on an expedition into the interior, but the
young man was kindly received by the secretary, who assured him there would be no doubt of
his obtaining a liberal grant of land to settle on. "But I came to get gold," replied Cortes, "not
to till the soil like a peasant."

On the governor's return, Cortes consented to give up his roving thoughts, at least for a time,
as the other laboured to convince him that he would be more likely to realise his wishes from

the slow, indeed, but sure, returns of husbandry, where the soil and the labourers were a free gift to the planter, than by taking his chance in the lottery of adventure, in which there were so many blanks to a prize. He accordingly received a grant of land, with a repartimiento of Indians, and was appointed notary of the town or settlement of Agua. His graver pursuits, however, did not prevent his indulgence of the amorous propensities which belong to the sunny clime where he was born; and this frequently involved him in affairs of honour, from which, though an expert swordsman, he carried away sears that accompanied him to his grave. He occasionally, moreover, found the means of breaking up the monotony of his way of life by engaging in the military expeditions which, under the command of Ovando's lieutenant, Diego Velasquez, were employed to suppress the insurrections of the natives. In this school the young adventurer first studied the wild tactics of Indian warfare; he became familiar with toil and danger, and with those deeds of cruelty which have too often, alas! stained the bright scutcheons of the Castilian chivalry in the New World. He was only prevented by illness — a most fortunate one, on this occasion — from embarking in Nicuessa's expedition, which furnished a tale of woe, not often matched in the annals of Spanish discovery. Providence reserved him for higher ends.

At length, in 1511, when Velasquez undertook the conquest of Cuba, Cortes willingly abandoned his quiet life for the stirring scenes there opened, and took part in the expedition. He displayed throughout the invasion an activity and courage that won him the approbation of the commander; while his free and cordial manners, his good humour, and lively sallies of wit made him the favourite of the soldiers. "He gave little evidence," says a contemporary, "of the great qualities which he afterwards showed." It is probable these qualities were not known to himself; while to a common observer his careless manners and jocund repartees might well seem incompatible with anything serious or profound; as the real depth of the current is not suspected under the light play and sunny sparkling of the surface.

After the reduction of the island, Cortes seems to have been held in great favour by Velasquez, now appointed its governor. According to Las Casas, he was made one of his secretaries. He still retained the same fondness for gallantry, for which his handsome person afforded obvious advantages, but which had more than once brought him into trouble in earlier life. Among the families who had taken up their residence in Cuba was one of the name of Xuarez, from Granada in Old Spain. It consisted of a brother, and four sisters remarkable for their beauty. With one of them, named Catalina, the susceptible heart of the young soldier became enamoured. How far the intimacy was carried is not quite certain. But it appears he gave his promise to marry her — a promise which, when the time came, and reason, it may be, had got the better of passion, he showed no alacrity in keeping. He resisted, indeed, all remonstrances to this effect from the lady's family, backed by the governor, and somewhat sharpened, no doubt, in the latter by the particular interest he took in one of the fair sisters, who is said not to have repaid it with ingratitude.

Whether the rebuke of Velasquez, or some other cause of disgust, rankled in the breast of Cortes, he now became cold toward his patron, and connected himself with a disaffected party tolerably numerous in the island. They were in the habit of meeting at his house and brooding over their causes of discontent, chiefly founded, it would appear, on what they conceived an ill requital of their services in the distribution of lands and offices. It may well be imagined, that it could have been no easy task for the ruler of one of these colonies, however discreet and well intentioned, to satisfy the indefinite cravings of speculators and adventurers, who swarmed, like so many famished harpies, in the track of discovery in the New World.

The malcontents determined to lay their grievances before the higher authorities in Hispaniola, from whom Velasquez had received his commission. The voyage was one of some hazard, as it was to be made in an open boat, across an arm of the sea, eighteen leagues wide; and they fixed on Cortes, with whose fearless spirit they were well acquainted, as the fittest man to undertake it. The conspiracy got wind, and came to the governor's ears before the departure of the envoy, whom he instantly caused to be seized, loaded with fetters, and placed in strict confinement. It is even said, he would have hung him, but for the interposition of his friends.

Cortes did not long remain in durance. He contrived to throw back one of the bolts of his fetters; and, after extricating his limbs, succeeded in forcing open a window with the irons so as to admit of his escape. He was lodged on the second floor of the building, and was able to let himself down to the pavement without injury, and unobserved. He then made the best of his way to a neighbouring church, where he claimed the privilege of sanctuary.

Velasquez, though incensed at his escape, was afraid to violate the sanctity of the place by employing force. But he stationed a guard in the neighbourhood, with orders to seize the fugitive, if he should forget himself so far as to leave the sanctuary. In a few days this happened. As Cortes was carelessly standing without the walls in front of the building, an alguacil suddenly sprung on him from behind and pinioned his arms, while others rushed in and secured him. This man, whose name was Juan Escudero, was afterwards hung by Cortes for some offence in New Spain.

The unlucky prisoner was again put in irons, and carried on board a vessel to sail the next morning for Hispaniola, there to undergo his trial. Fortune favoured him once more. He succeeded after much difficulty and no little pain, in passing his feet through the rings which shackled them. He then came cautiously on deck, and, covered by the darkness of the night, stole quietly down the side of the ship into a boat that lay floating below. He pushed off from the vessel with as little noise as possible. As he drew near the shore, the stream became rapid and turbulent. He hesitated to trust his boat to it; and, as he was an excellent swimmer, prepared to breast it himself, and boldly plunged into the water. The current was strong, but the arm of a man struggling for life was stronger; and after buffeting the waves till he was nearly exhausted, he succeeded in gaining a landing; when he sought refuge in the same sanctuary which had protected him before. The facility with which Cortes a second time effected his escape, may lead one to doubt the fidelity of his guards; who perhaps looked on him as the victim of persecution, and felt the influence of those popular manners which seem to have gained him friends in every society into which he was thrown.

For some reason not explained — perhaps from policy — he now relinquished his objections to the marriage with Catalina Xuarez. He thus secured the good offices of her family. Soon afterwards the governor himself relented, and became reconciled to his unfortunate enemy. A strange story is told in connection with this event. It is said, his proud spirit refused to accept the proffers of reconciliation made him by Velasquez; and that one evening, leaving the sanctuary, he presented himself unexpectedly before the latter in his own quarters, when on a military excursion at some distance from the capital. The governor, startled by the sudden apparition of his enemy completely armed before him, with some dismay inquired the meaning of it. Cortes answered by insisting on a full explanation of his previous conduct. After some hot discussion the interview terminated amicably; the parties embraced, and, when a messenger arrived to announce the escape of Cortes, he found him in the apartments of his Excellency, where, having retired to rest, both were actually sleeping in the same bed! The anecdote is repeated without distrust by more than one biographer of Cortes. It is not very probable, however, that a haughty irascible man like Velasquez should have given such uncommon proofs of condescension and familiarity to one, so far beneath him in station, with whom he had been so recently in deadly feud; nor, on the other hand, that Cortes should have had the silly temerity to brave the lion in his den, where a single nod would have sent him to the gibbet — and that too with as little compunction or fear of consequences as would have attended the execution of an Indian slave.

The reconciliation with the governor, however brought about, was permanent. Cortes, though not re-established in the office of secretary, received a liberal repartimiento of Indians, and an ample territory in the neighbourhood of St. Jago, of which he was soon after made alcalde. He now lived almost wholly on his estate, devoting himself to agriculture, with more zeal than formerly. He stocked his plantation with different kinds of cattle, some of which were first introduced by him into Cuba. He wrought, also, the gold mines which fell to his share, and which in this island promised better returns than those in Hispaniola. By this course of industry he found himself in a few years master of some two or three thousand castellanos, a large sum for one in his situation. "God, who alone knows at what cost of Indian lives it was obtained," exclaims Las Casas, "will take account of it!" His days glided smoothly away in these tranquil pursuits, and in the society of his beautiful wife, who, however ineligible as a connection, from the inferiority of her condition, appears to have fulfilled all the relations of a faithful and affectionate partner. Indeed, he was often heard to say at this time, as the good bishop above quoted remarks, "that he lived as happily with her as if she had been the daughter of a duchess." Fortune gave him the means in after life of verifying the truth of his assertion.

Such was the state of things, when Alvarado returned with the tidings of Grijalva's discoveries, and the rich fruits of his traffic with the natives. The news spread like wildfire throughout the island; for all saw in it the promise of more important results than any hitherto obtained. The governor, as already noticed, resolved to follow up the track of discovery with a more considerable armament; and he looked around for a proper person to share the expense of it, and to take the command.

Several hidalgos presented themselves, whom, from want of proper qualifications, or from his distrust of their assuming an independence of their employer, he one after another rejected. There were two persons in St. Jago in whom he placed great confidence — Amador de Lares, the contador, or royal treasurer, and his own secretary, Andres de Duero. Cortes was also in close intimacy with both these persons; and he availed himself of it to prevail on them to recommend him as a suitable person to be intrusted with the expedition. It is said, he reinforced the proposal by promising a liberal share of the proceeds of it. However this may be, the parties urged his selection by the governor with all the eloquence of which they were capable. That officer had had ample experience of the capacity and courage of the candidate. He knew, too, that he had acquired a fortune which would enable him to co-operate materially in fitting out the armament. His popularity in the island would speedily attract followers to his standard. All past animosities had long since been buried in oblivion, and the confidence he was now to repose in him would insure his fidelity and gratitude. He lent a willing ear, therefore, to the recommendation of his counsellors, and, sending for Cortes, announced his purpose of making him captaingeneral of the armada.

Cortes had now attained the object of his wishes — the object for which his soul had panted, ever since he had set foot in the New World. He was no longer to be condemned to a life of mercenary drudgery; nor to be cooped up within the precincts of a petty island; but he was to be placed on a new and independent theatre of action, and a boundless perspective was opened to his view, which might satisfy not merely the wildest cravings of avarice, but, to a bold aspiring spirit like his, the far more important cravings of ambition. He fully appreciated the importance of the late discoveries, and read in them the existence of the great empire in the far West, dark hints of which had floated from time to time in the islands, and of which more certain glimpses had been caught by those who had reached the continent. This was the country intimated to the "Great Admiral" in his visit to Honduras in 1502, and which he might have reached, had he held on a northern course, instead of striking to the south in quest of an imaginary strait. As it was, "he had but opened the gate," to use his own bitter expression, "for others to enter." The time had at length come when they were to enter it; and the young adventurer, whose magic lance was to dissolve the spell which had so long hung over these mysterious regions, now stood ready to assume the enterprise.

From this hour the deportment of Cortes seemed to undergo a change. His thoughts, instead of evaporating in empty levities or idle flashes of merriment, were wholly concentrated on the great object to which he was devoted. His elastic spirits were shown in cheering and stimulating the companions of his toilsome duties, and he was roused to a generous enthusiasm, of which even those who knew him best had not conceived him capable. He applied at once all the money in his possession to fitting out the armament. He raised more by the mortgage of his estates, and by giving his obligations to some wealthy merchants of the place, who relied for their reimbursement on the success of the expedition; and, when his own credit was exhausted, he availed himself of that of his friends.

The funds thus acquired he expended in the purchase of vessels, provisions, and military stores, while he invited recruits by offers of assistance to such as were too poor to provide for themselves, and by the additional promise of a liberal share of the anticipated profits.

All was now bustle and excitement in the little town of St. Jago. Some were busy in refitting the vessels and getting them ready for the voyage; some in providing naval stores; others in converting their own estates into money in order to equip themselves; every one seemed anxious to contribute in some way or other to the success of the expedition. Six ships, some of them of a large size, had already been procured; and three hundred recruits enrolled themselves in the course of a few days, eager to seek their fortunes under the banner of this daring and popular chieftain.

How far the governor contributed towards the expenses of the outfit is not very clear. If the friends of Cortes are to be believed, nearly the whole burden fell on him; since, while he supplied the squadron without remuneration, the governor sold many of his own stores at an exorbitant profit. Yet it does not seem probable that Velasquez, with such ample means at his command, should have thrown on his deputy the burden of the expedition; nor that the latter, had he done so, could have been in a condition to meet these expenses, amounting, as we are told, to more than twenty thousand gold ducats. Still it cannot be denied that an ambitious man like Cortes, who was to reap all the glory of the enterprise, would very naturally be less solicitous to count the gains of it, than his employer, who, inactive at home, and having no laurels to win, must look on the pecuniary profits as his only recompense. The question gave rise, some years later, to a furious litigation between the parties, with which it is not necessary at present to embarrass the reader.

It is due to Velasquez to state that the instructions delivered by him for the conduct of the expedition cannot be charged with a narrow or mercenary spirit. The first object of the voyage was to find Grijalva, after which the two commanders were to proceed in company together. Reports had been brought back by Cordova, on his return from the first visit to Yucatan, that six Christians were said to be lingering in captivity in the interior of the country. It was supposed they might belong to the party of the unfortunate Nicuessa, and orders were given to find them out, if possible, and restore them to liberty. But the great object of the expedition was barter with the natives. In pursuing this, special care was to be taken that they should receive no wrong, but be treated with kindness and humanity. Cortes was to bear in mind, above all things, that the object which the Spanish monarch had most at heart was the conversion of the Indians. He was to impress on them the grandeur and goodness of his royal master, to invite them "to give in their allegiance to him, and to manifest it by regaling him with such comfortable presents of gold, pearls, and precious stones as, by showing their own good will, would secure his favour and protection." He was to make an accurate survey of the coast, sounding its bays and inlets for the benefit of future navigators. He was to acquaint himself with the natural products of the country, with the character of its different races, their institutions and progress in civilisation; and he was to send home minute accounts of all these, together with such articles as he should obtain in his intercourse with them. Finally, he was to take the most careful care to omit nothing that might redound to the service of God or his sovereign.

Such was the general tenor of the instructions given to Cortes, and they must be admitted to provide for the interests of science and humanity, as wen as for those which had reference only to a commercial speculation. It may seem strange, considering the discontent shown by Velasquez with his former captain, Grijalva, for not colonising, that no directions should have been given to that effect here. But he bad not yet received from Spain the warrant for investing his agents with such powers; and that which had been obtained from the Hieronymite fathers in Hispaniola conceded only the right to traffic with the natives. The commission at the same time recognised the authority of Cortes as Captain General.

THE importance given to Cortes by his new position, and perhaps a somewhat more lofty bearing, gradually gave uneasiness to the naturally suspicious temper of Velasquez, who became apprehensive that his officer, when away where he would have the power, might also have the inclination, to throw off his dependence on him altogether. An accidental circumstance at this time heightened these suspicions. A mad fellow, his jester, one of those crack-brained wits — half wit, half fool — who formed in those days a common appendage to every great man's establishment, called out to the governor, as he was taking his usual walk one morning with Cortes towards the port, "Have a care, master Velasquez, or we shall have to go a hunting, some day or other, after this same captain of ours!" "Do you hear what the rogue says?" exclaimed the governor to his companion. "Do not heed him," said Cortes, "he is a saucy knave, and deserves a good whipping." The words sunk deep, however, in the mind of Velasquez — as, indeed, true jests are apt to stick.

There were not wanting persons about his Excellency, who fanned the latent embers of jealousy into a blaze. These worthy gentlemen, some of them kinsmen of Velasquez, who probably felt their own deserts somewhat thrown into the shade by the rising fortunes of Cortes, reminded the governor of his ancient quarrel with that officer, and of the little probability that affronts so keenly felt at the time could ever be forgotten. By these and similar suggestions, and by misconstructions of the present conduct of Cortes, they wrought on the passions of Velasquez to such a degree, that he resolved to intrust the expedition to other hands.

He communicated his design to his confidential advisers, Lares and Duero, and these trusty personages reported it without delay to Cortes, although, "to a man of half his penetration," says Las Casas, "the thing would have been readily divined from the governor's altered demeanour." The two functionaries advised their friend to expedite matters as much as possible, and to lose no time in getting his fleet ready for sea, if he would retain the command of it. Cortes showed the same prompt decision on this occasion, which more than once afterwards in a similar crisis gave the direction to his destiny.

He had not yet got his complement of men, nor of vessels; and was very inadequately provided with supplies of any kind. But he resolved to weigh anchor that very night. He waited on his officers, informed them of his purpose, and probably of the cause of it; and at midnight, when the town was hushed in sleep, they all went quietly on board, and the little squadron dropped down the bay. First, however, Cortes had visited the person whose business it was to supply the place with meat, and relieved him of all his stock on hand, notwithstanding his complaint that the city must suffer for it on the morrow, leaving him, at the same time, in payment, a massive gold chain of much value, which he wore round his neck.

Great was the amazement, of the good citizens of St. Jago, when, at dawn, they saw that the fleet, which they knew was so ill prepared for the voyage, had left its moorings and was busily getting under way. The tidings soon came to the ears of his Excellency, who, springing from his bed, hastily dressed himself, mounted his horse, and, followed by his retinue, galloped down to the quay. Cortes, as soon as he descried their approach, entered an armed boat, and came within speaking distance of the shore. "And is it thus you part from me!" exclaimed Velasquez; "a courteous way of taking leave, truly!" "Pardon me," answered Cortes, "time presses, and there are some things that should be done before they are even thought of. Has your Excellency any commands?" But the mortified governor had no commands to give; and Cortes, politely waving his hand, returned to his vessel, and the little fleet instantly made sail for the port of Macaca, about fifteen leagues distant. (November 18, 1518.) Velasquez rode back to his house to digest his chagrin as he best might; satisfied, probably, that he had made at least two blunders; one in appointing Cortes to the command — the other in attempting to deprive him of it. For, if it be true, that by giving our confidence by halves, we can scarcely hope to make a friend, it is equally true, that, by withdrawing it when given, we shall make an enemy.

This clandestine departure of Cortes has been severely criticised by some writers, especially by Las Casas. Yet much may be urged in vindication of his conduct. He had been appointed to the command by the voluntary act of the governor, and this had been fully ratified by the authorities of Hispaniola. He had at once devoted all his resources to the undertaking, incurring, indeed, a heavy debt in addition. He was now be deprived of his commission, without any misconduct having been alleged or at least proved against him. Such an event must overwhelm him in irretrievable ruin, to say nothing of the friends from whom he had so largely borrowed, and the followers who had embarked their fortunes in the expedition on the faith of his commanding it. There are few persons, probably, who under these circumstances would have felt called tamely to acquiesce in the sacrifice of their hopes to a groundless and arbitrary whim. The most to have been expected from Cortes was, that he should feel obliged to provide faithfully for the interests of his employer in the conduct of the enterprise. How far he felt the force of this obligation will appear in the sequel.

From Macaca, where Cortes laid in such stores as he could obtain from the royal farms, and which, he said, he considered as "a loan from the king," he proceeded to Trinidad; a more considerable town, on the southern coast of Cuba. Here he landed, and erecting his standard in front of his quarters, made proclamation, with liberal offers to all who would join the expedition. Volunteers came in daily, and among them more than a hundred of Grijalva's men, just returned from their voyage, and willing to follow up the discovery under an enterprising leader. The fame of Cortes attracted, also, a number of cavaliers of family and distinction, some of whom, having accompanied Grijalva, brought much information valuable for the present expedition. Among these hidalgos may be mentioned Pedro de Alvarado and his brothers, Christoval de Olid, Alonso de Avila, Juan Velasquez de Leon, a near relation of the governor, Alonso Hernandez de Puertocarrero, and Gonzalo de Sandoval — all of them men who took a most important part in the Conquest. Their presence was of great moment, as giving consideration to the enterprise; and, when they entered the little camp of the adventurers, the latter turned out to welcome them amidst lively strains of music and joyous salvos of artillery.

Cortes meanwhile was active in purchasing military stores and provisions. Learning that a trading vessel laden with grain and other commodities for the mines was off the coast, he ordered out one of his caravels to seize her and bring her into port. He paid the master in bills for both cargo and ship, and even persuaded this man, named Sedeno, who was wealthy, to join his fortunes to the expedition. He also despatched one of his officers, Diego de Ordaz, in quest of another ship, of which he had tidings, with instructions to seize it in like manner, and to meet him with it off Cape St. Antonio, the westerly point of the island. By this he effected another object, that of getting rid of Ordaz, who was one of the governor's household, and an inconvenient spy on his own actions.

While thus occupied, letters from Velasquez were received by the commander of Trinidad, requiring him to seize the person of Cortes, and to detain him, as he had been deposed from the command of the fleet, which was given to another. This functionary communicated his instructions to the principal officers in the expedition, who counselled him not to make the attempt, as it would undoubtedly lead to a commotion among the soldiers, that might end in laying the town in ashes. Verdugo thought it prudent to conform to this advice.

As Cortes was willing to strengthen himself by still further reinforcements, he ordered Alvarado with a small body of men to march across the country to the Havana, while he himself would sail round the westerly point of the island, and meet him there with the squadron. In this port he again displayed his standard, making the usual proclamation. He caused all the large guns to be brought on shore, and with the small arms and crossbows, to be put in order. As there was abundance of cotton raised in this neighbourhood, he had the jackets of the soldiers thickly quilted with it, for a defence against the Indian arrows, from which the troops in the former expeditions had grievously suffered. He distributed his men into eleven companies, each under the command of an experienced officer; and it was observed, that, although several of the cavaliers in the service were the personal friends and even kinsmen of Velasquez, he appeared to treat them all with perfect confidence.

His principal standard was of black velvet embroidered with gold, and emblazoned with a red cross amidst flames of blue and white, with this motto in Latin beneath: "Friends, let us follow the Cross; and under this sign, if we have faith, we shall conquer." He now assumed more state in his own person and way of living, introducing a greater number of domestics and officers into his household, and placing it on a footing becoming a man of high station. This state he maintained through the rest of his life.

Cortes at this time was thirty-three, or perhaps thirty-four years of age. In stature he was rather above the middle size. His complexion was pale; and his large dark eye gave an expression of gravity to his countenance, not to have been expected in one of his cheerful temperament. His figure was slender, at least until later life; but his chest was deep, his shoulders broad, his frame muscular and well-proportioned. It presented the union of agility and vigour which qualified him to excel in fencing, horsemanship, and the other generous exercises of chivalry. In his diet he was temperate, careless of what he ate, and drinking little; while to toil and privation he seemed perfectly indifferent. His dress, for he did not disdain the impression produced by such adventitious aids, was such as to set off his handsome person to advantage; neither gaudy nor striking, but rich. He wore few ornaments, and usually the same; but those were of great price. His manners, frank and soldier-like, concealed a most cool and calculating spirit. With his gayest humour there mingled a settled air of resolution, which made those who approached him feel they must obey; and which infused something like awe into the attachment of his most devoted followers. Such a combination, in which love was tempered by authority, was the one probably best calculated to inspire devotion in the rough and turbulent spirits among whom his lot was to be cast.

The character of Cortes seems to have undergone some change with change of circumstances; or to speak more correctly, the new scenes in which he was placed called forth qualities which before lay dormant in his bosom. There are some hardy natures that require the heats of excited action to unfold their energies; like the plants, which, closed to the mild influence of a temperate latitude, come to their full growth, and give forth their fruits, only in the burning atmosphere of the tropics.

Before the preparations were fully completed at the Havana, the commander of the place, Don Pedro Barba, received despatches from Velasquez ordering him to apprehend Cortes, and to prevent the departure of his vessels; while another epistle from the same source was delivered to Cortes himself, requesting him to postpone his voyage till the governor could communicate with him, as he proposed, in person. "Never," exclaims Las Casas, "did I see so little knowledge of affairs shown, as in this letter of Diego Velasquez — that he should have imagined that a man, who had so recently put such an affront on him, would defer his departure at his bidding!" It was, indeed, hoping to stay the flight of the arrow by a word, after it had left the bow.

The captain-general, however, during his short stay had entirely conciliated the good will of Barba. And, if that officer had had the inclination, he knew he had not the power, to enforce his principal's orders, in the face of a resolute soldiery, incensed at this ungenerous persecution of their commander, and "all of whom," in the words of the honest chronicler, Bernal Diaz, who bore part in the expedition, "officers and privates, would have cheerfully laid down their lives for him." Barba contented himself, therefore, with explaining to Velasquez the impracticability of the attempt, and at the same time endeavoured to traquillise his apprehensions by asserting his own confidence in the fidelity of Cortes. To this the latter added a communication of his own, in which he implored his Excellency to rely on his devotion to his interests, and concluded with the comfortable assurance that he and the whole fleet, God willing, would sail on the following morning.

Accordingly, on the 10th of February, 1519, the little squadron got under way, and directed its course towards Cape St. Antonio, the appointed place of rendezvous. When all were brought together, the vessels were found to be eleven in number; one of them, in which Cortes himself went, was of a hundred tons' burden, three others were from seventy to eighty tons, the remainder were caravels and open brigantines. The whole was put under the direction of

Antonio de Alaminos, as chief pilot; a veteran navigator, who, had acted as pilot to Columbus in his last voyage, and to Cordova and Grijalva in the former expeditions to Yucatan.

Landing on the Cape and mustering his forces, Cortes found they amounted to one hundred and ten mariners, five hundred and fifty-three soldiers, including thirty-two crossbow-men, and thirteen arquebusiers, besides two hundred Indians of the island, and a few Indian women for menial offices. He was provided with ten heavy guns, four lighter pieces called falconets, and with a good supply of ammunition. He had, besides, sixteen horses. They were not easily procured; for the difficulty of transporting them across the ocean in the flimsy craft of that day made them rare and incredibly dear in the islands. But Cortes rightfully estimated the importance of cavalry, however small in number, both for their actual service in the field, and for striking terror into the savages. With so paltry a force did he enter on a conquest which even his stout heart must have shrunk from attempting with such means, had he but foreseen half its real difficulties!

Before embarking, Cortes addressed his soldiers in a short but animated harangue. He told them they were about to enter on a noble enterprise, one that would make their name famous to after ages. He was leading them to countries more vast and opulent than any yet visited by Europeans. "I hold out to you a glorious prize," continued the orator, "but it is to be won by incessant toil. Great things are achieved only by great exertions and glory was never the reward of sloth. If I have laboured hard and staked my all on this undertaking, it is for the love of that renown, which is the noblest recompense of man. But, if any among you covet riches more, be but true to me, as I will be true to you and to the occasion, and I will make you masters of such as our countrymen have never dreamed of! You are few in number, but strong in resolution; and, if this does not falter, doubt not but that the Almighty, who has never deserted the Spaniard in his contest with the infidel, will shield you, though encompassed by a cloud of enemies; for your cause is a just cause, and you are to fight under the banner of the Cross. Go forward then," he concluded, "with alacrity and confidence, and carry to a glorious issue the work so auspiciously begun."

The rough eloquence of the general, touching the various chords of ambition, avarice, and religious zeal, sent a thrill through the bosoms of his martial audience; and, receiving it with acclamations, they seemed eager to press forward under a chief who was to lead them not so much to battle, as to triumph.

Cortes was well satisfied to find his own enthusiasm so largely shared by his followers. Mass was then celebrated with the solemnities usual with the Spanish navigators, when entering on their voyages of discovery. The fleet was placed under the immediate protection of St. Peter, the patron saint of Cortes; and, weighing anchor, took its departure on the eighteenth day of February, 1519, for the coast of Yucatan.

ORDERS were given for the vessels to keep as near together as possible, and to take the direction of the capitana, or admiral's ship, which carried a beacon-light in the stern during the night. But the weather, which had been favourable, changed soon after their departure, and one of those tempests set in, which at this season are often found in the latitudes of the West Indies. It fell with terrible force on the little navy, scattering it far asunder, dismantling some of the ships, and driving them all considerably south of their proposed destination.

Cortes, who had lingered behind to convoy a disabled vessel, reached the island of Cozumel last. On landing, he learned that one of his captains, Pedro de Alvarado, had availed himself of the short time he had been there to enter the temples, rifle them of their few ornaments, and, by his violent conduct, so far to terrify the simple natives, that they had fled for refuge into the interior of the island. Cortes, highly incensed at these rash proceedings, so contrary to the policy he had proposed, could not refrain from severely reprimanding his officer in the presence of the army. He commanded two Indian captives, taken by Alvarado, to be brought before him, and explained to them the pacific purpose of his visit. This he did through the assistance of his interpreter, Melchorejo, a native of Yucatan, who had been brought back by Grijalva, and who, during his residence in Cuba, had picked up some acquaintance with the Castilian. He then dismissed them loaded with presents, and with an invitation to their countrymen to return to their homes without fear of further annoyance. This humane policy succeeded. The fugitives, reassured, were not slow in coming back; and an amicable intercourse was established, in which Spanish cutlery and trinkets were exchanged for the gold ornaments of the natives; a traffic in which each party congratulated itself — a philosopher might think with equal reason — on outwitting the other.

The first object of Cortes was, to gather tidings of the unfortunate Christians who were reported to be still lingering in captivity on the neighbouring continent. From some traders in the islands he obtained such a confirmation of the report, that he sent Diego de Ordaz with two brigantines to the opposite coast of Yucatan, with instructions to remain there eight days. Some Indians went as messengers in the vessels, who consented to bear a letter to the captives, informing them of the arrival of their countrymen in Cozumel, with a liberal ransom for their release. Meanwhile the general proposed to make an excursion to the different parts of the island, that he might give employment to the restless spirits of the soldiers, and ascertain the resources of the country.

It was poor and thinly peopled. But everywhere he recognised the vestiges of a higher civilisation than what he had before witnessed in the Indian islands. The houses were some of them large, and often built of stone and lime. He was particularly struck with the temples, in which were towers constructed of the same solid materials, and rising several stories in height.

In the court of one of these he was amazed by the sight of a cross, of stone and lime, about ten palms high. It was the emblem of the God of rain. Its appearance suggested the wildest conjectures, not merely to the unlettered soldiers, but subsequently to the European scholar, who speculated on the character of the races that had introduced there the sacred symbol of Christianity. But no such inference, as we shall see hereafter, could be warranted. Yet it must be regarded as a curious fact, that the Cross should have been venerated as the object of religious worship both in the New World, and in regions of the Old, where the light of Christianity had never risen.

The next object of Cortes was to reclaim the natives from their gross idolatry, and to substitute a purer form of worship. In accomplishing this he was prepared to use force, if milder measures should be ineffectual. There was nothing which the Spanish government had more earnestly at heart, than the conversion of the Indians. It forms the constant burden of their instructions, and gave to the military expeditions in this Western Hemisphere somewhat of the air of a crusade. The cavalier who embarked in them entered fully into these chivalrous and devotional feelings. No doubt was entertained of the efficacy of conversion, however sudden might be the change, or however violent the means. The sword was a good argument when the tongue failed; and the spread of Mahometanism had shown that seeds sown by the hand of violence, far from perishing in the ground, would spring up and bear fruit to after time. If this were so in a bad cause, how much more would it be true in a good one! The Spanish cavalier felt he had a high mission to accomplish as a soldier of the Cross. However unauthorised or unrighteous the war into which he had entered may seem to us, to him it was a holy war. He was in arms against the infidel. Not to care for the soul of his benighted enemy was to put his own in jeopardy. The conversion of a single soul might cover a multitude of sins. It was not for morals that he was concerned, but for the faith. This, though understood in its most literal and limited sense, comprehended the whole scheme of Christian morality. Whoever died in the faith, however immoral had been his life, might be said to die in the Lord. Such was the creed of the Castilian knight of that day, as imbibed from the preachings of the pulpit, from cloisters and colleges at home, from monks and missionaries abroad — from all save one, Las Casas, whose devotion, kindled at a purer source, was not, alas! permitted to send forth its radiance far into the thick gloom by which he was encompassed.

No one partook more fully of the feelings above described than Hernan Cortes. He was, in truth, the very mirror of the times in which he lived, reflecting its motley characteristics, its speculative devotion, and practical licence — but with an intensity all his own. He was greatly scandalised at the exhibition of the idolatrous practices of the people of Cozumel, though untainted, as it would seem, with human sacrifices. He endeavoured to persuade them to embrace a better faith, through the agency of two ecclesiastics who attended the expedition — the licentiate Juan Diaz and Father Bartolome de Olmedo. The latter of these godly men afforded the rare example — rare in any age — of the union of fervent zeal with charity, while he beautifully illustrated in his own conduct the precepts which he taught. He remained with the army through the whole expedition, and by his wise and benevolent counsels was often enabled to mitigate the cruelties of the Conquerors, and to turn aside the edge of the sword from the unfortunate natives.

These two missionaries vainly laboured to persuade the people of Cozumel to renounce their abominations, and to allow the Indian idols, in which the Christians recognised the true lineaments of Satan, to be thrown down and demolished. The simple natives, filled with horror at the proposed profanation, exclaimed that these were the gods who sent them the sunshine and the storm, and, should any violence be offered, they would be sure to avenge it by sending their lightnings on the heads of its perpetrators.

Cortes was probably not much of a polemic. At all events, he preferred on the present occasion action to argument; and thought that the best way to convince the Indians of their error was to prove the falsehood of the prediction. He accordingly, without further ceremony, caused the venerated images to be rolled down the stairs of the great temple, amidst the groans and lamentations of the natives. An altar was hastily constructed, an image of the Virgin and Child placed over it, and mass was performed by Father Olmedo and his reverend companion for the first time within the walls of a temple in New Spain. The patient ministers tried once more to pour the light of the gospel into the benighted understandings of the islanders, and to expound the mysteries of the Catholic faith. The Indian interpreter must have afforded rather a dubious channel for the transmission of such abstruse doctrines. But they at length found favour with their auditors, who, whether overawed by the bold bearing of the invaders, or convinced of the impotence of deities that could not shield their own shrines from violation, now consented to embrace Christianity.

While Cortes was thus occupied with the triumphs of the Cross, he received intelligence that Ordaz had returned from Yucatan without tidings of the Spanish captives. Though much chagrined, the general did not choose to postpone longer his departure from Cozumel. The fleet had been well stored with provisions by the friendly inhabitants, and, embarking his troops, Cortes, in the beginning of March, took leave of its hospitable shores. The squadron had not proceeded far, however, before a leak in one of the vessels compelled them to return to the same port. The detention was attended with important consequences; so much so, indeed, that a writer of the time discerns in it "a great mystery and a miracle."

Soon after landing, a canoe with several Indians was seen making its way from the neighbouring shores of Yucatan. On reaching the island, one of the men inquired, in broken Castilian, "if he were among Christians"; and being answered in the affirmative, threw himself on his knees and returned thanks to Heaven for his delivery. He was one of the unfortunate captives for whose fate so much interest had been felt. His name was Jeronimo de Aguilar, a native of Ecija, in Old Spain, where he had been regularly educated for the church. He had been established with the colony at Darien, and on a voyage from that place to Hispaniola, eight years previous, was wrecked near the coast of Yucatan. He escaped with several of his companions in the ship's boat, where some perished from hunger and exposure, while others were sacrificed, on their reaching land, by the cannibal natives of the peninsula. Aguilar was preserved from the same dismal fate by escaping into the interior, where he fell into the hands of a powerful cacique, who, though he spared his life, treated him at first with great rigour. The patience of the captive, however, and his singular humility, touched the better feelings of the chieftain, who would have persuaded Aguilar to take a wife among his people, but the ecclesiastic steadily refused, in obedience to his vows. This admirable constancy excited the distrust of the cacique, who put his virtue to a severe test by various temptations, and much of the same sort as those with which the devil is said to have assailed St. Anthony. From all these fiery trials, however, like his ghostly predecessor, he came out unscorched. Continence is too rare and difficult a virtue with barbarians not to challenge their veneration, and the practice of it has made the reputation of more than one saint in the Old as well as the New World. Aguilar was now intrusted with the care of his master's household and his numerous wives. He was a man of discretion, as well as virtue; and his counsels were found so salutary that he was consulted on all important matters. In short, Aguilar became a great man among the Indians.

It was with much regret, therefore, that his master received the proposals for his return to his countrymen, to which nothing but the rich treasure of glass beads, hawk bells, and other jewels of like value, sent for his ransom, would have induced him to consent. When Aguilar reached the coast, there had been so much delay that the brigantines had sailed, and it was owing to the fortunate return of the fleet to Cozumel that he was enabled to join it.

On appearing before Cortes, the poor man saluted him in the Indian style, by touching the earth with his hand, and carrying it to his head. The commander, raising him up, affectionately embraced him, covering him at the same time with his own cloak, as Aguilar was simply clad in the habiliments of the country, somewhat too scanty for a European eye. It was long, indeed, before the tastes which he had acquired in the freedom of the forest could be reconciled to the constraints either of dress or manners imposed by the artificial forms of civilisation. Aguilar's long residence in the country had familiarised him with the Mayan dialects of Yucatan, and, as he gradually revived his Castilian, he became of essential importance as an interpreter. Cortes saw the advantage of this from the first, but he could not fully estimate all the consequences that were to flow from it.

The repairs of the vessels being at length completed, the Spanish commander once more took leave of the friendly natives of Cozumel, and set sail on the 4th of March. Keeping as near as possible to the coast of Yucatan, he doubled Cape Catoche, and with flowing sheets swept down the broad bay of Campeachy. He passed Potonchan, where Cordova had experienced a rough reception from the natives; and soon after reached the mouth of the Rio de Tabasco, or Grijalva, in which that navigator had carried on so lucrative a traffic. Though mindful of the great object of his voyage — the visit to the Aztec territories — he was desirous of acquainting himself with the resources of this country, and determined to ascend the river and visit the great town on its borders.

The water was so shallow, from the accumulation of sand at the mouth of the stream, that the general was obliged to leave the ships at anchor, and to embark in the boats with a part only of his forces. The banks were thickly studded with mangrove trees, that, with their roots shooting up and interlacing one another, formed a kind of impervious screen or net-work, behind which the dark forms of the natives were seen glancing to and fro with the most menacing looks and gestures. Cortes, much surprised at these unfriendly demonstrations, so unlike what he had reason to expect, moved cautiously up the stream. When he had reached an open place, where a large number of Indians were assembled, he asked, through his interpreter, leave to land, explaining at the same time his amicable intentions. But the Indians, brandishing their weapons, answered only with gestures of angry defiance. Though much chagrined, Cortes thought it best not to urge the matter further that evening, but withdrew to a neighbouring island, where he disembarked his troops, resolved to effect a landing on the following morning.

When day broke the Spaniards saw the opposite banks lined with a much more numerous array than on the preceding evening, while the canoes along the shore were filled with bands of armed warriors. Cortes now made his preparations for the attack. He first landed a detachment of a hundred men under Alonso de Avila, at a point somewhat lower down the stream, sheltered by a thick grove of palms, from which a road, as he knew, led to the town of Tabasco, giving orders to his officer to march at once on the place, while he himself advanced to assault it in front.

Then embarking the remainder of his troops, Cortes crossed the river in face of the enemy; but, before commencing hostilities, that he might "act with entire regard to justice, and in obedience to the instructions of the Royal Council," he first caused proclamation to be made through the interpreter, that he desired only a free passage for his men; and that he proposed to revive the friendly relations which had formerly subsisted between his countrymen and the natives. He assured them that if blood were spilt, the sin would be on their heads, and that resistance would be useless, since he was resolved at all hazards to take up his quarters that night in the town of Tabasco. This proclamation, delivered in lofty tone, and duly recorded by the notary, was answered by the Indians — who might possibly have comprehended one word in ten of it — with shouts of defiance and a shower of arrows.

Cortes, having now complied with all the requisitions of a loyal cavalier, and shifted the responsibility from his own shoulders to those of the Royal Council, brought his boats alongside of the Indian canoes. They grappled fiercely together and both parties were soon in the water, which rose above the girdle. The struggle was not long, though desperate. The superior strength of the Europeans prevailed, and they forced the enemy back to land. Here, however, they were supported by their countrymen, who showered down darts, arrows, and blazing billets of wood on the heads of the invaders. The banks were soft and slippery, and it was with difficulty the soldiers made good their footing. Cortes lost a sandal in the mud, but continued to fight barefoot, with great exposure of his person, as the Indians, who soon singled out the leader, called to one another, "Strike at the chief!"

At length the Spaniards gained the bank, and were able to come into something like order, when they opened a brisk fire from their arquebuses and crossbows. The enemy, astounded by the roar and flash of the firearms, of which they had had no experience, fell back, and retreated behind a breastwork of timber thrown across the way. The Spaniards, hot in the pursuit, soon carried these rude defences, and drove the Tabascans before them towards the town, where they again took shelter behind their palisades.

Meanwhile Avila had arrived from the opposite quarter, and the natives taken by surprise made no further attempt at resistance, but abandoned the place to the Christians. They had previously removed their families and effects. Some provisions fell into the hands of the victors, but little gold, "a circumstance," says Las Casas, "which gave them no particular satisfaction." It was a very populous place. The houses were mostly of mud, the better sort of stone and lime; affording proofs in the inhabitants of a superior refinement to that found in the islands, as their stout resistance had given evidence of superior valour.

Cortes, having thus made himself master of the town, took formal possession of it for the crown of Castile. He gave three cuts with his sword on a large ceiba tree, which grew in the place, and proclaimed aloud, that he took possession of the city in the name and on behalf of the Catholic sovereigns, and would maintain and defend the same with sword and buckler against all who should gainsay it. The same vaunting declaration was also made by the soldiers, and the whole was duly recorded and attested by the notary. This was the usual simple but chivalric form with which the Spanish cavaliers asserted the royal title to the conquered territories in the New World. It was a good title, doubtless, against the claims of any other European potentate.

The general took up his quarters that night in the courtyard of the principal temple. He posted his sentinels, and took all the precautions practised in wars with a civilised foe. Indeed, there was reason for them. A suspicious silence seemed to reign through the place and its neighbourhood; and tidings were brought that the interpreter, Melchorejo, had fled, leaving his Spanish dress hanging on a tree. Cortes was disquieted by the desertion of this man who would not only inform his countrymen of the small number of the Spaniards, but dissipate any illusions that might be entertained of their superior natures.

On the following morning, as no traces of the enemy were visible, Cortes ordered out a detachment under Alvarado, and another under Francisco de Lugo, to reconnoitre. The latter officer had not advanced a league before he learned the position of the Indians, by their attacking him in such force that he was fain to take shelter in a large stone building, where he was closely besieged. Fortunately the loud yells of the assailants, like most barbarous nations, seeking to strike terror by their ferocious cries, reached the ears of Alvarado and his men, who, speedily advancing to the relief of their comrades, enabled them to force a passage through the enemy. Both parties retreated closely pursued, on the town, when Cortes, marching out to their support, compelled the Tabascans to retire.

A few prisoners were taken in this skirmish. By them Cortes found his worst apprehensions verified. The country was everywhere in arms. A force consisting of many thousands had assembled from the neighbouring provinces, and a general assault was resolved on for the next day. To the general's inquiries why he had been received in so different a manner from his predecessor, Grijalva, they answered, that "the conduct of the Tabascans then had given great offence to the other Indian tribes, who taxed them with treachery and cowardice; so that they had promised, on any return of the white men, to resist them in the same manner as their neighbours had done."

Cortes might now well regret that he had allowed himself to deviate from the direct object of his enterprise, and to become intangled in a doubtful war which could lead to no profitable result. But it was too late to repent. He had taken the step, and had no alternative but to go forward. To retreat would dishearten his own men at the outset, impair their confidence in him as their leader, and confirm the arrogance of his foes, the tidings of whose success might precede him on his voyage, and prepare the way for greater mortifications and defeats. He did not hesitate as to the course he was to pursue; but, calling his officers together, announced his intention to give battle the following morning.

He sent back to the vessels such as were disabled by their wounds, and ordered the remainder of the forces to join the camp. Six of the heavy guns were also taken from the ships, together with all the horses. The animals were stiff and torpid from long confinement on board; but a few hours' exercise restored them to their strength and usual spirit. He gave the command of the artillery — if it may be dignified with the name — to a soldier named Mesa, who had acquired some experience as an engineer in the Italian wars. The infantry he put under the orders of Diego de Ordaz, and took charge of the cavalry himself. It consisted of some of the most valiant gentlemen of his little band, among whom may be mentioned Alvarado, Velasquez de Leon, Avila, Puertocarrero, Olid, Montejo. Having thus made all the necessary arrangements, and settled his plan of battle, he retired to rest — but not to slumber. His feverish mind, as may well be imagined, was filled with anxiety for the morrow, which might decide the fate of his expedition; and as was his wont on such occasions, he was frequently observed, during the night, going the rounds, and visiting the sentinels, to see that no one slept upon his post.

At the first glimmering of light he mustered his army, and declared his purpose not to abide, cooped up in the town, the assault of the enemy, but to march at once against him. For he well knew that the spirits rise with action, and that the attacking party gathers a confidence from the very movement, which is not felt by the one who is passively, perhaps anxiously, awaiting the assault. The Indians were understood to be encamped on a level ground a few miles distant from the city, called the plain of Ceutla. The general commanded that Ordaz should march with the foot, including the artillery, directly across the country, and attack them in front, while he himself would fetch a circuit with the horse, and turn their flank when thus engaged, or fall upon their rear.

These dispositions being completed, the little army heard mass and then sallied forth from the wooden walls of Tabasco. It was Lady-day, the 25th of March — long memorable in the annals of New Spain. The district around the town was chequered with patches of maize, and, on the lower level, with plantations of cacao — supplying the beverage, and perhaps the coin of the country, as in Mexico. These plantations, requiring constant irrigation, were fed by numerous canals and reservoirs of water, so that the country could not be traversed without great toil and difficulty. It was, however, intersected by a narrow path or causeway, over which the cannon could be dragged.

The troops advanced more than a league on their laborious march, without descrying the enemy. The weather was sultry, but few of them were embarrassed by the heavy mail worn by the European cavaliers at that period. Their cotton jackets, thickly quilted, afforded a tolerable protection against the arrows of the Indian, and allowed room for the freedom and activity of movement essential to a life of rambling adventure in the wilderness.

At length they came in sight of the broad plains of Ceutla, and beheld the dusky lines of the enemy stretching, as far as the eye could reach, along the edge of the horizon. The Indians had shown some sagacity in the choice of their position; and, as the weary Spaniards came slowly on, floundering through the morass, the Tabascans set up their hideous battle-cries, and discharged volleys of arrows, stones, and other missiles, which rattled like hail on the shields and helmets of the assailants. Many were severely wounded before they could gain the firm ground, where they soon cleared a space for themselves, and opened a heavy fire of artillery and musketry on the dense columns of the enemy, which presented a fatal mark for the balls. Numbers were swept down at every discharge; but the bold barbarians, far from being dismayed, threw up dust and leaves to hide their losses, and, sounding their war instruments, shot off fresh flights of arrows in return.

They even pressed closer on the Spaniards, and, when driven off by a vigorous charge, soon turned again, and, rolling back like the waves of the ocean, seemed ready to overwhelm the little band by weight of numbers. Thus cramped, the latter had scarcely room to perform their necessary evolutions, or even to work their guns with effect.

The engagement had now lasted more than an hour, and the Spaniards, sorely pressed, looked with great anxiety for the arrival of the horse — which some unaccountable impediments must have detained — to relieve them from their perilous position. At this crisis, the furthest columns of the Indian army were seen to be agitated and thrown into a disorder that rapidly spread through the whole mass. It was not long before the ears of the Christians were saluted with the cheering war-cry of "San Jago and San Pedro," and they beheld the bright helmets and swords of the Castilian chivalry flashing back the rays of the morning sun, as they dashed through the ranks of the enemy, striking to the right and left, and scattering dismay around them. The eye of faith, indeed, could discern the patron Saint of Spain himself, mounted on his grey war-horse, heading the rescue and trampling over the bodies of the fallen infidels!

The approach of Cortes had been greatly retarded by the broken nature of the ground. When he came up, the Indians were so hotly engaged, that he was upon them before they observed his approach. He ordered his men to direct their lances at the faces of their opponents, who, terrified at the monstrous apparition — for they supposed the rider and the horse, which they had never before seen, to be one and the same — were seized with a panic. Ordaz availed himself of it to command a general charge along the line, and the Indians, many of them throwing away their arms, fled without attempting further resistance.

Cortes was too content with the victory, to care to follow it up by dipping his sword in the blood of the fugitives. He drew off his men to a copse of palms which skirted the place, and, under their broad canopy, the soldiers offered up thanksgivings to the Almighty for the victory vouchsafed them. The field of battle was made the site of a town, called in honour of the day on which the action took place, Santa Maria de la Vitoria, long afterwards the capital of the province. The number of those who fought or fell in the engagement is altogether doubtful. Nothing, indeed, is more uncertain than numerical estimates of barbarians. And they gain nothing in probability, when they come, as in the present instance, from the reports of their enemies. Most accounts, however, agree that the Indian force consisted of five squadrons of eight thousand men each. There is more discrepancy as to the number of slain, varying from one to thirty thousand! In this monstrous discordance, the common disposition to exaggerate may lead us to look for truth in the neighbourhood of the smallest number. The loss of the Christians was inconsiderable; not exceeding — if we receive their own reports, probably, from the same causes, much diminishing the truth — two killed, and less than a hundred wounded! We may readily comprehend the feelings of the Conquerors, when they declared, that "Heaven must have fought on their side, since their own strength could never have prevailed against such a multitude of enemies!"

Several prisoners were taken in the battle, among them two chiefs. Cortes gave them their liberty, and sent a message by them to their countrymen, "that he would overlook the past, if they would come in at once, and tender their submission. Otherwise he would ride over the land, and put every living thing in it, man, woman, and child, to the sword!" With this formidable menace ringing in their ears, the envoys departed.

But the Tabascans had no relish for further hostilities. A body of inferior chiefs appeared the next day, clad in dark dresses of cotton, intimating their abject condition, and implored leave to bury their dead. It was granted by the general, with many assurances of his friendly disposition; but at the same time he told them, he expected their principal caciques, as he would treat with none other. These soon presented themselves, attended by a numerous train of vassals, who followed with timid curiosity to the Christian camp. Among their propitiatory gifts were twenty female slaves, which, from the character of one of them, proved of infinitely more consequence than was anticipated by either Spaniards or Tabascans. Confidence was soon restored; and was succeeded by a friendly intercourse, and the interchange of Spanish toys for the rude commodities of the country, articles of food, cotton, and a few gold ornaments of little value. When asked where the precious metal was procured, they pointed to the west, and answered "Culhua," "Mexico." The Spaniards saw this was no place for them to traffic, or to tarry in. — Yet here, they were not many leagues distant from a potent and opulent city, or what once had been so, the ancient Palenque. But its glory may have even then passed away, and its name have been forgotten by the surrounding nations.

Before his departure the Spanish commander did not omit to provide for one great object of his expedition, the conversion of the Indians. He first represented to the caciques, that he had been sent thither by a powerful monarch on the other side of the water, to whom he had now a right to claim their allegiance. He then caused the reverend fathers Olmedo and Diaz to enlighten their minds, as far as possible, in regard to the great truths of revelation, urging them to receive these in place of their own heathenish abominations. The Tabascans, whose perceptions were no doubt materially quickened by the discipline they had undergone, made but a faint resistance to either proposal. The next day was Palm Sunday, and the general resolved to celebrate their conversion by one of those pompous ceremonials of the Church, which should make a lasting impression on their minds.

A solemn procession was formed of the whole army with the ecclesiastics at their head, each soldier bearing a palm branch in his hand. The concourse was swelled by thousands of Indians of both sexes, who followed in curious astonishment at the spectacle. The long files bent their way through the flowery savannas that bordered the settlement, to the principal temple, where an altar was raised, and the image of the presiding deity was deposed to make room for that of the Virgin with the infant Saviour. Mass was celebrated by Father Olmedo, and the soldiers who were capable joined in the solemn chant. The natives listened in profound silence, and if we may believe the chronicler of the event who witnessed it, were melted into tears; while their hearts were penetrated with reverential awe for the God of those terrible beings who seemed to wield in their own hands the thunder and the lightning.

These solemnities concluded, Cortes prepared to return to his ships, well satisfied with the impression made on the new converts, and with the conquests he had thus achieved for Castile and Christianity. The soldiers, taking leave of their Indian friends, entered the boats with the palm branches in their hands, and descending the river re-embarked on board their vessels, which rode at anchor at its mouth. A favourable breeze was blowing, and the little navy, opening its sails to receive it, was soon on its way again to the golden shores of Mexico.

THE fleet held its course so near the shore, that the inhabitants could be seen on it; and, as it swept along the winding borders of the gulf, the soldiers, who had been on the former expedition with Grijalva, pointed out to their companions the memorable places on the coast. Here was the Rio de Alvarado, named after the gallant adventurer, who was present, also, in this expedition; there the Rio de Vanderas, in which Grijalva had carried on so lucrative a commerce with the Mexicans; and there the Isla de los Sacrificios, where the Spaniards first saw the vestiges of human sacrifice on the coast.

The fleet had now arrived off St. Juan de Ulua, the island so named by Grijalva. The weather was temperate and serene, and crowds of natives were gathered on the shore of the main land, gazing at the strange phenomenon, as the vessels glided along under easy sail on the smooth bosom of the waters. It was the evening of Thursday in Passion Week. The air came pleasantly off the shore, and Cortes, liking the spot, thought he might safely anchor under the lee of the island, which would shelter him from the nortes that sweep over these seas with fatal violence in the winter, sometimes even late in the spring.

The ships had not been long at anchor, when a light pirogue, filled with natives, shot off from the neighbouring continent, and steered for the general's vessel, distinguished by the royal ensign of Castile floating from the mast. The Indians came on board with a frank confidence, inspired by the accounts of the Spaniards spread by their countrymen who had traded with Grijalva. They brought presents of fruits and flowers and little ornaments of gold, which they gladly exchanged for the usual trinkets. Cortes was baffled in his attempts to hold a conversation with his visitors by means of the interpreter, Aguilar, who was ignorant of the language; the Mayan dialects, with which he was conversant, bearing too little resemblance to the Aztec. The natives supplied the deficiency, as far as possible, by the uncommon vivacity and significance of their gestures — the hieroglyphics of speech — but the Spanish commander saw with chagrin the embarrassments he must encounter in future for want of a more perfect medium of communication. In this dilemma, he was informed that one of the female slaves given to him by the Tabascan chiefs was a native Mexican, and understood the language. Her name — that given to her by the Spaniards — was Marina; and, as she was to exercise a most important influence on their fortunes, it is necessary to acquaint the reader with something of her character and history.

She was born at Painalla, in the province of Coatzacualco, on the south-eastern borders of the Mexican empire. Her father, a rich and powerful cacique, died when she was very young. Her mother married again, and, having a son, she conceived the infamous idea of securing to this offspring of her second union Marina's rightful inheritance. She accordingly feigned that the latter was dead, but secretly delivered her into the hands of some itinerant traders of Xicallanco. She availed herself, at the same time, of the death of a child of one of her slaves, to substitute the corpse for that of her own daughter, and celebrated the obsequies with mock solemnity. These particulars are related by the honest old soldier, Bernal Diaz, who knew the mother, and witnessed the generous treatment of her afterwards by Marina. By the merchants the Indian maiden was again sold to the cacique of Tabasco, who delivered her, as we have seen, to the Spaniards.

From the place of her birth she was well acquainted with the Mexican tongue, which, indeed, she is said to have spoken with great elegance. Her residence in Tabasco familiarised her with the dialects of that country, so that she could carry on a conversation with Aguilar, which he in turn rendered into the Castilian. Thus a certain, though somewhat circuitous channel was opened to Cortes for communicating with the Aztecs; a circumstance of the last importance to the success of his enterprise. It was not very long, however, before Marina, who had a lively genius, made herself so far mistress of the Castilian as to supersede the necessity of any other linguist. She learned it the more readily, as it was to her the language of love: Cortes, who appreciated the value of her services from the first, made her his interpreter, then his secretary, and, won by her charms, his mistress.

With the aid of his two intelligent interpreters, Cortes entered into conversation with his Indian visitors. He learned that they were Mexicans, or rather subjects of the great Mexican empire, of which their own province formed one of the comparatively recent conquests. The country was ruled by a powerful monarch, called Moctheuzoma, or by Europeans more commonly Montezuma, who dwelt on the mountain plains of the interior, nearly seventy leagues from the coast; their own province was governed by one of his nobles, named Teuhtlile, whose residence was eight leagues distant. Cortes acquainted them in turn with his own friendly views in visiting their country, and with his desire of an interview with the Aztec governor. He then dismissed them loaded with presents, having first ascertained that there was abundance of gold in the interior, like the specimens they had brought.

Cortes, pleased with the manners of the people, and the goodly reports of the land, resolved to take up his quarters here for the present. The next morning, April 21, being Good Friday, he landed with all his force, on the very spot where now stands the modern city of Vera Cruz. Little did the Conqueror imagine that the desolate beach, on which he first planted his foot, was one day to be covered by a flourishing city, the great mart of European and Oriental trade, the commercial capital of New Spain.

It was a wide and level plain, except where the sand had been drifted into hillocks by the perpetual blowing of the norte. On these sand-hills he mounted his little battery of guns, so as to give him the command of the country. He then employed the troops in cutting down small trees and bushes which grew near, in order to provide a shelter from the weather. In this he was aided by the people of the country, sent, as it appeared, by the governor of the district, to assist the Spaniards. With their help stakes were firmly set in the earth, and covered with boughs, and with mats and cotton carpets, which the friendly natives brought with them. In this way they secured, in a couple of days, a good defence against the scorching rays of the sun, which beat with intolerable fierceness on the sands. The place was surrounded by stagnant marshes, the exhalations from which, quickened by the heat into the pestilent malaria, have occasioned in later times wider mortality to Europeans than all the hurricanes on the coast. The bilious disorders, now the terrible scourge of the tierra caliente, were little known before the Conquest. The seeds of the poison seem to have been scattered by the hand of civilisation; for it is only necessary to settle a town, and draw together a busy European population, in order to call out the malignity of the venom which had before lurked in the atmosphere.

While these arrangements were in progress, the natives flocked in from the adjacent district, which was tolerably populous in the interior, drawn by a natural curiosity to see the wonderful strangers. They brought with them fruits, vegetables, flowers in abundance, game, and many dishes cooked after the fashion of the country, with little articles of gold and other ornaments. They gave away some as presents, and bartered others for the wares of the Spaniards; so that the camp, crowded with a motley throng of every age and sex, wore the appearance of a fair. From some of the visitors Cortes learned the intention of the governor to wait on him the following day.

This was Easter. Teuhtlile arrived, as he had announced, before noon. He was attended by a numerous train, and was met by Cortes, who conducted him with much ceremony to his tent, where his principal officers were assembled. The Aztec chief returned their salutations with polite, though formal courtesy. Mass was first said by father Olmedo, and the service was listened to by Teuhtlile and his attendants with decent reverence. A collation was afterwards served, at which the general entertained his guest with Spanish wines and confections. The interpreters were then introduced, and a conversation commenced between the parties.

The first inquiries of Teuhtlile were respecting the country of the strangers, and the purport of their visit. Cortes told him, that "he was the subject of a potent monarch beyond the seas, who ruled over an immense empire, and had kings and princes for his vassals! that, acquainted with the greatness of the Mexican emperor, his master had desired to enter into a communication with him, and had sent him as his envoy to wait on Montezuma with a present in token of his good will, and a message which he must deliver in person." He concluded by inquiring of Teuhtlile when he could be admitted to his sovereign's presence.

To this the Aztec noble somewhat haughtily replied, "How is it, that you have been here only two days, and demand to see the emperor?" He then added, with more courtesy, that "he was surprised to learn there was another monarch as powerful as Montezuma; but that if it were so, he had no doubt his master would be happy to communicate with him. He would send his couriers with the royal gift brought by the Spanish commander, and, so soon as he had learned Montezuma's will, would communicate it."

Teuhtlile then commanded his slaves to bring forward the present intended for the Spanish general. It consisted of ten loads of fine cotton, several mantles of that curious feather-work whose rich and delicate dyes might vie with the most beautiful painting, and a wicker basket filled with ornaments of wrought gold, all calculated to inspire the Spaniards with high ideas of the wealth and mechanical ingenuity of the Mexicans.

Cortes received these presents with suitable acknowledgments, and ordered his own attendants to lay before the chief the articles designed for Montezuma. These were an arm-chair richly carved and painted, a crimson cap of cloth, having a gold medal emblazoned with St. George and the dragon, and a quantity of collars, bracelets, and other ornaments of cut glass, which, in a country where glass was not to be had, might claim to have the value of real gems, and no doubt passed for such with the inexperienced Mexicans. Teuhtlile observed a soldier in the camp with a shining gilt helmet on his head, which he said reminded him of one worn by the god Quetzalcoatl in Mexico; and he showed a desire that Montezuma should see it. The coming of the Spaniards, as the reader will soon see, was associated with some traditions of this same deity. Cortes expressed his willingness that the casque should be sent to the emperor, intimating a hope that it would be returned filled with the gold dust of the country, that he might be able to compare its quality with that in his own! He further told the governor, as we are informed by his chaplain, "that the Spaniards were troubled with a disease of the heart, for which gold was a specific remedy!" "In short," says Las Casas, "he contrived to make his want of gold very clear to the governor."

While these things were passing, Cortes observed one of Teuhtlile's attendants busy with a pencil, apparently delineating some object. On looking at his work, he found that it was a sketch on canvas of the Spaniards, their costumes, arms, and, in short, different objects of interest, giving to each its appropriate form and colour. This was the celebrated picture-writing of the Aztecs, and, as Teuhtlile informed him, this man was employed in portraying the various objects for the eye of Montezuma, who would thus gather a more vivid notion of their appearance than from any description by words. Cortes was pleased with the idea; and, as he knew how much the effect would be heightened by converting still life into action, he ordered out the cavalry on the beach, the wet sands of which afforded a firm footing for the horses. The bold and rapid movements of the troops, as they went through their military exercises; the apparent ease with which they managed the fiery animals on which they were mounted; the glancing of their weapons, and the shrill cry of the trumpet, all filled the spectators with astonishment; but when they heard the thunders of the cannon, which Cortes ordered to be fired at the same time, and witnessed the volumes of smoke and flame issuing from these terrible engines, and the rushing sound of the balls, as they dashed through the trees of the neighbouring forest, shivering their branches into fragments, they were filled with consternation, from which the Aztec chief himself was not wholly free.

Nothing of all this was lost on the painters, who faithfully recorded, after their fashion, every particular; not omitting the ships — "the water-houses," as they called them, of the strangers — which, with their dark hulls and snow-white sails reflected from the water, were swinging lazily at anchor on the calm bosom of the bay. All was depicted with a fidelity, that excited in their turn the admiration of the Spaniards, who, doubtless unprepared for this exhibition of skill, greatly overestimated the merits of the execution.

These various matters completed, Teuhtlile with his attendants withdrew from the Spanish quarters, with the same ceremony with which he had entered them; leaving orders that his people should supply the troops with provisions and other articles requisite for their accommodation, till further instructions from the capital.

WE must now take leave of the Spanish camp in the tierra caliente, and transport ourselves to the distant capital of Mexico, where no little sensation was excited by the arrival of the wonderful strangers on the coast. The Aztec throne was filled at that time by Montezuma the Second, nephew of the last, and grandson of a preceding monarch. He had been elected to the regal dignity in 1502, in preference to his brothers, for his superior qualifications, both as a soldier and a priest — a combination of offices sometimes found in the Mexican candidates, as it was, more frequently, in the Egyptian. In early youth he had taken an active part in the wars of the empire, though of late he had devoted himself more exclusively to the services of the temple; and he was scrupulous in his attentions to all the burdensome ceremonial of the Aztec worship. He maintained a grave and reserved demeanour, speaking little and with prudent deliberation. His deportment was well calculated to inspire ideas of superior sanctity.

Montezuma displayed all the energy and enterprise in the commencement of his reign, which had been anticipated from him. His first expedition against a rebel province in the neighbourhood was crowned with success, and he led back in triumph a throng of captives for the bloody sacrifice that was to grace his coronation. This was celebrated with uncommon pomp. Games and religious ceremonies continued for several days, and among the spectators who flocked from distant quarters were some noble Tlascalans, the hereditary enemies of Mexico. They were in disguise, hoping thus to elude detection. They were recognised, however, and reported to the monarch. But he only availed himself of the information to provide them with honourable entertainment, and a good place for witnessing the games. This was a magnanimous act, considering the long cherished hostility between the nations.

In his first years, Montezuma was constantly engaged in war, and frequently led his armies in person. The Aztec banners were seen in the furthest provinces of the Gulf of Mexico, and the distant regions of Nicaragua and Honduras. The expeditions were generally successful; and the limits of the empire were more widely extended that at any preceding period.

Meanwhile the monarch was not inattentive to the interior concerns of the kingdom. He made some important changes in the courts of justice; and carefully watched over the execution of the laws, which he enforced with stern severity. He was in the habit of patrolling the streets of his capital in disguise, to make himself personally acquainted with the abuses in it. And with more questionable policy, it is said, he would sometimes try the integrity of his judges by tempting them with large bribes to swerve from their duty, and then call the delinquent to strict account for yielding to the temptation.

He liberally recompensed all who served him. He showed a similar munificent spirit in his public works, constructing and embellishing the temples, bringing water into the capital by a new channel, and establishing a hospital, or retreat for invalid soldiers, in the city of Colhuacan.

These acts, so worthy of a great prince, were counterbalanced by others of an opposite complexion. The humility, displayed so ostentatiously before his elevation, gave way to an intolerable arrogance. In his pleasure-houses, domestic establishment, and way of living, he assumed a pomp unknown to his predecessors. He secluded himself from public observation, or, when he went abroad, exacted the most slavish homage; while in the palace he would be served only, even in the most menial offices, by persons of rank. He, further, dismissed several plebeians, chiefly poor soldiers of merit, from the places they had occupied near the person of his predecessor, considering their attendance a dishonour to royalty. It was in vain that his oldest and sagest counsellors remonstrated on a conduct so impolitic.

While he thus disgusted his subjects by his haughty deportment, he alienated their affections by the imposition of grievous taxes. These were demanded by the lavish expenditure of his court. They fell with peculiar heaviness on the conquered cities. This oppression led to frequent insurrection and resistance; and the latter years of his reign present a scene of unintermitting hostility, in which the forces of one half of the empire were employed in suppressing the commotions of the other. Unfortunately there was no principle of amalgamation by which the new acquisitions could be incorporated into the ancient monarchy, as parts of one whole. Their interests, as well as sympathies, were different. Thus the more widely the Aztec empire was extended, the weaker it became, resembling some vast and ill-proportioned edifice, whose disjointed materials having no principle of cohesion, and tottering under their own weight, seem ready to fall before the first blast of the tempest.

In 1516, died the Tezcucan king, Nezahualpilli, in whom Montezuma lost his most sagacious counsellor. The succession was contested by his two sons, Cacama and Ixtlilxochitl. The former was supported by Montezuma. The latter, the younger of the princes, a bold, aspiring youth, appealing to the patriotic sentiment of his nation, would have persuaded them that his brother was too much in the Mexican interests to be true to his own country. A civil war ensued, and ended by a compromise, by which one half of the kingdom, with the capital, remained to Cacama, and the northern portion to his ambitious rival. Ixtlilxochitl became from that time the mortal foe of Montezuma.

A more formidable enemy still was the little republic of Tlascala, lying midway between the Mexican Valley and the coast. It had maintained its independence for more than two centuries against the allied forces of the empire. Its resources were unimpaired, its civilisation scarcely below that of its great rival states, and for courage and military prowess it had established a name inferior to none other of the nations of Anahuac.

Such was the condition of the Aztec monarchy, on the arrival of Cortes; — the people disgusted with the arrogance of the sovereign; the provinces and distant cities outraged by fiscal exactions; while potent enemies in the neighbourhood lay watching the hour when they might assail their formidable rival with advantage. Still the kingdom was strong in its internal resources, in the will of its monarch, in the long habitual deference to his authority — in short, in the terror of his name, and in the valour and discipline of his armies, grown grey in active service, and well drilled in all the tactics of Indian warfare. The time had now come when these imperfect tactics and rude weapons of the barbarian were to be brought into collision with the science and enginery of the most civilised nations of the globe.

During the latter years of his reign, Montezuma had rarely taken part in his military expeditions, which he left to his captains, occupying himself chiefly with his sacerdotal functions. Under no prince had the priesthood enjoyed greater consideration and immunities. The religious festivals and rites were celebrated with unprecedented pomp. The oracles were consulted on the most trivial occasions; and the sanguinary deities were propitiated by hecatombs of victims dragged in triumph to the capital from the conquered or rebellious provinces. The religion, or, to speak correctly, the superstition of Montezuma proved a principal cause of his calamities.

In a preceding chapter I have noticed the popular traditions respecting Quetzalcoatl, that deity with a fair complexion and flowing beard, so unlike the Indian physiognomy, who, after fulfilling his mission of benevolence among the Aztecs, embarked on the Atlantic Sea for the mysterious shores of Tlapallan. He promised, on his departure, to return at some future day with his posterity, and resume the possession of his empire. That day was looked forward to with hope or with apprehension, according to the interest of the believer, but with general confidence throughout the wide borders of Anahuac. Even after the Conquest, it still lingered among the Indian races, by whom it was as fondly cherished, as the advent of their king Sebastian continued to be by the Portuguese, or that of the Messiah by the Jews.

A general feeling seems to have prevailed in the time of Montezuma, that the period for the return of the deity, and the full accomplishment of his promise, was near at hand. This conviction is said to have gained ground from various preternatural occurrences, reported with more or less detail by all the most ancient historians. In 1510, the great lake of Tezcuco, without the occurrence of a tempest, or earthquake, or any other visible cause, became violently agitated, overflowed its banks, and, pouring into the streets of Mexico, swept off many of the buildings by the fury of the waters. In 1511, one of the turrets of the great temple took fire, equally without any apparent cause, and continued to burn in defiance of all attempts to extinguish it. In the following years, three comets were seen; and not long before the coming of the Spaniards a strange light broke forth in the east. It spread broad at its base on the horizon, and rising in a pyramidal form tapered off as it approached the zenith. It resembled a vast sheet or flood of fire, emitting sparkles, or, as an old writer expresses it, "seemed thickly powdered with stars." At the same time, low voices were heard in the air, and doleful wailings, as if to announce some strange, mysterious calamity! The Aztec monarch, terrified at the apparitions in the heavens, took council of Nezahualpilli, who was a great proficient in the subtle science of astrology. But the royal sage cast a deeper cloud over his spirit, by reading in these prodigies the speedy downfall of the empire.

Such are the strange stories reported by the chroniclers, in which it is not impossible to detect the glimmerings of truth. Nearly thirty years had elapsed since the discovery of the islands by Columbus, and more than twenty since his visit to the American continent. Rumours, more or less distinct, of this wonderful appearance of the white men, bearing in their hands the thunder and the lightning, so like in many respects to the traditions of Quetzalcoatl, would naturally spread far and wide among the Indian nations. Such rumours, doubtless, long before the landing of the Spaniards in Mexico, found their way up the grand plateau, filling the minds of men with anticipations of the near coming of the period when the great deity was to return and receive his own again.

When tidings were brought to the capital of the landing of Grijalva on the coast, in the preceding year, the heart of Montezuma was filled with dismay. He felt as if the destinies which had so long brooded over the royal line of Mexico were to be accomplished, and the sceptre was to pass away from his house for ever. Though somewhat relieved by the departure of the Spaniards, he caused sentinels to be stationed on the heights; and when the Europeans returned under Cortes, he doubtless received the earliest notice of the unwelcome event. It was by his orders, however, that the provincial governor had prepared so hospitable a reception for them. The hieroglyphical report of these strange visitors, now forwarded to the capital, revived all his apprehensions. He called without delay a meeting of his principal counsellors, including the kings of Tezcuco and Tlacopan, and laid the matter before them.

There seems to have been much division of opinion in that body. Some were for resisting the strangers at once, whether by fraud, or by open force. Others contended, that, if they were supernatural beings, fraud and force would be alike useless. If they were, as they pretended, ambassadors from a foreign prince, such a policy would be cowardly and unjust. That they were not of the family of Quetzalcoatl was argued from the fact, that they had shown themselves hostile to his religion; for tidings of the proceedings of the Spaniards in Tabasco, it seems, had already reached the capital. Among those in favour of giving them a friendly and honourable reception was the Tezcucan king, Cacama.

But Montezuma, taking counsel of his own ill-defined apprehensions, preferred a half-way course — as usual, the most impolitic. He resolved to send an embassy, with such a magnificent present to the strangers, as should impress them with high ideas of his grandeur and resources; while at the same time, he would forbid their approach to the capital. This was to reveal, at once, both his wealth and his weakness.

While the Aztec court was thus agitated by the arrival of the Spaniards, they were passing their time in the tierra caliente, not a little annoyed by the excessive heats and suffocating atmosphere of the sandy waste on which they were encamped. They experienced every alleviation that could be derived from the attentions of the friendly natives. These, by the governor's command, had constructed more than a thousand huts or booths of branches and matting which they occupied in the neighbourhood of the camp. Here they prepared various articles of food for the tables of Cortes and his officers, without any recompense; while the common soldiers easily obtained a supply for themselves, in exchange for such trifles as they brought with them for barter. Thus the camp was liberally provided with meat and fish dressed in many savoury ways, with cakes of corn, bananas, pine-apples, and divers luscious vegetables of the tropics, hitherto unknown to the Spaniards. The soldiers contrived, moreover, to obtain many little bits of gold, of no great value, indeed, from the natives; a traffic very displeasing to the partisans of Velasquez, who considered it an invasion of his rights. Cortes, however, did not think it prudent in this matter to baulk the inclinations of his followers.

At the expiration of seven, or eight days at most, the Mexican embassy presented itself before the camp. It may seem an incredibly short space of time, considering the distance of the capital was near seventy leagues. But it may be remembered that tidings were carried there by means of posts, as already noticed, in the brief space of four-and-twenty hours; and four or five days would suffice for the descent of the envoys to the coast, accustomed as the Mexicans were to long and rapid travelling. At all events, no writer states the period occupied by the Indian emissaries on this occasion as longer than that mentioned.

The embassy, consisting of two Aztec nobles, was accompanied by the governor, Teuhtlile, and by a hundred slaves, bearing the princely gifts of Montezuma. One of the envoys had been selected on account of the great resemblance which, as appeared from the painting representing the camp, he bore to the Spanish commander. And it is a proof of the fidelity of the painting, that the soldiers recognised the resemblance, and always distinguished the chief by the name of the "Mexican Cortes."

On entering the general's pavilion, the ambassadors saluted him and his officers, with the usual signs of reverence to persons of great consideration, touching the ground with their hands and then carrying them to their heads, while the air was filled with clouds of incense, which rose up from the censers borne by their attendants. Some delicately wrought mats of the country (petates) were then unrolled, and on them the slaves displayed the various articles they had brought. They were of the most miscellaneous kind; shields, helmets, cuirasses, embossed with plates and ornaments of pure gold; collars and bracelets of the same metal, sandals, fans, panaches and crests of variegated feathers, intermingled with gold and silver thread, and sprinkled with pearls and precious stones; imitations of birds and animals in wrought and cast gold and silver, of exquisite workmanship; curtains, coverlets, and robes of cotton, fine as silk, of rich and various dyes, interwoven with feather-work that rivalled the delicacy of painting. There were more than thirty loads of cotton cloth in addition. Among the articles was the Spanish helmet sent to the capital, and now returned filled to the brim with grains of gold. But the things which excited the most admiration were two circular plates of gold and silver, "as large as carriage-wheels." One, representing the sun, was richly carved with plants and animals — no doubt, denoting the Aztec century. It was thirty palms in circumference, and was valued at twenty thousand pesos de oro. The silver wheel, of the same size, weighed fifty marks.

When Cortes and his officers had completed their survey, the ambassadors courteously delivered the message of Montezuma. "It gave their master great pleasure," they said, "to hold this communication with so powerful a monarch as the King of Spain, for whom he felt the most profound respect. He regretted much that he could not enjoy a personal interview with the Spaniards, but the distance of his capital was too great; since the journey was beset with difficulties, and with too many dangers from formidable enemies, to make it possible. All that could be done, therefore, was for the strangers to return to their own land, with the proofs thus afforded them of his friendly disposition."

Cortes, though much chagrined at this decided refusal of Montezuma to admit his visit, concealed his mortification as he best might, and politely expressed his sense of the emperor's munificence. "It made him only the more desirous," he said, "to have a personal interview with him. He should feel it, indeed, impossible to present himself again before his own sovereign, without having accomplished this great object of his voyage; and one, who had sailed over two thousand leagues of ocean, held lightly the perils and fatigues of so short a journey by land." He once more requested them to become the bearers of his message to their master, together with a slight additional token of his respect.

This consisted of a few fine Holland shirts, a Florentine goblet, gilt and somewhat curiously enamelled, with some toys of little value — a sorry return for the solid magnificence of the royal present. The ambassadors may have thought as much. At least, they showed no alacrity in charging themselves either with the present. or the message; and, on quitting the Castilian quarters, repeated their assurance that the general's application would be unavailing.

The splendid treasure, which now lay dazzling the eyes of the Spaniards, raised in their bosoms very different emotions, according to the difference of their characters. Some it stimulated with the ardent desire to strike at once into the interior, and possess themselves of a country which teemed with such boundless stores of wealth. Others looked on it as the evidence of a power altogether too formidable to be encountered with their present insignificant force. They thought, therefore, it would be most prudent to return and report their proceedings to the governor of Cuba, where preparations could be made commensurate with so vast an undertaking. There can be little doubt as to the impression made on the bold spirit of Cortes, on which difficulties ever operated as incentives rather than discouragements to enterprise. But he prudently said nothing — at least in public — preferring that so important a movement should flow from the determination of his whole army, rather than from his own individual impulse.

Meanwhile the soldiers suffered greatly from the inconveniences of their position amidst burning sands and the pestilent effluvia of the neighbouring marshes, while the venomous insects of these hot regions left them no repose, day or night. Thirty of their number had already sickened and died; a loss that could in be afforded by the little band. To add to their troubles, the coldness of the Mexican chiefs had extended to their followers; and the supplies for the camp were not only much diminished, but the prices set on them were exorbitant. The position was equally unfavourable for the shipping, which lay in an open roadstead, exposed to the fury of the first norte which should sweep the Mexican Gulf.

The general was induced by these circumstances to despatch two vessels, under Francisco de Montejo, with Alaminos for his pilot, to explore the coast in a northerly direction, and see if a safer port and more commodious quarters for the army could not be found there.

After the lapse of ten days the Mexican envoys returned. They entered the Spanish quarters with the same formality as on the former visit, bearing with them an additional present of rich stuffs and metallic ornaments, which, though inferior in value to those before brought, were estimated at three thousand ounces of gold. Besides these, there were four precious stones of a considerable size, resembling emeralds, called by the natives chalchuites, each of which, as they assured the Spaniards, was worth more than a load of gold, and was designed as a mark of particular respect for the Spanish monarch. Unfortunately they were not worth as many loads of earth in Europe.

Montezuma's answer was in substance the same as before. It contained a positive prohibition for the strangers to advance nearer to the capital; and expressed the confidence, that, now they had obtained what they had most desired, they would return to their own country without unnecessary delay. Cortes received this unpalatable response courteously, though somewhat coldly, and, turning to his officers, exclaimed, "This is a rich and powerful prince indeed; yet it shall go hard, but we will one day pay him a visit in his capital!"

While they were conversing, the bell struck for vespers. At the sound, the soldiers, throwing themselves on their knees, offered up their orisons before the large wooden cross planted in the sands. As the Aztec chiefs gazed with curious surprise, Cortes thought it a favourable occasion to impress them with what he conceived to be a principal object of his visit to the country. Father Olmedo accordingly expounded, as briefly and clearly as he could, the great doctrines of Christianity, touching on the atonement, the passion, and the resurrection, and concluding with assuring his astonished audience, that it was their intention to extirpate the idolatrous practices of the nation, and to substitute the pure worship of the true God. He then put into their hands a little image of the Virgin with the infant Redeemer, requesting them to place it in their temples instead of their sanguinary deities. How far the Aztec lords comprehended the mysteries of the Faith, as conveyed through the double version of Aguilar and Marina, or how well they perceived the subtle distinctions between their own images and those of the Roman Church, we are not informed. There is a reason to fear, however, that the seed fell on barren ground; for, when the homily of the good father ended, they withdrew with an air of dubious reserve very different from their friendly manners at the first interview. The same night every hut was deserted by the natives, and the Spaniards saw themselves suddenly cut off from supplies in the midst of a desolate wilderness. The movement had so suspicious an appearance, that Cortes apprehended an attack would be made on his quarters, and took precautions accordingly. But none was meditated.

The army was at length cheered by the return of Montejo from his exploring expedition, after an absence of twelve days. He had run down the Gulf as far as Panuco, where he experienced such heavy gales, in attempting to double that headland, that he was driven back, and had nearly foundered. In the whole course of the voyage he had found only one place tolerably sheltered from the north winds. Fortunately, the adjacent country, well watered by fresh running streams, afforded a favourable position for the camp; and thither, after some deliberation, it was determined to repair.

CHAPTER 7. [1519] TROUBLES IN THE CAMP— PLAN FOR A COLONY— MANAGEMENT OF CORTES— MARCH TO CEMPOALLA— PROCEEDINGS WITH THE NATIVES— FOUNDATION OF VILLA RICA DE VERA CRUZ

THERE is no situation which tries so severely the patience and discipline of the soldier, as a life of idleness in camp, where his thoughts, instead of being bent on enterprise and action, are fastened on himself and the inevitable privations and dangers of his condition. This was particularly the case in the present instance, where, in addition to the evils of a scanty subsistence, the troops suffered from excessive heat, swarms of venomous insects, and the other annoyances of a sultry climate. They were, moreover, far from possessing the character of regular forces, trained to subordination under a commander whom they had long been taught to reverence and obey. They were soldiers of fortune, embarked with him in an adventure in which all seemed to have an equal stake, and they regarded their captain — the captain of a day — as little more than an equal.

There was a growing discontent among the men at their longer residence in this strange land. They were still more dissatisfied on learning the general's intention to remove to the neighbourhood of the port discovered by Montejo. "It was time to return," they said, "and report what had been done to the governor of Cuba, and not linger on these barren shores until they had brought the whole Mexican empire on their heads!" Cortes evaded their importunities as well as he could, assuring them there was no cause for despondency. "Everything so far had gone on prosperously, and, when they had taken up a more favourable position, there was no reason to doubt they might still continue the same profitable intercourse with the natives."

While this was passing, five Indians made their appearance in the camp one morning, and were brought to the general's tent. Their dress and whole appearance were different from those of the Mexicans. They wore rings of gold and gems of a bright blue stone in their ears and nostrils, while a gold leaf delicately wrought was attached to the under lip. Marina was unable to comprehend their language; but, on her addressing them in Aztec, two of them, it was found, could converse in that tongue. They said they were natives of Cempoalla, the chief town of the Totonacs, a powerful nation who had come upon the great plateau many centuries back, and descending its eastern slope, settled along the sierras and broad plains which skirt the Mexican Gulf towards the north. Their country was one of the recent conquests of the Aztecs, and they experienced such vexatious oppressions from their conquerors as made them very impatient of the yoke. They informed Cortes of these and other particulars. The fame of the Spaniards had reached their master, who sent these messengers to request the presence of the wonderful strangers in his capital.

This communication was eagerly listened to by the general, who, it will be remembered, was possessed of none of those facts, laid before the reader, respecting the internal condition of the kingdom, which he had no reason to suppose other than strong and united. An important truth now flashed on his mind, as his quick eye descried in this spirit of discontent a potent lever by the aid of which he might hope to overturn this barbaric empire. He received the mission of the Totonacs most graciously, and, after informing himself, as far as possible, of their dispositions and resources, dismissed them with presents, promising soon to pay a visit to their lord.

Meanwhile, his personal friends, among whom may be particularly mentioned Alonso Hernandez de Puertocarrero, Christoval de Olid, Alonso de Avila, Pedro de Alvarado and his brothers, were very busy in persuading the troops to take such measures as should enable Cortes to go foward in those ambitious plans for which he had no warrant from the powers of Velasquez. "To return now," they said, "was to abandon the enterprise on the threshold, which, under such a leader, must conduct to glory and incalculable riches. To return to Cuba would be to surrender to the greedy governor the little gains they had already got. The only way was to persuade the general to establish a permanent colony in the country, the government of which would take the conduct of matters into its own hands, and provide for the interests of its members. It was true, Cortes had no such authority from Velasquez. But the interests of the Sovereigns, which were paramount to every other, imperatively demanded it."

76

These conferences could not be conducted so secretly, though held by night, as not to reach the ears of the friends of Velasquez. They remonstrated against the proceedings, as insidious and disloyal. They accused the general of instigating them; and, calling on him to take measures without delay for the return of the troops to Cuba, announced their own intention to depart, with such followers as still remained true to the governor.

Cortes, instead of taking umbrage at this high-handed proceeding, or even answering in the same haughty tone, mildly replied, "that nothing was further from his desire than to exceed his instructions. He, indeed, preferred to remain in the country and continue his profitable intercourse with the natives. But, since the army thought otherwise, he should defer to their opinion, and give orders to return, as they desired." On the following morning, proclamation was made for the troops to hold themselves in readiness to embark at once on board the fleet, which was to sail for Cuba.

Great was the sensation caused by their general's order. Even many of those before clamorous for it, with the usual caprice of men whose wishes are too easily gratified, now regretted it. The partisans of Cortes were loud in their remonstrances. "They were betrayed by the general," they cried, and thronging round his tent, called on him to countermand his orders. "We came here," said they, "expecting to form a settlement, if the state of the country authorised it. Now it seems you have no warrant from the governor to make one. But there are interests, higher than those of Velasquez, which demand it. These territories are not his property, but were discovered for the Sovereigns; and it is necessary to plant a colony to watch over their interests, instead of wasting time in idle barter, or, still worse, of returning, in the present state of affairs, to Cuba. If you refuse," they concluded, "we shall protest against your conduct as disloyal to their Highnesses."

Cortes received this remonstrance with the embarrassed air of one by whom it was altogether unexpected. He modestly requested time for deliberation, and promised to give his answer on the following day. At the time appointed, he called the troops together, and made them a brief address. "There was no one," he said, "if he knew his own heart, more deeply devoted than himself to the welfare of his sovereigns, and the glory of the Spanish name. He had not only expended his all, but incurred heavy debts, to meet the charges of this expedition, and had hoped to reimburse himself by continuing his traffic with the Mexicans. But, if the soldiers thought a different course advisable, he was ready to postpone his own advantage to the good of the state." He concluded by declaring his willingness to take measures for settling a colony in the name of the Spanish Sovereigns, and to nominate a magistracy to preside over it.

For the alcaldes he selected Puertocarrero and Montejo, the former cavalier his fast friend, and the latter the friend of Velasquez, and chosen for that very reason; a stroke of policy which perfectly succeeded. The regidores, alguacil, treasurer, and other functionaries, were then appointed, all of them his personal friends and adherents. They were regularly sworn into office, and the new city received the title of Villa Rica de Vera Cruz, "The Rich Town of the True Cross"; a name which was considered as happily intimating that union of spiritual and temporal interests to which the arms of the Spanish adventurers in the New World were to be devoted. Thus, by a single stroke of the pen, as it were, the camp was transformed into a civil community, and the whole framework and even title of the city were arranged before the site of it had been settled.

The new municipality were not slow in coming together; when Cortes presented himself cap in hand, before that august body, and, laying the powers of Velasquez on the table, respectfully tendered the resignation of his office of Captain General, "which, indeed," he said, "had necessarily expired, since the authority of the governor was now superseded by that of the magistracy of Villa Rica de Vera Cruz." He then, with a profound obeisance, left the apartment.

The council, after a decent time spent in deliberation, again requested his presence. "There was no one," they said, "who, on mature reflection, appeared to them so well qualified to take charge of the interests of the community, both in peace and in war, as himself; and they unanimously named him, in behalf of their Catholic Highnesses, Captain General and Chief justice of the colony." He was further empowered to draw, on his own account, one fifth of the gold and silver which might hereafter be obtained by commerce or conquest from the natives.

Thus clothed with supreme civil and military jurisdiction, Cortes was not backward in exerting his authority. He found speedy occasion for it.

The transactions above described had succeeded each other so rapidly, that the governor's party seemed to be taken by surprise, and had formed no plan of opposition. When the last measure was carried, however, they broke forth into the most indignant and opprobrious invectives, denouncing the whole as a systematic conspiracy against Velasquez. These accusations led to recrimination from the soldiers of the other side, until from words they nearly proceeded to blows. Some of the principal cavaliers, among them Velasquez de Leon, a kinsman of the governor, Escobar his page, and Diego de Ordaz, were so active in instigating these turbulent movements that Cortes took the bold measure of putting them all in irons, and sending them on board the vessels. He then dispersed the common file by detaching many of them, with a strong party under Alvarado, to forage the neighbouring country, and bring home provisions for the destitute camp.

During their absence, every argument that cupidity or ambition could suggest was used to win the refractory to his views. Promises, and even gold, it is said, were liberally lavished; till, by degrees, their understandings were opened to a clearer view of the merits of the case. And when the foraging party re-appeared with abundance of poultry and vegetables, and the cravings of the stomach — that great laboratory of disaffection, whether in camp or capital — were appeased, good humour returned with good cheer, and the rival factions embraced one another as companions in arms, pledged to a common cause. Even the high-mettled hidalgos on board the vessels did not long withstand the general tide of reconciliation, but one by one gave in their adhesion to the new government. What is more remarkable is, that this forced conversion was not a hollow one, but from this time forward several of these very cavaliers become the most steady and devoted partisans of Cortes.

Such was the address of this extraordinary man, and such the ascendency which in a few months he had acquired over these wild and turbulent spirits! By this ingenious transformation of a military into a civil community, he had secured a new and effectual basis for future operations. He might now go forward without fear of cheek or control from a superior — at least from any other superior than the crown, under which alone he held his commission. In accomplishing this, instead of incurring the charge of usurpation, or of transcending his legitimate powers, he had transferred the responsibility, in a great measure, to those who had imposed on him the necessity of action. By this step, moreover, he had linked the fortunes of his followers indissolubly with his own. They had taken their chance with him, and, whether for weal or for woe, must abide the consequences. He was no longer limited to the narrow concerns of a sordid traffic, but sure of their co-operation, might now boldly meditate, and gradually disclose, those lofty schemes which he had formed in his own bosom for the conquest of an empire.

Harmony being thus restored, Cortes sent his heavy guns on board the fleet, and ordered it to coast along the shore to the north as far as Chiahuitztla, the town near which the destined port of the new city was situated; proposing, himself, at the head of his troops, to visit Cempoalla, on the march. The road lay for some miles across the dreary plains in the neighbourhood of the modern Vera Cruz. In this sandy waste no signs of vegetation met their eyes, which, however, were occasionally refreshed by glimpses of the blue Atlantic, and by the distant view of the magnificent Orizaba, towering with his spotless diadem of snow far above his colossal brethren of the Andes. As they advanced, the country gradually assumed a greener and richer aspect. They crossed a river, probably a tributary of the Rio de la Antigua, with difficulty, on rafts, and on some broken canoes that were lying on the banks. They now came in view of very different scenery — wide-rolling plains covered with a rich carpet of verdure, and overshadowed by groves of cocoas and feathery palms, among whose tall, slender stems were seen deer, and various wild animals with which the Spaniards were unacquainted. Some of the horsemen gave chase to the deer, and wounded, but did not succeed in killing them. They saw, also, pheasants and other birds; among them the wild turkey, the pride of the American forest, which the Spaniards described as a species of peacock.

On their route they passed through some deserted villages in which were Indian temples, where they found censers, and other sacred utensils, and manuscripts of the agave fibre, containing the picture-writing, in which, probably, their religious ceremonies were recorded. They now beheld, also, the hideous spectacle, with which they became afterwards familiar, of the mutilated corpses of victims who had been sacrificed to the accursed deities of the land. The Spaniards turned with loathing and indignation from a display of butchery, which formed so dismal a contrast to the fair scenes of nature by which they were surrounded.

They held their course along the banks of the river, towards its source, when they were met by twelve Indians, sent by the cacique of Cempoalla to show them the way to his residence. At night they bivouacked in an open meadow, where they were well supplied with provisions by their new friends. They left the stream on the following morning, and, striking northerly across the country, came upon a wide expanse of luxuriant plains and woodland, glowing in all the splendour of tropical vegetation. The branches of the stately trees were gaily festooned with clustering vines of the dark-purple grape, variegated convolvuli, and other flowering parasites of the most brilliant dyes. The undergrowth of prickly aloe, matted with wild rose and honeysuckle, made in many places an almost impervious thicket. Amid this wilderness of sweet-smelling buds and blossoms fluttered numerous birds of the parrot tribe, and clouds of butterflies, whose gaudy colours, nowhere so gorgeous as in the tierra caliente, rivalled those of the vegetable creation; while birds of exquisite song, the scarlet cardinal and the marvellous mockingbird, that comprehends in his own notes the whole music of a forest, filled the air with delicious melody. — The hearts of the stern Conquerors were not very sensible to the beauties of nature. But the magical charms of the scenery drew forth unbounded expressions of delight, and as they wandered through this "terrestrial paradise," as they called it, they fondly compared it to the fairest regions of their own sunny land.

As they approached the Indian city, they saw abundant signs of cultivation in the trim gardens and orchards that lined both sides of the road. They were now met by parties of the natives of either sex, who increased in numbers with every step of their progress. The women, as well as men, mingled fearlessly among the soldiers, bearing bunches and wreaths of flowers, with which they decorated the neck of the general's charger, and hung a chaplet of roses about his helmet. Flowers were the delight of this people. They bestowed much care in their cultivation, in which they were well seconded by a climate of alternate heat and moisture, stimulating the soil to the spontaneous production of every form of vegetable life. The same refined taste, as we shall see, prevailed among the warlike Aztecs.

Many of the women appeared, from their richer dress and numerous attendants, to be persons of rank. They were clad in robes of fine cotton, curiously coloured, which reached from the neck — in the inferior orders, from the waist — to the ankles. The men wore a sort of mantle of the same material, in the Moorish fashion, over their shoulders, and belts or sashes about the loins. Both sexes had jewels and ornaments of gold round their necks, while their ears and nostrils were perforated with rings of the same metal.

Just before reaching the town, some horsemen who had rode in advance returned with the amazing intelligence, "that they had been near enough to look within the gates, and found the houses all plated with burnished silver!" On entering the place, the silver was found to be nothing more than a brilliant coating of stucco, with which the principal buildings were covered; a circumstance which produced much merriment among the soldiers at the expense of their credulous comrades. Such ready credulity is a proof of the exalted state of their imaginations, which were prepared to see gold and silver in every object around them. The edifices of the better kind were of stone and lime, or bricks dried in the sun; the poorer were of clay and earth. All were thatched with palm-leaves, which, though a flimsy roof, apparently, for such structures, were so nicely interwoven as to form a very effectual protection against the weather.

The city was said to contain from twenty to thirty thousand inhabitants. This is the most moderate computation, and not improbable. Slowly and silently the little army paced the narrow and now crowded streets of Cempoalla, inspiring the natives with no greater wonder than they themselves experienced at the display of a policy and refinement so far superior to anything they had witnessed in the New World. The cacique came out in front of his residence to receive them. He was a tall and very corpulent man, and advanced leaning on two of his attendants. He received Cortes and his followers with great courtesy; and, after a brief interchange of civillties, assigned the army its quarters in a neighbouring temple, into the spacious courtyard of which a number of apartments opened, affording excellent accommodations for the soldiery.

Here the Spaniards were well supplied with provisions, meat cooked after the fashion of the country, and maize made into bread-cakes. The general received, also, a present of considerable value from the cacique, consisting of ornaments of gold and fine cottons. Notwithstanding these friendly demonstrations, Cortes did not relax his habitual vigilance, nor neglect any of the precautions of a good soldier. On his route, indeed, he had always marched in order of battle, well prepared against surprise. In his present quarters, he stationed his sentinels with like care, posted his small artillery so as to command the entrance, and forbade any soldier to leave the camp without orders, under pain of death.

The following morning, Cortes, accompanied by fifty of his men, paid a visit to the lord of Cempoalla in his own residence. It was a building of stone and lime, standing on a steep terrace of earth, and was reached by a flight of stone steps. It may have borne resemblance in its structure to some of the ancient buildings found in Central America. Cortes, leaving his soldiers in the courtyard, entered the mansion with one of his officers, and his fair interpreter, Dona Marina. A long conference ensued, from which the Spanish general gathered much light respecting the state of the country. He first announced to the chief, that he was the subject of a great monarch who dwelt beyond the waters; that he had come to the Aztec shores, to abolish the inhuman worship which prevailed there, and to introduce the knowledge of the true God. The cacique replied that their gods, who sent them the sunshine and the rain, were good enough for them; that he was the tributary of a powerful monarch also, whose capital stood on a lake far off among the mountains; a stern prince, merciless in his exactions, and, in case of resistance, or any offence, sure to wreak his vengeance by carrying off their young men and maidens to be sacrificed to his deities. Cortes assured him that he would never consent to such enormities; he had been sent by his sovereign to redress abuses and to punish the oppressor; and, if the Totonacs would be true to him, he would enable them to throw off the detested yoke of the Aztecs.

The cacique added, that the Totonac territory contained about thirty towns and villages, which could muster a hundred thousand warriors — a number much exaggerated. There were other provinces of the empire, he said, where the Aztec rule was equally odious; and between him and the capital lay the warlike republic of Tlascala, which had always maintained its independence of Mexico. The fame of the Spaniards had gone before them, and he was well acquainted with their terrible victory at Tabasco. But still he looked with doubt and alarm to a rupture with "the great Montezuma," as he always styled him; whose armies, on the least provocation, would pour down from the mountain regions of the west, and, rushing over the plains like a whirlwind, sweep off the wretched people to slavery and sacrifice!

Cortes endeavoured to reassure him, by declaring that a single Spaniard was stronger than a host of Aztecs. At the same time, it was desirable to know what nations would cooperate with him, not so much on his account, as theirs, that he might distinguish friend from foe, and know whom he was to spare in this war of extermination. Having raised the confidence of the admiring chief by this comfortable and politic vaunt, he took an affectionate leave, with the assurance that he would shortly return and concert measures for their future operations, when he had visited his ships in the adjoining port, and secured a permanent settlement there.

The intelligence gained by Cortes gave great satisfaction to his mind. It confirmd his former views, and showed, indeed, the interior of the monarchy to be in a state far more distracted than he had supposed. If he had before scarcely shrunk from attacking the Aztec empire in the true spirit of a knight-errant, with his single arm, as it were, what had he now to fear, when one half of the nation could be thus marshalled against the other? In the excitement of the moment, his sanguine spirit kindled with an enthusiasm which overleaped every obstacle. He communicated his own feelings to the officers about him, and, before a blow was struck, they already felt as if the banners of Spain were waving in triumph the towers of Montezuma!

Taking leave of the hospitable Indian on the following day, the Spaniards took the road to Chiahuitztla, about four leagues distant, near which was the port discovered by Montejo, where their ships were now riding at anchor. They were provided by the cacique with four hundred Indian porters, tamanes, as they were called, to transport the baggage. These men easily carried fifty pounds' weight five or six leagues in a day. They were in use all over the Mexican empire, and the Spaniards found them of great service, henceforth, in relieving the troops from this part of their duty. They passed through a country of the same rich, voluptuous character as that which they had lately traversed; and arrived early next morning at the Indian town, perched like a fortress on a bold, rocky eminence that commanded the Gulf. Most of the inhabitants had fled, but fifteen of the principal men remained, who received them in a friendly manner, offering the usual compliments of flowers and incense. The people of the place, losing their fears, gradually returned. While conversing with the chiefs, the Spaniards were joined by the worthy cacique of Cempoalla, borne by his men on a litter. He eagerly took part in their deliberations. The intelligence gained here by Cortes confirmed the accounts already gathered of the feelings and resources of the Totonac nation.

In the midst of their conference, they were interrupted by a movement among the people, and soon afterwards five men entered the great square or market-place, where they were standing. By their lofty port, their peculiar and much richer dress, they seemed not to be of the same race as these Indians. Their dark glossy hair was tied in a knot on the top of the head. They had bunches of flowers in their hands, and were followed by several attendants, some bearing wands with cords, other fans, with which they brushed away the flies and insects from their lordly masters. As these persons passed through the place, they cast a haughty look on the Spaniards, scarcely deigning to return their salutations. They were immediately joined, in great confusion, by the Totonac chiefs, who seemed anxious to conciliate them by every kind of attention.

The general, much astonished, inquired of Marina what it meant. She informed him, they were Aztec nobles, empowered to receive the tribute for Montezuma. Soon after, the chiefs returned with dismay painted on their faces. They confirmed Marina's statement, adding, that the Aztecs greatly resented the entertainment afforded the Spaniards without the emperor's permission; and demanded in expiation twenty young men and women for sacrifice to the gods. Cortes showed the strongest indignation at this insolence. He required the Totonacs not only to refuse the demand, but to arrest the persons of the collectors, and throw them into prison. The chiefs hesitated, but he insisted on it so peremptorily, that they at length complied, and the Aztecs were seized, bound hand and foot, and placed under a guard.

In the night, the Spanish general procured the escape of two of them, and had them brought secretly before him. He expressed his regret at the indignity they had experienced from the Totonacs; told them, he would provide means for their flight, and tomorrow would endeavour to obtain the release of their companions. He desired them to report this to their master, with assurances of the great regard the Spaniards entertained for him, notwithstanding his ungenerous behaviour in leaving them to perish from want on his barren shores. He then sent the Mexican nobles down to the port, whence they were carried to another part of the coast by water, for fear of the violence of the Totonacs. These were greatly incensed at the escape of the prisoners, and would have sacrificed the remainder at once, but for the Spanish commander, who evinced the utmost horror at the proposal, and ordered them to be sent for safe custody on board the fleet. Soon after, they were permitted to join their companions. — This artful proceeding, so characteristic of the policy of Cortes, had, as we shall see hereafter, all the effect intended on Montezuma.

By order of Cortes, messengers were despatched to the Totonac towns, to report what had been done, calling on them to refuse the payment of further tribute to Montezuma. But there was no need of messengers. The affrighted attendants of the Aztec lords had fled in every direction, bearing the tidings, which spread like wildfire through the country, of the daring insult offered to the majesty of Mexico. The astonished Indians, cheered with the sweet hope of regaining their ancient liberty, came in numbers to Chiahuitztla, to see and confer with the formidable strangers. The more timid, dismayed at the thoughts of encountering the power of Montezuma, recommended an embassy to avert his displeasure by timely concessions. But the dexterous management of Cortes had committed them too far to allow any reasonable expectation of indulgence from this quarter. After some hesitation, therefore, it was determined to embrace the protection of the Spaniards, and to make one bold effort for the recovery of freedom. Oaths of allegiance were taken by the chiefs to the Spanish sovereigns, and duly recorded by Godoy, the royal notary. Cortes, satisfied with the important acquisition of so many vassals to the crown, set out soon after for the destined port, having first promised to revisit Cempoalla, where his business was but partially accomplished.

The spot selected for the new city was only half a league distant, in a wide and fruitful plain, affording a tolerable haven for the shipping. Cortes was not long in determining the circuit of the walls, and the sites of the fort, granary, townhouse, temple, and other public buildings. The friendly Indians eagerly assisted, by bringing materials, stone, lime, wood, and bricks dried in the sun. Every man put his hand to the work. The general laboured with the meanest of the soldiers, stimulating their exertions by his example, as well as voice. In a few weeks the task was accomplished, and a town rose up, which, if not quite worthy of the aspiring name it bore, answered most of the purposes for which it was intended. It served as a good point d'appui for future operations; a place of retreat for the disabled, as well as for the army in case of reverses; a magazine for stores, and for such articles as might be received from or sent to the mother country; a port for the shipping; a position of sufficient strength to overawe the adjacent country.

It was the first colony — the fruitful parent of so many others — in New Spain. It was hailed with satisfaction by the simple natives, who hoped to repose in safety under its protecting shadow. Alas! they could not read the future, or they would have found no cause to rejoice in this harbinger of a revolution more tremendous than. any predicted by their bards and prophets. It was not the good Quetzalcoatl who had returned to claim his own again, bringing peace, freedom, and civilisation in his train. Their fetters, indeed, would be broken, and their wrongs be amply avenged on the proud head of the Aztec; but it was to be by that strong arm which should bow down equally the oppressor and the oppressed. The light of civilisation would be poured on their land; but it would be the light of a consuming fire, before which their barbaric glory, their institutions, their very existence and name as a nation, would wither and become extinct! Their doom was sealed when the white man. had set his foot on their soil.

WHILE the Spaniards were occupied with their new settlement, they were surprised by the presence of an embassy from Mexico. The account of the imprisonment of the royal collectors had spread rapidly through the country. When it reached the capital, all were filled with amazement at the unprecedented daring of the strangers. In Montezuma every other feeling, even that of fear, was swallowed up in indignation; and he showed his wonted energy in the vigorous preparations which he instantly made to punish his rebellious vassals, and to avenge the insult offered to the majesty of the empire. But when the Aztec officers liberated by Cortes reached the capital and reported the courteous treatment they had received from the Spanish commander, Montezuma's anger was mitigated, and his superstitious fears, getting the ascendency again, induced him to resume his former timid and conciliatory policy. He accordingly sent an embassy, consisting of two youths, his nephews, and four of the ancient nobles of his court, to the Spanish quarters. He provided them, in his usual munificent spirit, with a princely donation of gold, rich cotton stuffs, and beautiful mantles of the plumaje, or feather embroidery. The envoys, on coming before Cortes, presented him with the articles, at the same time offering the acknowledgments of their master for the courtesy he had shown in liberating his captive nobles. He was surprised and afflicted, however, that the Spaniards should have countenanced his faithless vassals in their rebellion. He had no doubt they were the strangers whose arrival had been so long announced by the oracles, and of the same lineage with himself. From deference to them he would spare the Totonacs, while they were present. But the time for vengeance would come.

Cortes entertained the Indian chieftains with frank hospitality. At the same time he took care to make such a display of his resources, as, while it amused their minds, should leave a deep impression of his power. He then, after a few trifling gifts, dismissed them with a conciliatory message to their master, and the assurance that he should soon pay his respects to him in his capital, where all misunderstanding between them would be readily adjusted.

The Totonac allies could scarcely credit their senses, when they gathered the nature of this interview. Notwithstanding the presence of the Spaniards, they had looked with apprehension to the consequences of their rash act; and their feelings of admiration were heightened into awe for the strangers who, at this distance, could exercise so mysterious an influence over the terrible Montezuma.

Not long after, the Spaniards received an application from the cacique of Cempoalla to aid him in a dispute in which he was engaged with a neighbouring city. Cortes marched with a part of his forces to his support. On the route, one Morla, a common soldier, robbed a native of a couple of fowls. Cortes, indignant at this violation of his orders before his face, and aware of the importance of maintaining a reputation for good faith with his allies, commanded the man to be hung up at once by the roadside, in face of the whole army. Fortunately for the poor wretch, Pedro de Alvarado, the future conqueror of Quiche, was present, and ventured to cut down the body while there was yet life in it. He, probably, thought enough had been done for example, and the loss of a single life, unnecessarily, was more than the little band could afford. The anecdote is characteristic, as showing the strict discipline maintained by Cortes over his men and the freedom assumed by his captains, who regarded him on terms nearly of equality — as a fellow-adventurer with themselves. This feeling of companionship led to a spirit of insubordination among them, which made his own post as commander the more delicate and difficult.

On reaching the hostile city, but a few leagues from the coast, they were received in an amicable manner; and Cortes, who was accompanied by his allies, had the satisfaction of reconciling these different branches of the Totonac family with each other, without bloodshed. He then returned to Cempoalla, where he was welcomed with joy by the people, who were now impressed with as favourable an opinion of his moderation and justice, as they had before been of his valour. In token of his gratitude, the Indian cacique delivered to the general eight

Indian maidens, richly dressed, wearing collars and ornaments of gold, with a number of female slaves to wait on them. They were daughters of the principal chiefs, and the cacique requested that the Spanish captains might take them as their wives. Cortes received the damsels courteously, but told the cacique they must first be baptised, as the sons of the Church could have no commerce with idolaters. He then declared that it was a great object of his mission to wean the natives from their heathenish abominations, and besought the Totonac lord to allow his idols to be cast down, and the symbols of the true faith to be erected in their place.

To this the other answered as before, that his gods were good enough for him; nor could all the persuasion of the general, nor the preaching of Father Olmedo, induce him to acquiesce. Mingled with his polytheism, he had conceptions of a Supreme and Infinite Being, Creator of the Universe, and his darkened understanding could not comprehend how such a Being could condescend to take the form of humanity, with its infirmities and ills, and wander about on earth, the voluntary victim of persecution from the hands of those whom his breath had called into existence. He plainly told the Spaniards that he would resist any violence offered to his gods, who would, indeed, avenge the act themselves, by the instant destruction of their enemies.

But the zeal of the Christians had mounted too high to be cooled by remonstrance or menace. During their residence in the land, the had witnessed more than once the barbarous rites of the natives, their cruel sacrifices of human victims, and their disgusting cannibal repasts. Their souls sickened at these abominations, and they agreed with one voice to stand by their general, when he told them, that "Heaven would never smile on their enterprise, if they countenanced such atrocities; and that, for his own part, he was resolved the Indian idols should be demolished that very hour, if it cost him his life." To postpone the work of conversion was a sin. In the enthusiasm of the moment, the dictates of policy and ordinary prudence were alike unheeded.

Scarcely waiting for his commands, the Spaniards moved towards one of the principal teocallis, or temples, which rose high on a pyramidal foundation, with a steep ascent of stone steps in the middle. The cacique, divining their purpose, instantly called his men to arms. The Indian warriors gathered from all quarters, with shrill cries and clashing of weapons; while the priests, in their dark cotton robes, with dishevelled tresses matted with blood, flowing wildly over their shoulders, rushed frantic among the natives, calling on them to protect their gods from violation! All was now confusion, tumult, and warlike menace, where so lately had been peace and the sweet brotherhood of nations.

Cortes took his usual prompt and decided measures. He caused the cacique and some of the principal inhabitants and priests to be arrested by his soldiers. He then commanded them to quiet the people, for, if an arrow was shot against a Spaniard, it should cost every one of them his life. Marina, at the same time, represented the madness of resistance, and reminded the cacique, that, if he now alienated the affections of the Spaniards, he would be left without a protector against the terrible vengeance of Montezuma. These temporal considerations seem to have had more weight with the Totonac chieftain than those of a more spiritual nature. He covered his face with his hands, exclaiming, that the gods would avenge their own wrongs.

The Christians were not slow in availing themselves of his tacit acquiescence. Fifty soldiers, at a signal from their general, sprang up the great stairway of the temple, entered the building on the summit, the walls of which were black with human gore, tore the huge wooden idols from their foundations, and dragged them to the edge of the terrace. Their fantastic forms and features, conveying a symbolic meaning, which was lost on the Spaniards, seemed in their eyes only the hideous lineaments of Satan. With great alacrity they rolled the colossal monsters down the steps of the pyramid, amidst the triumphant shouts of their own companions, and the groans and lamentations of the natives. They then consummated the whole by burning them in the presence of the assembled multitude.

The same effect followed as in Cozumel. The Totonacs, finding their deities incapable of preventing or even punishing this profanation of their shrines, conceived a mean opinion of their power, compared with that of the mysterious and formidable strangers. The floor and walls of the teocalli were then cleansed, by command of Cortes, from their, foul impurities; a fresh coating of stucco was laid on them by the Indian masons; and an altar was raised, surmounted by a lofty cross, and hung with garlands of roses. A procession was next formed, in which some of the principal Totonae priests, exchanging their dark mantles for robes of white, carried lighted candles in their hands; while an image of the Virgin, half smothered under the weight of flowers, was borne aloft, and, as the procession climbed the steps of the temple, was deposited above the altar. Mass was performed by Father Olmedo, and the impressive character of the ceremony and the passionate eloquence of the good priest touched the feelings of the motley audience, until Indians as well as Spaniards, if we may trust the chronicler, were melted into tears and audible sobs.

An old soldier named Juan de Torres, disabled by bodily infirmity, consented to remain and watch over the sanctuary and instruct the natives in its services. Cortes then, embracing his Totonac allies, now brothers in religion as in arms, set out once more for the Villa Rica, where he had some arrangements to complete, previous to his departure for the capital.

He was surprised to find that a Spanish vessel had arrived there in his absence, having on board twelve soldiers and two horses. It was under the command of a captain named Saucedo, a cavalier of the ocean, who had followed in the track of Cortes in quest of adventure. Though a small, they afforded a very seasonable, body of recruits for the little army. By these men, the Spaniards were informed that Velasquez, the governor of Cuba, had lately received a warrant from the Spanish government to establish a colony in the newly discovered countries.

Cortes now, resolved to put a plan in execution which he had been some time meditating. He knew that all the late acts of the colony, as well as his own authority, would fall to the ground without the royal sanction. He knew, too, that the interest of Velasquez, which was great at court, would, as soon as he was acquainted with his secession, be wholly employed to circumvent and crush him. He resolved to anticipate his movements, and to send a vessel to Spain, with despatches addressed to the emperor himself, announcing the nature and extent of his discoveries, and to obtain, if possible, the confirmation of his proceedings. In order to conciliate his master's good will, he further proposed to send him such a present as should suggest lofty ideas of the importance of his own services to the crown. To effect this, the royal fifth he considered inadequate. He conferred with his officers, and persuaded them to relinquish their share of the treasure. At his instance, they made a similar application to the soldiers; representing that it was the earnest wish of the general, who set the example by resigning his own fifth, equal to the share of the crown. It was but little that each man was asked to surrender, but the whole would make a present worthy of the monarch for whom it was intended. By this sacrifice they might hope to secure his indulgence for the past, and his favour for the future; a temporary sacrifice, that would be well repaid by the security of the rich possessions which awaited them in Mexico. A paper was then circulated among the soldiers, which all, who were disposed to relinquish their shares, were requested to sign. Those who declined should have their claims respected, and receive the amount due to them. No one refused to sign; thus furnishing another example of the extraordinary power obtained by Cortes over these rapacious spirits, who, at his call, surrendered up the very treasures which had been the great object of their hazardous enterprise!

He accompanied this present with a letter to the, emperor, in which he gave a full account of all that had befallen him since his departure from Cuba; of his various discoveries, battles, and traffic with the natives; their conversion to Christianity; his strange perils and sufferings; many particulars respecting the lands he had visited, and such as he could collect in regard to the great Mexican monarchy and its sovereign. He stated his difficulties with the governor of Cuba, the proceedings of the army in reference to colonisation, and besought the emperor to confirm their acts, as well as his own authority, expressing his entire confidence that he should be able, with the aid of his brave followers, to place the Castilian crown in possession of this great Indian empire.

This was the celebrated First Letter, as it is called, of Cortes, which has hitherto eluded every search that has been made for it in the libraries of Europe. Its existence is fully established by references to it, both in his own subsequent letters, and in the writings of contemporaries. Its general purport is given by his chaplain, Gomara. The importance of the document has doubtless been much overrated; and, should it ever come to light, it will probably be found to add little of interest to the matter contained in the letter from Vera Cruz, which has formed the basis of the preceding portion of our narrative. He had no sources of information beyond those open to the authors of the latter document. He was even less full and frank in his communications, if it be true, that he suppressed all notice of the discoveries of his two predecessors.

The magistrates of the Villa Rica, in their epistle, went over the same ground with Cortes; concluding with an emphatic representation of the misconduct of Velasquez, whose venality, extortion, and selfish devotion to his personal interests, to the exclusion of those of his sovereign's as well as of his own followers, they placed in a most clear and unenviable light. They implored the government not to sanction his interference with the new colony, which would be fatal to its welfare, but to commit the undertaking to Hernando Cortes, as the man most capable, by his experience and conduct, of bringing it to a glorious termination.

With this letter went also another in the name of the citizen-soldiers of Villa Rica, tendering their dutiful submission to the sovereigns, and requesting the confirmation of their proceedings, above all that of Cortes as their general.

The selection of the agents for the mission was a delicate matter, as on the result might depend the future fortunes of the colony and its commander. Cortes intrusted the affair to two cavaliers on whom he could rely: Francisco de Montejo, the ancient partisan of Velasquez, and Alonso Hernandez de Puertocarrero. The latter officer was a near kinsman of the Count of Medellin, and it was hoped his high connections might secure a favourable influence at court.

Together with the treasure, which seemed to verify the assertion that "the land teemed with gold as abundantly as that whence Solomon drew the same precious metal for his temple," several Indian manuscripts were sent. Some were of cotton, others of the Mexican agave. Their unintelligible characters, says a chronicler, excited little interest in the conquerors. As evidence of intellectual culture, however, they formed higher objects of interest to a philosophic mind, than those costly fabrics which attested only the mechanical ingenuity of the nation. Four Indian slaves were added as specimens of the natives. They had been rescued from the cages in which they were confined for sacrifice. One of the best vessels of the fleet was selected for the voyage, manned by fifteen seamen, and placed under the direction of the pilot Alaminos. He was directed to hold his course through the Bahama channel, north of Cuba, or Fernandina, as it was then called, and on no account to touch at that island, or any other in the Indian ocean. With these instructions, the good ship took its departure on the 26th of July, freighted with the treasures and the good wishes of the community of the Villa Rica de Vera Cruz.

After a quick run the emissaries made the island of Cuba, and, in direct disregard of orders, anchored before Marien on the northern side of the island. This was done to accommodate Montejo, who wished to visit a plantation owned by him in the neighbourhood. While off the port, a sailor got on shore, and, crossing the island to St. Jago, the capital, spread everywhere tidings of the expedition, until they reached the ears of Velasquez. It was the first intelligence which had been received of the armament since its departure; and, as the governor listened to the recital, it would not be easy to paint the mingled emotions of curiosity, astonishment, and wrath, which agitated his bosom. In the first sally of passion, he poured a storm of invective on the heads of his secretary and treasurer, the friends of Cortes, who had recommended him as the leader of the expedition. After somewhat relieving himself in this way, he despatched two fast-sailing vessels to Marien with orders to seize the rebel ship, and, in case of her departure, to follow and overtake her.

But before the ships could reach that port, the bird had flown, and was far on her way across the broad Atlantic. Stung with mortification at his fresh disappointment, Velasquez wrote letters of indignant complaint to the government at home, and to the fathers of St. Jerome, in Hispaniola, demanding redress. He obtained little satisfaction from the last. He resolved however, to take it into his own hands, and set about making formidable preparations for another squadron, which should be more than a match for that under his rebellious officer. He was indefatigable in his exertions, visiting every part of the island, and straining all his resources to effect his purpose. The preparations were on a scale that necessarily consumed many months.

Meanwhile the little vessel was speeding her prosperous way across the waters; and, after touching at one of the Azores, came safely into the harbour of St. Lucar, in the month of October. However long it may appear in the more perfect nautical science of our day, it was reckoned a fair voyage for that. Of what befell the commissioners on their arrival, their reception at court, and the sensation caused by their intelligence, I defer the account to a future chapter.

Shortly after the departure of the commissioners, an affair occurred of a most unpleasant nature. A number of persons, with the priest Juan Diaz at their head, ill-affected, from some cause or other, towards the administration of Cortes, or not relishing the hazardous expedition before them, laid a plan to seize one of the vessels, make the best of their way to Cuba, and report to the governor the fate of the armament. It was conducted with so much secrecy, that the party had got their provisions, water, and everything necessary for the voyage, on board, without detection; when the conspiracy was betrayed on the very night they were to sail by one of their own number, who repented the part he had taken in it. The general caused the persons implicated to be instantly apprehended. An examination was instituted. The guilt of the parties was placed beyond a doubt. Sentence of death was passed on two of the ringleaders; another, the pilot, was condemned to lose his feet, and several others to be whipped. The priest, probably the most guilty of the whole, claiming the usual benefit of clergy, was permitted to escape. One of those condemned to the gallows was named Escudero, the very alguacil who, the reader may remember, so stealthily apprehended Cortes before the sanctuary in Cuba. The general, on signing the death warrants, was heard to exclaim, "Would that I had never learned to write!"

The arrangements being now fully settled at the Villa Rica, Cortes sent forward Alvarado, with a large part of the army, to Cempoalla, where he soon after joined them with the remainder. The late affair of the conspiracy seems to have made a deep impression on his mind. It showed him that there were timid spirits in the camp on whom he could not rely, and who, he feared, might spread the seeds of disaffection among their companions. Even the more resolute, on any occasion of disgust or disappointment hereafter, might falter in purpose, and, getting possession of the vessels, abandon the enterprise. This was already too vast, and the odds were too formidable, to authorise expectation of success with diminution of numbers. Experience showed that this was always to be apprehended, while means of escape were at hand. The best chance for success was to cut off these means. He came to the daring resolution to destroy the fleet, without the knowledge of his army.

When arrived at Cempoalla, he communicated his design to a few of his devoted adherents, who entered warmly into his views. Through them he readily persuaded the pilots, by means of those golden arguments which weigh more than any other with ordinary minds, to make such a report of the condition of the fleet as suited his purpose. The ships, they said, were grievously racked by the heavy gales they had encountered, and, what was worse, the worms had eaten into their sides and bottoms until most of them were not sea-worthy, and some indeed, could scarcely now be kept afloat.

Cortes received the communication with surprise; "for he could well dissemble," observes Las Casas, with his usual friendly comment, "when it suited his interests." "If it be so," he exclaimed, "we must make the best of it! Heaven's will be done!" He then ordered five of the worst-conditioned to be dismantled, their cordage, sails, iron, and whatever was moveable, to be brought on shore, and the ships to be sunk. A survey was made of the others, and, on a similar report, four more were condemned in the same manner. Only one small vessel remained!

When the intelligence reached the troops in Cempoalla, it caused the deepest consternation. They saw themselves cut off by a single blow from friends, family, country! The stoutest hearts quailed before the prospect of being thus abandoned on a hostile shore, a handful of men arrayed against a formidable empire. When the news arrived of the destruction of the five vessels first condemned, they had acquiesced in it, as a necessary measure, knowing the mischievous activity of the insects in these tropical seas. But, when this was followed by the loss of the remaining four, suspicions of the truth flashed on their minds. They felt they were betrayed. Murmurs, at first deep, swelled louder and louder, menacing open mutiny. "Their general," they said, "had led them like cattle to be butchered in the shambles!" The affair wore a most alarming aspect. In no situation was Cortes ever exposed to greater danger from his soldiers.

His presence of mind did not desert him at this crisis. He called his men together, and employing the tones of persuasion rather than authority, assured them that a survey of the ships showed they were not fit for service. It he had ordered them to be destroyed, they should consider, also, that his was the greatest sacrifice, for they were his property — all, indeed, he possessed in the world. The troops on the other hand, would derive one great advantage from it, by the addition of a hundred able-bodied recruits, before required to man the vessels. But, even if the fleet had been saved, it could have been of little service in their present expedition; since they would not need it if they succeeded, while they would be too far in the interior to profit by it if they failed. He besought them to turn their thoughts in another direction. To be thus calculating chances and means of escape was unworthy of brave souls. They had set their hands to the work; to look back, as they advanced, would be their ruin. They had only to resume their former confidence in themselves and their general, and success was certain. "As for me," he concluded, "I have chosen my part. I will remain here, while there is one to bear me company. If there be any so craven, as to shrink from sharing the dangers of our glorious enterprise, let them go home, in God's name. There is still one vessel left. Let them take that and return to Cuba. They can tell there how they deserted their commander and their comrades, and patiently wait till we return loaded with the spoils of the Aztecs."

The politic orator had touched the right chord in the bosoms of the soldiers. As he spoke, their resentment gradually died away. The faded visions of future riches and glory, rekindled by his eloquence, again floated before their imaginations. The first shock over, they felt ashamed of their temporary distrust. The enthusiasm for their leader revived, for they felt that under his banner only they could hope for victory; and they testified the revulsion of their feelings by making the air ring with their shouts, "To Mexico! to Mexico!"

The destruction of his fleet by Cortes is, perhaps, the most remarkable passage in the life of this remarkable man. History, indeed, affords examples of a similar expedient in emergencies somewhat similar; but none where the chances of success were so precarious, and defeat would be so disastrous. Had he failed, it might well seem an act of madness. Yet it was the fruit of deliberate calculation. He had set fortune, fame, life itself, all upon the cast, and must abide the issue. There was no alternative in his mind but to succeed or perish. The measure he adopted greatly increased the chance of success. But to carry it into execution, in the face of an incensed and desperate soldiery, was an act of resolution that has few parallels in history.

BOOK 3. MARCH TO MEXICO

WHILE at Cempoalla, Cortes received a message from Escalante, his commander at Villa Rica, informing him there were four strange ships hovering off the coast, and that they took no notice of his repeated signals. This intelligence greatly alarmed the general, who feared they might be a squadron sent by the governor of Cuba to interfere with his movements. In much haste, he set out at the head of a few horsemen, and, ordering a party of light infantry to follow, posted back to Villa Rica. The rest of the army he left in charge of Alvarado and of Gonzalo de Sandoval, a young officer, who had begun to give evidence of the uncommon qualities which have secured to him so distinguished a rank among the conquerors of Mexico.

Escalante would have persuaded the general, on his reaching the town, to take some rest, and allow him to go in search of the strangers; but Cortes replied with the homely proverb, "A wounded hare takes no nap," and, without stopping to refresh himself or his men, pushed on three or four leagues to the north, where he understood the ships were at anchor. On the way, he fell in with three Spaniards, just landed from them. To his eager inquiries whence they came, they replied that they belonged to a squadron fitted out by Francisco de Garay, governor of Jamaica. This person, the year previous, had visited the Florida coast, and obtained from Spain — where he had some interest at court — authority over the countries he might discover in that vicinity. The three men, consisting of a notary and two witnesses, had been sent on shore to warn their countrymen under Cortes to desist from what was considered an encroachment on the territories of Garay. Probably neither the governor of Jamaica, nor his officers, had any very precise notion of the geography and limits of these territories.

Cortes saw at once there was nothing to apprehend from this quarter. He would have been glad, however, if he could, by any means have induced the crews of the ships to join his expedition. He found no difficulty in persuading the notary and his companions. But when he came in sight of the vessels, the people on board, distrusting the good terms on which their comrades appeared to be with the Spaniards, refused to send their boat ashore. In this dilemma, Cortes had recourse to a stratagem.

He ordered three of his own men to exchange dresses with the new comers. He then drew off his little band in sight of the vessels, affecting to return to the city. In the night, however, he came back to the same place, and lay in ambush, directing the disguised Spaniards, when the morning broke, and they could be discerned, to make signals to those on board. The artifice succeeded. A boat put off, filled with armed men, and three or four leaped on shore. But they soon detected the deceit, and Cortes, springing from his ambush, made them prisoners. Their comrades in the boat, alarmed, pushed off at once for the vessels, which soon got under weigh, leaving those on shore to their fate. Thus ended the affair. Cortes returned to Cempoalla, with the addition of half a dozen able-bodied recruits, and, what was of more importance, relieved in his own mind from the apprehension of interference with his operations.

He now made arrangements for his speedy departure from the Totonac capital. The forces reserved for the expedition amounted to about four hundred foot and fifteen horse, with seven pieces of artillery. He obtained, also, thirteen hundred Indian warriors, and a thousand tamanes, or porters, from the cacique of Cempoalla, to drag the guns, and transport the baggage. He took forty more of their principal men as hostages, as well as to guide him on the way, and serve him by their counsels among the strange tribes he was to visit. They were of essential service to him throughout the march.

The remainder of his Spanish force he left in garrison at Villa Rica de Vera Cruz, the command of which he had intrusted to the alguacil, Juan de Escalante, an officer devoted to his interests. The selection was judicious. It was important to place there a man who would resist any hostile interference from his European rivals, on the one hand, and maintain the present friendly relations with the natives, on the other. Cortes recommended the Totonac chiefs to apply to his officer, in case of any difficulty, assuring them that, so long as they remained faithful to their new sovereign and religion, they should find a sure protection in the Spaniards.

Before marching, the general spoke a few words of encouragement to his own men. He told them they were now to embark in earnest, on an enterprise which had been the great object of their desires; and that the blessed Saviour would carry them victorious through every battle with their enemies. "Indeed," he added, "this assurance must be our stay, for every other refuge is now cut off, but that afforded by the providence of God, and your own stout hearts." He ended by comparing their achievements to those of the ancient Romans, "in phrases of honeyed eloquence far beyond anything I can repeat," says the brave and simple-hearted Bernal Diaz, who heard them. Cortes was, indeed, master of that eloquence which went to the soldiers' hearts. For their sympathies were his, and he shared in that romantic spirit of adventure which belonged to them. "We are ready to obey you," they cried as with one voice. "Our fortunes, for better or worse, are cast with yours." Taking leave, therefore, of their hospitable Indian friends, the little army, buoyant with high hopes and lofty plans of conquest, set forward on the march to Mexico, the sixteenth of August, 1519.

After some leagues of travel over roads made nearly impassable by the summer rains, the troops began the gradual ascent — more gradual on the eastern than the western declivities of the Cordilleras — which leads up to the tableland of Mexico. At the close of the second day, they reached Xalapa, a place still retaining the same Aztec name that it has communicated to the drug raised in its environs, the medicinal virtues of which are now known throughout the world. Still winding their way upward, the army passed through settlements containing some hundreds of inhabitants each, and on the fourth day reached a "strong town," as Cortes terms it, standing on a rocky eminence, supposed to be that now known by the Mexican name of Naulinco. Here they were hospitably entertained by the inhabitants, who were friends of the Totonacs. Cortes endeavoured, through Father Olmedo, to impart to them some knowledge of Christian truths, which were kindly received, and the Spaniards were allowed to erect a cross in the place, for the future adoration of the natives. Indeed, the route of the army might be tracked by these emblems of man's salvation, raised wherever a willing population of Indians invited it.

The troops now entered a rugged defile, the Bishop's Pass, as it is called, capable of easy defence against an army. Very soon they experienced a most unwelcome change of climate. Cold winds from the mountains, mingled with rain, and, as they rose still higher, with driving sleet and hail, drenched their garments, and seemed to penetrate to their very bones. The Spaniards, indeed, partially covered by their armour and thick jackets of quilted cotton, were better able to resist the weather, though their long residence in the sultry regions of the valley made them still keenly sensible to the annoyance. But the poor Indians, natives of the tierra caliente, with little protection in the way of covering, sunk under the rude assault of the elements, and several of them perished on the road.

The aspect of the country was as wild and dreary as the climate. Their route wound along the spur of the huge Cofre of Perote, which borrows its name from the coffer-like rock on its summit. It is one of the great volcanoes of New Spain. It exhibits now, indeed, no vestige of a crater on its top, but abundant traces of volcanic action at its base, where acres of lava, blackened scoriae, and cinders, proclaim the convulsions of nature, while numerous shrubs and mouldering trunks of enormous trees, among the crevices, attest the antiquity of these events. Working their toilsome way across this scene of desolation, the path often led them along the border of precipices, down whose sheer depths of two or three thousand feet the shrinking eye might behold another climate, and see all the glowing vegetation of the tropics choking up the bottom of the ravines.

After three days of this fatiguing travel, the way-worn army emerged through another defile, the Sierra del Agua. They soon came upon an open reach of country, with a genial climate, such as belongs to the temperate latitudes of southern Europe. They had reached the level of more than seven thousand feet above the ocean, where the great sheet of tableland spreads out for hundreds of miles along the crests of the Cordilleras. The country showed signs of careful cultivation, but the products were, for the most part, not familiar to the eyes of the Spaniards. Fields and hedges of the various tribes of the cactus, the towering organum, and plantations of aloes with rich yellow clusters of flowers on their tall stems, affording drink and clothing to the Aztec, were everywhere seen. The plants of the torrid and temperate zones had disappeared, one after another, with the ascent into these elevated regions. The glossy and dark-leaved banana, the chief, as it is the cheapest, aliment of the countries below, had long since faded from the landscape. The hardy maize, however, still shone with its golden harvests in all the pride of cultivation, the great staple of the higher equally with the lower terraces of the plateau.

Suddenly the troops came upon what seemed the environs of a populous city, which, as they entered it, appeared to surpass even that of Cempoalla in the size and solidity of its structures. These were of stone and lime, many of them spacious and tolerably high. There were thirteen teocallis in the place; and in the suburbs they had seen a receptacle, in which, according to Bernal Diaz, were stored a hundred thousand skulls of human victims, all piled and ranged in order! He reports the number as one he had ascertained by counting them himself. Whatever faith we may attach to the precise accuracy of his figures, the result is almost equally startling. The Spaniards were destined to become familiar with this appalling spectacle, as they approached nearer to the Aztec capital.

The lord of the town ruled over twenty thousand vassals. He was tributary to Montezuma, and a strong Mexican garrison was quartered in the place. He had probably been advised of the approach of the Spaniards, and doubted how far it would be welcome to his sovereign. At all events, he gave them a cold reception, the more unpalatable after the extraordinary sufferings of the last few days. To the inquiry of Cortes, whether he were subject to Montezuma, he answered with real or affected surprise, "Who is there that is not a vassal to Montezuma?" The general told him, with some emphasis, that he was not. He then explained whence and why he came, assuring him that he served a monarch who had princes for his vassals as powerful as the Aztec monarch himself.

The cacique in turn fell nothing short of the Spaniard in the pompous display of the grandeur and resources of the Indian emperor. He told his guest that Montezuma could muster thirty great vassals, each master of a hundred thousand men! His revenues were immense, as every subject, however poor, paid something. They were all expended on his magnificent state, and in support of his armies. These were continually in the field, while garrisons were maintained in most of the large cities of the empire. More than twenty thousand victims, the fruit of his wars, were annually sacrificed on the altars of his gods! His capital, the cacique said, stood in a lake in the centre of a spacious valley. The lake was commanded by the emperor's vessels, and the approach to the city was by means of causeways, several miles long, connected in parts by wooden bridges, which, when raised, cut off all communication with the country. Some other things he added, in answer to queries of his guest, in which as the reader may imagine, the crafty or credulous cacique varnished over the truth with a lively colouring of romance. Whether romance or reality, the Spaniards could not determine. The particulars they gleaned were not of a kind to tranquillise their minds, and might well have made bolder hearts than theirs pause, ere they advanced. But far from it. "The words which we heard," says the stout old cavalier, so often quoted, "however they may have filled us with wonder, made us — such is the temper of the Spaniard — only the more earnest to prove the adventure, desperate as it might appear."

In a further conversation Cortes inquired of the chief whether his country abounded in gold, and intimated a desire to take home some, as specimens to his sovereign. But the Indian lord declined to give him any, saying it might displease Montezuma. "Should he command it," he added, "My gold, my person, and all I possess, shall be at your disposal." The general did not press the matter further.

The curiosity of the natives was naturally excited by the strange dresses, weapons, horses, and dogs of the Spaniards. Marina, in satisfying their inquiries, took occasion to magnify the prowess of her adopted countrymen, expatiating on their exploits and victories, and stating the extraordinary marks of respect they had received from Montezuma. This intelligence seems to have had its effect; for soon after, the cacique gave the general some curious trinkets of gold, of no great value, indeed, but as a testimony of his good will. He sent him, also, some female slaves to prepare bread for the troops, and supplied the means of refreshment and repose, more important to them, in the present juncture, than all the gold of Mexico.

The Spanish general, as usual, did not neglect the occasion to inculcate the great truths of revelation on his host, and to display the atrocity of the Indian superstitions. The cacique listened with civil, but cold indifference. Cortes, finding him unmoved, turned briskly round to his soldiers, exclaiming that now was the time to Plant the Cross! They eagerly seconded his pious purpose, and the same scenes might have been enacted as at Cempoalla, with, perhaps, very different results, had not Father Olmedo, with better judgment, interposed. He represented that to introduce the Cross among the natives, in their present state of ignorance and incredulity, would be to expose the sacred symbol to desecration, so soon as the backs of the Spaniards were turned. The only way was to wait patiently the season when more leisure should be afforded to instil into their minds a knowledge of the truth. The sober reasoning of the good father prevailed over the passions of the martial enthusiasts.

The Spanish commander remained in the city four or five days to recruit his fatigued and famished forces. Their route now opened on a broad and verdant valley, watered by a noble stream — a circumstance of not too frequent occurrence on the parched tableland of New Spain. All along the river, on both sides of it, an unbroken line of Indian dwellings, "so near as almost to touch one another," extended for three or four leagues; arguing a population much denser than at present. On a rough and rising ground stood a town, that might contain five or six thousand inhabitants, commanded by a fortress, which, with its walls and trenches, seemed to the Spaniards quite "on a level with similar works in Europe." Here the troops again halted, and met with friendly treatment.

Cortes now determined his future line of march. At the last place he had been counselled by the natives to take the route of the ancient city of Cholula, the inhabitants of which, subjects of Montezuma, were a mild race, devoted to mechanical and other peaceful arts, and would be likely to entertain him kindly. Their Cempoalla allies, however, advised the Spaniards not to trust the Cholulans, "a false and perfidious people," but to take the road to Tlascala, that valiant little republic which had so long maintained its independence against the arms of Mexico. The people were frank as they were fearless, and fair in their dealings. They had always been on terms of amity with the Totonacs, which afforded a strong guarantee for their amicable disposition on the present occasion.

The arguments of his Indian allies prevailed with the Spanish commander, who resolved to propitiate the good will of the Tlascalans by an embassy. He selected four of the principal Cempoallans for this, and sent by them a martial gift — a cap of crimson cloth, together with a sword and a crossbow, weapons which, it was observed, excited general admiration among the natives. He added a letter, in which he asked permission to pass through their country. He expressed his admiration of the valour of the Tlascalans, and of their long resistance to the Aztecs, whose proud empire he designed to humble. It was not to be expected that this epistle, indited in good Castilian, would be very intelligible to the Tlascalans. But Cortes communicated its import to the ambassadors. It mysterious characters might impress the natives with an idea of superior intelligence, and the letters serve instead of those hieroglyphical missives which formed the usual credentials of an Indian ambassador.

The Spaniards remained three days in this hospitable place, after the departure of the envoys, when they resumed their progress. Although in a friendly country, they marched always as if in a land of enemies, the horse and light troops in the van, with the heavy-armed and baggage in the rear, all in battle array. They were never without their armour, waking or sleeping, lying down with their weapons by their sides. This unintermitting and restless vigilance was, perhaps, more oppressive to the spirits than even bodily fatigue. But they were confident in their superiority in a fair field, and felt that the most serious danger they had to fear from Indian warfare was surprise. "We are few against many, brave companions," Cortes would say to them; "be prepared, then, not as if you were going to battle, but as if actually in the midst of it!"

The road taken by the Spaniards was the same which at present leads to Tlascala; not that, however, usually followed in passing from Vera Cruz to the capital, which makes a circuit considerably to the south, towards Puebla, in the neighbourhood of the ancient Cholula. They more than once forded the stream that rolls through this beautiful plain, lingering several days on the way, in hopes of receiving an answer from the Indian republic. The unexpected delay of the messengers could not be explained and occasioned some uneasiness.

As they advanced into a country of rougher and bolder features, their progress was suddenly arrested by a remarkable fortification. It was a stone wall nine feet in height, and twenty in thickness, with a parapet a foot and a half broad, raised on the summit for the protection of those who defended it. It had only one opening, in the centre, made by two semicircular lines of wall, overlapping each other for the space of forty paces, and affording a passageway between, ten paces wide, so contrived, therefore, as to be perfectly commanded by the inner wall. This fortification, which extended more than two leagues, rested at either end on the bold natural buttresses formed by the sierra. The work was built of immense blocks of stones nicely laid together without cement; and the remains still existing, among which are rocks of the whole breadth of the rampart, fully attest its solidity and size.

This singular structure marked the limits of Tlascala, and was intended, as the natives told the Spaniards, as a barrier against the Mexican invasions. The army paused, filled with amazement at the contemplation of this Cyclopean monument, which naturally suggested reflections on the strength and resources of the people who had raised it. It caused them, too, some painful solicitude as to the probable result of their mission to Tlascala, and their own consequent reception there. But they were too sanguine to allow such uncomfortable surmises long to dwell in their minds. Cortes put himself at the head of his cavalry, and calling out, "Forward, soldiers, the Holy Cross is our banner, and under that we shall conquer," led his little army through the undefended passage, and in a few moments they trod the soil of the free republic of Tlascala.

BEFORE advancing further with the Spaniards into the territory of Tlascala, it will be well to notice some traits in the character and institutions of the nation, in many respects the most remarkable in Anahuac. The Tlascalans belonged to the same great family with the Aztecs. They came on the grand plateau about the same time with the kindred races, at the close of the twelfth century, and planted themselves on the western borders of the lake of Tezcuco. Here they remained many years engaged in the usual pursuits of a bold and partially civilised people. From some cause or other, perhaps their turbulent temper, they incurred the enmity of surrounding tribes. A coalition was formed against them; and a bloody battle was fought on the plains of Poyauhtlan, in which the Tlascalans were completely victorious.

Disgusted, however, with residence among nations with whom they found so little favour, the conquering people resolved to migrate. They separated into three divisions, the largest of which, taking a southern course by the great volcan of Mexico, wound round the ancient city of Cholula, and finally settled in the district of country overshadowed by the sierra of Tlascala. The warm and fruitful valleys locked up in the embraces of this rugged brotherhood of mountains, afforded means of subsistence for an agricultural people, while the bold eminences of the sierra presented secure positions for their towns.

After the lapse of years, the institutions of the nation underwent an important change. The monarchy was divided first into two, afterwards into four separate states, bound together by a sort of federal compact, probably not very nicely defined. Each state, however, had its lord or supreme chief, independent in his own territories, and possessed of co-ordinate authority with the others in all matters concerning the whole republic. The affairs of government, especially all those relating to peace and war, were settled in a senate or council, consisting of the four lords with their inferior nobles.

The lower dignitaries held of the superior, each in his own district, by a kind of feudal tenure, being bound to supply his table, and enable him to maintain his state in peace, as well as to serve him in war. In return he experienced the aid and protection of his suzerain. The same mutual obligations existed between him and the followers among whom his own territories were distributed. Thus a chain of feudal dependencies was established, which, if not contrived with all the art and legal refinements of analogous institutions in the Old World, displayed their most prominent characteristics in its personal relations, the obligations of military service on the one hand, and protection on the other. This form of government, so different from that of the surrounding nations, subsisted till the arrival of the Spaniards. And it is certainly evidence of considerable civilisation, that so complex a polity should have so long continued undisturbed by violence or faction in the confederate states, and should have been found competent to protect the people in their rights, and the country from foreign invasion.

The lowest order of the people, however, do not seem to have enjoyed higher immunities than under the monarchical governments; and their rank was carefully defined by an appropriate dress, and by their exclusion from the insignia of the aristocratic orders.

The nation, agricultural in its habits, reserved its highest honours, like most other rude-unhappily also, civilised-nations, for military prowess. Public games were instituted, and prizes decreed to those who excelled in such manly and athletic exercises as might train them for the fatigues of war. Triumphs were granted to the victorious general, who entered the city, leading his spoils and captives in long procession, while his achievements were commemorated in national songs, and his effigy, whether in wood or stone, was erected in the temples. It was truly in the martial spirit of republican Rome.

An institution not unlike knighthood was introduced, very similar to one existing also among the Aztecs. The aspirant to the honours of this barbaric chivalry watched his arms and fasted fifty or sixty days in the temple, then listened to a grave discourse on the duties of his new profession. Various whimsical ceremonies followed, when his arms were restored to him; he was led in solemn procession through the public streets, and the inauguration was concluded by banquets and public rejoicings. The new knight was distinguished henceforth by certain peculiar privileges, as well as by a badge intimating his rank. It is worthy of remark, that this honour was not reserved exclusively for military merit; but was the recompense, also, of public services of other kinds, as wisdom in council, or sagacity and success in trade. For trade was held in as high estimation by the Tlascalans as by the other people of Anahuac.

The temperate climate of the tableland furnished the ready means for distant traffic. The fruitfulness of the soil was indicated by the name of the country — Tlascala signifying the "land of bread." Its wide plains, to the slopes of its rocky hills, waved with yellow harvests of maize, and with the bountiful maguey, a plant which, as we have seen, supplied the materials for some important fabrics. With these, as well as the products of agricultural industry, the merchant found his way down the sides of the Cordilleras, wandered over the sunny regions at their base, and brought back the luxuries which nature had denied to his own.

The various arts of civilisation kept pace with increasing wealth and public prosperity; at least these arts were cultivated to the same limited extent, apparently, as among the other people of Anahuac. The Tlascalan tongue, says the national historian, simple as beseemed that of a mountain region, was rough compared with the polished Tezcucan, or the popular Aztec dialect, and, therefore, not so well fitted for composition. But they made like proficiency with the kindred nations in the rudiments of science. Their calendar was formed on the same plan. Their religion, their architecture, many of their laws and social usages were the same, arguing a common origin for all. Their tutelary deity was the same ferocious war-god as that of the Aztecs, though with a different name; their temples, in like manner, were drenched with the blood of human victims, and their boards groaned with the same cannibal repasts.

Though not ambitious of foreign conquest, the prosperity of the Tlascalans, in time, excited the jealousy of their neighbours, and especially of the opulent state of Cholula. Frequent hostilities arose between them, in which the advantage was almost always on the side of the former. A still more formidable foe appeared in later days in the Aztecs; who could ill brook the independence of Tlascala, when the surrounding nations had acknowledged, one after another, their influence or their empire. Under the ambitious Axayacatl, they demanded of the Tlascalans the same tribute and obedience rendered by other people of the country. If it were refused, the Aztecs would raze their cities to their foundations, and deliver the land to their enemies.

To this imperious summons, the little republic proudly replied, "Neither they nor their ancestors had ever paid tribute or homage to a foreign power, and never would pay it. If their country was invaded, they knew how to defend it, and would pour out their blood as freely in defence of their freedom now, as their fathers did of yore, when they routed the Aztecs on the plains of Poyauhtlan!"

This resolute answer brought on them the forces of the monarchy. A pitched battle followed, and the sturdy republicans were victorious. From this period hostilities between the two nations continued with more or less activity, but with unsparing ferocity. Every captive was mercilessly sacrificed. The children were trained from the cradle to deadly hatred against the Mexicans; and, even in the brief intervals of war, none of those intermarriages took place between the people of the respective countries which knit together in social bonds most of the other kindred races of Anahuac.

In this struggle, the Tlascalans received an important support in the accession of the Othomis, or Otomies — as usually spelt by Castilian writers — a wild and warlike race originally spread over the tableland north of the Mexican valley. A portion of them obtained a settlement in the republic, and were speedily incorporated in its armies. Their courage and fidelity to the nation of their adoption showed them worthy of trust, and the frontier places were consigned to their keeping. The mountain barriers, by which Tlascala is encompassed, afforded many strong natural positions for defence against invasion. The country was open towards the east, where a valley, of some six miles in breadth, invited the approach of an enemy. But here it was, that the jealous Tlascalans erected the formidable rampart which had excited the admiration of the Spaniards, and which they manned with a garrison of Otomies.

Efforts for their subjugation were renewed on a greater scale, after the accession of Montezuma. His victorious arms had spread down the declivities of the Andes to the distant provinces of Vera Paz and Nicaragua, and his haughty spirit was chafed by the opposition of a petty state, whose territorial extent did not exceed ten leagues in breadth by fifteen in length. He sent an army against them under the command of a favourite son. His troops were beaten and his son was slain. The enraged and mortified monarch was roused to still greater preparations. He enlisted the forces of the cities bordering on his enemy, together with those of the empire, and with this formidable army swept over the devoted valleys of Tlascala. But the bold mountaineers withdrew into the recesses of their hills, and, coolly awaiting their opportunity, rushed like a torrent on the invaders, and drove them back, with dreadful slaughter, from their territories.

Still, notwithstanding the advantages gained over the enemy in the field, the Tlascalans were sorely pressed by their long hostilities with a foe so far superior to themselves in numbers and resources. The Aztec armies lay between them and the coast, cutting off all communication with that prolific region, and thus limited their supplies to the products of their own soil and manufacture. For more than half a century they had neither cotton, nor cacao, nor salt. Indeed, their taste had been so far affected by long abstinence from these articles, that it required the lapse of several generations after the Conquest to reconcile them to the use of salt at their meals. During the short intervals of war, it is said, the Aztec nobles, in the true spirit of chivalry, sent supplies of these commodities as presents, with many courteous expressions of respect, to the Tlascalan chiefs. This intercourse, we are assured by the Indian chronicler, was unsuspected by the people. Nor did it lead to any further correspondence, he adds, between the parties, prejudicial to the liberties of the republic, "which maintained its customs and good government inviolate, and the worship of its gods."

Such was the condition of Tlascala, at the coming of the Spaniards; holding, it might seem, a precarious existence under the shadow of the formidable power which seemed suspended like an avalanche over her head, but still strong in her own resources, stronger in the indomitable temper of her people; with a reputation established throughout the land for good faith and moderation in peace, for valour in war, while her uncompromising spirit of independence secured the respect even of her enemies. With such qualities of character, and with an animosity sharpened by long, deadly hostility with Mexico, her alliance was obviously of the last importance to the Spaniards, in their present enterprise. It was not easy to secure it.

The Tlascalans had been made acquainted with the advance and victorious career of the Christians, the intelligence of which had spread far and wide over the plateau. But they do not seem to have anticipated the approach of the strangers to their own borders. They were now much embarrassed by the embassy demanding a passage through their territories. The great council was convened, and a considerable difference of opinion prevailed in its members. Some, adopting the popular superstition, supposed the Spaniards might be the white and bearded men foretold by the oracles. At all events, they were the enemies of Mexico, and as such might co-operate with them in their struggle with the empire. Others argued that the strangers could have nothing in common with them. Their march throughout the land might be tracked by the broken images of the Indian gods, and desecrated temples. How did the Tlascalans even know that they were foes to Montezuma? They had received his embassies, accepted his presents, and were now in the company of his vassals on the way to his capital.

These last were the reflections of an aged chief, one of the four who presided over the republic. His name was Xicontecatl. He was nearly blind, having lived, as is said, far beyond the limits of a century. His son, an impetuous young man of the same name with himself, commanded a powerful army of Tlascalan and Otomie warriors, near the eastern frontier. It would be best, the old man said, to fall with this force at once on the Spaniards. If victorious, the latter would then be in their power. If defeated, the senate could disown the act as that of the general, not of the republic. The cunning counsel of the chief found favour with his hearers, though assuredly not in the spirit of chivalry, nor of the good faith for which his countrymen were celebrated. But with an Indian, force and stratagem, courage and deceit, were equally admissible in war, as they were among the barbarians of ancient Rome. — The Cempoallan envoys were to be detained under pretence of assisting at a religious sacrifice.

Meanwhile, Cortes and his gallant band, as stated in the preceding chapter, had arrived before the rocky rampart on the eastern confines of Tlascala. From some cause or other, it was not manned by its Otomie garrison, and the Spaniards passed in, as we have seen, without resistance. Cortes rode at the head of his body of horse, and, ordering the infantry to come on at a quick pace, went forward to reconnoitre. After advancing three or four leagues, he descried a small party of Indians, armed with sword and buckler, in the fashion of the country. They fled at his approach. He made signs for them to halt, but, seeing that they only fled the faster, he and his companions put spurs to their horses, and soon came up with them. The Indians, finding escape impossible, faced round, and, instead of showing the accustomed terror of the natives at the strange and appalling aspect of a mounted trooper, they commenced a furious assault on the cavaliers. The latter, however, were too strong for them, and would have cut their enemy to pieces without much difficulty, when a body of several thousand Indians appeared in sight, and coming briskly on to the support of their countrymen.

Cortes, seeing them, despatched one of his party, in all haste, to accelerate the march of his infantry. The Indians, after discharging their missiles, fell furiously on the little band of Spaniards. They strove to tear the lances from their grasp, and to drag the riders from the horses. They brought one cavalier to the ground, who afterwards died of his wounds, and they killed two of the horses, cutting through their necks with their stout broadswords — if we may believe the chronicler — at a blow. In the narrative of these campaigns, there is sometimes but one step — and that a short one — from history lo romance. The loss of the horses, so important and so few in number, was seriously felt by Cortes, who could have better spared the life of the best rider in the troop.

The struggle was a hard one. But the odds were as overwhelming as any recorded by the Spaniards in their own romances, where a handful of knights is arrayed against legions of enemies. The lances of the Christians did terrible execution here also; but they had need of the magic lance of Astolpho, that overturned myriads with a touch, to carry them safe through so unequal a contest. It was with no little satisfaction, therefore, that they beheld their comrades rapidly advancing to their support.

No sooner had the main body reached the field of battle, than, hastily forming, they poured such a volley from their muskets and crossbows as staggered the enemy. Astounded, rather than intimidated, by the terrible report of the firearms, now heard for the first time in these regions, the Indians made no further effort to continue the fight, but drew off in good order, leaving the road open to the Spaniards. The latter, too well satisfied to be rid of the annoyance, to care to follow the retreating foe, again held on their way.

Their route took them through a country sprinkled over with Indian cottages, amidst flourishing fields of maize and maguey, indicating an industrious and thriving peasantry. They were met here by two Tlascalans envoys, accompanied by two of the Cempoallans. The former, presenting themselves before the general, disavowed the assault on his troops as an unauthorised act, and assured him of a friendly reception at their capital. Cortes received the communication in a courteous manner, affecting to place more confidence in its good faith than he probably felt.

It was now growing late, and the Spaniards quickened their march, anxious to reach a favourable ground for encampment before nightfall. They found such a spot on the borders of a stream that rolled sluggishly across the plain. A few deserted cottages stood along the banks, and the fatigued and famished soldiers ransacked them in quest of food. All they could find was some tame animals resembling dogs. These they killed and dressed without ceremony, and, garnishing their unsavoury repast with the fruit of the tuna, the Indian fig, which grew wild in the neighbourhood, they contrived to satisfy the cravings of appetite. A careful watch was maintained by Cortes, and companies of a hundred men each relieved each other in mounting guard through the night. But no attack was made. Hostilities by night were contrary to the system of Indian tactics.

By break of day on the following morning, it being the 2nd of September, the troops were under arms. Besides the Spaniards, the whole number of Indian auxiliaries might now amount to three thousand; for Cortes had gathered recruits from the friendly places on his route; three hundred from the last. After hearing mass, they resumed their march. They moved in close array; the general had previously admonished the men not to lag behind, or wander from the ranks a moment, as stragglers would be sure to be cut off by their stealthy and vigilant enemy.

The horsemen rode three abreast, the better to give one another support; and Cortes instructed them in the heat of fight to keep together, and never to charge singly. He taught them how to carry their lances, that they might not be wrested from their hands by the Indians, who constantly attempted it. For the same reason they should avoid giving thrusts, but aim their weapons steadily at the faces of their foes.

They had not proceeded far, when they were met by the two remaining Cempoallan envoys, who with looks of terror informed the general, that they had been treacherously seized and confined, in order to be sacrificed at an approaching festival of the Tlascalans, but in the night had succeeded in making their escape. They gave the unwelcome tidings, also, that a large force of the natives was already assembled to oppose the progress of the Spaniards.

Soon after, they came in sight of a body of Indians, about a thousand, apparently all armed and brandishing their weapons, as the Christians approached, in token of defiance. Cortes, when he had come within hearing, ordered the interpreters to proclaim that he had no hostile intentions; but wished only to be allowed a passage through their country, which he had entered as a friend. This declaration he commanded the royal notary, Godoy, to record on the spot, that, if blood were shed, it might not be charged on the Spaniards. This pacific proclamation was met, as usual on such occasions, by a shower of darts, stones, and arrows, which fell like rain on the Spaniards, rattling on their stout harness, and in some instances penetrating to the skin. Galled by the smart of their wounds, they called on the general to lead them on, till he sounded the well-known battle-cry, "St. Jago, and at them!"

The Indians maintained their ground for a while with spirit, when they retreated with precipitation, but not in disorder. The Spaniards, whose blood was heated by the encounter, followed up their advantage with more zeal than prudence, suffering the wily enemy to draw them into a narrow glen or defile, intersected by a little stream of water, where the broken ground was impracticable for artillery, as well as for the movements of cavalry. Pressing forward with eagerness, to extricate themselves from their perilous position, to their great dismay, on turning an abrupt angle of the pass, they came in presence of a numerous army choking up the gorge of the valley, and stretching far over the plains beyond. To the astonished eyes of Cortes, they appeared a hundred thousand men, while no account estimates them at less than thirty thousand.

They presented a confused assemblage of helmets, weapons, and many-coloured plumes, glancing bright in the morning sun, and mingled with banners, above which proudly floated one that bore as a device the heron on a rock. It was the well-known ensign of the house of Titcala, and, as well as the white and yellow stripes on the bodies, and the like colours on the feather-mail of the Indians, showed that they were the warriors of Xicotencatl.

As the Spaniards came in sight, the Tlascalans set up a hideous war-cry, or rather whistle, piercing the ear with its shrillness, and which, with the beat of their melancholy drums, that could be heard for half a league or more, might well have filled the stoutest heart with dismay. This formidable host came rolling on towards the Christians, as if to overwhelm them by their very numbers. But the courageous band of warriors, closely serried together and sheltered under their strong panoplies, received the shock unshaken, while the broken masses of the enemy, chafing and heaving tumultuously around them, seemed to recede only to return with new and accumulated force.

Cortes, as usual, in the front of danger, in vain endeavoured, at the head of the horse, to open a passage for the infantry. Still his men, both cavalry and foot, kept their array unbroken, offering no assailable point to their foe. A body of the Tlascalans, however, acting in concert, assaulted a soldier named Moran, one of the best riders in the troop. They succeeded in dragging him from his horse, which they despatched with a thousand blows. The Spaniards, on foot, made a desperate effort to rescue their comrade from the hands of the enemy — and from the horrible doom of the captive. A fierce struggle now began over the body of the prostrate horse. Ten of the Spaniards were wounded, when they succeeded in retrieving the unfortunate cavalier from his assailants, but in so disastrous a plight that he died on the following day. The horse was borne off in triumph by the Indians, and his mangled remains were sent, a strange trophy, to the different towns of Tlascala. The circumstance troubled the Spanish commander, as it divested the animal of the supernatural terrors with which the superstition of the natives had usually surrounded it. To prevent such a consequence, he had caused the two horses, killed on the preceding day, to be secretly buried on the spot.

The enemy now began to give ground gradually, borne down by the riders, and trampled under the hoofs of their horses. Through the whole of this sharp encounter, the Indian allies were of great service to the Spaniards. They rushed into the water, and grappled their enemies, with the desperation of men who felt that "their only safety was in the despair of safety." "I see nothing but death for us," exclaimed a Cempoallan chief to Marina; "we shall never get through the pass alive." "The God of the Christians is with us," answered the intrepid woman; "and He will carry us safely through."

Amidst the din of battle the voice of Cortes was heard, cheering on his soldiers. "If we fail now," he cried, "the cross of Christ can never be planted in the land. Forward, comrades! When was it ever known that a Castilian turned his back on a foe?" Animated by the words and heroic bearing of their general, the soldiers, with desperate efforts, at length succeeded in forcing a passage through the dark columns of the enemy, and emerged from the defile on the open plain beyond.

Here they quickly recovered their confidence with their superiority. The horse soon opened a space for the manoeuvres of artillery. The close files of their antagonists presented a sure mark; and the thunders of the ordnance vomiting forth torrents of fire and sulphurous smoke, the wide desolation caused in their ranks, and the strangely mangled carcasses of the slain, filled the barbarians with consternation and horror. They had no weapons to cope with these terrible engines, and their clumsy missiles, discharged from uncertain hands, seemed to fall ineffectual on the charmed heads of the Christians. What added to their embarrassment was, the desire to carry off the dead and wounded from the field, a general practice among the people of Anahuac, but which necessarily exposed them, while thus employed, to still greater loss.

Eight of their principal chiefs had now fallen; and Xicotencatl, finding himself wholly unable to make head against the Spaniards in the open field, ordered a retreat. Far from the confusion of a panic-struck mob, so common among barbarians, the Tlascalan force moved off the ground with all the order of a well-disciplined army. Cortes, as on the preceding day, was too well satisfied with his present advantage to desire to follow it up. It was within an hour of sunset, and he was anxious before nightfall to secure a good position, where he might refresh his wounded troops, and bivouac for the night.

Gathering up his wounded, he held on his way, without loss of time; and before dusk reached a rocky eminence, called Tzompachtepetl, or "the hill of Tzompach," crowned by a sort of tower or temple. His first care was given to the wounded, both men and horses. Fortunately, an abundance of provisions was found in some neighbouring cottages; and the soldiers, at least all who were not disabled by their injuries, celebrated the victory of the day with feasting and rejoicing.

As to the number of killed or wounded on either side, it is matter of loosest conjecture. The Indians must have suffered severely, but the practice of carrying off the dead from the field made it impossible to know to what extent. The injury sustained by the Spaniards appears to have been principally in the number of their wounded. The great object of the natives of Anahuac in their battles was to make prisoners, who might grace their triumphs, and supply victims for sacrifice. To this brutal superstition the Christians were indebted, in no slight degree, for their personal preservation. To take the reports of the Conquerors, their own losses in action were always inconsiderable. But whoever has had occasion to consult the ancient chroniclers of Spain in relation to its wars with the infidel, whether Arab or American, will place little confidence in numbers.

The events of the day had suggested many topics for painful reflection to Cortes. He had nowhere met with so determined a resistance within the borders of Anahuac; nowhere had he encountered native troops so formidable for their, weapons, their discipline, and their valour. Far from manifesting the superstitious terrors felt by the other Indians at the strange arms and aspect of the Spaniards, the Tlascalans had boldly grappled with their enemy, and only yielded to the inevitable superiority of his military science. How important would the alliance of such a nation be in a struggle with those of their own race — for example, with the Aztecs! But how was he to secure this alliance? Hitherto, all overtures had been rejected with disdain; and it seemed probable, that every step of his progress in this populous land was to be fiercely contested. His army, especially the Indians, celebrated the events of the day with feasting and dancing, songs of merriment, and shouts of triumph. Cortes encouraged it, well knowing how important it was to keep up the spirits of his soldiers. But the sounds of revelry at length died away; and in the still watches of the night, many an anxious thought must have crowded on the mind of the general, while his little army lay buried in slumber in its encampment around the Indian hill.

THE Spaniards were allowed to repose undisturbed the following day, and to recruit their strength after the fatigue and hard fighting on the preceding. They found sufficient employment, however, in repairing and cleaning their weapons, replenishing their diminished stock of arrows, and getting everything in order for further hostilities, should the severe lesson they had inflicted on the enemy prove insufficient to discourage him. On the second day, as Cortes received no overtures from the Tlascalans, he determined to send an embassy to their camp, proposing a cessation of hostilities, and expressing his intention to visit their capital as a friend. He selected two of the principal chiefs taken in the late engagement as the bearers of the message.

Meanwhile, averse to leaving his men longer in a dangerous state of inaction, which the enemy might interpret as the result of timidity or exhaustion, he put himself at the head of the cavalry and such light troops as were most fit for service, and made a foray into the neighbouring country. It was a montainous region, formed by a. ramification of the great sierra of Tlascala, with verdant slopes and valleys teeming with maize and plantations of maguey, while the eminences were crowned with populous towns and villages. In one of these, he tells us, he found three thousand dwellings. In some places he met with a resolute resistance, and on these occasions took ample vengeance by laying the country waste with fire and sword. After a successful inroad he returned laden with forage and provisions, and driving before him several hundred Indian captives. He treated them kindly, however, when arrived in camp, endeavouring to make them understand that these acts of violence were not dictated by his own wishes, but by the unfriendly policy of their countrymen. In this way he hoped to impress the nation with the conviction of his power on the one hand, and of his amicable intentions, if met by them in the like spirit, on the other.

On reaching his quarters, he found the two envoys returned from the Tlascalan camp. They had fallen in with Xicotencatl at about two leagues' distance, where he lay encamped with a powerful force. The cacique gave them audience at the head of his troops. He told them to return with the answer, "That the Spaniards might pass on as soon as they chose to Tlascala; and, when they reached it, their flesh would be hewn from their bodies, for sacrifice to the gods! If they preferred to remain in their own quarters, he would pay them a visit there the next day." The ambassadors added, that the chief had an immense force with him, consisting of five battalions of ten thousand men each. They were the flower of the Tlascalan and Otomie warriors, assembled under the banners of their respective leaders, by command of the senate, who were resolved to try the fortunes of the state in a pitched battle, and strike one decisive blow for the extermination of the invaders.

This bold defiance fell heavily on the ears of the Spaniards, not prepared for so pertinacious a spirit in their enemy. They had had ample proof of his courage and formidable prowess. They were now, in their crippled condition, to encounter him with a still more terrible array of numbers. The war, too, from the horrible fate with which it menaced the vanquished, wore a peculiarly gloomy aspect that pressed heavily on their spirits. "We feared death," says the lion-hearted Diaz, with his usual simplicity, "for we were men." There was scarcely one in the army that did not confess himself that night to the reverend Father Olmedo, who was occupied nearly the whole of it with administering absolution, and with the other solemn offices of the Church. Armed with the blessed sacraments, the Catholic soldier lay tranquilly down to rest, prepared for any fate that might betide him under the banner of the Cross.

As a battle was now inevitable, Cortes resolved to march out and meet the enemy in the field. This would have a show of confidence, that might serve the double purpose of intimidating the Tlascalans, and inspiriting his own men, whose enthusiasm might lose somewhat of its heat, if compelled to await the assault of their antagonists, inactive in their own intrenchments. The sun rose bright on the following morning, the 5th of September, 1519, an eventful day in the history of Spanish Conquest. The general reviewed his army, and gave them, preparatory to marching, a few words of encouragement and advice.

CAPTURE OF THE CITY OF MEXICO BY CORTES

The infantry he instructed to rely on the point rather than the edge of their swords, and to endeavour to thrust their opponents through the body. The horsemen were to charge at half speed, with their lances aimed at the eyes of the Indians. The artillery the arquebusiers, and crossbowmen, were to support one another, some loading while others discharged their pieces, that there should be an unintermitted firing kept up through the action. Above all, they were to maintain their ranks close and unbroken, as on this depended their preservation.

They had not advanced a quarter of a league, when they came in sight of the Tlascalan army. Its dense array stretched far and wide over a vast plain or meadow ground, about six miles square. Its appearance justified the report which had been given of its numbers. Nothing could be more picturesque than the aspect of these Indian battalions, with the naked bodies of the common soldiers gaudily painted, the fantastic helmets of the chiefs glittering with gold and precious stones, and the glowing panoplies of feather-work which decorated their persons. Innumerable spears and darts tipped with points of transparent itztli or fiery copper, sparkled bright in the morning sun, like the phosphoric gleams playing on the surface of a troubled sea, while the rear of the mighty host was dark with the shadows of banners, on which were emblazoned the armorial bearings of the great Tlascalan and Otomie chieftains. Among these, the white heron on the rock, the cognisance of the house of Xicotencatl, was conspicuous, and, still more, the golden eagle with outspread wings, in the fashion of a Roman signum, richly ornamented with emeralds and silver work, the great standard of the republic of Tlascala.

The common file wore no covering except a girdle round the loins. Their bodies were painted with the appropriate colours of the chieftain whose banner they followed. The feather-mail of the higher class of warriors exhibited, also, a similar selection of colours for the like object, in the same manner as the colour of the tartan indicates the peculiar clan of the Highlander. The caciques and principal warriors were clothed in a quilted cotton tunic, two inches thick, which, fitting close to the body, protected also the thighs and the shoulders. Over this the wealthier Indians wore cuirasses of thin gold plate, or silver. Their legs were defended by leathern boots or sandals, trimmed with gold. But the most brilliant part of their costume was a rich mantle of the plumaje or feather-work, embroidered with curious art, and furnishing some resemblance to the gorgeous surcoat worn by the European knight over his armour in the Middle Ages. This graceful and picturesque dress was surmounted by a fantastic head-piece made of wood or leather, representing the head of some wild animal, and frequently displaying a formidable array of teeth. With this covering the warrior's head was enveloped, producing a most grotesque and hideous effect. From the crown floated a splendid panache of the richly variegated plumage of the tropics, indicating, by its form and colours, the rank and family of the wearer. To complete their defensive armour, they carried shields or targets, made sometimes of wood covered with leather, but more usually of a light frame of reeds quilted with cotton, which were preferred, as tougher and less liable to fracture than the former. They had other bucklers, in which the cotton was covered with an elastic substance, enabling them to be shut up in a more compact form, like a fan or umbrella. These shields were decorated with showy ornaments, according to the taste or wealth of the wearer, and fringed with a beautiful pendant of feather-work.

Their weapons were slings, bows and arrows, javelins, and darts. They were accomplished archers, and would discharge two or even three arrows at a time. But they most excelled in throwing the javelin. One species of this, with a thong attached to it, which remained in the slinger's hand, that he might recall the weapon, was especially dreaded by the Spaniards. These various weapons were pointed with bone, or the mineral itztli (obsidian), the hard vitreous substance already noticed, as capable of taking an edge like a razor, though easily blunted. Their spears and arrows were also frequently headed with copper. Instead of a sword, they bore a two-handed staff, about three feet and a half long, in which, at regular distances, were inserted, transversely, sharp blades of itztli — a formidable weapon, which, an eye-witness assures us, he had seen fell a horse at a blow.

Such was the costume of the Tlascalan warrior, and, indeed, of that great family of nations generally, who occupied the plateau of Anahuac. Some parts of it, as the targets and the cotton mail or escaupil, as it was called in Castilian, were so excellent, that they were subsequently adopted by the Spaniards, as equally effectual in the way of protection, and superior, on the score of lightness and convenience, to their own. They were of sufficient strength to turn an arrow, or the stroke of a javelin, although impotent as a defence against firearms. But what armour is not? Yet it is probably no exaggeration to say that, in convenience, gracefulness, and strength, the arms of the Indian warrior were not very inferior to those of the polished nations of antiquity.

As soon as the Castilians came in sight, the Tlascalans set up their yell of defiance, rising high above the wild barbaric minstrelsy of shell, atabal, and trumpet, with which they proclaimed their triumphant anticipations of victory over the paltry forces of the invaders. When the latter had come within bowshot, the Indians hurled a tempest of missiles, that darkened the sun for a moment as with a passing cloud, strewing the earth around with heaps of stones and arrows. Slowly and steadily the little band of Spaniards held on its way amidst this arrowy shower, until it had reached what appeared the proper distance for delivering its fire with full effect. Cortes then halted, and, hastily forming his troops, opened a general well-directed fire along the whole line. Every shot bore its errand of death; and the ranks of the Indians were mowed down faster than their comrades in the rear could carry off their bodies, according to custom, from the field. The balls in their passage through the crowded files, bearing splinters of the broken harness and mangled limbs of the warriors, scattered havoc and desolation in their path. The mob of barbarians stood petrified with dismay, till, at length, galled to desperation by their intolerable suffering, they poured forth simultaneously their hideous war-shriek, and rushed impetuously on the Christians.

On they came like an avalanche, or mountain torrent, shaking the solid earth, and sweeping away every obstacle in its path. The little army of Spaniards opposed a bold front to the overwhelming mass. But no strength could withstand it. They faltered, gave way, were borne along before it, and their ranks were broken and thrown into disorder. It was in vain the general called on them to close again and rally. His voice was drowned by the din of fight and the fierce cries of the assailants. For a moment, it seemed that all was lost. The tide of battle had turned against them, and the fate of the Christians was sealed.

But every man had that within his bosom which spoke louder than the voice of the general. Despair gave unnatural energy to his arms. The naked body of the Indian afforded no resistance to the sharp Toledo steel; and with their good swords, the Spanish infantry at length succeeded in staying the human torrent. The heavy guns from a distance thundered on the flank of the assailants, which, shaken by the iron tempest, was thrown into disorder. Their very numbers increased the confusion, as they were precipitated on the masses in front. The horse at the same moment, charging gallantly under Cortes, followed up the advantage, and at length compelled the tumultuous throng to fall back with greater precipitation and disorder than that with which they had advanced.

More than once in the course of the action, a similar assault was attempted by the Tlascalans, but each time with less spirit, and greater loss. They were too deficient in military science to profit by their vast superiority in numbers. They were distributed into companies, it is true, each serving under its own chieftain and banner. But they were not arranged by rank and file, and moved in a confused mass, promiscuously heaped together. They knew not how to concentrate numbers on a given point, or even how to sustain an assault, by employing successive detachments to support and relieve one another. A very small part only of their array could be brought into contact with an enemy inferior to them in amount of forces. The remainder of the army, inactive and worse than useless in the rear, served only to press tumultuously on the advance, and embarrass its movements by mere weight of numbers, while, on the least alarm, they were seized with a panic and threw the whole body into inextricable confusion. It was, in short, the combat of the ancient Greeks and Persians over again.

Still, the great numerical superiority of the Indians might have enabled them, at a severe cost of their own lives, indeed, to wear out, in time, the constancy of the Spaniards, disabled by wounds, and incessant fatigue. But, fortunately for the latter, dissensions arose among their enemies. A Tlascalan chieftain, commanding one of the great divisions, had taken umbrage at the haughty demeanour of Xicotencatl, who had charged him with misconduct or cowardice in the late action. The injured cacique challenged his rival to single combat. This did not take place. But, burning with resentment, he chose the present occasion to indulge it, by drawing off his forces, amounting to ten thousand men, from the field. He also persuaded another of the commanders to follow his example.

Thus reduced to about half his original strength, and that greatly crippled by the losses of the day, Xicotencatl could no longer maintain his ground against the Spaniards. After disputing the field with admirable courage for four hours, he retreated and resigned it to the enemy. The Spaniards were too much jaded, and too many were disabled by wounds, to allow them to pursue; and Cortes, satisfied with the decisive victory he had gained, returned in triumph to his position on the hill of Tzompach.

The number of killed in his own ranks had been very small, notwithstanding the severe loss inflicted on the enemy. These few he was careful to bury where they could not be discovered, anxious to conceal not only the amount of the slain, but the fact that the whites were mortal.

But very many of the men were wounded, and all the horses. The trouble of the Spaniards was much enhanced by the want of many articles important to them in their present exigency. They had neither oil, nor salt, which, as before noticed, was not to be obtained in Tlascala. Their clothing, accommodated to a softer climate, was ill adapted to the rude air of the mountains; and bows and arrows, as Bernal Diaz sarcastically remarks, formed an indifferent protection against the inclemency of the weather.

Still, they had much to cheer them in the events of the day; and they might draw from them a reasonable ground for confidence in their own resources, such as no other experience could have supplied. Not that the results could authorise anything like contempt for their Indian foe. Singly and with the same weapons, he might have stood his ground against the Spaniards. But the success of the day established the superiority of science and discipline over mere physical courage and numbers. It was fighting over again, as we have said, the old battle of the European and the Asiatic. But the handful of Greeks who routed the hosts of Xerxes and Darius, it must be remembered, had not so obvious an advantage on the score of weapons, as was enjoyed by the Spaniards in these wars. The use of firearms gave an ascendency which cannot easily be estimated; one so great, that a contest between nations equally civilised, which should be similar in all other respects to that between the Spaniards and the Tlascalans, would probably be attended with a similar issue. To all this must be added the effect produced by the cavalry. The nations of Anahuac had no large domesticated animals, and were unacquainted with any beast of burden. Their imaginations were bewildered when they beheld the strange apparition of the horse and his rider moving in unison and obedient to one impulse, as if possessed of a common nature; and as they saw the terrible animal, with his "neck clothed in thunder," bearing down their squadrons and trampling them in the dust, no wonder they should have regarded him with the mysterious terror felt for a supernatural being. A very little reflection on the manifold grounds of superiority, both moral and physical, possessed by the Spaniards in this contest, will surely explain the issue, without any disparagement to the courage or capacity of their opponents.

Cortes, thinking the occasion favourable, followed up the important blow he had struck by a new mission to the capital, bearing a message of similar import with that recently sent to the camp. But the senate was not yet sufficiently humbled. The late defeat caused, indeed, general consternation. Maxixcatzin, one of the four great lords who presided over the republic, reiterated with greater force the arguments before urged by him for embracing the proffered alliance of the strangers. The armies of the state had been beaten too often to allow any reasonable hope of successful resistance; and he enlarged on the generosity shown by the politic Conqueror to his prisoners — so unusual in Anahuac — as an additional motive for an alliance with men who knew how to be friends as well as foes.

But in these views he was overruled by the war-party, whose animosity was sharpened, rather than subdued, by the late discomfiture. Their hostile feelings were further exasperated by the younger Xicotencatl, who burned for an opportunity to retrieve his disgrace, and to wipe away the stain which had fallen for the first time on the arms of the republic.

In their perplexity they called in the assistance of the priests whose authority was frequently invoked in the deliberations of the American chiefs. The latter inquired, with some simplicity, of these interpreters of fate, whether the strangers were supernatural beings, or men of flesh and blood like themselves. The priests, after some consultation, are said to have made the strange answer, that the Spaniards, though not gods, were children of the sun; that they derived their strength from that luminary, and, when his beams were withdrawn, their powers would also fail. They recommended a night attack, therefore, as one which afforded the best chance of success. This apparently childish response may have had in it more of cunning than credulity. It was not improbably suggested by Xicotencatl himself, or by the caciques in his interest, to reconcile the people to a measure which was contrary to the military usages — indeed, it may be said, to the public law of Anahuac. Whether the fruit of artifice or superstition, it prevailed; and the Tlascalan general was empowered, at the head of a detachment of ten thousand warriors, to try the effect of an assault by night.

The affair was conducted with such secrecy that it did not reach the ears of the Spaniards. But their general was not one who allowed himself, sleeping or waking, to be surprised on his post. Fortunately the night appointed was illumined by the full beams of an autumnal moon; and one of the videttes perceived by its light, at a considerable distance, a large body of Indians moving towards the Christian lines. He was not slow in giving the alarm to the garrison.

The Spaniards slept, as has been said, with their arms by their side; while their horses, picketed near them, stood ready saddled, with the bridle hanging at the bow. In five minutes the whole camp was under arms, when they beheld the dusky columns of the Indians cautiously advancing over the plain, their heads just peering above the tall maize with which the land was partially covered. Cortes determined not to abide the assault in his intrenchments, but to sally out and pounce on the enemy when he had reached the bottom of the hill.

Slowly and stealthily the Indians advanced, while the Christian camp, hushed in profound silence, seemed to them buried in slumber. But no sooner had they reached the slope of the rising ground, than they were astounded by the deep battle-cry of the Spaniards, followed by the instantaneous apparition of the whole army, as they sallied forth from the works, and poured down the sides of the hill. Brandishing aloft their weapons, they seemed to the troubled fancies of the Tlascalans like so many spectres or demons hurrying to and fro in mid air, while the uncertain light magnified their numbers, and expanded the horse and his rider into gigantic and unearthly dimensions.

Scarcely waiting the shock of their enemy, the panic-struck barbarians let off a feeble volley of arrows, and, offering no other resistance, fled rapidly and tumultuously across the plain. The horse easily overtook the fugitives, riding them down and cutting them to pieces without mercy, until Cortes, weary with slaughter, called off his men, leaving the field loaded with the bloody trophies of victory.

The next day, the Spanish commander, with his usual policy after a decisive blow had been struck, sent a new embassy to the Tlascalan capital. The envoys received their instructions through the interpreter, Marina. That remarkable woman had attracted general admiration by the constancy and cheerfulness with which she endured all the privations of the camp. Far from betraying the natural weakness and timidity of her sex, she had shrunk from no hardship herself, and had done much to fortify the drooping spirits of the soldiers; while her sympathies, whenever occasion offered, had been actively exerted in mitigating the calamities of her Indian countrymen.

Through his faithful interpreter, Cortes communicated the terms of his message to the Tlascalan envoys. He made the same professions of amity as before, promising oblivion of all past injuries; but, if this proffer were rejected, he would visit their capital as a conqueror, raze every house in it to the ground, and put every inhabitant to the sword! He then dismissed the ambassadors with the symbolical presents of a letter in one hand, and an arrow in the other.

The envoys obtained respectful audience from the council of Tlascala, whom they found plunged in deep dejection by their recent reverses. The failure of the night attack had extinguished every spark of hope in their bosoms. Their armies had been beaten again and again, in the open field and in secret ambush. Stratagem and courage, all their resources, had alike proved ineffectual against a foe whose hand was never weary, and whose eye was never closed. Nothing remained but to submit. They selected four principal caciques, whom they intrusted with a mission to the Christian camp. They were to assure the strangers of a free passage through the country, and a friendly reception in the capital. The proffered friendship of the Spaniards was cordially embraced, with many awkward excuses for the past. The envoys were to touch at the Tlascalan camp on their way, and inform Xicotencatl of their proceedings. They were to require him, at the same time, to abstain from all further hostilities, and to furnish the white men with an ample supply of provisions.

But the Tlascalan deputies, on arriving at the quarters of that chief, did not find him in the humour to comply with these instructions. His repeated collisions with the Spaniards, or, it may be, his constitutional courage, left him inaccessible to the vulgar terrors of his countrymen. He regarded the strangers not as supernatural beings, but as men like himself. The animosity of a warrior had rankled into a deadly hatred from the mortifications he had endured at their hands, and his head teemed with plans for recovering his fallen honours, and for taking vengeance on the invaders of his country. He refused to disband any of the force, still

107

formidable, under his command; or to send supplies to the enemy's camp. He further induced the ambassadors to remain in his quarters, and relinquish their visit to the Spaniards. The latter, in consequence, were kept in ignorance of the movements in their favour which had taken place in the Tlascalan capital.

The conduct of Xicotencatl is condemned by Castilian writers as that of a ferocious and sanguinary barbarian. It is natural they should so regard it. But those who have no national prejudice to warp their judgments may come to a different conclusion. They may find much to admire in that high, unconquerable spirit, like some proud column, standing alone in its majesty amidst the fragments and ruins around it. They may see evidences of a clearsighted sagacity, which, piercing the thin veil of insidious friendship proffered by the Spaniards, and penetrating the future, discerned the coming miseries of his country; the noble patriotism of one who would rescue that country at any cost, and, amidst the gathering darkness, would infuse his own intrepid spirit into the hearts of his nation, to animate them to a last struggle for independence.

DESIROUS to keep up the terror of the Castilian name, by leaving the enemy no respite, Cortes on the same day that he despatched the embassy to Tlascala, put himself at the head of a small corps of cavalry and light troops to scour the neighbouring country. He was at that time so ill from fever, aided by medical treatment, that he could hardly keep his seat in the saddle. It was a rough country, and the sharp winds from the frosty summits of the mountains pierced the scanty covering of the troops, and chilled both men and horses. Four or five of the animals gave out, and the general, alarmed for their safety, sent them back to the camp. The soldiers, discouraged by this ill omen, would have persuaded him to return. But he made answer, "We fight under the banner of the Cross; God is stronger than nature," and continued his march.

It led through the same kind of chequered scenery of rugged hill and cultivated plain as that already described, well covered with towns and villages, some of them the frontier posts occupied by the Otomies. Practising the Roman maxim of lenity to the submissive foe, he took full vengeance on those who resisted, and, as resistance too often occurred, marked his path with fire and desolation. After a short absence, he returned in safety, laden with the plunder of a successful foray. It would have been more honourable to him had it been conducted with less rigour. The excesses are imputed by Bernal Diaz to the Indian allies, whom in the heat of victory it was found impossible to restrain. On whose head soever they fall, they seem to have given little uneasiness to the general, who declares in his letter to the Emperor Charles the Fifth, "As we fought under the standard of the Cross, for the true Faith, and the service of your Highness, Heaven crowned our arms with such success, that, while multitudes of the infidel were slain, little loss was suffered by the Castilians." The Spanish Conquerors, to judge from their writings, unconscious of any worldly motive lurking in the bottom of their hearts, regarded themselves as soldiers of the Church, fighting the great battle of Christianity; and in the same edifying and comfortable light are regarded by most of the national historians of a later day.

On his return to the camp, Cortes found a new cause of disquietude in the discontents which had broken out among the soldiery. Their patience was exhausted by a life of fatigue and peril, to which there seemed to be no end. The battles they had won against such tremendous odds had not advanced them a jot. The idea of their reaching Mexico, says the old soldier so often quoted, "was treated as jest by the whole army"; and the indefinite prospect of hostilities with the ferocious people among whom they were now cast, threw a deep gloom over their spirits.

Among the malcontents were a number of noisy, vapouring persons, such as are found in every camp, who, like empty bubbles, are sure to rise to the surface and make themselves seen in seasons of agitation. They were, for the most part, of the old faction of Velasquez, and had estates in Cuba, to which they turned many a wistful glance as they receded more and more from the coast. They now waited on the general, not in a mutinous spirit of resistance — for they remembered the lesson in Villa Rica — but with the design of frank expostulation, as with a brother adventurer in a common cause. The tone of familiarity thus assumed was eminently characteristic of the footing of equality on which the parties in the expedition stood with one another.

Their sufferings, they told him, were too great to be endured. All the men had received one, most of them two or three wounds. More than fifty had perished, in one way or another, since leaving Vera Cruz. There was no beast of burden but led a life preferable to theirs. For when the night came, the former could rest from his labours; but they, fighting or watching, had no rest, day nor night. As to conquering Mexico, the very thought of it was madness. If they had encountered such opposition from the petty republic of Tlascala, what might they not expect from the great Mexican empire? There was now a temporary suspension of hostilities. They should avail themselves of it to retrace their steps to Vera Cruz. It is true, the fleet there was destroyed; and by this act, unparalleled for rashness even in Roman annals, the general had become responsible for the fate of the whole army. Still there was one vessel left. That might be despatched to Cuba, for reinforcements and supplies; and, when these arrived, they would be enabled to resume operations with some prospect of success.

Cortes listened to this singular expostulation with perfect composure. He knew his men, and, instead of rebuke or harsher measures, replied in the same frank and soldier-like vein which they had affected.

There was much truth, he allowed, in what they said. The sufferings of the Spaniards had been great; greater than those recorded of any heroes in Greek or Roman story. So much the greater would be their glory. He had often been filled with admiration as he had seen his little host encircled by myriads of barbarians, and felt that no people but Spaniards could have triumphed over such formidable odds. Nor could they, unless the arm of the Almighty had been over them. And they might reasonably look for His protection hereafter; for was it not in His cause they were fighting? They had encountered dangers and difficulties, it was true; but they had not come here expecting a life of idle dalliance and pleasure. Glory, as he had told them at the outset, was to be won only by toil and danger. They would do him the justice to acknowledge that he had never shrunk from his share of both. "This was a truth," adds the honest chronicler, who heard and reports the dialogue — which no one could deny. But, if they had met with hardships, he continued, they had been everywhere victorious. Even now they were enjoying the fruits of this, in the plenty which reigned in the camp. And they would soon see the Tlascalans, humbled by their late reverses, suing for peace on any terms. To go back now was impossible. The very stones would rise up against them. The Tlascalans would hunt them in triumph down to the water's edge. And how would the Mexicans exult at this miserable issue of their vainglorious vaunts! Their former friends would become their enemies; and the Totonacs, to avert the vengeance of the Aztecs, from which the Spaniards could no longer shield them, would join in the general cry. There was no alternative, then, but to go forward in their career. And he besought them to silence their pusillanimous scruples, and, instead of turning their eyes towards Cuba, to fix them on Mexico, the great object of their enterprise.

While this singular conference was going on, many other soldiers had gathered round the spot; and the discontented party, emboldened by the presence of their comrades, as well as by the general's forbearance, replied, that they were far from being convinced. Another such victory as the last would be their ruin. They were going to Mexico only to be slaughtered. Until, at length, the general's patience being exhausted, he cut the argument short by quoting a verse from an old song, implying that it was better to die with honour, than to live disgraced; a sentiment which was loudly echoed by the greater part of his audience, who, notwithstanding their occasional murmurs, had no design to abandon the expedition, still less the commander, to whom they were passionately devoted. The malcontents, disconcerted by this rebuke, slunk back to their own quarters, muttering half-smothered execrations on the leader who had projected the enterprise, the Indians who had guided him, and their own countrymen who supported him in it.

Such were the difficulties that lay in the path of Cortes: a wily and ferocious enemy; a climate uncertain, often unhealthy; illness in his own person, much aggravated by anxiety as to the manner in which his conduct would be received by his sovereign; last, not least, disaffection among his soldiers, on whose constancy and union he rested for the success of his operations — the great lever by which he was to overturn the empire of Montezuma.

On the morning following this event, the camp was surprised by the appearance of a small body of Tlascalans, decorated with badges, the white colour of which intimated peace. They brought a quantity of provisions, and some trifling ornaments, which, they said, were sent by the Tlascalan general, who was weary of the war, and desired an accommodation with the Spaniards. He would soon present himself to arrange this in person. The intelligence diffused general joy, and the emissaries received a friendly welcome.

A day or two elapsed, and while a few of the party left the Spanish quarters, the others, about fifty in number, who remained, excited some distrust in the bosom of Marina. She communicated her suspicions to Cortes that they were spies. He caused several of them, in consequence, to be arrested, examined them separately, and ascertained that they were employed by Xicotencatl to inform him of the state of the Christian camp, preparatory to a meditated assault, for which he was mustering his forces. Cortes, satisfied of the truth of this, determined to make such an example of the delinquents as should intimidate his enemy from repeating the attempt. He ordered their hands to be cut off, and in that condition sent them back to their countrymen, with the message, "that the Tlascalans might come by day or night; they would find the Spaniards ready for them."

The doleful spectacle of their comrades returning in this mutilated state filled the Indian camp with horror and consternation. The haughty crest of their chief was humbled. From that moment, he lost his wonted buoyancy and confidence. His soldiers, filled with superstitious fear, refused to serve longer against a foe who could read their very thoughts, and divine their plans before they were ripe for execution.

The punishment inflicted by Cortes may well shock the reader by its brutality. But it should be considered in mitigation, that the victims of it were spies, and, as such, by the laws of war, whether among civilised or savage nations, had incurred the penalty of death. The amputation of the limbs was a milder punishment, and reserved for inferior offences. If we revolt at the barbarous nature of the sentence, we should reflect that it was no uncommon one at that day; not more uncommon, indeed, than whipping and branding with a hot iron were in our own country at the beginning of the present century, or than cropping the ears was in the preceding one. A higher civilisation, indeed, rejects such punishments as pernicious in themselves, and degrading to humanity. But in the sixteenth century, they were openly recognised by the laws of the most polished nations in Europe. And it is too much to ask of any man, still less one bred to the iron trade of war, to be in advance of the refinement of his age. We may be content, if, in circumstances so unfavourable to humanity, he does not fall below it.

All thoughts of further resistance being abandoned, the four delegates of the Tlascalan republic were now allowed to proceed on their mission. They were speedily followed by Xicotencatl himself, attended by a numerous train of military retainers. As they drew near the Spanish lines, they were easily recognised by the white and yellow colours of their uniforms, the livery of the house of Titcala. The joy of the army was great at this sure intimation of the close of hostilities; and it was with difficulty that Cortes was enabled to restore the men to tranquillity, and the assumed indifference which it was proper to maintain in the presence of an enemy.

The Spaniards gazed with curious eye on the valiant chief who had so long kept his enemies at bay, and who now advanced with the firm and fearless step of one who was coming rather to bid defiance than to sue for peace. He was rather above the middle size, with broad shoulders, and a muscular frame intimating great activity and strength. His head was large, and his countenance marked with the lines of hard service rather than of age, for he was but thirty-five. When he entered the presence of Cortes, he made the usual salutation, by touching the ground with his hand, and carrying it to his head; while the sweet incense of aromatic gums rolled up in clouds from the censers carried by his slaves.

Far from a pusillanimous attempt to throw the blame on the senate, he assumed the whole responsibility of the war. He had considered the white men, he said, as enemies, for they came with the allies and vassals of Montezuma. He loved his country, and wished to preserve the independence which she had maintained through her long wars with the Aztecs. He had been beaten. They might be the strangers who, it had been so long predicted, would come from the east, to take possession of the country. He hoped they would use their victory with moderation, and not trample on the liberties of the republic. He came now in the name of his nation, to tender their obedience to the Spaniards, assuring them they would find his countrymen as faithful in peace as they had been firm in war.

Cortes, far from taking umbrage, was filled with admiration at the lofty spirit which thus disdained to stoop beneath misfortunes. The brave man knows how to respect bravery in another. He assumed, however, a severe aspect, as he rebuked the chief for having so long persisted in bostilities. Had Xicotencatl believed the word of the Spaniards, and accepted their proffered friendship sooner, he would have spared his people much suffering, which they well merited by their obstinacy. But it was impossible, continued the general, to retrieve the past. He was willing to bury it in oblivion, and to receive the Tlascalans as vassals to the emperor, his master. If they proved true, they should find him a sure column of support; if false, he would take such vengeance on them as he had intended to take on their capital, had they not speedily given in their submission. — It proved an ominous menace for the chief to whom it was addressed.

The cacique then ordered his slaves to bring forward some trifling ornaments of gold and feather embroidery, designed as presents. They were of little value, he said, with a smile, for the Tlascalans were poor. They had little gold, not even cotton, nor salt; the Aztec emperor had left them nothing but their freedom and their arms. He offered this gift only as a token of his good will. "As such I receive it," answered Cortes, "and coming from the Tlascalans, set more value on it than I should from any other source, though it were a house full of gold"; a politic, as well as magnanimous reply, for it was by the aid of this good will that he was to win the gold of Mexico.

Thus ended the bloody war with the fierce republic of Tlascala, during the course of which, the fortunes of the Spaniards, more than once, had trembled in the balance. Had it been persevered in but a little longer, it must have ended in their confusion and ruin, exhausted as they were by wounds, watching, and fatigues, with the seeds of disaffection rankling among themselves. As it was, they came out of the fearful contest with untarnished glory. To the enemy, they seemed invulnerable, bearing charmed lives, proof alike against the accidents of fortune and the assaults of man. No wonder that they indulged a similar conceit in their own bosoms, and that the humblest Spaniard should have fancied himself the subject of a special interposition of providence, which shielded him in the hour of battle, and reserved him for a higher destiny.

While the Tlascalans were still in the camp, an embassy was announced from Montezuma. Tidings of the exploits of the Spaniards had spread far and wide over the plateau. The emperor, in particular, had watched every step of their progress, as they climbed the steeps of the Cordilleras, and advanced over the broad tableland on their summit. He had seen them, with great satisfaction, take the road to Tlascala, trusting that, if they were mortal men, they would find their graves there. Great was his dismay, when courier after courier brought him intelligence of their successes, and that the most redoubtable warriors on the plateau had been scattered like chaff by the swords of this handful of strangers.

His superstitious fears returned in full force. He saw in the Spaniards "the men of destiny" who were to take possession of his sceptre. In his alarm and uncertainty, he sent a new embassy to the Christian camp. It consisted of five great nobles of his court, attended by a train of two hundred slaves. They brought with them a present, as usual, dictated partly by fear, and, in part, by the natural munificence of his disposition. It consisted of three thousand ounces of gold, in grains, or in various manufactured articles, with several hundred mantles and dresses of embroidered cotton, and the picturesque feather-work. As they laid these at the feet of Cortes, they told him, they had come to offer the congratulations of their master on the late victories of the white men. The emperor only regretted that it would not be in his power to receive them in his capital, where the numerous population was so unruly, that their safety would be placed in jeopardy. The mere intimation of the Aztec emperor's wishes, in the most distant way, would have sufficed with the Indian nations. It had very little weight with the Spaniards; and the envoys, finding this puerile expression of them ineffectual, resorted to another argument, offering a tribute in their master's name to the Castilian sovereign, provided the Spaniards would relinquish their visit to his capital. This was a greater error; it was displaying the rich casket with one hand, which he was unable to defend with the other. Yet the author of this pusillanimous policy, the unhappy victim of superstition, was a monarch renowned among the Indian nations for his intrepidity and enterprise — the terror of Anahuac!

Cortes, while he urged his own sovereign's commands as a reason for disregarding the wishes of Montezuma, uttered expressions of the most profound respect for the Aztec prince, and declared that if he had not the means of requiting his munificence, as he could wish, at present, he trusted to repay him, at some future day, with good works!

The Mexican ambassadors were not much gratified with finding the war at an end, and a reconciliation established between their mortal enemies and the Spaniards. The mutual disgust of the two parties with each other was too strong to be repressed even in the presence of the general, who saw with satisfaction the evidences of a jealousy, which, undermining the strength of the Indian emperor, was to prove the surest source of his own success.

Two of the Aztec mission returned to Mexico, to acquaint their sovereign with the state of affairs in the Spanish camp. The others remained with the army, Cortes being willing that they should be personal spectators of the deference shown him by the Tlascalans. Still he did not hasten his departure for their capital. Not that he placed reliance on the injurious intimations of the Mexicans respecting their good faith. Yet he was willing to put this to some longer trial, and, at the same time, to re-establish his own health more thoroughly, before his visit. Meanwhile, messengers daily arrived from the city, pressing his journey, and were finally followed by some of the aged rulers of the republic, attended by a numerous retinue, impatient of his long delay. They brought with them a body of five hundred tamanes, or men of burden, to drag his cannon, and relieve his own forces from this fatiguing part of their duty. It was impossible to defer his departure longer; and after mass, and a solemn thanksgiving to the great Being who had crowned their arms with triumph, the Spaniards bade adieu to the quarters which they had occupied for nearly three weeks on the hill of Tzompach.

THE city of Tlascala, the capital of the republic of the same name, lay at the distance of about six leagues from the Spanish camp. The road led into a hilly region, exhibiting in every arable patch of ground the evidence of laborious cultivation. Over a deep barranca, or ravine, they crossed on a bridge of stone, which, according to tradition — a slippery authority — is the same still standing, and was constructed originally for the passage of the army. They passed some considerable towns on their route, where they experienced a full measure of Indian hospitality. As they advanced, the approach to a populous city was intimated by the crowds who flocked out to see and welcome the strangers; men and women in their picturesque dresses, with bunches and wreaths of roses, which they gave to the Spaniards, or fastened to the necks and caparisons of their horses, in the manner as at Cempoalla. Priests, with their white robes, and long matted tresses floating over them, mingled in the crowd, scattering volumes of incense from their burning censers. In this way, the multitudinous and motley procession defiled through the gates of the ancient capital of Tlascala. It was the 23rd of September, 1519.

The press was now so great, that it was with difficulty the police of the city could clear a passage for the army; while the azoteas, or flat-terraced roofs of the buildings, were covered with spectators, eager to catch a glimpse of the wonderful strangers. The houses were hung with festoons of flowers, and arches of verdant boughs, intertwined with roses and honeysuckle, were thrown across the streets. The whole population abandoned itself to rejoicing; and the air was rent with songs and shouts of triumph mingled with the wild music of the national instruments, that might have excited apprehensions in the breasts of the soldiery, had they not gathered their peaceful import from the assurance of Marina, and the joyous countenances of the natives.

With these accompaniments, the procession moved along the principal streets to the mansion of Xicotencatl, the aged father of the Tlascalan general, and one of the four rulers of the republic. Cortes dismounted from his horse, to receive the old chieftain's embrace. He was nearly blind; and satisfied, as far as he could, a natural curiosity respecting the person of the Spanish general, by passing his hand over his features. He then led the way to a spacious hall in his palace, where a banquet was served to the army. In the evening, they were shown to their quarters, in the buildings and open ground surrounding one of the principal teocallis; while the Mexican ambassadors, at the desire of Cortes, had apartments assigned them next to his own, that he might the better watch over their safety, in this city of their enemies.

Tlascala was one of the most important and populous towns on the tableland. Cortes, in his letter to the emperor, compares it to Granada, affirming that it was larger, stronger, and more populous than the Moorish capital, at the time of the conquest, and quite as well built. But notwithstanding we are assured by a most respectable writer at the close of the last century that its remains justify the assertion, we shall be slow to believe that its edifices could have rivalled those monuments of Oriental magnificence, whose light, aerial forms still survive after the lapse of ages, the admiration of every traveller of sensibility and taste. The truth is, that Cortes, like Columbus, saw objects through the warm medium of his own fond imagination, giving them a higher tone of colouring and larger dimensions than were strictly warranted by the fact. It was natural that the man who had made such rare discoveries should unconsciously magnify their merits to his own eyes and to those of others.

The houses were, for the most part, of mud or earth; the better sort of stone and lime, or bricks dried in the sun. They were unprovided with doors or windows, but in the apertures for the former hung mats fringed with pieces of copper or something which, by its tinkling sound, would give notice of any one's entrance. The streets were narrow and dark. The population must have been considerable if, as Cortes asserts, thirty thousand souls were often gathered in the market on a public day. These meetings were a sort of fairs, held, as usual in all the great towns, every fifth day, and attended by the inhabitants of the adjacent country, who brought there for sale every description of domestic produce and manufacture with which they were acquainted. They peculiarly excelled in pottery, which was considered as equal to the best in Europe. It is a further proof of civilised habits, that the Spaniards found barbers' shops, and baths, both of vapour and hot water, familiarly used by the inhabitants. A still higher proof of refinement may be discerned in a vigilant police which repressed everything like disorder among the people.

The city was divided into four quarters, which might rather be called so many separate towns, since they were built at different times, and separated from each other by high stone walls, defining their respective limits. Over each of these districts ruled one of the four great chiefs of the republic, occupying his own spacious mansion, and surrounded by his own immediate vassals. Strange arrangement — and more strange that it should have been compatible with social order and tranquillity! The ancient capital, through one quarter of which flowed the rapid current of the Zahuatl, stretched along the summits and sides of hills, at whose base are now gathered the miserable remains of its once flourishing population. Far beyond, to the south-west, extended the bold sierra of Tlascala, and the huge Malinche, crowned with the usual silver diadem of the highest Andes, having its shaggy sides clothed with dark green forests of firs, gigantic sycamores, and oaks whose towering stems rose to the height of forty or fifty feet, unencumbered by a branch. The clouds, which sailed over from the distant Atlantic, gathered round the lofty peaks of the sierra, and, settling into torrents, poured over the plains in the neighbourhood of the city, converting them, at such seasons, into swamps. Thunderstorms, more frequent and terrible here than in other parts of the tableland, swept down the sides of the mountains, and shook the frail tenements of the capital to their foundations. But, although the bleak winds of the sierra gave an austerity to the climate, unlike the sunny skies and genial temperature of the lower regions, it was far more favourable to the development of both the physical and moral energies. A bold and hardy peasantry was nurtured among the recesses of the hills, fit equally to cultivate the land in peace and to defend it in war. Unlike the spoiled child of Nature, who derives such facilities of subsistence from her too prodigal hand, as supersede the necessity of exertion on his own part, the Tlascalan earned his bread — from a soil not ungrateful, it is true — by the sweat of his brow. He led a life of temperance and toil. Cut off by his long wars with the Aztecs from commercial intercourse, he was driven chiefly to agricultural labour, the occupation most propitious to purity of morals and sinewy strength of constitution. His honest breast glowed with the patriotism — or local attachment to the soil, which is the fruit of its diligent culture; while he was elevated by a proud consciousness of independence, the natural birthright of the child of the mountains. — Such was the race with whom Cortes was now associated for the achievement of his great work.

Some days were given by the Spaniards to festivity, in which they were successively entertained at the hospitable boards of the four great nobles, in their several quarters of the city. Amidst these friendly demonstrations, however, the general never relaxed for a moment his habitual vigilance, or the strict discipline of the camp; and he was careful to provide for the security of the citizens by prohibiting, under severe penalties, any soldier from leaving his quarters without express permission. Indeed, the severity of his discipline provoked the remonstrance of more than one of his officers, as a superfluous caution; and the Tlascalan chiefs took some exception at it, as inferring an unreasonable distrust of them. But, when Cortes explained it, as in obedience to an established military system, they testified their admiration, and the ambitious young general of the republic proposed to introduce it, if possible, into his own ranks.

The Spanish commander, having assured himself of the loyalty of his new allies, next proposed to accomplish one of the great objects of his mission — their conversion to Christianity. By the advice of Father Olmedo, always opposed to precipitate measures, he had deferred this till a suitable opportunity presented itself for opening the subject. Such a one occurred when the chiefs of the state proposed to strengthen the alliance with the Spaniards, by the intermarriage of their daughters with Cortes and his officers. He told them this could not be, while they continued in the darkness of infidelity. Then, with the aid of the good friar, he expounded as well as he could the doctrines of the Faith; and, exhibiting the image of the

Virgin with the infant Redeemer, told them that there was the God, in whose worship alone they would find salvation, while that of their own false idols would sink them in eternal perdition.

It is unnecessary to burden the reader with a recapitulation of his homily, which contained, probably, dogmas quite as incomprehensible to the untutored Indian as any to be found in his own rude mythology. But, though it failed to convince his audience, they listened with a deferential awe. When he had finished, they replied, they had no doubt that the God of the Christians must be a good and a great God, and as such they were willing to give him a place among the divinities of Tlascala. The polytheistic system of the Indians, like that of the ancient Greeks, was of that accommodating kind which could admit within its elastic folds the deities of any other religion, without violence to itself. But every nation, they continued, must have its own appropriate and tutelary deities. Nor could they, in their old age, abjure the service of those who had watched over them from youth. It would bring down the vengeance of their gods, and of their own nation, who were as warmly attached to their religion as their liberties, and would defend both with the last drop of their blood!

It was clearly inexpedient to press the matter further, at present. But the zeal of Cortes, as usual, waxing warm by opposition, had now mounted too high for him to calculate obstacles; nor would he have shrunk, probably, from the crown of martyrdom in so good a cause. But fortunately, at least for the success of his temporal cause, this crown was not reserved for him.

The good monk, his ghostly adviser, seeing the course things were likely to take, with better judgment interposed to prevent it. He had no desire, he said, to see the same scenes acted over again as at Cempoalla. He had no relish for forced conversions. They could hardly be lasting. The growth of an hour might well die with the hour. Of what use was it to overturn the altar, if the idol remained enthroned in the heart? or to destroy the idol itself, if it were only to make room for another? Better to wait patiently the effect of time and teaching to soften the heart and open the understanding, without which there could be no assurance of a sound and permanent conviction. These rational views were enforced by the remonstrances of Alvarado, Velasquez de Leon, and those in whom Cortes placed most confidence; till, driven from his original purpose, the military polemic consented to relinquish the attempt at conversion, for the present, and to refrain from a repetition of the scenes, which, considering the different mettle of the population, might have been attended with very different results from those at Cozumel and Cempoalla.

But though Cortes abandoned the ground of conversion for the present, he compelled the Tlascalans to break the fetters of the unfortunate victims reserved for sacrifice; an act of humanity unhappily only transient in its effects, since the prisons were filled with fresh victims on his departure.

He also obtained permission for the Spaniards to perform the services of their own religion unmolested. A large cross was erected in one of the great courts or squares. Mass was celebrated every day in the presence of the army and of crowds of natives, who, if they did not comprehend its full import, were so far edified, that they learned to reverence the religion of their conquerors. The direct interposition of Heaven, however, wrought more for their conversion than the best homily of priest or soldier. Scarcely had the Spaniards left the city — the tale is told on very respectable authority — when a thin, transparent cloud descended and settled like a column on the cross, and, wrapping it round in its luminous folds, continued to emit a soft, celestial radiance through the night, thus proclaiming the sacred character of the symbol, on which was shed the halo of divinity!

The principle of toleration in religious matters being established, the Spanish general consented to receive the daughters of the caciques. Five or six of the most beautiful Indian maidens were assigned to as many of his principal officers, after they had been cleansed from the stains of infidelity by the waters of baptism. They received, as usual, on this occasion, good Castilian names, in exchange for the barbarous nomenclature of their own vernacular.

Among them, Xicotencatl's daughter, Dona Luisa, as she was called after her baptism, was a princess of the highest estimation and authority in Tlascala. She was given by her father to Alvarado, and their posterity intermarried with the noblest families of Castile. The frank and joyous manners of this cavalier made him a great favourite with the Tlascalans; and his bright open countenance, fair complexion, and golden locks, gave him the name of Tonatiuh, the "Sun." The Indians often pleased their fancies by fastening a sobriquet, or some characteristic epithet, on the Spaniards. As Cortes was always attended, on public occasions, by Dona Marina, or Malinche, as she was called by the natives, they distinguished him by the same name. By these epithets, originally bestowed in Tlascala, the two Spanish captains were popularly designated among the Indian nations.

While these events were passing, another embassy arrived from the court of Mexico. It was charged, as usual, with a costly donative of embossed gold plate, and rich embroidered stuffs of cotton and feather-work. The terms of the message might well argue a vacillating and timid temper in the monarch, did they not mask a deeper policy. He now invited the Spaniards to his capital, with the assurance of a cordial welcome. He besought them to enter into no alliance with the base and barbarous Tlascalans; and he invited them to take the route of the friendly city of Cholula, where arrangements, according to his orders, were made for their reception.

The Tlascalans viewed with deep regret the general's proposed visit to Mexico. Their reports fully confirmd all he had before heard of the power and ambition of Montezuma. His armies, they said, were spread over every part of the continent. His capital was a place of great strength, and as, from its insular position, all communication could be easily cut off with the adjacent country, the Spaniards, once entrapped there, would be at his mercy. His policy, they represented, was as insidious as his ambition was boundless. "Trust not his fair words," they said, "his courtesies, and his gifts. His professions are hollow, and his friendships are false." When Cortes remarked, that he hoped to bring about a better understanding between the emperor and them, they replied, it would be impossible; however smooth his words, he would hate them at heart.

They warmly protested, also, against the general's taking the route of Cholula. The inhabitants, not brave in the open field, were more dangerous from their perfidy and craft. They were Montezuma's tools, and would do his bidding. The Tlascalans seemed to combine with this distrust a superstitious dread of the ancient city, the headquarters of the religion of Anahuac. It was here that the god Quetzalcoatl held the pristine seat of his empire. His temple was celebrated throughout the land, and the priests were confidently believed to have the power, as they themselves boasted, of opening an inundation from the foundations of his shrine, which should bury their enemies in the deluge. The Tlascalans further reminded Cortes, that while so many other and distant places had sent to him at Tlascala, to testify their good will, and offer their allegiance to his sovereign, Cholula, only six leagues distant, had done neither. The last suggestion struck the general more forcibly than any of the preceding. He instantly despatched a summons to the city requiring a formal tender of its submission.

Among the embassies from different quarters which had waited on the Spanish commander, while at Tlascala, was one from Ixtlilxochitl, son of the great Nezahualpilli, and an unsuccessful competitor with his elder brother — as noticed in a former part of our narrative — for the crown of Tezcuco. Though defeated in his pretensions, he had obtained a part of the kingdom, over which he ruled with a deadly feeling of animosity towards his rival, and to Montezuma, who had sustained him. He now offered his services to Cortes, asking his aid, in return, to place him on the throne of his ancestors. The politic general returned such an answer to the aspiring young prince, as might encourage his expectations, and attach him to his interests. It was his aim to strengthen his cause by attracting to himself every particle of disaffection that was floating through the land.

It was not long before deputies arrived from Cholula, profuse in their expressions of good will, and inviting the presence of the Spaniards in their capital. The messengers were of low degree, far beneath the usual rank of ambassadors. This was pointed out by the Tlascalans; and Cortes regarded it as a fresh indignity. He sent in consequence a new summons, declaring, if they did not instantly send him a deputation of their principal men, he would deal with them as rebels to his own sovereign, the rightful lord of these realms! The menace had the desired effect. The Cholulans were not inclined to contest, at least for the present, his magnificent pretensions. Another embassy appeared in the camp, consisting of some of the highest nobles; who repeated the invitation for the Spaniards to visit their city, and excused their own tardy appearance by apprehensions for their personal safety in the capital of their enemies. The explanation was plausible, and was admitted by Cortes.

The Tlascalans were now more than ever opposed to his projected visit. A strong Aztec force, they had ascertained, lay in the neighbourhood of Cholula, and the people were actively placing their city in a posture of defence. They suspected some insidious scheme concerted by Montezuma to destroy the Spaniards.

These suggestions disturbed the mind of Cortes, but did not turn him from his purpose. He felt a natural curiosity to see the venerable city so celebrated in the history of the Indian nations. He had, besides, gone too far to recede — too far, at least, to do so without a show of apprehension, implying a distrust in his own resources, which could not fail to have a bad effect on his enemies, his allies, and his own men. After a brief consultation with his officers, he decided on the route to Cholula.

It was now three weeks since the Spaniards had taken up their residence within the hospitable walls of Tlascala; and nearly six since they entered her territory. They had been met on the threshold as an enemy, with the most determined hostility. They were now to part with the same people, as friends and allies; fast friends, who were to stand by them, side by side, through the whole of their arduous struggle. The result of their visit, therefore, was of the last importance, since on the co-operation of these brave and warlike republicans, greatly depended the ultimate success of the expedition.

THE ancient city of Cholula, capital of the republic of that name, lay nearly six leagues south of Tlascala, and about twenty east, or rather south-east of Mexico. It was said by Cortes to contain twenty thousand houses within the walls, and as many more in the environs. Whatever was its real number of inhabitants, it was unquestionably, at the time of the Conquest, one of the most populous and flourishing cities in New Spain.

It was of great antiquity, and was founded by the primitive races who overspread the land before the Aztecs. We have few particulars of its form of government, which seems to have been cast on a republican model similar to that of Tlascala. This answered so well, that the state maintained its independence down to a very late period, when, if not reduced to vassalage by the Aztecs, it was so far under their control as to enjoy few of the benefits of a separate political existence. Their connection with Mexico brought the Cholulans into frequent collision with their neighbours and kindred, the Tlascalans. But, although far superior to them in refinement and the various arts of civilisation, they were no match in war for the bold mountaineers, the Swiss of Anahuac. The Cholulan capital was the great commercial emporium of the plateau. The inhabitants excelled in various mechanical arts, especially that of working in metals, the manufacture of cotton and agave cloths, and of a delicate kind of pottery, rivalling, it was said, that of Florence in beauty. But such attention to the arts of a polished and peaceful community naturally indisposed them to war, and disqualified them for coping with those who made war the great business of life. The Cholulans were accused of effeminacy, and were less distinguished — it is the charge of their rivals — by their courage than their cunning.

But the capital, so conspicuous for its refinement and its great antiquity, was even more venerable for the religious traditions which invested it. It was here that the god Quetzalcoatl paused in his passage to the coast, and passed twenty years in teaching the Toltec inhabitants the arts of civilisation. He made them acquainted with better forms of government, and a more spiritualised religion, in which the only sacrifices were the fruits and flowers of the season. It is not easy to determine what he taught, since, his lessons have been so mingled with the licentious dogmas of his own priests, and the mystic commentaries of the Christian missionary. It is probable that he was one of those rare and gifted beings, who dissipating the darkness of the age by the illumination of their own genius, are deified by a grateful posterity, and placed among the lights of heaven.

It was in honour of this benevolent deity, that the stupendous mound was erected on which the traveller still gazes with admiration as the most colossal fabric in New Spain, rivalling in dimensions, and somewhat resembling in form, the pyramidal structures of ancient Egypt. The date of its erection is unknown, for it was found there when the Aztecs entered on the plateau. It had the form common to the Mexican teocallis, that of a truncated pyramid, facing with its four sides the cardinal points, and divided into the same number of terraces. Its original outlines, however, have been effaced by the action of time and of the elements, while the exuberant growth of shrubs and wild flowers, which have mantled over its surface, give it the appearance of one of those symmetrical elevations thrown up by the caprice of nature, rather than by the industry of man. It is doubtful, indeed, whether the interior be not a natural hill, though it seems not improbable that it is an artificial composition of stone and earth, deeply incrusted, as is certain, in every part, with alternate strata of brick and clay.

The perpendicular height of the pyramid is one hundred and seventy-seven feet. Its base is one thousand four hundred and twenty-three feet long, twice as long as that of the great pyramid of Cheops. It may give some idea of its dimensions to state, that its base, which is square, covers about forty-four acres, and the platform on its truncated summit, embraces more than one. It reminds us of those colossal monuments of brickwork, which are still seen in ruins on the banks of the Euphrates, and, in much higher preservation, on those of the Nile.

On the summit stood a sumptuous temple, in which was the image of the mystic deity, "god of the air," with ebon features, unlike the fair complexion which he bore upon earth, wearing a mitre on his head waving with plumes of fire, with a resplendent collar of gold round his neck, pendants of mosaic turquoise in his ears, a jewelled sceptre in one hand, and a shield curiously painted, the emblem of his rule over the winds, in the other. The sanctity of the place, hallowed by hoary tradition, and the magnificence of the temple and its services, made it an object of veneration throughout the land, and pilgrims from the furthest corners of Anahuac came to offer up their devotions at the shrine of Quetzalcoatl. The number of these was so great, as to give an air of mendicity to the motley population of the city; and Cortes, struck with the novelty, tells us that he saw multitudes of beggars such as are to be found in the enlightened capitals of Europe; — a whimsical criterion of civilisation which must place our own prosperous land somewhat low in the scale.

Cholula was not the resort only of the indigent devotee. Many of the kindred races had temples of their own in the city, in the same manner as some Christian nations have in Rome, and each temple was provided with its own peculiar ministers for the service of the deity to whom it was consecrated. In no city was there seen such a concourse of priests, so many processions, such pomp of ceremonial sacrifice, and religious festivals. Cholula was, in short, what Mecca is among Mahometans, or Jerusalem among Christians; it was the Holy City of Anahuac.

The religious rites were not performed, however, in the pure spirit originally prescribed by its tutelary deity. His altars, as well as those of the numerous Aztec gods, were stained with human blood; and six thousand victims are said to have been annually offered up at their sanguinary shrines. The great number of these may be estimated from the declaration of Cortes, that he counted four hundred towers in the city; yet no temple had more than two, many only one. High above the rest rose the great "Pyramid of Cholula," with its undying fires flinging their radiance over the capital, and proclaiming to the nations that there was the mystic worship — alas! how corrupted by cruelty and superstition — of the good deity who was one day to return and resume his empire over the land.

But it is time to return to Tlascala. On the appointed morning the Spanish army took up its march to Mexico by the way of Cholula. It was followed by crowds of the citizens, filled with admiration at the intrepidity of men who, so few in number, would venture to brave the great Montezuma in his capital. Yet an immense body of warriors offered to share the dangers of the expedition; but Cortes, while he showed his gratitude for their good will, selected only six thousand of the volunteers to bear him company. He was unwilling to encumber himself with an unwieldy force that might impede his movements; and probably did not care to put himself so far in the power of allies whose attachment was too recent to afford sufficient guaranty for their fidelity.

After crossing some rough and hilly ground, the army entered on the wide plain which spreads out for miles around Cholula. At the elevation of more than six thousand feet above the sea they beheld the rich products of various climes growing side by side, fields of towering maize, the juicy aloe, the chilli or Aztec pepper, and large plantations of the cactus, on which the brilliant cochineal is nourished. Not a rood of land but was under cultivation; and the soil — an uncommon thing on the tableland — was irrigated by numerous streams and canals, and well shaded by woods, that have disappeared before the rude axe of the Spaniards. Towards evening they reached a small stream, on the banks of which Cortes determined to take up his quarters for the night, being unwilling to disturb the tranquillity of the city by introducing so large a force into it at an unseasonable hour.

Here he was soon joined by a number of Cholulan caciques and their attendants, who came to view and welcome the strangers. When they saw their Tlascalan enemies in the camp, however, they exhibited signs of displeasure, and intimated an apprehension that their presence in the town might occasion disorder. The remonstrance seemed reasonable to Cortes, and he accordingly commanded his allies to remain in their present quarters, and to join him as he left the city on the way to Mexico.

On the following morning he made his entrance at the head of his army into Cholula, attended by no other Indians than those from Cempoalla, and a handful of Tlascalans to take charge of the baggage. His allies, at parting, gave him many cautions respecting the people he was to visit, who, while they affected to despise them as a nation of traders, employed the dangerous arms of perfidy and cunning. As the troops drew near the city, the road was lined with swarms of people of both sexes and every age — old men tottering with infirmity, women with children in their arms, all eager to catch a glimpse of the strangers, whose persons, weapons, and horses were objects of intense curiosity to eyes which had not hitherto ever encountered them in battle. The Spaniards, in turn, were filled with admiration at the aspect of the Cholulans, much superior in dress and general appearance to the nations they had hitherto seen. They were particularly struck with the costume of the higher classes, who wore fine embroidered mantles, resembling the graceful albornoz, or Moorish cloak, in their texture and fashion. They showed the same delicate taste for flowers as the other tribes of the plateau, decorating their persons with them, and tossing garlands and bunches among the soldiers. An immense number of priests mingled. with the crowd, swinging their aromatic censers, while music from various kinds of instruments gave a lively welcome to the visitors, and made the whole scene one of gay, bewildering enchantment. If it did not have the air of a triumphal procession so much as at Tlascala, where the melody of instruments was drowned by the shouts of the multitude, it gave a quiet assurance of hospitality and friendly feeling not less grateful.

The Spaniards were also struck with the cleanliness of the city, the width and great regularity of the streets, which seemed to have been laid out on a settled plan, with the solidity of the houses, and the number and size of the pyramidal temples. In the court of one of these, and its surrounding buildings, they were quartered.

They were soon visited by the principal lords of the place, who seemed solicitous to provide them with accommodations. Their table was plentifully supplied, and, in short, they experienced such attentions as were calculated to dissipate their suspicions, and made them impute those of their Tlascalan friends to prejudice and old national hostility.

In a few days the scene changed. Messengers arrived from Montezuma, who, after a short and unpleasant intimation to Cortes that his approach occasioned much disquietude to their master, conferred separately with the Mexican ambassadors still in the Castilian camp, and then departed, taking one of the latter along with them. From this time, the deportment of their Cholulan hosts underwent a visible alteration. They did not visit the quarters as before, and, when invited to do so, excused themselves on pretence of illness. The supply of provisions was stinted, on the ground that they were short of maize. These symptoms of alienation, independently of temporary embarrassment, caused serious alarm in the breast of Cortes, for the future. His apprehensions were not allayed by the reports of the Cempoallans, who told him, that in wandering round the city they had seen several streets barricaded; the azoteas, or flat roofs of the houses, loaded with huge stones and other missiles, as if preparatory to an assault; and in some places they had found holes covered over with branches, and upright stakes planted within, as if to embarrass the movements of the cavalry. Some Tlascalans coming in also from their camp, informed the general that a great sacrifice, mostly of children, had been offered up in a distant quarter of the town, to propitiate the favour of the gods, apparently for some intended enterprise. They added, that they had seen numbers of the citizens leaving the city with their women and children, as if to remove them to a place of safety. These tidings confirmed the worst suspicions of Cortes, who had no doubt that some hostile scheme was in agitation. If he had felt any, a discovery by Marina, the good angel of the expedition, would have turned these doubts into certainty.

The amiable manners of the Indian girl had won her the regard of the wife of one of the caciques, who repeatedly urged Marina to visit her house, darkly intimating that in this way she would escape the fate that awaited the Spaniards. The interpreter, seeing the importance of obtaining further intelligence at once, pretended to be pleased with the proposal, and affected, at the same time, great discontent with the white men, by whom she was detained in captivity. Thus throwing the credulous Cholulan off her guard, Marina gradually insinuated herself into her confidence, so far as to draw from her a full account of the conspiracy.

It originated, she said, with the Aztec emperor, who had sent rich bribes to the great caciques, and to her husband among others, to secure them in his views. The Spaniards were to be assaulted as they marched out of the capital, when entangled in its streets, in which numerous impediments had been placed to throw the cavalry into disorder. A force of twenty thousand Mexicans was already quartered at no great distance from the city, to support the Cholulans in the assault. It was confidently expected that the Spaniards, thus embarrassed in their movements, would fall an easy prey to the superior strength of their enemy. A sufficient number of prisoners was to be reserved to grace the sacrifices of Cholula; the rest were to be led in fetters to the capital of Montezuma.

While this conversation was going on, Marina occupied herself with putting up such articles of value and wearing apparel as she proposed to take with her in the evening, when she could escape unnoticed from the Spanish quarters to the house of her Cholulan friend, who assisted her in the operation. Leaving her visitor thus employed, Marina found an opportunity to steal away for a few moments, and, going to the general's apartment, disclosed to him her discoveries. He immediately caused the cacique's wife to be seized, and on examination she fully confirmed the statement of his Indian mistress.

The intelligence thus gathered by Cortes filled him with the deepest alarm. He was fairly taken in the snare. To fight or to fly seemed equally difficult. He was in a city of enemies, where every house might be converted into a fortress, and where such embarrassments were thrown in the way, as might render the manoeuvres of his artillery and horse nearly impracticable. In addition to the wily Cholulans, he must cope, under all these disadvantages, with the redoubtable warriors of Mexico. He was like a traveller who has lost his way in the darkness among precipices, where any step may dash him to pieces, and where to retreat or to advance is equally perilous.

He was desirous to obtain still further confirmation and particulars of the conspiracy. He accordingly induced two of the priests in the neighbourhood, one of them a person of much influence in the place, to visit his quarters. By courteous treatment, and liberal largesses of the rich presents he had received from Montezuma — thus turning his own gifts against the giver — he drew from them a full confirmation of the previous report. The emperor had been in a state of pitiable vacillation since the arrival of the Spaniards. His first orders to the Cholulans were, to receive the strangers kindly. He had recently consulted his oracles anew, and obtained for answer, that Cholula would be the grave of his enemies; for the gods would be sure to support him in avenging the sacrilege offered to the Holy City. So confident were the Aztecs of success, that numerous manacles, or poles with thongs which served as such, were already in the place to secure the prisoners.

Cortes, now feeling himself fully possessed of the facts, dismissed the priests, with injunctions of secrecy, scarcely necessary. He told them it was his purpose to leave the city on the following morning, and requested that they would induce some of the principal caciques to grant him an interview in his quarters. He then summoned a council of his officers, though, as it seems, already determined as to the course he was to take.

The members of the council were differently affected by the startling intelligence, according to their different characters. The more timid, disheartened by the prospect of obstacles which seemed to multiply as they drew nearer the Mexican capital, were for retracing their steps, and seeking shelter in the friendly city of Tlascala. Others, more persevering, but prudent, were for taking the more northerly route originally recommended by their allies. The greater part supported the general, who was ever of opinion that they had no alternative but to advance. Retreat would be ruin. Half-way measures were scarcely better; and would infer a timidity which must discredit them with both friend and foe. Their true policy was to rely on themselves; to strike such a blow as should intimidate their enemies, and show them that the Spaniards were as incapable of being circumvented by artifice, as of being crushed by weight of numbers and courage in the open field.

When the caciques, persuaded by the priests, appeared before Cortes, he contented himself with gently rebuking their want of hospitality, and assured them the Spaniards would be no longer a burden to their city, as he proposed to leave it early on the following morning. He requested, moreover, that they would furnish a reinforcement of two thousand men to transport his artillery and baggage. The chiefs, after some consultation, acquiesced in a demand which might in some measure favour their own designs.

On their departure, the general summoned the Aztec ambassadors before him. He briefly acquainted them with his detection of the treacherous plot to destroy his army, the contrivance of which, he said, was imputed to their master, Montezuma. It grieved him much, he added, to find the emperor implicated in so nefarious a scheme, and that the Spaniards must now march as enemies against the prince, whom they had hoped to visit as a friend.

The ambassadors, with earnest protestations, asserted their entire ignorance of the conspiracy; and their belief that Montezuma was equally innocent of a crime, which they charged wholly on the Cholulans. It was clearly the policy of Cortes to keep on good terms with the Indian monarch; to profit as long as possible by his good offices; and to avail himself of his fancied security — such feelings of security as the general could inspire him with — to cover his own future operations. He affected to give credit, therefore, to the assertion of the envoys, and declared his unwillingness to believe that a monarch, who had rendered the Spaniards so many friendly offices, would now consummate the whole by a deed of such unparalleled baseness. The discovery of their twofold duplicity, he added, sharpened his resentment against the Cholulans, on whom he would take such vengeance as should amply requite the injuries done both to Montezuma and the Spaniards. He then dismissed the ambassadors, taking care, notwithstanding this show of confidence, to place a strong guard over them, to prevent communication with the citizens.

That night was one of deep anxiety to the army. The ground they stood on seemed loosening beneath their feet, and any moment might be the one marked for their destruction. Their vigilant general took all possible precautions for their safety, increasing the number of the sentinels, and posting his guns in such a manner as to protect the approaches to the camp. His eyes, it may well be believed, did not close during the night. Indeed every Spaniard lay down in his arms, and every horse stood saddled and bridled, ready for instant service. But no assault was meditated by the Indians, and the stillness of the hour was undisturbed except by the occasional sounds heard in a populous city, even when buried in slumber, and by the hoarse cries of the priests from the turrets of the teocallis, proclaiming through their trumpets the watches of the night.

WITH the first streak of morning light, Cortes was seen on horseback, directing the movements of his little band. The strength of his forces he drew up in the great square or court, surrounded partly by buildings, as before noticed, and in part by a high wall. There were three gates of entrance, at each of which he placed a strong guard. The rest of his troops, with his great guns, he posted without the enclosure, in such a manner as to command the avenues, and secure those within from interruption in their bloody work. Orders had been sent the night before to the Tlascalan chiefs to hold themselves ready, at a concerted signal, to march into the city and join the Spaniards.

The arrangements were hardly completed, before the Cholulan caciques appeared, leading a body of levies, tamanes, even more numerous than had been demanded. They were marched at once into the square, commanded, as we have seen, by the Spanish infantry, which was drawn up under the walls. Cortes then took some of the caciques aside. With a stern air, he bluntly charged them with the conspiracy, showing that he was well acquainted with all the particulars. He had visited their city, he said, at the invitation of their emperor; had come as friend; had respected the inhabitants and their property; and, to avoid all cause of umbrage, had left a great part of his forces without the walls. They had received him with a show of kindness and hospitality, and, reposing on this, he had been decoyed into the snare, and found this kindness only a mask to cover the blackest perfidy.

The Cholulans were thunderstruck at the accusation. An undefined awe crept over them as they gazed on the mysterious strangers, and felt themselves in the presence of beings who seemed to have the power of reading the thoughts scarcely formed in their bosoms. There was no use in prevarication or denial before such judges. They confessed the whole, and endeavoured to excuse themselves by throwing the blame on Montezuma. Cortes, assuming an air of higher indignation at this, assured them that the pretence should not serve, since, even if well founded, it would be no justification; and he would now make such an example of them for their treachery, that the report of it should ring throughout the wide borders of Anahuac!

The fatal signal, the discharge of an arquebuse was then given. In an instant every musket and crossbow was levelled at the unfortunate Cholulans in the courtyard, and a frightful volley poured into them as they stood crowded together like a herd of deer in the centre. They were taken by surprise, for they had not heard the preceding dialogue with the chiefs. They made scarcely any resistance to the Spaniards, who followed up the discharge of their pieces by rushing on them with their swords; and, as the half-naked bodies of the natives afforded no protection, they hewed them down with as much ease as the reaper mows down the ripe corn in harvest time. Some endeavoured to scale the walls, but only afforded a surer mark to the arquebusiers and archers. Others threw themselves into the gateways, but were received on the long pikes of the soldiers who guarded them. Some few had better luck in hiding themselves under the heaps of slain with which the ground was soon loaded.

While this work of death was going on, the countrymen of the slaughtered Indians, drawn together by the noise of the massacre, had commenced a furious assault on the Spaniards from without. But Cortes had placed his battery of heavy guns in a position that commanded the avenues, and swept off the files of the assailants as they rushed on. In the intervals between the discharges, which, in the imperfect state of the science in that day, were much longer than in ours, he forced back the press by charging with the horse into the midst. The steeds, the guns, the weapons of the Spaniards, were all new to the Cholulans. Notwithstanding the novelty of the terrific spectacle, the flash of firearms mingling with the deafening roar of the artillery, as its thunders reverberated among the buildings, the despairing Indians pushed on to take the places of their fallen comrades.

While this fierce struggle was going forward, the Tlascalans, hearing the concerted signal, had advanced with quick pace into the city. They had bound, by order of Cortes, wreaths of sedge round their heads, that they might the more surely be distinguished from the Cholulans. Coming up in the very heat of the engagement, they fell on the defenceless rear of the townsmen, who, trampled down under the heels of the Castilian cavalry on one side, and galled by their vindictive enemies on the other, could no longer maintain their ground. They gave way, some taking refuge in the nearest buildings, which, being partly of wood, were speedily set on fire. Others fled to the temples. One strong party, with a number of priests at its head, got possession of the great teocalli. There was a vulgar tradition, already alluded to, that, on removal of part of the walls, the god would send forth an inundation to overwhelm his enemies. The superstitious Cholulans with great difficulty succeeded in wrenching away some of the stones in the walls of the edifice. But dust, not water followed. Their false gods deserted them in the hour of need. In despair they flung themselves into the wooden turrets that crowned the temple, and poured down stones, javelins, and burning arrows on the Spaniards, as they climbed the great staircase, which, by a flight of one hundred and twenty steps, scaled the face of the pyramid. But the fiery shower fell harmless on the steel bonnets of the Christians, while they availed themselves of the burning shafts to set fire to the wooden citadel, which was speedily wrapt in flames. Still the garrison held out, and though quarter, it is said, was offered, only one Cholulan availed himself of it. The rest threw themselves headlong from the parapet, or perished miserably in the flames.

All was now confusion and uproar in the fair city which had so lately reposed in security and peace. The groans of the dying, the frantic supplications of the vanquished for mercy, were mingled with the loud battle-cries of the Spaniards, as they rode down their enemy, and with the shrill whistle of the Tlascalans, who gave full scope to the long cherished rancour of ancient rivalry. The tumult was still further swelled by the incessant rattle of musketry, and the crash of falling timbers, which sent up a volume of flame that outshone the ruddy light of morning, making altogether a hideous confusion of sights and sounds, that converted the Holy City into a Pandemonium. As resistance slackened, the victors broke into the houses and sacred places, plundering them of whatever valuables they contained, plate, jewels, which were found in some quantity, wearing apparel and provisions, the two last coveted even more than the former by the simple Tlascalans, thus facilitating a division of the spoil, much to the satisfaction of their Christian confederates. Amidst this universal licence, it is worthy of remark, the commands of Cortes were so far respected that no violence was offered to women or children, though these, as well as numbers of the men, were made prisoners, to be swept into slavery by the Tlascalans. These scenes of violence had lasted some hours, when Cortes, moved by the entreaties of some Cholulan chiefs, who had been reserved from the massacre, backed by the prayers of the Mexican envoys, consented, out of regard, as he said, to the latter, the representatives of Montezuma, to call off the soldiers, and put a stop, as well as he could, to further outrage. Two of the caciques were also permitted to go to their countrymen with assurances of pardon and protection to all who would return to their obedience.

These measures had their effect. By the joint efforts of Cortes and the caciques, the tumult was with much difficulty appeased. The assailants, Spaniards and Indians, gathered under their respective banners, and the Cholulans, relying on the assurance of their chiefs, gradually returned to their homes.

The first act of Cortes was, to prevail on the Tlascalan chiefs to liberate their captives. Such was their deference to the Spanish commander, that they acquiesced, though not without murmurs, contenting themselves, as they best could, with the rich spoil rifled from the Cholulans, consisting of various luxuries long since unknown in Tlascala. His next care was to cleanse the city from its loathsome impurities, particularly from the dead bodies which lay festering in heaps in the streets and great square. The general, in his letter to Charles the Fifth, admits three thousand slain; most accounts say six, and some swell the amount yet higher. As the eldest and principal cacique was among the number, Cortes assisted the Cholulans in installing a successor in his place. By these pacific measures, confidence was gradually restored. The people in the environs, reassured, flocked into the capital to supply the place of the diminished population. The markets were again opened; and the usual avocations of an orderly, industrious community were resumed. Still, the long piles of black and smouldering ruins proclaimed the hurricane which had so lately swept over the city, and the walls surrounding the scene of slaughter in the great square, which were standing more than fifty years after the event, told the sad tale of the Massacre of Cholula.

This passage in their history is one of those that have left a dark stain on the memory of the Conquerors. Nor can we contemplate at this day, without a shudder, the condition of this fair and flourishing capital thus invaded in its privacy, and delivered over to the excesses of a rude and ruthless soldiery. But, to judge the action fairly, we must transport ourselves to the age when it happened. The difficulty that meets us in the outset is, to find a justification of the right of conquest at all. But it should be remembered, that religious infidelity, at this period, and till a much later, was regarded — no matter whether founded on ignorance or education, whether hereditary or acquired, heretical or pagan — as a sin to be punished with fire and faggot in this world, and eternal suffering in the next. Under this code, the territory of the heathen, wherever found, was regarded as a sort of religious waif, which, in default of a legal proprietor, was claimed and taken possession of by the Holy See, and as such was freely given away, by the head of the church, to any temporal potentate whom he pleased, that would assume the burden of conquest. Thus, Alexander the Sixth generously granted a large portion of the Western Hemisphere to the Spaniards, and of the Eastern to the Portuguese. These lofty pretensions of the successors of the humble fisherman of Galilee, far from being nominal, were acknowledged and appealed to as conclusive in controversies between nations.

With the right of conquest, thus conferred, came also the obligation, on which it may be said to have been founded, to retrieve the nations sitting in darkness from eternal perdition. This obligation was acknowledged by the best and the bravest, the gownsman in his closet, the missionary, and the warrior in the crusade. However much it may have been debased by temporal motives and mixed up with worldly considerations of ambition and avarice, it was still active in the mind of the Christian conqueror. We have seen how far paramount it was to every calculation of personal interest in the breast of Cortes. The concession of the pope then, founded on and enforcing the imperative duty of conversion, was the assumed basis — and, in the apprehension of that age, a sound one — of the right of conquest.

The right could not, indeed, be construed to authorise any unnecessary act of violence to the natives. The present expedition, up to the period of its history at which we are now arrived, had probably been stained with fewer of such acts than almost any similar enterprise of the Spanish discoverers in the New World. Throughout the campaign, Cortes had prohibited all wanton injuries to the natives, in person or property, and had punished the perpetrators of them with exemplary severity. He had been faithful to his friends, and, with perhaps a single exception, not unmerciful to his foes. Whether from policy or principle, it should be recorded to his credit, though, like every sagacious mind, he may have felt that principle and policy go together.

He had entered Cholula as a friend, at the invitation of the Indian emperor, who had a real, if not avowed, control over the state. He had been received as a friend, with every demonstration of good will; when, without any offence of his own or his followers, he found they were to be the victims of an insidious plot — that they were standing on a mine which might be sprung at any moment, and bury them all in its ruins. His safety, as he truly considered, left no alternative but to anticipate the blow of his enemies. Yet who can doubt that the punishment thus inflicted was excessive — that the same end might have been attained by directing the blow against the guilty chiefs, instead of letting it fall on the ignorant rabble, who but obeyed the commands of their masters? But when was it ever seen, that fear, armed with power, was scrupulous in the exercise of it? or that the passions of a fierce soldiery, inflamed by conscious injuries, could be regulated in the moment of explosion?

But whatever be thought of this transaction in a moral view, as a stroke of policy it was unquestionable. The nations of Anahuac had beheld, with admiration mingled with awe, the little band of Christian warriors steadily advancing along the plateau in face of every obstacle, overturning army after army with as much ease, apparently, as the good ship throws off the angry billows from her bows; or rather like the lava, which rolling from their own volcanoes, holds on its course unchecked by obstacles, rock, tree, or building, bearing them along, or crushing and consuming them in its fiery path. The prowess of the Spaniards —"the white gods," as they were often called — made them to be thought invincible. But it was not till their arrival at Cholula that the natives learned how terrible was their vengeance — and they trembled!

None trembled more than the Aztec emperor on his throne among the mountains. He read in these events the dark character traced by the finger of Destiny. He felt his empire melting away like a morning mist. He might well feel so. Some of the most important cities in the neighbourhood of Cholula, intimidated by the fate of that capital, now sent their envoys to the Castilian camp, tendering their allegiance, and propitiating the favour of the strangers by rich presents of gold and slaves. Montezuma, alarmed at these signs of defection, took counsel again of his impotent deities; but, although the altars smoked with fresh hecatombs of human victims, he obtained no cheering response. He determined, therefore, to send another embassy to the Spaniards, disavowing any participation in the conspiracy of Cholula.

Meanwhile Cortes was passing his time in that capital. He thought that the impression produced by the late scenes, and by the present restoration of tranquillity, offered a fair opportunity for the good work of conversion. He accordingly urged the citizens to embrace the Cross, and abandon the false guardians who had abandoned them in their extremity. But the traditions of centuries rested on the Holy City, shedding a halo of glory around it as "the sanctuary of the gods," the religious capital of Anahuac. It was too much to expect that the people would willingly resign this preeminence, and descend to the level of an ordinary community. Still Cortes might have pressed the matter, however unpalatable, but for the renewed interposition of the wise Olmedo, who persuaded him to postpone it till after the reduction of the whole country.

During the occurrence of these events, envoys arrived from Mexico. They were charged, as usual, with a rich present of plate and ornaments of gold; among others, artificial birds in imitation of turkeys, with plumes of the same precious metal. To these were added fifteen hundred cotton dresses of delicate fabric. The emperor even expressed his regret at the catastrophe of Cholula, vindicated himself from any share in the conspiracy, which, he said, had brought deserved retribution on the heads of its authors, and explained the existence of an Aztec force in the neighbourhood, by the necessity of repressing some disorders there.

One cannot contemplate this pusillanimous conduct of Montezuma without mingled feelings of pity and contempt. It is not easy to reconcile his assumed innocence of the plot with many circumstances connected with it. But it must be remembered here and always, that his history is to be collected solely from Spanish writers, and such of the natives as flourished after the Conquest, when the country had become a colony of Spain. It is the hard fate of this unfortunate monarch, to be wholly indebted for his portraiture to the pencil of his enemies.

More than a fortnight had elapsed since the entrance of the Spaniards into Cholula, and Cortes now resolved, without loss of time, to resume his march towards the capital. His rigorous reprisals had so far intimidated the Cholulans, that he felt assured he should no longer leave an active enemy in his rear, to annoy him in case of retreat. He had the satisfaction, before his departure, to heal the feud — in outward appearance, at least — that had so long subsisted between the Holy City and Tlascala, and which, under the revolution which so soon changed the destinies of the country, never revived.

It was with some disquietude that he now received an application from his Cempoallan allies to be allowed to withdraw from the expedition, and return to their own homes. They had incurred too deeply the — resentment of the Aztec emperor, by their insults to his collectors, and by their co-operation with the Spaniards, to care to trust themselves in his capital. It was in vain Cortes endeavoured to re-assure them by promises of his protection. Their habitual distrust and dread of "the great Montezuma" were not to be overcome. The general learned their determination with regret, for they had been of infinite service to the cause by their staunch fidelity and courage. All this made it the more difficult for him to resist their reasonable demand. Liberally recompensing their services, therefore, from the rich wardrobe and treasures of the emperor, he took leave of his faithful followers, before his own departure from Cholula. He availed himself of their return to send letters to Juan de Escalante, his lieutenant at Vera Cruz, acquainting him with the successful progress of the expedition. He enjoined on that officer to strengthen the fortifications of the place, so as the better to resist any hostile interference from Cuba — an event for which Cortes was ever on the watch — and to keep down revolt among the natives. He especially commended the Totonacs to his protection, as allies whose fidelity to the Spaniards exposed them, in no slight degree, to the vengeance of the Aztecs.

EVERYTHING being now restored to quiet in Cholula, the allied army of Spaniards and Tlascalans set forward in high spirits, and resumed the march on Mexico. The road lay through the beautiful savannas and luxuriant plantations that spread out for several leagues in every direction. On the march they were met occasionally by embassies from the neighbouring places, anxious to claim the protection of the white men, and to propitiate them by gifts, especially of gold, for which their appetite was generally known throughout the country.

Some of these places were allies of the Tlascalans, and all showed much discontent with the oppressive rule of Montezuma. The natives cautioned the Spaniards against putting themselves in his power by entering his capital; and they stated, as evidence of his hostile disposition, that he had caused the direct road to it to be blocked up, that the strangers might be compelled to choose another, which, from its narrow passes and strong positions, would enable him to take them at great disadvantage.

The information was not lost on Cortes, who kept a strict eye on the movements of the Mexican envoys, and redoubled his own precautions against surprise. Cheerful and active, he was ever where his presence was needed, sometimes in the van, at others in the rear, encouraging the weak, stimulating the sluggish, and striving to kindle in the breasts of others the same courageous spirit which glowed in his own. At night he never omitted to go the rounds, to see that every man was at his post. On one occasion his vigilance had well nigh proved fatal to him. He approached so near a sentinel that the man, unable to distinguish his person in the dark, levelled his crossbow at him, when, fortunately, an exclamation of the general, who gave the watchword of the night, arrested a movement which might else have brought the campaign to a close, and given a respite for some time longer to the empire of Montezuma.

The army came at length to the place mentioned by the friendly Indians, where the road forked, and one arm of it was found, as they had foretold, obstructed with large trunks of trees and huge stones which had been strewn across it. Cortes inquired the meaning of this from the Mexican ambassadors. They said it was done by the emperor's orders, to prevent their taking a route which, after some distance, they would find nearly impracticable for the cavalry. They acknowledged, however, that it was the most direct road; and Cortes, declaring that this was enough to decide him in favour of it, as the Spaniards made no account of obstacles, commanded the rubbish to be cleared away. The event left little doubt in the general's mind of the meditated treachery of the Mexicans. But he was too politic to betray his suspicions.

They were now leaving the pleasant champaign country, as the road wound up the bold sierra which separates the great plateaus of Mexico and Puebla. The air, as they ascended, became keen and piercing; and the blasts, sweeping down the frozen sides of the mountains, made the soldiers shiver in their thick harness of cotton, and benumbed the limbs of both men and horses.

They were passing between two of the highest mountains on the North American continent, Popocatepetl, "the hill that smokes," and Iztaccihuatl, or "white woman,"— a name suggested, doubtless, by the bright robe of snow spread over its broad and broken surface. A puerile superstition of the Indians regarded these celebrated mountains as gods, and Iztaccihuatl as the wife of her more formidable neighbour. A tradition of a higher character described the northern volcano as the abode of the departed spirits of wicked rulers, whose fiery agonies in their prison-house caused the fearful bellowings and convulsions in times of eruption.

The army held on its march through the intricate gorges of the sierra. The route was nearly the same as that pursued at the present day by the courier from the capital to Puebla, by the way of Mecameca. It was not that usually taken by travellers from Vera Cruz, who follow the more circuitous road round the northern base of Iztaccihuatl, as less fatiguing than the other, though inferior in picturesque scenery and romantic points of view. The icy winds, that now swept down the sides of the mountains, brought with them a tempest of arrowy sleet and snow, from which the Christians suffered even more than the Tlascalans, reared from infancy among the wild solitudes of their own native hills. As night came on, their sufferings would have been intolerable, but they luckily found a shelter in the commodious stone buildings which the Mexican government had placed at stated intervals along the roads for the accommodation of the traveller and their own couriers.

The troops, refreshed by a night's rest, succeeded, early on the following day, in gaining the crest of the sierra of Ahualco, which stretches like a curtain between the two great mountains on the north and south. Their progress was now comparatively easy, and they marched forward with a buoyant step, as they felt they were treading the soil of Montezuma.

They had not advanced far, when, turning an angle of the sierra, they suddenly came on a view which more than compensated the toils of the preceding day. It was that of the Valley of Mexico, or Tenochtitlan, as more commonly called by the natives; which, with its picturesque assemblage of water, woodland, and cultivated plains, its shining cities and shadowy hills, was spread out like some gay and gorgeous panorama before them. In the highly rarefied atmosphere of these upper regions, even remote objects have a brilliancy of colouring and distinctness of outline which seem to annihilate distance. Stretching far away at their feet were seen noble forests of oak, sycamore, and cedar, and beyond, yellow fields of maize and the towering maguey, intermingled with orchards and blooming gardens; for flowers, in such demand for their religious festivals, were even more abundant in this populous valley than in other parts of Anahuac. In the centre of the great basin were beheld the lakes, occupying then a much larger portion of its surface than at present; their borders thickly studded with towns and hamlets, and, in the midst — like some Indian empress with her coronal of pearls — the fair city of Mexico, with her white towers and pyramidal temples, reposing, as it were, on the bosom of the waters — the far-famed "Venice of the Aztecs." High over all rose the royal hill of Chapoltepec, the residence of the Mexican monarchs, crowned with the same grove of gigantic cypresses which at this day fling their broad shadows over the land. In the distance beyond the blue waters of the lake, and nearly screened by intervening foliage, was seen a shining speck, the rival capital of Tezcuco, and, still further on, the dark belt of porphyry, girding the Valley around, like a rich setting which Nature had devised for the fairest of her jewels.

Such was the beautiful vision which broke on the eyes of the Conquerors. And even now, when so sad a change has come over the scene; when the stately forests have been laid low, and the soil, unsheltered from the fierce radiance of a tropical sun, is in many places abandoned to sterility; when the waters have retired, leaving a broad and ghastly margin white with the incrustation of salts, while the cities and hamlets on their borders have mouldered into ruins; — even now that desolation broods over the landscape, so indestructible are the lines of beauty which Nature has traced on its features, that no traveller, however cold, can gaze on them with any other emotions than those of astonishment and rapture.

What, then, must have been the emotions of the Spaniards, when, after working their toilsome way into the upper air, the cloudy tabernacle parted before their eyes, and they beheld these fair scenes in all their pristine magnificence and beauty! It was like the spectacle which greeted the eyes of Moses from the summit of Pisgah, and, in the warm glow of their feelings, they cried out, "It is the promised land!"

But these feelings of admiration were soon followed by others of a very different complexion; as they saw in all this the evidences of a civilisation and power far superior to anything they had yet encountered. The more timid, disheartened by the prospect, shrunk from a contest so unequal, and demanded, as they had done on some former occasions, to be led back again to Vera Cruz. Such was not the effect produced on the sanguine spirit of the general. His avarice was sharpened by the display of the dazzling spoil at his feet; and, if he felt a natural anxiety at the formidable odds, his confidence was renewed, as he gazed on the lines of his veterans, whose weather-beaten visages and battered armour told of battles won and difficulties surmounted, while his bold barbarians, with appetites whetted by the view of their enemy's country, seemed like eagles on the mountains, ready to pounce upon their prey. By argument, entreaty, and menace, he endeavoured to restore the faltering courage of the soldiers, urging them not to think of retreat, now that they had reached the goal for which they had panted, and the golden gates were open to receive them. In these efforts he was well seconded by the brave cavaliers, who held honour as dear to them as fortune; until the dullest spirits caught somewhat of the enthusiasm of their leaders, and the general had the satisfaction to see his hesitating columns, with their usual buoyant step, once more on their march down the slopes of the sierra.

With every step of their progress, the woods became thinner; patches of cultivated land more frequent; and hamlets were seen in the green and sheltered nooks, the inhabitants of which, coming out to meet them, gave the troops a kind reception. Everywhere they heard complaints of Montezuma, especially of the unfeeling manner in which he carried off their young men to recruit his armies, and their maidens for his harem. These symptoms of discontent were noticed with satisfaction by Cortes, who saw that Montezuma's "Mountain throne," as it was called, was indeed seated on a volcano, with the elements of combustion so active within, that it seemed as if any hour might witness an explosion. He encouraged the disaffected natives to rely on his protection, as he had come to redress their wrongs. He took advantage, moreover, of their favourable dispositions to scatter among them such gleams of spiritual light as time and the preaching of Father Olmedo could afford.

He advanced by easy stages, somewhat retarded by the crowd of curious inhabitants gathered on the highways to see the strangers, and halting at every spot of interest or importance. On the road he was met by another embassy from the capital. It consisted of several Aztec lords, freighted, as usual, with a rich largess of gold, and robes of delicate furs and feathers. The message of the emperor was couched in the same deprecatory terms as before. He even condescended to bribe the return of the Spaniards, by promising, in that event, four loads of gold to the general, and one to each of the captains, with a yearly tribute to their sovereign. So effectually had the lofty and naturally courageous spirit of the barbarian monarch been subdued by the influence of superstition!

But the man whom the hostile array of armies could not daunt, was not to be turned from his purpose by a woman's prayers. He received the embassy with his usual courtesy, declaring, as before, that he could not answer it to his own sovereign, if he were now to return without visiting the emperor in his capital. It would be much easier to arrange matters by a personal interview than by distant. negotiation. The Spaniards came in the spirit of peace. Montezuma would so find it, but, should their presence prove burdensome to him, it would be easy for them to relieve him of it.

The Aztec monarch, meanwhile, was a prey to the most dismal apprehensions. It was intended that the embassy above noticed should reach the Spaniards before they crossed the mountains. When he learned that this was accomplished, and that the dread strangers were on their march across the valley, the very threshold of his capital, the last spark of hope died away in his bosom. Like one who suddenly finds himself on the brink of some dark and yawning gulf, he was too much bewildered to be able to rally his thoughts, or even to comprehend his situation. He was the victim of an absolute destiny, against which no foresight or precautions could have availed. It was as if the strange beings, who had thus invaded his shores, had dropped from some distant planet, so different were they from all he had ever seen, in appearance and manners; so superior — though a mere handful in numbers — to the banded nations of Anahuac in strength and science, and all the fearful accompaniments of war! They were now in the valley. The huge mountain-screen, which nature had so kindly drawn around it for its defence, had been overleaped. The golden visions of security and repose, in which he had so long indulged, the lordly sway descended from his ancestors, his broad imperial domain, were all to pass away. It seemed like some terrible dream — from which he was now, alas! to awake to a still more terrible reality.

In a paroxysm of despair he shut himself up in his palace, refused food, and sought relief in prayer and in sacrifice. But the oracles were dumb. He then adopted the more sensible expedient of calling a council of his principal and oldest nobles. Here was the same division of opinion which had before prevailed. Cacama, the young king of Tezcuco, his nephew, counselled him to receive the Spaniards courteously, as ambassadors, so styled by themselves, of a foreign prince. Cuitlahua, Montezuma's more warlike brother, urged him to muster his forces on the instant, and drive back the invaders from his capital, or die in its defence. But the monarch found it difficult to rally his spirits for this final struggle. With downcast eye and dejected mien he exclaimed, "Of what avail is resistance when the gods have declared themselves against us! Yet I mourn most for the old and infirm, the women and children, too feeble to fight or to fly. For myself and the brave men around me, we must bare our breasts to the storm, and meet it as we may!" Such are the sorrowful and sympathetic tones in which the Aztec emperor is said to have uttered the bitterness of his grief. He would have acted a more glorious part had he put his capital in a posture of defence, and prepared, like the last of the Palaeologi, to bury himself under its ruins.

He straightway prepared to send a last embassy to the Spaniards, with his nephew, the lord of Tezcuco, at its head, to welcome them to Mexico.

The Christian army, meanwhile, had advanced as far as Amaquemecan, a well-built town of several thousand inhabitants. They were kindly received by the cacique, lodged in large commodious stone buildings, and at their departure presented, among other things, with gold to the amount of three thousand castellanos. Having halted there a couple of days, they descended among flourishing plantations of maize and of maguey, the latter of which might be called the Aztec vineyards, towards the lake of Chalco. Their first resting-place was Ajotzinco, a town of considerable size, with a great part of it then standing on piles in the water. It was the first specimen which the Spaniards had seen of this maritime architecture. The canals, which intersected the city instead of streets, presented an animated scene from the number of barks which glided up and down, freighted with provisions and other articles for the inhabitants. The Spaniards were particularly struck with the style and commodious structure of the houses, built chiefly of stone, and with the general aspect of wealth, and even elegance which prevailed there.

Though received with the greatest show of hospitality, Cortes found some occasion for distrust in the eagerness manifested by the people to see and approach the Spaniards. Not content with gazing at them in the roads, some even made their way stealthily into their quarters, and fifteen or twenty unhappy Indians were shot down by the sentinels as spies. Yet there appears, as well as we can judge at this distance of time, to have been no real ground for such suspicion. The undisguised jealousy of the court, and the cautions he had received from his allies, while they very properly put the general on his guard, seem to have given an unnatural acuteness, at least in the present instance, to his perceptions of danger.

Early on the following morning, as the army was preparing to leave the place, a courier came, requesting the general to postpone his departure till after the arrival of the king of Tezcuco, who was advancing to meet him. It was not long before he appeared, borne in a palanquin or litter, richly decorated with plates of gold and precious stones, having pillars curiously wrought, supporting a canopy of green plumes, a favourite colour with the Aztec princes. He was accompanied by a numerous suite of nobles and inferior attendants. As he came into the presence of Cortes, the lord of Tezcuco descended from his palanquin, and the obsequious officers swept the ground before him as he advanced. He appeared to be a young man of about twenty-five years of age, with a comely presence, erect and stately in his deportment. He made the Mexican salutation usually addressed to persons of high rank, touching the earth with his right hand, and raising it to his head. Cortes embraced him as he rose, when the young prince informed him that he came as the representative of Montezuma, to bid the Spaniards welcome to his capital. He then presented the general with three pearls of uncommon size and lustre. Cortes, in return, threw over Cacama's neck a chain of cut glass, which, where glass was a rare as diamonds, might be admitted to have a value as real as the latter. After this interchange of courtesies, and the most friendly and respectful assurances on the part of Cortes, the Indian prince withdrew, leaving the Spaniards strongly impressed with the superiority of his state and bearing over anything they had hitherto seen in the country.

Resuming its march, the army kept along the southern borders of the lake of Chalco, overshadowed at that time by noble woods, and by orchards glowing with autumnal fruits, of unknown names, but rich and tempting hues. More frequently it passed through cultivated fields waving with the yellow harvest, and irrigated by canals introduced from the neighbouring lake; the whole showing a careful and economical husbandry, essential to the maintenance of a crowded population.

Leaving the main land, the Spaniards came on the great dike or causeway, which stretches some four or five miles in length, and divides lake Chalco from Xochimilco on the west. It was a lance in breadth in the narrowest part, and in some places wide enough for eight horsemen to ride abreast. It was a solid structure of stone and lime, running directly through the lake, and struck the Spaniards as one of the most remarkable works which they had seen in the country.

As they passed along, they beheld the gay spectacle of multitudes of Indians darting up and down in their light pirogues, eager to catch a glimpse of the strangers, or bearing the products of the country to the neighbouring cities. They were amazed, also, by the sight of the chinampas, or floating gardens — those wandering islands of verdure, to which we shall have occasion to return hereafter — teeming with flowers and vegetables, and moving like rafts over the waters. All round the margin, and occasionally far in the lake, they beheld little towns and villages, which, half concealed by the foliage, and gathered in white clusters round the shore, looked in the distance like companies of wild swans riding quietly on the waves. A scene so new and wonderful filled their rude hearts with amazement. It seemed like enchantment; and they could find nothing to compare it with, but the magical pictures in the Amadis de Gaula. Few pictures, indeed, in that or any other legend of chivalry, could surpass the realities of their own experience. The life of the adventurer in the New World was romance put into action. What wonder, then, if the Spaniard of that day, feeding his imagination with dreams of enchantment at home, and with its realities abroad, should have displayed a Quixotic enthusiasm — a romantic exaltation of character, not to be comprehended by the colder spirits of other lands!

Midway across the lake the army halted at the town of Cuitlahuac, a place of moderate size, but distinguished by the beauty of the buildings — the most beautiful, according to Cortes, that he had yet seen in the country. After taking some refreshment at this place, they continued their march along the dike. Though broader in this northern section, the troops found themselves much embarrassed by the throng of Indians, who, not content with gazing on them from the boats, climbed up the causeway, and lined the sides of the roads. The general, afraid that his ranks might be disordered, and that too great familiarity might diminish a salutary awe in the natives, was obliged to resort not merely to command but menace, to clear a passage. He now found, as he advanced, a considerable change in the feelings shown towards the government. He heard only of the pomp and magnificence, nothing of the oppressions of Montezuma. Contrary to the usual fact, it seemed that the respect for the court was greatest in its immediate neighbourhood.

From the causeway, the army descended on that narrow point of land which divides the waters of the Chalco from the Tezcucan lake, but which in those days was overflowed for many a mile, now laid bare. Traversing this peninsula, they entered the royal residence of Iztapalapan, a place containing twelve or fifteen thousand houses, according to Cortes. It was governed by Cuitlahua, the emperor's brother, who, to do greater honour to the general, had invited the lords of some neighbouring cities, of the royal house of Mexico, like himself, to be present at the interview. This was conducted with much ceremony, and, after the usual presents of gold and delicate stuffs, a collation was served to the Spaniards in one of the great halls of the palace. The excellence of the architecture here, also, excited the admiration of the general, who does not hesitate, in the glow of his enthusiasm, to pronounce some of the buildings equal to the best in Spain. They were of stone, and the spacious apartments had roofs of odorous cedar-wood, while the walls were tapestried with fine cottons stained with brilliant colours.

But the pride of Iztapalapan, on which its lord had freely lavished his care and his revenues, was its celebrated gardens. They covered an immense tract of land; were laid out in regular squares, and the paths intersecting them were bordered with trellises, supporting creepers and aromatic shrubs, that loaded the air with their perfumes. The gardens were stocked with fruit-trees, imported from distant places, and with the gaudy family of flowers which belong to the Mexican Flora, scientifically arranged, and growing luxuriant in the equable temperature of the tableland. The natural dryness of the atmosphere was counteracted by means of aqueducts and canals, that carried water into all parts of the grounds.

In one quarter was an aviary, filled with numerous kinds of birds, remarkable in this region both for brilliancy of plumage and of song. The gardens were intersected by a canal communicating with the lake of Tezcuco, and of sufficient size for barges to enter from the latter. But the most elaborate piece of work was a huge reservoir of stone, filled to a considerable height with water, well supplied with different sorts of fish. This basin was sixteen hundred paces in circumference, and was surrounded by a walk, made also of stone, wide enough for four persons to go abreast. The sides were curiously sculptured, and a flight of steps led to the water below, which fed the aqueducts above noticed, or, collected into fountains, diffused a perpetual moisture.

Such are the accounts transmitted of these celebrated gardens, at a period when similar horticultural establishments were unknown in Europe; and we might well doubt their existence in this semi-civilised land, were it not a matter of such notoriety at the time, and so explicitly attested by the invaders. But a generation had scarcely passed after the Conquest before a sad change came over these scenes so beautiful. The town itself was deserted, and the shore of the lake was strewed with the wreck of buildings which once were its ornament and its glory. The gardens shared the fate of the city. The retreating waters withdrew the means of nourishment, converting the flourishing plains into a foul and unsightly morass, the haunt of loathsome reptiles; and the water-fowl built her nest in what had once been the palaces of princes!

In the city of Iztapalapan, Cortes took up his quarters for the night. We may imagine what a crowd of ideas must have pressed on the mind of the Conqueror, as, surrounded by these evidences of civilisation, he prepared, with his handful of followers, to enter the capital of a monarch, who, as he had abundant reason to know, regarded him with distrust and aversion. This capital was now but a few miles distant, distinctly visible from Iztapalapan. And as its long lines of glittering edifices, struck by the rays of the evening sun, trembled on the dark blue waters of the lake, it looked like a thing of fairy creation, rather than the work of mortal hands. Into this city of enchantment Cortes prepared to make his entry on the following morning.

WITH the first faint streak of dawn, the Spanish general was up, mustering his followers. They gathered, with beating hearts, under their respective banners as the trumpet sent forth its spirit-stirring sounds across water and woodland, till they died away in distant echoes among the mountains. The sacred flames on the altars of numberless teocallis, dimly seen through the grey mists of morning, indicated the site of the capital, till temple, tower, and palace were fully revealed in the glorious illumination which the sun, as he rose above the eastern barrier, poured over the beautiful valley. It was the 8th of November; a conspicuous day in history, as that on which the Europeans first set foot in the capital of the Western World.

Cortes, with his little body of horse formed a sort of advanced guard to the army. Then came the Spanish infantry, who in a summer campaign had acquired the discipline and the weather-beaten aspect of veterans. The baggage occupied the centre; and the rear was closed by the dark files of Tlascalan warriors. The whole number must have fallen short of seven thousand; of which less than four hundred were Spaniards.

For a short distance, the army kept along the narrow tongue of land that divides the Tezcucan from the Chalcan waters, when it entered the great dike which, with the exception of an angle near the commencement, stretches in a perfectly straight line across the salt floods of Tezcuco to the gates of the capital. It was the same causeway, or rather the basis of that which still forms the great southern avenue of Mexico. The Spaniards had occasion more than ever to admire the mechanical science of the Aztecs, in the geometrical precision with which the work was executed, as well as the solidity of its construction. It was composed of huge stones well laid in cement; and wide enough, throughout its whole extent, for ten horsemen to ride abreast.

They saw, as they passed along, several large towns, resting on piles, and reaching far into the water — a kind of architecture which found great favour with the Aztecs, being in imitation of that of their metropolis. The busy population obtained a good subsistence from the manufacture of salt, which they extracted from the waters of the great lake. The duties on the traffic were a considerable source of revenue to the crown.

Everywhere the Conquerors beheld the evidence of a. crowded and thriving population, exceeding all they had yet seen. The temples and principal buildings of the cities were covered with a hard white stucco, which glistened like enamel in the level beams of the morning. The margin of the great basin was more thickly gemmed, than that of Chalco, with towns and hamlets. The water was darkened by swarms of canoes filled with Indians, who clambered up the sides of the causeway, and gazed with curious astonishment on the strangers. And here, also, they beheld those fairy islands of flowers, overshadowed occasionally by trees of considerable size, rising and falling with the gentle undulation of the billows. At the distance of half a league from the capital, they encountered a solid work, or curtain of stone, which traversed the dike. It was twelve feet high, was strengthened by towers at the extremities, and in the centre was a battlemented gateway, which opened a passage to the troops. It was called the Fort of Xoloc, and became memorable in after times as the position occupied by Cortes in the famous siege of Mexico.

Here they were met by several hundred Aztec chiefs, who came out to announce the approach of Montezuma, and to welcome the Spaniards to his capital. They were dressed in the fanciful gala costume of the country, with the Maxtlatl, or cotton sash, around their loins, and a broad mantle of the same material, or of the brilliant feather-embroidery, flowing gracefully down their shoulders. On their necks and arms they displayed collars and bracelets of turquoise mosaic, with which delicate plumage was curiously mingled, while their ears, under-lips, and occasionally their noses, were garnished with pendants formed of precious stones, or crescents of fine gold As each cacique made the usual formal salutation of the country separately to the general, the tedious ceremony delayed the march more than an hour. After this, the army experienced no further interruption till it reached a bridge near the gates of the city. It was built of wood, since replaced by one of stone, and was thrown across an opening of the dike, which furnished an outlet to the waters, when agitated by the winds, or swollen by a sudden influx in the rainy season. It was a drawbridge; and the Spaniards, as they crossed it, felt how truly they were committing themselves to the mercy of Montezuma, who, by thus cutting off their communications with the country, might hold them prisoners in his capital.

In the midst of these unpleasant reflections, they beheld the glittering retinue of the emperor emerging from the great street which led through the heart of the city. Amidst a crowd of Indian nobles, preceded by three officers of state, bearing golden wands, they saw the royal palanquin blazing with burnished gold. It was borne on the shoulders of nobles, and over it a canopy of gaudy feather-work, powdered with jewels, and fringed with silver, was supported by four attendants of the same rank. They were bare-footed, and walked with a slow, measured pace, and with eyes bent on the ground. When the train had come within a convenient distance, it halted, and Montezuma, descending from his litter, came forward leaning on the arms of the lords of Tezcuco and Iztapalapan, his nephew and brother, both of whom, as we have seen, had already been made known to the Spaniards. As the monarch advanced under the canopy, the obsequious attendants strewed the ground with cotton tapestry, that his imperial feet might not be contaminated by the rude soil. His subjects of high and low degree, who lined the sides of the causeway, bent forward with their eyes fastened on the ground as he passed, and some of the humbler class prostrated themselves before him. Such was the homage paid to the Indian despot, showing that the slavish forms of oriental adulation were to be found among the rude inhabitants of the Western World.

Montezuma wore the girdle and ample square cloak, tilmatli, of his nation. It was made of the finest cotton, with the embroidered ends gathered in a knot round his neck. His feet were defended by sandals having soles of gold, and the leathern thongs which bound them to his ankles were embossed with the same metal. Both the cloak and sandals were sprinkled with pearls and precious stones, among which the emerald and the chalchiuitl — a green stone of higher estimation than any other among the Aztecs — were conspicuous. On his head he wore no other ornament than a panache of plumes of the royal green, which floated down his back, the badge of military rather than of regal rank.

He was at this time about forty years of age. His person was tall and thin, but not ill made. His hair, which was black and straight, was not very long; to wear it short was considered unbecoming persons of rank. His beard was thin; his complexion somewhat paler than is often found in his dusky, or rather copper-coloured race. His features, though serious in their expression, did not wear the look of melancholy, indeed, of dejection, which characterises his portrait, and which may well have settled on them at a later period. He moved with dignity, and his whole demeanour, tempered by an expression of benignity not to have been anticipated from the reports circulated of his character, was worthy of a great prince. Such is the portrait left to us of the celebrated Indian emperor, in this first interview with the white men.

The army halted as he drew near. Cortes, dismounting, threw his reins to a page, and, supported by a few of the principal cavaliers, advanced to meet him. The interview must have been one of uncommon interest to both. In Montezuma Cortes beheld the lord of the broad realms he had traversed, whose magnificence and power had been the burden of every tongue. In the Spaniard, on the other hand, the Aztec prince saw the strange being whose history seemed to be so mysteriously connected with his own; the predicted one of his oracles; whose achievements proclaimed him something more than human. But, whatever may have been the monarch's feelings, he so far suppressed them as to receive his guest with princely courtesy, and to express his satisfaction at personally seeing him in his capital. Cortes responded by the most profound expressions of respect, while he made ample acknowledgments for the substantial proofs which the emperor had given the Spaniards of his munificence. He then hung round Montezuma's neck a sparkling chain of coloured crystal, accompanying this with a movement as if to embrace him, when he was restrained by the two Aztec lords, shocked at the menaced profanation of the sacred person of their master. After the interchange of these civilities, Montezuma appointed his brother to conduct the Spaniards to their residence in the capital, and again entering his litter, was borne off amidst prostrate crowds in the same state in which he had come. The Spaniards quickly followed, and with colours flying and music playing, soon made their entrance into the southern quarter of Tenochtitlan.

Here, again, they found fresh cause for admiration in the grandeur of the city, and the superior style of its architecture. The dwellings of the poorer class were, indeed, chiefly of reeds and mud. But the great avenue through which they were now marching was lined with the houses of the nobles, who were encouraged by the emperor to make the capital their residence. They were built of a red porous stone drawn from quarries in the neighbourhood, and, though they rarely rose to a second story, often covered a large space of ground. The flat roofs, azoteas, were protected by stone parapets, so that every house was a fortress. Sometimes these roofs resembled parterres of flowers, so thickly were they covered with them, but more frequently these were cultivated in broad terraced gardens, laid out between the edifices. Occasionally a great square or market-place intervened, surrounded by its porticoes of stone and stucco; or a pyramidal temple reared its colossal bulk, crowned with its tapering sanctuaries, and altars blazing with inextinguishable fires. The great street facing the southern causeway, unlike most others in the place, was wide, and extended some miles in nearly a straight line, as before noticed, through the centre of the city. A spectator standing at one end of it, as his eye ranged along the deep vista of temples, terraces, and gardens, might clearly discern the other, with the blue mountains in the distance, which, in the transparent atmosphere of the tableland, seemed almost in contact with the buildings.

But what most impressed the Spaniards was the throngs of people who swarmed through the streets and on the canals, filling every doorway and window, and clustering on the roofs of the buildings. "I well remember the spectacle," exclaims Bernal Diaz; "it seems now, after so many years, as present to my mind as if it were but yesterday." But what must have been the sensations of the Aztecs themselves, as they looked on the portentous pageant! as they heard, now for the first time, the well-cemented pavement ring under the iron tramp of the horses — the strange animals which fear had clothed in such supernatural terrors; as they gazed on the children of the East, revealing their celestial origin in their fair complexions; saw the bright falchions and bonnets of steel, a metal to them unknown, glancing like meteors in the sun, while sounds of unearthly music — at least, such as their rude instruments had never wakened — floated in the air! But every other emotion was lost in that of deadly hatred, when they beheld their detested enemy, the Tlascalan, stalking in defiance as it were through their streets, and staring around with looks of ferocity and wonder, like some wild animal of the forest, who had strayed by chance from his native fastnesses into the haunts of civilisation.

As they passed down the spacious street, the troops repeatedly traversed bridges suspended above canals, along which they saw the Indian barks gliding swiftly with their little cargoes of fruits and vegetables for the markets of Tenochtitlan. At length, they halted before a broad area near the centre of the city, where rose the huge pyramidal pile dedicated to the patron war-god of the Aztecs, second only in size, as well as sanctity, to the temple of Cholula, and covering the same ground now in part occupied by the great cathedral of Mexico.

Facing the western gate of the inclosure of the temple stood a low range of stone buildings, spreading over a wide extent of ground, the palace of Axayacatl, Montezuma's father, built by that monarch about fifty years before. It was appropriated as the barracks of the Spaniards. The emperor himself was in the courtyard, waiting to receive them. Approaching Cortes, he took from a vase of flowers, borne by one of his slaves, a massy collar, in which the shell of a species of craw-fish, much prized by the Indians, was set in gold, and connected by heavy links of the same metal. From this chain depended eight ornaments, also of gold, made in resemblance of the same shellfish, a span in length each, and of delicate workmanship; for the Aztec goldsmiths were confessed to have shown skill in their craft, not inferior to their brethren of Europe. Montezuma, as he hung the gorgeous collar round the general's neck, said, "This palace belongs to you, Malinche" (the epithet by which he always addressed him), "and your brethren. Rest after your fatigues, for you have much need to do so, and in a little while I will visit you again." So saying, he withdrew with his attendants, evincing, in this act, a delicate consideration not to have been expected in a barbarian.

Cortes' first care was to inspect his new quarters. The building, though spacious, was low, consisting of one floor, except indeed in the centre, where it rose to an additional story. The apartments were of great size, and afforded accommodations, according to the testimony of the Conquerors themselves, for the whole army! The hardy mountaineers of Tlascala were, probably, not very fastidious, and might easily find a shelter in the out-buildings, or under temporary awnings in the ample courtyards. The best apartments were hung with gay cotton draperies, the floors covered with mats or rushes. There were, also, low stools made of single pieces of wood elaborately carved, and in most of the apartments beds made of the palm-leaf, woven into a thick mat, with coverlets, and sometimes canopies of cotton. These mats were the only beds used by the natives, whether of high or low degree.

After a rapid survey of this gigantic pile, the general assigned to his troops their respective quarters, and took as vigilant precautions for security, as if he had anticipated a siege, instead of a friendly entertainment. The place was encompassed by a stone wall of considerable thickness, with towers or heavy buttresses at intervals, affording a good means of defence. He planted his cannon so as to command the approaches, stationed his sentinels along the works, and, in short, enforced in every respect as strict military discipline as had been observed in any part of the march. He well knew the importance to his little band, at least for the present, of conciliating the good will of the citizens; and to avoid all possibility of collision he prohibited any soldier from leaving his quarters without orders, under pain of death. Having taken these precautions, he allowed his men to partake of the bountiful collation which had been prepared for them.

They had been long enough in the country to become reconciled to, if not to relish, the peculiar cooking of the Aztecs. The appetite of the soldier is not often dainty, and on the present occasion it cannot be doubted that the Spaniards did full justice to the savoury productions of the royal kitchen. During the meal they were served by numerous Mexican slaves, who were indeed, distributed through the palace, anxious to do the bidding of the strangers. After the repast was concluded, and they had taken their siesta, not less important to a Spaniard than food itself, the presence of the emperor was again announced.

Montezuma was attended by a few of his principal nobles. He was received with much deference by Cortes; and, after the parties had taken their seats, a conversation commenced between them through the aid of Dona Marina, while the cavaliers and Aztec chieftains stood around in respectful silence.

Montezuma made many inquiries concerning the country of the Spaniards, their sovereign, the nature of his government, and especially their own motives in visiting Anahuac. Cortes explained these motives by the desire to see so distinguished a monarch, and to declare to him the true Faith professed by the Christians. With rare discretion, he contented himself with dropping this hint for the present, allowing it to ripen in the mind of the emperor till a future conference. The latter asked, whether those white men, who in the preceding year had landed on the eastern shores of his empire, were their countrymen. He showed himself well-informed of the proceedings of the Spaniards from their arrival in Tabasco to the present time, information of which had been regularly transmitted in the hieroglyphical paintings. He was curious, also, in regard to the rank of his visitors in their own country; inquiring, if they were the kinsmen of the sovereign. Cortes replied, they were kinsmen of one another, and subjects of their great monarch, who held them all in peculiar estimation. Before his departure, Montezuma made himself acquainted with the names of the principal cavaliers, and the position they occupied. in the army.

At the conclusion of the interview, the Aztec prince commanded his attendants to bring forward the presents prepared for his guests. They consisted of cotton dresses, enough to supply every man, it is said, including the allies, with a suit! And he did not fail to add the usual accompaniment of gold chains and other ornaments, which he distributed in profusion among the Spaniards. He then withdrew with the same ceremony with which he had entered, leaving every one deeply impressed with his munificence and his affability, so unlike what they had been taught to expect by what they now considered an invention of the enemy.

That evening, the Spaniards celebrated their arrival in the Mexican capital by a general discharge of artillery. The thunders of the ordnance reverberating among the buildings and shaking them to their foundations, the stench of the sulphureous vapour that rolled in volumes above the walls of the encampment, reminding the inhabitants of the explosions of the great volcan, filled the hearts of the superstitious Aztecs with dismay. It proclaimed to them, that their city held in its bosom those dread beings whose path had been marked with desolation, and who could call down the thunderbolts to consume their enemies! It was doubtless the policy of Cortes to strengthen this superstitious feeling as far as possible, and to impress the natives, at the outset, with a salutary awe of the supernatural powers of the Spaniards.

On the following morning, the general requested permission to return the emperor's visit, by waiting on him in his palace. This was readily granted, and Montezuma sent his officers to conduct the Spaniards to his presence. Cortes dressed himself in his richest habit, and left the quarters attended by Alvarado, Sandoval, Velasquez, and Ordaz, together with five or six of the common file.

The royal habitation was at no great distance. It was a vast, irregular pile of low stone buildings, like that garrisoned by the Spaniards. So spacious was it indeed, that, as one of the Conquerors assures us, although he had visited it more than once, for the express purpose, he had been too much fatigued each time by wandering through the apartments ever to see the whole of it. It was built of the red porous stone of the country, tetzontli, was ornamented with marble, and on the facade over the principal entrance were sculptured the arms or device of Montezuma, an eagle bearing an ocelot in his talons.

In the courts through which the Spaniards passed, fountains of crystal water were playing, fed from the copious reservoir on the distant hill of Chapoltepec, and supplying in their turn more than a hundred baths in the interior of the palace. Crowds of Aztec nobles were sauntering up and down in these squares, and in the outer halls, loitering away their hours in attendance on the court. The apartments were of immense size, though not lofty. The ceilings were of various sorts of odoriferous wood ingeniously carved; the floors covered with mats of the palm-leaf. The walls were hung with cotton richly stained, with the skins of wild animals, or gorgeous draperies of feather-work wrought in imitation of birds, insects, and flowers, with the nice art and glowing radiance of colours that might compare with the tapestries of Flanders. Clouds of incense rolled up from censers, and diffused intoxicating odours through the apartments. The Spaniards might well have fancied themselves in the voluptuous precincts of an Eastern harem, instead of treading the halls of a wild barbaric chief in the Western World.

On reaching the hall of audience, the Mexican officers took off their sandals, and covered their gay attire with a mantle of nequen, a coarse stuff made of the fibres of the maguey, worn only by the poorest classes. This act of humiliation was imposed on all, except the members of his own family, who approached the sovereign. Thus bare-footed, with downcast eyes, and formal obeisance, they ushered the Spaniards into the royal presence.

They found Montezuma seated at the further end of a spacious saloon, and surrounded by a few of his favourite chiefs. He received them kindly, and very soon Cortes, without much ceremony, entered on the subject which was uppermost in his thoughts. He was fully aware of the importance of gaining the royal convert, whose example would have such an influence on the conversion of his people. The general, therefore, prepared to display the whole store of his theological science, with the most winning arts of rhetoric he could command, while the interpretation was conveyed through the silver tones of Marina, as inseparable from him, on these occasions, as his shadow.

He set forth, as clearly as he could, the ideas entertained by the Church in regard to the holy mysteries of the Trinity, the Incarnation, and the Atonement. From this he ascended to the origin of things, the creation of the world, the first pair, paradise, and the fall of man. He assured Montezuma, that the idols he worshipped were Satan under different forms. A sufficient proof of it was the bloody sacrifices they imposed, which he contrasted with the pure and simple rite of the mass. Their worship would sink him in perdition. It was to snatch his soul, and the souls of his people, from the flames of eternal fire by opening to them a purer faith, that the Christians had come to his land. And he earnestly besought him not to neglect the occasion, but to secure his salvation by embracing the Cross, the great sign of human redemption.

The eloquence of the preacher was wasted on the insensible heart of his royal auditor. It doubtless lost somewhat of its efficacy, strained through the imperfect interpretation of so recent a neophyte as the Indian damsel. But the doctrines were too abstruse in themselves to be comprehended at a glance by the rude intellect of a barbarian. And Montezuma may have, perhaps, thought it was not more monstrous to feed on the flesh of a fellow-creature, than on that of the Creator himself. He was, besides, steeped in the superstitions of his country from his cradle. He had been educated in the straitest sect of her religion; had been himself a priest before his election to the throne; and was now the head both of the religion and the state. Little probability was there that such a man would be open to argument or persuasion, even from the lips of a more practised polemic than the Spanish commander. How could he abjure the faith that was intertwined with the dearest affections of his heart, and the very elements of his being? How could he be false to the gods who had raised him to such prosperity and honours, and whose shrines were intrusted to his especial keeping?

He listened, however, with silent attention, until the general had concluded his homily. He then replied, that he knew the Spaniards, had held this discourse wherever they had been. He doubted not their God was, as they said, a good being. His gods, also, were good to him. Yet what his visitor said of the creation of the world was like what he had been taught to believe. It was not worth while to discourse further of the matter. His ancestors, he said, were not the original proprietors of the land. They had occupied it but a few ages, and had been led there by a great Being, who; after giving them laws and ruling over the nation for a time, had withdrawn to the regions where the sun rises. He had declared, on his departure, that he or his descendants would again visit them and resume his empire. The wonderful deeds of the Spaniards, their fair complexions, and the quarter whence they came, all showed they were his descendants. If Montezuma had resisted their visit to his capital, it was because he had heard such accounts Of their cruelties — that they sent the lightning to consume his people, or crushed them to pieces under the hard feet of the ferocious animals on which they rode. He was now convinced that these were idle tales; that the Spaniards were kind and generous in their natures; they were mortals of a different race, indeed, from the Aztecs, wiser, and more valiant — and for this he honoured them.

"You, too," he added, with a smile, "have been told, perhaps, that I am a god, and dwell in palaces of gold and silver. But you see, it is false. My houses, though large, are of stone and wood like those of others; and as to my body," he said, baring his tawny arm, "you see it is flesh and bone like yours. It is true, I have a great empire, inherited from my ancestors; lands, and gold, and silver. But your sovereign beyond the waters is, I know, the rightful lord of all. I rule in his name. You, Malinche, are his ambassador; you and your brethren shall share these things with me. Rest now from your labours. You are here in your own dwellings, and everything shall be provided for your subsistence. I will see that your wishes shall be obeyed in the same way as my own." As the monarch concluded these words, a few natural tears suffused his eyes, while the image of ancient independence, perhaps, flitted across his mind.

Cortes, while he encouraged the idea that his own sovereign was the great Being indicated by Montezuma, endeavoured to comfort the monarch by the assurance that his master had no desire to interfere with his authority, otherwise than, out of pure concern for his welfare, to effect his conversion and that of his people to Christianity. Before the emperor dismissed his visitors he consulted his munificent spirit, as usual, by distributing rich stuffs and trinkets of gold among them, so that the poorest soldier, says Bernal Diaz, one of the party, received at least two heavy collars of the precious metal for his share. The iron hearts of the Spaniards were touched with the emotion displayed by Montezuma, as well as by his princely spirit of liberality. As they passed him, the cavaliers, with bonnet in hand, made him the most profound obeisance, and, "on the way home," continues the same chronicler, "we could discourse of nothing but the gentle breeding and courtesy of the Indian monarch, and of the respect we entertained for him."

Speculations of a graver complexion must have pressed on the mind of the general, as he saw around him the evidences of a civilisation, and consequently power, for which even the exaggerated reports of the natives — discredited from their apparent exaggeration — had not prepared him. In the pomp and burdensome ceremonial of the court, he saw that nice system of subordination and profound reverence for the monarch which characterise the semi-civilised empires of Asia. In the appearance of the capital, its massy, yet elegant architecture, its luxurious social accommodations, its activity in trade, he recognised the proofs of the intellectual progress, mechanical skill, and enlarged resources, of an old and opulent community; while the swarms in the streets attested the existence of a population capable of turning these resources to the best account.

In the Aztec he beheld a being unlike either the rude republican Tlascalan, or the effeminate Cholulan; but combining the courage of the one with the cultivation of the other. He was in the heart of a great capital, which seemed like an extensive fortification, with its dikes and its drawbridges, where every house might be easily converted into a castle. Its insular position removed it from the continent, from which, at the mere nod of the sovereign, all communication might be cut off, and the whole warlike population be at once precipitated on him and his handful of followers. What could superior science avail against such odds?

As to the subversion of Montezuma's empire, now that he had seen him in his capital, it must have seemed a more doubtful enterprise than ever. The recognition which the Aztec prince had made of the feudal supremacy, if I may so say, of the Spanish sovereign, was not to be taken too literally. Whatever show of deference he be disposed to pay the latter, under the influence of his present — perhaps temporary-delusion, it was not to be supposed that he would so easily relinquish his actual power and possessions, or that his people would consent to it. Indeed, his sensitive apprehensions in regard to this very subject, on the coming of the Spaniards, were sufficient proof of the tenacity with which he clung to his authority. It is true that Cortes had a strong lever for future operations in the superstitious reverence felt for himself both by prince and people. It was undoubtedly his policy to maintain this sentiment unimpaired in both, as far as possible. But, before settling any plan of operations, it was necessary to make himself personally acquainted with the topography and local advantages of the capital, the character of its population, and the real nature and amount of its resources. With this view, he asked the emperor's permission to visit the principal public edifices.

BOOK 4. RESIDENCE IN MEXICO

THE ancient city of Mexico covered the same spot occupied by the modern capital. The great causeways touched it in the same points; the streets ran in much the same direction, nearly from north to south, and from east to west; the cathedral in the plaza mayor stands on same ground that was covered by the temple of the Aztec war-god; and the four principal quarters of the town are still known among the Indians by their ancient names. Yet an Aztec of the days of Montezuma, could he behold the modern metropolis; which has risen with such phoenix-like splendour from the ashes of the old, would not recognise its site as that of his own Tenochtitlan. For the latter was encompassed by the salt floods of Tezcuco, which flowed in ample canals through every part of the city; while the Mexico of our day stands high and dry on the mainland, nearly a league distant, at its centre, from the water. The cause of this apparent change in its position is the diminution of the lake, which, from the rapidity of evaporation in these elevated regions, had become perceptible before the Conquest, but which has since been greatly accelerated by artificial causes.

The chinampas, that archipelago of wandering islands, to which our attention was drawn in the last chapter, have also nearly disappeared. These had their origin in the detached masses of earth, which, loosening from the shores, were still held together by the fibrous roots with which they were penetrated. The primitive Aztecs, in their poverty of land, availed themselves of the hint thus afforded by nature. They constructed rafts of reeds, rushes, and other fibrous materials, which, tightly knit together, formed a sufficient basis for the sediment that they drew up from the bottom of the lake. Gradually islands were formed, two or three hundred feet in length, and three or four feet in depth, with a rich stimulated soil, on which the economical Indian raised his vegetables and flowers for the markets of Tenochtitlan. Some of these chinampas were even firm enough to allow the growth of small trees, and to sustain a hut for the residence of the person that had charge of it, who, with a long pole resting on the sides or the bottom of the shallow basin, could change the position of his little territory at pleasure, which with its rich freight of vegetable stores was seen moving like some enchanted island over the water.

The ancient dikes were three in number. That of Iztapalapan, by which the Spaniards entered, approaching the city from the south. That of Tepejacac, on the north, which, continuing the principal street, might be regarded, also, as a continuation of the first causeway. Lastly, the dike of Tlacopan, connecting the island-city with the continent on the west. This last causeway, memorable for the disastrous retreat of the Spaniards, was about two miles in length. They were all built in the same substantial manner, of lime and stone, were defended by drawbridges, and were wide enough for ten or twelve horsemen to ride abreast.

The rude founders of Tenochtitlan built their frail tenements of reeds and rushes on the group of small islands in the western part of the lake. In process of time, these were supplanted by more substantial buildings. A quarry in the neighbourhood, of a red porous amygdaloid, tetzontli, was opened, and a light, brittle stone drawn from it, and wrought with little difficulty. Of this their edifices were constructed, with some reference to architectural solidity, if not elegance. Mexico, as already noticed, was the residence of the great chiefs, whom the sovereign encouraged, or rather compelled, from obvious motives of policy, to spend part of the year in the capital. It was also the temporary abode of the great lords of Tezcuco and Tlacopan, who shared nominally, at least, the sovereignty of the empire. The mansions of these dignitaries, and of the principal nobles, were on a scale of rude magnificence corresponding with their state. They were low, indeed; seldom of more than one floor, never exceeding two. But they spread over a wide extent of ground; were arranged in a quadrangular form, with a court in the centre, and were surrounded by porticoes embellished with porphyry and jasper, easily found in the neighbourhood, while not unfrequently a fountain of crystal water in the centre shed a grateful coolness over the atmosphere. The dwellings of the common people were also placed on foundations of stone, which rose to the height of a few feet, and were then succeeded by courses of unbaked bricks, crossed occasionally by wooden rafters. Most of the streets were mean and narrow. Some few, however, were wide and of great length. The principal street, conducting from the great southern causeway, penetrated in a straight line the whole length of the city, and afforded a noble vista, in which the long lines of low stone edifices were broken occasionally by intervening gardens, rising on terraces, and displaying all the pomp of Aztec horticulture.

The great streets, which were coated with a hard cement, were intersected by numerous canals. Some of these were flanked by a solid way, which served as a foot-walk for passengers, and as a landing-place where boats might discharge their cargoes. Small buildings were erected at intervals, as stations for the revenue officers who collected the duties on different articles of merchandise. The canals were traversed by numerous bridges, many of which could be raised affording the means of cutting off communication between different parts of the city.

From the accounts of the ancient capital, one is reminded of those acquatic cities in the Old World, the positions of which have been selected from similar motives of economy and defence; above all, of Venice — if it be not rash to compare the rude architecture of the American Indian with the marble palaces and temples — alas, how shorn of their splendour! — which crowned the once proud mistress of the Adriatic. The example of the metropolis was soon followed by the other towns in the vicinity. Instead of resting their foundations on terra firma, they were seen advancing far into the lake, the shallow waters of which in some parts do not exceed four feet in depth. Thus an easy means of intercommunication was opened, and the surface of this inland "sea," as Cortes styles it, was darkened by thousands of canoes — an Indian term — industriously engaged in the traffic between these little communities. How gay and picturesque must have been the aspect of the lake in those days, with its shining cities, and flowering islets rocking, as it were, at anchor on the fair bosom of its waters!

The population of Tenochtitlan, at the time of the Conquest, is variously stated. No contemporary writer estimates it at less than sixty thousand houses, which, by the ordinary rules of reckoning, would give three hundred thousand souls. If a dwelling often contained, as is asserted, several families, it would swell the amount considerably higher. Nothing is more uncertain than estimates of numbers among barbarous communities, who necessarily live in a more confused and promiscuous manner than civilised, and among whom no regular system is adopted for ascertaining the population. The concurrent testimony of the Conquerors; the extent of the city, which was said to be nearly three leagues in circumference; the immense size of its great market-place; the long lines of edifices, vestiges of whose ruins may still be found in the suburbs, miles from the modern city; the fame of the metropolis throughout Anahuac, which, however, could boast many large and populous places; lastly, the economical husbandry and the ingenious contrivances to extract aliment from the most unpromising sources — all attest a numerous population, far beyond that of the present capital.

A careful police provided for the health and cleanliness of the city. A thousand persons are said to have been daily employed in watering and sweeping the streets, so that a man — to borrow the language of an old Spaniard —"could walk through them with as little danger of soiling his feet as his hands." The water, in a city washed on all sides by the salt floods, was extremely brackish. A liberal supply of the pure element, however, was brought from Chapoltepec, "the grasshopper's hill," less than a league distant. it was brought through an earthen pipe, along a dike constructed for the purpose. That there might be no failure in so essential an article, when repairs were going on, a double course of pipes was laid. In this way a column of water the size of a man's body was conducted into the heart of the capital, where it fed the fountains and reservoirs of the principal mansions. Openings were made in the aqueduct as it crossed the bridges, and thus a supply was furnished to the canoes below, by means of which it was transported to all parts of the city.

While Montezuma encouraged a taste for architectural magnificence in his nobles, he contributed his own share towards the embellishment of the city. It was in his reign that the famous calendarstone, weighing, probably, in its primitive state, nearly fifty tons, was transported from its native quarry, many leagues distant, to the capital, where it still forms one of the most curious monuments of Aztec science. Indeed, when we reflect on the difficulty of hewing such a stupendous mass from its hard basaltic bed without the aid of iron tools, and that of transporting it such a distance across land and water without the help of animals, we may feel admiration at the mechanical ingenuity and enterprise of the people who accomplished it.

Not content with the spacious residence of his father, Montezuma erected another on a yet more magnificent scale. It occupied the ground partly covered by the private dwellings on one side of the plaza mayor of the modern city. This building, or, as it might more correctly be styled, pile of buildings, spread over an extent of ground so vast, that, as one of the Conquerors assures us, its terraced roof might have afforded ample room for thirty knights to run their courses in a regular tourney. I have already noticed its interior decorations, its fanciful draperies, its roofs inlaid with cedar and other odoriferous woods, held together without a nail, and probably without a knowledge of the arch, its numerous and spacious apartments, which Cortes, with enthusiastic hyperbole, does not hesitate to declare superior to anything of the kind in Spain.

Adjoining the principal edifices were others devoted to various objects. One was an armoury, filled with the weapons and military dresses worn by the Aztecs, all kept in the most perfect order, ready for instant use. The emperor was himself very expert in the management of the maquahuitl, or Indian sword, and took great delight in witnessing athletic exercises, and the mimic representation of war by his young nobility. Another building was used as a granary, and others as warehouses for the different articles of food and apparel contributed by the districts charged with the maintenance of the royal household.

There were also edifices appropriated to objects of quite another kind. One of these was an immense aviary, in which birds of splendid plumage were assembled from all parts of the empire. Here was the scarlet cardinal, the golden pheasant, the endless parrot-tribe with their rainbow hues (the royal green predominant), and that miniature miracle of nature, the humming-bird, which delights to revel among the honeysuckle bowers of Mexico. Three hundred attendants had charge of this aviary, who made themselves acquainted with the appropriate food of its inmates, oftentimes procured at great cost, and in the moulting season were careful to collect the beautiful plumage, which, with its many-coloured tints, furnished the materials for the Aztec painter.

A separate building was reserved for the fierce birds of prey; the voracious vulture-tribes and eagles of enormous size, whose home was in the snowy solitudes of the Andes. No less than five hundred turkeys, the cheapest meat in Mexico, were allowed for the daily consumption of these tyrants of the feathered race.

Adjoining this aviary was a menagerie of wild animals, gathered from the mountain forests, and even from the remote swamps of the tierra caliente. The resemblance of the different species to those in the Old World, with which no one of them, however, was identical, led to a perpetual confusion the nomenclature of the Spaniards, as it has since done in that of better instructed naturalists. The collection was still further swelled by a great number of reptiles and serpents, remarkable for their size and venomous qualities, among which the Spaniards beheld the fiery little animal "with the castanets in his tail," the terror of the American wilderness. The serpents were confined in long cages, lined with down or feathers, or in troughs of mud and water. The beasts and birds of prey were provided with apartments large enough to allow of their moving about, and secured by a strong lattice-work, through which light and air were freely admitted. The whole was placed under the charge of numerous keepers, who acquainted themselves with the habits of their prisoners, and provided for their comfort and cleanliness. With what deep interest would the enlightened naturalist of that day — an Oviedo, or a Martyr, for example — have surveyed this magnificent collection, in which the various tribes which roamed over the Western wilderness, the unknown races of an unknown world, were, brought into one view! How would they have delighted to study the peculiarities of these new species, compared with those of their own hemisphere, and thus have risen to some comprehension of the general laws by which Nature acts in all her works! The rude followers of Cortes did not trouble themselves with such refined speculations. They gazed on the spectacle with a vague curiosity, not unmixed with awe; and, as they listened to the wild cries of the ferocious animals and the hissings of the serpents, they almost fancied themselves in the infernal regions.

I must not omit to notice a strange collection of human monsters, dwarfs, and other unfortunate persons, in whose organisation Nature had capriciously deviated from her regular laws. Such hideous anomalies were regarded by the Aztecs as a suitable appendage of state. It is even said they were in some cases the result of artificial means, employed by unnatural parents, desirous to secure a provision for their offspring by thus qualifying them for a place in the royal museum!

Extensive gardens were spread out around these buildings, filled with fragrant shrubs and flowers, and especially with medicinal plants. No country has afforded more numerous species of these last, than New Spain; and their virtues were perfectly understood by the Aztecs, with whom medical botany may be said to have been studied as a science. Amidst this labyrinth of sweet-scented groves and shrubberies, fountains of pure water might be seen throwing up their sparkling jets, and scattering refreshing dews over the blossoms. Ten large tanks, well stocked with fish, afforded a retreat on their margins to various tribes of water-fowl, whose habits were so carefully consulted, that some of these ponds were of salt water, as that which they most loved to frequent. A tessellated pavement of marble inclosed the ample basins, which were overhung by light and fanciful pavilions, that admitted the perfumed breezes of the gardens, and offered a grateful shelter to the monarch and his mistresses in the sultry heats of summer.

But the most luxurious residence of the Aztec monarch, at that season, was the royal hill of Chapoltepec, a spot consecrated, moreover, by the ashes of his ancestors. It stood in a westerly direction from the capital, and its base was, in his day, washed by the waters of the Tezcuco. On its lofty crest of porphyritic rock there now stands the magnificent, though desolate, castle erected by the young viceroy Galvez, at the close of the seventeenth century. The view from its windows is one of the finest in the environs of Mexico. The landscape is not disfigured here, as in many other quarters, by the white and barren patches, so offensive to the sight; but the eye wanders over an unbroken expanse of meadows and cultivated fields, waving with rich harvests of European grain. Montezuma's gardens stretched for miles around the base of the hill. Two statues of that monarch and his father, cut in bas relief in the porphyry, were spared till the middle of the last century; and the grounds are still shaded by gigantic cypresses, more than fifty feet in circumference, which were centuries old at the time of the Conquest. The place is now a tangled wilderness of wild shrubs, where the myrtle mingles its dark, glossy leaves with the red berries and delicate foliage of the pepper-tree. Surely there is no spot better suited to awaken meditation on the past; none where the traveller, as he sits under those stately cypresses grey with the moss of ages, can so fitly ponder on the sad destinies of the Indian races and the monarch who once held his courtly revels under the shadow of their branches.

The domestic establishment of Montezuma was on the same scale of barbaric splendour as everything else about him. He could boast as many wives as are found in the harem of an Eastern sultan. They were lodged in their own apartments, and provided with every accommodation, according to their ideas, for personal comfort and cleanliness. They passed their hours in the usual feminine employments of weaving and embroidery, especially in the graceful feather-work, for which such rich materials were furnished by the royal aviaries. They conducted themselves with strict decorum, under the supervision of certain aged females, who acted in the respectable capacity of duennas, in the same manner as in the religious houses attached to the teocallis. The palace was supplied with numerous baths, and Montezuma set the example, in his own person, of frequent ablutions. He bathed, at least once, and changed his dress four times, it is said, every day. He never put on the same apparel a second time, but gave it away to his attendants. Queen Elizabeth, with a similar taste for costume, showed a less princely spirit in hoarding her discarded suits.

Besides his numerous female retinue, the halls and antechambers were filled with nobles in constant attendance on his person, who served also as a sort of bodyguard. It had been usual for plebeians of merit to fill certain offices in the palace. But the haughty Montezuma refused to be waited upon by any but men of noble birth. They were not unfrequently the sons of the great chiefs, and remained as hostages in the absence of their fathers; thus serving the double purpose of security and state.

His meals the emperor took alone. The well-matted floor of a large saloon was covered with hundreds of dishes. Sometimes Montezuma himself, but more frequently his steward, indicated those which he preferred, and which were kept hot by means of chafingdishes. The royal bill of fare comprehended, besides domestic animals, game from the distant forests, and fish which, the day before, were swimming in the Gulf of Mexico! They were dressed in manifold ways, for the Aztec artistes, as we have already had occasion to notice, had penetrated deep into the mysteries of culinary science.

The meats were served by the attendant nobles, who then resigned the office of waiting on the monarch to maidens selected for their personal grace and beauty. A screen of richly gilt and carved wood was drawn around him, so as to conceal him from vulgar eyes during the repast. He was seated on a cushion, and the dinner was served on a low table, covered with a delicate cotton cloth. The dishes were of the finest ware of Cholula. He had a service of gold, which was reserved for religious celebrations. Indeed, it would scarcely have comported with even his princely revenues to have used it on ordinary occasions, when his table equipage was not allowed to appear a second time, but was given away to his attendants. The saloon was lighted by torches made of a resinous wood, which sent forth a sweet odour, and probably not a little smoke, as they burned. At his meal, he was attended by five or six of his ancient counsellors, who stood at a respectful distance, answering his questions, and occasionally rejoiced by some of the viands with which he complimented them from his table.

This course of solid dishes was succeeded by another of sweetmeats and pastry, for which the Aztec cooks, provided with the important requisites of maize-flour, eggs, and the rich sugar of the aloe, were famous. Two girls were occupied at the further end of the apartment, during dinner, in preparing fine rolls and wafers, with which they garnished the board from time to time. The emperor took no other beverage than the chocolatl, a potation of chocolate, flavoured with vanilla and other spices, and so prepared as to be reduced to a froth of the consistency of honey, which gradually dissolved in the mouth. This beverage, if so it could be called, was served in golden goblets, with spoons of the same metal or of tortoise-shell finely wrought. The emperor was exceedingly fond of it, to judge from the quantity — no less than fifty jars or pitchers being prepared for his own daily consumption! Two thousand more were allowed for that of his household.

The general arrangement of the meal seems to have been not very unlike that of Europeans. But no prince in Europe could boast a dessert which could compare with that of the Aztec emperor: for it was gathered fresh from the most opposite climes; and his board displayed the products of his own temperate region, and the luscious fruits of the tropics, plucked the day previous, from the green groves of the tierra caliente, and transmitted with the speed of steam, by means of couriers, to the capital. It was as if some kind fairy should crown our banquets with the spicy products that but yesterday were growing in a sunny isle of the far-off Indian seas!

After the royal appetite was appeased, water was handed to him by the female attendants in a silver basin, in the same manner as had been done before commencing his meal; for the Aztecs were as constant in their ablutions, at these times, as any nation of the East. Pipes were then brought, made of a varnished and richly gilt wood, from which he inhaled, sometimes through the nose, at others through the mouth, the fumes of an intoxicating weed, called "tobacco," mingled with liquid-amber. While this soothing process of fumigation was going on, the emperor enjoyed the exhibitions of his mountebanks and jugglers, of whom a regular corps was attached to the palace. No people, not even those of China or Hindostan, surpassed the Aztecs in feats of agility and legerdemain.

Sometimes he amused himself with his jester; for the Indian monarch had his jesters, as well as his more refined brethren of Europe at that day. Indeed, he used to say, that more instruction was to be gathered from them than from wiser men, for they dared to tell the truth. At other times, he witnessed the graceful dances of his women, or took delight in listening to music — if the rude minstrelsy of the Mexicans deserve that name — accompanied by a chant, in slow and solemn cadence, celebrating the heroic deeds of great Aztec warriors or of his own princely line.

When he had sufficiently refreshed his spirits with these diversions, he composed himself to sleep, for in his siesta he was as regular as a Spaniard. On awaking, he gave audience to ambassadors from foreign states, or his own tributary cities, or to such caciques as had suits to prefer to him. They were introduced by the young nobles in attendance, and, whatever might be their rank, unless of the blood royal, they were obliged to submit to the humiliation of shrouding their rich dresses under the coarse mantle of nequen, and entering bare-footed, with downcast eyes, into the presence. The emperor addressed few and brief remarks to the suitors, answering them generally by his secretaries; and the parties retired with the same reverential obeisance, taking care to keep their faces turned towards the monarch. Well might Cortes exclaim that no court, whether of the Grand Seignior or any other infidel, ever displayed so pompous and elaborate a ceremonial!

Besides the crowd of retainers already noticed, the royal household was not complete without a host of artisans constantly employed in the erection or repair of buildings, besides a great number of jewellers and persons skilled in working metals, who found abundant demand for their trinkets among the dark-eyed beauties of the harem. The imperial mummers and jugglers were also very numerous, and the dancers belonging to the palace occupied a particular district of the city, appropriated exclusively to them.

The maintenance of this little host, amounting to some thousands of individuals, involved a heavy expenditure, requiring accounts of a complicated, and, to a simple people, it might well be, embarrassing nature. Everything, however, was conducted with perfect order; and all the various receipts and disbursements were set down in the picture-writing of the country. The arithmetical characters were of a more refined and conventional sort than those for narrative purposes; and a separate apartment was fired with hieroglyphical ledgers, exhibiting a complete view of the economy of the palace. The care of all this was intrusted to a treasurer, who acted as sort of major-domo in the household, having a general superintendence over all its concerns. This responsible office, on the arrival of the Spaniards, was in the hands of a trusty cacique named Tapia.

Such is the picture of Montezuma's domestic establishment and way of living, as delineated by the conquerors, and their immediate followers, who had the best means of information, too highly coloured, it may be, by the proneness to exaggerate, which was natural to those who first witnessed a spectacle so striking to the imagination, so new and unexpected. I have thought it best to present the full details, trivial though they may seem to the reader, as affording a curious picture of manners, so superior in point of refinement to those of the other aboriginal tribes on the North American continent. Nor are they, in fact, so trivial, when we reflect, that in these details of private life we possess a surer measure of civilisation, than in those of a public nature.

In surveying them we are strongly reminded of the civilisation of the East; not of that higher, intellectual kind which belonged to the more polished Arabs and the Persians, but that semi-civilisation which has distinguished, for example, the Tartar races, among whom art, and even science, have made, indeed, some progress in their adaptation to material wants and sensual gratification, but little in reference to the higher and more ennobling interests of humanity. It is characteristic of such a people to find a puerile pleasure in a dazzling and ostentatious pageantry; to mistake show for substance, vain pomp for power; to hedge round the throne itself with a barren and burdensome ceremonial, the counterfeit of real majesty.

Even this, however, was an advance in refinement compared with the rude manners of the earlier Aztecs. The change may, doubtless, be referred in some degree to the personal influence of Montezuma. In his younger days, he had tempered the fierce habits of the soldier with the milder profession of religion. In later life, he had withdrawn himself still more from the brutalising occupations of war, and his manners acquired a refinement tinctured, it may be added, with an effeminacy unknown to his martial predecessors.

The condition of the empire, too, under his reign, was favourable to this change. The dismemberment of the Tezcucan kingdom, on the death of the great Nezahualpilli, had left the Aztec monarchy without a rival; and it soon spread its colossal arms over the furthest limits of Anahuac. The aspiring mind of Montezuma rose with the acquisition of wealth and power; and he displayed the consciousness of new importance by the assumption of unprecedented state.

He affected a reserve unknown to his predecessors; withdrew his person from the vulgar eye, and fenced himself round with an elaborate and courtly etiquette. When he went abroad, it was in state, on some public occasion, usually to the great temple, to take part in the religious services; and, as he passed along, he exacted from his people, as we have seen, the homage of an adulation worthy of an oriental despot. His haughty demeanour touched the pride of his more potent vassals, particularly those who at a distance felt themselves nearly independent of his authority.

His exactions, demanded by the profuse expenditure of his palace, scattered broadcast the seeds of discontent; and, while the empire seemed towering in its most palmy and prosperous state, the canker had eaten deepest into its heart.

FOUR days had elapsed since the Spaniards made their entry into Mexico. Whatever schemes their commander may have revolved in his mind, he felt that he could determine on no plan of operations till he had seen more of the capital, and ascertained by his own inspection the nature of its resources. He accordingly, as was observed at the close of the last book, sent to Montezuma, asking permission to visit the great teocalli, and some other places in the city.

The friendly monarch consented without difficulty. He even prepared to go in person to the great temple, to receive his guests there — it may be, to shield the shrine of his tutelar deity from any attempted profanation. He was acquainted, as we have already seen, with the proceedings of the Spaniards on similar occasions in the course of their march. — Cortes put himself at the head of his little corps of cavalry, and nearly all the Spanish foot, as usual, and followed the caciques sent by Montezuma to guide him. They proposed first to conduct him to the great market of Tlatelolco in the western part of the city.

On the way, the Spaniards were struck, in the same manner as they had been on entering the capital, with the appearance of the inhabitants, and their great superiority in the style and quality of their dress, over the people of the lower countries. The tilmatli, or cloak, thrown over the shoulders, and tied round the neck, made of cotton of different degrees of fineness, according to the condition of the wearer, and the ample sash around the loins, were often wrought in rich and elegant figures, and edged with a deep fringe or tassel. As the weather was now growing cool, mantles of fur or of the gorgeous feather-work were sometimes substituted. The latter combined the advantage of great warmth with beauty. The Mexicans had also the art of spinning a fine thread of the hair of the rabbit and other animals, which they wove into a delicate web that took a permanent dye.

The women, as in other parts of the country, seemed to go about as freely as the men. They wore several skirts or petticoats of different lengths, with highly ornamented borders, and sometimes over them loose flowing robes, which reached to the ankles. These also were made of cotton, for the wealthier classes, of a fine texture, prettily embroidered. No veils were worn here, as in some other parts of Anahuac, where they were made of the aloe thread, or of the light web of hair above noticed. The Aztec women had their faces exposed; and their dark raven tresses floated luxuriantly over their shoulders, revealing features which, although of a dusky or rather cinnamon hue, were not unfrequently pleasing, while touched with the serious, even sad expression characteristic of the national physiognomy.

On drawing near to the tianguez, or great market, the Spaniards were astonished at the throng of people pressing towards it, and, on entering the place, their surprise was still further heightened by the sight of the multitudes assembled there, and the dimensions of the inclosure, thrice as large as the celebrated square of Salamanca. Here were met together traders from all parts, with the products and manufactures peculiar to their countries; the goldsmiths of Azcapotzalco; the potters and jewellers of Cholula, the painters of Tezcuco, the stone-cutters of Tenajocan, the hunters of Xilotepec, the fishermen of Cuitlahuac, the fruiterers of the warm countries, the mat and chair-makers of Quauhtitlan, and the florists of Xochimilco — all busily engaged in recommending their respective wares, and in chaffering with purchasers.

The market-place was surrounded by deep porticoes, and the several articles had each its own quarter allotted to it. Here might be seen cotton piled up in bales, or manufactured into dresses and articles of domestic use, as tapestry, curtains, coverlets, and the like. The richly-stained and nice fabrics reminded Cortes of the alcayceria, or silk-market of Granada. There was the quarter assigned to the goldsmiths, where the purchaser might find various articles of ornament or use formed of the precious metals, or curious toys, such as we have already had occasion to notice, made in imitation of birds and fishes, with scales and feathers alternately of gold and silver, and with movable heads and bodies. These fantastic little trinkets were often garnished with precious stones, and showed a patient, puerile ingenuity in the manufacture, like that of the Chinese.

In an adjoining quarter were collected specimens of pottery, coarse and fine, vases of wood elaborately carved, varnished or gilt, of curious and sometimes graceful forms. There were also hatchets made of copper alloyed with tin, the substitute, and, as it proved, not a bad one, for iron. The soldier found here all the implements of his trade. The casque fashioned into the head of some wild animal, with its grinning defences of teeth, and bristling crest dyed with the rich tint of the cochineal; the escaupil, or quilted doublet of cotton, the rich surcoat of feather-mail, and weapons of all sorts, copper-headed lances and arrows, and the broad maquahuitl, the Mexican sword, with its sharp blades of itztli. Here were razors and mirrors of this same hard and polished mineral which served so many of the purposes of steel with the Aztecs. In the square were also to be found booths occupied by barbers, who used these same razors in their vocation. For the Mexicans, contrary to the popular and erroneous notions respecting the aborigines of the New World, had beards, though scanty ones. Other shops or booths were tenanted by apothecaries, well provided with drugs, roots, and different medicinal preparations. In other places, again, blank books or maps for the hieroglyphical picture-writing were to be seen, folded together like fans, and made of cotton, skins, or more commonly the fibres of the agave, the Aztec papyrus.

Under some of the porticoes they saw hides raw and dressed, and various articles for domestic or personal use made of the leather. Animals, both wild and tame, were offered for sale, and near them, perhaps, a gang of slaves, with collars round their necks, intimating they were likewise on sale — a spectacle unhappily not confined to the barbarian markets of Mexico, though the evils of their condition were aggravated there by the consciousness that a life of degradation might be consummated at any moment by the dreadful doom of sacrifice.

The heavier materials for building, as stone, lime, timber, were considered too bulky to be allowed a place in the square, and were deposited in the adjacent streets on the borders of the canals. It would be tedious to enumerate all the various articles, whether for luxury or daily use, which were collected from all quarters in this vast bazaar. I must not omit to mention, however, the display of provisions, one of the most attractive features of the tianguez; meats of all kinds, domestic poultry, game from the neighbouring mountains, fish from the lakes and streams, fruits in all the delicious abundance of these temperate regions, green vegetables, and the unfailing maize. There was many a viand, too, ready dressed, which sent up its savoury steams provoking the appetite of the idle passenger; pastry, bread of the Indian corn, cakes, and confectionery. Along with these were to be seen cooling or stimulating beverages, the spicy foaming chocolatl — with its delicate aroma of vanilla, and the inebriating pulque, the fermented juice of the aloe. All these commodities, and every stall and portico, were set out, or rather smothered, with flowers, showing, on a much greater scale, indeed, a taste similar to that displayed in the markets of modern Mexico. Flowers seem to be the spontaneous growth of this luxuriant soil; which, instead of noxious weeds, as in other regions, is ever ready, without the aid of man, to cover up its nakedness with this rich and variegated livery of nature.

As to the numbers assembled in the market, the estimates differ, as usual. The Spaniards often visited the place, and no one states the amount at less than forty thousand! Some carry it much higher. Without relying too much on the arithmetic of the Conquerors, it is certain that on this occasion, which occurred every fifth day, the city swarmed with a motley crowd of strangers, not only from the vicinity, but from many leagues around; the causeways were thronged, and the lake was darkened by canoes filled with traders flocking to the great tianguez. It resembled indeed the periodical fairs in Europe, not as they exist now, but as they existed in the Middle Ages, when, from the difficulties of intercommunication, they served as the great central marts for commercial intercourse, exercising a most important and salutary influence on the community.

The exchanges were conducted partly by barter, but more usually in the currency of the country. This consisted of bits of tin stamped with a character like a T, bags of cacao, the value of which was regulated by their size, and lastly quills filled with gold dust. Gold was part of the regular currency, it seems, in both hemispheres. In their dealings it is singular that they should have had no knowledge of scales and weights. The quantity was determined by measure and number.

The most perfect order reigned throughout this vast assembly. Officers patrolled the square, whose business it was to keep the peace, to collect the duties imposed on the different articles of merchandise, to see that no false measures or fraud of any kind were used, and to bring offenders at once to justice. A court of twelve judges sat in one part of the tianguez, clothed with those ample and summary powers, which, in despotic countries, are often delegated even to petty tribunals. The extreme severity with which they exercised these powers, in more than one instance, proves that they were not a dead letter.

The tianguez of Mexico was naturally an object of great interest, as well as wonder, to the Spaniards. For in it they saw converged into one focus, as it were, all the rays of civilisation scattered throughout the land. Here they beheld the various evidences of mechanical skill, of domestic industry, the multiplied resources, of whatever kind, within the compass of the natives. It could not fail to impress them with high ideas of the magnitude of these resources, as well as of the commercial activity and social subordination by which the whole community was knit together; and their admiration is fully evinced by the minuteness and energy of their descriptions.

From this bustling scene, the Spaniards took their way to the great teocalli, in the neighbourhood of their own quarters. It covered, with the subordinate edifices, as the reader has already seen, the large tract of ground now occupied by the cathedral, part of the market-place, and some of the adjoining streets. It was the spot which had been consecrated to the same object, probably, ever since the foundation of the city. The present building, however, was of no great antiquity, having been constructed by Ahuitzotl, who celebrated its dedication in 1486, by that hecatomb of victims, of which such incredible reports are to be found in the chronicles.

It stood in the midst of a vast area, encompassed by a wall of stone and lime, about eight feet high, ornamented on the outer side by figures of serpents, raised in relief, which gave it the name of the coatepantli, or "wall of serpents." This emblem was a common one in the sacred sculpture of Anahuac, as well as of Egypt. The wall, which was quadrangular, was pierced by huge battlemented gateways, opening on the four principal streets of the capital. Over each of the gates was a kind of arsenal, filled with arms and warlike gear; and, if we may credit the report of the Conquerors, there were barracks adjoining, garrisoned by ten thousand soldiers, who served as a sort of military police for the capital, supplying the emperor with a strong arm in case of tumult or sedition.

The teocalli itself was a solid pyramidal structure of earth and pebbles, coated on the outside with hewn stones, probably of the light, porous kind employed in the buildings of the city. It was probably square, with its sides facing the cardinal points. It was divided into five bodies or stories, each one receding so as to be of smaller dimensions than that immediately below it; the usual form of the Aztec teocallis, as already described, and bearing obvious resemblance to some of the primitive pyramidal structures in the Old World. The ascent was by a flight of steps on the outside, which reached to the narrow terrace or platform at the base of the second story, passing quite round the building, when a second stairway conducted to a similar landing at the base of the third. The breadth of this walk was just so much space as was left by the retreating story next above it. From this construction the visitor was obliged to pass round the whole edifice four times, in order to reach the top. This had a most imposing effect in the religious ceremonials, when the pompous procession of priests with their wild minstrelsy came sweeping round the huge sides of the pyramid, as they rose higher and higher in the presence of gazing multitudes, towards the summit.

The dimensions of the temple cannot be given with any certainty. The Conquerors judged by the eye, rarely troubling themselves with anything like an accurate measurement. It was, probably, not much less than three hundred feet square at the base; and, as the Spaniards counted a hundred and fourteen steps, was probably less than one hundred feet in height.

When Cortes arrived before the teocalli, he found two priests and several caciques commissioned by Montezuma to save him the fatigue of the ascent by bearing him on their shoulders, in the same manner as had been done to the emperor. But the general declined the compliment, preferring to march up at the head of his men. On reaching the summit, they found it a vast area, paved with broad flat stones. The first object that met their view was a large block of jasper, the peculiar shape of which showed it was the stone on which the bodies of the unhappy victims were stretched for sacrifice. Its convex surface, by raising the breast, enabled the priest to perform his diabolical task more easily, of removing the heart. At the other end of the area were two towers or sanctuaries, consisting of three stories, the lower one of stone and stucco, the two upper of wood elaborately carved. In the lower division stood the images of their gods; the apartments above were filled with utensils for their religious services, and with the ashes of some of their Aztec princes, who had fancied this airy sepulchre. Before each sanctuary stood an altar with that undying fire upon it, the extinction of which boded as much evil to the empire, as that of the Vestal flame would have done in ancient Rome. Here, also, was the huge cylindrical drum made of serpents' skins, and struck only on extraordinary occasions, when it sent forth a melancholy sound that might be heard for miles — a sound of woe in after times to the Spaniards.

Montezuma, attended by the high-priest, came forward to receive Cortes as he mounted the area. "You are weary, Malinche," said he to him, "with climbing up our great temple." But Cortes, with a politic vaunt, assured him "the Spaniards were never weary!" Then, taking him by the hand, the emperor pointed out the localities of the neighbourhood. The temple on which they stood, rising high above all other edifices in the capital, afforded the most elevated as well as central point of view. Below them the city lay spread out like a map, with its streets and canals intersecting each other at right angles, its terraced roofs blooming like so many parterres of flowers. Every place seemed alive with business and bustle; canoes were glancing up and down the canals, the streets were crowded with people in their gay, picturesque costume, while from the marketplace they had so lately left, a confused hum of many sounds and voices rose upon the air. They could distinctly trace the symmetrical plan of the city, with its principal avenues issuing, as it were, from the four gates of the coatepantli; and connecting themselves with the causeways, which formed the grand entrances to the capital. This regular and beautiful arrangement was imitated in many of the inferior towns, where the great roads converged towards the chief teocalli, or cathedral, as to a common focus. They could discern the insular position of the metropolis, bathed on all sides by the salt floods, of the Tezcuco, and in the distance the clear fresh waters of the Chalco; far beyond stretched a wide prospect of fields and waving woods, with the burnished walls of many a lofty temple rising high above the trees, and crowning the distant hill-tops. The view reached in an unbroken line to the very base of the circular range of mountains, whose frosty peaks glittered as if touched with fire in the morning ray; while long, dark wreaths of vapour, rolling up from the hoary head of Popocatepetl, told that the destroying element was, indeed, at work in the bosom of the beautiful valley.

Cortes was filled with admiration at this grand and glorious spectacle, and gave utterance to his feelings in animated language to the emperor, the lord of these flourishing domains. His thoughts, however, soon took another direction; and, turning to Father Olmedo, who stood by his side, he suggested that the area would afford a most conspicuous position for the Christian Cross, if Montezuma would but allow it to be planted there. But the discreet ecclesiastic, with the good sense which on these occasions seems to have been so lamentably deficient in his commander, reminded him that such a request, at present, would be exceedingly ill-timed, as the Indian monarch had shown no dispositions as yet favourable to Christianity.

Cortes then requested Montezuma to allow him to enter the sanctuaries, and behold the shrines of his gods. To this the latter, after a short conference with the priests, assented, and conducted the Spaniards into the building. They found themselves in a spacious apartment incrusted on the sides with stucco, on which various figures were sculptured, representing the Mexican calendar, perhaps, or the priestly ritual. At one end of the saloon was a recess with a roof of timber richly carved and gilt. Before the altar in this sanctuary stood the colossal image of Huitzilopochtli, the tutelary deity and war-god of the Aztecs. His countenance was distorted into hideous lineaments of symbolical import. In his right hand he wielded a bow, and in his left a bunch of golden arrows, which a mystic legend had connected with the victories of his people. The huge folds of a serpent, consisting of pearls and precious stones, were coiled round his waist, and the same rich materials were profusely sprinkled over his person. On his left foot were the delicate feathers of the humming-bird, which, singularly enough, gave its name to the dread deity. The most conspicuous ornament was a chain of gold and silver hearts alternate, suspended round his neck, emblematical of the sacrifice in which he most delighted. A more unequivocal evidence of this was afforded by three human hearts smoking and almost palpitating, as if recently torn from the victims, and now lying on the altar before him!

The adjoining sanctuary was dedicated to a milder deity. This was Tezcatlipoca, next in honour to that invisible Being, the Supreme God, who was represented by no image, and confined by no temple. It was Tezcatlipoca who created the world, and watched over it with a providential care. He was represented as a young man, and his image, of polished black stone, was richly garnished with gold plates and ornaments; among which a shield, burnished like a mirror, was the most characteristic emblem, as in it he saw reflected all the doings of the world. But the homage to this god was not always of a more refined or merciful character than that paid to his carnivorous brother; for five bleeding hearts were also seen in a golden platter on his altar.

The walls of both these chapels were stained with human gore. "The stench was more intolerable," exclaims Diaz, "than that of the slaughter-houses in Castile!" And the frantic forms of the priests, with their dark robes clotted with blood, as they flitted to and fro, seemed to the Spaniards to be those of the very ministers of Satan!

From this foul abode they gladly escaped into the open air; when Cortes, turning to Montezuma, said with a smile, "I do not comprehend how a great and wise prince like you can put faith in such evil spirits as these idols, the representatives of the devil! If you will but permit us to erect here the true Cross, and place the images of the blessed Virgin and her Son in your sanctuaries, you will soon see how your false gods will shrink before them!"

Montezuma was greatly shocked at this sacrilegious address. "These are the gods," he answered, "who have led the Aztecs on to victory since they were a nation, and who send the seed-time and harvest in their seasons. Had I thought you would have offered them this outrage, I would not have admitted you into their presence!"

Cortes, after some expressions of concern at having wounded the feelings of the emperor, took his leave. Montezuma remained, saying that he must expiate, if possible, the crime of exposing the shrines of the divinities to such profanation by the strangers.

On descending to the court, the Spaniards took a leisurely survey of the other edifices in the inclosure. The area was protected by a smooth stone pavement, so polished, indeed, that it was with difficulty the horses could keep their legs. There were several other teocallis, built generally on the model of the great one, though of much inferior size, dedicated to the different Aztec deities. On their summits were the altars crowned with perpetual flames, which, with those on the numerous temples in other quarters of the capital, shed a brilliant illumination over its streets, through the long nights.

Among the teocallis in the inclosure was one consecrated to Quetzalcoatl, circular in its form, and having an entrance in imitation of a dragon's mouth, bristling with sharp fangs and dropping with blood. As the Spaniards cast a furtive glance into the throat of this horrible monster, they saw collected there implements of sacrifice and other abominations of fearful import. Their bold hearts shuddered at the spectacle, and they designated the place not inaptly as the "Hell."

One other structure may be noticed as characteristic of the brutish nature of their religion. This was a pyramidal mound or tumulus, having a complicated framework of timber on its broad summit. On this was strung an immense number of human skulls, which belonged to the victims, mostly prisoners of war, who had perished on the accursed stone of sacrifice. One of the soldiers had the patience to count the number of these ghastly trophies, and reported it to be one hundred and thirty-six thousand! Belief might well be staggered, did not the Old World present a worthy counterpart in the pyramidal Golgothas which commemorated the triumphs of Tamerlane.

There were long ranges of buildings in the inclosure, appropriated as the residence of the priests and others engaged in the offices of religion. The whole number of them was said to amount to several thousand. Here were, also, the principal seminaries for the instruction of youth of both sexes, drawn chiefly from the higher and wealthier classes. The girls were taught by elderly women, who officiated as priestesses in the temples, a custom familiar also to Egypt. The Spaniards admit that the greatest care for morals, and the most blameless deportment, were maintained in these institutions. The time of the pupils was chiefly occupied, as in most monastic establishments, with the minute and burdensome ceremonial of their religion. The boys were likewise taught such elements of science as were known to their teachers, and the girls initiated in the mysteries of embroidery and weaving, which they employed in decorating the temples. At a suitable age they generally went forth into the world to assume the occupations fitted to their condition, though some remained permanently devoted to the services of religion.

The spot was also covered by edifices of a still different character. There were granaries filled with the rich produce of the churchlands, and with the first-fruits and other offerings of the faithful. One large mansion was reserved for strangers of eminence, who were on a pilgrimage to the great teocalli. The inclosure was ornamented with gardens, shaded by ancient trees, and watered by fountains and reservoirs from the copious streams of Chapoltepec. The little community was thus provided with almost everything requisite for its own maintenance and the services of the temple.

It was a microcosm of itself — a city within a city; and, according to the assertion of Cortes, embraced a tract of ground large enough for five hundred houses. It presented in this brief compass the extremes of barbarism, blended with a certain civilisation, altogether characteristic of the Aztecs. The rude Conquerors saw only the evidence of the former. In the fantastic and symbolical features of the deities, they beheld the literal lineaments of Satan; in the rites and frivolous ceremonial, his own especial code of damnation; and in the modest deportment and careful nurture of the inmates of the seminaries, the snares by which he was to beguile his deluded victims. Before a century had elapsed, the descendants of these same Spaniards discerned in the mysteries of the Aztec religion the features, obscured and defaced, indeed, of the Jewish and Christian revelations! Such were the opposite conclusions of the unlettered soldier and of the scholar. A philosopher, untouched by superstition, might well doubt which of the two was the most extraordinary.

The sight of the Indian abominations seems to have kindled in the Spaniards a livelier feeling for their own religion; since, on the following day, they asked leave of Montezuma to convert one of the halls in their residence into a chapel, that they might celebrate the services of the Church there. The monarch, in whose bosom the feelings of resentment seem to have soon subsided, easily granted their request, and sent some of his own artisans to aid them in the work.

While it was in progress, some of the Spaniards observed what appeared to be a door recently plastered over. It was a common rumour that Montezuma still kept the treasures of his father, King Axayacatl, in this ancient palace. The Spaniards, acquainted with this fact, felt no scruple in gratifying their curiosity by removing the plaster. As was anticipated, it concealed a door. On forcing this, they found the rumour was no exaggeration. They beheld a large hall filled with rich and beautiful stuffs, articles of curious workmanship of various kinds, gold and silver in bars and in the ore, and many jewels of value. It was the private hoard of Montezuma, the contributions, it may be, of tributary cities, and once the property of his father. "I was a young man," says Diaz, who was one of those that obtained a sight of it, "and it seemed to me as if all the riches of the world were in that room!" The Spaniards, notwithstanding their elation at the discovery of this precious deposit, seem to have felt some commendable scruples as to appropriating it to their own use — at least for the present. And Cortes, after closing up the wall as it was before, gave strict injunctions that nothing should be said of the matter, unwilling that the knowledge of its existence by his guests should reach the ears of Montezuma.

Three days sufficed to complete the chapel; and the Christians had the satisfaction to see themselves in possession of a temple where they might worship God in their own way, under the protection of the Cross, and the blessed Virgin. Mass was regularly performed by the fathers, Olmedo and Diaz, in the presence of the assembled army, who were most earnest and exemplary in their devotions, partly, says the chronicler above quoted, from the propriety of the thing, and partly for its edifying influence on the benighted heathen.

THE Spaniards had been now a week in Mexico. During this time, they had experienced the most friendly treatment from the emperor. But the mind of Cortes was far from easy. He felt that it was quite uncertain how long this amiable temper would last. A hundred circumstances might occur to change it. He might very naturally feel the maintenance of so large a body too burdensome on his treasury. The people of the capital might become dissatisfied at the presence of so numerous an armed force within their walls. Many causes of disgust might arise betwixt the soldiers and the citizens. Indeed, it was scarcely possible that a rude, licentious soldiery, like the Spaniards, could be long kept in subjection without active employment. The danger was even greater with the Tlascalans, a fierce race now brought into daily contact with the nation who held them in loathing and detestation. Rumours were already rife among the allies, whether well-founded or not, of murmurs among the Mexicans, accompanied by menaces of raising the bridges.

Even should the Spaniards be allowed to occupy their present quarters unmolested, it was not advancing the great object of the expedition. Cortes was not a whit nearer gaining the capital, so essential to his meditated subjugation of the country; and any day he might receive tidings that the Crown, or, what he most feared, the governor of Cuba, had sent a force of superior strength to wrest from him a conquest but half achieved. Disturbed by these anxious reflections, he resolved to extricate himself from his embarrassment by one bold stroke. But he first submitted the affair to a council of the officers in whom he most confided, desirous to divide with them the responsibility of the act, and no doubt, to interest them more heartily in its execution, by making it in some measure the result of their combined judgments.

When the general had briefly stated the embarrassments of their position, the council was divided in opinion. All admitted the necessity of some instant action. One party were for retiring secretly from the city, and getting beyond the causeways before their march could be intercepted. Another advised that it should be done openly, with the knowledge of the emperor, of whose good will they had had so many proofs. But both these measures seemed alike impolitic. A retreat under these circumstances, and so abruptly made, would have the air of a flight. It would be construed into distrust of themselves; and anything like timidity on their part would be sure not only to bring on them the Mexicans, but the contempt of their allies, who would, doubtless, join in the general cry.

As to Montezuma, what reliance could they place on the protection of a prince so recently their enemy, and who, in his altered bearing, must have taken counsel of his fears rather than his inclinations?

Even should they succeed in reaching the coast, their situation would be little better. It would be proclaiming to the world that, after all their lofty vaunts, they were unequal to the enterprise. Their only hopes of their sovereign's favour, and of pardon for their irregular proceedings, were founded on success. Hitherto, they had only made the discovery of Mexico; to retreat would be to leave conquest and the fruits of it to another. — In short, to stay and to retreat seemed equally disastrous.

In this perplexity, Cortes proposed an expedient, which none but the most daring spirit, in the most desperate extremity, would have conceived. This was, to march to the royal palace, and bring Montezuma to the Spanish quarters, by fair means if they could persuade him, by force if necessary — at all events, to get possession of his person. With such a pledge, the Spaniards would be secure from the assault of the Mexicans, afraid by acts of violence to compromise the safety of their prince. If he came by his own consent, they would be deprived of all apology for doing so. As long as the emperor remained among the Spaniards, it would be easy, by allowing him a show of sovereignty, to rule in his name, until they had taken measures for securing their safety, and the success of their enterprise. The idea of employing a sovereign as a tool for the government of his own kingdom, if a new one in the age of Cortes, is certainly not so in ours.

A plausible pretext for the seizure of the hospitable monarch — for the most barefaced action seeks to veil itself under some show of decency — was afforded by a circumstance of which Cortes had received intelligence at Cholula. He had left, as we have seen, a faithful officer, Juan de Escalante, with a hundred and fifty men in garrison at Vera Cruz, on his departure for the capital. He had not been long absent, when his lieutenant received a message from an Aztec chief named Quauhpopoca, governor of a district to the north of the Spanish settlement, declaring his desire to come in person and tender his allegiance to the Spanish authorities at Vera Cruz. He requested that four of the white men might be sent to protect him against certain unfriendly tribes through which his road lay. This was not an uncommon request, and excited no suspicion in Escalante. The four soldiers were sent; and on their arrival two of them were murdered by the false Aztec. The other two made their way back to the garrison.

The commander marched at once, with fifty of his men, and several thousand Indian allies, to take vengeance on the cacique. A pitched battle followed. The allies fled from the redoubted Mexicans. The few Spaniards stood firm, and with the aid of the firearms and the blessed Virgin, who was distinctly seen hovering over their ranks in the van, they made good the field against the enemy. It cost them dear, however, since seven or eight Christians were slain, and among them the gallant Escalante himself, who died of his injuries soon after his return to the fort. The Indian prisoners captured in the battle spoke of the whole proceeding as having taken place at the instigation of Montezuma.

One of the Spaniards fell into the hands of the natives, but soon after perished of his wounds. His head was cut off and sent to the Aztec emperor. It was uncommonly large and covered with hair; and, as Montezuma gazed on the ferocious features, rendered more horrible by death, he seemed to read in them the dark lineaments of the destined destroyers of his house. He turned from it with a shudder, and commanded that it should be taken from the city, and not offered at the shrine of any of his gods.

Although Cortes had received intelligence of this disaster at Cholula, he had concealed it within his own breast, or communicated it to very few only of his most trusty officers, from apprehension of the ill effect it might have on the spirits of the common soldiers.

The cavaliers whom Cortes now summoned to the council were men of the same mettle with their leader. Their bold chivalrous spirit seemed to court danger for its own sake. If one or two, less adventurous, were startled by the proposal he made, they were soon overruled by the others, who, no doubt, considered that a desperate disease required as desperate a remedy.

That night, Cortes was heard pacing his apartment to and fro, like a man oppressed by thought, or agitated by strong emotion. He may have been ripening in his mind the daring scheme for the morrow. In the morning the soldiers heard mass as usual, and Father Olmedo invoked the blessing of Heaven on their hazardous enterprise. Whatever might be the cause in which he was embarked, the heart of the Spaniard was cheered with the conviction that the Saints were on his side.

Having asked an audience from Montezuma, which was readily granted, the general made the necessary arrangements for his enterprise. The principal part of his force was drawn up in the courtyard, and he stationed a considerable detachment in the avenues leading to the palace, to cheek any attempt at rescue by the populace. He ordered twenty-five or thirty of the soldiers to drop in at the palace, as if by accident, in groups of three or four at a time, while the conference was going on with Montezuma. He selected five cavaliers, in whose courage and coolness he placed most trust, to bear him company; Pedro de Alvarado, Gonzalo de Sandoval, Francisco de Lugo, Velasquez de Leon, and Alonso de Avila — brilliant names in the annals of the Conquest. All were clad, as well as the common soldiers, in complete armour, a circumstance of too familiar occurrence to excite suspicion.

The little party were graciously received by the emperor, who soon, with the aid of the interpreters, became interested in a sportive conversation with the Spaniards, while he indulged his natural munificence by giving them presents of gold and jewels. He paid the Spanish general the particular compliment of offering him one of his daughters as his wife; an honour which the latter respectfully declined, on the ground that he was already accommodated with one in Cuba, and that his religion forbade a plurality.

When Cortes perceived that a sufficient number of his soldiers were assembled, he changed his playful manner, and with a serious tone briefly acquainted Montezuma with the treacherous proceedings in the tierra caliente, and the accusation of him as their author. The emperor listened to the charge with surprise; and disavowed the act, which he said could only have been imputed to him by his enemies. Cortes expressed his belief in his declaration, but added, that, to prove it true, it would be necessary to send for Quauhpopoca and his accomplices, that they might be examined and dealt with according to their deserts. To this Montezuma made no objection. Taking from his wrist, to which it was attached, a precious stone, the royal signet, on which was cut the figure of the war-god, he gave it to one of his nobles, with orders to show it to the Aztec governor, and require his instant presence in the capital, together with all those who had been accessory to the murder of the Spaniards. If he resisted, the officer was empowered to call in the aid of the neighbouring towns to enforce the mandate.

When the messenger had gone, Cortes assured the monarch that this prompt compliance with his request convinced him of his innocence. But it was important that his own sovereign should be equally convinced of it. Nothing would promote this so much as for Montezuma to transfer his residence to the palace occupied by the Spaniards, till on the arrival of Quauhpopoca the affair could be fully investigated. Such an act of condescension would, of itself, show a personal regard for the Spaniards, incompatible with the base conduct alleged against him, and would fully absolve him from all suspicion!

Montezuma listened to this proposal, and the flimsy reasoning with which it was covered, with looks of profound amazement. He became pale as death; but in a moment his face flushed with resentment, as with the pride of offended dignity, he exclaimed, "Men was it ever heard that a great prince, like myself, voluntarily left his own palace to become a prisoner in the hands of strangers!"

Cortes assured him he would not go as a prisoner. He would experience nothing but respectful treatment from the Spaniards; would be surrounded by his own household, and hold intercourse with his people as usual. In short, it would be but a change of residence, from one of his palaces to another, a circumstance of frequent occurrence with him. — It was in vain. "If I should consent to such a degradation," he answered, "my subjects never would!" When further pressed, he offered to give up one of his sons and of his daughters to remain as hostages with the Spaniards, so that he might be spared this disgrace.

Two hours passed in this fruitless discussion, till a high-mettled cavalier, Velasquez de Leon, impatient of the long delay, and seeing that the attempt, if not the deed, must ruin them, cried out, "Why do we waste words on this barbarian? We have gone too far to recede now. Let us seize him, and, if he resists, plunge our swords into his body!" The fierce tone and menacing gestures with which this was uttered alarmed the monarch, who inquired of Marina what the angry Spaniard said. The interpreter explained it in as gentle a manner as she could, beseeching him "to accompany the white men to their quarters, where he would be treated with all respect and kindness, while to refuse them would but expose himself to violence, perhaps to death." Marina, doubtless, spoke to her sovereign as she thought, and no one had better opportunity of knowing the truth than herself.

This last appeal shook the resolution of Montezuma. It was in vain that the unhappy prince looked around for sympathy or support. As his eyes wandered over the stern visages and iron forms of the Spaniards, he felt that his hour was indeed come; and, with a voice scarcely audible from emotion, he consented to accompany the strangers — to quit the palace, whither he was never more to return. Had he possessed the spirit of the first Montezuma, he would have called his guards around him, and left his life-blood on the threshold, sooner than have been dragged a dishonoured captive across it. But his courage sank under circumstances. He felt he was the instrument of an irresistible Fate!

No sooner had the Spaniards got his consent, than orders were given for the royal litter. The nobles, who bore and attended it, could scarcely believe their senses, when they learned their master's purpose. But pride now came to Montezuma's aid, and, since he must go, he

159

preferred that it should appear to be with his own free-will. As the royal retinue, escorted by the Spaniards, marched through the street with downcast eyes and dejected mien, the people assembled in crowds, and a rumour ran among them, that the emperor was carried off by force to the quarters of the white men. A tumult would have soon arisen but for the intervention of Montezuma himself, who called out to the people to disperse, as he was visiting his friends of his own accord; thus sealing his ignominy by a declaration which deprived his subjects of the only excuse for resistance. On reaching the quarters, he sent out his nobles with similar assurances to the mob, and renewed orders to return to their homes.

He was received with ostentatious respect by the Spaniards, and selected the suite of apartments which best pleased him. They were soon furnished with fine cotton tapestries, feather-work, and all the elegances of Indian upholstery. He was attended by such of his household as he chose, his wives and his pages, and was served with his usual pomp and luxury at his meals. He gave audience, as in his own palace, to his subjects, who were admitted to his presence, few, indeed, at a time, under the pretext of greater order and decorum. From the Spaniards themselves he met with a formal deference. No one, not even the general himself, approached him without doffing his casque, and rendering the obeisance due to his rank. Nor did they ever sit in his presence, without being invited by him to do so.

With all this studied ceremony and show of homage, there was one circumstance which too clearly proclaimed to his people that their sovereign was a prisoner. In the front of the palace a patrol of sixty men was established, and the same number in the rear. Twenty of each corps mounted guard at once, maintaining a careful watch day and night. Another body, under command of Velasquez de Leon, was stationed in the royal antechamber. Cortes punished any departure from duty, or relaxation of vigilance, in these sentinels, with the utmost severity. He felt, as, indeed, every Spaniard must have felt, that the escape of the emperor now would be their ruin. Yet the task of this unintermitting watch sorely added to their fatigues. "Better this dog of a king should die," cried a soldier one day, "than that we should wear out our lives in this manner." The words were uttered in the hearing of Montezuma, who gathered something of their import, and the offender was severely chastised by order of the general. Such instances of disrespect, however, were very rare. Indeed, the amiable deportment of the monarch, who seemed to take pleasure in the society of his jailers, and who never allowed a favour or attention from the meanest soldier to go unrequited, inspired the Spaniards with as much attachment as they were capable of feeling — for a barbarian.

Things were in this posture, when the arrival of Quauhpopoca from the coast was announced. He was accompanied by his son and fifteen Aztec chiefs. He had travelled all the way, borne, as became his high rank, in a litter. On entering Montezuma's presence, he threw over his dress the coarse robe of nequen, and made the usual humiliating acts of obeisance. The poor parade of courtly ceremony was the more striking when placed in contrast with the actual condition of the parties.

The Aztec governor was coldly received by his master, who referred the affair (had he the power to do otherwise?) to the examination of Cortes. It was, doubtless, conducted in a sufficiently summary manner. To the general's query, whether the cacique was the subject of Montezuma, he replied, "And what other sovereign could I serve?" Implying that his sway was universal. He did not deny his share in the transaction, nor did he seek to shelter himself under the royal authority, till sentence of death was passed on him and his followers, when they all laid the blame of their proceedings on Montezuma. They were condemned to be burnt alive in the area before the palace. The funeral piles were made of heaps of arrows, javelins, and other weapons, drawn by the emperor's permission from the arsenals round the great teocalli, where they had been stored to supply means of defence in times of civic tumult or insurrection. By this politic precaution, Cortes proposed to remove a ready means of annoyance in case of hostilities with the citizens.

To crown the whole of these extraordinary proceedings, Cortes, while preparations for the execution were going on, entered the emperor's apartment, attended by a soldier bearing fetters in his hands. With a severe aspect, he charged the monarch with being the original contriver of the violence offered to the Spaniards, as was now proved by the declaration of his own instruments. Such a crime, which merited death in a subject, could not be atoned for, even by a sovereign, without some punishment. So saying, he ordered the soldier to fasten the fetters on Montezuma's ankles. He coolly waited till it was done; then, turning his back on the monarch, quitted the room.

Montezuma was speechless under the infliction of this last insult. He was like one struck down by a heavy blow, that deprives him of all his faculties. He offered no resistance. But, though he spoke not a word, low, ill-suppressed moans, from time to time, intimated the anguish of his spirit. His attendants, bathed in tears, offered him their consolations. They tenderly held his feet in their arms, and endeavoured, by inserting their shawls and mantles, to relieve them from the pressure of the iron. But they could not reach the iron which had penetrated into his soul. He felt that he was no more a king.

Meanwhile, the execution of the dreadful doom was going forward in the courtyard. The whole Spanish force was under arms, to check any interruption that might be offered by the Mexicans. But none was attempted. The populace gazed in silent wonder, regarding it as the sentence of the emperor. The manner of the execution, too, excited less surprise, from their familiarity with similar spectacles, aggravated, indeed, by additional horrors, in their own diabolical sacrifices. The Aztec lord and his companions, bound hand and foot to the blazing piles, submitted without a cry or a complaint to their terrible fate. Passive fortitude is the virtue of the Indian warriors; and it was the glory of the Aztec, as of the other races on the North American continent, to show how the spirit of the brave man may triumph over torture and the agonies of death.

When the dismal tragedy was ended, Cortes re-entered Montezuma's apartment. Kneeling down, he unclasped his shackles with his own hand, expressing at the same time his regret that so disagreeable a duty as that of subjecting him to such a punishment had been imposed on him. This last indignity had entirely crushed the spirit of Montezuma; and the monarch, whose frown, but a week since, would have made the nations of Anahuac tremble to their remotest borders, was now craven enough to thank his deliverer for his freedom, as for a great and unmerited boon!

Not long after, the Spanish general, conceiving that his royal captive was sufficiently humbled, expressed his willingness that he should return, if he inclined, to his own palace. Montezuma declined it; alleging, it is said, that his nobles had more than once importuned him to resent his injuries by taking arms against the Spaniards; and that, were he in the midst of them, it would be difficult to avoid it, or to save his capital from bloodshed and anarchy. The reason did honour to his heart, if it was the one which influenced him. It is probable that he did not care to trust his safety to those haughty and ferocious chieftains who had witnessed the degradation of their master, and must despise his pusillanimity, as a thing unprecedented in an Aztec monarch.

Whatever were his reasons, it is certain that he declined the offer; and the general, in a well-feigned, or real ecstasy, embraced him, declaring "that he loved him as a brother, and that every Spaniard would be zealously devoted to his interests, since he had shown himself so mindful of theirs!" Honeyed words, "which," says the shrewd old chronicler who was present, "Montezuma was wise enough to know the worth of."

The events recorded in this chapter are certainly some of the most extraordinary on the page of history. That a small body of men, like the Spaniards, should have entered the palace of a mighty prince, have seized his person in the midst of his vassals, have borne him off a captive to their quarters — that they should have put to an ignominious death before his face his high officers, for executing probably his own commands, and have crowned the whole by putting the monarch in irons like a common malefactor — that this should have been done, not to a drivelling dotard in the decay of his fortunes, but to a proud monarch in the plenitude of his power, in the very heart of his capital, surrounded by thousands and tens of thousands who trembled at his nod, and would have poured out their blood like water in his defence — that all this should have been done by a mere handful of adventurers, is a thing too extravagant, altogether too improbable, for the pages of romance! It is, nevertheless, literally true.

THE settlement of La Villa Rica de Vera Cruz was of the last importance to the Spaniards. It was the port by which they were to communicate with Spain; the strong post on which they were to retreat in case of disaster, and which was to bridle their enemies and give security to their allies; the point d'appui for all their operations in the country. It was of great moment, therefore, that the care of it should be intrusted to proper hands.

A cavalier, named Alonso de Grado, had been sent by Cortes to take the place made vacant by the death of Escalante. He was a person of greater repute in civil than military matters, and would be more likely, it was thought, to maintain peaceful relations with the natives, than a person of more belligerant spirit. Cortes made — what was rare with him — a bad choice. He soon received such accounts of troubles in the settlement from the exactions and negligence of the new governor, that he resolved to supersede him.

He now gave the command to Gonzalo de Sandoval, a young cavalier, who had displayed through the whole campaign singular intrepidity united with sagacity and discretion, while the good humour with which he bore every privation, and his affable manners, made him a favourite with all, privates as well as officers. Sandoval accordingly left the camp for the coast. Cortes did not mistake his man a second time.

Notwithstanding the actual control exercised by the Spaniards through their royal captive, Cortes felt some uneasiness, when he reflected that it was in the power of the Indians, at any time, to cut off his communications with the surrounding country, and hold him a prisoner in the capital. He proposed, therefore, to build two vessels of sufficient size to transport his forces across the lake, and thus to render himself independent of the causeways. Montezuma was pleased with the idea of seeing those wonderful "water-houses," of which he had heard so much, and readily gave permission to have the timber in the royal forests felled for the purpose. The work was placed under the direction of Martin Lopez, an experienced ship-builder. Orders were also given to Sandoval to send up from the coast a supply of cordage, sails, iron, and other necessary materials, which had been judiciously saved on the destruction of the fleet.

The Aztec emperor, meanwhile, was passing his days in the Spanish quarters in no very different manner from what he had been accustomed to in his own palace. His keepers were too well aware of the value of their prize, not to do everything which could make his captivity comfortable, and disguise it from himself. But the chain will gall, though wreathed with roses. After Montezuma's breakfast, which was a light meal of fruits or vegetables, Cortes or some of his officers usually waited on him, to learn if he had any commands for them. He then devoted some time to business. He gave audience to those of his subjects who had petitions to prefer, or suits to settle. The statement of the party was drawn up on the hieroglyphic scrolls, which were submitted to a number of counsellors or judges, who assisted him with their advice on these occasions. Envoys from foreign states or his own remote provinces and cities were also admitted, and the Spaniards were careful that the same precise and punctilious etiquette should be maintained towards the royal puppet, as when in the plenitude of his authority.

After business was despatched, Montezuma often amused himself with seeing the Castilian troops go through their military exercises. He, too, had been a soldier, and in his prouder days led armies in the field. It was very natural he should take an interest in the novel display of European tactics and discipline. At other times he would challenge Cortes or his officers to play at some of the national games. A favourite one was called totoloque, played with golden balls aimed at a target or mark of the same metal. Montezuma usually staked something of value — precious stones or ingots of gold. He lost with good humour; indeed it was of little consequence whether he won or lost, since he generally gave away his winnings to his attendants. He had, in truth, a most munificent spirit. His enemies accused him of avarice. But, if he were avaricious, it could have been only that he might have the more to give away.

Each of the Spaniards had several Mexicans, male and female, who attended to his cooking and various other personal offices. Cortes, considering that the maintenance of this host of menials was a heavy tax on the royal exchequer, ordered them to be dismissed, excepting one to be retained for each soldier. Montezuma, on learning this, pleasantly remonstrated with the general on his careful economy, as unbecoming a royal establishment and, countermanding the order, caused additional accommodations to be provided for the attendants, and their pay to be doubled.

On another occasion, a soldier purloined some trinkets of gold from the treasure kept in the chamber, which, since Montezuma's arrival in the Spanish quarters, had been re-opened. Cortes would have punished the man for the theft, but the emperor interfering said to him, "Your countrymen are welcome to the gold and other articles, if you will but spare those belonging to the gods." Some of the soldiers, making the most of his permission, carried off several hundred loads of fine cotton to their quarters. When this was represented to Montezuma, he only replied, "What I have once given I never take back again."

While thus indifferent to his treasures, he was keenly sensitive to personal slight or insult. When a common soldier once spoke to him angrily, the tears came into the monarch's eyes, as it made him feel the true character of his impotent condition. Cortes, on becoming acquainted with it, was so much incensed, that he ordered the soldier to be hanged; but, on Montezuma's intercession, commuted this severe sentence for a flogging. The general was not willing that any one but himself should treat his royal captive with indignity. Montezuma was desired to procure a further mitigation of the punishment. But he refused, saying, "that, if a similar insult had been offered by any one of his subjects to Malinche, he would have resented it in like manner."

Such instances of disrespect were very rare. Montezuma's amiable and inoffensive manners, together with his liberality, the most popular of virtues with the vulgar, made him generally beloved by the Spaniards. The arrogance, for which he had been so distinguished in his prosperous days, deserted him in his fallen fortunes. His character in captivity seems to have undergone something of that change which takes place in the wild animals of the forest, when caged within the walls of the menagerie.

The Indian monarch knew the name of every man in the army, and was careful to discriminate his proper rank. For some he showed a strong partiality. He obtained from the general a favourite page, named Orteguilla, who, being in constant attendance on his person, soon learned enough of the Mexican language to be of use to his countrymen. Montezuma took great pleasure, also, in the society of Velasquez de Leon, the captain of his guard, and Pedro de Alvarado, Tonatiuh, or "the Sun," as he was called by the Aztecs, from his yellow hair and sunny countenance. The sunshine, as events afterwards showed, could sometimes be the prelude to a terrible tempest.

Notwithstanding the care taken to cheat him of the tedium of captivity, the royal prisoner cast a wistful glance now and then beyond the walls of his residence to the ancient haunts of business or pleasure. He intimated a desire to offer up his devotions at the great temple, where he was once so constant in his worship. The suggestion startled Cortes. It was too reasonable, however, for him to object to it, without wholly discarding the appearance which he was desirous to maintain. But he secured Montezuma's return by sending an escort with him of a hundred and fifty soldiers under the same resolute cavaliers who had aided in his seizure. He told him also, that, in case of any attempt to escape, his life would instantly pay the forfeit. Thus guarded, the Indian prince visited the teocalli, where he was received with the usual state, and, after performing his devotions, he returned again to his quarters.

It may well be believed that the Spaniards did not neglect the opportunity afforded by his residence with them, of instilling into him some notions of the Christian doctrine. Fathers Diaz and Olmedo exhausted all their battery of logic and persuasion to shake his faith in his idols, but in vain. He, indeed, paid a most edifying attention, which gave promise of better things. But the conferences always closed with the declaration, that "the God of the Christians was good, but the gods of his own country were the true gods for him." It is said, however, they extorted a promise from him, that he would take part in no more human sacrifices. Yet such sacrifices were of daily occurrence in the great temples of the capital; and the people were too blindly attached to their bloody abominations for the Spaniards to deem it safe, for the present at least, openly to interfere.

Montezuma showed, also, an inclination to engage in the pleasures of the chase, of which he once was immoderately fond. He had large forests reserved for the purpose on the other side of the lake. As the Spanish brigantines were now completed, Cortes proposed to transport him and his suite across the water in them. They were of a good size, strongly built. The largest was mounted with four falconets, or small guns. It was protected by a gaily-coloured awning stretched over the deck, and the royal ensign of Castile floated proudly from the mast. On board of this vessel, Montezuma, delighted with the opportunity of witnessing the nautical skill of the white men, embarked with a train of Aztec nobles and a numerous guard of Spaniards. A fresh breeze played on the waters, and the vessel soon left behind it the swarms of light pirogues which darkened their surface. She seemed like a thing of life in the eyes of the astonished natives, who saw her, as if disdaining human agency, sweeping by with snowy pinions as if on the wings of the wind, while the thunders from her sides now for the first time breaking on the silence of this "inland sea," showed that the beautiful phantom was clothed in terror.

The royal chase was well stocked with game; some of which the emperor shot with arrows, and others were driven by the numerous attendants into nets. In these woodland exercises, while he ranged over his wild domain, Montezuma seemed to enjoy again the sweets of liberty. It was but the shadow of liberty, however; as in his quarters, at home, he enjoyed but the shadow of royalty. At home or abroad, the eye of the Spaniard was always upon him.

But while he resigned himself without a struggle to his inglorious fate, there were others who looked on it with very different emotions. Among them was his nephew Cacama, lord of Tezcuco, a young man not more than twenty-five years of age, but who enjoyed great consideration from his high personal qualities, especially his intrepidity of character. He was the same prince who had been sent by Montezuma to welcome the Spaniards on their entrance into the valley; and, when the question of their reception was first debated in the council, had advised to admit them honourably as ambassadors of a foreign prince, and, if they should prove different from what they pretended, it would be time enough then to take up arms against them. That time, he thought, had now come.

In a former part of this work, the reader has been made acquainted with the ancient history of the Acolhuan or Tezcucan monarchy, once the proud rival of the Aztec in power, and greatly its superior in civilisation. Under its last sovereign, Nezahualpilli, its territory is said to have been grievously clipped by the insidious practices of Montezuma, who fomented dissensions and insubordination among his subjects. On the death of the Tezcucan prince, the succession was contested, and a bloody war ensued between his eldest son, Cacama, and an ambitious younger brother, Ixtlilxochitl. This was followed by a partition of the kingdom, in which the latter chieftain held the mountain districts north of the capital, leaving the residue to Cacama. Though shorn of a large part of his hereditary domain, the city was itself so important, that the lord of Tezcuco still held a high rank among the petty princes of the valley. His capital, at the time of the Conquest, contained, according to Cortes, a hundred and fifty thousand inhabitants. It was embellished with noble buildings, rivalling those of Mexico itself.

The young Tezcucan chief beheld, with indignation and no slight contempt, the abject condition of his uncle. He endeavoured to rouse him to manly exertion, but in vain. He then set about forming a league with several of the neighbouring caciques to rescue his kinsman, and to break the detested yoke of the strangers. He called on the lord of Iztapalapan, Montezuma's brother, the lord of Tlacopan, and some others of most authority, all of whom entered heartily into his views. He then urged the Aztec nobles to join them, but they expressed an unwillingness to take any step not first sanctioned by the emperor. They entertained, undoubtedly, a profound reverence for their master; but it seems probable that jealousy of the personal views of Cacama had its influence on their determination. Whatever were their motives, it is certain, that, by this refusal, they relinquished the best opportunity ever presented for retrieving their sovereign's independence, and their own.

These intrigues could not be conducted so secretly as not to reach the ears of Cortes, who, with his characteristic promptness, would have marched at once on Tezcuco, and trodden out the spark of "rebellion," before it had time to burst into a flame. But from this he was dissuaded by Montezuma, who represented that Cacama was a man of resolution, backed by a powerful force, and not to be put down without a desperate struggle. He consented, therefore, to negotiate, and sent a message of amicable expostulation to the cacique. He received a haughty answer in return. Cortes rejoined in a more menacing tone, asserting the supremacy of his own sovereign, the emperor of Castile. To this Cacama replied, "He acknowledged no such authority; he knew nothing of the Spanish sovereign nor his people, nor did he wish to know anything of them." Montezuma was not more successful in his application to Cacama to come to Mexico, and allow him to mediate his differences with the Spaniards, with whom he assured the prince he was residing as a friend. But the young lord of Tezcuco was not to be so duped. He understood the position of his uncle, and replied, "that, when he did visit his capital, it would be to rescue it, as well as the emperor himself, and their common gods, from bondage. He should come, not with his hand in his bosom, but on his sword — to drive out the detested strangers who had brought such dishonour on their country."

Cortes, incensed at this tone of defiance, would again have put himself in motion to punish it, but Montezuma interposed with his more politic arts. He had several of the Tezcucan nobles, he said, in his pay; and it would be easy, through their means, to secure Cacama's person, and thus break up the confederacy at once, without bloodshed. The maintaining of corps of stipendiaries in the courts of neighbouring princes was a refinement which showed that the western barbarian understood the science of political intrigue, as well as some of his royal brethren on the other side of the water.

By the contrivance of these faithless nobles, Cacama was induced to hold a conference, relative to the proposed invasion, in a villa which overhung the Tezcucan lake, not far from his capital. Like most of the principal edifices, it was raised so as to admit the entrance of boats beneath it. In the midst of the conference, Cacama was seized by the conspirators, hurried on board a bark in readiness for the purpose, and transported to Mexico. When brought into Montezuma's presence, the high-spirited chief abated nothing of his proud and lofty bearing. He taxed his uncle with his perfidy, and a pusillanimity so unworthy of his former character, and of the royal house from which he was descended. By the emperor he was referred to Cortes, who, holding royalty but cheap in an Indian prince, put him in fetters.

THE TEMPLE OF THE SUN

There was at this time in Mexico a brother of Cacama, a stripling much younger than himself. At the instigation of Cortes, Montezuma, pretending that his nephew had forfeited the sovereignty by his late rebellion, declared him to be deposed, and appointed Cuicuitzca in his place. The Aztec sovereigns had always been allowed a paramount authority in questions relating to the succession. But this was a most unwarrantable exercise of it. The Tezcucans acquiesced, however, with a ready ductility, which showed their allegiance hung but lightly on them, or, what is more probable, that they were greatly in awe of the Spaniards; and the new prince was welcomed with acclamations to his capital.

Cortes still wanted to get into his hands the other chiefs who had entered into the confederacy with Cacama. This was no difficult matter. Montezuma's authority was absolute, everywhere but in his own palace. By his command, the caciques were seized, each in his own

167

city, and brought in chains to Mexico, where Cortes placed them in strict confinement with their leader.

He had now triumphed over all his enemies. He had set his foot on the necks of princes; and the great chief of the Aztec empire was but a convenient tool in his hands for accomplishing his purposes. His first use of this power was to ascertain the actual resources of the monarchy. He sent several parties of Spaniards, guided by the natives, to explore the regions where gold was obtained. It was gleaned mostly from the beds of rivers, several hundred miles from the capital.

His next object was to learn if there existed any good natural harbour for shipping on the Atlantic coast, as the road of Vera Cruz left no protection against the tempests that at certain seasons swept over these seas. Montezuma showed him a chart on which the shores of the Mexican Gulf were laid down with tolerable accuracy. Cortes, after carefully inspecting it, sent a commission, consisting of ten Spaniards, several of them pilots, and some Aztecs, who descended to Vera Cruz, and made a careful survey of the coast for nearly sixty leagues south of that settlement, as far as the great river Coatzacualco, which seemed to offer the best, indeed the only, accommodations for a safe and suitable harbour. A spot was selected as the site of a fortified post, and the general sent a detachment of a hundred and fifty men, under Velasquez de Leon, to plant a colony there.

He also obtained a grant of an extensive tract of land in the fruitful province of Oaxaca, where he proposed to lay out a plantation for the Crown. He stocked it with the different kinds of domesticated animals peculiar to the country, and with such indigenous grains and plants as would afford the best articles for export. He soon had the estate under such cultivation, that he assured his master, the emperor, Charles the Fifth, it was worth twenty thousand ounces of gold.

CORTES now felt his authority sufficiently assured to demand from Montezuma a formal recognition of the supremacy of the Spanish emperor. The Indian monarch had intimated his willingness to acquiesce in this, on their very first interview. He did not object, therefore, to call together his principal caciques for the purpose. When they were assembled, he made them an address, briefly stating the object of the meeting. They were all acquainted, he said, with the ancient tradition, that the great Being, who had once ruled over the land, had declared, on his departure, that he should return at some future time and resume his sway. That time had now arrived. The white men had come from the quarter where the sun rises, beyond the ocean, to which the good deity had withdrawn. They were sent by their master to reclaim the obedience of his ancient subjects. For himself he was ready to acknowledge his authority. "You have been faithful vassals of mine," continued Montezuma, "during the many years that I have sat on the throne of my fathers. I now expect that you will show me this last act of obedience by acknowledging the great king beyond the waters to be your lord, also, and that you will pay him tribute in the same manner as you have hitherto done to me." As he concluded, his voice was stifled by his emotion, and the tears fell fast down his cheeks.

His nobles, many of whom, coming from a distance, had not kept pace with the changes which had been going on in the capital, were filled with astonishment as they listened to his words, and beheld the voluntary abasement of their master, whom they had hitherto reverenced as the omnipotent lord of Anahuac. They were the more affected, therefore, by the sight of his distress. His will, they told him, had always been their law. It should be now; and, if he thought the sovereign of the strangers was the ancient lord of their country, they were willing to acknowledge him as such still. The oaths of allegiance were then administered with all due solemnity, attested by the Spaniards present, and a full record of the proceedings was drawn up by the royal notary, to be sent to Spain. There was something deeply touching in the ceremony by which an independent and absolute monarch, in obedience less to the dictates of fear than of conscience, thus relinquished his hereditary rights in favour of an unknown and mysterious power. It even moved those hard men who were thus unscrupulously availing themselves of the confiding ignorance of the natives; and, though "it was in the regular way of their own business," says an old chronicler, "there was not a Spaniard who could look on the spectacle with a dry eye!"

The rumour of these strange proceedings was soon circulated through the capital and the country. Men read in them the finger of Providence. The ancient tradition of Quetzalcoatl was familiar to all; and where it had slept scarcely noticed in the memory, it was now revived with many exaggerated circumstances. It was said to be part of the tradition, that the royal line of the Aztecs was to end with Montezuma; and his name, the literal signification of which is "sad" or "angry lord," was construed into an omen of his evil destiny.

Having thus secured this great feudatory to the crown of Castile, Cortes suggested that it would be well for the Aztec chiefs to send his sovereign such a gratuity as would conciliate his good will by convincing him of the loyalty of his new vassals. Montezuma consented that his collectors should visit the principal cities and provinces, attended by a number of Spaniards, to receive the customary tributes, in the name of the Castilian sovereign. In a few weeks most of them returned, bringing back large quantities of gold and silver plate, rich stuffs, and the various commodities in which the taxes were usually paid.

To this store Montezuma added, on his own account, the treasure of Axayacatl, previously noticed, some part of which had been already given to the Spaniards. It was the fruit of long and careful hoarding — of extortion, it may be — by a prince who little dreamed of its final destination. When brought into the quarters, the gold alone was sufficient to make three great heaps. It consisted partly of native grains; part had been melted into bars; but the greatest portion was in utensils, and various kinds of ornaments and curious toys, together with imitations of birds, insects, or flowers, executed with uncommon truth and delicacy. There were also quantities of collars, bracelets, wands, fans, and other trinkets, in which the gold and feather-work were richly powdered with pearls and precious stones. Many of the articles were even more admirable for the workmanship than for the value of the materials; such, indeed — if we may take the report of Cortes to one who would himself have soon an opportunity to judge of its veracity, and whom it would not be safe to trifle with — as no monarch in Europe could boast in his dominions!

Magnificent as it was, Montezuma expressed his regret that the treasure was no larger. But he had diminished it, he said, by his former gifts to the white men. "Take it," he added, "Malinche, and let it be recorded in your annals, that Montezuma sent his present to your master."

The Spaniards gazed with greedy eyes on the display of riches, now their own, which far exceeded an hitherto seen in the New World, and fell nothing short of the El Dorado which their glowing imaginations had depicted. It may be that they felt somewhat rebuked by the contrast which their own avarice presented to the princely munificence of the barbarian chief. At least, they seemed to testify their sense of his superiority by the respectful homage which they rendered him, as they poured forth the fulness of their gratitude. They were not so scrupulous, however, as to manifest any delicacy in appropriating to themselves the donative, a small part of which was to find its way into the royal coffers. They clamoured loudly for an immediate division of the spoil, which the general would have postponed till the tributes from the remote provinces had been gathered in. The goldsmiths of Azcapotzalco were sent for to take in pieces the larger and coarser ornaments, leaving untouched those of more delicate workmanship. Three days were consumed in this labour, when the heaps of gold were cast into ingots, and stamped with the royal arms.

Some difficulty occurred in the division of the treasure, from the want of weights, which, strange as it appears, considering their advancement in the arts, were, as already observed, unknown to the Aztecs. The deficiency was soon supplied by the Spaniards, however, with scales and weights of their own manufacture, probably not the most exact. With the aid of these they ascertained the value of the royal fifth to be thirty-two thousand and four hundred pesos de oro. Diaz swells it to nearly four times that amount. But their desire of securing the emperor's favour makes it improbable that the Spaniards should have defrauded the exchequer of any part of its due; while, as Cortes was responsible for the sum admitted in his letter, he would be still less likely to overstate it. His estimate may be received as the true one.

The whole amounted, therefore, to one hundred and sixty-two thousand pesos de oro, independently of the fine ornaments and jewellery, the value of which Cortes computes at five hundred thousand ducats more. There were, besides, five hundred marks of silver, chiefly in plate, drinking cups, and other articles of luxury. The inconsiderable quantity of the silver, as compared with the gold, forms a singular contrast to the relative proportions of the two metals since the occupation of the country by the Europeans. The whole amount of the treasure, reduced to our own currency, and making allowance for the change in the value of gold since the beginning of the sixteenth century, was about six million three hundred thousand dollars, or one million four hundred and seventeen thousand pounds sterling; a sum large enough to show the incorrectness of the popular notion that little or no wealth was found in Mexico. It was, indeed, small in comparison with that obtained by the conquerors in Peru. But few European monarchs of that day could boast a larger treasure in their coffers. Many of them, indeed, could boast little or nothing in their coffers. Maximilian of Germany, and the more prudent Ferdinand of Spain, left scarcely enough to defray their funeral expenses.

The division of the spoil was a work of some difficulty. A perfectly equal division of it among the Conquerors would have given them more than three thousand pounds sterling a-piece; a magnificent booty! But one fifth was to be deducted for the crown. An equal portion was reserved for the general, pursuant to the tenor of his commission. A large sum was then allowed to indemnify him and the governor of Cuba for the charges of the expedition and the loss of the fleet, The garrison of Vera Cruz was also to be provided for. Ample compensation was made to the principal cavaliers. The cavalry, arquebusiers, and crossbowmen, each received double pay. So that when the turn of the common soldiers came, there remained not more than a hundred pesos de oro for each; a sum so insignificant, in comparison with their expectations, that several refused to accept it.

Loud murmurs now rose among the men. "Was it for this," they said, "that we left our homes and families, perilled our lives, submitted to fatigue and famine, and all for so contemptible a pittance! Better to have stayed in Cuba, and contented ourselves with the gains of a safe and easy traffic. When we gave up our share of the gold at Vera Cruz, it was on the assurance that we should be amply requited in Mexico. We have indeed, found the riches we expected; but no sooner seen, than they are snatched from us by the very men who pledged us their faith!" The malcontents even went so far as to accuse their leaders of appropriating to themselves several of the richest ornaments, before the partition had been made; an accusation that receives some countenance from a dispute which arose between Mexia, the treasurer for the crown, and Velasquez de Leon, a relation of the governor, and a favourite of Cortes. The treasurer accused this cavalier of purloining certain pieces of plate before they were submitted to the royal stamp. From words the parties came to blows. They were good swordsmen; several wounds were given on both sides, and the affair might have ended fatally, but for the interference of Cortes, who placed both under arrest.

He then used all his authority and insinuating eloquence to calm the passions of his men. It was a delicate crisis. He was sorry, he said, to see them so unmindful of the duty of loyal soldiers, and cavaliers of the Cross, as to brawl like common banditti over their booty. The division, he assured them, had been made on perfectly fair and equitable principles. As to his own share, it was no more than was warranted by his commission. Yet, if they thought it too much, he was willing to forego his just claims, and divide with the poorest soldier. Gold, however welcome, was not the chief object of his ambition. If it were theirs, they should still reflect, that the present treasure was little in comparison with what awaited them hereafter; for had they not the whole country and its mines at their disposal? It was only necessary that they should not give an opening to the enemy, by their discord, to circumvent and to crush them. With these honeyed words, of which he had good store for all fitting occasions, says an old soldier, for whose benefit, in part, they were intended, he succeeded in calming the storm for the present; while in private he took more effectual means, by presents judiciously administered, to mitigate the discontents of the importunate and refractory. And, although there were a few of more tenacious temper, who treasured this in their memories against a future day, the troops soon returned to their usual subordination. This was one of those critical conjunctures which taxed all the address and personal authority of Cortes. He never shrunk from them, but on such occasions was true to himself. At Vera Cruz, he had persuaded his followers to give up what was but the earnest of future gains. Here he persuaded them to relinquish these gains themselves. It was snatching the prey from the very jaws of the lion. Why did he not turn and rend him?

To many of the soldiers, indeed, it mattered little whether their share of the booty were more or less. Gaming is a deep-rooted passion in the Spaniard, and the sudden acquisition of riches furnished both the means and the motive for its indulgence. Cards were easily made out of old parchment drumheads, and in a few days most of the prize-money, obtained with so much toil and suffering, had changed hands, and many of the improvident soldiers closed the campaign as poor as they had commenced it. Others, it is true, more prudent, followed the example of their officers, who, with the aid of the royal jewellers, converted their gold into chains, services of plate, and other portable articles of ornament or use.

Cortes seemed now to have accomplished the great objects of the expedition. The Indian monarch had declared himself the feudatory of the Spanish. His authority, his revenues, were at the disposal of the general. The conquest of Mexico seemed to be achieved, and that without a blow. But it was far from being achieved. One important step yet remained to be taken, towards which the Spaniards had hitherto made little progress — the conversion of the natives. With all the exertions of Father Olmedo, backed by the polemic talents of the general, neither Montezuma nor his subjects showed any disposition to abjure the faith of their fathers. The bloody exercises of their religion, on the contrary, were celebrated with all the usual circumstance and pomp of sacrifice before the eyes of the Spaniards.

171

Unable further to endure these abominations, Cortes, attended by several of his cavaliers, waited on Montezuma. He told the emperor that the Christians could no longer consent to have the services of their religion shut up within the narrow walls of the garrison. They wished to spread its light far abroad, and to open to the people a full participation in the blessings of Christianity. For this purpose they requested that the great teocalli should be delivered up, as a fit place where their worship might be conducted in the presence of the whole city.

Montezuma listened to the proposal with visible consternation. Amidst all his troubles he had leaned for support on his own faith, and, indeed, it was in obedience to it that he had shown such deference to the Spaniards as the mysterious messenger predicted by the oracles. "Why," said he, "Malinche, why will you urge matters to an extremity, that must surely bring down the vengeance of our gods, and stir up an insurrection among my people, who will never endure this profanation of their temples?"

Cortes, seeing how greatly he was moved, made a sign to his officers to withdraw. When left alone with the interpreters, he told the emperor that he would use his influence to moderate the zeal of his followers, and persuade them to be contented with one of the sanctuaries of the teocalli. If that were not granted, they should be obliged to take it by force, and to roll down the images of his false deities in the face of the city. "We fear not for our lives," he added, "for, though our numbers are few, the arm of the true God is over us." Montezuma, much agitated, told him that he would confer with the priests.

The result of the conference was favourable to the Spaniards, who were allowed to occupy one of the sanctuaries as a Place of worship. The tidings spread great joy throughout the camp. They might now go forth in open day and publish their religion to the assembled capital. No time was lost in availing themselves of the permission. The sanctuary was cleansed of its disgusting impurities An altar was raised, surmounted by a crucifix and the image of the Virgin. Instead of the gold and jewels which blazed on the neighbouring pagan shrine, its walls were decorated with fresh garlands of flowers; and an old soldier was stationed to watch over the chapel, and guard it from intrusion.

When these arrangements were completed, the whole army moved in solemn procession up the winding ascent of the pyramid. Entering the sanctuary, and clustering round its portals, they listened reverently to the service of the mass, as it was performed by the fathers Olmedo and Diaz. And as the beautiful Te Deum rose towards heaven, Cortes and his soldiers, kneeling on the ground, with tears streaming from their eyes, poured forth their gratitude to the Almighty for this glorious triumph of the Cross.

It was a striking spectacle — that of these rude warriors lifting up their orisons on the summit of this mountain temple, in the very capital of heathendom, on the spot especially dedicated to its unhallowed mysteries. Side by side, the Spaniard and the Aztec knelt down in prayer; and the Christian hymn mingled its sweet tones of love and mercy with the wild chant raised by the Indian priest in honour of the war-god of Anahuac! It was an unnatural union, and could not long abide.

A nation will endure any outrage sooner than that on its religion. This is an outrage both on its principles and its prejudices; on the ideas instilled into it from childhood, which have strengthened with its growth, until they become a part of its nature — which have to do with its highest interests here, and with the dread hereafter. Any violence to the religious sentiment touches all alike, the old and the young, the rich and the poor, the noble and the plebeian. Above all, it touches the priests, whose personal consideration rests on that of their religion; and who, in a semi-civilised state of society, usually hold an unbounded authority. Thus it was with the Brahmins of India, the Magi of Persia, the Roman Catholic clergy in the Dark Ages, the priests of ancient Egypt and Mexico.

The people had borne with patience all the injuries and affronts hitherto put on them by the Spaniards. They had seen their sovereign dragged as a captive from his own palace; his ministers butchered before his eyes; his treasures seized and appropriated; himself in a manner deposed from his royal supremacy. All this they had seen without a struggle to prevent it. But the profanation of their temples touched a deeper feeling, of which the priesthood were not slow to take advantage.

The first intimation of this change of feeling was gathered from Montezuma himself. Instead of his usual cheerfulness, he appeared grave and abstracted, and instead of seeking, as he was wont, the society of the Spaniards, seemed rather to shun it. It was noticed, too, that conferences were more frequent between him and the nobles, and especially the priests. His little page, Orteguilla, who had now picked up a tolerable acquaintance with the Aztec, contrary to Montezuma's usual practice, was not allowed to attend him at these meetings. These circumstances could not fail to awaken most uncomfortable apprehensions in the Spaniards.

Not many days elapsed, however, before Cortes received an invitation, or rather a summons, from the emperor, to attend him in his apartment. The general went with some feelings of anxiety and distrust, taking with him Olid, captain of the guard, and two or three other trusty cavaliers. Montezuma received them with cold civility, and, turning to the general, told him that all his predictions had come to pass. The gods of his country had been offended by the violation of their temples. They had threatened the priests that they would forsake the city, if the sacrilegious strangers were not driven from it, or rather sacrificed on the altars, in expiation of their crimes. The monarch assured the Christians, it was from regard to their safety that he communicated this; and, "if you have any regard for it yourselves," he concluded, "you will leave the country without delay. I have only to raise my finger, and every Aztec in the land will rise in arms against you." There was no reason to doubt his sincerity; for Montezuma, whatever evils had been brought on him by the white men, held them in reverence as a race more highly gifted than his own, while for several, as we have seen, he had conceived an attachment, flowing, no doubt, from their personal attentions and deferences to himself.

Cortes was too much master of his feelings to show how far he was startled by this intelligence. He replied with admirable coolness, that he should regret much to leave the capital so precipitately, when he had no vessels to take him from the country. If it were not for this, there could be no obstacle to his leaving it at once. He should also regret another step to which he should be driven, if he quitted it under these circumstances — that of taking the emperor along with him.

Montezuma was evidently troubled by this last suggestion. He inquired how long it would take to build the vessels, and finally consented to send a sufficient number of workmen to the coast, to act under the orders of the Spaniards; meanwhile, he would use his authority to restrain the impatience of the people, under the assurance that the white men would leave the land, when the means for it were provided. He kept his word. A large body of Aztec artisans left the capital with the most experienced Castilian ship-builders, and, descending to Vera Cruz, began at once to fell the timber and build a sufficient number of ships to transport the Spaniards back to their own country. The work went forward with apparent alacrity. But those who had the direction of it, it is said, received private instructions from the general to interpose as many delays as possible, in hopes of receiving in the meantime such reinforcements from Europe as would enable him to maintain his ground.

The whole aspect of things was now changed in the Castilian quarters. Instead of the security and repose in which the troops had of late indulged, they felt a gloomy apprehension of danger, not the less oppressive to the spirits, that it was scarcely visible to the eye; — like the faint speck just descried above the horizon by the voyager in the tropics, to the common gaze seeming only a summer cloud, but which to the experienced mariner bodes the coming of the hurricane. Every precaution that prudence could devise was taken to meet it. The soldier, as he threw himself on his mats for repose, kept on his armour. He ate, drank, slept, with his weapons by his side. His horse stood ready caparisoned, day and night, with the bridle hanging at the saddle-bow. The guns were carefully planted, so as to command the great avenues. The sentinels were doubled, and every man, of whatever rank, took his turn in mounting guard. The garrison was in a state of siege. Such was the uncomfortable position of the army when, in the beginning of May, 1520, six months after their arrival in the capital, tidings came from the coast, which gave greater alarm to Cortes, than even the menaced insurrection of the Aztecs.

173

BEFORE explaining the nature of the tidings alluded to in the preceding chapter, it will be necessary to cast a glance over some of the transactions of an earlier period. The vessel, which, as the reader may remember, bore the envoys Puertocarrero and Montejo with the despatches from Vera Cruz, after touching, contrary to orders, at the northern coast of Cuba, and spreading the news of the late discoveries, held on its way uninterrupted towards Spain, and early in October, 1519, reached the little port of San Lucar. Great was the sensation caused by her arrival and the tidings which she brought; a sensation scarcely inferior to that created by the original discovery of Columbus. For now, for the first time, all the magnificent anticipations formed of the New World seemed destined to be realised.

Unfortunately, there was a person in Seville, at this time, named Benito Martin, chaplain of Velasquez, the governor of Cuba. No sooner did this man learn the arrival of the envoys, and the particulars of their story, than he lodged a complaint with the Casa de Contratacion — the Royal India House — charging those on board the vessel with mutiny and rebellion against the authorities of Cuba, as well as with treason to the crown. In consequence of his representations, the ship was taken possession of by the public officers, and those on board were prohibited from moving their own effects, or anything else from her. The envoys were not even allowed the funds necessary for the expenses of the voyage, nor a considerable sum remitted by Cortes to his father, Don Martin. In this embarrassment they had no alternative but to present themselves, as speedily as possible, before the emperor, deliver the letters with which they had been charged by the colony, and seek redress for their own grievances. They first sought out Martin Cortes, residing at Medellin, and with him made the best of their way to court.

Charles the Fifth was then on his first visit to Spain after his accession. It was not a long one; long enough, however, to disgust his subjects, and, in a great degree, to alienate their affections. He had lately received intelligence of his election to the imperial crown of Germany. From that hour, his eyes were turned to that quarter. His stay in the Peninsula was prolonged only that he might raise supplies for appearing with splendour on the great theatre of Europe. Every act showed too plainly that the diadem of his ancestors was held lightly in comparison with the imperial bauble in which neither his countrymen nor his own posterity could have the slightest interest. The interest was wholly personal.

Contrary to established usage, he had summoned the Castilian cortes to meet at Compostella, a remote town in the north, which presented no other advantage than that of being near his place of embarkation. On his way thither he stopped some time at Tordesillas, the residence of his unhappy mother, Joanna "The Mad." It was here that the envoys from Vera Cruz presented themselves before him, in March, 1520. At nearly the same time, the treasures brought over by them reached the court, where they excited unbounded admiration. Hitherto, the returns from the New World had been chiefly in vegetable products, which, if the surest, are also the. slowest, sources of wealth. Of gold they had as yet seen but little, and that in its natural state, or wrought into the rudest trinkets. The courtiers gazed with astonishment on the large masses of the precious metal, and the delicate manufacture of the various articles, especially of the richly-tinted feather-work. And, as they listened to the accounts, written and oral, of the great Aztec empire, they felt assured that the Castilian ships had, at length, reached the golden Indies, which hitherto had seemed to recede before them.

In this favourable mood there is little doubt the monarch would have granted the petition of the envoys, and confirmed the irregular proceedings of the Conquerors, but for the opposition of a person who held the highest office in the Indian department. This was Juan Rodriguez de Fonseca, formerly dean of Seville, now bishop of Burgos. He was a man of noble family, and had been intrusted with the direction of the colonial concerns, on the discovery of the New World. On the establishment of the Royal Council of the Indies by Ferdinand the Catholic, he had been made its president, and had occupied that post ever since. His long continuance in a position of great importance and difficulty is evidence of capacity for business. It was no uncommon thing in that age to find ecclesiastics in high civil, and even military employments. Fonseca appears to have been an active, efficient person, better suited to a secular than to a religious vocation. He had, indeed, little that was religious in his temper; quick to take offence, and slow to forgive. His resentments seem to have been nourished and perpetuated like a part of his own nature. Unfortunately his peculiar position enabled him to display them towards some of the most illustrious men of his time. From pique at some real or fancied slight from Columbus, he had constantly thwarted the plans of the great navigator. He had shown the same unfriendly feeling towards the admiral's son, Diego, the heir of his honours; and he now, and from this time forward, showed a similar spirit towards the Conqueror of Mexico. The immediate cause of this was his own personal relations with Velasquez, to whom a near relative was betrothed.

Through this prelate's representations, Charles, instead of a favourable answer to the envoys, postponed his decision till he should arrive at Coruna, the place of embarkation. But here he was much pressed by the troubles which his impolitic conduct had raised, as well as by preparations for his voyage. The transaction of the colonial business, which, long postponed, had greatly accumulated on his hands, was reserved for the last week in Spain. But the affairs of the "young admiral" consumed so large a portion of this, that he had no time to give to those of Cortes; except, indeed, to instruct the board at Seville to remit to the envoys so much of their funds as was required to defray the charges of the voyage. On the 16th of May, 1520, the impatient monarch bade adieu to his distracted kingdom, without one attempt to settle the dispute between his belligerent vassals in the New World, and without an effort to promote the magnificent enterprise which was to secure to him the possession of an empire. What a contrast to the policy of his illustrious predecessors, Ferdinand and Isabella!

The governor of Cuba, meanwhile, without waiting for support from home, took measures for redress into his own hands. We have seen, in a preceding chapter, how deeply he was moved by the reports of the proceedings of Cortes and of the treasures which his vessel was bearing to Spain. Rage, mortification, disappointed avarice, distracted his mind. He could not forgive himself for trusting the affair to such hands. On the very week in which Cortes had parted from him to take charge of the fleet, a capitulation had been signed by Charles the Fifth, conferring on Velasquez the title of adelantado, with great augmentation of his original powers. The governor resolved, without loss of time, to send such a force to the Aztec coast, as should enable him to assert his new authority to its full extent, and to take vengeance on his rebellious officer. He began his preparations as early as October. At first, he proposed to assume the command in person. But his unwieldy size, which disqualified him for the fatigues incident to such an expedition, or, according to his own account, tenderness for his Indian subjects, then wasted by an epidemic, induced him to devolve the command on another.

The person whom he selected was a Castilian hidalgo, named Panfilo de Narvaez. He had assisted Velasquez in the reduction of Cuba, where his conduct cannot be wholly vindicated from the charge of inhumanity, which too often attaches to the early Spanish adventurers. From that time he continued to hold important posts under the government, and was a decided favourite with Velasquez. He was a man of some military capacity, though negligent and lax in his discipline. He possessed undoubted courage, but it was mingled with an arrogance, or rather overweening confidence in his own powers, which made him deaf to the suggestions of others more sagacious than himself. He was altogether deficient in that prudence and calculating foresight demanded in a leader who was to cope with an antagonist like Cortes.

The governor and his lieutenant were unwearied in their efforts to assemble an army. They visited every considerable town in the island, fitting out vessels, laying in stores and ammunition, and encouraging volunteers to enlist by liberal promises. But the most effectual bounty was the assurance of the rich treasures that awaited them in the golden regions of Mexico. So confident were they in this expectation, that all classes and ages vied with one another in eagerness to embark in the expedition, until it seemed as if the whole white population would desert the island, and leave it to its primitive occupants.

The report of these proceedings soon spread through the islands, and drew the attention of the Royal Audience of St. Domingo. This body was intrusted, at that time, not only with the highest judicial authority in the colonies, but with a civil jurisdiction, which, as "the Admiral" complained, encroached on his own rights. The tribunal saw with alarm the proposed expedition of Velasquez, which, whatever might be its issue in regard to the parties, could not fail to compromise the interests of the crown. They chose accordingly one of their number, the licentiate Ayllon, a man of prudence and resolution, and despatched him to Cuba, with instructions to interpose his authority, and stay, if possible, the proceedings of Velasquez.

On his arrival, he found the governor in the western part of the island, busily occupied in getting the fleet ready for sea. The licentiate explained to him the purport of his mission, and the views entertained of the proposed enterprise by the Royal Audience. The conquest of a powerful country like Mexico required the whole force of the Spaniards, and, if one half were employed against the other, nothing but ruin could come of it. It was the governor's duty, as a good subject, to forego all private animosities, and to sustain those now engaged in the great work by sending them the necessary supplies. He might, indeed, proclaim his own powers, and demand obedience to them. But, if this were refused, he should leave the determination of his dispute to the authorised tribunals, and employ his resources in prosecuting discovery in another direction, instead of hazarding all by hostilities with his rival.

This admonition, however sensible and salutary, was not at all to the taste of the governor. He professed, indeed, to have no intention of coming to hostilities with Cortes. He designed only to assert his lawful jurisdiction over territories discovered under his own auspices. At the same time he denied the right of Ayllon or of the Royal Audience to interfere in the matter. Narvaez was still more refractory; and, as the fleet was now ready, proclaimed his intention to sail in a few hours. In this state of things, the licentiate, baffled in his first purpose of staying the expedition, determined to accompany it in person, that he might prevent, if possible, by his presence, an open rupture between the parties.

The squadron consisted of eighteen vessels, large and small. It carried nine hundred men, eighty of whom were cavalry, eighty more arquebusiers, one hundred and fifty crossbowmen, with a number of heavy guns, and a large supply of ammunition and military stores. There were, besides, a thousand Indians, natives of the island, who went probably in a menial capacity. So gallant an armada — with one exception, the great fleet under Ovando, 1501, in which Cortes had intended to embark for the New World — never before rode in the Indian seas. None to compare with it had ever been fitted out in the Western World.

Leaving Cuba early in March, 1520, Narvaez held nearly the same course as Cortes, and running down what was then called the "Island of Yucatan," after a heavy tempest, in which some of his smaller vessels foundered, anchored, April 23, off San Juan de Ulua. It was the place where Cortes also had first landed; the sandy waste covered by the present city of Vera Cruz.

Here the commander met with a Spaniard, one of those sent by the general from Mexico, to ascertain the resources of the country, especially its mineral products. This man came on board the fleet, and from him the Spaniards gathered the particulars of all that had occurred since the departure of the envoys from Vera Cruz — the march into the interior, the bloody battles with the Tlascalans, the occupation of Mexico, the rich treasures found in it, and the seizure of the monarch, by means of which, concluded the soldier, "Cortes rules over the land like its own sovereign, so that a Spaniard may travel unarmed from one end of the country to the other, without insult or injury." His audience listened to this marvellous report with speechless amazement, and the loyal indignation of Narvaez waxed stronger and stronger, as he learned the value of the prize which had been snatched from his employer.

He now openly proclaimed his intention to march against Cortes, and punish him for his rebellion. He made this vaunt so loudly, that the natives who had flocked in numbers to the camp, which was soon formed on shore, clearly comprehended that the new comers were not friends, but enemies, of the preceding. Narvaez determined, also — though in opposition to the counsel of the Spaniard, who quoted the example of Cortes — to establish a settlement on this unpromising spot: and he made the necessary arrangements to organise a municipality. He was informed by the soldier of the existence of the neighbouring colony at Villa Rica, commanded by Sandoval, and consisting of a few invalids, who, he was assured, would surrender on the first summons. Instead of marching against the place, however, he determined to send a peaceful embassy to display his powers, and demand the submission of the garrison.

These successive steps gave serious displeasure to Ayllon, who saw they must lead to inevitable collision with Cortes. But it was in vain he remonstrated, and threatened to lay the proceedings of Narvaez before the government. The latter, chafed by his continued opposition and sour rebuke, determined to rid himself of a companion who acted as a spy on his movements. He caused him to be seized and sent back to Cuba. The licentiate had the address to persuade the captain of the vessel to change her destination for St. Domingo; and, when he arrived there, a formal report of his proceedings, exhibiting in strong colours the disloyal conduct of the governor and his lieutenant, was prepared and despatched by the Royal Audience to Spain.

Sandoval, meanwhile, had not been inattentive to the movements of Narvaez. From the time of his first appearance on the coast, that vigilant officer, distrusting the object of the armament, had kept his eye on him. No sooner was he apprised of the landing of the Spaniards, than the commander of Villa Rica sent off his few disabled soldiers to a place of safety in the neighbourhood. He then put his works in the best posture of defence that he could, and prepared to maintain the place to the last extremity. His men promised to stand by him, and, the more effectually to fortify the resolution of any who might falter, he ordered a gallows to be set up in a conspicuous part of the town! The constancy of his men was not put to the trial.

The only invaders of the place were a priest, a notary, and four other Spaniards, selected for the mission already noticed, by Narvaez. The ecclesiastic's name was Guevara. On coming before Sandoval, he made him a formal address, in which he pompously enumerated the services and claims of Velasquez, taxed Cortes and his adherents with rebellion, and demanded of Sandoval to tender his submission as a loyal subject to the newly constituted authority of Narvaez.

The commander of La Villa Rica was so much incensed at this unceremonious mention of his companions in arms, that he assured the reverend envoy, that nothing but respect for his cloth saved him from the chastisement he merited. Guevara now waxed wroth in his turn, and called on the notary to read the proclamation. But Sandoval interposed, promising that functionary, that, if he attempted to do so, without first producing a warrant of his authority from the crown, he should be soundly flogged. Guevara lost all command of himself at this, and stamping on the ground repeated his orders in a more peremptory tone than before. Sandoval was not a man of many words; he simply remarked, that the instrument should be read to the general himself in Mexico. At the same time, he ordered his men to procure a number of sturdy tamanes, or Indian porters, on whose backs the unfortunate priest and his companions were bound like so many bales of goods. They were then placed under a guard of twenty Spaniards, and the whole caravan took its march for the capital. Day and night they travelled, stopping only to obtain fresh relays of carriers; and as they passed through populous towns, forests and cultivated fields, vanishing as soon as seen, the Spaniards, bewildered by the strangeness of the scene, as well as of their novel mode of conveyance, hardly knew whether they were awake or in a dream. In this way, at the end of the fourth day, they reached the Tezcucan lake in view of the Aztec capital.

Its inhabitants had already been made acquainted with the fresh arrival of white men on the coast. Indeed, directly on their landing, intelligence had been communicated to Montezuma, who is said does not seem probable) to have concealed it some days from Cortes. At length, inviting him to an interview, he told him there was no longer any obstacle to his leaving the country, as a fleet was ready for him. To the inquiries of the astonished general, Montezuma replied by pointing to a hieroglyphical map sent him from the coast, on which the ships, the Spaniards themselves, and their whole equipment, were minutely delineated. Cortes, suppressing all emotions but those of pleasure, exclaimed, "Blessed be the Redeemer for his mercies!" On returning to his quarters, the tidings were received by the troops with loud shouts, the firing of cannon, and other demonstrations of joy. They hailed the new comers as a reinforcement from Spain. Not so their commander. From the first, he suspected them to be sent by his enemy, the governor of Cuba. He communicated his suspicions to his officers, through whom they gradually found their way among the men. The tide of joy was instantly checked. Alarming apprehensions succeeded, as they dwelt on the probability of this suggestion, and on the strength of the invaders. Yet their constancy did not desert them; and they pledged themselves to remain true to their cause, and, come what might, to stand by their leader. It was one of those occasions, that proved the entire influence which Cortes held over these wild adventurers. All doubts were soon dispelled by the arrival of the prisoners from Villa Rica.

One of the convoy, leaving the party in the suburbs, entered the city, and delivered a letter to the general from Sandoval, acquainting him with all the particulars. Cortes instantly sent to the prisoners, ordered them to be released, and furnished them with horses to make their entrance into the capital — a more creditable conveyance than the backs of tamanes. On their arrival, he received them with marked courtesy, apologised for the rude conduct of his officers, and seemed desirous by the most assiduous attentions to soothe the irritation of their minds. He showed his good will still further by lavishing presents on Guevara and his associates, until he gradually wrought such a change in their dispositions, that, from enemies, he converted them into friends, and drew forth many important particulars respecting not merely the designs of their leader, but the feelings of his army. The soldiers, in general, they said, far from desiring a rupture with those of Cortes, would willingly co-operate with them, were it not for their commander. They had no feelings of resentment to gratify. Their object was gold. The personal influence of Narvaez was not great, and his arrogance and penurious temper had already gone far to alienate from him the affections of his followers. These hints were not lost on the general.

He addressed a letter to his rival in the most conciliatory terms. He besought him not to proclaim their animosity to the world, and, by kindling a spirit of insubordination in the natives, unsettle all that had been so far secured. A violent collision must be prejudicial even to the victor, and might be fatal to both. It was only in union that they could look for success. He was ready to greet Narvaez as a brother in arms, to share with him the fruits of conquest, and, if he could produce a royal commission, to submit to his authority. Cortes well knew he had no such commission to show.

Soon after the departure of Guevara and his comrades, the general determined to send a special envoy of his own. The person selected for this delicate office was Father Olmedo, who, through the campaign, had shown a practical good sense, and a talent for affairs, not always to be found in persons of his spiritual calling. He was intrusted with another epistle to Narvaez, of similar import with the preceding. Cortes wrote, also, to the licentiate Ayllon, with whose departure he was not acquainted, and to Andres de Duero, former secretary of Velasquez, and his own friend, who had come over in the present fleet. Olmedo was instructed to converse with these persons in private, as well as with the principal officers and soldiers, and, as far as possible, to infuse into them a spirit of accommodation. To give greater weight to his arguments, he was furnished with a liberal supply of gold.

During this time, Narvaez had abandoned his original design of planting a colony on the sea-coast, and had crossed the country to Cempoalla, where he had taken up his quarters. He was here when Guevara returned, and presented the letter of Cortes.

Narvaez glanced over it with a look of contempt, which was changed into one of stern displeasure, as his envoy enlarged on the resources and formidable character of his rival, counselling him, by all means, to accept his proffers of amity. A different effect was produced on the troops, who listened with greedy ears to the accounts given of Cortes, his frank and liberal manners, which they involuntarily contrasted with those of their own commander, the wealth in his camp, where the humblest private could stake his ingot and chain of gold at play, where all revelled in plenty, and the life of the soldier seemed to be one long holiday. Guevara had been admitted only to the sunny side of the picture.

The impression made by these accounts was confirmed by the presence of Olmedo. The ecclesiastic delivered his missives, in like manner, to Narvaez, who ran through their contents with feelings of anger which found vent in the most opprobrious invectives against his rival; while one of his captains, named Salvatierra, openly avowed his intention to cut off the rebel's ears, and broil them for his breakfast! Such impotent sallies did not alarm the stout-hearted friar, who soon entered into communication with many of the officers and soldiers, whom he found better inclined to an accommodation. His insinuating eloquence, backed by his liberal largesses, gradually opened a way into their hearts, and a party was formed under the very eye of their chief, better affected to his rival's interests than to his own. The intrigue could not be conducted so secretly as wholly to elude the suspicions of Narvaez, who would have arrested Olmedo and placed him under confinement, but for the interposition of Duero. He put a stop to his further machinations by sending him back again to his master. But the poison was left to do its work.

Narvaez made the same vaunt as at his landing, of his design to march against Cortes and apprehend him as a traitor. The Cempoallans learned with astonishment that their new guests, though the countrymen, were enemies of their former. Narvaez also proclaimd his intention to release Montezuma from captivity, and restore him to his throne. It is said he received a rich present from the Aztec emperor, who entered into a correspondence with him. That Montezuma should have treated him with his usual munificence, supposing him to be the friend of Cortes, is very probable. But that he should have entered into a secret communication, hostile to the general's interests, is too repugnant to the whole tenor of his conduct, to be lightly admitted.

These proceedings did not escape the watchful eye of Sandoval. He gathered the particulars partly from deserters, who fled to Villa Rica, and partly from his own agents, who in the disguise of natives mingled in the enemy's camp. He sent a full account of them to Cortes, acquainted him with the growing defection of the Indians, and urged him to take speedy measures for the defence of Villa Rica, if he would not see it fall into the enemy's hands. The general felt that it was time to act.

Yet the selection of the course to be pursued was embarrassing in the extreme. If he remained in Mexico and awaited there the attack of his rival, it would give the latter time to gather round him the whole forces of the empire, including those of the capital itself, all willing, no doubt, to serve under the banners of a chief who proposed the liberation of their master. The odds were too great to be hazarded.

If he marched against Narvaez, he must either abandon the city and the emperor, the fruit of all his toils and triumphs, or, by leaving a garrison to hold them in awe, must cripple his strength, already far too weak to cope with that of his adversary. Yet on this latter course he decided. He trusted less, perhaps, to an open encounter of arms, than to the influence of his personal address and previous intrigues, to bring about an amicable arrangement. But he prepared himself for either result.

In the preceding chapter, it was mentioned that Velasquez de Leon was sent with a hundred and fifty men to plant a colony on one of the great rivers emptying into the Mexican Gulf. Cortes, on learning the arrival of Narvaez, had despatched a messenger to his officer to acquaint him with the fact, and to arrest his further progress. But Velasquez had already received notice of it from Narvaez himself, who, in a letter written soon after his landing, had adjured him in the name of his kinsman, the governor of Cuba, to quit the banners of Cortes, and come over to him. That officer, however, had long since buried the feelings of resentment which he had once nourished against his general, to whom he was now devotedly attached, and who had honoured him throughout the campaign with particular regard. Cortes had early seen the importance of securing this cavalier to his interests. Without waiting for orders, Velasquez abandoned his expedition, and commenced a countermarch on the capital, when he received the general's commands to wait him in Cholula.

Cortes had also sent to the distant province of Chinantla, situated far to the south-east of Cholula, for a reinforcement of two thousand natives. They were a bold race, hostile to the Mexicans, and had offered their services to him since his residence in the metropolis. They used a long spear in battle, longer, indeed, than that borne by the Spanish or German infantry. Cortes ordered three hundred of their double-headed lances to be made for him, and to be tipped with copper instead of itztli. With this formidable weapon he proposed to foil the cavalry of his enemy.

The command of the garrison, in his absence, he instructed to Pedro de Alvarado — the Tonatiuh of the Mexicans — a man possessed of many commanding qualities, of an intrepid, though somewhat arrogant spirit, and his warm personal friend. He inculcated on him moderation and forbearance. He was to keep a close watch on Montezuma, for on the possession of the royal person rested all their authority in the land. He was to show him the deference alike due to his high station, and demanded by policy. He was to pay uniform respect to the usages and the prejudices of the people; remembering that though his small force would be large enough to overawe them in times of quiet, yet, should they be once roused, it would be swept away like chaff before the whirlwind.

From Montezuma he exacted a promise to maintain the same friendly relations with his lieutenant which he had preserved towards himself. This, said Cortes, would be most grateful to his own master, the Spanish sovereign. Should the Aztec prince do otherwise, and lend himself to any hostile movement, he must be convinced that he would fall the first victim of it.

The emperor assured him of his continued good will. He was much perplexed, however, by the recent events. Were the at his court, or those just landed, the true representatives of their sovereign? Cortes, who had hitherto maintained a reserve on the subject, now told him that the latter were indeed his countrymen, but traitors to his master. As such it was his painful duty to march against them, and, when he had chastised their rebellion, he should return, before his departure from the land, in triumph to the capital. Montezuma offered to support him with five thousand Aztec warriors; but the general declined it, not choosing to encumber himself with a body of doubtful, perhaps disaffected, auxiliaries.

He left in garrison, under Alvarado, one hundred and forty men, two-thirds of his whole force. With these remained all the artillery, the greater part of the little body of horse, and most of the arquebusiers. He took with him only seventy soldiers, but they were men of the most mettle in the army and his staunch adherents. They were lightly armed, and encumbered with as little baggage as possible. Everything depended on celerity of movement.

Montezuma, in his royal litter, borne on the shoulders of his nobles, and escorted by the whole Spanish infantry, accompanied the general to the causeway. There, embracing him in the most cordial manner, they parted, with all the external marks of mutual regard. — It was about the middle of May, 1520, more than six months since the entrance of the Spaniards into Mexico.

During this time they had lorded it over the land with absolute sway. They were now leaving the city in hostile array, not against an Indian foe, but their own countrymen.

It was the beginning of a long career of calamity — chequered, indeed, by occasional triumphs — which was yet to be run before the Conquest could be completed.

TRAVERSING the southern causeway, by which they had entered the capital, the little party were soon on their march across the beautiful valley. They climbed the mountain-screen which Nature has so ineffectually drawn around it; passed between the huge volcanoes that, like faithless watch-dogs on their posts, have long since been buried in slumber; threaded the intricate defiles where they had before experienced such bleak and tempestuous weather; and, emerging on the other side, descended the eastern slope which opens on the wide expanse of the fruitful plateau of Cholula.

They heeded little of what they saw on their rapid march, nor whether it was cold or hot. The anxiety of their minds made them indifferent to outward annoyances; and they had fortunately none to encounter from the natives, for the name of Spaniard was in itself a charm — a better guard than helm or buckler to the bearer.

In Cholula, Cortes had the inexpressible satisfaction of meeting Velasquez de Leon, with the hundred and twenty soldiers intrusted to his command for the formation of a colony. That faithful officer had been some time at Cholula, waiting for the general's approach. Had he failed, the enterprise of Cortes must have failed also. The idea of resistance, with his own handful of followers, would have been chimerical. As it was, his little band was now trebled, and acquired a confidence in proportion.

Cordially embracing their companions in arms, now knit together more closely than ever by the sense of a great and common danger, the combined troops traversed with quick step the streets of the sacred city, where many a dark pile of ruins told of their disastrous visit on the preceding autumn. They kept the high road to Tlascala; and, at not many leagues' distance from that capital, fell in with Father Olmedo and his companions on their return from the camp of Narvaez. The ecclesiastic bore a letter from that commander, in which he summoned Cortes and his followers to submit to his authority, as captain-general of the country, menacing them with condign punishment, in case of refusal or delay. Olmedo gave many curious particulars of the state of the enemy's camp. Narvaez he described as puffed up by authority, and negligent of precautions against a foe whom he held in contempt. He was surrounded by a number of pompous conceited officers, who ministered to his vanity, and whose braggart tones, the good father, who had an eye for the ridiculous, imitated, to the no small diversion of Cortes and the soldiers. Many of the troops, he said, showed no great partiality for their commander, and were strongly disinclined to a rupture with their countrymen; a state of feeling much promoted by the accounts they had received of Cortes, by his own arguments and promises, and by the liberal distribution of the gold with which he had been provided. In addition to these matters, Cortes gathered much important intelligence respecting the position of the enemy's force, and his general plan of operations.

At Tlascala, the Spaniards were received with a frank and friendly hospitality. It is not said whether any of the Tlascalan allies accompanied them from Mexico. If they did, they went no further than their native city. Cortes requested a reinforcement of six hundred fresh troops to attend him on his present expedition. It was readily granted; but, before the army had proceeded many miles on its route, the Indian auxiliaries fell off, one after another, and returned to their city. They had no personal feeling of animosity to gratify in the present instance, as in a war against Mexico. It may be, too, that although intrepid in a contest with the bravest of the Indian races, they had too fatal experience of the prowess of the white men to care to measure swords with them again. At any rate, they deserted in such numbers that Cortes dismissed the remainder at once, saying, good-humouredly, "He had rather part with them then, than in the hour of trial."

The troops soon entered on that wild district in the neighbourhood of Perote, strewed with the wreck of volcanic matter, which forms so singular a contrast to the general character of beauty with which the scenery is stamped. It was not long before their eyes were gladdened by the approach of Sandoval and about sixty soldiers from the garrison of Vera Cruz, including several deserters from the enemy. It was a most important reinforcement, not more on account of the numbers of the men than of the character of the commander. He had been compelled to fetch a circuit, in order to avoid falling in with the enemy, and had forced his way through thick forests and wild mountain passes, till he had fortunately, without accident, reached the appointed place of rendezvous, and stationed himself once more under the banner of his chieftain. At the same place, also, Cortes was met by Tobillos, a Spaniard whom he had sent to procure the lances from Chinantla. They were perfectly well made, after the pattern which had been given; double-headed spears, tipped with copper, and of great length.

Cortes now took a review of his army — if so paltry a force may be called an army — and found their numbers were two hundred and sixty-six, only five of whom were mounted. A few muskets and crossbows were sprinkled among them. In defensive armour they were sadly deficient. They were for the most part cased in the quilted doublet of the country, thickly stuffed with cotton, the escaupil, recommended by its superior lightness, but which, though competent to turn the arrow of the Indian, was ineffectual against a musket-ball. Most of this cotton mail was exceedingly out of repair, giving evidence, in its unsightly gaps, of much rude service, and hard blows. Few, in this emergency, but would have given almost any price — the best of the gold chains which they wore in tawdry display over their poor habiliments — for a steel morion or cuirass, to take the place of their own hacked and battered armour.

The troops now resumed their march across the tableland, until, reaching the eastern slope, their labours were lightened, as they descended towards the broad plains of the tierra caliente, spread out like a boundless ocean of verdure below them. At some fifteen leagues' distance from Cempoalla, where Narvaez, as has been noticed, had established his quarters, they were met by another embassy from that commander. It consisted of the priest, Guevara, Andres de Duero, and two or three others. Duero, the fast friend of Cortes, had been the person most instrumental, originally, in obtaining him his commission from Velasquez. They now greeted each other with a warm embrace, and it was not till after much preliminary conversation on private matters, that the secretary disclosed the object of his visit.

He bore a letter from Narvaez, couched in terms somewhat different from the preceding. That officer required, indeed, the acknowledgment of his paramount authority in the land, but offered his vessels to transport all who desired it, from the country, together with their treasures and effects, without molestation or inquiry. The more liberal tenor of these terms was, doubtless, to be ascribed to the influence of Duero. The secretary strongly urged Cortes to comply with them, as the most favourable that could be obtained, and as the only alternative affording him a chance of safety in his desperate condition. "For, however valiant your men may be, how can they expect," he asked, "to face a force so much superior in numbers and equipment as that of their antagonists?" But Cortes had set his fortunes on the cast, and he was not the man to shrink from it. "If Narvaez bears a royal commission," he returned, "I will readily submit to him. But he has produced none. He is a deputy of my rival, Velasquez. For myself I am a servant of the king, I have conquered the country for him; and for him I and my brave followers will defend it, to the last drop of our blood. If we fall, it will be glory enough to have perished in the discharge of our duty."

His friend might have been somewhat puzzled to comprehend how the authority of Cortes rested on a different ground from that of Narvaez; and if they both held of the same superior, the governor of Cuba, why that dignitary should not be empowered to supersede his own officer in case of dissatisfaction, and appoint a substitute. But Cortes here reaped the full benefit of that legal fiction, if it may be so termed, by which his commission, resigned to the self-constituted municipality of Vera Cruz, was again derived through that body from the crown. The device, indeed, was too palpable to impose on any but those who chose to be blinded.

Duero had arranged with his friend in Cuba, when he took command of the expedition, that he himself was to have a liberal share of the profits. It is said that Cortes confirmed this arrangement at the present juncture, and made it clearly for the other's interest that be should prevail in the struggle with Narvaez. This was an important point, considering the position of the secretary. From this authentic source the general derived much information respecting the designs of Narvaez, which had escaped the knowledge of Olmedo. On the departure of the envoys, Cortes intrusted them with a letter for his rival, a counterpart of that which he had received from him. This show of negotiation intimated a desire on his part to postpone if not avoid hostilities, which might the better put Narvaez off his guard. In the letter he summoned that commander and his followers to present themselves before him without delay, and to acknowledge his authority as the representative of his sovereign. He should otherwise be compelled to proceed against them as rebels to the crown! With this missive, the vaunting tone of which was intended quite as much for his own troops as the enemy, Cortes dismissed the envoys. They returned to disseminate among their comrades their admiration of the general and of his unbounded liberality, of which he took care they should experience full measure, and they dilated on the riches of his adherents, who, over their wretched attire, displayed with ostentatious profusion, jewels, ornaments of gold, collars, and massive chains winding several times round their necks and bodies, the rich spoil of the treasury of Montezuma.

The army now took its way across the level plains of the tierra caliente. Coming upon an open reach of meadow, of some extent, they were, at length, stopped by a river or rather stream, called Rio de Canoas, "the River of Canoes," of no great volume ordinarily, but swollen at this time by excessive rains; it had rained hard that day. The river was about a league distant from the camp of Narvaez. Before seeking out a practical ford, by which to cross it, Cortes allowed his men to recruit their exhausted strength by stretching themselves on the ground. The shades of evening had gathered round; and the rising moon, wading through dark masses of cloud, shone with a doubtful and interrupted light. It was evident that the storm had not yet spent its fury. Cortes did not regret this. He had made up his mind to an assault that very night, and in the darkness and uproar of the tempest his movements would be most effectually concealed.

Before disclosing his design, he addressed his men in one of those stirring, soldierly harangues, to which he had recourse in emergencies of great moment, as if to sound the depths of their hearts, and, where any faltered, to re-animate them with his own heroic spirit. He briefly recapitulated the great events of the campaign, the dangers they had surmounted, the victories they had achieved over the most appalling odds, the glorious spoil they had won. But of this they were now to be defrauded; not by men holding a legal warrant from the crown, but by adventurers, with no better title than that of superior force. They had established a claim on the gratitude of their country and their sovereign. This claim was now to be dishonoured; their very services were converted into crimes, and their names branded with infamy as those of traitors. But the time had at last come for vengeance. God would not desert the soldier of the Cross. Those, whom he had carried victorious through greater dangers, would not be left to fail now. And, if they should fail, better to die like brave men on the field of battle, than, with fame and fortune cast away, to perish ignominiously like slaves on the gibbet. — This last point he urged upon his hearers; well knowing there was not one among them so dull as not to be touched by it.

They responded with hearty acclamations, and Velasquez de Leon, and de Lugo, in the name of the rest, assured their commander, if they failed, it should be his fault, not theirs. They would follow wherever he led. — The general was fully satisfied with the temper of his soldiers, as he felt that his difficulty lay not in awakening their enthusiasm, but in giving it a right direction. One thing is remarkable. He made no allusion to the defection which he knew existed in the enemy's camp. He would have his soldiers, in this last pinch, rely on nothing but themselves.

He announced his purpose to attack the enemy that very night, when he should be buried in slumber, and the friendly darkness might throw a veil over their own movements, and conceal the poverty of their numbers. To this the troops, jaded though they were by incessant marching, and half famished, joyfully assented. In their situation, suspense was the worst of evils. He next distributed the commands among his captains. To Gonzalo de Sandoval he assigned the important office of taking Narvaez. He was commanded, as alguacil mayor, to seize the person of that officer as a rebel to his sovereign, and, if he made resistance, to kill him on the spot. He was provided with sixty picked men to aid him in this difficult task, supported by several of the ablest captains, among whom were two of the Alvarados, de Avila and Ordaz. The largest division of the force was placed under Christoval de Olid, or according to some authorities, Pizarro, one of that family so renowned in the subsequent conquest of Peru. He was to get possession of the artillery, and to cover the assault of Sandoval by keeping those of the enemy at bay, who would interfere with it. Cortes reserved only a body of twenty men for himself, to act on any point that occasion might require. The watchword was Espiritu Santo, it being the evening of Whitsunday. Having made these arrangements, he prepared to cross the river.

During the interval thus occupied by Cortes, Narvaez had remained at Cempoalla, passing his days in idle and frivolous amusement. From this he was at length roused, after the return of Duero, by the remonstrances of the old cacique of the city. "Why are you so heedless?" exclaimed the latter; "do you think Malinche is so? Depend on it, he knows your situation exactly, and, when you least dream of it, he will be upon you."

Alarmed at these suggestions and those of his friends, Narvaez at length put himself at the head of his troops, and, on the very day on which Cortes arrived at the River of Canoes, sallied out to meet him. But, when he had reached this barrier, Narvaez saw no sign of an enemy. The rain, which fell in torrents, soon drenched the soldiers to the skin. Made somewhat effeminate by their long and luxurious residence at Cempoalla, they murmured at their uncomfortable situation. "Of what use was it to remain there fighting with the elements? There was no sign of an enemy, and little reason to apprehend his approach in such tempestuous weather. It would be wiser to return to Cempoalla, and in the morning they should be all fresh for action, should Cortes make his appearance."

Narvaez took counsel of these advisers, or rather of his own inclinations. Before retracing his steps, he provided against surprise, by stationing a couple of sentinels at no great distance from the river, to give notice of the approach of Cortes. He also detached a body of forty horse in another direction, by which he thought it not improbable the enemy might advance on Cempoalla. Having taken these precautions, he fell back again before night on his own quarters.

He there occupied the principal teocalli. It consisted of a stone building on the usual pyramidal basis; and the ascent was by a flight of steep steps on one of the faces of the pyramid. In the edifice or sanctuary above he stationed himself with a strong party of arquebusiers and crossbowmen. Two other teocallis in the same area were garrisoned by large detachments of infantry. His artillery, consisting of seventeen or eighteen small guns, he posted in the area below, and protected it by the remainder of his cavalry. When he had thus distributed his forces, he returned to his own quarters, and soon after to repose, with as much indifference as if his rival had been on the other side of the Atlantic, instead of a neighbouring stream.

That stream was now converted by the deluge of waters into a furious torrent. It was with difficulty that a practicable ford could be found. The slippery stones, rolling beneath the feet, gave way at every step. The difficulty of the passage was much increased by the darkness and driving tempest. Still, with their long pikes, the Spaniards contrived to make good their footing, at least, all but two, who were swept down by the fury of the current. When they had reached the opposite side, they had new impediments to encounter in traversing a road never good, now made doubly difficult by the deep mire and the tangled brushwood with which it was overrun.

Here they met with a cross, which had been raised by them on their former march into the interior. They hailed it as a good omen; and Cortes, kneeling before the blessed sign, confessed his sins, and declared his great object to be the triumph of the holy Catholic faith. The army followed his example, and, having made a general confession, received absolution from Father Olmedo, who invoked the blessing of heaven on the warriors who had consecrated their swords to the glory of the Cross. Then rising up and embracing one another, as companions in the good cause, they found themselves wonderfully invigorated and refreshed. The incident is curious, and well illustrates the character of the time — in which war, religion, and rapine were so intimately blended together. Adjoining the road was a little coppice; and Cortes, and the few who had horses, dismounting, fastened the animals to the trees, where they might find some shelter from the storm. They deposited there, too, their baggage and such superfluous articles as would encumber their movement. The general then gave them a few last words of advice. "Everything," said he, "depends on obedience. Let no man, from desire of distinguishing himself, break his ranks. On silence, despatch, and, above all, obedience to your officers, the success of our enterprise depends."

Silently and stealthily they held on their way without beat of drum or sound of trumpet, when they suddenly came on the two sentinels who had been stationed by Narvaez to give notice of their approach. This had been so noiseless, that the videttes were both of them surprised on their posts, and one only, with difficulty, effected his escape. The other was brought before Cortes. Every effort was made to draw from him some account of the present position of Narvaez. But the man remained obstinately silent; and, though threatened with the gibbet, and having a noose actually drawn round his neck, his Spartan heroism was not be vanquished. Fortunately no change had taken place in the arrangements of Narvaez since the intelligence previously derived from Duero.

The other sentinel, who had escaped, carried the news of the enemy's approach to the camp. But his report was not credited by the lazy soldiers, whose slumbers he had disturbed. "He had been deceived by his fears," they said, "and mistaken the noise of the storm, and the waving of the bushes, for the enemy. Cortes and his men were far enough on the other side of the river, which they would be slow to cross in such a night." Narvaez himself shared in the same blind infatuation, and the discredited sentinel slunk abashed to his own quarters, vainly menacing them with the consequences of their incredulity.

Cortes, not doubting that the sentinel's report must alarm the enemy's camp, quickened his pace. As he drew near, he discerned a light in one of the lofty towers of the city. "It is the quarters of Narvaez," he exclaimed to Sandoval, "and that light must be your beacon." On entering the suburbs, the Spaniards were surprised to find no one stirring, and no symptom of alarm. Not a sound was to be heard, except the measured tread of their own footsteps, half-drowned in the howling of the tempest. Still they could not move so stealthily as altogether to elude notice, as they defiled through the streets of this populous city. The tidings were quickly conveyed to the enemy's quarters, where, in an instant, all was bustle and confusion. The trumpets sounded to arms. The dragoons sprang to their steeds, the artillerymen to their guns. Narvaez hastily buckled on his armour, called his men around him, and summoned those in the neighbouring teocallis, to join him in the area. He gave his orders with coolness; for, however wanting in prudence, he was not deficient in presence of mind or courage.

All this was the work of a few minutes. But in those minutes the Spaniards had reached the avenue leading to the camp. Cortes ordered his men to keep close to the walls of the buildings, that the cannon-shot might have free range. No sooner had they presented themselves before the inclosure than the artillery of Narvaez opened a general fire. Fortunately the pieces were pointed so high that most of the balls passed over their heads, and three men only were struck down. They did not give the enemy time to reload. Cortes shouting the watchword of the night, "Espiritu Santo! Espiritu Santo! Upon them!" in a moment Olid and his division rushed on the artillerymen, whom they pierced or knocked down with their pikes, and got possession of their guns. Another division engaged the cavalry, and made a diversion in favour of Sandoval, who with his gallant little band sprang up the great stairway of the temple. They were received with a shower of missiles, arrows and musketballs, which, in the hurried aim, and the darkness of the night, did little mischief. The next minute the assailants were on the platform, engaged hand to hand with their foes. Narvaez fought bravely in the midst, encouraging his followers. His standard-bearer fell by his side, run through the body. He himself received several wounds; for his short sword was not match for the long pikes of the assailants. At length, he received a blow from a spear, which struck out his left "Santa Maria!" exclaimed the unhappy man, "I am slain!" The cry was instantly taken up by the followers of Cortes, who shouted, "Victory!"

Disabled, and half-mad with agony from his wound, Narvaez was withdrawn by his men into the sanctuary. The assailants endeavoured to force an entrance, but it was stoutly defended. At length a soldier, getting possession of a torch, or firebrand, flung it on the thatched roof, and in a few moments the combustible materials of which it was composed were in a blaze. Those within were driven out by the suffocating heat and smoke. A soldier, named Farfan, grappled with the wounded commander, and easily brought him to the ground; when he was speedily dragged down the steps, and secured with fetters. His followers, seeing@ the fate of their chief, made no further resistance.

During this time, Cortes and the troops of Olid had been engaged with the cavalry, and had discomfited them, after some ineffectual attempts on the part of the latter to break through the dense array of pikes, by which several of their number were unhorsed and some of them slain. The general then prepared to assault the other teocallis, first summoning the garrisons to surrender. As they refused, he brought up the heavy guns to bear on them, thus turning the artillery against its own masters. He accompanied this menacing movement with offers of the most liberal import; an amnesty of the past, and a full participation in all the advantages of the Conquest. One of the garrisons was under the command of Salvatierra, the same officer who talked of cutting off the ears of Cortes. From the moment he had learned the fate of his own general, the hero was seized with a violent fit of illness which disabled him from further action. The garrison waited only for one discharge of the ordnance, when they accepted the terms of capitulation. Cortes, it is said, received, on this occasion, a support from an unexpected auxiliary. The air was filled with cocuyos — a species of large beetle which emits an intense phosphoric light from its body, strong enough to enable one to read by it. These wandering fires, seen in the darkness of the night, were converted by the excited imaginations of the besieged, into an army with matchlocks. Such is the report of an eye-witness. But the facility with which the enemy surrendered may quite as probably to be referred to the cowardice of the commander, and the disaffection of the soldiers, not unwilling to come under the banners of Cortes.

The body of cavalry posted, it will be remembered, by Narvaez on one of the roads to Cempoalla, to intercept his rival, having learned what had been passing, were not long in tendering their submission. Each of the soldiers in the conquered army was required, in token of his obedience, to deposit his arms in the hands of the alguacils, and to take the oaths to Cortes as Chief justice and Captain General of the colony.

The number of the slain is variously reported. It seems probable that no more than twelve perished on the side of the vanquished, and of the victors half that number. The small amount may be explained by the short duration of the action, and the random aim of the missiles in the darkness. The number of the wounded was much more considerable.

The field was now completely won. A few brief hours had sufficed to change the condition of Cortes from that of a wandering outlaw at the head of a handful of needy adventurers, a rebel with a price upon his head, to that of an independent chief, with a force at his disposal strong enough not only to secure his present conquests, but to open a career for still loftier ambition. While the air rung with the acclamations of the soldiery, the victorious general, assuming a deportment corresponding with his change of fortune, took his seat in a chair of state, and, with a rich embroidered mantle thrown over his shoulders, received, one by one, the officers and soldiers, as they came to tender their congratulations. The privates were graciously permitted to kiss his hand. The officers he noticed with words of compliment or courtesy; and, when Duero, Bermudez the treasurer, and some others of the vanquished party, his old friends, presented themselves, he cordially embraced them.

Narvaez, Salvatierra, and two or three of the hostile leaders were led before him in chains. It was a moment of deep humiliation for the former commander, in which the anguish of the body, however keen, must have been forgotten in that of the spirit. "You have great reason, Senor Cortes," said the discomfited warrior, "to thank fortune for having given you the day so easily, and put me in your power."—"I have much to be thankful for," replied the general; "but for my victory over you, I esteem it as one of the least of my achievements since my coming into the country!" He then ordered the wounds of the prisoners to be cared for, and sent them under a strong guard to Vera Cruz.

Notwithstanding the proud humility of his reply, Cortes could scarcely have failed to regard his victory over Narvaez as one of the most brilliant achievements in his career. With a few scores of followers, badly clothed, worse fed, wasted by forced marches, under every personal disadvantage, deficient in weapons and military stores, he had attacked in their own quarters, routed, and captured the entire force of the enemy, thrice his superior in numbers, well provided with cavalry and artillery, admirably equipped, and complete in all the munitions of war! The amount of troops engaged on either side was, indeed, inconsiderable. But the proportions are not affected by this: and the relative strength of the parties made a result so decisive one of the most remarkable events in the annals of war.

THE tempest that had raged so wildly during the night passed away with the morning, which rose bright and unclouded on the field of battle. As the light advanced, it revealed more strikingly the disparity of the two forces so lately opposed to each other. Those of Narvaez could not conceal their chagrin; and murmurs of displeasure became audible, as they contrasted their own superior numbers and perfect appointments with the way-worn visages and rude attire of their handful of enemies! It was with some satisfaction, therefore, that the general beheld his dusky allies from Chinantla, two thousand in number, arrive upon the field. They were a fine athletic set of men; and, as they advanced in a sort of promiscuous order, so to speak, with their gay banners of feather-work, and their lances tipped with itztli and copper, glistering in the morning sun, they had something of an air of military discipline. They came too late for the action, indeed, but Cortes was not sorry to exhibit to his new followers the extent of his resources in the country. As he had now no occasion for his Indian allies, after a courteous reception and a liberal recompense, he dismissed them to their homes.

He then used his utmost endeavours to allay the discontent of the troops. He addressed them in his most soft and insinuating tones, and was by no means frugal of his promises. He suited the action to the word. There were few of them but had lost their accoutrements, or their baggage, or horses taken and appropriated by the victors. This last article was in great request among the latter, and many a soldier, weary with the long marches hitherto made on foot, had provided himself, as he imagined, with a much more comfortable as well as creditable conveyance for the rest of the campaign. The general now commanded everything to be restored. "They were embarked in the same cause," he said, "and should share with one another equally." He went still further; and distributed among the soldiers of Narvaez a quantity of gold and other precious commodities gathered from the neighbouring tribes, or found in his rival's quarters.

These proceedings, however politic in reference to his new followers, gave great disgust to his old. "Our commander," they cried, "has forsaken his friends for his foes. We stood by him in his hour of distress, and are rewarded with blows and wounds, while the spoil goes to our enemies!" The indignant soldiery commissioned the priest Olmedo and Alonso de Avila to lay their complaints before Cortes. The ambassadors stated them without reserve, comparing their commander's conduct to the ungrateful proceeding of Alexander, who, when he gained a victory, usually gave away more to his enemies than to the troops who enabled him to beat them. Cortes was greatly perplexed. Victorious or defeated, his path seemed equally beset with difficulties!

He endeavoured to soothe their irritation by pleading the necessity of the case. "Our new comrades," he said, "are formidable from their numbers; so much so, that we are even now much more in their power than they are in ours. Our only security is to make them not merely confederates, but friends. On any cause of disgust, we shall have the whole battle to fight over again; and, if they are united, under a much greater disadvantage than before. I have considered your interests," he added, "as much as my own. All that I have is yours. But why should there be any ground for discontent, when the whole country, with its riches, is before us? And our augmented strength must henceforth secure the undisturbed control of it!"

But Cortes did not rely wholly on argument for the restoration of tranquillity. He knew this to be incompatible with inaction; and be made arrangements to divide his forces at once, and to employ them on distant services. He selected a detachment of two hundred men, under Diego de Ordaz, whom he ordered to form the settlement before meditated on the Coatzacualco. A like number was sent with Velasquez de Leon, to secure the province of Panuco, some three degrees to the north, on the Mexican Gulf. Twenty in each detachment were drafted from his own veterans.

Two hundred men he despatched to Vera Cruz, with orders to have the rigging, iron, and everything portable on board of the fleet of Narvaez, brought on shore, and the vessels completely dismantled. He appointed a person named Cavallero superintendent of the marine, with instructions that if any ships hereafter should enter the port, they should be dismantled in like manner, and their officers imprisoned on shore.

But while he was thus occupied with new schemes of discovery and conquest, he received such astounding intelligence from Mexico, as compelled him to concentrate all his faculties and his forces on that one point. The city was in a state of insurrection. No sooner had the struggle with his rival been decided, than Cortes despatched a courier with the tidings to the capital. In less than a fortnight, the same messenger returned with letters from Alvarado, conveying the alarming information that the Mexicans were in arms, and had vigorously assaulted the Spaniards in their own quarters. The enemy, he added, had burned the brigantines, by which Cortes had secured the means of retreat in case of the destruction of the bridges. They had attempted to force the defences, and had succeeded in partially undermining them, and they had overwhelmed the garrison with a tempest of missiles, which had killed several, and wounded a great number. The letter concluded with beseeching his commander to hasten to their relief, if he would save them, or keep his hold on the capital.

These tidings were a heavy blow to the general — the heavier, it seemed, coming, as they did, in the hour of triumph, when he had thought to have all his enemies at his feet. There was no room for hesitation. To lose their footing in the capital, the noblest city in the Western World, would be to lose the country itself, which looked up to it as its head. He opened the matter fully to his soldiers, calling on all who would save their countrymen to follow him. All declared their readiness to go; showing an alacrity, says Diaz, which some would have been slow to manifest, had they foreseen the future.

Cortes now made preparations for instant departure. He countermanded the orders previously given to Velasquez and Ordaz, and directed them to join him with their forces at Tlascala. He recalled the troops from Vera Cruz, leaving only a hundred men in garrison there, under command of one Rodrigo Rangre: for he could not spare the services of Sandoval at this crisis. He left his sick and wounded at Cempoalla, under charge of a small detachment, directing that they should follow as soon as they were in marching order. Having completed these arrangements, he set out from Cempoalla, well supplied with provisions by its hospitable cacique, who attended him some leagues on his way. The Totonac chief seems to have had an amiable facility of accommodating himself to the powers that were in the ascendant.

Nothing worthy of notice occurred during the first part of the march. The troops everywhere met with a friendly reception from the peasantry, who readily supplied their wants. Some time before reaching Tlascala, the route lay through a country thinly settled, and the army experienced considerable suffering from want of food, and still more from that of water. Their distress increased to an alarming degree, as, in the hurry of their march, they travelled with the meridian sun beating fiercely on their heads. Several faltered by the way, and, throwing themselves down by the roadside, seemed incapable of further effort, and almost indifferent to life.

In this extremity, Cortes sent forward a small detachment of horse to procure provisions in Tlascala, and speedily followed in person. On arriving, he found abundant supplies already prepared by the hospitable natives. They were sent back to the troops; the stragglers were collected one by one; refreshments were administered; and the army, restored in strength and spirits, entered the republican capital.

Here they gathered little additional news respecting the events in Mexico, which a popular rumour attributed to the secret encouragement and machinations of Montezuma. Cortes was commodiously lodged in the quarters of Maxixca, one of the four chiefs of the republic. They readily furnished him with two thousand troops. There was no want of heartiness, when the war was with their ancient enemy, the Aztec.

The Spanish commander, on reviewing his forces, after the junction with his two captains, found that they amounted to about a thousand foot, and one hundred horse, besides the Tlascalan levies. In the infantry were nearly a hundred arquebusiers, with as many crossbowmen; and the part of the army brought over by Narvaez was admirably equipped. It was inferior, however, to his own veterans in what is better than any outward appointments — military training, and familiarity with the peculiar service in which they were engaged.

Leaving these friendly quarters, the Spaniards took a more northerly route, as more direct than that by which they had before penetrated into the valley. It was the road to Tezcuco. It still compelled them to climb the same bold range of the Cordilleras, which attains its greatest elevation in the two mighty volcans at whose base they had before travelled. As they descended into the populous plains, their reception by the natives was very different from that which they had experienced on the preceding visit. There were no groups of curious peasantry to be seen gazing at them as they passed, and offering their simple hospitality. The supplies they asked were not refused, but granted with an ungracious air, that showed the blessing of their giver did not accompany them. This air of reserve became still more marked as the army entered the suburbs of the ancient capital of the Acolhuas. No one came forth to greet them, and the population seemed to have dwindled away — so many of them were withdrawn to the neighbouring scene of hostilities at Mexico. Their cold reception was a sensible mortification to the veterans of Cortes, who, judging from the past, had boasted to their new comrades of the sensation their presence would excite among the natives. The cacique of the place, who, as it may be remembered, had been created through the influence of Cortes, was himself absent. The general drew an ill omen from all these circumstances, which even raised an uncomfortable apprehension in his mind respecting the fate of the garrison in Mexico.

But his doubts were soon dispelled by the arrival of a messenger in a canoe from that city, whence he had escaped through the remissness of the enemy, or, perhaps, with their connivance. He brought despatches from Alvarado, informing his commander that the Mexicans had for the last fortnight desisted from active hostilities, and converted their operations into a blockade. The garrison had suffered greatly, but Alvarado expressed his conviction that the siege would be raised, and tranquillity restored, on the approach of his countrymen. Montezuma sent a messenger, also, to the same effect. At the same time, he exculpated himself from any part in the late hostilities, which he said had not only been conducted without his privity, but contrary to his inclination and efforts.

The Spanish general, having halted long enough to refresh his wearied troops, took up his march along the southern margin of the lake, which led him over the same causeway by which he had before entered the capital. It was the day consecrated to St. John the Baptist, the 24th of June, 1520. But how different was the scene from that presented on his former entrance! No crowds now lined the roads, no boats swarmed on the lake, filled with admiring spectators. A single pirogue might now and then be seen in the distance, like a spy stealthily watching their movements, and darting away the moment it had attracted notice. A death-like stillness brooded over the scene — a stillness that spoke louder to the heart than the acclamations of multitudes.

Cortes rode on moodily at the head of his battalions, finding abundant food for meditation, doubtless, in this change of circumstances. As if to dispel these gloomy reflections, he ordered his trumpets to sound, and their clear, shrill notes, borne across the waters, told the inhabitants of the beleaguered fortress that their friends were at hand. They were answered by a joyous peal of artillery, which seemed to give a momentary exhilaration to the troops, as they quickened their pace, traversed the great drawbridges, and once more found themselves within the walls of the imperial city.

The appearance of things here was not such as to allay their apprehensions. In some places they beheld the smaller bridges removed, intimating too plainly, now that their brigantines were destroyed, how easy it would be cut off their retreat. The town seemed even more deserted than Tezcuco. Its once busy and crowded population had mysteriously vanished. And, as the Spaniards defiled through the empty streets, the tramp of their horses' feet upon the pavement was answered by dull and melancholy echoes that fell heavily on their hearts. With saddened feelings they reached the great gates of the palace of Axayacatl. The gates were thrown open, and Cortes and his veterans, rushing in, were cordially embraced by their companions in arms, while both parties soon forgot the present in the interesting recapitulation of the past.

The first inquiries of the general were respecting the origin of the tumult. The accounts were various. Some imputed it to the desire of the Mexicans to release their sovereign from confinement; others to the design of cutting off the garrison while crippled by the absence of Cortes and their countrymen. All agreed, however, in tracing the immediate cause to the violence of Alvarado. It was common for the Aztecs to celebrate an annual festival in May, in honour of their patron war-god. It was called the "incensing of Huitzilopochtli," and was commemorated by sacrifice, religious songs, and dances, in which most of the nobles engaged, for it was one of the great festivals which displayed the pomp of the Aztec ritual. As it was held in the court of the teocalli, in the immediate neighbourhood of the Spanish quarters, and as a part of the temple itself was reserved for a Christian chapel, the caciques asked permission of Alvarado to perform their rites there. They requested also to be allowed the presence of Montezuma. This latter petition Alvarado declined, in obedience to the injunctions of Cortes; but acquiesced in the former, on condition that the Aztecs should celebrate no human sacrifices, and should come without weapons.

They assembled accordingly on the day appointed, to the number of six hundred, at the smallest computation. They were dressed in their most magnificent gala costumes, with their graceful mantles of feather-work, sprinkled with precious stones, and their necks, arms and legs ornamented with collars and bracelets of gold. They had that love of gaudy splendour which belongs to semi-civilised nations, and on these occasions displayed all the pomp and profusion of their barbaric wardrobes.

Alvarado and his soldiers attended as spectators, some of them taking their station at the gates, as if by chance, and others mingling in the crowd. They were all armed, a circumstance which, as it was usual, excited no attention. The Aztecs were soon engrossed by the exciting movement of the dance, accompanied by their religious chant, and wild, discordant minstrelsy. While thus occupied, Alvarado and his men, at a concerted signal, rushed with drawn swords on their victims. Unprotected by armour or weapons of any kind, they were hewn down without resistance by their assailants, who, in their bloody work, says a contemporary, showed no touch of pity or compunction. Some fled to the gates, but were caught on the long pikes of the soldiers. Others, who attempted to scale the Coatepantli, or Wall of Serpents, as it was called, which surrounded the area, shared the like fate, or were cut to pieces, or shot by the ruthless soldiery. The pavement, says a writer of the age, ran with streams of blood, like water in a heavy shower. Not an Aztec of all that gay company was left alive! It was repeating the dreadful scene of Cholula, with the disgraceful addition, that the Spaniards, not content with slaughtering their victims, rifled them of the precious ornaments on their persons! On this sad day fell the flower of the Aztec nobility. Not a family of note but had mourning and desolation brought within its walls; and many a doleful ballad, rehearsing the tragic incidents of the story, and adapted to the plaintive national airs, continued to be chanted by the natives long after the subjugation of the country.

Various explanations have been given of this atrocious deed; but few historians have been content to admit that of Alvarado himself. According to this, intelligence had been obtained through his spies — some of them Mexicans — of an intended rising of the Indians. The celebration of this festival was fixed on as the period for its execution, when the caciques would be met together, and would easily rouse the people to support them. Alvarado, advised of all this, had forbidden them to wear arms at their meeting. While affecting to comply, they had secreted their weapons in the neighbouring arsenals, whence they could readily withdraw them. But his own blow, by anticipating theirs, defeated the design, and, as he confidently hoped, would deter the Aztecs from a similar attempt in future.

Such is the account of the matter given by Alvarado. But, if true, why did he not verify his assertion by exposing the arms thus secreted? Why did he not vindicate his conduct in the eyes of the Mexicans generally, by publicly avowing the treason of the nobles, as was done by Cortes at Cholula? The whole looks much like an apology devised after the commission of the deed, to cover up its atrocity.

Some contemporaries assign a very different motive for the massacre, which, according to them, originated in the cupidity of the Conquerors, as shown by their plundering the bodies of their victims. Bernal Diaz, who, though not present, had conversed familiarly with those who were, vindicates them from the charge of this unworthy motive. According to him, Alvarado struck the blow in order to intimidate the Aztecs from any insurrectionary movement. But whether he had reason to apprehend such, or even affected to do so before the massacre, the old chronicler does not inform us.

On reflection, it seems scarcely possible that so foul a deed, and one involving so much hazard to the Spaniards themselves, should have been perpetrated from the mere desire of getting possession of the baubles worn on the persons of the natives. It is more likely this was an after-thought, suggested to the rapacious soldiery by the display of the spoil before them. It is not improbable that Alvarado may have gathered rumours of a conspiracy among the nobles — rumours, perhaps, derived through the Tlascalans, their inveterate foes, and for that reason very little deserving of credit. He proposed to defeat it by imitating the example of his commander at Cholula. But he omitted to imitate his leader in taking precautions against the subsequent rising of the populace. And he grievously miscalculated, when he confounded the bold and warlike Aztec with the effeminate Cholulan.

No sooner was the butchery accomplished, than the tidings spread like wildfire through the capital. Men could scarcely credit their senses. All they had hitherto suffered, the desecration of their temples, the imprisonment of their sovereign, the insults heaped on his person, all were forgotten in this one act. Every feeling of long smothered hostility and rancour now burst forth in the cry for vengeance. Every former sentiment of superstitious dread was merged in that of inextinguishable hatred. It required no effort of the priests — though this was not wanting — to fan these passions into a blaze. The city rose in arms to a man; and on the following dawn, almost before the Spaniards could secure themselves in their defences, they were assaulted with desperate fury. Some of the assailants attempted to scale the walls; others succeeded in partially undermining and in setting fire to the works. Whether they would have succeeded in carrying the place by storm is doubtful. But, at the prayers of the garrison, Montezuma himself interfered, and mounting the battlements addressed the populace, whose fury he endeavoured to mitigate by urging considerations for his own safety. They respected their monarch so far as to desist from further attempts to storm the fortress, but changed their operations into a regular blockade. They threw up works around the palace to prevent the egress of the Spaniards. They suspended the tianguez, or market, to preclude the possibility of their enemy's obtaining supplies; and they then quietly sat down, with feelings of sullen desperation, waiting for the hour when famine should throw their victims into their hands.

The condition of the besieged, meanwhile, was sufficiently distressing. Their magazines of provisions, it is true, were not exhausted; but they suffered greatly from want of water, which, within the inclosure, was exceedingly brackish, for the soil was saturated with the salt of the surrounding element. In this extremity, they discovered, it is said, a spring of fresh water in the area. Such springs were known in some other parts of the city; but, discovered first under these circumstances, it was accounted as nothing less than a miracle. Still they suffered much from their past encounters. Seven Spaniards, and many Tlascalans, had fallen, and there was scarcely one of either nation who had not received several wounds. In this situation, far from their own countrymen, without expectation of succour from abroad, they seemed to have no alternative before them, but a lingering death by famine, or one more dreadful on the altar of sacrifice. From this gloomy state they were relieved by the coming of their comrades.

Cortes calmly listened to the explanation made by Alvarado. But, before it was ended, the conviction must have forced itself on his mind, that he had made a wrong selection for this important post. Yet the mistake was natural. Alvarado was a cavalier of high family, gallant and chivalrous, and his warm personal friend. He had talents for action, was possessed of firmness and intrepidity, while his frank and dazzling manners made the Tonatiuh an especial favourite with the Mexicans. But, underneath this showy exterior, the future conqueror of Guatemala concealed a heart rash, rapacious, and cruel. He was altogether destitute of that moderation, which, in the delicate position he occupied, was a quality of more worth than all the rest.

When Alvarado had concluded his answers to the several interrogatories of Cortes, the brow of the latter darkened, as he said to his lieutenant, "You have done badly. You have been false to your trust. Your conduct has been that of a madman!" And, turning abruptly on his heel, he left him in undisguised displeasure.

Yet this was not a time to break with one so popular, and in many respects so important to him, as this captain, much less to inflict on him the punishment he merited. The Spaniards were like mariners labouring in a heavy tempest, whose bark nothing but the dexterity of the pilot, and the hearty co-operation of the crew, can save from foundering. Dissensions at such a moment must be fatal. Cortes, it is true, felt strong in his present resources. He now found himself at the head of a force which could scarcely amount to less than twelve hundred and fifty Spaniards, and eight thousand native warriors, principally Tlascalans. But, though relying on this to overawe resistance, the very augmentations of numbers increased the difficulty of subsistence. Discontented with himself, disgusted with his officer, and embarrassed by the disastrous consequences in which Alvarado's intemperance had involved him, he became irritable, and indulged in a petulance by no means common; for, though a man of lively passions by nature, he held them habitually under control.

On the day that Cortes arrived, Montezuma had left his own quarters to welcome him. But the Spanish commander, distrusting, as it would seem, however unreasonably, his good faith, received him so coldly that the Indian monarch withdrew, displeased and dejected, to his apartment. As the Mexican populace made no show of submission, and brought no supplies to the army, the general's ill-humour with the emperor continued. When, therefore, Montezuma sent some of the nobles to ask an interview with Cortes, the latter, turning to his own officers, haughtily exclaimed, "What have I to do with this dog of a king, who suffers us to starve before his eyes!"

His captains, among whom were Olid, de Avila, and Velasquez de Leon, endeavoured to mitigate his anger, reminding him, in respectful terms, that, had it not been for the emperor, the garrison might even now have been overwhelmed by the enemy. This remonstrance only chafed him the more. "Did not the dog," he asked, repeating the opprobrious epithet, "betray us in his communications with Narvaez? And does he not now suffer his markets to be closed, and leave us to die of famine?" Then, turning fiercely to the Mexicans he said, "Go, tell your master and his people to open the markets, or we will do it for them, at their cost!" The chiefs, who had gathered the import of his previous taunt on their sovereign, from his tone and gesture, or perhaps from some comprehensions of his language, left his presence swelling with resentment; and, in communicating his message, took care it should lose none of its effect.

Shortly after, Cortes, at the suggestion, it is said, of Montezuma, released his brother Cuitlahua, lord of Iztapalapan, who, it will be remembered, had been seized on suspicion of co-operating with the chief of Tezcuco in his meditated revolt. It was thought he might be of service in allaying the present tumult, and bringing the. populace to a better state of feeling. But he returned no more to the fortress. He was a bold, ambitious prince, and the injuries he had received from the Spaniards rankled deep in his bosom. He was presumptive heir to the crown, which, by the Aztec laws of succession, descended much more frequently in a collateral than in a direct line. The people welcomed him as the representative of their reign, and chose him to supply the place of Montezuma during his captivity. Cuitlahua willingly accepted the post of honour and of danger. He was an experienced warrior, and exerted himself to reorganise the disorderly levies, and to arrange a more efficient plan of operations. The effect was soon visible.

Cortes, meanwhile, had so little doubt of his ability to overawe the insurgents, that he wrote to that effect to the garrison of Villa Rica, by the same despatches in which he informed them of his safe arrival in the capital. But scarcely had his messenger been gone half an hour, when he returned breathless with terror, and covered with wounds.

"The city," he said, "was all in arms! The drawbridges were raised, and the enemy would soon be upon them!" He spoke truth. It was not long before a hoarse, sullen sound became audible, like that of the roaring of distant waters. It grew louder and louder; till, from the parapet surrounding the inclosure, the great avenues which led to it might be seen dark with the masses of warriors, who came rolling on in a confused tide towards the fortress. At the same time the terraces and azoteas or flat roofs, in the neighbourhood, were thronged with combatants brandishing their missiles, who seemed to have risen up as if by magic! It was a spectacle to appal the stoutest. — But the dark storm to which it was the prelude, and which gathered deeper and deeper round the Spaniards during the remainder of their residence in the capital, must form the subject of a separate book.

BOOK 5. EXPULSION FROM MEXICO

THE palace of Axayacatl, in which the Spaniards were quartered, was, as the reader may remember, a vast, irregular pile of stone buildings, having but one floor, except in the centre, where another story was added, consisting of a suite of apartments which rose like turrets on the main building of the edifice. A vast area stretched around, encompassed by a stone wall of no great height. This was supported by towers or bulwarks at certain intervals, which gave it some degree of strength, not, indeed, as compared with European fortifications, but sufficient to resist the rude battering enginery of the Indians. The parapet had been pierced here and there with embrasures for the artillery, which consisted of thirteen guns; and smaller apertures were made in other parts for the convenience of the arquebusiers. The Spanish forces found accommodations within the great building; but the numerous body of Tlascalan auxiliaries could have had no other shelter than what was afforded by barracks or sheds hastily constructed for the purpose in the spacious courtyard. Thus crowded into a small compact compass, the whole army could be assembled at a moment's notice; and, as the Spanish commander was careful to enforce the strictest discipline and vigilance, it was scarcely possible that he could be taken by surprise. No sooner, therefore, did the trumpet call to arms, as the approach of the enemy was announced, than every soldier was at his post, the cavalry mounted, the artillerymen at their guns, and the archers and arquebusiers stationed so as to give the assailants a warm reception.

On they came, with the companies, or irregular masses, into which the multitude was divided, rushing forward each in its own dense column, with many a gay banner displayed, and many a bright gleam of light reflected from helmet, arrow, and spear-head, as they were tossed about in their disorderly array. As they drew near the inclosure, the Aztecs set up a hideous yell, or rather that shrill whistle used in fight by the nations of Anahuac, which rose far above the sound of shell and atabal, and their other rude instruments of warlike melody. They followed this by a tempest of missiles — stones, darts, and arrows — which fell thick as rain on the besieged, while volleys of the same kind descended from the crowded terraces of the neighbourhood.

The Spaniards waited until the foremost column had arrived within the best distance for giving effect to their fire, when a general discharge of artillery and arquebuses swept the ranks of the assailants, and mowed them down by hundreds. The Mexicans were familiar with the report of these formidable engines, as they had been harmlessly discharged on some holiday festival; but never till now had they witnessed their murderous power. They stood aghast for a moment, as with bewildered looks they staggered under the fury of the fire; but, soon rallying, the bold barbarians uttered a piercing cry, and rushed forward over the prostrate bodies of their comrades. A second and a third volley checked their career, and threw them into disorder, but still they pressed on, letting off clouds of arrows; while their comrades on the roofs of the houses took more deliberate aim at the combatants in the courtyard. The Mexicans were particularly expert in the use of the sling; and the stones which they hurled from their elevated positions on the heads of their enemies did even greater execution than the arrows. They glanced, indeed, from the mail-covered bodies of the cavaliers, and from those who were sheltered under the cotton panoply, or escaupil. But some of the soldiers, especially the veterans of Cortes, and many of their Indian allies, had but slight defences, and suffered greatly under this stony tempest.

The Aztecs, meanwhile, had advanced close under the walls of the intrenchment; their ranks broken and disordered, and their limbs mangled by the unintermitting fire of the Christians. But they still pressed on, under the very muzzle of the guns. They endeavoured to scale the parapet, which from its moderate height was in itself a work of no great difficulty. But the moment they showed their heads above the rampart, they were shot down by the unerring marksmen within, or stretched on the ground by a blow of a Tlascalan maquahuitl. Nothing daunted, others soon appeared to take the place of the fallen, and strove, by raising themselves on the writhing bodies of their dying comrades, or by fixing their spears in the crevices of the wall, to surmount the barrier. But the attempt proved equally vain.

Defeated here, they tried to effect a breach in the parapet by battering it with heavy pieces of timber. The works were not constructed on those scientific principles by which one part is made to overlook and protect another. The besiegers, therefore, might operate at their pleasure, with but little molestation from the garrison within, whose guns could not be brought into a position to bear on them, and who could mount no part of their own works for their defence, without exposing their persons to the missiles of the whole besieging army. The parapet, however, proved too strong for the efforts of the assailants. In their despair, they endeavoured to set the Christian quarters on fire, shooting burning arrows into them, and climbing up so as to dart their firebrands through the embrasures. The principal edifice was of stone. But the temporary defences of the Indian allies, and other parts of the exterior works, were of wood. Several of these took fire, and the flame spread rapidly among the light combustible materials. This was a disaster for which the besieged were wholly unprepared. They had little water, scarcely enough for their own consumption. They endeavoured to extinguish the flames by heaping on earth; but in vain. Fortunately the great building was of materials which defied the destroying element. But the fire raged in some of the outworks, connected with the parapet, with a fury which could only be checked by throwing down a part of the wall itself, thus laying open a formidable breach. This, by the general's order, was speedily protected by a battery of heavy guns, and a file of arquebusiers, who kept up an incessant volley through the opening on the assailants.

The fight now raged with fury on both sides. The walls around the palace belched forth an unintermitting sheet of flame and smoke. The groans of the wounded and dying were lost in the fiercer battle-cries of the combatants, the roar of the artillery, the sharper rattle of the musketry, and the hissing sound of Indian missiles. It was the conflict of the European with the American; of civilised man with the barbarian; of the science of the one with the rude weapons and warfare of the other. And as the ancient walls of Tenochtitlan shook under the thunders of the artillery — it announced that the white man, the destroyer, had set his foot within her precincts.

Night at length came, and drew her friendly mantle over the contest. The Aztec seldom fought by night. It brought little repose, however, to the Spaniards, in hourly expectation of an assault; and they found abundant occupation in restoring the breaches in their defences, and in repairing their battered armour. The ferocity shown by the Mexicans seems to have been a thing for which Cortes was wholly unprepared. His past experience, his uninterrupted career of victory with a much feebler force at his command, had led him to underrate the military efficiency, if not the valour, of the Indians. The apparent facility with which the Mexicans had acquiesced in the outrages on their sovereign and themselves, had led him to hold their courage, in particular, too lightly. He could not believe the present assault to be anything more than a temporary ebullition of the populace, which would soon waste itself by its own fury. And he proposed, on the following day, to sally out and inflict such chastisement on his foes as should bring them to their senses, and show who was master in the capital.

With early dawn, the Spaniards were up and under arms; but not before their enemies had given evidence of their hostility by the random missiles, which, from time to time, were sent into the inclosure. As the grey light of morning advanced, it showed the besieging army far from being diminished in numbers, filling up the great square and neighbouring avenues, in more dense array than on the preceding evening. Instead of a confused, disorderly rabble, it had the appearance of something like a regular force, with its battalions distributed under their respective banners, the devices of which showed a contribution from the principal cities and districts in the valley. High above the rest was conspicuous the ancient standard of Mexico, with its well-known cognisance, an eagle pouncing on an ocelot, emblazoned on a rich mantle of feather-work. Here and there priests might be seen mingling in the ranks of the besiegers, and, with frantic gestures, animating them to avenge their insulted deities.

The greater part of the enemy had little clothing save the Maxtlatl, or sash, round the loins. They were variously armed, with long spears tipped with copper, or flint, or sometimes merely pointed and hardened in the fire. Some were provided with slings, and others with darts having two or three points, with long strings attached to them, by which, when discharged, they could be torn away again from the body of the wounded. This was a formidable weapon, much dreaded by the Spaniards. Those of a higher order wielded the terrible maquahuitl, with its sharp and brittle blades of obsidian. Amidst the motley bands of warriors, were seen many whose showy dress and air of authority intimated persons of high military consequence. Their breasts were protected by plates of metal, over which was thrown the gay surcoat of feather-work. They wore casques resembling, in their form, the head of some wild and ferocious animal, crested with bristly hair, or overshadowed by tall and graceful plumes of many a brilliant colour. Some few were decorated with the red fillet bound round the hair, having tufts of cotton attached to it, which denoted by their number that of the victories they had won, and their own pre-eminent rank among the warriors of the nation. The motley assembly showed that priest, warrior, and citizen had all united to swell the tumult.

Before the sun had shot his beams into the Castilian quarters, the enemy were in motion, evidently preparing to renew the assault of the preceding day. The Spanish commander determined to anticipate them by a vigorous sortie, for which he had already made the necessary dispositions. A general discharge of ordnance and musketry sent death far and wide into the enemy's ranks, and, before they had time to recover from their confusion, the gates were thrown open, and Cortes, sallying out at the head of his cavalry, supported by a large body of infantry and several thousand Tlascalans, rode at full gallop against them. Taken thus by surprise, it was scarcely possible to offer much resistance. Those who did were trampled down under the horses' feet, cut to pieces with the broadswords, or pierced with the lances of the riders. The infantry followed up the blow, and the rout for the moment was general.

But the Aztecs fled only to take refuge behind a barricade, or strong work of timber and earth, which had been thrown across the great street through which they were pursued. Rallying on the other side, they made a gallant stand, and poured in turn a volley of their light weapons on the Spaniards, who, saluted with a storm of missiles at the same time, from the terraces of the houses, were checked in their career, and thrown into some disorder.

Cortes, thus impeded, ordered up a few pieces of heavy ordnance, which soon swept away the barricades, and cleared a passage for the army. But it had lost the momentum acquired in its rapid advance. They enemy had time to rally and to meet the Spaniards on more equal terms. They were attacked in flank, too, as they advanced, by fresh battalions, who swarmed in from the adjoining streets and lanes. The canals were alive with boats filled with warriors, who, with their formidable darts, searched every crevice or weak place in the armour of proof, and made havoc on the unprotected bodies of the Tlascalans. By repeated and vigorous charges, the Spaniards succeeded in driving the Indians before them; though many, with a desperation which showed they loved vengeance better than life, sought to embarrass the movements of their horses by clinging to their legs, or more successfully strove to pull the riders from their saddles. And woe to the unfortunate cavalier who was thus dismounted — to be despatched by the brutal maquahuitl, or to be dragged on board a canoe to the bloody altar of sacrifice!

But the greatest annoyance which the Spaniards endured from the missiles from the azoteas, consisting often of large stones, hurled with a force that would tumble the stoutest rider from his saddle. Galled in the extreme by these discharges, against which even their shields afforded no adequate protection, Cortes ordered fire to be set to the buildings. This was no very difficult matter, since, although chiefly of stone, they were filled with mats, canework, and other combustible materials, which were soon in a blaze. But the buildings stood separated from one another by canals and drawbridges, so that the flames did not easily communicate to the neighbouring edifices. Hence the labour of the Spaniards was incalculably increased, and their progress in the work of destruction — fortunately for the city — was comparatively slow. They did not relax their efforts, however, till several hundred houses had been consumed, and the miseries of a conflagration, in which the wretched inmates perished equally with the defenders, were added to the other horrors of the scene.

The day was now far spent. The Spaniards had been everywhere victorious. But the enemy, though driven back on every point, still kept the field. When broken by the furious charges of the cavalry, he soon rallied behind the temporary defences, which, at different intervals, had been thrown across the streets, and, facing about, renewed the fight with undiminished courage, till the sweeping away of the barriers by the cannon of the assailants left a free passage for the movements of their horse. Thus the action was a succession of rallying and retreating, in which both parties suffered much, although the loss inflicted on the Indians was probably tenfold greater than that of the Spaniards. But the Aztecs could better afford the loss of a hundred lives than their antagonists that of one. And while the Spaniards showed an array broken, and obviously thinned in numbers, the Mexican army, swelled by the tributary levies which flowed in upon it from the neighbouring streets, exhibited, with all its losses, no sign of diminution. At length, sated with carnage, and exhausted by toil and hunger, the Spanish commander drew off his men, and sounded a retreat.

On his way back to his quarters, he beheld his friend, the secretary Duero, in a street adjoining, unhorsed, and hotly engaged with a body of Mexicans, against whom he was desperately defending himself with his poniard. Cortes, roused at the sight, shouted his war-cry, and, dashing into the midst of the enemy, scattered them like chaff by the fury of his onset; then recovering his friend's horse, he enabled him to remount, and the two cavaliers, striking their spurs into their steeds, burst through their opponents and joined the main body of the army.

The undaunted Aztecs hung on the rear of their retreating foes, annoying them at every step by fresh flights of stones and arrows; and when the Spaniards had re-entered their fortress, the Indian host encamped around it, showing the same dogged resolution as on the preceding evening. Though true to their ancient habits of inaction during the night, they broke the stillness of the hour by insulting cries and menaces, which reached the ears of the besieged. "The gods have delivered you, at last, into our hands," they said; "Huitzilopochtli has long cried for his victims. The stone of sacrifice is ready. The knives are sharpened. The wild beasts in the palace are roaring for their offal. And the cages," they added, taunting the Tlascalans with their leanness, "are waiting for the false sons of Anahuac, who are to be fattened for the festival." These dismal menaces, which sounded fearfully in the ears of the besieged, who understood too well their import, were mingled with piteous lamentations for their sovereign, whom they called on the Spaniards to deliver up to them.

Cortes suffered much from a severe wound which he had received in the hand in the late action. But the anguish of his mind must have been still greater, as he brooded over the dark prospect before him. He had mistaken the character of the Mexicans. Their long and patient endurance had been a violence to their natural temper, which, as their whole history proves, was arrogant and ferocious beyond that of most of the races of Anahuac. The restraint which, in deference to their monarch, more than to their own fears, they had so long put on their natures, being once removed, their passions burst forth with accumulated violence. The Spaniards had encountered in the Tlascalan an open enemy, who had no grievance to complain of, no wrong to redress. He fought under the vague apprehension only of some coming evil to his country. But the Aztec, hitherto the proud lord of the land, was goaded by insult and injury, till he had reached that pitch of self-devotion, which made fife cheap, in comparison with revenge.

Considerations of this kind may have passed through the mind of Cortes, as he reflected on his own impotence to restrain the fury of the Mexicans, and resolved in despite of his late supercilious treatment of Montezuma, to employ his authority to allay the tumult — an authority so successfully exerted in behalf of Alvarado, at an earlier stage of the insurrection. He was the more confirmed in his purpose, on the following morning, when the assailants, redoubling their efforts, succeeded in scaling the works in one quarter, and effecting an entrance into the inclosure. It is true, they were met with so resolute a spirit, that not a man of those who entered was left alive. But in the impetuosity of the assault, it seemed, for a few moments, as if the place was to be carried by storm.

Cortes now sent to the Aztec emperor to request his interposition with his subjects in behalf of the Spaniards. But Montezuma was not in the humour to comply. He had remained moodily in his quarters ever since the general's return. Disgusted with the treatment he had received, he had still further cause for mortification in finding himself the ally of those who were the open enemies of his nation. From his apartment he had beheld the tragical scenes in his capital, and seen another, Cuitlahua, the presumptive heir to his throne, whom Cortes had released a few days previous, taking the place which he should have occupied at the head of his warriors, and fighting the battles of his country. Distressed by his position, indignant at those who had placed him in it, he coldly answered, "What have I to do with Malinche? I do not wish to hear from him. I desire only to die. To what a state has my willingness to serve him reduced me!" When urged still further to comply by Olid and Father Olmedo, he added, "It is of no use. They will neither believe me, nor the false words and promises of Malinche. You will never leave these walls alive." On being assured, however, that the Spaniards would willingly depart, if a way were opened to them by their enemies, he at length — moved, probably, more by the desire to spare the blood of his subjects than of the Christians — consented to expostulate with his people.

In order to give the greater effect to his presence, he put on his imperial robes. The tilmatli, his mantle of white and blue, flowed over his shoulders, held together by its rich clasp of the green chalchuitl. The same precious gem, with emeralds of uncommon size, set in gold, profusely ornamented other parts of his dress. His feet were shod with the golden sandals, and his brows covered by the copilli, or Mexican diadem, resembling in form the pontifical tiara. Thus attired, and surrounded by a guard of Spaniards and several Aztec nobles, and preceded by the golden wand, the symbol of sovereignty, the Indian monarch ascended the central turret of the palace. His presence was instantly recognised by the people, and, as the royal retinue advanced along the battlements, a change, as if by magic, came over the scene. The clang of instruments, the fierce cries of the assailants, were hushed, and a death-like stillness pervaded the whole assembly, so fiercely agitated but a few moments before by the wild tumult of war! Many prostrated themselves on the ground; others bent the knee; and all turned with eager expectation towards the monarch, whom they had been taught to reverence with slavish awe, and from whose countenance they had been wont to turn away as from the intolerable splendours of divinity! Montezuma saw his advantage; and, while he stood thus confronted with his awe-struck people, he seemed to recover all his former authority and confidence as he felt himself to be still a king. With a calm voice, easily heard over the silent assembly, he is said by the Castilian writers to have thus addressed them:

"Why do I see my people here in arms against the palace of my fathers? Is it that you think your sovereign a prisoner, and wish to release him? If so, you have acted rightly. But you are mistaken. I am no prisoner. The strangers are my guests. I remain with them only from choice, and can leave them when I list. Have you come to drive them from the city? That is unnecessary. They will depart of their own accord, if you will open a way for them. Return to your homes, then. Lay down your arms. Show your obedience to me who have a right to it. The white men shall go back to their own land; and all shall be well again within the walls of Tenochtitlan."

As Montezuma announced himself the friend of the detested strangers, a murmur ran through the multitude; a murmur of contempt for the pusillanimous prince who could show himself so insensible to the insults and injuries for which the nation was in arms! The swollen tide of their passions swept away all the barriers of ancient reverence, and, taking a new direction, descended on the head of the unfortunate monarch, so far degenerated from his warlike ancestors. "Base Aztec," they exclaimed, "woman, coward, the white men have made you a woman — fit only to weave and spin!" These bitter taunts were soon followed by still more hostile demonstrations. A chief, it is said, of high rank, bent a bow or brandished a javelin with an air of defiance against the emperor, when, in an instant, a cloud of stones and arrows descended on the spot where the royal train was gathered. The Spaniards appointed to protect his person had been thrown off their guard by the respectful deportment of the people during their lord's address. They now hastily interposed their bucklers. But it was too late. Montezuma was wounded by three of the missiles one of which, a stone, fell with such violence on his head, near the temple, as brought him senseless to the ground. The Mexicans, shocked at their own sacrilegious act, experienced a sudden revulsion of feeling, and setting up a dismal cry, dispersed panic-struck in different directions. Not one of the multitudinous array remained in the great square before the palace!

The unhappy prince, meanwhile, was borne by his attendants to his apartments below. On recovering from the insensibility caused by the blow, the wretchedness of his condition broke upon him. He had tasted the last bitterness of degradation. He had been reviled, rejected, by his people. The meanest of the rabble had raised their hands against him. He had nothing more to live for. It was in vain that Cortes and his officers endeavoured to soothe the anguish of his spirit and fill him with better thoughts. He spoke not a word in answer. His wound, though dangerous, might still, with skilful treatment, not prove mortal. But Montezuma refused all the remedies prescribed for it. He tore off the bandages as often as they were applied, maintaining all the while the most determined silence. He sat with eyes dejected, brooding over his fallen fortunes, over the image of ancient majesty and present humiliation. He had survived his honour. But a spark of his ancient spirit seemed to kindle in his bosom, as it was clear he did not mean to survive his disgrace. — From this painful scene the Spanish general and his followers were soon called away by the new dangers which menaced the garrison.

OPPOSITE to the Spanish quarters, at only a few rods' distance, stood the great teocalli of Huitzilopochtli. This pyramidal mound, with the sanctuaries that crowned it, rising altogether to the height of near a hundred and fifty feet, afforded an elevated position that completely commanded the palace of Axayacatl, occupied by the Christians. A body of five or six hundred Mexicans, many of them nobles and warriors of the highest rank, had got possession of the teocalli, whence they discharged such a tempest of arrows on the garrison, that no one could leave his defences for a moment without imminent danger; while the Mexicans, under shelter of the sanctuaries, were entirely covered from the fire of the besieged. It was obviously necessary to dislodge the enemy, if the Spaniards would remain longer in their quarters.

Cortes assigned this service to his chamberlain Escobar, giving him a hundred men for the purpose, with orders to storm the teocalli, and set fire to the sanctuaries. But that officer was thrice repulsed in the attempt, and, after the most desperate efforts, was obliged to return with considerable loss and without accomplishing his object.

Cortes, who saw the immediate necessity of carrying the place, determined to lead the storming party himself. He was then suffering much from the wound in his left hand, which had disabled it for the present. He made the arm serviceable, however, by fastening his buckler to it, and, thus crippled, sallied out at the head of three hundred chosen cavaliers, and several thousand of his auxiliaries.

In the courtyard of the temple he found a numerous body of Indians prepared to dispute his passage. He briskly charged them, but the flat, smooth stones of the pavement were so slippery that the horses lost their footing and many of them fell. Hastily dismounting, they sent back the animals to their quarters, and, renewing the assault, the Spaniards succeeded without much difficulty in dispersing the Indian warriors, and opening a free passage for themselves to the teocalli.

Cortes, having cleared a way for the assault, sprang up the lower stairway, followed by Alvarado, Sandoval, Ordaz, and the other gallant cavaliers of his little band, leaving a file of arquebusiers and a strong corps of Indian allies to hold the enemy in check at foot of the monument. On the first landing, as well as on the several galleries above, and on the summit, the Aztec warriors were drawn up to dispute his passage. From their elevated position they showered down volleys of lighter missiles, together with heavy stones, beams, and burning rafters, which, thundering along the stairway, overturned the ascending Spaniards, and carried desolation through their ranks. The more fortunate, eluding or springing over these obstacles, succeeded in gaining the first terrace, where, throwing themselves on their enemies. they compelled them, after a short resistance, to fall back. The assailants pressed on, effectually supported by a brisk fire of the musketeers from below, which so much galled the Mexicans in their exposed situation, that they were glad to take shelter on the broad summit of the teocalli.

Cortes and his comrades were close upon their rear, and the two parties soon found themselves face to face on this aerial battle-field, engaged in mortal combat in presence of the whole city, as well as of the troops in the courtyard, who paused, as if by mutual consent, from their own hostilities, gazing in silent expectation on the issue of those above. The area, though somewhat smaller than the base of the teocalli, was large enough to afford a fair field of fight for a thousand combatants. It was paved with broad, flat stones. No impediment occurred over its surface, except the huge sacrificial block, and the temples of stone which rose to the height of forty feet, at the further extremity of the arena. One of these had been consecrated to the Cross; the other was still occupied by the Mexican war-god. The Christian and the Aztec contended for their religions under the very shadow of their respective shrines; while the Indian priests, running to and fro, with their hair wildly streaming over their sable mantles, seemed hovering in mid air, like so many demons of darkness urging on the work of slaughter!

The parties closed with the desperate fury of men who had no hope but in victory. Quarter was neither asked nor given; and to fly was impossible. The edge of the area was unprotected by parapet or battlement. The least slip would be fatal; and the combatants, as they struggled in mortal agony, were sometimes seen to roll over the sheer sides of the precipice together. Many of the Aztecs, seeing the fate of such of their comrades as fell into the hands of the Spaniards, voluntarily threw themselves headlong from the lofty summit and were dashed in pieces on the pavement.

The battle lasted with unintermitting fury for three hours. The number of the enemy was double that of the Christians; and it seemed as if it were a contest which must be determined by numbers and brute force, rather than by superior science. But it was not so. The invulnerable armour of the Spaniard, his sword of matchless temper, and his skill in the use of it, gave him advantages which far outweighed the odds of physical strength and numbers. After doing all that the courage of despair could enable men to do, resistance grew fainter and fainter on the side of the Aztecs. One after another they had fallen. Two or three priests only survived to be led away in triumph by the victors. Every other combatant was stretched a corpse on the bloody arena, or had been hurled from the giddy heights. Yet the loss of the Spaniards was not inconsiderable. It amounted to forty-five of their best men, and nearly all the remainder were more or less injured in the desperate conflict.

The victorious cavaliers now rushed towards the sanctuaries. The lower story was of stone; the two upper were of wood. Penetrating into their recesses, they had the mortification to find the image of the Virgin and the Cross removed. But in the other edifice they still beheld the grim figure of Huitzilopochtli, with the censer of smoking hearts, and the walls of his oratory reeking with gore — not improbably of their own countrymen! With shouts of triumph the Christians tore the uncouth monster from his niche, and tumbled him, in the presence of the horror-struck Aztecs, down the steps of the teocalli. They then set fire to the accursed building. The flame speedily ran up the slender towers, sending forth an ominous light over city, lake, and valley, to the remotest hut among the mountains. It was the funeral pyre of paganism, and proclaimed the fall of that sanguinary religion which had so long hung like a dark cloud over the fair regions of Anahuac! No achievement in the war struck more awe into the Mexicans than this storming of the great temple, in which the white men seemed to bid defiance equally to the powers of God and man.

Having accomplished this good work, the Spaniards descended the winding slopes of the teocalli with more free and buoyant step, as if conscious that the blessing of Heaven now rested on their arms. They passed through the dusky files of Indian warriors in the courtyard, too much dismayed by the appalling scenes they had witnessed to offer resistance; and reached their own quarters in safety. That very night they followed up the blow by a sortie on the sleeping town, and burned three hundred houses, the horrors of conflagration being made still more impressive by occurring at the hour when the Aztecs, from their own system of warfare, were least prepared for them.

Hoping to find the temper of the natives somewhat subdued by these reverses, Cortes now determined, with his usual policy, to make them a vantage-ground for proposing terms of accommodation. He accordingly invited the enemy to a parley, and, as the principal chiefs, attended by their followers, assembled in the great square, he mounted the turret before occupied by Montezuma, and made signs that he would address them. Marina, as usual, took her place by his side, as his interpreter. The multitude gazed with earnest curiosity on the Indian girl, whose influence with the Spaniards was well known, and whose connection with the general, in particular, had led the Aztecs to designate him by her Mexican name of Malinche. Cortes, speaking through the soft, musical tones of his mistress, told his audience they must now be convinced that they had nothing further to hope from opposition to the Spaniards. They had seen their gods trampled in the dust, their altars broken, their dwellings burned, their warriors falling on all sides. "All this," continued he, "you have brought on yourselves by your rebellion. Yet for the affection the sovereign, whom you have unworthily treated, still bears you, I would willingly stay my hand, if you will lay down your arms, and return once more to your obedience. But, if you do not," he concluded, "I will make your city a heap of ruins, and leave not a soul alive to mourn over it!"

But the Spanish commander did not yet comprehend the character of the Aztecs, if he thought to intimidate them by menaces. Calm in their exterior and slow to move, they were the more difficult to pacify when roused; and now that they had been stirred to their inmost depths, it was no human voice that could still the tempest. It may be, however, that Cortes did not so much misconceive the character of the people. He may have felt that an authoritative tone was the only one he could assume with any chance of effect, in his present position, in which milder and more conciliatory language would, by intimating a consciousness of inferiority, have too certainly defeated its own object.

It was true, they answered, he had destroyed their temples, broken in pieces their gods, massacred their countrymen. Many more, doubtless, were yet to fall under their terrible swords. But they were content so long as for every thousand Mexicans they could shed the blood of a single white man! "Look out," they continued, "on our terraces and streets, see them still thronged with warriors as far as your eyes can reach. Our numbers are scarcely diminished by our losses. Yours, on the contrary, are lessening every hour. You are perishing from hunger and sickness. Your provisions and water are failing. You must soon fall into our hands. The bridges are broken down, and you cannot escape! There will be too few of you left to glut the vengeance of our gods!" As they concluded, they sent a volley of arrows over the battlements, which compelled the Spaniards to descend and take refuge in their defences.

The fierce and indomitable spirit of the Aztecs filled the besieged with dismay. All, then, that they had done and suffered, their battles by day, their vigils by night, the perils they had braved, even the victories they had won, were of no avail. It was too evident that they had no longer the spring of ancient superstition to work upon in the breasts of the natives, who, like some wild beast that has burst the bonds of his keeper, seemed now to swell and exult in the full consciousness of their strength. The annunciation respecting the bridges fell like a knell on the ears of the Christians. All that they had heard was too true — and they gazed on one another with looks of anxiety and dismay.

The same consequences followed, which sometimes take place among the crew of a shipwrecked vessel. Subordination was lost in the dreadful sense of danger. A spirit of mutiny broke out, especially among the recent levies drawn from the army of Narvaez. They had come into the country from no motive of ambition, but attracted simply by the glowing reports of its opulence, and they had fondly hoped to return in a few months with their pockets well lined with the gold of the Aztec monarch. But how different had been their lot! From the first hour of their landing, they had experienced only trouble and disaster, privations of every description, sufferings unexampled, and they now beheld in perspective a fate yet more appalling. Bitterly did they lament the hour when they left the sunny fields of Cuba for these cannibal regions! And heartily did they curse their own folly in listening to the call of Velasquez, and still more in embarking under the banner of Cortes!

They now demanded with noisy vehemence to be led instantly from the city, and refused to serve longer in defence of a place where they were cooped up like sheep in the shambles, waiting only to be dragged to slaughter. In all this they were rebuked by the more orderly soldier-like conduct of the veterans of Cortes. These latter had shared with their general the day of his prosperity, and they were not disposed to desert him in the tempest. It was, indeed, obvious, on a little reflection, that the only chance of safety, in the existing crisis, rested on subordination and union; and that even this chance must be greatly diminished under any other leader than their present one.

Thus pressed by enemies without and by factions within, that leader was found, as usual, true to himself. Circumstances so appalling as would have paralysed a common mind, only stimulated his to higher action, and drew forth all its resources. He combined what is most rare, singular coolness and constancy of purpose, with a spirit of enterprise that might well be called romantic. His presence of mind did not now desert him. He calmly surveyed his condition, and weighed the difficulties which surrounded him, before coming to a decision. Independently of the hazard of a retreat in the face of a watchful and desperate foe, it was a deep mortification to surrender up the city, where he had so long lorded it as a master; to abandon the rich treasures which he had secured to himself and his followers; to forego the very means by which he had hoped to propitiate the favour of his sovereign, and secure an amnesty for his irregular proceedings. This, he well knew, must, after all, be dependent on success. To fly now was to acknowledge himself further removed from the conquest than ever.

What a close was this to a career so auspiciously begun! What a contrast to his magnificent vaunts! What a triumph would it afford to his enemies! The governor of Cuba would be amply revenged.

But, if such humiliating reflections crowded on his mind, the alternative of remaining, in his present crippled condition, seemed yet more desperate. With his men daily diminishing in strength and numbers, their provisions reduced so low that a small daily ration of bread was all the sustenance afforded to the soldier under his extraordinary fatigues, with the breaches every day widening in his feeble fortifications, with his ammunition, in fine, nearly expended, it would be impossible to maintain the place much longer — and none but men of iron constitutions and tempers, like the Spaniards, could have held it out so long — against the enemy. The chief embarrassment was as to the time and manner in which it would be expedient to evacuate the city. The best route seemed to be that of Tlacopan (Tacuba). For the causeway, the most dangerous part of the road, was but two miles long in that direction, and would therefore place the fugitives much sooner than either of the other great avenues on terra firma. Before his final departure, however, he proposed to make another sally in that direction, in order to reconnoitre the ground, and, at the same time, divert the enemy's attention from his real purpose by a show of active operations.

For some days his workmen had been employed in constructing a military machine of his own invention. It was called a manta, and was contrived somewhat on the principle of the mantelets used in the wars of the Middle Ages. It was, however, more complicated, consisting of a tower made of light beams and planks, having two chambers, one over the other. These were to be filled with musketeers, and the sides were provided with loop-holes, through which a fire could be kept up on the enemy. The great advantage proposed by this contrivance was, to afford a defence to the troops against the missiles hurled from the terraces. These machines, three of which were made, rested on rollers, and were provided with strong ropes, by which they were to be dragged along the streets by the Tlascalan auxiliaries.

The Mexicans gazed with astonishment on this warlike machinery, and, as the rolling fortresses advanced, belching forth fire and smoke from their entrails, the enemy, incapable of making an impression on those within, fell back in dismay. By bringing the mantas under the walls of the houses, the Spaniards were enabled to fire with effect on the mischievous tenants of the azoteas, and when this did not silence them, by letting a ladder, or light drawbridge, fall on the roof from the top of the manta, they opened a passage to the terrace, and closed with the combatants hand to hand. They could not, however, thus approach the higher buildings, from which the Indian warriors threw down such heavy masses of stone and timber as dislodged the planks that covered the machines, or, thundering against their sides, shook the frail edifices to their foundations, threatening all within with indiscriminate ruin. Indeed, the success of the experiment was doubtful, when the intervention of a canal put a stop to their further progress.

The Spaniards now found the assertion of their enemies too well confirmed. The bridge which traversed the opening had been demolished; and, although the canals which intersected the city were in general of no great width or depth, the removal of the bridges not only impeded the movements of the general's clumsy machines, but effectually disconcerted those of his cavalry. Resolving to abandon the mantas, he gave orders to fill up the chasm with stone, timber, and other rubbish drawn from the ruined buildings, and to make a new passage-way for the army. While this labour was going on, the Aztec slingers and archers on the other side of the opening kept up a galling discharge on the Christians, the more defenceless from the nature of their occupation. When the work was completed, and a safe passage secured, the Spanish cavaliers rode briskly against the enemy, who, unable to resist the shock of the steel-clad column, fell back with precipitation to where another canal afforded a similar strong position for defence.

There were no less than seven of these canals, intersecting the great street of Tlacopan, and at every one the same scene was renewed, the Mexicans making a gallant stand, and inflicting some loss, at each, on their persevering antagonists. These operations consumed two days, when, after incredible toil, the Spanish general had the satisfaction to find the line of communication completely re-established through the whole length of the avenue, and the principal bridges placed under strong detachments of infantry. At this juncture, when he had driven the foe before him to the furthest extremity of the street, where it touches on the causeway, he was informed that the Mexicans, disheartened by their reverses, desired to open a parley with him respecting the terms of an accommodation, and that their chiefs awaited his return for that purpose at the fortress. Overjoyed at the intelligence, he instantly rode back, attended by Alvarado, Sandoval, and about sixty of the cavaliers, to his quarters.

The Mexicans proposed that he should release the two priests captured in the temple, who might be the bearers of his terms, and serve as agents for conducting the negotiation. They were accordingly sent with the requisite instructions to their countrymen. But they did not return. The whole was an artifice of the enemy, anxious to procure the liberation of their religious leaders, one of whom was their teoteuctli, or high-priest, whose presence was indispensable in the probable event of a new coronation.

Cortes, meanwhile, relying on the prospects of a speedy arrangement, was hastily taking some refreshment with his officers, after the fatigues of the day, when he received the alarming tidings that the enemy were in arms again, with more fury than ever; that they had overpowered the detachments posted under Alvarado at three of the bridges, and were busily occupied in demolishing them. Stung with shame at the facility with which he had been duped by his wily foe, or rather by his own sanguine hopes, Cortes threw himself into the saddle, and, followed by his brave companions, galloped back at full speed to the scene of action. The Mexicans recoiled before the impetuous charge of the Spaniards. The bridges were again restored; and Cortes and his chivalry rode down the whole extent of the great street, driving the enemy, like frightened deer, at the points of their lances. But before he could return on his steps, he had the mortification to find, that the indefatigable foe, gathering from the adjoining lanes and streets, had again closed on his infantry, who, worn down by fatigue, were unable to maintain their position, at one of the principal bridges. New swarms of warriors now poured in on all sides, overwhelming the little band of Christian cavaliers with a storm of stones, darts, and arrows, which rattled like hail on their armour and on that of their well-barbed horses. Most of the missiles, indeed, glanced harmless from the good panoplies of steel, or thick quilted cotton; but, now and then, one better aimed penetrated the joints of the harness, and stretched the rider on the ground.

The confusion became greater around the broken bridge. Some of the horsemen were thrown into the canal, and their steeds floundered wildly about without a rider. Cortes himself, at this crisis, did more than any other to cover the retreat of his followers. While the bridge was repairing, he plunged boldly into the midst of the barbarians, striking down an enemy at every vault of his charger, cheering on his own men, and spreading terror through the ranks of his opponents by the well-known sound of his battle-cry. Never did he display greater hardihood, or more freely expose his person, emulating, says an old chronicler, the feats of the Roman Cocles. In this way he stayed the tide of assailants, till the last man had crossed the bridge, when, some of the planks having given way, he was compelled to leap a chasm of full six feet in width, amidst a cloud of missiles, before he could place himself in safety. A report ran through the army that the general was slain. It soon spread through the city, to the great joy of the Mexicans, and reached the fortress, where the besieged were thrown into no less consternation. But, happily for them, it was false. He, indeed, received two severe contusions on the knee, but in other respects remained uninjured. At no time, however, had he been in such extreme danger; and his escape, and that of his companions, were esteemed little less than a miracle.

The coming of night dispersed the Indian battalions, which, vanishing like birds of ill-omen from the field, left the well-contested pass in possession of the Spaniards. They returned, however, with none of the joyous feelings of conquerors to their citadel, but with slow step and dispirited, with weapons hacked, armour battered, and fainting under the loss of blood, fasting, and fatigue. In this condition they had yet to learn the tidings of a fresh misfortune in the death of Montezuma.

The Indian monarch had rapidly declined, since he had received his injury, sinking, however, quite as much under the anguish of a wounded spirit, as under disease. He continued in the same moody state of insensibility as that already described; holding little communication with those around him, deaf to consolation, obstinately rejecting all medical remedies, as well as nourishment. Perceiving his end approach, some of the cavaliers present in the fortress, whom the kindness of his manners had personally attached to him, were anxious to save the soul of the dying prince from the sad doom of those who perish in the darkness of unbelief. They accordingly waited on him, with Father Olmedo at their head, and in the most earnest manner implored him to open his eyes to the error of his creed, and consent to be baptised. But Montezuma — whatever may have been suggested to the contrary — seems never to have faltered in his hereditary faith, or to have contemplated becoming an apostate; for surely he merits that name in its most odious application, who, whether Christian or pagan, renounces his religion without conviction of its falsehood. Indeed, it was a too implicit reliance on its oracles, which had led him to give such easy confidence to the Spaniards. His intercourse with them had, doubtless, not sharpened his desire to embrace their communion; and the calamities of his country he might consider as sent by his gods to punish him for his hospitality to those who had desecrated and destroyed their shrines.

When Father Olmedo, therefore, kneeling at his side, with the uplifted crucifix, affectionately besought him to embrace the sign of man's redemption, he coldly repulsed the priest, exclaiming, "I have but a few moments to live; and will. not at this hour desert the faith of my fathers." One thing, however, seemed to press heavily on Montezuma's mind. This was the fate of his children, especially of three daughters, whom he had by his two wives; for there were certain rites of marriage, which distinguished the lawful wife from the concubine. Calling Cortes to his bedside, he earnestly commended these children to his care, as "the most precious jewels that he could leave him." He besought the general to interest his master, the emperor, in their behalf, and to see that they should not be left destitute, but be allowed some portion of their rightful inheritance. "Your lord will do this," he concluded, "if it were only for the friendly offices I have rendered the Spaniards, and for the love I have shown them — though it has brought me to this condition! But for this I bear them no ill-will." Such, according to Cortes himself, were the words of the dying monarch. Not long after, on the 30th of June, 1520, he expired in the arms of some of his own nobles, who still remained faithful in their attendance on his person.

Montezuma, at the time of his death, was about forty-one years old, of which he reigned eighteen. His person and manners have been already described. He left a numerous progeny by his various wives, most of whom, having lost their consideration after the Conquest, fell into obscurity as they mingled with the mass of the Indian population. Two of them, however, a son and a daughter, who embraced Christianity, became the founders of noble houses in Spain. The government, willing to show its gratitude for the large extent of empire derived from their ancestor, conferred on them ample estates, and important hereditary honours; and the Counts of Montezuma and Tula, intermarrying with the best blood of Castile, intimated by their names and titles their illustrious descent from the royal dynasty of Mexico.

Montezuma's death was a misfortune to the Spaniards. While he lived, they had a precious pledge in their hands, which, in extremity they might possibly have turned to account. Now the last link was snapped which connected them with the natives of the country. But independently of interested feelings, Cortes and his officers were much affected by his death from personal considerations; and, when they gazed on the cold remains of the ill-starred monarch, they may have felt a natural compunction as they contrasted his late flourishing condition with that to which his friendship for them had now reduced him.

The Spanish commander showed all respect for his memory. His body, arrayed in its royal robes, was laid decently on a bier, and borne on the shoulders of his nobles to his subjects in the city. What honours, if any, indeed, were paid to his remains, is uncertain. A sound of wailing, distinctly heard in the western quarters of the capital, was interpreted by the Spaniards into the moans of a funeral procession, as it bore the body to be laid among those of his ancestors, under the princely shades of Chapoltepec. Others state, that it was removed to a burial-place in the city named Copalco, and there burnt with the usual solemnities and signs of lamentation by his chiefs, but not without some unworthy insults from the Mexican populace. Whatever be the fact, the people, occupied with the stirring scenes in which they were engaged, were probably not long mindful of the monarch, who had taken no share in their late patriotic movements. Nor is it strange that the very memory of his sepulchre should be effaced in the terrible catastrophe which afterwards overwhelmed the capital, and swept away every landmark from its surface.

THERE was no longer any question as to the expediency of evacuating the capital. The only doubt was as to the time of doing so, and the route. The Spanish commander called a council of officers to deliberate on these matters. It was his purpose to retreat on Tlascala, and in that capital to decide according to circumstances on his future operations. After some discussion, they agreed on the causeway of Tlacopan as the avenue by which to leave the city. It would, indeed, take them back by a circuitous route, considerably longer than either of those by which they had approached the capital. But, for that reason, it would be less likely to be guarded, as least suspected; and the causeway, itself being shorter than either of the other entrances, would sooner place the army in comparative security on the main land.

There was some difference of opinion in respect to the hour of departure. The day-time, it was argued by some, would be preferable, since it would enable them to see the nature and extent of their danger, and to provide against it. Darkness would be much more likely to embarrass their own movements than those of the enemy, who were familiar with the ground. A thousand impediments would occur in the night, which might prevent their acting in concert, or obeying, or even ascertaining, the orders of the commander. But, on the other hand, it was urged, that the night presented many obvious advantages in dealing with a foe who rarely carried his hostilities beyond the day. The late active operations of the Spaniards had thrown the Mexicans off their guard, and it was improbable they would anticipate so speedy a departure of their enemies. With celerity and caution they might succeed, therefore, in making their escape from the town, possibly over the causeway, before their retreat should be discovered; and, could they once get beyond that pass of peril, they felt little apprehension for the rest.

These views were fortified, it is said, by the counsels of a soldier named Botello, who professed the mysterious science of judicial astrology. He had gained credit with the army by some predictions which had been verified by the events; those lucky hits which make chance pass for calculation with the credulous multitude. This man recommended to his countrymen by all means to evacuate the place in the night, as the hour most propitious to them, although he should perish in it. The event proved the astrologer better acquainted with his own horoscope than with that of others.

It is possible Botello's predictions had some weight in determining the opinion of Cortes. Superstition was the feature of the age, and the Spanish general, as we have seen, had a full measure of its bigotry. Seasons of gloom, moreover, dispose the mind to a ready acquiescence in the marvellous. It is, however, quite as probable that he made use of the astrologer's opinion, finding it coincided with his own, to influence that of his men, and inspire them with higher confidence. At all events, it was decided to abandon the city that very night.

The general's first care was to provide for the safe transportation of the treasure. Many of the common soldiers had converted their share of the prize, as we have seen, into gold chains, collars, or other ornaments, which they easily carried about their persons. But the royal fifth, together with that of Cortes himself, and much of the rich booty of the principal cavaliers had been converted into bars and wedges of solid gold, and deposited in one of the strong apartments of the palace. Cortes delivered the share belonging to the crown to the royal officers, assigning them one of the strongest horses, and a guard of Castilian soldiers to transport it. Still, much of the treasure belonging both to the crown and to individuals was necessarily abandoned, from the want of adequate means of conveyance. The metal lay scattered in shining heaps along the floor, exciting the cupidity of the soldiers. "Take what you will of it," said Cortes to his men. "Better you should have it than these Mexican hounds. But be careful not to overload yourselves. He travels safest in the dark night who travels lightest." His own more wary followers took heed to his counsel, helping themselves to a few articles of least bulk, though, it might be, of greatest value. But the troops of Narvaez, pining for riches, of which they had heard so much, and hitherto seen so little, showed no such discretion. To them it seemed as if the very mines of Mexico were turned up before them, and, rushing on the treacherous spoil, they greedily loaded themselves with as much of it, not merely as they could accommodate about their persons, but as they could stow away in wallets, boxes, or any other mode of conveyance at their disposal.

Cortes next arranged the order of march. The van, composed of two hundred Spanish foot, he placed under the command of the valiant Gonzalo de Sandoval, supported by Diego de Ordaz, Francisco de Lugo, and about twenty other cavaliers. The rear-guard, constituting the strength of the infantry, was intrusted to Pedro de Alvarado and Velasquez de Leon. The general himself took charge of the "battle," or centre, in which went the baggage, some of the heavy guns, most of which, however, remained in the rear, the treasure, and the prisoners. These consisted of a son and two daughters of Montezuma, Cacama, the deposed lord of Tezcuco, and several other nobles, whom Cortes retained as important pledges in his future negotiations with the enemy. The Tlascalans were distributed pretty equally among the three divisions; and Cortes had under his immediate command a hundred picked soldiers, his own veterans most attached to his service, who, with Christoval de Olid, Francisco de Morla, Alonso de Avila, and two or three other cavaliers, formed a select corps, to act wherever occasion might require.

The general had already superintended the construction of a portable bridge to be laid over the open canals in the causeway. This was given in charge to an officer named Magarino, with forty soldiers under his orders, all pledged to defend the passage to the last extremity. The bridge was to be taken up when the entire army had crossed one of the breaches, and transported to the next. There were three of these openings in the causeway, and most fortunate would it have been for the expedition, if the foresight of the commander had provided the same number of bridges. But the labour would have been great, and time was short.

At midnight the troops were under arms, in readiness for the march. Mass was performed by Father Olmedo, who invoked the protection of the Almighty through the awful perils of the night. The gates were thrown open, and, on the first of July, 1520, the Spaniards for the last time sallied forth from the walls of the ancient fortress, the scene of so much suffering and such indomitable courage.

The night was cloudy, and a drizzling rain, which fell without intermission, added to the obscurity. The great square before the palace was deserted, as, indeed, it had been since the fall of Montezuma. Steadily, and as noiselessly as possible, the Spaniards held their way along the great street of Tlacopan, which so lately had resounded to the tumult of battle. All was now hushed in silence; and they were only reminded of the past by the occasional presence of some solitary corpse, or a dark heap of the slain, which too plainly told where the strife had been hottest. As they passed along the lanes and alleys which opened into the great street, or looked down the canals, whose polished surface gleamed with a sort of ebon lustre through the obscurity of night, they easily fancied that they discerned the shadowy forms of their foe lurking in ambush, and ready to spring on them. But it was only fancy; and the city slept undisturbed even by the prolonged echoes of the tramp of the horses, and the hoarse rumbling of the artillery and baggage trains. At length a lighter space beyond the dusky line of buildings showed the van of the army that it was emerging on the open causeway. They might well have congratulated themselves on having thus escaped the dangers of an assault in the city itself, and that a brief time would place them in comparative safety on the opposite shore. But the Mexicans were not all asleep.

As the Spaniards drew near the spot where the street opened on the causeway, and were preparing to lay the portable bridge across the uncovered breach which now met their eyes, several Indian sentinels, who had been stationed at this, as at the other approaches to the city, took the alarm, and fled, rousing their countrymen by their cries. The priests, keeping their night watch on the summit of the teocallis, instantly caught the tidings and sounded their shells, while the huge drum in the desolite temple of the war-god sent forth those solemn tones, which, heard only in seasons of calamity, vibrated through every corner of the capital. The Spaniards saw that no time was to be lost. The bridge was brought forward and fitted with all possible expedition. Sandoval was the first to try its strength, and, riding across, was followed by his little body of chivalry, his infantry, and Tlascalan allies, who formed the first division of the army. Then came Cortes and his squadrons, with the baggage, ammunition wagons, and a part of the artillery. But before they had time to defile across the narrow passage, a gathering sound was heard, like that of a mighty forest agitated by the winds. It grew louder and louder, while on the dark waters of the lake was heard a splashing noise, as of many oars. Then came a few stones and arrows striking at random among the hurrying troops. They fell every moment faster and more furious, till they thickened into a terrible tempest, while the very heavens were rent with the yells and war-cries of myriads of combatants, who seemed all at once to be swarming over land and lake!

The Spaniards pushed steadily on through this arrowy sleet, though the barbarians, dashing their canoes against the sides of the causeway, clambered up and broke in upon their ranks. But the Christians, anxious only to make their escape, declined all combat except for self-preservation. The cavaliers, spurring forward their steeds, shook off their assailants, and rode over their prostrate bodies, while the men on foot with their good swords or the butts of their pieces drove them headlong again down the sides of the dike.

But the advance of several thousand men, marching, probably, on a front of not more than fifteen or twenty abreast, necessarily required much time, and the leading files had already reached the second breach in the causeway before those in the rear had entirely traversed the first. Here they halted; as they had no means of effecting a passage, smarting all the while under unintermitting volleys from the enemy, who were clustered thick on the waters around this second opening. Sorely distressed, the vanguard sent repeated messages to the rear to demand the portable bridge. At length the last of the army had crossed, and Magarino and his sturdy followers endeavoured to raise the ponderous framework. But it stuck fast in the sides of the dike. In vain they strained every nerve. The weight of so many men and horses, and above all of the heavy artillery, had wedged the timbers so firmly in the stones and earth, that it was beyond their power to dislodge them. Still they laboured amidst a torrent of missiles, until, many of them slain, and all wounded, they were obliged to abandon the attempt.

The tidings soon spread from man to man, and no sooner was their dreadful import comprehended, than a cry of despair arose, which for a moment drowned all the noise of conflict. All means of retreat were cut off. Scarcely hope was left. The only hope was in such desperate exertions as each could make for himself. Order and subordination were at an end. Intense danger produced intense selfishness. Each thought only of his own life. Pressing forward, he trampled down the weak and the wounded, heedless whether it were friend or foe. The leading files, urged on by the rear, were crowded on the brink of the gulf. Sandoval, Ordaz, and the other cavaliers dashed into the water. Some succeeded in swimming their horses across; others failed, and some, who reached the opposite bank, being overturned in the ascent, rolled headlong with their steeds into the lake. The infantry followed pellmell, heaped promiscuously on one another, frequently pierced by the shafts, or struck down by the war-clubs of the Aztecs; while many an unfortunate victim was dragged half-stunned on board their canoes, to be reserved for a protracted, but more dreadful death.

The carnage raged fearfully along the length of the causeway. Its shadowy bulk presented a mark of sufficient distinctness for the enemy's missiles, which often prostrated their own countrymen in the blind fury of the tempest. Those nearest the dike, running their canoes alongside, with a force that shattered them to pieces, leaped on the land and grappled with the Christians, until both came rolling down the side of the causeway together. But the Aztec fell among his friends, while his antagonist was borne away in triumph to the sacrifice. The struggle was long and deadly. The Mexicans were recognised by their white cotton tunics, which showed faint through the darkness. Above the combatants rose a wild and discordant clamour, in which horrid shouts of vengeance were mingled with groans of agony, with invocations of the saints and the blessed Virgin, and with the screams of women; for there were several women, both native and Spaniards, who had accompanied the Christian camp. Among these, one named Maria de Estrada is particularly noticed for the courage she displayed, battling with broadsword and target like the staunchest of the warriors.

The opening in the causeway, meanwhile, was filled up with the wreck of matter which had been forced into it, ammunition wagons, heavy guns, bales of rich stuffs scattered over the waters, chests of solid ingots, and bodies of men and horses, till over this dismal ruin a passage was gradually formed, by which those in the rear were enabled to clamber to the other side. Cortes, it is said, found a place that was fordable, where halting with the water up to his saddle-girths, he endeavoured to check the confusion, and lead his followers by a safer path to the opposite bank. But his voice was lost in the wild uproar, and finally, hurrying on with the tide, he pressed forward with a few trusty cavaliers, who remained near his person, to the van; but not before he had seen his favourite page, Juan de Salazar, struck down, a corpse, by his side. Here he found Sandoval and his companions, halting before the third and last breach, endeavouring to cheer on their followers to surmount it. But their resolution faltered. It was wide and deep; though the passage was not so closely beset by the enemy as the preceding ones. The cavaliers again set the example by plunging into the water. Horse and foot followed as they could, some swimming, others with dying grasp clinging to the manes and tails of the struggling animals. Those fared best, as the general had predicted, who travelled lightest; and many were the unfortunate wretches, who, weighed down by the fatal gold which they loved so well, were buried with it in the salt floods of the lake. Cortes, with his gallant comrades, Olid, Morla, Sandoval, and some few others, still kept in the advance, leading his broken remnant off the fatal causeway. The din of battle lessened in the distance; when the rumour reached them, that the rear-guard would be wholly overwhelmed without speedy relief. It seemed almost an act of desperation; but the generous hearts of the Spanish cavaliers did not stop to calculate danger when the cry for succour reached them. Turning their horses' bridles, they galloped back to the theatre of action, worked their way through the press, swam the canal, and placed themselves in the thick of the melee on the opposite bank.

The first grey of the morning was now coming over the waters. It showed the hideous confusion of the scene which had been shrouded in the obscurity of night. The dark masses of combatants, stretching along the dike, were seen struggling for mastery, until the very causeway on which they stood appeared to tremble, and reel to and fro, as if shaken by an earthquake; while the bosom of the lake, as far as the eye could reach, was darkened by canoes crowded with warriors, whose spears and bludgeons, armed with blades of "volcanic glass," gleamed in the morning light.

The cavaliers found Alvarado unhorsed, and defending himself with a poor handful of followers against an overwhelming tide of the enemy. His good steed, which had borne him through many a hard fight, had fallen under him. He was himself wounded in several places, and was striving in vain to rally his scattered column, which was driven to the verge of the canal by the fury of the enemy, then in possession of the whole rear of the causeway, where they were reinforced every hour by fresh combatants from the city. The artillery in the earlier part of the engagement had not been idle, and its iron shower, sweeping along the dike, had mowed down the assailants by hundreds. But nothing could resist their impetuosity. The front ranks, pushed on by those behind, were at length forced up to the pieces, and, pouring over them like a torrent, overthrew men and guns in one general ruin. The resolute charge of the Spanish cavaliers, who had now arrived, created a temporary check, and gave time for their countrymen to make a feeble rally. But they were speedily borne down by the returning flood. Cortes and his companions were compelled to plunge again into the lake — though all did not escape. Alvarado stood on the brink for a moment, hesitating what to do. Unhorsed as he was, to throw himself into the water in the face of the hostile canoes that now swarmed around the opening, afforded but a desperate chance of safety. He had but a second for thought. He was a man of powerful frame, and despair gave him unnatural energy. Setting his long lance firmly on the wreck which strewed the bottom of the lake, he sprung forward with all his might, and cleared the wide gap at a leap! Aztecs and Tlascalans gazed in stupid amazement, exclaiming, as they beheld the incredible feat, "This is truly the Tonatiuh — the child of the Sun!"— The breadth of the opening is not given. But it was so great, that the valorous Captain Diaz, who well remembered the place, says the leap was impossible to any man. Other contemporaries, however, do not discredit the story.

Cortes and his companions now rode forward to the front, where the troops in a loose, disorderly manner, were marching off the fatal causeway. A few only of the enemy hung on their rear, or annoyed them by occasional flights of arrows from the lake. The attention of the Aztecs was diverted by the rich spoil that strewed the battle-ground; fortunately for the Spaniards, who, had their enemy pursued with the same ferocity with which he had fought, would, in their crippled condition, have been cut off, probably to a man. But little molested, therefore, they were allowed to defile through the adjacent village, or suburbs, it might be called, of Popotla.

The Spanish commander there dismounted from his jaded steed, and, sitting down on the steps of an Indian temple, gazed mournfully on the broken files as they passed before him. What a spectacle did they present! The cavalry, most of them dismounted, were mingled with the infantry, who dragged their feeble limbs along with difficulty; their shattered mail and tattered garments dripping with the salt ooze, showing through their rents many a bruise and ghastly wound; their bright arms soiled, their proud crests and banners gone, the baggage, artillery — all, in short, that constitutes the pride and panoply of glorious war, for ever lost. Cortes, as he looked wistfully on their thinned and disordered ranks, sought in vain for many a familiar face, and missed more than one dear companion who had stood side by side with him through all the perils of the Conquest. Though accustomed to control his emotions, or, at least, to conceal them, the sight was too much for him. He covered his face with his hands, and the tears which trickled down revealed too plainly the anguish of his soul.

He found some consolation, however, in the sight of several of the cavaliers on whom he most relied. Alvarado, Sandoval, Olid, Ordaz, Avila, were yet safe. He had the inexpressible satisfaction, also, of learning the safety of the Indian interpreter, Marina, so dear to him, and so important to the army. She had been committed with a daughter of a Tlascalan chief, to several of that nation. She was fortunately placed in the van, and her faithful escort had carried her securely through all the dangers of the night. Aguilar, the other interpreter, had also escaped; and it was with no less satisfaction that Cortes learned the safety of the ship-builder, Martin Lopez. The general's solicitude for the fate of this man, so indispensable, as he proved, to the success of his subsequent operations, showed that amidst all his affliction, his indomitable spirit was looking forward to the hour of vengeance.

Meanwhile, the advancing column had reached the neighbouring city of Tlacopan (Tacuba), once the capital of an independent principality. There it halted in the great street, as if bewildered and altogether uncertain what course to take. Cortes, who had hastily mounted and rode on to the front again, saw the danger of remaining in a populous place, where the inhabitants might sorely annoy the troops from the azoteas, with little risk to themselves. Pushing forward, therefore, he soon led them into the country. There he endeavoured to reform his disorganised battalions, and bring them to something like order.

Hard by, at no great distance on the left, rose an eminence, looking towards a chain of mountains which fences in the valley on the west. It was called the Hill of Otoncalpolco, and sometimes the Hill of Montezuma. It was crowned with an Indian teocalli, with its large outworks of stone covering an ample space, and by its strong position, which commanded the neighbouring plain, promised a good place of refuge for the exhausted troops. But the men, disheartened and stupefied by their late reverses, seemed for the moment incapable of further exertion; and the place was held by a body of armed Indians. Cortes saw the necessity of dislodging them, if he would save the remains of his army from entire destruction. The event showed he still held a control over their wills stronger than circumstances themselves. Cheering them on, and supported by his gallant cavaliers, he succeeded in infusing into the most sluggish something of his own intrepid temper, and led them up the ascent in face of the enemy. But the latter made slight resistance, and after a few feeble volleys of missiles which did little injury, left the ground to the assailants.

It was covered by a building of considerable size, and furnished ample accommodations for the diminished numbers of the Spaniards. They found there some provisions; and more, it is said, were brought to them in the course of the day from some friendly Otomie villages in the neighbourhood. There was, also, a quantity of fuel in the courts, destined to the uses of the temple. With this they made fires to dry their drenched garments, and busily employed themselves in dressing one another's wounds, stiff and extremely painful from exposure and long exertion. Thus refreshed, the weary soldiers threw themselves down on the floor and courts of the temple, and soon found the temporary oblivion which Nature seldom denies even in the greatest extremity of suffering.

There was one eye in that assembly, however, which we may well believe did not so speedily close. For what agitating thoughts must have crowded on the mind of their commander, as he beheld his poor remnant of followers thus huddled together in this miserable bivouac! And this was all that survived of the brilliant array with which but a few weeks since he had entered the capital of Mexico! Where now were his dreams of conquest and empire? And what was he but a luckless adventurer, at whom the finger of scorn would be uplifted as a madman? Whichever way he turned, the horizon was almost equally gloomy, with scarcely one light spot to cheer him. He had still a weary journey before him, through perilous and unknown paths, with guides of whose fidelity he could not be assured. And how could he rely on his reception at Tlascala, the place of his destination; the land of his ancient enemies; where, formerly as a foe, and now as a friend, he had brought desolation to every family within its borders?

Yet these agitating and gloomy reflections, which might have crushed a common mind, had no power over that of Cortes; or rather, they only served to renew his energies, and quicken his perceptions, as the war of the elements purifies and gives elasticity to the atmosphere. He looked with an unblenching eye on his past reverses; but, confident in his own resources, he saw a light through the gloom which others could not. Even in the shattered relics which lay around him, resembling in their haggard aspect and wild attire a horde of famished outlaws, he discerned the materials out of which to reconstruct his ruined fortunes. In the very hour of discomfiture and general despondency, there is no doubt that his heroic spirit was meditating the plan of operations which he afterwards pursued with such dauntless constancy.

The loss sustained by the Spaniards on this fatal night, like every other event in the history of the Conquest, is reported with the greatest discrepancy. If we believe Cortes' own letter, it did not exceed one hundred and fifty Spaniards and two thousand Indians. But the general's bulletins, while they do full justice to the difficulties to be overcome, and the importance of the results, are less scrupulous in stating the extent either of his means or of his losses. Thoan Cano, one of the cavaliers present, estimates the slain at eleven hundred and seventy Spaniards, and eight thousand allies. But this is a greater number than we have allowed for the whole army. Perhaps we may come nearest the truth by taking the computation of Gomara, the chaplain of Cortes, who had free access doubtless, not only to the general's papers, but to other authentic sources of information. According to him, the number of Christians killed and missing was four hundred and fifty, and that of natives four thousand. This, with the loss sustained in the conflicts of the previous week, may have reduced the former to something more than a third, and the latter to a fourth, or, perhaps, fifth, of the original force with which they entered the capital. The brunt of the action fell on the rear-guard, few of whom escaped. It was formed chiefly of the soldiers of Narvaez, who fell the victims in some measure of their cupidity. Forty-six of the cavalry were cut off, which with previous losses reduced the number in this branch of the service to twenty-three, and some of these in very poor condition. The greater part of the treasure, the baggage, the general's papers, including his accounts, and a minute diary of transactions since leaving Cuba — which, to posterity, at least, would have been of more worth than the gold — had been swallowed up by the waters. The ammunition, the beautiful little train of artillery, with which Cortes had entered the city, were all gone. Not a musket even remained, the men having thrown them away, eager to disencumber themselves of all that might retard their escape on that disastrous night. Nothing, in short, of their military apparatus was left, but their swords, their crippled cavalry, and a few damaged crossbows, to assert the superiority of the European over the barbarian.

The prisoners, including, as already noticed, the children of Montezuma and the cacique of Tezcuco, all perished by the hands of their ignorant countrymen, it is said, in the indiscriminate fury of the assault. There were, also, some persons of consideration among the Spaniards, whose names were inscribed on the same bloody roll of slaughter. Such was Francisco de Morla, who fell by the side of Cortes, on returning with him to the rescue. But the greatest loss was that of Juan Velasquez de Leon, who, with Alvarado, had command of the rear. It was the post of danger on that night, and he fell, bravely defending it, at an early part of the retreat. There was no cavalier in the army, with the exception, perhaps, of Sandoval and Alvarado, whose loss would have been so deeply deplored by the commander. Such were the disastrous results of this terrible passage of the causeway; more disastrous than those occasioned by any other reverse which has stained the Spanish arms in the New World; and which have branded the night on which it happened, in the national annals, with the name of the noche triste, "the sad or melancholy night."

THE Mexicans, during the day which followed the retreat of the Spaniards, remained, for the most part, quiet in their own capital, where they found occupation in cleansing the streets and causeways from the dead, which lay festering in heaps that might have bred a pestilence. They may have been employed, also, in paying the last honours to such of their warriors as had fallen, solemnising the funeral rites by the sacrifice of their wretched prisoners, who, as they contemplated their own destiny, may well have envied the fate of their companions who left their bones on the battle-field. It was most fortunate for the Spaniards, in their extremity, that they had this breathing-time allowed them by the enemy. But Cortes knew that he could not calculate on its continuance, and, feeling how important it was to get the start of his vigilant foe, he ordered his troops to be in readiness to resume their march by midnight. Fires were left burning, the better to deceive the enemy; and at the appointed hour, the little army, without sound of drum or trumpet, but with renewed spirits, sallied forth from the gates of the teocalli.

It was arranged that the sick and wounded should occupy the centre, transported on litters, or on the backs of the tamanes, while those who were strong enough to keep their seats should mount behind the cavalry. The able-bodied soldiers were ordered to the front and rear, while others protected the flanks, thus affording all the security possible to the invalids.

The retreating army held on its way unmolested under cover of the darkness. But, as morning dawned, they beheld parties of the natives moving over the heights, or hanging at a distance, like a cloud of locusts on their rear. They did not belong to the capital; but were gathered from the neighbouring country, where the tidings of their rout had already penetrated. The charm, which had hitherto covered the white men, was gone.

The Spaniards, under the conduct of their Tlascalan guides, took a circuitous route to the north, passing through Quauhtitlan, and round lake Tzompanco (Zumpango), thus lengthening their march, but keeping at a distance from the capital. From the eminences, as they passed along, the Indians rolled down heavy stones, mingled with volleys of darts and arrows on the heads of the soldiers. Some were even bold enough to descend into the plain and assault the extremities of the column. But they were soon beaten off by the horse, and compelled to take refuge among the hills, where the ground was too rough for the rider to follow. Indeed, the Spaniards did not care to do so, their object being rather to fly than to fight.

In this way they slowly advanced, halting at intervals to drive off their assailants when they became too importunate, and greatly distressed by their missiles and their desultory attacks. At night, the troops usually found shelter in some town or hamlet, whence the inhabitants, in anticipation of their approach, had been careful to carry off all the provisions. The Spaniards were soon reduced to the greatest straits for subsistence. Their principal food was the wild cherry, which grew in the woods or by the roadside. Fortunate were they if they found a few ears of corn unplucked. More frequently nothing was left but the stalks; and with them, and the like unwholesome fare, they were fain to supply the cravings of appetite. When a horse happened to be killed, it furnished an extraordinary banquet; and Cortes himself records the fact of his having made one of a party who thus sumptuously regaled themselves, devouring the animal even to his hide.

The wretched soldiers, faint with famine and fatigue, were sometimes seen to drop down lifeless on the road. Others loitered behind unable to keep up with the march, and fell into the hands of the enemy, who followed in the track of the army like a flock of famished vultures, eager to pounce on the dying and the dead. Others, again, who strayed too far, in their eagerness to procure sustenance, shared the same fate. The number of these, at length, and the consciousness of the cruel lot for which they were reserved, compelled Cortes to introduce stricter discipline, and to enforce it by sterner punishments than he had hitherto done — though too often ineffectually, such was the indifference to danger, under the overwhelming pressure of present calamity.

Through these weary days Cortes displayed his usual serenity and fortitude. He was ever in the post of danger, freely exposing himself in encounters with the enemy; in one of which he received a severe wound in the head, that afterwards gave him much trouble. He fared no better than the humblest soldier, and strove, by his own cheerful countenance and counsels, to fortify the courage of those who faltered, assuring them that their sufferings would soon be ended by their arrival in the hospitable "land of bread." His faithful officers co-operated with him in these efforts; and the common file, indeed, especially his own veterans, must be allowed, for the most part, to have shown a full measure of the constancy and power of endurance so characteristic of their nation — justifying the honest boast of an old chronicler, "that there was no people so capable of supporting hunger as the Spaniards, and none of them who were ever more severely tried than the soldiers of Cortes." A similar fortitude was shown by the Tlascalans, trained in a rough school that made them familiar with hardships and privations. Although they sometimes threw themselves on the ground, in the extremity of famine, imploring their gods not to abandon them, they did their duty as warriors; and, far from manifesting coldness towards the Spaniards as the cause of their distresses, seemed only the more firmly knit to them by the sense of a common suffering.

On the seventh morning, the army had reached the mountain rampart which overlooks the plains of Otompan, or Otumba, as commonly called, from the Indian city — now a village — situated in them. The distance from the capital is hardly nine leagues. But the Spaniards had travelled more than thrice that distance, in their circuitous march round the lakes. This had been performed so slowly, that it consumed a week; two nights of which had been passed in the same quarters, from the absolute necessity of rest. It was not, therefore, till the 7th of July that they reached the heights commanding the plains which stretched far away towards the territory of Tlascala, in full view of the venerable pyramids of Teotihuacan, two of the most remarkable monuments of the antique American civilisation now existing north of the Isthmus. During all the preceding day, they had seen parties of the enemy hovering like dark clouds above the highlands, brandishing their weapons, and calling out in vindictive tones, "Hasten on! You will soon find yourselves where you cannot escape!" words of mysterious import, which they were made fully to comprehend on the following morning.

As the army was climbing the mountain steeps which shut in the Valley of Otompan, the videttes came in with the intelligence, that a powerful body was encamped on the other side, apparently awaiting their approach. The intelligence was soon confirmed by their own eyes, as they turned the crest of the sierra, and saw spread out, below, a mighty host, filling up the whole depth of the valley, and giving to it the appearance, from the white cotton mail of the warriors, of being covered with snow. It consisted of levies from the surrounding country, and especially the populous territory of Tezcuco, drawn together at the instance of Cuitlahua, Montezuma's successor, and now concentrated on this point to dispute the passage of the Spaniards. Every chief of note had taken the field with his whole array gathered under his standard, proudly displaying all the pomp and rude splendour of his military equipment. As far as the eye could reach, were to be seen shields and waving banners, fantastic helmets, forests of shining spears, the bright feather-mail of the chief, and the coarse cotton panoply of his follower, all mingled together in wild confusion, and tossing to and fro like the billows of a troubled ocean. It was a sight to fill the stoutest heart among the Christians with dismay, heightened by the previous expectation of soon reaching the friendly land which was to terminate their wearisome pilgrimage. Even Cortes, as he contrasted the tremendous array before him with his own diminished squadrons, wasted by disease and enfeebled by hunger and fatigue, could not escape the conviction that his last hour had arrived.

But his was not the heart to despond; and he gathered strength from the very extremity of his situation. He had no room for hesitation; for there was no alternative left to him. To escape was impossible. He could not retreat on the capital, from which he had been expelled. He must advance — cut through the enemy, or perish. He hastily made his dispositions for the fight. He gave his force as broad a front as possible, protecting it on each flank by his little body of horse, now reduced to twenty. Fortunately, he had not allowed the invalids, for the last two days, to mount, behind the riders, from a desire to spare the horses, so that these were now in tolerable condition; and, indeed, the whole army had been refreshed by halting, as we have seen, two nights and a day in the same place, a delay, however, which had allowed the enemy time to assemble in such force to dispute its progress.

Cortes instructed his cavaliers not to part with their lances, and to direct them at the face. The infantry were to thrust, not strike, with their swords; passing them, at once, through the bodies of their enemies. They were, above all, to aim at the leaders, as the general well knew how much depends on the life of the commander in the wars of barbarians, whose want of subordination makes them impatient of any control but that to which they are accustomed.

He then addressed to his troops a few words of encouragement, as customary with him on the eve of an engagement. He reminded them of the victories they had won with odds nearly as discouraging as the present; thus establishing the superiority of science and discipline over numbers. Numbers, indeed, were of no account, where the arm of the Almighty was on their side. And he bade them have full confidence, that He, who had carried them safely through so many perils, would not now abandon them and his own good cause, to perish by the hand of the infidel. His address was brief, for he read in their looks that settled resolve which rendered words unnecessary. The circumstances of their position spoke more forcibly to the heart of every soldier than any eloquence could have done, filling it with that feeling of desperation, which makes the weak arm strong, and turns the coward into a hero. After they had earnestly commended themselves, therefore, to the protection of God, the Virgin, and St. James, Cortes led his battalions straight against the enemy.

It was a solemn moment — that in which the devoted little band, with steadfast countenances, and their usual intrepid step, descended on the plain to be swallowed up, as it were, in the vast ocean of their enemies. The latter rushed on with impetuosity to meet them, making the mountains ring to their discordant yells and battle-cries, and sending forth volleys of stones and arrows which for a moment shut out the light of day. But, when the leading files of the two armies closed, the superiority of the Christians was felt, as their antagonists, falling back before the charges of cavalry, were thrown into confusion by their own numbers who pressed on them from behind. The Spanish infantry followed up the blow, and a wide lane was opened in the ranks of the enemy, who, receding on all sides, seemed willing to allow a free passage for their opponents. But it was to return on them with accumulated force, as, rallying, they poured upon the Christians, enveloping the little army on all sides, which with its bristling array of long swords and javelins, stood firm — in the words of a contemporary — like an islet against which the breakers, roaring and surging, spend their fury in vain. The struggle was desperate of man against man. The Tlascalan seemed to renew his strength, as he fought almost in view of his own native hills; as did the Spaniard, with the horrible doom of the captive before his eyes. Well did the cavaliers do their duty on that day; charging, in little bodies of four or five abreast, deep into the enemy's ranks, riding over the broken files, and by this temporary advantage giving strength and courage to the infantry. Not a lance was there which did not reek with the blood of the infidel. Among the rest, the young captain Sandoval is particularly commemorated for his daring prowess. Managing his fiery steed with easy horsemanship, he darted, when least expected, into the thickest of the melee, overturning the staunchest warriors, and rejoicing in danger, as if it were his natural element.

But these gallant displays of heroism served only to ingulf the Spaniards deeper and deeper in the mass of the enemy, with scarcely any more chance of cutting their way through his dense and interminable battalions, than of hewing a passage with their swords through the mountains. Many of the Tlascalans and some of the Spaniards had fallen, and not one but had been wounded. Cortes himself had received a second cut on the head, and his horse was so much injured that he was compelled to dismount, and take one from the baggage train, a strong-boned animal, who carried him well through the turmoil of the day. The contest had now lasted several hours. The sun rode high in the heavens, and shed an intolerable fervour over the plain. The Christians, weakened by previous sufferings, and faint with loss of blood, began to relax in their desperate exertions. Their enemies, constantly supported by fresh relays from the rear, were still in good heart, and, quick to perceive their advantage, pressed with redoubled force on the Spaniards. The horse fell back, crowded on the foot; and the latter, in vain seeking a passage amidst the dusky throngs of the enemy, who now closed up the rear, were thrown into some disorder. The tide of battle was setting rapidly against the Christians.

The fate of the day would soon be decided; and all that now remained for them seemed to be to sell their lives as dearly as possible.

At this critical moment, Cortes, whose restless eye had been roving round the field in quest of any object that might offer him the means of arresting the coming ruin, rising in his stirrups, descried at a distance, in the midst of the throng, the chief who, from his dress and military cortege, he knew must be the commander of the barbarian forces. He was covered with a rich surcoat of feather-work; and a panache of beautiful plumes, gorgeously set in gold and precious stones, floated above his head. Rising above this, and attached to his back, between the shoulders, was a short staff bearing a golden net for a banner — the singular, but customary, symbol of authority for an Aztec commander. The cacique, whose name was Cihuaca, was borne on a litter, and a body of young warriors, whose gay and ornamented dresses showed them to be the flower of the Indian nobles, stood round as a guard of his person and the sacred emblem.

The eagle eye of Cortes no sooner fell on this personage, than it lighted up with triumph. Turning quickly round to the cavaliers at his side, among whom were Sandoval, Olid, Alvarado, and Avila, he pointed out the chief, exclaiming, "There is our mark! Follow and support me!" Then crying his war-cry, and striking his iron heel into his weary steed, he plunged headlong into the thickest of the press. His enemies fell back, taken by surprise and daunted by the ferocity of the attack. Those who did not were pierced through with his lance, or borne down by the weight of his charger. The cavaliers followed close in the rear. On they swept, with the fury of a thunderbolt, cleaving the solid ranks asunder, strewing their path with the dying and the dead, and bounding over every obstacle in their way. In a few minutes they were in the presence of the Indian commander, and Cortes, overturning his supporters, sprung forward with the strength of a lion, and, striking him through with his lance, hurled him to the ground. A young cavalier, Juan de Salamanca, who had kept close by his general's side, quickly dismounted and despatched the fallen chief. Then tearing away his banner, he presented it to Cortes, as a trophy to which he had the best claim. It was all the work of a moment. The guard, overpowered by the suddenness of the onset, made little resistance, but, flying, communicated their own panic to their comrades. The tidings of the loss soon spread over the field. The Indians, filled with consternation, now thought only of escape. In their blind terror, their numbers augmented their confusion. They trampled on one another, fancying it was the enemy in their rear.

The Spaniards and Tlascalans were not slow to avail themselves of the marvellous change in their affairs. Their fatigue, their wounds, hunger, thirst, all were forgotten in the eagerness for vengeance; and they followed up the flying foe, dealing death at every stroke, and taking ample retribution for all they had suffered in the bloody marshes of Mexico. Long did they pursue, till, the enemy having abandoned the field, they returned sated with slaughter to glean the booty which he had left. It was great, for the ground was covered with the bodies of chiefs, at whom the Spaniards, in obedience to the general's instructions, had particularly aimed; and their dresses displayed all the barbaric pomp of ornament, in which the Indian warrior delighted. When his men had thus indemnified themselves, in some degree, for their late reverses, Cortes called them again under their banners; and, after offering up a grateful acknowledgment to the Lord of Hosts for their miraculous preservation, they renewed their march across the now deserted valley. The sun was declining in the heavens, but before the shades of evening had gathered around, they reached an Indian temple on an eminence, which afforded a strong and commodious position for the night.

Such was the famous battle of Otompan, or Otumba, as commonly called, from the Spanish corruption of the name. It was fought on the 8th of July, 1520. The whole amount of the Indian force is reckoned by Castilian writers at two hundred thousand! that of the slain at twenty thousand! Those who admit the first part of the estimate will find no difficulty in receiving the last. Yet it was, undoubtedly, one of the most remarkable victories ever achieved in the New World.

ON the following morning the army broke up its encampment at an early hour. The enemy do not seem to have made an attempt to rally. Clouds of skirmishers, however, were seen during the morning, keeping at a respectful distance, though occasionally venturing near enough to salute the Spaniards with a volley of missiles.

On a rising ground they discovered a fountain, a blessing not too often met with in these arid regions, and gratefully commemorated by the Christians, for the refreshment afforded by its cool and abundant waters. A little further on, they descried the rude works which served as the bulwark and boundary of the Tlascalan territory. At the sight, the allies sent up a joyous shout of congratulation, in which the Spaniards heartily joined, as they felt they were soon to be on friendly and hospitable ground.

But these feelings were speedily followed by others of a different nature; and, as they drew nearer the territory, their minds were disturbed with the most painful apprehensions, as to their reception by the people among whom they were bringing desolation and mourning, and who might so easily, if ill-disposed take advantage of their present crippled condition. "Thoughts like these," says Cortes, "weighed as heavily on my spirit as any which I ever experienced in going to battle with the Aztecs." Still he put, as usual, a good face on the matter, and encouraged his men to confide in their allies, whose past conduct had afforded every ground for trusting to their fidelity in future. He cautioned them, however, as their own strength was so much impaired, to be most careful to give no umbrage, or ground for jealousy, to their high-spirited allies. "Be but on your guard," continued the intrepid general, "and we have still stout hearts and strong hands to carry us through the midst of them!" With these anxious surmises, bidding adieu to the Aztec domain, the Christian army crossed the frontier, and once more trod the soil of the republic.

The first place at which they halted was the town of Huejotlipan, a place of about twelve or fifteen thousand inhabitants. They were kindly greeted by the people, who came out to receive them, inviting the troops to their habitations, and administering all the relief of their simple hospitality; yet not so disinterested as to prevent their expecting a share of the plunder. Here the weary forces remained two or three days, when the news of their arrival having reached the capital, not more than four or five leagues distant, the old chief, Maxixca, their efficient friend on their former visit, and Xicontencatl, the young warrior who, it will be remembered, had commanded the troops of his nation in their bloody encounters with the Spaniards, came with a numerous concourse of the citizens to welcome the fugitives to Tlascala. Maxixca, cordially embracing the Spanish commander, testified the deepest sympathy for his misfortunes. That the white men could so long have withstood the confederated power of the Aztecs was proof enough of their marvellous prowess. "We have made common cause together," said the lord of Tlascala — "and we have common injuries to avenge; and, come weal or come woe, be assured we will prove true and loyal friends, and stand by you to the death."

This cordial assurance and sympathy, from one who exercised a control over the public counsels beyond any other ruler, effectually dispelled the doubts that lingered in the mind of Cortes. He readily accepted his invitation to continue his march at once to the capital, where he would find so much better accommodation for his army, than in a small town on the frontier. The sick and wounded, placed in hammocks, were borne on the shoulders of the friendly natives; and, as the troops drew near the city, the inhabitants came flocking out in crowds to meet them, rending the air with joyous acclamations and wild bursts of their rude Indian minstrelsy. Amidst the general jubilee, however, were heard sounds of wailing and sad lament, as some unhappy relative or friend, looking earnestly into the diminished files of their countrymen, sought in vain for some dear and familiar countenance, and, as they turned disappointed away, gave utterance to their sorrow in tones that touched the heart of every soldier in the army. With these mingled accompaniments of joy and woe — the motley web of human life — the way-worn columns of Cortes at length re-entered the republican capital.

The general and his suite were lodged in the rude, but spacious, palace of Maxixca. The rest of the army took up their quarters in the district over which the Tlascalan lord presided. Here they continued several weeks, until, by the attentions of the hospitable citizens, and such medical treatment as their humble science could supply, the wounds of the soldiers were healed, and they recovered from the debility to which they had been reduced by their long and unparalleled sufferings. Cortes was one of those who suffered severely. He lost the use of two of the fingers of his left hand. He had received, besides, two injuries on the head; one of which was so much exasperated by his subsequent fatigues and excitement of mind, that it assumed an alarming appearance. A part of the bone was obliged to be removed. A fever ensued, and for several days the hero, who had braved danger and death in their most terrible forms, lay stretched on his bed, as helpless as an infant. His excellent constitution, however, got the better of disease, and he was, at length, once more enabled to resume his customary activity. — The Spaniards, with politic generosity, requited the hospitality of their hosts by sharing with them the spoils of their recent victory; and Cortes especially rejoiced the heart of Maxixca, by presenting him with the military trophy which he had won from the Indian commander.

But while the Spaniards were thus recruiting their health and spirits under the friendly treatment of their allies, and recovering the confidence and tranquillity of mind which had sunk under their hard reverses, they received tidings, from time to time, which showed that their late disaster had not been confined to the Mexican capital. On his descent from Mexico to encounter Narvaez, Cortes had brought with him a quantity of gold, which he left for safe keeping at Tlascala. To this was added a considerable sum collected by the unfortunate Velasquez de Leon, in his expedition to the coast, as well as contributions from other sources. From the unquiet state of the capital, the general thought it best, on his return there, still to leave the treasure under the care of a number of invalid soldiers, who, when in marching condition, were to rejoin him in Mexico. A party from Vera Cruz, consisting of five horsemen and forty foot, had since arrived at Tlascala, and, taking charge of the invalids and treasure, undertook to escort them to the capital. He now learned they had been intercepted on the route, and all cut off, with the entire loss of the treasure. Twelve other soldiers, marching in the same direction, had been massacred in the neighbouring province of Tepeaca; and accounts continually arrived of some unfortunate Castilian, who, presuming the respect hitherto shown to his countrymen, and ignorant of the disasters in the capital, had fallen a victim to the fury of the enemy.

These dismal tidings filled the mind of Cortes with gloomy apprehensions for the fate of the settlement at Villa Rica — the last of their hopes. He despatched a trusty messenger, at once, to that place; and had the inexpressible satisfaction to receive a letter in return from the commander of the garrison, acquainting him with the safety of the colony, and its friendly relations with the neighbouring Totonacs. It was the best guarantee of the fidelity of the latter, that they had offended the Mexicans too deeply to be forgiven.

While the affairs of Cortes wore so gloomy an aspect without, he had to experience an annoyance scarcely less serious from the discontents of his followers. Many of them had fancied that their late appalling reverses would put an end to the expedition; or, at least, postpone all thoughts of resuming it for the present. But they knew little of Cortes who reasoned thus. Even while tossing on his bed of sickness, he was ripening in his mind fresh schemes for retrieving his honour, and for recovering the empire which had been lost more by another's rashness than his own. This was apparent, as he became convalescent, from the new regulations he made respecting the army, as well as from the orders sent to Vera Cruz for fresh reinforcements.

The knowledge of all this occasioned much disquietude to the disaffected soldiers. They were, for the most part, the ancient followers of Narvaez, on whom, as we have seen, the brunt of war had fallen the heaviest. Many of them possessed property in the islands, and had embarked on this expedition chiefly from the desire of increasing it. But they had gathered neither gold nor glory in Mexico. Their present service filled them only with disgust; and the few, comparatively, who had been so fortunate as to survive, languished to return to their rich mines and pleasant farms in Cuba, bitterly cursing the day when they had left them.

Finding their complaints little heeded by the general, they prepared a written remonstrance, in which they made their demand more formally. They represented the rashness of persisting in the enterprise in his present impoverished state, without arms or ammunition, almost without men; and this too, against a powerful enemy, who had been more than a match for him, with all the strength of his late resources. It was madness to think of it. The attempt would bring them all to the sacrifice-block. Their only course was to continue their march to Vera Cruz. Every hour of delay might be fatal. The garrison in that Place might be overwhelmed from want of strength to defend itself; and thus their last hope would be annihilated. But, once there, they might wait in comparative security for such reinforcements as would join them from abroad; while, in case of failure, they could the more easily make their escape. They concluded with insisting on being permitted to return, at once, to the port of Villa Rica. This petition, or rather remonstrance, was signed by all the disaffected soldiers, and, after being formally attested by the royal notary, was presented to Cortes.

It was a trying circumstance for him. What touched him most nearly was, to find the name of his friend, the secretary Duero, to whose good offices he had chiefly owed his command, at the head of the paper. He was not, however, to be shaken from his purpose for a moment; and while all outward resources seemed to be fading away, and his own friends faltered or failed him, he was still true to himself. He knew that to retreat to Vera Cruz would be to abandon the enterprise. Once there, his army would soon find a pretext and a way for breaking up, and returning to the islands. All his ambitious schemes would be blasted. The great prize, already once in his grasp, would then be lost for ever. He would be a ruined man.

In his celebrated letter to Charles the Fifth, he says, that, in reflecting on his position, he felt the truth of the old adage, "that fortune favours the brave. The Spaniards were the followers of the Cross; and, trusting in the infinite goodness and mercy of God, he could not believe that He would suffer them and His own good cause thus to perish among the heathen. He was resolved, therefore, not to descend to the coast, but at all hazards to retrace his steps and beard the enemy again in his capital."

It was in the same resolute tone that he answered his discontented followers. He urged every argument which could touch their pride or honour as cavaliers. He appealed to that ancient Castilian valour which had never been known to falter before an enemy; besought them not to discredit the great deeds which had made their name ring throughout Europe; not to leave the emprise half achieved, for others more daring and adventurous to finish. How could they with any honour, he asked, desert their allies whom they had involved in the war, and leave them unprotected to the vengeance of the Aztecs? To retreat but a single step towards Villa Rica would be to proclaim their own weakness. It would dishearten their friends, and give confidence to their foes. He implored them to resume the confidence in him which they had ever shown, and to reflect that, if they had recently met with reverses, he had up to that point accomplished all, and more than all, that he had promised. It would be easy now to retrieve their losses, if they would have patience, and abide in this friendly land until the reinforcements, which would be ready to come in at his call, should enable them to act on the offensive. If, however, there were any so insensible to the motives which touch a brave man's heart, as to prefer ease at home to the glory of this great achievement, he would not stand in their way. Let them go in God's name. Let them leave their general in his extremity. He should feel stronger in the service of a few brave spirits, than if surrounded by a host of the false or the faint-hearted.

The disaffected party, as already noticed, was chiefly drawn from the troops of Narvaez. When the general's own veterans heard this appeal, their blood warmed with indignation at the thoughts of abandoning him or the cause at such a crisis. They pledged themselves to stand by him to the last; and the malcontents silenced, if not convinced, by this generous expression of sentiment from their comrades, consented to postpone their departure for the present, under the assurance, that no obstacle should be thrown in their way, when a more favourable season should present itself.

Scarcely was this difficulty adjusted, when Cortes was menaced with one more serious, in the jealousy springing up between his soldiers and their Indian allies. Notwithstanding the demonstrations of regard by Maxixca and his immediate followers, there were others of the nation who looked with an evil eye on their guests, for the calamities in which they had involved them; and they tauntingly asked, if, in addition to this, they were now to be burdened by the presence and maintenance of the strangers? The sallies of discontent were not so secret as altogether to escape the ears of the Spaniards, in whom they occasioned no little disquietude. They proceeded, for the most part, it is true, from persons of little consideration, since the four great chiefs of the republic appear to have been steadily secured to the interests of Cortes. But they derived some importance from the countenance of the warlike Xicotencatl, in whose bosom still lingered the embers of that implacable hostility which he had displayed so courageously on the field of battle; and sparkles of this fiery temper occasionally gleamed forth in the intimate intercourse into which he was now reluctantly brought with his ancient opponents.

Cortes, who saw with alarm the growing feelings of estrangement, which must sap the very foundations on which he was to rest the lever for future operations, employed every argument which suggested itself to restore the confidence of his own men. He reminded them of the good services they had uniformly received from the great body of the nation. They had a sufficient pledge of the future constancy of the Tlascalans in their long cherished hatred of the Aztecs, which the recent disasters they had suffered from the same quarter could serve only to sharpen. And he urged with much force, that, if any evil designs had been meditated by them against the Spaniards, the Tlascalans would doubtless have taken advantage of their late disabled condition, and not waited till they had recovered their strength and means of resistance.

While Cortes was thus endeavouring, with somewhat doubtful success, to stifle his own apprehensions, as well as those in the bosoms of his followers, an event occurred which happily brought the affair to an issue, and permanently settled the relations in which the two parties were to stand to each other. This will make it necessary to notice some events which had occurred in Mexico since the expulsion of the Spaniards.

On Montezuma's death, his brother Cuitlahua, lord of Iztapalapan, conformably to the usage regulating the descent of the Aztec crown, was chosen to succeed him. He was an active prince, of large experience in military affairs, and, by the strength of his character, was well fitted to sustain the tottering fortunes of the monarchy. He appears, morever, to have been a man of liberal, and what may be called enlightened taste, to judge from the beautiful gardens which he had filled with rare exotics, and which so much attracted the admiration of the Spaniards in his city of Iztapalapan. Unlike his predecessor, he held the white men in detestation; and had probably the satisfaction of celebrating his own coronation by the sacrifice of many of them. From the moment of his release from the Spanish quarters, were he had been detained by Cortes, he entered into the patriotic movements of his people. It was he who conducted the assaults both in the streets of the city, and on the "Melancholy Night"; and it was at his instigation that the powerful force had been assembled to dispute the passage of the Spaniards in the Vale of Otumba.

Since the evacuation of the capital, he had been busily occupied in repairing the mischief it had received — restoring the buildings and the bridges, and putting it in the best posture of defence. He had endeavoured to improve the discipline and arms of his troops. He introduced the long spear among them, and, by attaching the swordblades taken from the Christians to long poles, contrived a weapon that should be formidable against cavalry. He summoned his vassals, far and near, to hold themselves in readiness to march to the relief of the capital, if necessary, and, the better to secure their good will, relieved them from some of the burdens usually laid on them. But he was now to experience the instability of a government which rested not on love, but on fear. The vassals in the neighbourhood of the valley remained true to their allegiance; but others held themselves aloof, uncertain what course to adopt; while others, again, in the more distant provinces, refused obedience altogether, considering this a favourable moment for throwing off the yoke which had so long galled them.

In this emergency, the government sent a deputation to its ancient enemies, the Tlascalans. It consisted of six Aztec nobles, bearing a present of cotton cloth, salt, and other articles, rarely seen, of late years, in the republic. The lords of the state, astonished at this unprecedented act of condescension in their ancient foe, called the council or senate of the great chiefs together, to give the envoys audience.

Before this body, the Aztecs stated the purpose of their mission. They invited the Tlascalans to bury all past grievances in oblivion, and to enter into a treaty with them. All the nations of Anahuac should make common cause in defence of their country against the white men. The Tlascalans would bring down on their own heads the wrath of the gods, if they longer harboured the strangers who had violated and destroyed their temples. If they counted on the support and friendship of their guests, let them take warning from the fate of Mexico, which had received them kindly within its walls and which, in return, they had filled with blood and ashes. They conjured them, by their reverence for their common religion, not to suffer the white men, disabled as they now were, to escape from their hands, but to sacrifice them at once to the gods, whose temples they had profaned. In that event, they proffered them their alliance, and the renewal of that friendly traffic which would restore to the republic the possession of the comforts and luxuries of which it had been so long deprived.

The proposals of the ambassadors produced different effects on their audience. Xicotencatl was for embracing them at once. Far better was it, he said, to unite with their kindred, with those who held their own language, their faith and usages, than to throw themselves into the arms of the fierce strangers, who, however they might talk of religion, worshipped no god but gold. This opinion was followed by that of the younger warriors, who readily caught the fire of his enthusiasm. But the elder chiefs, especially his blind old father, one of the four rulers of the state, who seem to have been all heartily in the interests of the Spaniards, and one of them, Maxixca, their staunch friend, strongly expressed their aversion to the proposed alliance with the Aztecs. They were always the same, said the latter — fair in speech, and false in heart. They now proffered friendship to the Tlascalans. But it was fear which drove them to it, and, when that fear was removed, they would return to their old hostility. Who was it, but these insidious foes, that had so long deprived the country of the very necessaries of life, of which they were now so lavish in their offers? Was it not owing to the white men that the nation at length possessed them? Yet they were called on to sacrifice the white men to the gods! — the warriors who, after fighting the battles of the Tlascalans, now threw themselves on their hospitality. But the gods abhorred perfidy. And were not their guests the very beings whose coming had been so long predicted by the oracles? Let us avail ourselves of it, he concluded, and unite and make common cause with them, until we have humbled our haughty enemy.

This discourse provoked a sharp rejoinder from Xicotencatl, tin the passion of the elder chieftain got the better of his patience, and, substituting force for argument, he thrust his younger antagonist with some violence from the council chamber. A proceeding so contrary to the usual decorum of Indian debate astonished the assembly. But, far from bringing censure on its author, it effectually silenced opposition. Even the hot-headed followers of Xicotencatl shrunk from supporting a leader who had incurred such a mark of contemptuous displeasure from the ruler whom they most venerated. His own father openly condemned him; and the patriotic young warrior, gifted with a truer foresight into futurity than his countrymen, was left without support in the council, as he had formerly been on the field of battle. — The proffered alliance of the Mexicans was unanimously rejected; and the envoys, fearing that even the sacred character with which they were invested might not protect them from violence, made their escape secretly from the capital.

The result of the conference was of the last importance to the Spaniards, who, in their present crippled condition, especially if taken unawares, would have been, probably, at the mercy of the Tlascalans. At all events, the union of these latter with the Aztecs would have settled the fate of the expedition; since, in the poverty of his own resources, it was only by adroitly playing off one part of the Indian population against the other, that Cortes could ultimately hope for success.

THE Spanish commander, reassured by the result of the deliberations in the Tlascalan senate, now resolved on active operations, as the best means of dissipating the spirit of faction and discontent inevitably fostered by a life of idleness. He proposed to exercise his troops, at first, against some of the neighbouring tribes who had laid violent hands on such of the Spaniards as, confiding in their friendly spirit, had passed through their territories. Among these were the Tepeacans, a people often engaged in hostility with the Tlascalans, and who, as mentioned in a preceding chapter, had lately massacred twelve Spaniards in their march to the capital. An expedition against them would receive the ready support of his allies, and would assert the dignity of the Spanish name, much dimmed in the estimation of the natives by the late disasters.

The Tepeacans were a powerful tribe of the same primitive stock as the Aztecs, to whom they acknowledged allegiance. They had transferred this to the Spaniards, on their first march into the country, intimidated by the bloody defeats of their Tlascalan neighbours. But, since the troubles in the capital, they had again submitted to the Aztec sceptre. Their capital, now a petty village, was a flourishing city at the time of the Conquest, situated in the fruitful plains that stretch far away towards the base of Orizaba. The province contained, moreover, several towns of considerable size, filled with a bold and warlike population.

As these Indians had once acknowledged the authority of Castile, Cortes and his officers regarded their present conduct in the light of rebellion, and, in a council of war, it was decided that those engaged in the late massacre had fairly incurred the doom of slavery. Before proceeding against them, however, the general sent a summons requiring their submission, and offering full pardon for the past, but, in case of refusal, menacing them with the severest retribution. To this the Indians, now in arms, returned a contemptuous answer, challenging the Spaniards to meet them in fight, as they were in want of victims for their sacrifices.

Cortes, without further delay, put himself at the head of his small corps of Spaniards, and a large reinforcement of Tlascalan warriors. They were led by the young Xicotencatl, who now appeared willing to bury his recent animosity, and desirous to take a lesson in war under the chief who had so often foiled him in the field.

The Tepeacans received their enemy on their borders. A bloody battle followed, in which the Spanish horse were somewhat embarrassed by the tall maize that covered part of the plain. They were successful in the end, and the Tepeacans, after holding their ground like good warriors, were at length routed with great slaughter. A second engagement, which took place a few days after, was followed by like decisive results; and the victorious Spaniards with their allies, marching straightway on the city of Tepeaca, entered it in triumph. No further resistance was attempted by the enemy, and the whole province, to avoid further calamities, eagerly tendered its submission. Cortes, however, inflicted the meditated chastisement on the places implicated in the massacre. The inhabitants were branded with a hot iron as slaves, and, after the royal fifth had been reserved, were distributed between his own men and the allies. The Spaniards were familiar with the system of repartimientos established in the islands; but this was the first example of slavery in New Spain. It was justified, in the opinion of the general and his military casuists, by the aggravated offences of the party. The sentence, however, was not countenanced by the crown, which, as the colonial legislation abundantly shows, was ever at issue with the craving and mercenary spirit of the colonist.

Satisfied with this display of his vengeance, Cortes now established his head-quarters at Tepeaca, which, situated in a cultivated country, afforded easy means for maintaining an army, while its position on the Mexican frontier made it a good point d'appui for future operations.

The Aztec government, since it had learned the issue of its negotiations at Tlascala, had been diligent in fortifying its frontier in that quarter. The garrisons usually maintained there were strengthened, and large bodies of men were marched in the same direction, with orders to occupy the strong positions on the borders. The conduct of these troops was in their usual style of arrogance and extortion, and greatly disgusted the inhabitants of the country.

Among the places thus garrisoned by the Aztecs was Quauhquechollan a city containing thirty thousand inhabitants, according to the historians, and lying to the south-west twelve leagues or more from the Spanish quarters. It stood at the extremity of a deep valley, resting against a bold range of hills, or rather mountains, and flanked by two rivers with exceedingly high and precipitous banks. The only avenue by which the town could be easily approached, was protected by a stone wall more than twenty feet high, and of great thickness. Into this place, thus strongly defended by art as well as by nature, the Aztec emperor had thrown a garrison of several thousand warriors, while a much more formidable force occupied the heights commanding the city.

The cacique of this strong post, impatient of the Mexican yoke, sent to Cortes, inviting him to march to his relief, and promising a co-operation of the citizens in an assault on the Aztec quarters. The general eagerly embraced the proposal, and arranged with the cacique that, on the appearance of the Spaniards, the inhabitants should rise on the garrison. Everything succeeded as he had planned. No sooner had the Christian battalions defiled on the plain before the town, than the inhabitants attacked the garrison with the utmost fury. The latter, abandoning the outer defences of the place, retreated to their own quarters in the principal teocalli, where they maintained a hard struggle with their adversaries. In the heat of it, Cortes, at the head of his little body of horse, rode into the place, and directed the assault in person. The Aztecs made a fierce defence. But fresh troops constantly arriving to support the assailants, the works were stormed, and every one of the garrison was put to the sword.

The Mexican forces, meanwhile, stationed on the neighbouring eminences, had marched down to the support of their countrymen in the town, and formed in order of battle in the suburbs, where they were encountered by the Tlascalan levies. "They mustered," says Cortes, speaking of the enemy, "at least thirty thousand men, and it was a brave sight for the eye to look on — such a beautiful array of warriors glistening with gold and jewels and variegated feather-work!" The action was well contested between the two Indian armies. The suburbs were set on fire, and, in the midst of the flames, Cortes and his squadrons, rushing on the enemy, at length broke their array, and compelled them to fall back in disorder into the narrow gorge of the mountain, from which they had lately descended. The pass was rough and precipitous. Spaniards and Tlascalans followed close in the rear, and the light troops, scaling the high wall of the valley, poured down on the enemy's flanks. The heat was intense, and both parties were so much exhausted by their efforts, that it was with difficulty, says the chronicler, that the one could pursue, or the other fly. They were not too weary, however, to slay. The Mexicans were routed with terrible slaughter. They found no pity from their Indian foes, who had a long account of injuries to settle with them. Some few sought refuge by flying higher up into the fastnesses of the sierra. They were followed by their indefatigable enemy, until, on the bald summit of the ridge, they reached the Mexican encampment. It covered a wide tract of ground. Various utensils, ornamented dresses, and articles of luxury, were scattered round, and the number of slaves in attendance showed the barbaric pomp with which the nobles of Mexico went to their campaigns. It was a rich booty for the victors, who spread over the deserted camp, and loaded themselves with the spoil, until the gathering darkness warned them to descend.

Cortes followed up the blow by assaulting the strong town of Itzocan, held also by a Mexican garrison, and situated in the depths of a green valley watered by artificial canals, and smiling in all the rich abundance of this fruitful region of the plateau. The place, though stoutly defended, was stormed and carried; the Aztecs were driven across a river which ran below the town, and, although the light bridges that traversed it were broken down in the flight, whether by design or accident, the Spaniards, fording and swimming the stream as they could, found their way to the opposite bank, following up the chase with the eagerness of bloodhounds. Here, too, the booty was great; and the Indian auxiliaries flocked by thousands to the banners of the chief who so surely led them on to victory and plunder.

Soon afterwards, Cortes returned to his head-quarters at Tepeaca. Thence he detached his officers on expeditions which were usually successful. Sandoval, in particular, marched against a large body of the enemy lying between the camp and Vera Cruz; defeated them in two decisive battles, and thus restored the communications with the port.

The result of these operations was the reduction of that populous and cultivated territory which lies between the great volcan, on the west, and the mighty skirts of Orizaba, on the east. Many places, also, in the neighbouring province of Mixtecapan, acknowledged the authority of the Spaniards, and others from the remote region of Oaxaca sent to claim their protection. The conduct of Cortes towards his allies had gained him great credit for disinterestedness and equity. The Indian cities in the adjacent territory appealed to him, as their umpire, in their differences with one another, and cases of disputed succession in their governments were referred to his arbitration. By his discreet and moderate policy, he insensibly acquired an ascendency over their counsels, which had been denied to the ferocious Aztec. His authority extended wider and wider every day; and a new empire grew up in the very heart of the land, forming a counterpoise to the colossal power which had so long overshadowed it.

Cortes now felt himself strong enough to put in execution the plans for recovering the capital, over which he had been brooding ever since the hour of his expulsion. He had greatly undervalued the resources of the Aztec monarchy. He was now aware, from bitter experience, that, to vanquish it, his own forces, and all he could hope to muster, would be incompetent, without a very extensive support from the Indians themselves. A large army, would, moreover, require large supplies for its maintenance, and these could not be regularly obtained, during a protracted siege, without the friendly co-operation of the natives. On such support he might now safely calculate from Tlascala, and the other Indian territories, whose warriors were so eager to serve under his banners. His past acquaintance with them had instructed him in their national character and system of war; while the natives who had fought under his command, if they had caught little of the Spanish tactics, had learned to act in concert with the white men, and to obey him implicitly as their commander. This was a considerable improvement in such wild and disorderly levies, and greatly augmented the strength derived from numbers.

Experience showed, that in a future conflict with the capital it would not do to trust to the causeways, but that to succeed, he must command the lake. He proposed, therefore, to build a number of vessels, like those constructed under his orders in Montezuma's time, and afterwards destroyed by the inhabitants. For this he had still the services of the same experienced ship-builder, Martin Lopez, who, as we have seen, had fortunately escaped the slaughter of the "Melancholy Night." Cortes now sent this man to Tlascala, with orders to build thirteen brigantines, which might be taken to pieces and carried on the shoulders of the Indians to be launched on the waters of Lake Tezcuco. The sails, rigging, and iron-work, were to be brought from Vera Cruz, where they had been stored since their removal from the dismantled ships. It was a bold conception, that of constructing a fleet to be transported across forest and mountain before it was launched on its destined waters! But it suited the daring genius of Cortes, who, with the co-operation of his staunch Tlascalan confederates, did not doubt his ability to carry it into execution.

It was with no little regret, that the general learned at this time the death of his good friend Maxixca, the old lord of Tlascala, who had stood by him so steadily in the hour of adversity. He had fallen a victim to that terrible epidemic, the small-pox, which was now sweeping over the land like fire over the prairies, smiting down prince and peasant, and adding another to the long train of woes that followed the march of the white men. It was imported into the country, it is said, by a Negro slave, in the fleet of Narvaez. It first broke out in Cempoalla. The poor natives, ignorant of the best mode of treating the loathsome disorder, sought relief in their usual practice of bathing in cold water, which greatly aggravated their trouble. From Cempoalla it spread rapidly over the neighbouring country, and, penetrating through Tlascala, reached the Aztec capital, where Montezuma's successor, Cuitlahua, fell one of its first victims. Thence it swept down towards the borders of the Pacific, leaving its path strewn with the dead bodies of the natives, who, in the strong language of a contemporary, perished in heaps like cattle stricken with the murrain. It does not seem to have been fatal to the Spaniards, many of whom, probably, had already had the disorder.

The death of Maxixca was deeply regretted by the troops, who lost in him a true and most efficient ally. With his last breath, he commended them to his son and successor, as the great beings whose coming into the country had been so long predicted by the oracles. He expressed a desire to die in the profession of the Christian faith. Cortes no sooner learned his condition than he despatched Father Olmedo to Tlascala. The friar found that Maxixca had already caused a crucifix to be placed before his sick couch, as the object of his adoration. After explaining, as intelligibly as he could, the truths of revelation, he baptised the dying chieftain; and the Spaniards had the satisfaction to believe that the soul of their benefactor was exempted from the doom of eternal perdition that hung over the unfortunate Indian who perished in his unbelief.

Their late brilliant successes seem to have reconciled most of the disaffected soldiers to the prosecution of the war. There were still a few among them, the secretary Duero, Bermudez the treasurer, and others high in office, or wealthy hidalgos, who looked with disgust on another campaign, and now loudly reiterated their demand of a free passage to Cuba. To this Cortes, satisfied with the support on which he could safely count, made no further objection. Having once given his consent, he did all in his power to facilitate their departure, and provide for their comfort. He ordered the best ship at Vera Cruz to be placed at their disposal, to be well supplied with provisions and everything necessary for the voyage, and sent Alvarado to the coast to superintend the embarkation. He took the most courteous leave of them, with assurances of his own unalterable regard. But, as the event proved, those who could part from him at this crisis had little sympathy with his fortunes; and we find Duero not long afterwards in Spain, supporting the claims of Velasquez before the emperor, in opposition to those of his former friend and commander.

The loss of these few men was amply compensated by the arrival of others, whom fortune most unexpectedly threw in his way. The first of these came in a small vessel sent from Cuba by the governor, Velasquez, with stores for the colony at Vera Cruz. He was not aware of the late transactions in the country, and of the discomfiture of his officer. In the vessel came despatches, it is said, from Fonseca, Bishop of Burgos, instructing Narvaez to send Cortes, if he had not already done so, for trial to Spain. The alcalde of Vera Cruz, agreeably to the general's instructions, allowed the captain of the bark to land, who had no doubt that the country was in the hands of Narvaez. He was undeceived by being seized, together with his men, so soon as they had set foot on shore. The vessel was then secured; and the commander and his crew, finding out their error, were persuaded without much difficulty to join their countrymen in Tlascala.

A second vessel, sent soon after by Velasquez, shared the same fate, and those on board consented also to take their chance in the expedition under Cortes.

About the same time, Garay, the governor of Jamaica, fitted out three ships with an armed force to plant a colony on the Panuco, a river which pours into the Gulf a few degrees north of Villa Rica. Garay persisted in establishing this settlement, in contempt of the claims of Cortes, who had already entered into a friendly communication with the inhabitants of that region. But the crews experienced such a rough reception from the natives on landing, and lost so many men, that they were glad to take to their vessels again. One of these foundered in a storm. The others put into the port of Vera Cruz to restore the men, much weakened by hunger and disease. Here they were kindly received, their wants supplied, their wounds healed; when they were induced, by the liberal promises of Cortes, to abandon the disastrous service of their employer, and enlist under his own prosperous banner. The reinforcements obtained from these sources amounted to full a hundred and fifty men, well provided with arms and ammunition, together with twenty horses. By this strange concurrence of circumstances, Cortes saw himself in possession of the supplies he most needed; that, too, from the hands of his enemies, whose costly preparations were thus turned to the benefit of the very man whom they were designed to ruin.

His good fortune did not stop here. A ship from the Canaries touched at Cuba, freighted with arms and military stores for the adventurers in the New World. Their commander heard there of the recent discoveries in Mexico, and, thinking it would afford a favourable market for him, directed his course to Vera Cruz. He was not mistaken. The alcalde, by the general's orders, purchased both ship and cargo; and the crews, catching the spirit of adventure, followed their countrymen into the interior. There seemed to be a magic in the name of Cortes, which drew all who came within hearing of it under his standard.

Having now completed the arrangements for settling his new conquests, there seemed to be no further reason for postponing his departure to Tlascala. He was first solicited by the citizens of Tepeaca to leave a garrison with them, to protect them from the vengeance of the Aztecs. Cortes acceded to the request, and, considering the central position of the town favourable for maintaining his conquests, resolved to plant a colony there. For this object he selected sixty of his soldiers, most of whom were disabled by wounds or infirmity. He appointed the alcaldes, regidores, and other functionaries of a civic magistracy. The place be called Segura de la Frontera or Security of the Frontier. It received valuable privileges as a city, a few years later, from the emperor Charles the Fifth; and rose to some consideration in the age of the Conquest. But its consequence soon after declined. Even its Castilian name, with the same caprice which has decided the fate of more than one name in our own country, was gradually supplanted by its ancient one, and the little village of Tepeaca is all that now commemorates the once flourishing Indian capital, and the second Spanish colony in Mexico.

While at Segura, Cortes wrote that celebrated letter to the emperor — the second in the series — so often cited in the preceding pages. It takes up the narrative with the departure from Vera Cruz, and exhibits in a brief and comprehensive form the occurrences up to the time at which we are now arrived. In the concluding page, the general, after noticing the embarrassments under which he labours, says, in his usual manly spirit, that he holds danger and fatigue light in comparison with the attainment of his object; and that he is confident a short time will restore the Spaniards to their former position, and repair all their losses.

He notices the resemblance of Mexico, in many of its features and productions, to the mother country, and requests that it may henceforth be called, "New Spain of the Ocean Sea." He finally requests that a commission may be sent out at once, to investigate his conduct, and to verify the accuracy of his statements.

This letter, which was printed at Seville the year after its reception, has been since reprinted and translated more than once. It excited a great sensation at the court, and among the friends of science generally. The previous discoveries of the New World had disappointed the expectations which had been formed after. the solution of the grand problem of its existence. They had brought to light only rude tribes, which, however gentle and inoffensive in their manners, were still in the primitive stages of barbarism. Here was an authentic account of a vast nation, potent and populous, exhibiting an elaborate social polity, well advanced in the arts of civilisation, occupying a soil that teemed with mineral treasures and with a boundless variety of vegetable products, stores of wealth, both natural and artificial, that seemed, for the first time, to realise the golden dreams in which the great discoverer of the New World had so fondly, and in his own day so fallaciously, indulged. Well might the scholar of that age exult in the revelation of these wonders, which so many had long, but in vain, desired to see.

With this letter went another to the emperor, signed, as it would seem, by nearly every officer and soldier in the camp. It expatiated on the obstacles thrown in the way of the expedition by Velasquez and Narvaez, and the great prejudice this had caused to the royal interests. It then set forth the services of Cortes, and besought the emperor to confirm him in his authority, and not to allow any interference with one who, from his personal character, his intimate knowledge of the land and its people, and the attachment of his soldiers, was the man best qualified in all the world to achieve the conquest of the country.

It added not a little to the perplexities of Cortes, that he was still in entire ignorance of the light in which his conduct was regarded in Spain. He had not even heard whether his despatches, sent the year preceding from Vera Cruz, had been received. Mexico was as far removed from all intercourse with the civilised world, as if it had been placed at the antipodes. Few vessels had entered, and none had been allowed to leave its ports. The governor of Cuba, an island distant but a few days' sail, was yet ignorant, as we have seen, of the fate of his armament. On the arrival of every new vessel or fleet on these shores, Cortes might well doubt whether it brought aid to his undertaking, or a royal commission to supersede him. His sanguine spirit relied on the former; though the latter was much the more probable, considering the intimacy of his enemy, the governor, with Bishop Fonseca. It was the policy of

Cortes, therefore, to lose no time; to push forward his preparations, lest another should be permitted to snatch the laurel now almost within his grasp. Could he but reduce the Aztec capital, he felt that he should be safe; and that, in whatever light his irregular proceedings might now be viewed, his services in that event would far more than counterbalance them in the eyes both of the crown and of the country.

The general wrote, also, to the Royal Audience at St. Domingo, in order to interest them in his cause. He sent four vessels to the same island, to obtain a further supply of arms and ammunition; and, the better to stimulate the cupidity of adventurers, and allure them to the expedition, he added specimens of the beautiful fabrics of the country, and of its precious metals. The funds for procuring these important supplies were probably derived from the plunder gathered in the late battles, and the gold which, as already remarked, had been saved from the general wreck by the Castilian convoy.

It was the middle of December, when Cortes, having completed all his arrangements, set out on his return to Tlascala, ten or twelve leagues distant. He marched in the van of the army, and took the way of Cholula. How different was his condition from that in which he had left the republican capital not five months before! His march was a triumphal procession, displaying the various banners and military ensigns taken from the enemy, long files of captives, and all the rich spoils of conquest gleaned from many a hard-fought field. As the army passed through the towns and villages, the inhabitants poured out to greet them, and, as they drew near to Tlascala, the whole population, men, women, and children, came forth celebrating their return with songs, dancing, and music. Arches decorated with flowers were thrown across the streets through which they passed, and a Tlascalan orator addressed the general, on his entrance into the city, in a lofty panegyric on his late achievements, proclaiming him the "avenger of the nation." Amidst this pomp and triumphal show, Cortes and his principal officers were seen clad in deep mourning in honour of their friend Maxixca. And this tribute of respect to the memory of their venerated ruler touched the Tlascalans more sensibly than all the proud display of military trophies.

The general's first act was to confirm the son of his deceased friend in the succession, which had been contested by an illegitimate brother. The youth was but twelve years of age; and Cortes prevailed on him without difficulty to follow his father's example, and receive baptism. He afterwards knighted him with his own hand; the first instance, probably, of the order of chivalry being conferred on an American Indian. The elder Xicotencatl was also persuaded to embrace Christianity; and the example of their rulers had its obvious effect in preparing the minds of the people for the reception of the truth. Cortes, whether from the suggestions of Olmedo, or from the engrossing nature of his own affairs, did not press the work of conversion further at this time, but wisely left the good seed, already sown, to ripen in secret, till time should bring forth the harvest.

The Spanish commander, during his short stay in Tlascala, urged forward the preparations for the campaign. He endeavoured to drill the Tlascalans, and give them some idea of European discipline and tactics. He caused new arms to be made, and the old ones to be put in order. Powder was manufactured with the aid of sulphur obtained by some adventurous cavaliers from the smoking throat of Popocatepetl. The construction of the brigantines went forward prosperously under the direction of Lopez, with the aid of the Tlascalans. Timber was cut in the forests, and pitch, an article unknown to the Indians, was obtained from the pines on the neighbouring Sierra de Malinche. The rigging and other appurtenances were transported by the Indian tamanes from Villa Rica; and by Christmas, the work was so far advanced, that it was no longer necessary for Cortes to delay the march to Mexico.

WHILE the events related in the preceding chapter were passing, an important change had
taken place in the Aztec monarchy. Montezuma's brother and successor, Cuitlahua, had
suddenly died of the small-pox after a brief reign of four months — brief, but glorious, for it
had witnessed the overthrow of the Spaniards and their expulsion from Mexico. On the death
of their warlike chief, the electors were convened, as usual, to supply the vacant throne. It was
an office of great responsibility in the dark hour of their fortunes.

The choice fell on Quauhtemotzin, or Guatemozin, as euphoniously corrupted by the
Spaniards. He was nephew to the two last monarchs, and married his cousin, the beautiful
princess Tecuichpo, Montezuma's daughter. "He was not more than twenty-five years old,
and elegant in his person for an Indian," says one who had seen him often; "valiant, and so terrible,
that his followers trembled in his presence." He did not shrink from the perilous post that was
offered to him; and, as he saw the tempest gathering darkly around, he prepared to meet it like
a man. Though young, he had ample experience in military matters, and had distinguished
himself above all others in the bloody conflicts of the capital.

By means of his spies, Guatemozin made himself acquainted with the movements of the
Spaniards, and their design to besiege the capital. He prepared for it by sending away the
useless part of the population, while he called in his potent vassals from the neighbourhood.
He continued the plans of his predecessor for strengthening the defences of the city, reviewed
his troops, and stimulated them by prizes to excel in their exercises. He made harangues to his
soldiers to rouse them to a spirit of desperate resistance. He encouraged his vassals throughout
the empire to attack the white men wherever they were to be met with, setting a price on their
heads, as well as the persons of all who should be brought alive to him in Mexico. And it was
no uncommon thing for the Spaniards to find hanging up in the temples of the conquered
places the arms and accoutrements of their unfortunate countrymen who had been seized and
sent to the capital for sacrifice. Such was the young monarch who was now called to the
tottering throne of the Aztecs; worthy, by his bold and magnanimous nature, to sway the
sceptre of his country, in the most flourishing period of her renown; and now, in her distress,
devoting himself in the true spirit of a patriotic prince to uphold her falling fortunes, or bravely
perish with them.

We must now return to the Spaniards in Tlascala, where we left them preparing to resume
their march on Mexico. Their commander had the satisfaction to see his troops tolerably
complete in their appointments; varying, indeed, according to the condition of the different
reinforcements which had arrived from time to time; but on the whole, superior to those of the
army with which he had first invaded the country. His whole force fell little short of six
hundred men; forty of whom were cavalry, together with eighty arquebusiers and
crossbowmen. The rest were armed with sword and target, and with the copper-headed pike of
Chinantla. He had nine cannon of a moderate calibre, and was indifferently supplied with
powder.

As his forces were drawn up in order of march, Cortes rode through the ranks, exhorting his
soldiers, as usual with him on these occasions, to be true to themselves, and the enterprise in
which they were embarked. He told them, they were to march against rebels, who had once
acknowledged allegiance to the Spanish sovereign; against barbarians, the enemies of their
religion. They were to fight the battles of the Cross and of the crown; to fight their own battles,
to wipe away the stain from their arms, to avenge their injuries, and the loss of the dear
companions who had been butchered on the field or on the accursed altar of their sacrifice.
Never was there a war which offered higher incentives to the Christian cavalier; a war which
opened to him riches and renown in this life, and an imperishable glory in that to come. They
answered with acclamations, that they were ready to die in defence of the faith; and would

either conquer, or leave their bones with those of their countrymen, in the waters of the Tezcuco.

The army of the allies next passed in review before the general. It is variously estimated by writers from a hundred and ten to a hundred and fifty thousand soldiers! The palpable exaggeration, no less than the discrepancy, shows that little reliance can be placed on any estimate. It is certain, however, that it was a multitudinous array, consisting not only of the flower of the Tlascalan warriors, but of those of Cholula, Tepeaca, and the neighbouring territories, which had submitted to the Castilian crown.

Cortes, with the aid of Marina, made a brief address to his Indian allies. He reminded them that he was going to fight their battles against their ancient enemies. He called on them to support him in a manner worthy of their renowned republic. To those who remained at home, he committed the charge of aiding in the completion of the brigantines, on which the success of the expedition so much depended; and he requested that none would follow his banner, who were not prepared to remain till the final reduction of the capital. This address was answered by shouts, or rather yells, of defiance, showing the exultation felt by his Indian confederates at the prospect of at last avenging their manifold wrongs, and humbling their haughty enemy.

Before setting out on the expedition, Cortes published a code of ordinances, as he terms them, or regulations for the army, too remarkable to be passed over in silence. The preamble sets forth that in all institutions, whether divine or human — if the latter have any worth — order is the great law. The ancient chronicles inform us, that the greatest captains in past times owed their successes quite as much to the wisdom of their ordinances, as to their own valour and virtue. The situation of the Spaniards eminently demanded such a code; a mere handful of men as they were, in the midst of countless enemies, most cunning in the management of their weapons and in the art of war. The instrument then reminds the army that the conversion of the heathen is the work most acceptable in the eye of the Almighty, and one that will be sure to receive his support. It calls on every soldier to regard this as the prime object of the expedition, without which the war would be manifestly unjust, and every acquisition made by it a robbery.

The general solemnly protests, that the principal motive which operates in his own bosom, is the desire to wean the natives from their gloomy idolatry, and to impart to them the knowledge of a purer faith; and next, to recover for his master, the emperor, the dominions which of right belong to him.

The ordinances then prohibit all blasphemy against God or the saints. Another law is directed against gaming, to which the Spaniards in all ages have been peculiarly addicted. Cortes, making allowance for the strong national propensity, authorises it under certain limitations; but prohibits the use of dice altogether. Then follow other laws against brawls and private combats, against Personal taunts and the irritating sarcasms of rival companies; rules for the more perfect discipline of the troops, whether in camp or the field. Among others is one prohibiting any captain, under pain of death, from charging the enemy without orders; a practice noticed as most pernicious and of too frequent occurrence — showing the impetuous spirit and want of true military subordination in the bold cavaliers who followed the standard of Cortes.

The last ordinance prohibits any man, officer or private, from securing to his own use any of the booty taken from the enemy, whether it be gold, silver, precious stones, feather-work, stuffs, slaves, or other commodity, however or wherever obtained, in the city or in the field; and requires him to bring it forthwith to the presence of the general, or the officer appointed to receive it. The violation of this law was punished with death and confiscation of property. So severe an edict may be thought to prove that, however much the Conquistador may have been influenced by spiritual considerations, he was by no means insensible to those of a temporal character.

These provisions were not suffered to remain a dead letter. The Spanish commander, soon after their proclamation, made an example of two of his own slaves, whom he hanged for plundering the natives. A similar sentence was passed on a soldier for the like offence, though he allowed him to be cut down before the sentence was entirely executed. Cortes knew well the character of his followers; rough and turbulent spirits, who required to be ruled with an iron hand. Yet he was not eager to assert his authority on light occasions. The intimacy into which they were thrown by their peculiar situation, perils, and sufferings, in which all equally shared, and a common interest in the adventure, induced a familiarity between men and officers, most unfavourable to military discipline. The general's own manners, frank and liberal, seemed to invite this freedom, which on ordinary occasions he made no attempt to repress; perhaps finding it too difficult, or at least impolitic, since it afforded a safety-valve for the spirits of a licentious soldiery, that, if violently coerced, might have burst forth into open mutiny. But the limits of his forbearance were clearly defined; and any attempt to overstep them, or to violate the established regulations of the camp, brought a sure and speedy punishment on the offender. By thus tempering severity with indulgence, masking an iron will under the open bearing of a soldier — Cortes established a control over his band of bold and reckless adventurers, such as a pedantic martinet, scrupulous in enforcing the minutiae of military etiquette, could never have obtained.

The ordinances, dated on the twenty-second of December, were proclaimed to the assembled army on the twenty-sixth. Two days afterwards, the troops were on their march. Notwithstanding the great force mustered by the Indian confederates, the Spanish general allowed but a small part of them now to attend him. He proposed to establish his head-quarters at some place on the Tezcucan lake, whence he could annoy the Aztec capital, by reducing the surrounding country, cutting off the supplies, and thus placing the city in a state of blockade.

The direct assault on Mexico itself he intended to postpone, until the arrival of the brigantines should enable him to make it with the greatest advantage. Meanwhile, he had no desire to encumber himself with a superfluous multitude, whom it would be difficult to feed; and he preferred to leave them at Tlascala, whence they might convey the vessels, when completed, to the camp, and aid him in his future operations.

Three routes presented themselves to Cortes, by which he might penetrate into the valley. He chose the most difficult, traversing the bold sierra which divides the eastern plateau from the western, and so rough and precipitous, as to be scarcely practicable for the march of an army. He wisely judged, that he should be less likely to experience annoyance from the enemy in this direction, as they might naturally confide in the difficulties of the ground.

The first day the troops advanced five or six leagues, Cortes riding in the van at the head of his little body of cavalry. They halted at the village of Tetzmellocan, at the base of the mountain chain which traverses the country, touching at its southern limit the mighty Iztaccihuatl, or "White Woman,"— white with the snows of ages. At this village they met with a friendly reception, and on the following morning began the ascent of the sierra.

It was night before the way-worn soldiers reached the bald crest of the sierra, where they lost no time in kindling their fires; and, huddling round their bivouacs, they warmed their frozen limbs, and prepared their evening repast. With the earliest dawn, the troops were again in motion. Mass was said, and they began their descent, more difficult and painful than their ascent on the day preceding; for, in addition to the natural obstacles of the road, they found it strewn with huge pieces of timber and trees, obviously felled for the purpose by the natives. Cortes ordered up a body of light troops to clear away the impediments, and the army again resumed its march, but with the apprehension that the enemy had prepared an ambuscade, to surprise them when they should be entangled in the pass. They moved cautiously forward, straining their vision to pierce the thick gloom of the forests, where the wily foe might be lurking. But they saw no living thing, except only the wild inhabitants of the woods, and flocks of the zopilote, the voracious vulture of the country, which, in anticipation of a bloody banquet, hung like a troop of evil spirits on the march of the army.

At length, the army emerged on an open level, where the eye, unobstructed by intervening wood or hill-top, could range far and wide over the Valley of Mexico. The magnificent vision, new to many of the spectators, filled them with rapture. Even the veterans of Cortes could not withhold their admiration, though this was soon followed by a bitter feeling, as they recalled the sufferings which had befallen them within these beautiful, but treacherous precincts. It made us feel, says the lion-hearted Conqueror in his letters, that "we had no choice but victory or death; and our minds once resolved, we moved forward with as light a step as if we had been going on an errand of certain pleasure."

As the Spaniards advanced, they beheld the neighbouring hilltops blazing with beacon-fires, showing that the country was already alarmed and mustering to oppose them. The general called on his men to be mindful of their high reputation; to move in order, closing up their ranks, and to obey implicitly the commands of their officers. At every turn among the hills, they expected to meet the forces of the enemy drawn up to dispute their passage. And, as they were allowed to pass the defiles unmolested, and drew near to the open plains, they were prepared to see them occupied by a formidable host, who would compel them to fight over again the battle of Otumba. But, although clouds of dusky warriors were seen, from time to time, hovering on the highlands, as if watching their progress, they experienced no interruption, till they reached a barranca, or deep ravine, through which flowed a little river, crossed by a bridge partly demolished. On the opposite side a considerable body of Indians was stationed, as if to dispute the passage, but whether distrusting their own numbers, or intimidated by the steady advance of the Spaniards, they offered them no annoyance, and were quickly dispersed by a few resolute charges of cavalry. The army then proceeded, without molestation, to a small town, called Coatepec, where they halted for the night. Before retiring to his own quarters, Cortes made the rounds of the camp, with a few trusty followers, to see that all was safe. He seemed to have an eye that never slumbered, and a frame incapable of fatigue. It was the indomitable spirit within, which sustained him.

Yet he may well have been kept awake through the watches of the night, by anxiety and doubt. He was now but three leagues from Tezcuco, the far-famed capital of the Acolhuans. He proposed to establish his head-quarters, if possible, at this place. Its numerous dwellings would afford ample accommodations for his army. An easy communication with Tlascala, by a different route from that which he had traversed, would furnish him with the means of readily obtaining supplies from that friendly country, and for the safe transportation of the brigantines, when finished, to be launched on the waters of the Tezcuco. But he had good reason to distrust the reception he should meet with in the capital; for an important revolution had taken place there, since the expulsion of the Spaniards from Mexico, of which it will be necessary to give some account.

The reader will remember that the cacique of that place, named Cacama, was deposed by Cortes, during his first residence in the Aztec metropolis, in consequence of a projected revolt against the Spaniards, and that the crown had been placed on the head of a younger brother, Cuicuitzea. The deposed prince was among the prisoners carried away by Cortes, and perished with the others, in the terrible passage of the causeway, on the noche triste. His brother, afraid, probably, after the flight of the Spaniards, of continuing with the Aztecs, accompanied his friends in their retreat, and was so fortunate as to reach Tlascala in safety.

Meanwhile, a second son of Nezahualpilli, named Coanaco, claimed the crown, on his elder brother's death, as his own rightful inheritance. As he heartily joined his countrymen and the Aztecs in their detestation of the white men, his claims were sanctioned by the Mexican emperor. Soon after his accession, the new lord of Tezcuco had an opportunity of showing his loyalty to his imperial patron in an effectual manner.

A body of forty-five Spaniards, ignorant of the disasters in Mexico, were transporting thither a large quantity of gold, at the very time their countrymen were on the retreat to Tlascala. As they passed through the Tezcucan territory, they were attacked by Coanaco's orders, most of them massacred on the spot, and the rest sent for sacrifice to Mexico. The arms and accoutrements of these unfortunate men were hung up as trophies in the temples, and their skins, stripped from their dead bodies, were suspended over the bloody shrines, as the most acceptable offering to the offended deities.

Some months after this event, the exiled prince, Cuicuitzca, wearied with his residence in Tlascala, and pining for his former royal state, made his way back secretly to Tezcuco, hoping, it would seem, to raise a party there in his favour. But if such were his expectations, they were sadly disappointed; for no sooner had he set foot in the capital, than he was betrayed to his brother, who, by the advice of Guatemozin, put him to death, as a traitor to his country. — Such was the posture of affairs in Tezcuco, when Cortes, for the second time, approached its gates; and well might he doubt, not merely the nature of his reception there, but whether he would be permitted to enter it at all, without force of arms.

These apprehensions were dispelled the following morning, when, before the troops were well under arms, an embassy was announced from the lord of Tezcuco. It consisted of several nobles, some of whom were known to the companions of Cortes. They bore a golden flag in token of amity, and a present of no great value to Cortes. They brought also a message from the cacique, imploring the general to spare his territories, inviting him to take up his quarters in his capital, and promising on his arrival to become the vassal of the Spanish sovereign.

Cortes dissembled the satisfaction with which he listened to these overtures, and sternly demanded of the envoys an account of the Spaniards who had been massacred, insisting, at the same time, on the immediate restitution of the plunder. But the Indian nobles excused themselves, by throwing the whole blame upon the Aztec emperor, by whose orders the deed had been perpetrated, and who now had possession of the treasure. They urged Cortes not to enter the city that day, but to pass the night in the suburbs, that their master might have time to prepare suitable accommodations for him. The Spanish commander, however, gave no heed to this suggestion, but pushed forward his march, and, at noon, on the 31st of December, 1520, entered, at the head of his legions, the venerable walls of Tezcuco.

He was struck, as when he before visited this populous city, with the solitude and silence which reigned throughout its streets. He was conducted to the palace of Nezahualpilli, which was assigned as his quarters. It was an irregular pile of low buildings, covering a wide extent of ground, like the royal residence occupied by the troops in Mexico. It was spacious enough to furnish accommodations, not only for all the Spaniards, says Cortes, but for twice their number. He gave orders on his arrival, that all regard should be paid to the persons and property of the citizens; and forbade any Spaniard to leave his quarters under pain of death.

Alarmed at the apparent desertion of the place, as well as by the fact that none of its principal inhabitants came to welcome him, Cortes ordered some soldiers to ascend the neighbouring teocalli and survey the city. They soon returned with the report, that the inhabitants were leaving it in great numbers, with their families and effects, some in canoes upon the lake, others on foot towards the mountains. The general now comprehended the import of the cacique's suggestion, that the Spaniards should pass the night in the suburbs — in order to secure time for evacuating the city. He feared that the chief himself might have fled. He lost no time in detaching troops to secure the principal avenues, where they were to turn back the fugitives, and arrest the cacique, if he were among the number. But it was too late. Coanaco was already far on his way across the lake to Mexico.

Cortes now determined to turn this event to his own account, by placing another ruler on the throne, who should be more subservient to his interests. He called a meeting of the few principal persons still remaining in the city, and by their advice and ostensible election advanced a brother of the late sovereign to the dignity, which they declared vacant. The prince, who consented to be baptised, was a willing instrument in the hands of the Spaniards. He survived but a few months, and was succeeded by another member of the royal house, named Ixtlilxochitl, who, indeed, as general of his armies, may be said to have held the reins of government in his hands during his brother's lifetime. As this person was intimately associated with the Spaniards in their subsequent operations, to the success of which he essentially contributed, it is proper to give some account of his earlier history, which, in truth, is as much enveloped in the marvellous, as that of any fabulous hero of antiquity.

He was son, by a second queen, of the great Nezahualpilli. Some alarming prodigies at his birth, and the gloomy aspect of the planets, led the astrologers, who cast his horoscope, to advise the king, his father, to take away the infant's life, since, if he lived to grow up, he was destined to unite with the enemies of his country, and overturn its institutions and religion. But the old monarch replied, says the chronicler, that the time had arrived when the sons of Quetzalcoatl were to come from the East to take possession of the land; and, if the Almighty had selected his child to co-operate with them in the work, His will be done.

As the boy advanced in years, he exhibited a marvellous precocity not merely of talent, but of mischievous activity, which afforded an alarming prognostic for the future. When about twelve years old, be formed a little corps of followers of about his own age, or somewhat older, with whom he practised the military exercises of his nation, conducting mimic fights and occasionally assaulting the peaceful burghers, and throwing the whole city as well as palace into uproar and confusion. Some of his father's ancient counsellors, connecting this conduct with the predictions at his birth, saw in it such alarming symptoms, that they repeated the advice of the astrologers, to take away the prince's life, if the monarch would not see his kingdom one day given up to anarchy. This unpleasant advice was reported to the juvenile offender, who was so much exasperated by it, that he put himself at the head of a party of his young desperadoes, and, entering the house of the offending counsellors, dragged them forth, and administered to them the garrote — the mode in which capital punishment was inflicted in Tezcuco.

He was seized and brought before his father. When questioned as to his extraordinary conduct, he cooly replied, "that he had done no more than he had a right to do. The guilty ministers had deserved their fate, by endeavouring to alienate his father's affections from him, for no other reason than his too great fondness for the profession of arms — the most honourable profession in the state, and the one most worthy of a prince. If they had suffered death, it was no more than they had intended for him." The wise Nezahualpilli, says the chronicler, found much force in these reasons; and, as he saw nothing low and sordid in the action, but rather the ebulliton of a daring spirit, which in after life might lead to great things, he contented himself with bestowing a grave admonition on the juvenile culprit. Whether this admonition had any salutary effect on his subsequent demeanour, we are not informed. It is said, however, that as he grew older he took an active part in the wars of his country, and when no more than seventeen had won for himself the insignia of a valiant and victorious captain.

On his father's death, he disputed the succession with his elder brother, Cacama. The country was menaced with a civil war, when the affair was compromised by his brother's ceding to him that portion of his territories which lay among the mountains. On the arrival of the Spaniards, the young chieftain-for he was scarcely twenty years of age-made, as we have seen, many friendly demonstrations towards them, induced, no doubt, by his hatred of Montezuma, who had supported the pretensions of Cacama. It was not, however, till his advancement to the lordship of Tezcuco, that he showed the full extent of his good will. From that hour, he became the fast friend of the Christians, supporting them with his personal authority, and the whole strength of his military array and resources, which, although much shorn of their ancient splendour since the days of his father, were still considerable, and made him a most valuable ally. His important services have been gratefully commemorated by the Castilian historians; and history should certainly not defraud him of his just meed of glory — the melancholy glory of having contributed more than any other chieftain of Anahuac to rivet the chains round the necks of his countrymen.

BOOK 6. SIEGE AND SURRENDER OF MEXICO

THE city of Tezcuco was the best position, probably, which Cortes could have chosen for the head-quarters of the army. It supplied all the accommodation for lodging a numerous body of troops, and all the facilities for subsistence, incident to a large and populous town. It furnished, moreover, a multitude of artisans and labourers for the uses of the army. Its territories, bordering on the Tlascalan, afforded a ready means of intercourse with the country of his allies, while its vicinity to Mexico enabled the general, without much difficulty, to ascertain the movements in that capital. Its central situation, in short, opened facilities for communication with all parts of the valley, and made it an excellent Point d'appui for his future operations.

The first care of Cortes was to strengthen himself in the palace assigned to him, and to place his quarters in a state of defence, which might secure them against surprise, not only from the Mexicans, but from the Tezcucans themselves. Since the election of their new ruler, a large part of the population had returned to their homes, assured of protection in person and property. But the Spanish general, notwithstanding their show of submission, very much distrusted its sincerity; for he knew that many of them were united too intimately with the Aztecs, by marriage and other social relations, not to have their sympathies engaged in their behalf. The young monarch, however, seemed wholly in his interest; and, to secure him more effectually, Cortes placed several Spaniards near his person, whose ostensible province it was to instruct him in their language and religion, but who were in reality to watch over his conduct, and prevent his correspondence with those who might be unfriendly to the Spanish interests.

Tezcuco stood about half a league from the lake. It would be necessary to open a communication with it, so that the brigantines, when put together in the capital, might be launched upon its waters. It was proposed, therefore, to dig a canal, reaching from the gardens of Nezahualcoyotl, as they were called from the old monarch who planned them, to the edge of the basin. A little stream or rivulet, which flowed in that direction, was to be deepened sufficiently for the purpose; and eight thousand Indian labourers were forthwith employed on this great work, under the direction of the young Ixtlilxochitl.

Meanwhile Cortes received messages from several places in the neighbourhood, intimating their desire to become the vassals of his sovereign, and to be taken under his protection. The Spanish commander required, in return, that they should deliver up every Mexican who should set foot in their territories. Some noble Aztecs, who had been sent on a mission to these towns, were consequently delivered into his hands. He availed himself of it to employ them as bearers of a message to their master, the emperor. In it he deprecated the necessity of the present hostilities. Those who had most injured him, he said, were no longer among the living. He was willing to forget the past; and invited the Mexicans, by a timely submission, to save their capital from the horrors of a siege. Cortes had no expectation of producing any immediate result by this appeal. But he thought it might lie in the minds of the Mexicans, and that, if there was a party among them disposed to treat with him, it might afford them encouragement, as showing his own willingness to co-operate with their views. At this time, however, there was no division of opinion in the capital. The whole population seemed animated by a spirit of resistance, as one man.

In a former page I have mentioned that it was the plan of Cortes, on entering the valley, to commence operations by reducing the subordinate cities before striking at the capital itself, which, like some goodly tree, whose roots had been severed one after another, would be thus left without support against the fury of the tempest. The first point of attack which he selected was the ancient city of Iztapalapan; a place containing fifty thousand inhabitants, according to his own account, and situated about six leagues distant, on the narrow tongue of land which divides the waters of the great salt lake from those of the fresh. It was the private domain of the last sovereign of Mexico; where, as the reader may remember, he entertained the white men the night before their entrance into the capital, and astonished them by the display of his princely gardens. To this monarch they owed no good will, for he had conducted the operations on the noche triste. He was, indeed, no more; but the people of his city entered heartily into his hatred of the strangers, and were now the most loyal vassals of the Mexican crown.

In a week after his arrival at his new quarters, Cortes, leaving the command of the garrison to Sandoval, marched against this Indian city, at the head of two hundred Spanish foot, eighteen horse, and between three and four thousand Tlascalans. Within two leagues of their point of destination, they were encountered by a strong Aztec force, drawn up to dispute their progress. Cortes instantly gave them battle. The barbarians showed their usual courage; but, after some hard fighting, were compelled to give way before the steady valour of the Spanish infantry, backed by the desperate fury of the Tlascalans, whom the sight of an Aztec seemed to inflame almost to madness. The enemy retreated in disorder, closely followed by the Spaniards. When they had arrived within half a league of Iztapalapan, they observed a number of canoes filled with Indians, who appeared to be labouring on the mole which hemmed in the waters of the salt lake. Swept along in the tide of pursuit, they gave little heed to it, but, following up the chase, entered pell-mell with the fugitives into the city.

The houses stood some of them on dry ground, some on piles in the water. The former were deserted by the inhabitants, most of whom had escaped in canoes across the lake, leaving, in their haste, their effects behind them. The Tlascalans poured at once into the vacant dwellings and loaded themselves with booty; while the enemy, making the best of their way through this part of the town, sought shelter in the buildings erected over the water, or among the reeds which sprung from its shallow bottom. In the houses were many of the citizens also, who still lingered with their wives and children, unable to find the means of transporting themselves from the scene of danger.

Cortes, supported by his own men, and by such of the allies as could be brought to obey his orders, attacked the enemy in this last place of their retreat. Both parties fought up to their girdles in the water. A desperate struggle ensued, as the Aztec fought with the fury of a tiger driven to bay by the huntsmen. It was all in vain. The enemy was overpowered in every quarter. The citizen shared the fate of the soldier, and a pitiless massacre succeeded, without regard to sex or age. Cortes endeavoured to stop it. But it would have been as easy to call away the starving wolf from the carcass he was devouring, as the Tlascalan who had once tasted the blood of an enemy. More than six thousand, including women and children, according to the Conqueror's own statement, perished in the conflict.

Darkness meanwhile had set in; but it was dispelled in some measure by the light of the burning houses, which the troops had set on fire in different parts of the town. Their insulated position, it is true, prevented the flames from spreading from one building to another, but the solitary masses threw a strong and lurid glare over their own neighbourhood, which gave additional horror to the scene. As resistance was now at an end, the soldiers abandoned themselves to pillage, and soon stripped the dwellings of every portable article of any value.

While engaged in this work of devastation, a murmuring sound was heard as of the hoarse rippling of waters, and a cry soon arose among the Indians that the dikes were broken! Cortes now comprehended the business of the men whom he had seen in the canoes at work on the mole which fenced in the great basin of Lake Tezcuco. It had been pierced by the desperate Indians, who thus laid the country under an inundation, by suffering the waters of the salt lake to spread themselves over the lower level, through the opening. Greatly alarmed, the general called his men together, and made all haste to evacuate the city. Had they remained three hours longer, he says, not a soul could have escaped. They came staggering under the weight of booty, wading with difficulty through the water, which was fast gaining upon them. For some distance their path was illumined by the glare of the burning buildings. But, as the light faded away in distance, they wandered with uncertain steps, sometimes up to their knees, at others up to their waists, in the water, through which they floundered on with the greatest difficulty. As they reached the opening in the dike, the stream became deeper, and flowed out with such a current that the men were unable to maintain their footing. The Spaniards, breasting the flood, forced their way through; but many of the Indians, unable to swim, were borne down by the waters. All the plunder was lost. The powder was spoiled; the arms and clothes of the soldiers were saturated with the brine, and the cold night wind, as it blew over them, benumbed their weary limbs till they could scarcely drag them along. At dawn they beheld the lake swarming with canoes, full of Indians, who had anticipated their disaster, and who now saluted them with showers of stones, arrows, and other deadly missiles. Bodies of light troops, hovering in the distance, disquieted the flanks of the army in like manner. The Spaniards had no desire to close with the enemy. They only wished to regain their comfortable quarters in Tezcuco, where they arrived on the same day, more disconsolate and fatigued than after many a long march and hard-fought battle.

The close of the expedition, so different from its brilliant commencement, greatly disappointed Cortes. His numerical loss had, indeed, not been great; but this affair convinced him how much he had to apprehend from the resolution of a people, who were prepared to bury their country under water rather than to submit. Still, the enemy had little cause for congratulation, since, independently of the number of slain, they had seen one of their most flourishing cities sacked, and in part, at least, laid in ruins — one of those, too, which in its public works displayed the nearest approach to civilisation. Such are the triumphs of war!

The expedition of Cortes, notwithstanding the disasters which chequered it, was favourable to the Spanish cause. The fate of Iztapalapan struck a terror throughout the valley. The consequences were soon apparent in the deputations sent by the different places eager to offer their submission. Its influence was visible, indeed, beyond the mountains. Among others, the people of Otumba, the town near which the Spaniards had gained their famous victory, sent to tender their allegiance, and to request the protection of the powerful strangers. They excused themselves, as usual, for the part they had taken in the late hostilities, by throwing the blame on the Aztecs.

But the place of most importance which thus claimed their protection, was Chalco, situated on the eastern extremity of the lake of that name. It was an ancient city, people by a kindred tribe of the Aztecs, and once their formidable rival. The Mexican emperor, distrusting their loyalty, had placed a garrison within their walls to hold them in check. The rulers of the city now sent a message secretly to Cortes, proposing to put themselves under his protection, if he would enable them to expel the garrison.

The Spanish commander did not hesitate; but instantly detached a considerable force under Sandoval for this object. On the march his rear-guard, composed of Tlascalans, was roughly handled by some light troops of the Mexicans. But he took his revenge in a pitched battle, which took place with the main body of the enemy at no great distance from Chalco. They were drawn up on a level ground, covered with green crops of maize and maguey. Sandoval, charging the enemy at the head of his cavalry, threw them into disorder. But they quickly rallied, formed again, and renewed the battle with greater spirit than ever. In a second attempt he was more fortunate; and, breaking through their lines by a desperate onset, the brave cavalier succeeded, after a warm but ineffectual struggle on their part, in completely routing and driving them from the field. The conquering army continued its march to Chalco, which the Mexican garrison had already evacuated, and was received in triumph by the assembled citizens, who seemed eager to testify their gratitude for their deliverance from the Aztec yoke. After taking such measures as he could for the permanent security of the place, Sandoval returned to Tezcuco, accompanied by the two young lords of the city, sons of the late cacique.

They were courteously received by Cortes; and they informed him that their father had died full of years, a short time before. With his last breath he had expressed his regret that he should not have lived to see Malinche. He believed that the white men were the beings predicted by the oracles, as one day to come from the East and take possession of the land; and he enjoined it on his children, should the strangers return to the valley, to render them their homage and allegiance. The young caciques expressed their readiness to do so; but, as this must bring on them the vengeance of the Aztecs, they implored the general to furnish a sufficient force for their protection.

Cortes received a similar application from various other towns, which were disposed, could they do so with safety, to throw off the Mexican yoke. But he was in no situation to comply with their request. He now felt, more sensibly than ever, the incompetency of his means to his undertaking. "I assure your Majesty," he writes in his letter to the emperor, "the greatest uneasiness which I feel after all my labours and fatigues, is from my inability to succour and support our Indian friends, your Majesty's loyal vassals." Far from having a force competent to this, he had scarcely enough for his own protection. His vigilant enemy had an eye on all his movements, and, should he cripple his strength by sending away too many detachments, or by employing them at too great a distance, would be prompt to take advantage of it. His only expeditions, hitherto, had been in the neighbourhood, where the troops, after striking some sudden and decisive blow, might speedily regain their quarters. The utmost watchfulness was maintained there, and the Spaniards lived in as constant preparation for an assault, as if their camp was pitched under the walls of Mexico.

On two occasions the general had sallied forth and engaged the enemy in the environs of Tezcuco. At one time a thousand canoes, filled with Aztecs, crossed the lake to gather in a large crop of Indian corn nearly ripe, on its borders. Cortes thought it important to secure this for himself. He accordingly marched out and gave battle to the enemy, drove them from the field, and swept away the rich harvest to the granaries of Tezcuco. Another time a strong body of Mexicans had established themselves in some neighbouring towns friendly to their interests. Cortes, again sallying, dislodged them from their quarters, beat them in several skirmishes, and reduced the places to obedience. But these enterprises demanded all his resources, and left him nothing to spare for his allies. In this exigency, his fruitful genius suggested an expedient for supplying the deficiency of his means.

Some of the friendly cities without the valley, observing the numerous beacon-fires on the mountains, inferred that the Mexicans were mustering in great strength, and that the Spaniards must be hard pressed in their new quarters. They sent messengers to Tezcuco, expressing their apprehension, and offering reinforcements, which the general, when he set out on his march, had declined. He returned many thanks for the proffered aid; but, while he declined it for himself, as unnecessary, he indicated in what manner their services might be effectual for the defence of Chalco and the other places which had invoked his protection. But his Indian allies were in deadly feud with these places, whose inhabitants had too often fought under the Aztec banner not to have been engaged in repeated wars with the people beyond the mountains.

Cortes set himself earnestly to reconcile these differences. He told the hostile parties that they should be willing to forget their mutual wrongs, since they bad entered into new relations. They were now vassals of the same sovereign, engaged in a common enterprise against a formidable foe who had so long trodden them in the dust. Singly they could do little, but united they might protect each other's weakness, and hold their enemy at bay till the Spaniards could come to their assistance. These arguments finally prevailed; and the politic general had the satisfaction to see the high-spirited and hostile tribes forego their long-cherished rivalry, and, resigning the pleasures of revenge, so dear to the barbarian, embrace one another as friends and champions in a common cause. To this wise policy the Spanish commander owed quite as much of his subsequent successes, as to his arms.

Thus the foundations of the Mexican empire were hourly loosening, as the great vassals around the capital, on whom it most relied, fell off one after another from their allegiance. The Aztecs, properly so called, formed but a small part of the population of the valley. This was principally composed of cognate tribes, members of the same great family of the Nahuatlacs, who had come upon the plateau at nearly the same time. They were mutual rivals, and were reduced one after another by the more warlike Mexican, who held them in subjection, often by open force, always by fear. Fear was the great principle of cohesion which bound together the discordant members of the monarchy, and this was now fast dissolving before the influence of a power more mighty than that of the Aztec. This, it is true, was not the first time that the conquered races had attempted to recover their independence; but all such attempts had failed for want of concert. It was reserved for the commanding genius of Cortes to extinguish their old hereditary feuds, and, combining their scattered energies, to animate them with a common principle of action.

Encouraged by this state of things, the Spanish general thought it a favourable moment to press his negotiations with the capital. He availed himself of the presence of some noble

Mexicans, taken in the late action with Sandoval, to send another message to their master. It was in substance a repetition of the first with a renewed assurance, that, if the city would return to its allegiance to the Spanish crown, the authority of Guatemozin should be confirmed, and the persons and property of his subjects be respected. To this communication no reply was made. The young Indian emperor had a spirit as dauntless as that of Cortes himself. On his head descended the full effects of that vicious system of government bequeathed to him by his ancestors. But, as he saw his empire crumbling beneath him, he sought to uphold it by his own energy and resources. He anticipated the defection of some vassals by establishing garrisons within their walls. Others he conciliated by exempting them from tributes, or greatly lightening their burdens, or by advancing them to posts of honour and authority in the state. He showed, at the same time, his implacable animosity towards the Christians, by commanding that every one taken within his dominions should be sent to the capital, where he was sacrificed with all the barbarous ceremonies prescribed by the Aztec ritual.

While these occurrences were passing, Cortes received the welcome intelligence, that the brigantines were completed and waiting to be transported to Tezcuco. He detached a body for the service, consisting of two hundred Spanish foot and fifteen horse, which he placed under the command of Sandoval. This cavalier had been rising daily in the estimation both of the general and of the army. Though one of the youngest officers in the service, he possessed a cool head and a ripe judgment, which fitted him for the most delicate and difficult undertakings. Sandoval was a native Of Medellin, the birth-place of Cortes himself. He was warmly attached to his commander, and had on all occasions proved himself worthy of his confidence. He was a man of few words, showing his worth rather by what he did, than what he said. His honest, soldier-like deportment made him a favourite with the troops, and had its influence even on his enemies. He unfortunately died in the flower of his age. But he discovered talents and military skill, which, had he lived to later life, would undoubtedly have placed his name on the roll with those of the greatest captains of his nation.

Sandoval's route was to lead him by Zoltepec, a city where the massacre of the forty-five Spaniards, already noticed, had been perpetrated. The cavalier received orders to find out the guilty parties, if possible, and to punish them for their share in the transaction.

When the Spaniards arrived at the spot, they found that the inhabitants, who had previous notice of their approach, had all fled. In the deserted temples they discovered abundant traces of the fate of their countrymen; for, besides their arms and clothing, and the hides of their horses, the heads of several soldiers, prepared in such a way that they could be well preserved, were found suspended as trophies of the victory. In a neighbouring building, traced with charcoal on the walls, they found the following inscription in Castilian: "In this place the unfortunate Juan Juste, with many others of his company, was imprisoned." This hidalgo was one of the followers of Narvaez, and had come with him into the country in quest of gold, but had found, instead, an obscure and inglorious death. The eyes of the soldiers were suffused with tears, as they gazed on the gloomy record, and their bosoms swelled with indignation, as they thought of the horrible fate of the captives. Fortunately the inhabitants were not then before them. Some few, who subsequently fell into their hands, were branded as slaves. But the greater part of the population, who threw themselves, in the most abject manner, on the mercy of the Conquerors, imputing the blame of the affair to the Aztecs, the Spanish commander spared, from pity, or contempt.

He now resumed his march on Tlascala; but scarcely had he crossed the borders of the republic, when he descried the flaunting banners of the convoy which transported the brigantines, as it was threading its way through the defiles of the mountains. Great was his satisfaction at the spectacle, for he had feared a detention of some days at Tlascala, before the preparations for the march could be completed.

There were thirteen vessels in all, of different sizes. They had been constructed under the direction of the experienced shipbuilder, Martin Lopez, aided by three of four Spanish carpenters and the friendly natives, some of whom showed no mean degree of imitative skill. The brigantines, when completed, had been fairly tried on the waters of the Zahuapan. They were then taken to pieces, and, as Lopez was impatient of delay, the several parts, the timbers, anchors, iron-work, sails, and cordage were placed on the shoulders of the tamanes, and, under a numerous military escort, were thus far advanced on the way to Tezcuco. Sandoval dismissed a part of the Indian convoy, as superfluous.

Twenty thousand warriors he retained, dividing them into two equal bodies for the protection of the tamanes in the centre. His own little body of Spaniards be distributed in like manner. The Tlascalans in the van marched under the command of a chief who gloried in the name of Chichemecatl. For some reason Sandoval afterwards changed the order of march, and placed this division in the rear — an arrangement which gave great umbrage to the doughty warrior that led it, who asserted his right to the front, the place which he and his ancestors had always occupied, as the post of danger. He was somewhat appeased by Sandoval's assurance that it was for that very reason he had been transferred to the rear, the quarter most likely to be assailed by the enemy. But even then he was greatly dissatisfied, on finding that the Spanish commander was to march by his side, grudging, it would seem, that any other should share the laurel with himself.

Slowly and painfully, encumbered with their heavy burden, the troops worked their way over steep eminences, and rough mountainpasses, presenting, one might suppose in their long line of march, many a vulnerable point to an enemy. But, although small parties of warriors were seen hovering at times on their flanks and rear, they kept at a respectful distance, not caring to encounter so formidable a foe. On the fourth day the warlike caravan arrived in safety before Tezcuco.

Their approach was beheld with joy by Cortes and the soldiers, who hailed it as a signal of a speedy termination of the war. The general, attended by his officers, all dressed in their richest attire, came out to welcome the convoy. It extended over a space of two leagues, and so slow was its progress that six hours elapsed before the closing files had entered the city. The Tlascalan chiefs displayed their wonted bravery of apparel, and the whole array, composed of the flower of their warriors, made a brilliant appearance. They marched by the sound of atabal and comet, and, as they traversed the streets of the capital amidst the acclamations of the soldiery, they made the city ring with the shouts of "Castile and Tlascala, long live our sovereign, the emperor."

"It was a marvellous thing," exclaims the Conqueror, in his letters, "that few have seen, or even heard of — this transportation of thirteen vessels of war on the shoulders of men, for nearly twenty leagues across the mountains!" It was, indeed, a stupendous achievement, and not easily matched in ancient or modern story; one which only a genius like that of Cortes could have devised, or a daring spirit like his have so successfully executed. Little did he foresee, when he ordered the destruction of the fleet which first brought him to the country, and with his usual forecast commanded the preservation of the iron-work and rigging — little did he foresee the important uses for which they were to be reserved. So important, that on their preservation may be said to have depended the successful issue of his great enterprise.

IN the course of three or four days, the Spanish general furnished the Tlascalans with the opportunity so much coveted, and allowed their boiling spirits to effervesce in active operations. He had, for some time, meditated an expedition to reconnoitre the capital and its environs, and to chastise, on the way, certain places which had sent him insulting messages of defiance, and which were particularly active in their hostilities. He disclosed his design to a few only of his principal officers, from his distrust of the Tezcucans, whom he suspected to be in correspondence with the enemy.

Early in the spring, he left Tezcuco, at the head of three hundred and fifty Spaniards and the whole strength of his allies. He took with him Alvarado and Olid, and intrusted the charge of the garrison to Sandoval. Cortes had practical acquaintance with the incompetence of the first of these cavaliers for so delicate a post, during his short, but disastrous, rule in Mexico.

But all his precautions had not availed to shroud his designs from the vigilant foe, whose eye was on all his movements; who seemed even to divine his thoughts, and to be prepared to thwart their execution. He had advanced but a few leagues, when he was met by a considerable body of Mexicans, drawn up to dispute his progress. A sharp skirmish took place, in which the enemy were driven from the ground, and the way was left open to the Christians. They held a circuitous route to the north, and their first point of attack was the insular town of Xaltocan, situated on the northern extremity of the lake of that name, now called San Christobal. The town was entirely surrounded by water, and communicated with the main land by means of causeways, in the same manner as the Mexican capital. Cortes, riding at the head of his cavalry, advanced along the dike, till he was brought to a stand by finding a wide opening in it, through which the waters poured so as to be altogether impracticable, not only for horse, but for infantry. The lake was covered with canoes, filled with Aztec warriors, who, anticipating the movement of the Spaniards, had come to the aid of the city. They now began a furious discharge of stones and arrows on the assailants, while they were themselves tolerably well protected from the musketry of their enemy by the light bulwarks, with which, for that purpose, they had fortified their canoes.

The severe volleys of the Mexicans did some injury to the Spaniards and their allies, and began to throw them into disorder, crowded as they were on the narrow causeway, without the means of advancing, when Cortes ordered a retreat. This was followed by renewed tempests of missiles, accompanied by taunts and fierce yells of defiance. The battle-cry of the Aztec, like the war-whoop of the North American Indian, was an appalling note, according to the Conqueror's own acknowledgment, in the ears of the Spaniards. At this juncture, the general fortunately obtained information from a deserter, one of the Mexican allies, of a ford, by which the army might traverse the shallow lake, and penetrate the place. He instantly detached the greater part of the infantry on the service, posting himself with the remainder, and with the horse, at the entrance of the passage, to cover the attack and prevent any interruption in the rear.

The soldiers, under the direction of the Indian guide, forded the lake without much difficulty, though in some places the water came above their girdles. During the passage, they were annoyed by the enemy's missiles; but when they had gained the dry level, they took ample revenge, and speedily put all who resisted to the sword. The greater part, together with the townsmen, made their escape in the boats. The place was now abandoned to pillage. The troops found in it many women, who had been left to their fate; and these, together with a considerable quantity of cotton stuffs, gold, and articles of food, fell into the hands of the victors, who, setting fire to the deserted city, returned in triumph to their comrades.

Continuing his circuitous route, Cortes presented himself successively before three other places, each of which had been deserted by the inhabitants in anticipation of his arrival. The principal of these, Azcapotzalco, had once been the capital of an independent state. It was now the great slave-market of the Aztecs, where their unfortunate captives were brought, and disposed of at public sale. It was also the quarter occupied by the jewellers; and the place whence the Spaniards obtained the goldsmiths who melted down the rich treasures received from Montezuma. But they found there only a small supply of the precious metals, or, indeed, of anything else of value, as the people had been careful to remove their effects. They spared the buildings, however, in consideration of their having met with no resistance.

During the nights, the troops bivouacked in the open fields, maintaining the strictest watch, for the country was all in arms, and beacons were flaming on every hill-top, while dark masses of the enemy were occasionally descried in the distance. The Spaniards were now traversing the most opulent region of Anahuac. Cities and villages were scattered over hill and valley, all giving token of a dense and industrious population. It was the general's purpose to march at once on Tacuba, and establish his quarters in that ancient capital for the present. He found a strong force encamped under its walls, prepared to dispute his entrance. Without waiting for their advance, he rode at full gallop against them with his little body of horse. The arquebuses and crossbows opened a lively volley on their extended wings, and the infantry, armed with their swords and copper-headed lances, and supported by the Indian battalions, followed up the attack of the horse with an alacrity which soon put the enemy to flight. Cortes led his troops without further opposition into the suburbs of Tacuba, the ancient Tlacopan, where he established himself for the night.

On the following morning, he found the indefatigable Aztecs again under arms, and, on the open ground before the city, prepared to give him battle. He marched out against them, and, after an action hotly contested, though of no long duration, again routed them. They fled towards the town, but were driven through the streets at the point of the lance, and were compelled, together with the inhabitants, to evacuate the place. The city was then delivered over to pillage; and the Indian allies, not content with plundering the houses of everything portable within them, set them on fire, and in a short time a quarter of the town — the poorer dwellings, probably, built of light, combustible materials — was in flames.

Cortes proposed to remain in his present quarters for some days, during which time he established his own residence in the ancient palace of the lords of Tlacopan. It was a long range of low buildings, like most of the royal residences in the country, and offered good accommodations for the Spanish forces. During his halt here, there was not a day on which the army was not engaged in one or more rencontres with the enemy. They terminated almost uniformly in favour of the Spaniards, though with more or less injury to them and to their allies. One encounter, indeed, had nearly been attended with more fatal consequences.

The Spanish general, in the heat of pursuit, had allowed himself to be decoyed upon the great causeway — the same which had once been so fatal to his army. He followed the flying foe, until he had gained the further side of the nearest bridge, which had been repaired since the disastrous action of the noche triste. When thus far advanced, the Aztecs, with the rapidity of lightning, turned on him, and he beheld a large reinforcement in their rear, all fresh on the field, prepared to support their countrymen. At the same time, swarms of boats, unobserved in the eagerness of the chase, seemed to start up as if by magic, covering the waters around. The Spaniards were now exposed to a perfect hailstorm of missiles, both from the causeway and the lake; but they stood unmoved amidst the tempest, when Cortes, too late perceiving his error, gave orders for the retreat. Slowly, and with admirable coolness, his men receded, step by step, offering a resolute front to the enemy. The Mexicans came on with their usual vociferation, making the shores echo to their war-cries, and striking at the Spaniards with their long pikes, and with poles, to which the swords taken from the Christians had been fastened. A cavalier, named Volante, bearing the standard of Cortes, was felled by one of their weapons, and, tumbling into the lake, was picked up by the Mexican boats. He was a man of a muscular frame, and, as the enemy were dragging him off, he succeeded in extricating himself from their grasp, and clenching his colours in his hand, with a desperate effort sprang back upon the causeway. At length, after some hard fighting, in which many of the Spaniards were wounded, and many of their allies slain, the troops regained the land, where Cortes, with a full heart, returned thanks to Heaven for what he might well regard as a providential deliverance. It was a salutary lesson; though he should scarcely have needed one, so soon after the affair of Iztapalapan, to warn him of the wily tactics of his enemy.

It had been one of Cortes' principal objects in this expedition to obtain an interview, if possible, with the Aztec emperor, or with some of the great lords at his court, and to try if some means for an accommodation could not be found, by which he might avoid the appeal to arms. An occasion for such a parley presented itself, when his forces were one day confronted with those of the enemy, with a broken bridge interposed between them. Cortes, riding in advance of his people, intimated by signs his peaceful intent, and that he wished to confer with the Aztecs. They respected the signal, and, with the aid of his interpreter, he requested, that, if there were any great chief among them, he would come forward and hold a parley with him. The Mexicans replied, in derision, they were all chiefs, and bade him speak openly whatever he had to tell them. As the general returned no answer, they asked, why he did not make another visit to the capital, and tauntingly added, "Perhaps Malinche does not expect to find there another Montezuma, as obedient to his command as the former." Some of them complimented the Tlascalans with the epithet of women, who, they said, would never have ventured so near the capital, but for the protection of the white men.

The animosity of the two nations was not confined to these harmless, though bitter jests, but showed itself in regular cartels of defiance, which daily passed between the principal chieftains. These were followed by combats, in which one or more champions fought on a side, to vindicate the honour of their respective countries. A fair field of fight was given to the warriors, who conducted those combats, a l'outrance, with the punctilio of a European tourney; displaying a valour worthy of the two boldest of the races of Anahuac, and a skill in the management of their weapons, which drew forth the admiration of the Spaniards.

Cortes had now been six days in Tacuba. There was nothing further to detain him, as he had accomplished the chief objects of his expedition. He had humbled several of the places which had been most active in their hostility; and he had revived the credit of the Castilian arms, which had been much tarnished by their former reverses in this quarter of the valley. He had also made himself acquainted with the condition of the capital, which he found in a better posture of defence than he had imagined. All the ravages of the preceding year seemed to be repaired, and there was no evidence, even to his experienced eye, that the wasting hand of war had so lately swept over the land. The Aztec troops, which swarmed through the valley, seemed to be well appointed, and showed an invincible spirit, as if prepared to resist to the last. It is true, they had been beaten in every encounter. In the open field they were no match for the Spaniards, whose cavalry they could never comprehend, and whose firearms easily penetrated the cotton mail, which formed the stoutest defence of the Indian warrior. But, entangled in the long streets and narrow lanes of the metropolis, where every house was a citadel, the Spaniards, as experience had shown, would lose much of their superiority. With the Mexican emperor, confident in the strength of his preparations, the general saw there was no probability of effecting an accommodation. He saw, too, the necessity of the most careful preparations on his own part — indeed, that he must strain his resources to the utmost, before he could safely venture to rouse the lion in his lair.

The Spaniards returned by the same route by which they had come. Their retreat was interpreted into a flight by the natives, who hung on the rear of the army, uttering vainglorious vaunts, and saluting the troops with showers of arrows, which did some mischief. Cortes resorted to one of their own stratagems to rid himself of this annoyance. He divided his cavalry into two or three small parties, and concealed them among some thick shrubbery, which fringed both sides of the road. The rest of the army continued its march. The Mexicans followed, unsuspicious of the ambuscade, when the horse, suddenly darting from their place of concealment, threw the enemy's flanks into confusion, and the retreating columns of infantry, facing about suddenly, commenced a brisk attack, which completed their consternation. It was a broad and level plain, over which the panic-struck Mexicans made the best of their way, without attempting resistance; while the cavalry, riding them down and piercing the fugitives with their lances, followed up the chase for several miles, in what Cortes calls a truly beautiful style. The army experienced no further annoyance from the enemy.

On their arrival at Tezcuco, they were greeted with joy by their comrades, who had received no tidings of them during the fortnight which had elapsed since their departure. The Tlascalans, immediately on their return, requested the general's permission to carry back to their own country the valuable booty which they had gathered in their foray — a request which, however unpalatable, he could not refuse.

The troops had not been in quarters more than two or three days, when an embassy arrived from Chalco, again soliciting the protection of the Spaniards against the Mexicans, who menaced them from several points in their neighbourhood. But the soldiers were so much exhausted by unintermitted vigils, forced marches, battles, and wounds, that Cortes wished to give them a breathing-time to recruit, before engaging in a new expedition. He answered the application of the Chalcans, by sending his missives to the allied cities, calling on them to march to the assistance of their confederate. It is not to be supposed that they could comprehend the import of his despatches. But the paper, with its mysterious characters, served for a warrant to the officer who bore it, as the interpreter of the general's commands.

But, although these were implicitly obeyed, the Chalcans felt the danger so pressing, that they soon repeated their petition for the Spaniards to come in person to their relief. Cortes no longer hesitated; for he was well aware of the importance of Chalco, not merely on its own account, but from its position, which commanded one of the great avenues to Tlascala, and to Vera–Cruz, the intercourse with which should run no risk of interruption. Without further loss of time, therefore, he detached a body of three hundred Spanish foot and twenty horse, under the command of Sandoval, for the protection of the city.

That active officer soon presented himself before Chalco, and, strengthened by the reinforcement of its own troops and those of the confederate towns, directed his first operations against Huaxtepec, a place of some importance, lying two leagues or more to the south among the mountains. It was held by a strong Mexican force, watching their opportunity to make a descent upon Chalco. The Spaniards found the enemy drawn up at a distance from the town, prepared to receive them. The ground was broken and tangled with bushes, unfavourable to the cavalry, which in consequence soon fell into disorder; and Sandoval, finding himself embarrassed by their movements, ordered them, after sustaining some loss, from the field. In their place he brought up his musketeers and crossbowmen, who poured a rapid fire into the thick columns of the Indians. The rest of the infantry, with sword and pike, charged the flanks of the enemy, who, bewildered by the shock, after sustaining considerable slaughter, fell back in an irregular manner, leaving the field of battle to the Spaniards.

The victors proposed to bivouac there for the night. But, while engaged in preparations for their evening meal, they were aroused by the cry of "To arms, to arms! the enemy is upon us!" In an instant the trooper was in his saddle, the soldier grasped his musket or his good toledo, and the action was renewed with greater fury than before. The Mexicans had received a reinforcement from the city. But their second attempt was not more fortunate than their first; and the victorious Spaniards, driving their antagonists before them, entered and took possession of the town itself, which had already been evacuated by the inhabitants.

Sandoval took up his quarters in the dwelling of the lord of the place, surrounded by gardens, which rivalled those of Iztapalapan in magnificence, and surpassed them in extent. They are said to have been two leagues in circumference, having pleasure-houses, and numerous tanks stocked with various kinds of fish; and they were embellished with trees, shrubs, and plants, native and exotic, some selected for their beauty and fragrance, others for their medicinal properties. They were scientifically arranged; and the whole establishment displayed a degree of horticultural taste and knowledge, of which it would not have been easy to find a counterpart, at that day, in the more civilised communities of Europe. Such is the testimony not only of the rude Conquerors, but of men of science, who visited these beautiful repositories in the day of their glory.

After halting two days to refresh his forces in this agreeable spot, Sandoval marched on Jacapichtla, about six miles to the eastward. It was a town, or rather fortress, perched on a rocky eminence, almost inaccessible from its steepness. It was garrisoned by a Mexican force, who rolled down on the assailants, as they attempted to scale the heights, huge fragments of rock, which, thundering over the sides of the precipice, carried ruin and desolation in their path. The Indian confederates fell back in dismay from the attempt. But Sandoval, indignant that any achievement should be too difficult for a Spaniard, commanded his cavaliers to dismount, and, declaring that he "would carry the place or die in the attempt," led on his men with the cheering cry of "St. Iago." With renewed courage, they now followed their gallant leader up the ascent, under a storm of lighter missiles, mingled with huge masses of stone, which, breaking into splinters, overturned the assailants, and made fearful havoc in their ranks. Sandoval, who had been wounded on the preceding day, received a severe contusion on the head, while more than one of his brave comrades were struck down by his side. Still they clambered up, sustaining themselves by the bushes or projecting pieces of rock, and seemed to force themselves onward as much by the energy of their wills, as by the strength of their bodies.

After incredible toil, they stood on the summit, face to face with the astonished garrison. For a moment they paused to recover breath, then sprang furiously on their foes. The struggle was short but desperate. Most of the Aztecs were put to the sword. Some were thrown headlong over the battlements, and others, letting themselves down the precipice, were killed on the borders of a little stream that wound round its base, the waters of which were so polluted with blood, that the victors were unable to slake their thirst with them for a full hour!

Sandoval, having now accomplished the object of his expedition, by reducing the strongholds which had so long held the Chalcans in awe, returned in triumph to Tezcuco. Meanwhile, the Aztec emperor, whose vigilant eye had been attentive to all that had passed, thought that the absence of so many of its warriors afforded a favourable opportunity for recovering Chalco. He sent a fleet of boats for this purpose across the lake, with a numerous force under the command of some of his most valiant chiefs. Fortunately the absent Chalcans reached their city before the arrival of the enemy; but, though supported by their Indian allies, they were so much alarmed by the magnitude of the hostile array, that they sent again to the Spaniards, invoking their aid.

The messengers arrived at the same time with Sandoval and his army. Cortes was much puzzled by the contradictory accounts. He suspected some negligence in his lieutenant, and, displeased with his precipitate return in this unsettled state of the affair, ordered him back at once, with such of his forces as were in fighting condition. Sandoval felt deeply injured by this proceeding, but he made no attempt at exculpation, and, obeying his commander in silence, put himself at the head of his troops, and made a rapid countermarch on the Indian city.

Before he reached it, a battle had been fought between the Mexicans and the confederates, in which the latter, who had acquired unwonted confidence from their recent successes, were victorious. A number of Aztec nobles fell into their hands in the engagement, whom they delivered to Sandoval to be carried off as prisoners to Tezcuco. On his arrival there, the cavalier, wounded by the unworthy treatment he had received, retired to his own quarters without presenting himself before his chief.

During his absence, the inquiries of Cortes had satisfied him of his own precipitate conduct, and of the great injustice he had done his lieutenant. There was no man in the army on whose services he set so high a value, as the responsible situations in which he had placed him plainly showed; and there was none for whom he seems to have entertained a greater personal regard. On Sandoval's return, therefore, Cortes instantly sent to request his attendance; when, with a soldier's frankness, he made such an explanation as soothed the irritated spirit of the cavalier — a matter of no great difficulty, as the latter had too generous a nature, and too earnest a devotion to his commander and the cause in which they were embarked, to harbour a petty feeling of resentment in his bosom.

During the occurrence of these events, the work was going forward actively on the canal, and the brigantines were within a fortnight of their completion. The greatest vigilance was required, in the mean time, to prevent their destruction by the enemy, who had already made three ineffectual attempts to burn them on the stocks. The precautions which Cortes thought it necessary to take against the Tezcucans themselves, added not a little to his embarrassment.

At this time he received embassies from different Indian states, some of them on the remote shores of the Mexican Gulf, tendering their allegiance and soliciting his protection. For this he was partly indebted to the good offices of Ixtlilxochitl, who, in consequence of his brother's death, was now advanced to the sovereignty of Tezcuco. This important position greatly increased his consideration and authority through the country, of which he freely availed himself to bring the natives under the dominion of the Spaniards.

The general received also at this time the welcome intelligence of the arrival of three vessels at Villa Rica, with two hundred men on board, well provided with arms and ammunition, and with seventy or eighty horses. It was a most seasonable reinforcement. From what quarter it came is uncertain; most probably, from Hispaniola. Cortes, it may be remembered, had sent for supplies to that place; and the authorities of the island, who had general jurisdiction over the affairs of the colonies, had shown themselves, on more than one occasion, well inclined towards him, probably considering him, under all circumstances, as better fitted than any other man to achieve the conquest of the country.

The new recruits soon found their way to Tezcuco; as the communications with the port were now open and unobstructed. Among them were several cavaliers of consideration, one of whom, Julian de Alderete, the royal treasurer, came over to superintend the interests of the crown.

NOTWITHSTANDING the relief which had been afforded to the people of Chalco, it was so ineffectual, that envoys from that city again arrived at Tezcuco, bearing a hieroglyphical chart, on which were depicted several strong places in their neighbourhood, garrisoned by the Aztecs, from which they expected annoyance. Cortes determined this time to take the affair into his own hands, and to scour the country so effectually, as to place Chalco, if possible, in a state of security. He did not confine himself to this object, but proposed, before his return, to pass quite round the great lakes, and reconnoitre the country to the south of them, in the same manner as he had before done to the west. In the course of his march, he would direct his arms against some of the strong places from which the Mexicans might expect support in the siege. Two or three weeks must elapse before the completion of the brigantines; and, if no other good resulted from the expedition, it would give active occupation to his troops, whose turbulent spirits might fester into discontent in the monotonous existence of a camp.

He selected for the expedition thirty horse and three hundred Spanish infantry, with a considerable body of Tlascalan and Tezcucan warriors. The remaining garrison he left in charge of the trusty Sandoval, who, with the friendly lord of the capital, would watch over the construction of the brigantines, and protect them from the assaults of the Aztecs.

On the fifth of April he began his march, and on the following day arrived at Chalco, where he was met by a number of the confederate chiefs. With the aid of his faithful interpreters, Dona Marina and Aguilar, he explained to them the objects of his present expedition; stated his purpose soon to enforce the blockade of Mexico, and required their co-operation with the whole strength of their levies. To this they readily assented; and he soon received a sufficient proof of their friendly disposition in the forces which joined him on the march, amounting, according to one of the army, to more than had ever before followed his banner.

Taking a southerly direction, the troops, after leaving Chalco, struck into the recesses of the wild sierra, which, with its bristling peaks, serves as a formidable palisade to fence round the beautiful valley; while, within its rugged arms, it shuts up many a green and fruitful pasture of its own. As the Spaniards passed through its deep gorges, they occasionally wound round the base of some huge cliff or rocky eminence, on which the inhabitants had built their town in the same manner as was done by the people of Europe in the feudal ages; a position which, however favourable to the picturesque, intimates a sense of insecurity as the cause of it, which may reconcile us to the absence of this striking appendage of the landscape in our own more fortunate country.

The occupants of these airy pinnacles took advantage of their situation to shower down stones and arrows on the troops, as they defiled through the narrow passes of the sierra. Though greatly annoyed by their incessant hostilities, Cortes held on his way, till, winding round the base of a castellated cliff, occupied by a strong garrison of Indians, he was so severely pressed, that he felt to pass on without chastising the aggressors would imply a want of strength, which must disparage him in the eyes of his allies. Halting in the valley, therefore, he detached a small body of light troops to scale the heights, while he remained with the main body of the army below, to guard against surprise from the enemy.

The lower region of the rocky eminence was so steep, that the soldiers found it no easy matter to ascend, scrambling, as well as they could, with hand and knee. But, as they came into the more exposed view of the garrison, the latter rolled down huge masses of rock, which, bounding along the declivity, and breaking into fragments, crushed the foremost assailants, and mangled their limbs in a frightful manner. Still they strove to work their way upward, now taking advantage of some gulley, worn by the winter torrent, now sheltering themselves behind a projecting cliff, or some straggling tree, anchored among the crevices of the mountain. It was all in vain. For no sooner did they emerge again into open view, than the rocky avalanche thundered on their heads with a fury against which steel helm and cuirass were as little defence as gossamer. All the party were more or less wounded. Eight of the number were killed on the spot — a loss the little band could ill afford — and the gallant ensign Corral, who led the advance, saw the banner in his hand torn into shreds. Cortes, at length convinced of the impracticability of the attempt, at least without a more severe loss than he was disposed to incur, commanded a retreat. It was high time; for a large body of the enemy were on full march across the valley to attack him.

He did not wait for their approach, but gathering his broken files together, headed his cavalry, and spurred boldly against them. On the level plain, the Spaniards were on their own ground. The Indians, unable to sustain the furious onset, broke, and fell back before it. The fight soon became a rout, and the fiery cavaliers, dashing over them at full gallop, or running them through with their lances, took some revenge for their late discomfiture. The pursuit continued for some miles, till the nimble foe made their escape into the rugged fastnesses of the sierra, where the Spaniards did not care to follow. The weather was sultry, and, as the country was nearly destitute of water, the men and horses suffered extremely. Before evening they reached a spot overshadowed by a grove of wild mulberry trees, in which some scanty springs afforded a miserable supply to the army.

Near the place rose another rocky summit of the sierra, garrisoned by a stronger force than the one which they had encountered in the former part of the day; and at no great distance stood a second fortress at a still greater height, though considerably smaller than its neighbour. This was also tenanted by a body of warriors, who, as well as those of the adjoining cliff, soon made active demonstration of their hostility by pouring down missiles on the troops below. Cortes, anxious to retrieve the disgrace of the morning, ordered an assault on the larger, and, as it seemed, more practicable eminence. But, though two attempts were made with great resolution, they were repulsed with loss to the assailants. The rocky sides of the hill had been artificially cut and smoothed, so as greatly to increase the natural difficulties of the ascent. — The shades of evening now closed around; and Cortes drew off his men to the mulberry grove, where he took up his bivouac for the night, deeply chagrined at having been twice foiled by the enemy on the same day.

During the night, the Indian force, which occupied the adjoining height, passed over to their brethren, to aid them in the encounter, which they foresaw would be renewed on the following morning. No sooner did the Spanish general, at the break of day, become aware of this manoeuvre, than, with his usual quickness, he took advantage of it. He detached a body of musketeers and crossbowmen to occupy the deserted eminence, purposing, as soon as this was done, to lead the assault in person against the other. It was not long before the Castilian banner was seen streaming from the rocky pinnacle, when the general instantly led up his men to the attack. And, while the garrison were meeting them resolutely on that quarter, the detachment on the neighbouring heights poured into the Place a well-directed fire, which so much distressed the enemy, that, in a very short time, they signified their willingness to capitulate.

On entering the place, the Spaniards found that a plain of some extent ran along the crest of the sierra, and that it was tenanted, not only by men, but by women and their families, with their effects. No violence was offered by the victors to the property or persons of the vanquished, and the knowledge of his lenity induced the Indian garrison, who had made so stout a resistance on the morning of the preceding day, to tender their submission.

After a halt of two days in this sequestered region, the army resumed its march in a south-westerly direction on Huaxtepec, the same city which had surrendered to Sandoval. Here they were kindly received by the cacique, and entertained in his magnificent gardens, which Cortes and his officers, who had not before seen them, compared with the best in Castile. Still threading the wild mountain mazes, the army passed through Jauhtepec and several other places, which were abandoned at their approach. As the inhabitants, however, hung in armed bodies on their flanks and rear, doing them occasionally some mischief, the Spaniards took their revenge by burning the deserted towns.

Thus holding on their fiery track, they descended the bold slope of the Cordilleras, which, on the south, are far more precipitous than on the Atlantic side. Indeed, a single day's journey is sufficient to place the traveller on a level several thousand feet lower than that occupied by him in the morning; thus conveying him in a few hours through the climates of many degrees of latitude. On the ninth day of their march, the troops arrived before the strong city of Quauhnahuac, or Cuernavaca, as since called by the Spaniards. It was the ancient capital of the Tlahuicas, and the most considerable place for wealth and population in this part of the country. It was tributary to the Aztecs, and a garrison of this nation was quartered within its walls. The town was singularly situated, on a projecting piece of land, encompassed by barrancas, or formidable ravines, except on one side, which opened on a rich and well cultivated country. For, though the place stood at an elevation of between five and six thousand feet above the level of the sea, it had a southern exposure so sheltered by the mountain barrier on the north, that its climate was as soft and genial as that of a much lower region.

The Spaniards, on arriving before this city, the limit of their southerly progress, found themselves separated from it by one of the vast barrancas before noticed, which resembled one of those frightful rents not unfrequent in the Mexican Andes, the result, no doubt, of some terrible convulsion in earlier ages. The rocky sides of the ravine sunk perpendicularly down, and so bare as scarcely to exhibit even a vestige of the cactus or of the other hardy plants with which Nature in these fruitful regions so gracefully covers up her deformities. At the bottom of the ravine was seen a little stream, which, oozing from the stony bowels of the sierra, tumbled along its narrow channel, and contributed by its perpetual moisture to the exuberant fertility of the valley. This rivulet, which at certain seasons of the year was swollen to a torrent, was traversed at some distance below the town, where the sloping sides of the barranca afforded a more practicable passage, by two rude bridges, both of which had been broken in anticipation of the coming of the Spaniards. The latter had now arrived on the brink of the chasm. It was, as has been remarked, of no great width, and the army drawn up on its borders was directly exposed to the archery of the garrison, on whom its own fire made little impression, protected as they were by their defences.

The general, annoyed by his position, sent a detachment to seek a passage lower down, by which the troops might be landed on the other side. But although the banks of the ravine became less formidable as they descended, they found no means of crossing the river, till a path unexpectedly presented itself, on which, probably, no one before hid ever been daring enough to venture.

From the cliffs on the opposite sides of the barranca, two huge trees shot up to an enormous height, and, inclining towards each other, interlaced their boughs so as to form a sort of natural bridge. Across this avenue, in mid air, a Tlascalan conceived it would not be difficult to pass to the opposite bank. The bold mountaineer succeeded in the attempt, and was soon followed by several others of his countrymen, trained to feats of agility and strength among their native hills. The Spaniards imitated their example. It was a perilous effort for an armed man to make his way over this aerial causeway, swayed to and fro by the wind, where the brain might become giddy, and where a single false movement of hand or foot would plunge him into the abyss below. Three of the soldiers lost their hold and fell. The rest, consisting of some twenty or thirty Spaniards, and a considerable number of Tlascalans, alighted in safety on the other bank. There hastily forming, they marched with all speed on the city. The enemy, engaged in their contest with the Castilians on the opposite brink of the ravine, were taken by surprise — which, indeed, could scarcely have been exceeded if they had seen their foe drop from the clouds on the field of battle.

They made a brave resistance, however, when fortunately the Spaniards succeeded in repairing one of the dilapidated bridges in such a manner as to enable both cavalry and foot to cross the river, though with much delay. The horse under and Andres de Tapia, instantly rode up to the succour of their countrymen. They were soon followed by Cortes at the head of the remaining battalions; and the enemy, driven from one point to another, were compelled to evacuate the city, and to take refuge among the mountains. The buildings in one quarter of the town were speedily wrapt in flames. The place was abandoned to pillage, and, as it was one of the most opulent marts in the country, it amply compensated the victors for the toil and danger they had encountered. The trembling caciques, returning soon after to the city, appeared before Cortes, and deprecating his resentment by charging the blame, as usual, on the Mexicans, threw themselves on his mercy. Satisfied with their submission, he allowed no further violence to the inhabitants.

Having thus accomplished the great object of his expedition across the mountains, the Spanish commander turned his face northwards, to recross the formidable barrier which divided him from the valley. The ascent, steep and laborious, was rendered still more difficult by fragments of rock and loose stones which encumbered the passes. The weather was sultry, and, as the stony soil was nearly destitute of water, the troops suffered severely from thirst. Several of them, indeed, fainted on the road, and a few of the Indian allies perished from exhaustion. The line of march must have taken the army across the eastern shoulder of the mountain, called the Cruz del Marques, or Cross of the Marquess, from a huge stone cross, erected there to indicate the boundary of the territories granted by the crown to Cortes, as Marquess of the Valley. Much, indeed, of the route lately traversed by the troops lay across the princely domain subsequently assigned to the Conqueror.

The point of attack selected by the general was Xochimilco, or the "field of flowers," as its name implies, from the floating gardens which rode at anchor, as it were, on the neighbouring waters. It was one of the most potent and wealthy cities in the Mexican valley, and a staunch vassal of the Aztec crown. It stood, like the capital itself, partly in the water, and was approached in that quarter by causeways of no great length. The town was composed of houses like those of most other places of like magnitude in the country, mostly of cottages or huts made of clay and the light bamboo, mingled with aspiring teocallis, and edifices of stone, belonging to the more opulent classes.

As the Spaniards advanced, they were met by skirmishing parties of the enemy, who, after dismissing a light volley of arrows, rapidly retreated before them. As they took the direction of Xochimilco, Cortes inferred that they were prepared to resist him in considerable force. It exceeded his expectations.

On traversing the principal causeway, he found it occupied, at the further extremity, by a numerous body of warriors, who, stationed on the opposite sides of a bridge, which had been broken, were prepared to dispute his passage. They had constructed a temporary barrier of palisades, which screened them from the fire of the musketry. But the water in its neighbourhood was very shallow. and the cavaliers and infantry, plunging into it, soon made their way, swimming or wading, as they could, in face of a storm of missiles, to the landing, near the town. Here they closed with the enemy, and, hand to hand, after a sharp struggle, drove them back on the city; a few, however, taking the direction of the open country, were followed up by the cavalry. The great mass hotly pursued by the infantry, were driven through street and lane, without much further resistance. Cortes, with a few followers, disengaging himself from the tumult, remained near the entrance of the city. He had not been there long, when he was assailed by a fresh body of Indians, who suddenly poured into the place from a neighbouring dike. The general, with his usual fearlessness, threw himself into the midst, in hopes to check their advance. But his own followers were too few to support him, and he was overwhelmed by the crowd of combatants. His horse lost his footing and fell; and Cortes, who received a severe blow on the head before he could rise, was seized and dragged off in triumph by the Indians. At this critical moment, a Tlascalan, who perceived the general's extremity, sprang, like one of the wild ocelots of his own foreata, into the midst of the assailants, and endeavoured to tear him from their grasp. Two of the general's servants also speedily came to the rescue, and Cortes, with their aid and that of the brave Tlascalan, succeeded in regaining his feet and shaking off his enemies. To vault into the saddle and brandish his good lance was but the work of a moment. Others of his men quickly came up, and the clash of arms reaching the ears of the Spaniards who had gone in pursuit, they returned, and, after a desperate conflict, forced the enemy from the city. Their retreat, however, was intercepted by the cavalry returning from the country, and, thus hemmed in between the opposite columns, they were cut to pieces, or saved themselves only by plunging into the lake. This was the greatest personal danger which Cortes had yet encountered. His life was in the power of the barbarians, and, had it not been for their eagerness to take him prisoner, he must undoubtedly have lost it. To the same cause may be frequently attributed the preservation of the Spaniards in these engagements.

It was not yet dusk when Cortes and his followers re-entered the city; and the general's first act was to ascend a neighbouring teocalli and reconnoitre the surrounding country. He there beheld a sight which might have troubled a bolder spirit than his. The surface of the salt lake was darkened with canoes, and the causeway, for many a mile, with Indian squadrons, apparently on their march towards the Christian camp. In fact, no sooner had Guatemozin been apprised of the arrival of the white men at Xochimilco, than he mustered his levies in great force to relieve the city. They were now on their march, and, as the capital was but four leagues distant, would arrive soon after nightfall.

Cortes made active preparations for the defence of his quarters. He stationed a corps of pikemen along the landing where the Aztecs would be likely to disembark. He doubled the sentinels, and, with his principal officers, made the rounds repeatedly in the course of the night. In addition to other causes for watchfulness, the bolts of the crossbowmen were nearly exhausted, and the archers were busily employed in preparing and adjusting shafts to the copper heads, of which great store bad been provided for the army. There was little sleep in the camp that night.

It passed away, however, without molestation from the enemy. Though not stormy, it was exceedingly dark. But, although the Spaniards on duty could see nothing, they distinctly heard the sound of many oars in the water, at no great distance from the shore. Yet those on board the canoes made no attempt to land, distrusting, or advised, it may be, of the preparations made for their reception. With early dawn, they were under arms, and, without waiting for movement of the Spaniards, poured into the city and attacked them in their own quarters.

The Spaniards, who were gathered in the area round one of the teocallis, were taken at disadvantage in the town, where the narrow lanes and streets, many of them covered with a smooth and slippery cement, offered obvious impediments to the manoeuvres of cavalry. But Cortes hastily formed his muskeeters and crossbowmen, and poured such a lively, well directed fire into the enemy's ranks, as threw him into disorder, and compelled him to recoil. The infantry, with their long pikes, followed up the blow; and the horse, charging at full speed, as the retreating Aztecs emerged from the city, drove them several miles along the main land.

At some distance, however, they were met by a strong reinforcement of their countrymen, and rallying, the tide of battle turned, and the cavaliers, swept along by it, gave the rein to their steeds, and rode back at full gallop towards the town. They had not proceeded very far, when they came upon the main body of the army, advancing rapidly to their support. Thus strengthened, they once more returned to the charge, and the rival hosts met together in full career, with the shock of an earthquake. For a time, victory seemed to hang in the balance, as the mighty press reeled to and fro under the opposite impulse, and a confused shout rose up towards heaven, in which the war-whoop of the savage was mingled with the battle-cry of the Christian — a still stranger sound on these sequestered shores. But, in the end, Castilian valour, or rather Castilian arms and discipline, proved triumphant. The enemy faltered, gave way, and recoiling step by step, the retreat soon terminated in a rout, and the Spaniards, following up the flying foe, drove them from the field with such dreadful slaughter, that they made no further attempt to renew the battle.

The victors were now undisputed masters of the city. It was a wealthy place, well stored with Indian fabrics, cotton, gold, feather-work, and other articles of luxury and use, affording a rich booty to the soldiers. While engaged in the work of plunder, a party of the enemy, landing from their canoes, fell on some of the stragglers laden with merchandise, and made four of them prisoners. It created a greater sensation among the troops than if ten times that number had fallen on the field. Indeed, it was rare that a Spaniard allowed himself to be taken alive. In the present instance the unfortunate men were taken by surprise. They were hurried to the capital, and soon after sacrificed; when their arms and legs were cut off, by the command of the ferocious young chief of the Aztecs, and sent round to the different cities, with the assurance, that this should be the fate of the enemies of Mexico!

From the prisoners taken in the late engagement, Cortes learned that the forces already sent by Guatemozin formed but a small part of his levies; that his policy was to send detachment after detachment, until the Spaniards, however victorious they might come off from the contest with each individually, would, in the end, succumb from mere exhaustion, and thus be vanquished, as it were, by their own victories.

The soldiers having now sacked the city, Cortes did not care to await further assaults from the enemy in his present quarters. On the fourth morning after his arrival, he mustered his forces on a neighbouring plain. They came many of them reeling under the weight of their plunder. The general saw this with uneasiness. They were to march, he said, through a populous country, all in arms to dispute their passage. To secure their safety, they should move as light and unencumbered as possible. The sight of so much spoil would sharpen the appetite of their enemies, and draw them on, like a flock of famished eagles after their prey. But his eloquence was lost on his men; who plainly told him they had a right to the fruit of their victories, and that what they had won with their swords, they knew well enough how to defend with them.

Seeing them thus bent on their purpose, the general did not care to baulk their inclinations. He ordered the baggage to the centre, and placed a few of the cavalry over it; dividing the remainder between the front and rear, in which latter post, as that most exposed to attack, he also stationed his arquebusiers and crossbowmen. Thus prepared, he resumed his march; but first set fire to the combustible buildings of Xochimilco, in retaliation for the resistance he had met there. The light of the burning city streamed high into the air, sending its ominous glare far and wide across the waters, and telling the inhabitants on their margin, that the fatal strangers so long predicted by their oracles had descended like a consuming flame upon their borders.

Small bodies of the enemy were seen occasionally at a distance, but they did not venture to attack the army on its march, which before noon brought them to Cojohuacan, a large town about two leagues distant from Xochimilco. One could scarcely travel that distance in this populous quarter of the valley without meeting with a place of considerable size, oftentimes the capital of what had formerly been an independent state. The inhabitants, members of different tribes, and speaking dialects somewhat different, belonged to the same great family of nations who had come from the real or imaginary region of Aztlan, in the far north-west. Gathered round the shores of their Alpine sea, these petty communities continued, after their incorporation with the Aztec monarchy, to maintain a spirit of rivalry in their intercourse with one another, which — as with the cities on the Mediterranean, in the feudal ages — quickened their mental energies, and raised the Mexican Valley higher in the scale of civilisation than most other quarters of Anahuac.

The town at which the army had now arrived was deserted by its inhabitants; and Cortes halted two days there to restore his troops, and give the needful attention to the wounded. He made use of the time to reconnoitre the neighbouring ground, and taking with him a strong detachment, descended on the causeway which led from Cojohuacan to the great avenue Iztapalapan. At the point of intersection, called Xoloc, he found a strong barrier or fortification, behind which a Mexican force was intrenched. Their archery did some mischief to the Spaniards, as they came within bow-shot. But the latter, marching intrepidly forward in face of the arrowy shower, stormed the works, and, after an obstinate struggle, drove the enemy from their position. Cortes then advanced some way on the great causeway of Iztapalapan; but he beheld the further extremity darkened by a numerous array of warriors, and as he did not care to engage in unnecessary hostilities, especially as his ammunition was nearly exhausted, he fell back and retreated to his own quarters.

The following day, the army continued its march, taking the road to Tacuba, but a few miles distant. On the way it experienced much annoyance from straggling parties of the enemy, who, furious at the sight of the booty which the invaders were bearing away, made repeated attacks on their flanks and rear. Cortes retaliated, as on the former expedition, by one of their own stratagems, but with less success than before; for, pursuing the retreating enemy too hotly, he fell with his cavalry into an ambuscade, which they had prepared for him in their turn. He was not yet a match for their wily tactics. The Spanish cavaliers were enveloped in a moment by their subtle foe, and separated from the rest of the army. But, spurring on their good steeds, and charging in a solid column together, they succeeded in breaking through the Indian array, and in making their escape, except two individuals, who fell into the enemy's hands. They were the general's own servants, who had followed him faithfully through the whole campaign, and he was deeply affected by their loss; rendered the more distressing by the consideration of the dismal fate that awaited them. When the little band rejoined the army, which had halted in some anxiety at their absence, under the walls of Tacuba, the soldiers were astonished at the dejected mien of their commander, which too visibly betrayed his emotion.

The sun was still high in the heavens, when they entered the ancient capital of the Tepanecs. The first care of Cortes was to ascend the principal teocalli, and survey the surrounding country. It was an admirable point of view, commanding the capital, which lay but little more than a league distant, and its immediate environs. Cortes was accompanied by Alderete, the treasurer, and some other cavaliers, who had lately joined his banner. The spectacle was still new to them; and, as they gazed on the stately city, with its broad lake covered with boats and barges hurrying to and fro, some laden with merchandise, or fruits and vegetables, for the markets of Tenochtitlan, others crowded with warriors, they could not withhold their admiration at the life and activity of the scene, declaring that nothing but the hand of Providence could have led their countrymen safe through the heart of this powerful empire.

Tacuba was the point which Cortes had reached on his former expedition round the northern side of the valley. He had now, therefore, made the entire circuit of the great lake; had reconnoitred the several approaches to the capital, and inspected with his own eyes the dispositions made on the opposite quarters for its defence. He had no occasion to prolong his stay in Tacuba, the vicinity of which to Mexico must soon bring on him its whole warlike population.

Early on the following morning, he resumed his march, taking the route pursued in the former expedition, north of the small lakes. He met with less annoyance from the enemy than on the preceding days; a circumstance owing in some degree, perhaps, to the state of the weather, which was exceedingly tempestuous. The soldiers, with their garments heavy with moisture, ploughed their way with difficulty through the miry roads flooded by the torrents. On one occasion, as their military chronicler informs us, the officers neglected to go the rounds of the camp at night, and the sentinels to mount guard, trusting to the violence of the storm for their protection. Yet the fate of Narvaez might have taught them not to put their faith in the elements.

At Acolman, in the Acolhuan territory, they were met by Sandoval, with the friendly cacique of Tezcuco, and several cavaliers, among whom were some recently arrived from the islands.

They cordially greeted their countrymen, and communicated the tidings that the canal was completed, and that the brigantines, rigged and equipped, were ready to be launched on the bosom of the lake.

There seemed to be no reason, therefore, for longer postponing operations against Mexico. — With this welcome intelligence, Cortes and his victorious legions made their entry for the last time into the Acolhuan capital, having consumed just three weeks in completing the circuit of the valley.

AT the very time when Cortes was occupied with reconnoitring the valley, preparatory to his siege of the capital, a busy faction in Castile was labouring to subvert his authority and defeat his plans of conquest altogether. The fame of his brilliant exploits had spread not only through the isles, but to Spain and many parts of Europe, where a general admiration was felt for the invincible energy of the man, who with his single arm as it were, could so long maintain a contest with the powerful Indian empire. The absence of the Spanish monarch from his dominions, and the troubles of the country, can alone explain the supine indifference shown by the government to the prosecution of this great enterprise. To the same causes it may be ascribed, that no action was had in regard to the suits of Velasquez and Narvaez, backed as they were by so potent an advocate as Bishop Fonseca, president of the Council of the Indies. The reins of government had fallen into the hands of Adrian of Utrecht, Charles' preceptor, and afterwards Pope — a man of learning, and not without sagacity, but slow and timid in his policy, and altogether incapable of that decisive action which suited the bold genius of his predecessor, Cardinal Ximenes.

In the spring of 1521, however, a number of ordinances passed the Council of the Indies, which threatened an important innovation in the affairs of New Spain. It was decreed, that the Royal Audience of Hispaniola should abandon the proceedings already instituted against Narvaez, for his treatment of the commissioner Ayllon; that that unfortunate commander should be released from his confinement at Vera Cruz; and that an arbitrator should be sent to Mexico, with authority to investigate the affairs — and conduct of Cortes, and to render ample justice to the governor of Cuba. There were not wanting persons at court, who looked with dissatisfaction, on these proceedings, as an unworthy requital of the services of Cortes, and who thought the present moment, at any rate, not the most suitable for taking measures which might discourage the general, and, perhaps, render him desperate. But the arrogant temper of the Bishop of Burgos overruled all objections; and the ordinances having been approved by the Regency, were signed by that body, April 11, 1521. A person named Tapia, one of the functionaries of the Audience of St. Domingo, was selected as the new commissioner to be despatched to Vera Cruz. Fortunately circumstances occurred which postponed the execution of the design for the present, and permitted Cortes to go forward unmolested in his career of conquest.

But, while thus allowed to remain, for the present at least, in possession of authority, he was assailed by a danger nearer home, which menaced not only his authority, but his life. This was a conspiracy in the army, of a more dark and dangerous character than any hitherto formed there. It was set on foot by a common soldier, named Antonio Villafana, a native of Old Castile, of whom nothing is known but his share in this transaction. He was one of the troop of Narvaez — that leaven of disaffection, which had remained with the army, swelling with discontent on every light occasion, and ready at all times to rise into mutiny. They had voluntarily continued in the service after the secession of their comrades at Tlascala; but it was from the same mercenary hopes with which they had originally embarked in the expedition — and in these they were destined still to be disappointed. They had little of the true spirit of adventure, which distinguished the old companions of Cortes; and they found the barren laurels of victory but a sorry recompense for all their toils and sufferings.

With these men were joined others, who had causes of personal disgust with the general; and others, again, who looked with disgust on the result of the war. The gloomy fate of their countrymen, who had fallen into the enemy's hands, filled them with dismay. They felt themselves the victims of a chimerical spirit in their leader, who, with such inadequate means, was urging to extremity so ferocious and formidable a foe; and they shrunk with something like apprehension from thus pursuing the enemy into his own haunts, where he would gather tenfold energy from despair.

These men would have willingly abandoned the enterprise, and returned to Cuba; but how could they do it? Cortes had control over the whole route from the city to the sea-coast; and not a vessel could leave its ports without his warrant. Even if he were put out of the way, there were others, his principal officers, ready to step into his place, and avenge the death of their commander. It was necessary to embrace these, also, in the scheme of destruction; and it was proposed, therefore, together with Cortes, to assassinate Sandoval, Olid, Alvarado, and two or three others most devoted to his interests. The conspirators would then raise the cry of liberty, and doubted not that they should be joined by the greater part of the army, or enough, at least, to enable them to work their own pleasure. They proposed to offer the command, on Cortes' death, to Francisco Verdugo, a brother-inlaw of Velasquez. He was an honourable cavalier, and not privy to their design. But they had little doubt that he would acquiesce in the command, thus, in a manner, forced upon him, and this would secure them the protection of the governor of Cuba, who, indeed, from his own hatred of Cortes, would be disposed to look with a lenient eye on their proceedings.

The conspirators even went so far as to appoint the subordinate officers, an alguacil mayor, in place of Sandoval, a quarter-master-general to succeed Olid, and some others. The time fixed for the execution of the plot was soon after the return of Cortes from his expedition. A parcel, pretended to have come by a fresh arrival from Castile, was to be presented to him while at table, and, when he was engaged in breaking open the letters, the conspirators were to fall on him and his officers, and despatch them with their poniards. Such was the iniquitous scheme devised for the destruction of Cortes and the expedition. But a conspiracy, to be successful, especially when numbers are concerned, should allow but little time to elapse between its conception and its execution.

On the day previous to that appointed for the perpetration of the deed, one, of the party, feeling a natural compunction at the commission of the crime, went to the general's quarters, and solicited a private interview with him. He threw himself at his commander's feet, and revealed all the particulars relating to the conspiracy, adding, that in Villafana's possession a paper would be found, containing the names of his accomplices. Cortes, thunderstruck at the disclosure, lost not a moment in profiting by it. He sent for Alvarado, Sandoval, and other officers marked out by the conspirator, and, after communicating the affair to them, went at once with them to Villafana's quarters, attended by four alguacils.

They found him in conference with three or four friends, who were instantly taken from the apartment, and placed in custody. Villafana, confounded at this sudden apparition of his commander, had barely time to snatch a paper, containing the signatures of the confederates, from his bosom, and attempt to swallow it. But Cortes arrested his arm, and seized the paper. As he glanced his eye rapidly over the fatal list, he was much moved at finding there the names of more than one who had some claim to consideration in the army. He tore the scroll in pieces, and ordered Villafana, to be taken into custody. He was immediately tried by a military court hastily got together, at which the general himself presided. There seems to have been no doubt of the man's guilt. He was condemned to death, and, after allowing him time for confession and absolution, the sentence was executed by hanging him from the window of his own quarters.

Those ignorant of the affair were astonished at the spectacle; and the remaining conspirators were filled with consternation when they saw that their plot was detected, and anticipated a similar fate for themselves. But they were mistaken. Cortes pursued the matter no further. A little reflection convinced him, that to do so would involve him in the most disagreeable, and even dangerous, perplexities. And, however much the parties implicated in so foul a deed might deserve death, he could ill afford the loss even of the guilty, with his present limited numbers. He resolved, therefore, to content himself with the punishment of the ringleader.

He called his troops together, and briefly explained to them the nature of the crime for which Villafana had suffered. He had made no confession, he said, and the guilty secret had perished with him. He then expressed his sorrow, that any should have been found in their ranks capable of so base an act, and stated his own unconsciousness of having wronged any individual among them; but, if he had done so, he invited them frankly to declare it, as he was most anxious to afford them all the redress in his power. But there was no one of his audience, whatever might be his grievances, who cared to enter his complaint at such a moment; least of all were the conspirators willing to do so, for they were too happy at having, as they fancied, escaped detection, to stand forward now in the ranks of the malcontents. The affair passed off, therefore, without further consequences.

As was stated at the close of the last chapter, the Spaniards, on their return to quarters, found the construction of the brigantines completed, and that they were fully rigged, equipped, and ready for service. The canal, also, after having occupied eight thousand men for nearly two months, was finished.

It was a work of great labour; for it extended half a league in length, was twelve feet wide, and as many deep. The sides were strengthened by palisades of wood, or solid masonry. At intervals dams and locks were constructed, and part of the opening was through the hard rock. By this avenue the brigantines might now be safely introduced on the lake.

Cortes was resolved that so auspicious an event should be celebrated with due solemnity. On the 28th of April, the troops were drawn up under arms, and the whole population of Tezcuco assembled to witness the ceremony. Mass was performed, and every man in the army, together with the general, confessed and received the sacrament. Prayers were offered up by Father Olmedo, and a benediction invoked on the little navy, the first worthy of the name ever launched on American waters. The signal was given by the firing of a cannon, when the vessels, dropping down the canal one after another, reached the lake in good order; and as they emerged on its ample bosom, with music sounding, and the royal ensign of Castile proudly floating from their masts, a shout of admiration arose from the countless multitudes of spectators, which mingled with the roar of artillery and musketry from the vessels and the shore! It was a novel spectacle to the simple natives; and they gazed with wonder on the gallant ships, which, fluttering like sea-birds on their snowy pinions, bounded lightly over the waters, as if rejoicing in their element. It touched the stern hearts of the Conquerors with a glow of rapture, and, as they felt that Heaven had blessed their undertaking, they broke forth, by general accord, into the noble anthem of the Te Deum. But there was no one of that vast multitude for whom the sight had deeper interest than their commander. For he looked on it as the work, in a manner, of his own hands; and his bosom swelled with exultation, as he felt he was now possessed of a power strong enough to command the lake, and to shake the haughty towers of Tenochtitlan.

The general's next step was to muster his forces in the great square of the capital. He found they amounted to eighty-seven horse, and eight hundred and eighteen foot, of which one hundred and eighteen were arquebusiers and crossbowmen. He had three large field-pieces of iron, and fifteen lighter guns or falconets of brass. The heavier cannon had been transported from Vera Cruz to Tezcuco, a little while before, by the faithful Tlascalans. He was well supplied with shot and balls, with about ten hundredweight of powder, and fifty thousand copper-headed arrows, made after a pattern furnished by him to the natives. The number and appointments of the army much exceeded what they had been at any time since the flight from Mexico, and showed the good effects of the late arrivals from the Islands. Indeed, taking the fleet into the account, Cortes had never before been in so good a condition for carrying on his operations. Three hundred of the men were sent to man the vessels, thirteen, or rather twelve, in number, one of the smallest having been found, on trial, too dull a sailer to be of service. Half of the crews were required to navigate the ships. There was some difficulty in finding hands for this, as the men were averse to the employment. Cortes selected those who came from Palos, Moguer, and other maritime towns, and notwithstanding their frequent claims of exemption, as hidalgos, from this menial occupation, he pressed them into the service. Each vessel mounted a piece of heavy ordnance, and was placed under an officer of respectability, to whom Cortes gave a general code of instructions for the government of the little navy, of which he proposed to take the command in person.

He had already sent to his Indian confederates, announcing his purpose of immediately laying siege to Mexico, and called on them to furnish their promised levies within the space of ten days at furthest. The Tlascalans he ordered to join him at Tezcuco; the others were to assemble at Chalco, a more convenient place of rendezvous for the operations in the southern quarter of the valley. The Tlascalans arrived within the time prescribed, led by the younger

Xicotencatl, supported by Chichemecatl, the same doughty warrior who had convoyed the brigantines to Tezcuco. They came fifty thousand strong, according to Cortes, making a brilliant show with their military finery, and marching proudly forward under the great national banner, emblazoned with a spread eagle, the arms of the republic. With as blithe and manly a step as if they were going to the battle-ground, they defiled through the gates of the capital, making its walls ring with the friendly shouts of "Castile and Tlascala."

The observations which Cortes had made in his late tour of reconnaissance had determined him to begin the siege by distributing his forces into three separate camps, which he proposed to establish at the extremities of the principal causeways. By this arrangement the troops would be enabled to move in concert on the capital, and be in the best position to intercept its supplies from the surrounding country. The first of these points was Tacuba, commanding the fatal causeway of the noche triste. This was assigned to Pedro de Alvarado, with a force consisting, according to Cortes' own statement, of thirty horse, one hundred and sixty-eight Spanish infantry, and five and twenty thousand Tlascalans. Christoval de Olid had command of the second army, of much the same magnitude, which was to take up its position at Cojohuacan, the city, it will be remembered, overlooking the short causeway connected with that of Iztapalapan. Gonzalo de Sandoval had charge of the third division, of equal strength with each of the two preceding, but which was to draw its Indian levies from the forces assembled at Chalco. This officer was to march on Iztapalapan, and complete the destruction of that city, begun by Cortes soon after his entrance into the valley. It was too formidable a post to remain in the rear of the army. The general intended to support the attack with his brigantines, after which the subsequent movements of Sandoval would be determined by circumstances.

Having announced his intended dispositions to his officers, the Spanish commander called his troops together, and made one of those brief and stirring harangues with which he was wont on great occasions to kindle the hearts of his soldiery. "I have taken the last step," he said; "I have brought you to the goal for which you have so long panted. A few days will place you before the gates of Mexico — the capital from which you were driven with so much ignominy. But we now go forward under the smiles of Providence. Does any one doubt it? Let him but compare our present condition with that in which we found ourselves not twelve months since, when, broken and dispirited, we sought shelter within the walls of Tlascala; nay, with that in which we were but a few months since, when we took up our quarters in Tezcuco. Since that time our strength has been nearly doubled. We are fighting the battles of the Faith, fighting for our honour, for riches, for revenge. I have brought you face to face with your foe. It is for you to do the rest."

The address of the bold chief was answered by the thundering acclamations of his followers, who declared that every man would do his duty under such a leader; and they only asked to be led against the enemy. Cortes then caused the regulations for the army, published at Tlascala, to be read again to the troops, with the assurance that they should be enforced to the letter.

It was arranged that the Indian forces should precede the Spanish by a day's march, and should halt for their confederates on the borders of the Tezcucan territory. A circumstance occurred soon after their departure, which gave bad augury for the future. A quarrel had arisen in the camp at Tezcuco between a Spanish soldier and a Tlascalan chief, in which the latter was badly hurt. He was sent back to Tlascala, and the matter was hushed up, that it might not reach the ears of the general, who, it was known, would not pass it over lightly. Xicotencatl was a near relative of the injured party, and on the first day's halt, he took the opportunity to leave the army, with a number of his followers, and set off for Tlascala. Other causes are assigned for his desertion. It is certain that, from the first, he looked on the expedition with an evil eye, and had predicted that no good would come of it. He came into it with reluctance, as, indeed, he detested the Spaniards in his heart.

His partner in the command instantly sent information of the affair to the Spanish general, still encamped at Tezcuco. Cortes, who saw at once the mischievous consequences of this defection at such a time, detached a party of Tlascalan and Tezcucan Indians after the fugitive, with instructions to prevail on him, if possible, to return to his duty. They overtook him on the road, and remonstrated with him on his conduct, contrasting it with that of his countrymen generally, and of his own father in particular, the steady friend of the white men. "So much the worse," replied the chieftain; "if they had taken my counsel, they would never have become the dupes of the perfidious strangers." Finding their remonstrances received only with anger or contemptuous taunts, the emissaries returned without accomplishing their object.

Cortes did not hesitate on the course he was to pursue. "Xicotencatl," he said, "had always been the enemy of the Spaniards, first in the field, and since in the council-chamber; openly, or in secret, still the same — their implacable enemy. There was no use in parleying with the false-hearted Indian." He instantly despatched a small body of horse with an alguacil to arrest the chief, wherever he might be found, even though it were in the streets of Tlascala, and to bring him back to Tezcuco. At the same time he sent information of Xicotencatl's proceedings to the Tlascalan senate, adding, that desertion among the Spaniards was punished with death.

The emissaries of Cortes punctually fulfilled his orders. They arrested the fugitive chief — whether in Tlascala or in its neighbourhood is uncertain — and brought him a prisoner to Tezcuco, where a high gallows, erected in the great square, was prepared for his reception. He was instantly led to the place of execution; his sentence and the cause for which he suffered were publicly proclaimed, and the unfortunate cacique expiated his offence by the vile death of a malefactor. His ample property, consisting of lands, slaves, and some gold, was all confiscated to the Castilian crown.

Thus perished Xicotencatl, in the flower of his age — as dauntless a warrior as ever led an Indian army to battle. He was the first chief who successfully resisted the arms of the invaders; and, had the natives of Anahuac generally been animated with a spirit like his, Cortes would probably never have set foot in the capital of Montezuma. He was gifted with a clearer insight into the future than his countrymen; for he saw that the European was an enemy far more to be dreaded than the Aztec. Yet, when he consented to fight under the banner of the white men, he had no right to desert it, and he incurred the penalty prescribed by the code of savage as well as of civilised nations. It is said, indeed, that the Tlascalan senate aided in apprehending him, having previously answered Cortes, that his crime was punishable with death by their own laws. It was a bold act, however, thus to execute him in the midst of his people; for he was a powerful chief, heir to one of the four seigniories of the republic. His chivalrous qualities made him popular, especially with the younger part of his countrymen; and his garments were torn into shreds at his death, and distributed as sacred relics among them. Still, no resistance was offered to the execution of the sentence, and no commotion followed it. He was the only Tlascalan who ever swerved from his loyalty to the Spaniards.

According to the plan of operations settled by Cortes, Sandoval, with his division, was to take a southern direction; while Alvarado and Olid would make the northern circuit of the lakes. These two cavaliers, after getting possession of Tacuba, were to advance to Chapoltepec, and demolish the great aqueduct there, which supplied Mexico with water. On the 10th of May, they commenced their march; but at Acolman, where they halted for the night, a dispute arose between the soldiers of the two divisions, respecting their quarters. From words they came to blows, and a defiance was even exchanged between the leaders, who entered into the angry feelings of their followers. Intelligence of this was soon communicated to Cortes, who sent at once to the fiery chiefs, imploring them, by their regard for him and the common cause, to lay aside their differences, which must end in their own ruin, and that of the expedition. His remonstrance prevailed, at least, so far as to establish a show of reconciliation between the parties. But was not a man to forget, or easily to forgive; and Alvarado, though frank and liberal, had an impatient temper, much more easily excited than appeased. They were never afterwards friends.

The Spaniards met with no opposition on their march. The principal towns were all abandoned by the inhabitants, who had gone to strengthen the garrison of Mexico, or taken refuge with their families among the mountains. Tacuba was in like manner deserted, and the troops once more established themselves in their old quarters in the lordly city of the Tepanecs.

Their first undertaking was, to cut off the pipes that conducted the water from the royal streams of Chapoltepec to feed the numerous tanks and fountains which sparkled in the courtyards of the capital. The aqueduct, partly constructed of brickwork, and partly of stone and mortar, was raised on a strong, though narrow, dike, which transported it across an arm of the lake; and the whole work was one of the most pleasing monuments of Mexican civilisation. The Indians, well aware of its importance, had stationed a large body of troops for its protection. A battle followed, in which both sides suffered considerably, but the Spaniards were victorious. A part of the aqueduct was demolished, and during the siege no water found its way again to the capital through this channel.

On the following day the combined forces descended on the fatal causeway, to make themselves masters, if possible, of the nearest bridge. They found the dike covered with a swarm of warriors, as numerous as on the night of their disaster, while the surface of the lake was dark with the multitude of canoes. The intrepid Christians strove to advance under a perfect hurricane of missiles from the water and the land, but they made slow progress. Barricades thrown across the causeway embarrassed the cavalry, and rendered it nearly useless. The sides of the Indian boats were fortified with bulwarks, which shielded the crews from the arquebuses and crossbows; and, when the warriors on the dike were hard pushed by the pikemen, they threw themselves fearlessly into the water, as if it were their native element, and re-appearing along the sides of the dike, shot off their arrows and javelins with fatal execution. After a long and obstinate struggle, the Christians were compelled to fall back on their own quarters with disgrace, and — including the allies — with nearly as much damage as they had inflicted on the enemy. Olid, disgusted with the result of the engagement, inveighed against his companion, as having involved them in it by his wanton temerity, and drew off his forces the next morning to his own station at Cojohuacan.

The camps, separated by only two leagues, maintained an easy communication with each other. They found abundant employment in foraging the neighbouring country for provisions, and in repelling the active sallies of the enemy; on whom they took their revenge by cutting off his supplies. But their own position was precarious, and they looked with impatience for the arrival of the brigantines under Cortes. It was in the latter part of May that took up his quarters at Cojohuacan; and from that time may be dated the commencement of the siege of Mexico.

NO sooner had Cortes received intelligence that his two officers had established themselves in their respective posts, than he ordered Sandoval to march on Iztapalapan. The cavalier's route led him through a country for the most part friendly; and at Chalco his little body of Spaniards was swelled by the formidable muster of Indian levies, who awaited there his approach. After this junction, he continued his march without opposition till he arrived before the hostile city, under whose walls he found a large force drawn up to receive him. A battle followed, and the natives, after maintaining their ground sturdily for some time, were compelled to give way, and to seek refuge either on the water or in that part of the town which hung over it. The remainder was speedily occupied by the Spaniards.

Meanwhile Cortes had set sail with his flotilla, intending to support his lieutenant's attack by water. On drawing near the southern shore of the lake, he passed under the shadow of an insulated peak, since named from him the "Rock of the Marquess." It was held by a body of Indians, who saluted the fleet, as it passed, with showers of stones and arrows. Cortes, resolving to punish their audacity, and to clear the lake of his troublesome enemy, instantly landed with a hundred and fifty of his followers. He placed himself at their head, scaled the steep ascent, in the face of a driving storm of missiles, and, reaching the summit, put the garrison to the sword. There was a number of women and children, also, gathered in the place, whom he spared.

On the top of the eminence was a blazing beacon, serving to notify to the inhabitants of the capital when the Spanish fleet weighed anchor. Before Cortes had regained his brigantine, the canoes and piraguas of the enemy had left the harbours of Mexico, and were seen darkening the lake for many a rood. There were several hundred of them, all crowded with warriors, and advancing rapidly by means of their oars over the calm bosom of the waters.

Cortes, who regarded his fleet, to use his own language, as "the key of the war," felt the importance of striking a decisive blow in the first encounter with the enemy. It was with chagrin, therefore, that he found his sails rendered useless by the want of wind. He calmly waited the approach of the Indian squadron, which, however, lay on their oars, at something more than musket-shot distance, as if hesitating to encounter these leviathans of their waters. At this moment, a light air from land rippled the surface of the lake; it gradually freshened into a breeze, and Cortes, taking advantage of the friendly succour, which he may be excused, under all the circumstances, for regarding as especially sent him by Heaven, extended his line of battle and bore down, under full press of canvas, on the enemy.

The latter no sooner encountered the bows of their formidable opponents, than they were overturned and sent to the bottom by the shock, or so much damaged that they speedily filled and sank. The water was covered with the wreck of broken canoes, and with the bodies of men struggling for life in the waves, and vainly imploring their companions to take them on board their overcrowded vessels. The Spanish fleet, as it dashed through the mob of boats, sent off its volleys to the right and left with a terrible effect, completing the discomfiture of the Aztecs. The latter made no attempt at resistance, scarcely venturing a single flight of arrows, but strove with all their strength to regain the port from which they had so lately issued. They were no match in the chase, any more than in the fight, for their terrible antagonist, who, borne on the wings of the wind, careered to and fro at his pleasure, dealing death widely around him, and making the shores ring with the thunders of his ordnance. A few only of the Indian flotilla succeeded in recovering the port, and, gliding up the canals, found a shelter in the bosom of the city, where the heavier burden of the brigantines made it impossible for them to follow. This victory, more complete than even the sanguine temper of Cortes had prognosticated, proved the superiority of the Spaniards, and left them, henceforth, undisputed masters of the Aztec sea.

It was nearly dusk when the squadron, coasting along the great southern causeway, anchored off the point of junction, called Xoloc, where the branch from Cojohuacan meets the principal dike. The avenue widened at this point, so as to afford room for two towers, or turreted temples, built of stone, and surrounded by walls of the same material, which presented altogether a position of some strength, and, at the present moment, was garrisoned by a body of Aztecs. They were not numerous; and Cortes, landing with his soldiers, succeeded without much difficulty in dislodging the enemy, and in getting possession of the works.

It seems to have been originally the general's design to take up his own quarters with at Cojohuacan. But, if so, he now changed his purpose, and wisely fixed on this spot, as the best position for his encampment. It was but half a league distant from the capital; and, while it commanded its great southern avenue, had a direct communication with the garrison at Cojohuacan, through which he might receive supplies from the surrounding country. Here, then, he determined to establish his head-quarters. He at once caused his heavy iron cannon to be transferred from the brigantines to the causeway, and sent orders to to join him with half his force, while Sandoval was instructed to abandon his present quarters, and advance to Cojohuacan, whence he was to detach fifty picked men of his infantry to the camp of Cortes. Having made these arrangements, the general busily occupied himself with strengthening the works at Xoloc, and putting them in the best posture of defence.

The two principal avenues to Mexico, those on the south and the west, were now occupied by the Christians. There still remained a third, the great dike of Tepejacac, on the north, which, indeed, taking up the principal street, that passed in a direct line through the heart of the city, might be regarded as a continuation of the dike of Iztapalapan. By this northern route a means of escape was still left open to the besieged, and they availed themselves of it, at present, to maintain their communications with the country, and to supply themselves with provisions. Alvarado, who observed this from his station at Tacuba, advised his commander of it, and the latter instructed Sandoval to take up his position on the causeway. That officer, though suffering at the time from a severe wound received from a lance in one of the late skirmishes, hastened to obey; and thus, by shutting up its only communication with the surrounding country, completed the blockade of the capital.

But Cortes was not content to wait patiently the effects of a dilatory blockade, which might exhaust the patience of his allies, and his own resources. He determined to support it by such active assaults on the city as should still further distress the besieged, and hasten the hour of surrender. For this purpose he ordered a simultaneous attack, by the two commanders at the other stations, on the quarters nearest their encampments.

On the day appointed, his forces were under arms with the dawn. Mass, as usual, was performed; and the Indian confederates, as they listened with grave attention to the stately and imposing service, regarded with undisguised admiration the devotional reverence shown by the Christians, whom, in their simplicity, they looked upon as little less than divinities themselves. The Spanish infantry marched in the van, led on by Cortes, attended by a number of cavaliers, dismounted like himself. They had not moved far upon the causeway, when they were brought to a stand by one of the open breaches, that had formerly been traversed by a bridge. On the further side a solid rampart of stone and lime had been erected, and behind this a strong body of Aztecs were posted, who discharged on the Spaniards, as they advanced, a thick volley of arrows. The latter vainly endeavoured to dislodge them with their firearms and crossbows; they were too well secured behind their defences.

Cortes then ordered two of the brigantines, which had kept along, one on each side of the causeway, in order to co-operate with the army, to station themselves so as to enfilade the position occupied by the enemy. Thus placed between two well-directed fires, the Indians were compelled to recede. The soldiers on board the vessels, springing to land, bounded like deer up the sides of the dike. They were soon followed by their countrymen under Cortes, who, throwing themselves into the water, swam the undefended chasm, and joined in pursuit of the enemy. The Mexicans fell back, however, in something like order, till they reached another opening in the dike, like the former, dismantled of its bridge, and fortified in the same manner by a bulwark of stone, behind which the retreating Aztecs, swimming across the chasm, and reinforced by fresh bodies of their countrymen, again took shelter.

They made good their post till, again assailed by the cannonade from the brigantines, they were compelled to give way. In this manner breach after breach was carried, and, at every fresh instance of success, a shout went up from the crews of the vessels, which, answered by the long files of the Spaniards and their confederates on the causeway, made the valley echo to its borders.

Cortes had now reached the end of the great avenue, where it entered the suburbs. There he halted to give time for the rearguard to come up with him. It was detained by the labour of filling up the breaches in such a manner as to make a practicable passage for the artillery and horse, and to secure one for the rest of the army on its retreat. This important duty was intrusted to the allies, who executed it by tearing down the ramparts on the margins, and throwing them into the chasms, and, when this was not sufficient — for the water was deep around the southern causeway — by dislodging the great stones and rubbish from the dike itself, which was broad enough to admit of it, and adding them to the pile, until it was raised above the level of the water.

The street on which the Spaniards now entered, was the great avenue that intersected the town from north to south, and the same by which they had first visited the capital. It was broad and perfectly straight, and, in the distance, dark masses of warriors might be seen gathering to the support of their countrymen, who were prepared to dispute the further progress of the Spaniards. The sides were lined with buildings, the terraced roofs of which were also crowded with combatants, who, as the army advanced, poured down a pitiless storm of missiles on their heads, which glanced harmless, indeed, from the coat of mail, but too often found their way through the more common escaupil of the soldier, already gaping with many a ghastly rent. Cortes, to rid himself of this annoyance for the future, ordered his Indian pioneers to level the principal buildings, as they advanced; in which work of demolition, no less than in the repair of the breaches, they proved of inestimable service.

The Spaniards, meanwhile, were steadily, but slowly, advancing, as the enemy recoiled before the rolling fire of musketry, though turning at intervals to discharge their javelins and arrows against their pursuers. In this way they kept along the great street, until their course was interrupted by a wide ditch or canal, once traversed by a bridge, of which only a few planks now remained. These were broken by the Indians the moment they had crossed, and a formidable array of spears were instantly seen bristling over the summit of a solid rampart of stone, which protected the opposite side of the canal. Cortes was no longer supported by his brigantines, which the shallowness of the canals prevented from penetrating into the suburbs. He brought forward his arquebusiers, who, protected by the targets of their comrades, opened a fire on the enemy. But the balls fell harmless from the bulwarks of stone; while the assailants presented but too easy a mark to their opponents.

The general then caused the heavy guns to be brought up, and opened a lively cannonade, which soon cleared a breach in the works, through which the musketeers and crossbowmen poured in their volleys thick as hail. The Indians now gave way in disorder after having held their antagonists at bay for two hours. The latter, jumping into the shallow water, scaled the opposite bank without further resistance, and drove the enemy along the street towards the square, where the sacred pyramid reared its colossal bulk high over the other edifices of the city.

It was a spot too familiar to the Spaniards. On one side stood the palace of Axacayatl, their old quarters, the scene to many of them of so much suffering. Opposite was the pile of low, irregular, buildings, once the residence of the unfortunate Montezuma; while the third side of the square was flanked by the Coatepantli, or Wall of Serpents, which encompassed the great teocalli with its little city of holy edifices. The Spaniards halted at the entrance of the square, as if oppressed, and for a moment overpowered, by the bitter recollections that crowded on their minds. But their intrepid leader, impatient at their hesitation, loudly called on them to advance before the Aztecs had time to rally; and grasping his target in one hand, and waving his sword high above his head with the other, he cried his war-cry of "St. Jago," and led them at once against the enemy.

The Mexicans, intimidated by the presence of their detested foe, who, in spite of all their efforts had again forced his way into the heart of their city, made no further resistance, but retreated, or rather fled, for refuge into the sacred inclosure of the teocalli, where the numerous buildings scattered over its ample area afforded many good points of defence. A few priests, clad in their usual wild and blood-stained vestments, were to be seen lingering on the terraces which wound round the stately sides of the pyramid, chanting hymns in honour of their god, and encouraging the warriors below to battle bravely for his altars.

The Spaniards poured through the open gates into the area, and a small party rushed up the winding corridors to its summit. No vestige now remained there of the Cross, or of any other symbol of the pure faith to which it had been dedicated. A new effigy of the Aztec war-god had taken the place of the one demolished by the Christians, and raised its fantastic and hideous form in the same niche which had been occupied by its predecessor. The Spaniards soon tore away its golden mask and the rich jewels with which it was bedizened, and hurling the struggling priests down the sides of the pyramid, made the best of their way to their comrades in the area. It was full time.

The Aztecs, indignant at the sacrilegious outrage perpetrated before their eyes, and gathering courage from the inspiration of the place, under the very presence of their deities, raised a yell of horror and vindictive fury, as, throwing themselves into something like order, they sprang by a common impulse on the Spaniards. The latter, who had halted near the entrance, though taken by surprise, made an effort to maintain their position at the gateway. But in vain; for the headlong rush of the assailants drove them at once into the square, where they were attacked by other bodies of Indians, pouring in from the neighbouring streets. Broken, and losing their presence of mind, the troops made no attempt to rally, but, crossing the square, and abandoning the cannon planted there to the enemy, they hurried down the great street of Iztapalapan. Here they were soon mingled with the allies, who choked up the way, and who, catching the panic of the Spaniards, increased the confusion, while the eyes of the fugitives, blinded by the missiles that rained on them from the azoteas, were scarcely capable of distinguishing friend from foe. In vain Cortes endeavoured to stay the torrent, and to restore order. His voice was drowned in the wild uproar, as he was swept away, like driftwood, by the fury of the current.

All seemed to be lost; — when suddenly sounds were heard in an adjoining street, like the distant tramp of horses galloping rapidly over the pavement. They drew nearer and nearer, and a body of cavalry soon emerged on the great square. Though but a handful in number, they plunged boldly into the thick of the enemy. We have often had occasion to notice the superstitious dread entertained by the Indians of the horse and his rider. And, although the long residence of the cavalry in the capital had familiarised the natives, in some measure, with their presence, so long a time had now elapsed since they had beheld them, that all their former mysterious terrors revived in full force; and, when thus suddenly assailed in flank by the formidable apparition, they were seized with a panic, and fell into confusion. It soon spread to the leading files, and Cortes, perceiving his advantage, turned with the rapidity of lightning, and, at this time supported by his followers, succeeded in driving the enemy with some loss back into the inclosure.

It was now the hour of vespers, and, as night must soon overtake them, he made no further attempt to pursue his advantage. Ordering the trumpets, therefore, to sound a retreat, he drew off his forces in good order, taking with him the artillery which had been abandoned in the square. The allies first went off the ground, followed by the Spanish infantry, while the rear was protected by the horse, thus reversing the order of march on their entrance. The Aztecs hung on the closing files, and though driven back by frequent charges of the cavalry, still followed in the distance, shooting off their ineffectual missiles, and filling the air with wild cries and howling, like a herd of ravenous wolves disappointed of their prey. It was late before the army reached its quarters at Xoloc.

Cortes had been well supported by Alvarado and Sandoval in this assault on the city; though neither of these commanders had penetrated the suburbs, deterred, perhaps, by the difficulties of the passage, which, in Alvarado's case, were greater than those presented to Cortes, from the greater number of breaches with which the dike in his quarter was intersected. Something was owing, too, to the want of brigantines, until Cortes supplied the deficiency by detaching half of his little navy to the support of his officers. Without their co-operation, however, the general himself could not have advanced so far, nor, perhaps, have succeeded at all in setting foot within the city. The success of this assault spread consternation, not only among the Mexicans, but their vassals, as they saw that the formidable preparations for defence were to avail little against the white man, who had so soon, in spite of them, forced his way into the very heart of the capital. Several of the neighbouring places, in consequence, now showed a willingness to shake off their allegiance, and claimed the protection of the Spaniards. Among these, were the territory of Xochimilco, so roughly treated by the invaders, and some tribes of Otomies, a rude but valiant people, who dwelt on the western confines of the valley. Their support was valuable, not so much from the additional reinforcement which it brought, as from the greater security it gave to the army, whose outposts were perpetually menaced by these warlike barbarians.

Thus strengthened, Cortes prepared to make another attack upon the capital, and that before it should have time to recover from the former. Orders were given to his lieutenants on the other causeways, to march at the same time, and co-operate with him, as before, in the assault. It was conducted in precisely the same manner as on the previous entry, the infantry taking the van, and the allies and cavalry following. But, to the great dismay of the Spaniards, they found two-thirds of the breaches restored to their former state, and the stones and other materials, with which they had been stopped, removed by the indefatigable enemy. They were again obliged to bring up the cannon, the brigantines ran alongside, and the enemy was dislodged, and driven from post to post, in the same manner as on the preceding attack. In short, the whole work was to be done over again. It was not till an hour after noon that the army had won a footing in the suburbs.

Here their progress was not so difficult as before; for the buildings from the terraces of which they had experienced the most annoyance had been swept away. Still it was only step by step that they forced a passage in face of the Mexican militia, who disputed their advance with the same spirit as before. Cortes, who would willingly have spared the inhabitants, if he could have brought them to terms, saw them with regret, as he says, thus desperately bent on a war of extermination. He conceived that there would be no way more likely to affect their minds, than by destroying at once some of the principal edifices, which they were accustomed to venerate as the pride and ornament of the city.

Marching into the great square, he selected, as the first to be destroyed, the old palace of Axayacatl, his former barracks. The ample range of low buildings was, it is true, constructed of stone; but the interior, as well as outworks, its turrets, and roofs, were of wood. The Spaniards, whose associations with the pile were of so gloomy a character, sprang to the work of destruction with a satisfaction like that which the French mob may have felt in the demolition of the Bastile. Torches and firebrands were thrown about in all directions; the lower parts of the building were speedily on fire, which, running along the inflammable bangings and woodwork of the interior, rapidly spread to the second floor. There the element took freer range, and, before it was visible from without, sent up from every aperture and crevice a dense column of vapour, that hung like a funeral pall over the city. This was dissipated by a bright sheet of flame, which enveloped all the upper regions of the vast pile, till, the supporters giving way, the wide range of turreted chambers fell, amidst clouds of dust and ashes, with an appalling crash, that for a moment stayed the Spaniards in the work of devastation.

The Aztecs gazed with inexpressible horror on this destruction of the venerable abode of their monarchs, and of the monuments of their luxury and splendour. Their rage was exasperated almost to madness, as they beheld their hated foes, the Tlascalans, busy in the work of desolation, and aided by the Tezcucans, their own allies, and not unfrequently their kinsmen. They vented their fury in bitter execrations, especially on the young prince Ixtlilxochitl, who, marching side by side with Cortes, took his full share in the dangers of the day. The warriors from the housetops poured the most approbrious epithets on him as he passed, denouncing him as false-hearted traitor; false to his country and his blood — reproaches not altogether unmerited, as his kinsman, who chronicles the circumstance, candidly confesses. He gave little heed to their taunts, however, holding on his way with the dogged resolution of one true to the cause in which he was embarked; and, when he entered the great square, he grappled with the leader of the Aztec forces, wrenched a lance from his grasp, won by the latter from the Christians, and dealt him a blow with his mace, or maquahuitl, which brought him lifeless to the ground.

The Spanish commander, having accomplished the work of destruction, sounded a retreat, sending on the Indian allies, who blocked up the way before him. The Mexicans, maddened by their losses, in wild transports of fury hung close on his rear, and though driven back by the cavalry, still returned, throwing themselves desperately under the horses, striving to tear the riders from their saddles, and content to throw away their own lives for one blow at their enemy. Fortunately the greater part of their militia was engaged with the assailants on the opposite quarters of the city; but, thus crippled, they pushed the Spaniards under Cortes so vigorously, that few reached the camp that night without bearing on their bodies some token of the desperate conflict.

On the following day, and, indeed, on several days following, the general repeated his assaults with as little care for repose, as if he and his men had been made of iron. On one occasion he advanced some way down the street of Tacuba, in which he carried three of the bridges, desirous, if possible, to open a communication with Alvarado, posted on the contiguous causeway. But the Spaniards in that quarter had not penetrated beyond the suburbs, still impeded by the severe character of the ground, and wanting, it may be, somewhat of that fiery impetuosity which the soldier feels who fights under the eye of his chief.

In each of these assaults, the breaches were found more or less restored to their original state by the pertinacious Mexicans, and the materials, which had been deposited in them with so much labour, again removed. It may seem strange, that Cortes did not take measures to guard against the repetition of an act which caused so much delay and embarrassment to his operations. He notices this in his letter to the emperor, in which he says that to do so would have required, either that he should have established his quarters in the city itself, which would have surrounded him with enemies, and cut off his communications with the country; or that he should have posted a sufficient guard of Spaniards — for the natives were out of the question — to protect the breaches by night, a duty altogether beyond the strength of men engaged in so arduous a service through the day.

Yet this was the course adopted by Alvarado; who stationed, at night, a guard of forty soldiers for the defence of the opening nearest to the enemy. This was relieved by a similar detachment in a few hours, and this again by a third, the two former still lying on their post; so that, on an alarm, a body of one hundred and twenty soldiers was ready on the spot to repel an attack. Sometimes, indeed, the whole division took up their bivouac in the neighbourhood of the breach, resting on their arms, and ready for instant action.

But a life of such incessant toil and vigilance was almost too severe even for the stubborn constitutions of the Spaniards. "Through the long night," exclaims Diaz, who served in Alvarado's division, "we kept our dreary watch; neither wind, nor wet, nor cold availing anything. There we stood, smarting, as we were, from the wounds we had received in the fight of the preceding day." It was the rainy season, which continues in that country from July to September; and the surface of the causeways, flooded by the storms, and broken up by the constant movement of such large bodies of men, was converted into a marsh, or rather quagmire, which added inconceivably to the distresses of the army.

The troops under Cortes were scarcely in a better situation. But few of them could find shelter in the rude towers that garnished the works of Xoloc. The greater part were compelled to bivouac in the open air, exposed to all the inclemency of the weather. Every man, unless his wounds prevented it, was required by the camp regulations to sleep on his arms; and they were often roused from their hasty slumbers by the midnight call to battle. For Guatemozin, contrary to the usual practice of his countrymen, frequently selected the hours of darkness to aim a blow at the enemy. "In short," exclaims the veteran soldier above quoted, "so unintermitting were our engagements, by day and by night, during the three months in which we lay before the capital, that to recount them all would but exhaust the reader's patience, and make him to fancy he was perusing the incredible feats of a knight-errant of romance."

The Aztec emperor conducted his operations on a systematic plan, which showed some approach to military science. He not unfrequently made simultanious attacks on the three several divisions of the Spaniards established on the causeways, and on the garrisons at their extremities. To accomplish this, he enforced the service not merely of his own militia of the capital, but of the great towns in the neighbourhood, who all moved in concert, at the well-known signal of the beacon-fire, or of the huge. drum struck by the priests on the summit of the temple. One of these general attacks, it was observed, whether from accident or design, took place on the eve of St. John the Baptist, the anniversary of the day on which the Spaniards made their second entry into the Mexican capital.

Notwithstanding the severe drain on his forces by this incessant warfare, the young monarch contrived to relieve them in some degree by different detachments, who took the place of one another. This was apparent from the different uniforms and military badges of the Indian battalions, who successively came and disappeared from the field. At night a strict guard was maintained in the Aztec quarters, a thing not common with the nations of the plateau. The outposts of the hostile armies were stationed within sight of each other. That of the Mexicans was usually placed in the neighbourhood of some wide breach, and its position was marked by a large fire in front. The hours for relieving guard were intimated by the shrill Aztec whistle, while bodies of men might be seen moving behind the flame, which threw a still ruddier glow over the cinnamon-coloured skins of the warriors.

While thus active on land, Guatemozin was not idle on the water. He was too wise, indeed, to cope with the Spanish navy again in open battle; but he resorted to stratagem, so much more congenial to Indian warfare. He placed a large number of canoes in ambuscade among the tall reeds which fringed the southern shores of the lake, and caused piles, at the same time, to be driven into the neighbouring shallows. Several piraguas, or boats of a larger size, then issued forth, and rowed near the spot where the Spanish brigantines were moored. Two of the smallest vessels, supposing the Indian barks were conveying provisions to the besieged, instantly stood after them, as had been foreseen. The Aztec boats fled for shelter to the reedy thicket, where their companions lay in ambush. The Spaniards, following, were soon entangled among the palisades under the water. They were instantly surrounded by the whole swarm of Indian canoes, most of the men were wounded, several, including the two commanders, slain, and one of the brigantines fell — a useless prize — into the hands of the victors. Among the slain was Pedro Barba, captain of the crossbowmen, a gallant officer, who had highly distinguished himself in the Conquest. This disaster occasioned much mortification to Cortes. It was a salutary lesson that stood him in good stead during the remainder of the war.

It may appear extraordinary that Guatemozin should have been able to provide for the maintenance of the crowded population now gathered in the metropolis, especially as the avenues were all in the possession of the besieging army. But, independently of the preparations made with this view before the siege and of the loathsome sustenance daily furnished by the victims for sacrifice, supplies were constantly obtained from the surrounding country across the lake. This was so conducted, for a time, as in a great measure to escape observation; and even when the brigantines were commanded to cruise day and night, and sweep the waters of the boats employed in this service, many still contrived, under cover of the darkness, to elude the vigilance of the cruisers, and brought their cargoes into port. It was not till the great towns in the neighbourhood cast off their allegiance that the supply began to fall, from the failure of its sources. The defection was more frequent, as the inhabitants became convinced that the government, incompetent to its own defence, must be still more so to theirs: and the Aztec metropolis saw its great vassals fall off, one after another, as the tree, over which decay is stealing, parts with its leaves at the first blast of the tempest.

The cities, which now claimed the Spanish general's protection, supplied the camp with an incredible number of warriors; a number which, if we admit Cortes' own estimate, one hundred and fifty thousand, could have only served to embarrass his operations on the long extended causeways. These levies were distributed among the three garrisons at the terminations of the causeways; and many found active employment in foraging the country for provisions, and yet more in carrying on hostilities against the places still unfriendly to the Spaniards.

Cortes found further occupation for them in the construction of barracks for his troops, who suffered greatly from exposure to the incessant rains of the season, which were observed to fall more heavily by night than by day. Quantities of stone and timber were obtained from the buildings that had been demolished in the city. They were transported in the brigantines to the causeway, and from these materials a row of huts or barracks was constructed, extending on either side of the works of Xoloc.

By this arrangement, ample accommodations were furnished for the Spanish troops and their Indian attendants, amounting in all to about two thousand. The great body of the allies, with a small detachment of horse and infantry, were quartered at the neighbouring post of Cojohuacan, which served to protect the rear of the encampment, and to maintain its communications with the country. A similar disposition of forces took place in the other divisions of the army, under Alvarado and Sandoval, though the accommodations provided for the shelter of the troops on their causeways were not so substantial as those for the division of Cortes.

The Spanish camp was supplied with provisions from the friendly towns in the neighbourhood, and especially from Tezcuco. They consisted of fish, the fruits of the country, particularly a sort of fig borne by the tuna (cactus opuntia), and a species of cherry, or something much resembling it, which grew abundant at this season. But their principal food was the tortillas, cakes of Indian meal, still common in Mexico, for which bakehouses were established, under the care of the natives, in the garrison towns commanding the causeways. The aries, as appears too probable, reinforced their frugal fare with an occasional banquet of human flesh, for which the battle-field unhappily afforded them too much facility, and which, however shocking to the feelings of Cortes, he did not consider himself in a situation at that moment to prevent.

Thus the tempest, which had been so long mustering, broke at length in all its fury on the Aztec capital. Its unhappy inmates beheld the hostile legions encompassing them about with their glittering files stretching as far as the eye could reach. They saw themselves deserted by their allies and vassals in their utmost need; the fierce stranger penetrating into their secret places, violating their temples, plundering their palaces, wasting the fair city by day, firing its suburbs by night, and intrenching himself in solid edifices under their walls as if determined never to withdraw his foot while one stone remained upon another. All this they saw, yet their spirits were unbroken; and, though famine and pestilence were beginning to creep over them, they still showed the same determined front to their enemies. Cortes, who would gladly have spared the town and its inhabitants, beheld this resolution with astonishment. He intimated more than once, by means of the prisoners whom he released, his willingness to grant them fair terms of capitulation. Day after day, he fully expected his proffers would be accepted. But day after day he was disappointed. He had yet to learn how tenacious was the memory of the Aztecs; and that, whatever might be the horrors of their present situation, and their fears for the future, they were all forgotten in their hatred of the white man.

FAMINE was now gradually working its way into the heart of the beleaguered city. It seemed certain that, with this strict blockade, the crowded population must in the end be driven to capitulate, though no arm should be raised against them. But it required time; and the Spaniards, though constant and enduring by nature, began to be impatient of hardships scarcely inferior to those experienced by the besieged. In some respects their condition was even worse, exposed, as they were, to the cold, drenching rains, which fen with little intermission, rendering their situation dreary and disastrous in the extreme.

In this state of things there were many who would willingly have shortened their sufferings, and taken the chance of carrying the place by a coup de main. Others thought it would be best to get possession of the great market of Tlatelolco, which, from its situation in the north-western part of the city, might afford the means of communication with the camps of both Alvarado and Sandoval. This place, encompassed by spacious porticos, would furnish accommodations for a numerous host; and, once established in the capital, the Spaniards would be in a position to follow up the blow with far more effect than at a distance.

These arguments were pressed by several of the officers, particularly by Alderete, the royal treasurer, a person of much consideration, not only from his rank, but from the capacity and zeal he had shown in the service. In deference to their wishes, Cortes summoned a council of war, and laid the matter before it. The treasurer's views were espoused by most of the high-mettled cavaliers, who looked with eagerness to any change of their present forlorn and wearisome life; and Cortes, thinking it probably more prudent to adopt the less expedient course, than to enforce a cold and reluctant obedience to his own opinion, suffered himself to be overruled.

A day was fixed for the assault, which was to be made simultaneously by the two divisions under Alvarado and the commander-inchief. Sandoval was instructed to draw off the greater part of his forces from the northern causeway, and to unite himself with Alvarado, while seventy picked soldiers were to be detached to the support of Cortes.

On the appointed morning, the two armies, after the usual celebration of mass, advanced along their respective causeways against the city. They were supported, in addition to the brigantines, by a numerous fleet of Indian boats, which were to force a passage up the canals, and by a countless multitude of allies, whose very numbers served in the end to embarrass their operations. After clearing the suburbs, three avenues presented themselves, which all terminated in the square of Tlatelolco. The principal one, being of much greater width than the other two, might rather be called a causeway than a street, since it was flanked by deep canals on either side. Cortes divided his force into three bodies. One of them he placed under Alderete, with orders to occupy the principal street. A second he gave in charge to Andres de Tapia and Jorge de Alvarado; the former a cavalier of courage and capacity, the latter, a younger brother of Don Pedro and possessed of the intrepid spirit which belonged to that chivalrous family. These were to penetrate by one of the parallel streets, while the general himself, at the head of the third division, was to occupy the other. A small body of cavalry, with two or three field-pieces, was stationed as a reserve in front of the great street of Tacuba, which was designated as the rallying point for the different divisions.

Cortes gave the most positive instructions to his captains not to advance a step without securing the means of retreat, by carefully filling up the ditches, and the openings in the causeway. The neglect of this precaution by Alvarado, in an assault which he had made on the city but a few days before, had been attended with such serious consequences to his army, that Cortes rode over, himself, to his officer's quarters, for the purpose of publicly reprimanding him for his disobedience of orders. On his arrival at the camp, however, he found that his offending captain had conducted the affair with so much gallantry, that the intended reprimand — though well deserved — subsided into a mild rebuke.

The arrangements being completed, the three divisions marched at once up the several streets. Cortes, dismounting, took the van of his own squadron, at the head of his infantry. The Mexicans fell back as he advanced, making less resistance than usual. The Spaniards pushed on, carrying one barricade after another, and carefully filling up the gaps with rubbish, so as to secure themselves a footing. The canoes supported the attack, by moving along the canals, and grappling with those of the enemy; while numbers of the nimble-footed Tlascalans, scaling the terraces, passed on from one house to another, where they were connected, hurling the defenders into the streets below. The enemy, taken apparently by surprise, seemed incapable of withstanding for a moment the fury of the assault; and the victorious Christians, cheered on by the shouts of triumph which arose from their companions in the adjoining streets, were only the more eager to be first at the destined goal.

Indeed, the facility of his success led the general to suspect that he might be advancing too fast; that it might be a device of the enemy to draw them into the heart of the city, and then surround or attack them in the rear. He had some misgivings, moreover, lest his too ardent officers, in the heat of the chase, should, notwithstanding his commands, have overlooked the necessary precaution of filling up the breaches. He accordingly brought his squadron to a halt, prepared to baffle any insidious movement of his adversary. Meanwhile he received more than one message from Alderete, informing him that he had nearly gained the market. This only increased the general's apprehension, that, in the rapidity of his advance, he might have neglected to secure the ground. He determined to trust no eyes but his own, and, taking a small body of troops, proceeded to reconnoitre the route followed by the treasurer.

He had not proceeded far along the great street, or causeway, when his progress was arrested by an opening ten or twelve paces wide, and filled with water, at least two fathoms deep, by which a communication was formed between the canals on the opposite sides. A feeble attempt had been made to stop the gap with the rubbish of the causeway, but in too careless a manner to be of the least service; and a few straggling stones and pieces of timber only showed that the work had been abandoned almost as soon as begun. To add to his consternation, the general observed that the sides of the causeway in this neighbourhood had been pared off, and, as was evident, very recently. He saw in all this the artifice of the cunning enemy; and had little doubt that his hot-headed officer had rushed into a snare deliberately laid for him. Deeply alarmed, he set about repairing the mischief as fast as possible, by ordering his men to fill up the yawning chasm.

But they had scarcely begun their labours, when the hoarse echoes of conflict in the distance were succeeded by a hideous sound of mingled yells and war-whoops, that seemed to rend the very heavens. This was followed by a rushing noise, as of the tread of thronging multitudes, showing that the tide of battle was turned back from its former course, and was rolling on towards the spot where Cortes and his little band of cavaliers were planted.

His conjecture proved too true. Alderete had followed the retreating Aztecs with an eagerness which increased with every step of his advance. He had carried the barricades, which had defended the breach, without much difficulty, and, as he swept on, gave orders. that the opening should be stopped. But the blood of the high-spirited cavaliers was warmed by the chase, and no one cared to be detained by the ignoble occupation of filling up the ditches, while he could gather laurels so easily in the fight; and they all pressed on, exhorting and cheering one another with the assurance of being the first to reach the square of Tlatelolco. In this way they suffered themselves to be decoyed into the heart of the city; when suddenly the horn of Guatemozin sent forth a long and piercing note from the summit of a neighbouring teocalli. In an instant, the flying Aztecs, as if maddened by the blast, wheeled about, and turned on their pursuers. At the same time, countless swarms of warriors from the adjoining streets and lanes poured in upon the flanks of the assailants, filling the air with the fierce, unearthly cries which bad reached the ears of Cortes, and drowning, for a moment, the wild dissonance which reigned in the other quarters of the capital.

The army, taken by surprise, and shaken by the fury of the assault, were thrown into the utmost disorder. Friends and foes, white men and Indians, were mingled together in one promiscuous mass; spears, swords, and war-clubs were brandished together in the air. Blows fell at random. In their eagerness to escape, they trod down one another. Blinded by the missiles, which now rained on them from the azoteas, they staggered on, scarcely knowing in what direction, or fell, struck down by hands which they could not see. On they came like a rushing torrent sweeping along some steep declivity, and rolling in one confused tide towards the open breach, on the further side of which stood Cortes and his companions, horror-struck at the sight of the approaching ruin. The foremost files soon plunged into the gulf, treading one another under the flood, some striving ineffectually to swim, others, with more success, to clamber over the heaps of their suffocated comrades. Many, as they attempted to scale the opposite sides of the slippery dike, fell into the water, or were hurried off by the warriors in the canoes, who added to the horrors of the rout by the fresh storm of darts and javelins which they poured on the fugitives.

Cortes, meanwhile, with his brave followers, kept his station undaunted on the other side of the breach. "I had made up my mind," he says, "to die rather than desert my poor followers in their extremity!" With outstretched hands he endeavoured to rescue as many as he could from the watery grave, and from the more appalling fate of captivity. He as vainly tried to restore something like presence of mind and order among the distracted fugitives. His person was too well known to the Aztecs, and his position now made him a conspicuous mark for their weapons. Darts, stones, and arrows fell around him as thick as hail, but glanced harmless from his steel helmet and armour of proof. At length a cry of "Malinche, Malinche!" arose among the enemy; and six of their number, strong and athletic warriors, rushing on him at once, made a violent effort to drag him on board their boat. In the struggle he received a severe wound in the leg, which, for the time, disabled it. There seemed to be no hope for him; when a faithful follower, Christoval de Olea, perceiving his general's extremity, threw himself on the Aztecs, and with a blow cut off the arm of one savage, and then plunged his sword in the body of another. He was quickly supported by a comrade named Lerma, and by a Tlascalan chief, who, fighting over the prostrate body of Cortes, despatched three more of the assailants, though the heroic Olea paid dearly for his self-devotion, as he fell mortally wounded by the side of his general.

The report soon spread among the soldiers that their commander was taken; and Quinones, the captain of his guard, with several others pouring in to the rescue, succeeded in disentangling Cortes from the grasp of his enemies who were struggling with him in the water, and raising him in their arms, placed him again on the causeway. One of his pages, meanwhile, had advanced some way through the press, leading a horse for his master to mount. But the youth received a wound in the throat from a javelin, which prevented him from effecting his object. Another of his attendants was more successful. It was Guzman, his chamberlain; but as he held the bridle, while Cortes was assisted into the saddle, he was snatched away by the Aztecs, and with the swiftness of thought, hurried off by their canoes. The general still lingered, unwilling to leave the spot, whilst his presence could be of the least service. But the faithful Quinones, taking his horse by the bridle, turned his head from the breach, exclaiming at the same time, that "his master's life was too important to the army to be thrown away there."

Cortes at length succeeded in regaining the firm ground, and reaching the open place before the great street of Tacuba. Here, under a sharp fire of the artillery, he rallied his broken squadrons, and charging at the head of the little body of horse, which, not having been brought into action, were still fresh, he beat off the enemy. He then commanded the retreat of the two other divisions. The scattered forces again united; and the general, sending forward his Indian confederates, took the rear with a chosen body of cavalry to cover the retreat of the army, which was effected with but little additional loss.

Andres de Tapia was despatched to the western causeway to acquaint Alvarado and Sandoval with the failure of the enterprise. Meanwhile the two captains had penetrated far into the city. Cheered by the triumphant shouts of their countrymen in the adjacent streets, they had pushed on with extraordinary vigour, that they might not be outstripped in the race of glory. They had almost reached the market-place, which lay nearer to their quarters than to the general's, when they heard the blast from the dread horn of Guatemozin, followed by the overpowering yell of the barbarians, which had so startled the ears of Cortes: till at length the sounds the receding conflict died away in the distance. The two captains now understood that the day must have gone hard with their countrymen. They soon had further proof of it, when the victorious Aztecs, returning from the pursuit of Cortes, joined their forces to those engaged with Sandoval and Alvarado, and fell on them with redoubled fury. At the same time they rolled on the ground two or three of the bloody heads of the Spaniards, shouting the name of "Malinche." The captains, struck with horror at the spectacle, though they gave little credit to the words of the enemy — instantly ordered a retreat. The fierce barbarians followed up the Spaniards to their very intrenchments. But here they were met, first by the cross fire of the brigantines, which, dashing through the palisades planted to obstruct their movements, completely enfiladed the causeway, and next by that of the small battery erected in front of the camp, which, under the management of a skilful engineer, named Medrano, swept the whole length of the defile. Thus galled in front and on flank, the shattered columns of the Aztecs were compelled to give way and take shelter under the defences of the city.

The greatest anxiety now prevailed in the camp, regarding the fate of Cortes, for Tapia had been detained on the road by scattered parties of the enemy, whom Guatemozin had stationed there to interrupt the communications between the camps. He arrived, at length, however, though bleeding from several wounds. His intelligence, while it re-assured the Spaniards as to the general's personal safety, was not calculated to allay their uneasiness in other respects.

Sandoval, in particular, was desirous to acquaint himself with the actual state of things, and the further intentions of Cortes. Suffering as he was from three wounds, which he had received in that day's fight, he resolved to visit in person the quarters of the commander-inchief. It was mid-day — for the busy scenes of the morning had occupied but a few hours, when Sandoval remounted the good steed, on whose strength and speed he knew he could rely.

On arriving at the camp, he found the troops there much worn and dispirited by the disaster of the morning. They had good reason to be so. Besides the killed, and a long file of wounded, sixty-two Spaniards, with a multitude of allies, had fallen alive into the hands of the enemy. The loss of two field-pieces and seven horses crowned their own disgrace and the triumphs of the Aztecs.

Cortes, it was observed, had borne himself throughout this trying day with his usual intrepidity and coolness. It was with a cheerful countenance, that he now received his lieutenant; but a shade of sadness was visible through this outward composure, showing how the catastrophe of the puente cuidada, "the sorrowful bridge," as he mournfully called it, lay heavy at his heart.

To the cavalier's anxious inquiries, as to the cause of the disaster, he replied: "It is for my sins that it has befallen me, son Sandoval"; for such was the affectionate epithet with which Cortes often addressed his best-beloved and trusty officer. He then explained to him the immediate cause, in the negligence of the treasurer. Further conversation followed, in which the general declared his purpose to forego active hostilities for a few days. "You must take my place," continued, "for I am too much crippled at present to discharge my duties. You must watch over the safety of the camps. Give especial heed to Alvarado's. He is a gallant soldier, I know it well; but I doubt the Mexican hounds may, some hour, take him at disadvantage." These few words showed the general's own estimate of his two lieutenants; both equally brave and chivalrous; but the one uniting with these qualities the circumspection so essential to success in perilous enterprises, in which the other was signally deficient. It was under the training of Cortes that he learned to be a soldier. The general, having concluded his instructions, affectionately embraced his lieutenant, and dismissed him to his quarters.

It was late in the afternoon when he reached them; but the sun was still lingering above the western hills, and poured his beams wide over the valley, lighting up the old towers and temples of Tenochtitlan with a mellow radiance that little harmonised with the dark scenes of strife in which the city had so lately been involved. The tranquillity of the hour, however, was on a sudden broken by the strange sounds of the great drum in the temple of the war-god — sounds which recalled the noche triste, with all its terrible images, to the minds of the Spaniards, for that was the only occasion on which they had ever heard them. They intimated some solemn act of religion within the unhallowed precincts of the teocalli; and the soldiers, startled by the mournful vibrations, which might be heard for leagues across the valley, turned their eyes to the quarter whence they proceeded. They there beheld a long procession winding up the huge sides of the pyramid; for the camp of Alvarado was pitched scarcely a mile from the city, and objects are distinctly visible, at a great distance, in the transparent atmosphere of the tableland.

As the long file of priests and warriors reached the flat summit of the teocalli, the Spaniards saw the figures of several men stripped to their waists, some of whom, by the whiteness of their skins, they recognised as their own countrymen. They were the victims for sacrifice. Their heads were gaudily decorated with coronals of plumes, and they carried fans in their hands. They were urged along by blows, and compelled to take part in the dances in honour of the Aztec war-god. The unfortunate captives, then stripped of their sad finery, were stretched one after another on the great stone of sacrifice. On its convex surface, their breasts were heaved up conveniently for the diabolical purpose of the priestly executioner, who cut asunder the ribs by a strong blow with his sharp razor of itztli, and thrusting his hand into the wound, tore away the heart, which, hot and reeking, was deposited on the golden censer before the idol. The body of the slaughtered victim was then hurled down the steep stairs of the pyramid, which, it may be remembered, were placed at the same angle of the pile, one flight below another; and the mutilated remains were gathered up by the savages beneath, who soon prepared with them the cannibal repast which completed the work of abomination!

We may imagine with what sensations the stupefied Spaniards must have gazed on this horrid spectacle, so near that they could almost recognise the persons of their unfortunate friends, see the struggles and writhing of their bodies, hear — or fancy that they heard — their screams of agony! yet so far removed that they could render them no assistance. Their limbs trembled beneath them, as they thought what might one day be their own fate; and the bravest among them, who had hitherto gone to battle, as careless and lighthearted, as to the banquet or the ball-room, were unable, from this time forward, to encounter their ferocious enemy without a sickening feeling, much akin to fear, coming over them.

The five following days passed away in a state of inaction, except indeed, so far as was necessary to repel the sorties, made from time to time, by the militia of the capital. The Mexicans, elated with their success, meanwhile abandoned themselves to jubilee; singing, dancing and feasting on the mangled relics of their wretched victims. Guatemozin sent several heads of the Spaniards, as well as of the horses, round the country, calling on his old vassals to forsake the banners of the white men, unless they would share the doom of the enemies of Mexico. The priests now cheered the young monarch and the people with the declaration, that the dread Huitzilopochtli, their offended deity, appeased by the sacrifices offered up on his altars, would again take the Aztecs under his protection, and deliver their enemies, before the expiration of eight days, into their hands.

This comfortable prediction, confidently believed by the Mexicans, was thundered in the ears of the besieging army in tones of exultation and defiance. However it may have been contemned by the Spaniards, it had a very different effect on their allies. The latter had begun to be disgusted with a service so full of peril and suffering, and already protracted far beyond the usual term of Indian hostilities. They had less confidence than before in the Spaniards. Experience had shown that they were neither invincible nor immortal, and their recent reverses made them even distrust the ability of the Christians to reduce the Aztec metropolis. They recalled to mind the ominous words of Xicotencatl, that "no sacrilegious a war could come to no good for the people of Anahuac." They felt that their arm was raised against the gods of their country. The prediction of the oracle fell heavy on their hearts. They had little doubt of its fulfilment, and were only eager to turn away the bolt from their own heads by a timely secession from the cause.

They took advantage, therefore, of the friendly cover of night to steal away from their quarters. Company after company deserted in this manner, taking the direction of their respective homes. Those belonging to the great towns of the valley, whose allegiance was the most recent, were the first to cast it off. Their example was followed by the older confederates, the militia of Cholula, Tepeaca, Tezcuco, and even the faithful Tlascala. There were, it is true, some exceptions to these, and among them, Ixtlilxochitl, the younger lord of Tezcuco, and Chichemecatl, the valiant Tlascalan chieftain, who, with a few of their immediate followers, still remained true to the banner under which they had. enlisted. But their number was insignificant. The Spaniards beheld with dismay the mighty array, on which they relied for support, thus silently melting away before the breath of superstition. Cortes alone maintained a cheerful countenance. He treated the prediction with contempt, as an invention of the priests, and sent his messengers after the retreating squadrons, beseeching them to postpone their departure, or at least to halt on the road, till the time, which would soon elapse, should show the falsehood of the prophecy.

The affairs of the Spaniards, at this crisis, must be confessed to have worn a gloomy aspect. Deserted by their allies, with their ammunition nearly exhausted, cut off from the customary supplies from the neighbourhood, harassed by unintermitting vigils and fatigues, smarting under wounds, of which every man in the army had his share, with an unfriendly country in their rear, and a mortal foe in front, they might well be excused for faltering in their enterprise. Night after night fresh victims were led up to the great altar of sacrifice; and while the city blazed with the illuminations of a thousand bonfires on the terraced roofs of the dwellings, and in the areas of the temples, the dismal pageant was distinctly visible from the camp below. One of the last of the sufferers was Guzman, the unfortunate chamberlain of Cortes, who lingered in captivity eighteen days before he met his doom.

Amidst all the distresses and multiplied embarrassments of their situation, the Spaniards still remained true to their purpose. They relaxed in no degree the severity of the blockade. Their camps still occupied the only avenues to the city; and their batteries, sweeping the long defiles at every fresh assault of the Aztecs, mowed down hundreds of the assailants. Their brigantines still rode on the waters, cutting off the communication with the shore. It is true, indeed, the loss of the auxiliary canoes left a passage open for the occasional introduction of supplies to the capital. But the whole amount of these supplies was small; and its crowded population, while exulting in their temporary advantage, and the delusive assurances of their priests, were beginning to sink under the withering grasp of an enemy within, more terrible than the one which lay before their gates.

CHAPTER 7. [1521] SUCCESS OF THE SPANIARDS— FRUITLESS OFFERS TO GUATEMOZIN— BUILDINGS RAZED TO THE GROUND— TERRIBLE FAMINE— THE TROOPS GAIN THE MARKET— PLACE

THUS passed away the eight days prescribed by the oracle; and the sun, which rose upon the ninth, beheld the fair city still beset on every side by the inexorable foe. It was a great mistake of the Aztec priests — one not uncommon with false prophets, anxious to produce a startling impression on their followers — to assign so short a term for the fulfilment of their prediction.

The Tezcucan and Tlascalan chiefs now sent to acquaint their troops with the failure of the prophecy, and to recall them to the Christian camp. The Tlascalans, who had halted on the way, returned, ashamed of their credulity, and with ancient feelings of animosity, heightened by the artifice of which they had been the dupes. Their example was followed by many of the other confederates. In a short time the Spanish general found himself at the head of an auxiliary force, which, if not so numerous as before, was more than adequate to all his purposes. He received them with politic benignity; and, while he reminded them that they had been guilty of a great crime in thus abandoning their commander, he was willing to overlook it in consideration of their past services. They must be aware that these services were not necessary to the Spaniards, who had carried on the siege with the same vigour during their absence as when they were present. But he was unwilling that those who had shared the dangers of the war with him, should not also partake of its triumphs, and be present at the fall of their enemy, which he promised, with a confidence better founded than that of the priests in their prediction, should not be long delayed.

Yet the menaces and machinations of Guatemozin were still not without effect in the distant provinces. Before the full return of the confederates, Cortes received an embassy from Cuernavaca, ten or twelve leagues distant, and another from some friendly towns of the Otomies, still further off, imploring his protection against their formidable neighbours, who menaced them with hostilities as allies of the Spaniards. As the latter were then situated, they were in a condition to receive succour much more than to give it. Most of the officers were accordingly opposed to granting a request, the compliance with which must still further impair their diminished strength. But Cortes knew the importance, above all, of not betraying his own inability to grant it. "The greater our weakness," he said, "the greater need have we to cover it under a show of strength."

He immediately detached Tapia with a body of about a hundred men in one direction, and Sandoval with a somewhat larger force in the other, with orders that their absence should not in any event be prolonged beyond ten days. The two capitains executed their commission promptly and effectually. They each met and defeated his adversary in a pitched battle; laid waste the hostile territories, and returned within the time prescribed. They were soon followed by ambassadors from the conquered places, soliciting the alliance of the Spaniards; and the affair terminated by an accession of new confederates, and, what was more important, a conviction in the old, that the Spaniards were both willing and competent to protect them.

Fortune, who seldom dispenses her frowns or her favours singlehanded, further showed her good will to the Spaniards at this time, by sending a vessel into Vera Cruz laden with ammunition and military stores. It was part of the fleet destined for the Florida coast by the romantic old knight, Ponce de Leon. The cargo was immediately taken by the authorities of the port, and forwarded, without delay, to the camp, where it arrived most seasonably, as the want of powder, in particular, had begun to be seriously felt. With strength thus renovated, Cortes determined to resume active operations, but on a plan widely differing from that pursued before.

In the former deliberations on the subject, two courses, as we have seen, presented themselves to the general. One was, to intrench himself in the heart of the capital, and from this point carry on hostilities; the other was the mode of proceeding hitherto followed. Both were open to serious objections, which he hoped would be obviated by the one now adopted. This was, to advance no step without securing the entire safety of the army, not only on its immediate retreat, but in its future inroads. Every breach in the causeway, every canal in the streets, was to be filled up in so solid a manner, that the work should not be again disturbed. The materials for this were to be furnished by the buildings, every one of which, as the army advanced, whether public or private, hut, temple, or palace, was to be demolished! Not a building in their path was to be spared. They were all indiscriminately to be levelled, until, in the Conqueror's own language, "the water should be converted into dry land," and a smooth and open ground be afforded for the manoeuvres of the cavalry and artillery.

Cortes came to this terrible determination with great difficulty. He sincerely desired to spare the city, "the most beautiful thing in the world," as he enthusiastically styles it, and which would have formed the most glorious trophy of his conquest. But, in a place where every house was a fortress, and every street was cut up by canals so embarrassing to his movements, experience proved it was vain to think of doing so, and becoming master of it. There was as little hope of a peaceful accommodation with the Aztecs, who, so far from being broken by all they had hitherto endured, and the long perspective of future woes, showed a spirit as haughty and implacable as ever.

The general's intentions were learned by the Indian allies with unbounded satisfaction; and they answered his call for aid by thousands of pioneers, armed with their coas, or hoes of the country, all testifying the greatest alacrity in helping on the work of destruction. In a short time the breaches in the great causeways were filled up so effectually that they were never again molested. Cortes himself set the example by carrying stones and timber with. his own hands. The buildings in the suburbs were then thoroughly levelled, the canals were filled up with the rubbish, and a wide space around the city was thrown open to the manoeuvres of the cavalry, who swept over it free and unresisted. The Mexicans did not look with indifference on these preparations to lay waste their town, and leave them bare and unprotected against the enemy. They made incessant efforts to impede the labours of the besiegers, but the latter, under cover of their guns, which kept up an unintermitting fire, still advanced in the work of desolation.

The gleam of fortune, which had so lately broken out on the Mexicans, again disappeared; and the dark mist, after having been raised for a moment, settled on the doomed capital more heavily than before. Famine, with all her hideous train of woes, was making rapid strides among its accumulated population. The stores provided for the siege were exhausted. The casual supply of human victims, or that obtained by some straggling pirogue from the neighbouring shores, was too inconsiderable to be widely felt. Some forced a scanty sustenance from a mucilaginous substance, gathered in small quantities on the surface of the lake and canals. Others appeased the cravings of appetite by devouring rats, lizards, and the like loathsome reptiles, which had not yet deserted the starving city. Its days seemed to be already numbered. But the page of history has many an example, to show that there are no limits to the endurance of which humanity is capable, when animated by hatred and despair.

With the sword thus suspended over it, the Spanish commander, desirous to make one more effort to save the capital, persuaded three Aztec nobles, taken in one of the late actions, to bear a message from him to Guatemozin; though they undertook it with reluctance, for fear of the consequences to themselves. Cortes told the emperor, that all had now been done that brave men could do in defence of their country. There remained no hope, no chance of escape for the Mexicans. Their provisions were exhausted; their communications were cut off; their vassals had deserted them; even their gods had betrayed them. They stood alone, with the nations of Anahuac banded against them. There was no hope, but in immediate surrender. He besought the young monarch to take compassion on his brave subjects, who were daily perishing before his eyes; and on the fair city, whose stately buildings were fast crumbling into ruins. "Return to the allegiance," he concludes, "which you once proffered to the sovereign of Castile. The past shall be forgotten. The persons and property — in short, all the rights of the Aztecs shall be respected. You shall be confirmed in your authority, and Spain will once more take your city under her protection."

The eye of the young monarch kindled, and his dark cheek flushed with sudden anger, as he listened to proposals so humiliating. But, though his bosom glowed with the fiery temper of the Indian, he had the qualities of a "gentle cavalier," says one of his enemies, who knew him well. He did no harm to the envoys; but, after the heat of the moment had passed off, he gave the matter a calm consideration, and called a council of his wise men and warriors to deliberate upon it. Some were for accepting the proposals, as offering the only chance of preservation. But the priests took a different view of the matter. They knew that the ruin of their own order must follow the triumph of Christianity. "Peace was good," they said, "but not with the white men." They reminded Guatemozin of the fate of his uncle Montezuma, and the requital he had met with for all his hospitality: of the seizure and imprisonment of Cacama, the cacique of Tezcuco; of the massacre of the nobles by Alvarado; of the insatiable avarice of the invaders, which had stripped the country of its treasures; of their profanation of the temples; of the injuries and insults which they had heaped without measure on the people and their religion. "Better," they said, "to trust in the promises of their own gods, who had so long watched over the nation. Better, if need be, give up our lives at once for our country, than drag them out in slavery and suffering among the false strangers."

The eloquence of the priests, artfully touching the various wrongs of his people, roused the hot blood of Guatemozin. "Since it is so," he abruptly exclaimed, "let us think only of supplying the wants of the people. Let no man, henceforth, who values his life, talk of surrender. We can at least die like warriors."

The Spaniards waited two days for the answer to their embassy. At length, it came in a general sortie of the Mexicans, who, pouring through every gate of the capital, like a river that has burst its banks, swept on, wave upon wave, to the very intrenchments of the besiegers, threatening to overwhelm them by their numbers! Fortunately, the position of the latter on the dikes secured their flanks, and the narrowness of the defile gave their small battery of guns all the advantages of a larger one. The fire of artillery and musketry blazed without intermission along the several causeways, belching forth volumes of sulphurous smoke, that, rolling heavily over the waters, settled dark around the Indian city, and hid it from the surrounding country. The brigantines thundered, at the same time. on the flanks of the columns, which, after some ineffectual efforts to maintain themselves, rolled back in wild confusion, till their impotent fury died away in sullen murmurs within the capital.

Cortes now steadily pursued the plan he had laid down for the devastation of the city. Day after day the several armies entered by their respective quarters; Sandoval probably directing his operations against the north-eastern district. The buildings made of the porous tetzontli, though generally low, were so massy and extensive, and the canals were so numerous, that their progress was necessarily slow. They, however, gathered fresh accessions of strength every day from the numbers who flocked to the camp from the surrounding country, and who joined in the work of destruction with a hearty good will, which showed their eagerness to break the detested yoke of the Aztecs. The latter raged with impotent anger as they beheld their lordly edifices, their temples, all they had been accustomed to venerate, thus ruthlessly swept away; their canals, constructed with so much labour, and what to them seemed science, filled up with rubbish; their flourishing city, in short, turned into a desert, over which the insulting foe now rode triumphant. They heaped many a taunt on the Indian allies. "Go on," they said, bitterly; "the more you destroy, the more you will have to build up again hereafter. If we conquer, you shall build for us; and if your white friends conquer, they will make you do as much for them." The event justified the prediction.

The division of Cortes had now worked its way as far north as the great street of Tacuba, which opened a communication with Alvarado's camp, and near which stood the palace of Guatemozin. It was a spacious stone pile, that might well be called a fortress. Though deserted by its royal master, it was held by a strong body of Aztecs, who made a temporary defence, but of little avail against the battering enginery of the besiegers. It was soon set on fire, and its crumbling walls were levelled in the dust, like those other stately edifices of the capital, the boast and admiration of the Aztecs, and some of the fairest fruits of their civilisation. "It was a sad thing to witness their destruction," exclaims Cortes; "but it was part of our plan of operations, and we had no alternative."

These operations had consumed several weeks, so that it was now drawing towards the latter part of July. During this time, the blockade had been maintained with the utmost rigour, and the wretched inhabitants were suffering all the extremities of famine. Some few stragglers were taken, from time to time, in the neighbourhood of the Christian camp, whither they had wandered in search of food. They were kindly treated by command of Cortes, who was in hopes to induce others to follow their example, and thus to afford a means of conciliating the inhabitants, which might open the way to their submission. But few were found willing to leave the shelter of the capital, and they preferred to take their chance with their suffering countrymen, rather than trust themselves to the mercies of the besiegers.

From these few stragglers, however, the Spaniards heard a dismal tale of woe, respecting the crowded population in the interior of the city. All the ordinary means of sustenance had long since failed, and they now supported life as they could, by means of such roots as they could dig from the earth, by gnawing the bark of trees, by feeding on the grass — on anything, in short, however loathsome, that could allay the craving of appetite. Their only drink was the brackish water of the soil, saturated with the salt lake. Under this unwholesome diet, and the diseases engendered by it, the population was gradually wasting away. Men sickened and died every day, in all the excruciating torments produced by hunger, and the wan and emaciated survivors seemed only to be waiting for their time.

The Spaniards had visible confirmation of all this, as they penetrated deeper into the city, and approached the district of Tlatelolco now occupied by the besieged. They found the ground turned up in quest of roots and weeds, the trees stripped of their green stems, their foliage, and their bark. Troops of famished Indians flitted in the distance, gliding like ghosts among the scenes of their former residence. Dead bodies lay unburied in the streets and courtyards, or filled up the canals. It was a sure sign of the extremity of the Aztecs; for they held the burial of the dead as a solemn and imperative duty. In the early part of the siege, they had religiously attended to it. In its later stages, they were still careful to withdraw the dead from the public eye, by bringing their remains within the houses. But the number of these, and their own sufferings, had now so fearfully increased, that they had grown indifferent to this, and they suffered their friends and their kinsmen to lie and moulder on the spot where they drew their last breath!

As the invaders entered the dwellings, a more appalling spectacle presented itself; — the floors covered with the prostrate forms of the miserable inmates, some in the agonies of death, others festering in their corruption; men, women, and children, inhaling the poisonous atmosphere, and mingling promiscuously together; mothers, with their infants in their arms perishing of hunger before their eyes, while they were unable to afford them the nourishment of nature; men crippled by their wounds, with their bodies frightfully mangled, vainly attempting to crawl away, as the enemy entered. Yet, even in this state, they scorned to ask for mercy, and glared on the invaders with the sullen ferocity of the wounded tiger, that the huntsmen have tracked to his forest cave. The Spanish commander issued strict orders that mercy should be shown to these poor and disabled victims. But the Indian allies made no distinction. An Aztec, under whatever circumstances, was an enemy; and, with hideous shouts of triumph, they pulled down the burning buildings on their heads, consuming the living and the dead in one common funeral pile!

Yet the sufferings of the Aztecs, terrible as they were, did not incline them to submission. There were many, indeed, who, from greater strength of constitution, or from the more favourable circumstances in which they were placed, still showed all their wonted energy of body and mind, and maintained the same undaunted and resolute demeanour as before. They fiercely rejected all the overtures of Cortes, declaring they would rather die than surrender, and, adding with a bitter tone of exultation, that the invaders would be at least disappointed in their expectations of treasure, for it was buried where they could never find it!

Cortes had now entered one of the great avenues leading to the market-place of Tlatelolco, the quarter towards which the movements of Alvarado were also directed. A single canal only lay in his way, but this was of great width and stoutly defended by the Mexican archery. At this crisis, the army one evening, while in their intrenchments on the causeway, were surprised by an uncommon light, that arose from the huge teocalli in that part of the city, which, being at the north, was the most distant from their own position. This temple, dedicated to the dread war-god, was inferior only to the pyramid in the great square; and on it the Spaniards had more than once seen their unhappy countrymen led to slaughter. They now supposed that the enemy were employed in some of their diabolical ceremonies, when the flame, mounting higher and higher, showed that the sanctuaries themselves were on fire. A shout of exultation at the sight broke forth from the assembled soldiers, as they assured one another that their countrymen under Alvarado had got possession of the building.

It was indeed true. That gallant officer, whose position on the western causeway placed him near the district of Tlatelolco, had obeyed his commander's instructions to the letter, razing every building to the ground in his progress, and filling up the ditches with their ruins. He, at length, found himself before the great teocalli in the neighbourhood of the market. He ordered a company, under a cavalier named Gutierre de Badajoz, to storm the place, which was defended by a body of warriors, mingled with priests, still more wild and ferocious than the soldiery. The garrison, rushing down the winding terraces, fell on the assailants with such fury, as compelled them to retreat in confusion, and with some loss. Alvarado ordered another detachment to their support. This last was engaged, at the moment, with a body of Aztecs, who hung on its rear as it wound up the galleries of the teocalli. Thus hemmed in between two enemies, above and below, the position of the Spaniards was critical. With sword and buckler, they plunged desperately on the ascending Mexicans, and drove them into the courtyard below, where Alvarado plied them with such lively volleys of musketry, as soon threw them into disorder and compelled them to abandon the ground. Being thus rid of annoyance in the rear, the Spaniards returned to the charge. They drove the enemy up the heights of the pyramid, and, reaching the broad summit, a fierce encounter followed in mid-air — such an encounter as takes place where death is the certain consequence of defeat. It ended as usual, in the discomfiture of the Aztecs, who were either slaughtered on the spot still wet with the blood of their own victims, or pitched headlong down the sides of the pyramid.

The Spaniards completed their work by firing the sanctuaries, that the place might be no more polluted by these abominable rites. The flame crept slowly up the lofty pinnacles, in which stone was mingled with wood, till, at length, bursting into one bright blaze, it shot up its spiral volume to such a height, that it was seen from the most distant quarters of the valley. It was this which had been hailed by the soldiers of Cortes.

The commander-inchief and his division, animated by the spectacle, made, in their entrance on the following day, more determined efforts to place themselves alongside of their companions under Alvarado. The broad canal, above noticed as the only impediment now lying in his way, was to be traversed; and on the further side, the emaciated figures of the Aztec warriors were gathered in numbers to dispute the passage. They poured down a storm of missiles on the heads of the Indian labourers, while occupied with filling up the wide gap with the ruins of the surrounding buildings. Still they toiled on in defiance of the arrowy shower, fresh numbers taking the place of those who fell. And when at length the work was completed, the cavalry rode over the rough plain at full charge against the enemy, followed by the deep array of spearmen, who bore down all opposition with their invincible phalanx.

The Spaniards now found themselves on the same ground with Alvarado's division. Soon afterwards that chief, attended by several of his staff, rode into their lines, and cordially embraced his countrymen and companions in arms, for the first time since the beginning of the siege. They were now in the neighbourhood of the market. Cortes, taking with him a few of his cavaliers, galloped into it. It was a vast inclosure, as the reader has already seen, covering many an acre. The flat roofs of the piazzas were now covered with crowds of men and women, who gazed in silent dismay on the steel-clad horsemen, that profaned these precincts with their presence for the first time since their expulsion from the capital. The multitude, composed for the most part, probably, of unarmed citizens, seemed taken by surprise; at least, they made no show of resistance; and the general, after leisurely viewing the ground, was permitted to ride back unmolested to the army.

On arriving there, he ascended the teocalli, from which the standard of Castile, supplanting the memorials of Aztec superstition, was now triumphantly floating. The Conqueror, as he strode among the smoking embers on the summit, calmly surveyed the scene of desolation below. The palaces, the temples, the busy marts of industry and trade, the glittering canals, covered with their rich freights from the surrounding country, the royal pomp of groves and gardens, all the splendours of the imperial city, the capital of the Western World, for ever gone — and in their place a barren wilderness! How different the spectacle which the year before had met his eye, as it wandered over the scenes from the heights of the neighbouring teocalli, with Montezuma at his side! Seven-eighths of the city were laid in ruins, with the occasional exception, perhaps, of some colossal temple. The remaining eighth, comprehending the district of Tlatelolco, was all that now remained to the Aztecs, whose population — still large after all its losses — was crowded into a compass that would hardly have afforded accommodation for a third of their numbers.

THERE was no occasion to resort to artificial means to precipitate the ruin of the Azecs. It was accelerated every hour by causes more potent than those arising from mere human agency. There they were — pent up in their close and suffocating quarters, nobles, commoners, and slaves, men, women, and children, some in houses, more frequently in hovels — for this part of the city was not the best — others in the open air in canoes, or in the streets, shivering in the cold rains of night, and scorched by the burning heat of day. The ordinary means of sustaining life were long since gone. They wandered about in search of anything, however unwholesome or revolting, that might mitigate the fierce gnawings of hunger. Some hunted for insects and worms on the borders of the lake, or gathered the salt weeds and moss from its bottom, while at times they might be seen casting a wistful look at the hills beyond, which many of them had left to share the fate of their brethren in the capital.

To their credit, it is said by the Spanish writers, that they were not driven in their extremity to violate the laws of nature by feeding on one another. But unhappily this is contradicted by the Indian authorities, who state that many a mother, in her agony, devoured the offspring which she had no longer the means of supporting. This is recorded of more than one siege in history; and it is the more probable here, where the sensibilities must have been blunted by familiarity with the brutal practices of the national superstition.

But all was not sufficient, and hundreds of famished wretches died every day from extremity of suffering. Some dragged themselves into the houses, and drew their last breath alone, and in silence. Others sank down in the public streets. Wherever they died, there they were left. There was no one to bury or to remove them. Familiarity with the spectacle made men indifferent to it. They looked on in dumb despair, waiting for their own turn. There was no complaint, no lamentation, but deep, unutterable woe.

If in other quarters of the town the corpses might be seen scattered over the streets, here they were gathered in heaps. "They lay so thick," says Bernal Diaz, "that one could not tread except among the bodies." "A man could not set his foot down," says Cortes, yet more strongly, "unless on the corpse of an Indian!" They were piled one upon another, the living mingled with the dead. They stretched themselves on the bodies of their friends, and lay down to sleep there. Death was everywhere. The city was a vast charnel-house, in which all was hastening to decay and decomposition. A poisonous steam arose from the mass of putrefaction, under the action of alternate rain and heat, which so tainted the whole atmosphere, that the Spaniards, including the general himself, in their brief visits to the quarter, were made ill by it, and it bred a pestilence that swept off even greater numbers than the famine.

In the midst of these awful scenes, the young emperor of the Aztecs remained, according to all accounts, calm and courageous. With his fair capital laid in ruins before his eyes, his nobles and faithful subjects dying around him, his territory rent away, foot by foot, till scarce enough remained for him to stand on, he rejected every invitation to capitulate, and showed the same indomitable spirit as at the commencement of the siege. When Cortes, in the hope that the extremities of the besieged would incline them to listen to an accommodation, persuaded a noble prisoner to bear to Guatemozin his proposals to that effect, the fierce young monarch, according to the general, ordered him at once to be sacrificed. It is a Spaniard, we must remember, who tells the story.

Cortes, who had suspended hostilities for several days, in the vain hope that the distresses of the Mexicans would bend them to submission, now determined to drive them to it by a general assault. Cooped up, as they were, within a narrow quarter of the city, their position favoured such an attempt. He commanded Alvarado to hold himself in readiness, and directed Sandoval-who, besides the causeway, had charge of the fleet, which lay off the Tlatelolcan district — to support the attack by a cannonade on the houses near the water. He then led his forces into the city, or rather across the horrid waste that now encircled it.

On entering the Indian precincts, he was met by several of the chiefs, who, stretching forth their emaciated arms, exclaimed, "You are the children of the Sun. But the Sun is swift in his course. Why are you, then, so tardy? Why do you delay so long to put an end to our miseries? Rather kill us at once, that we may go to our god Huitzilopochtli, who waits for us in heaven to give us rest from our sufferings!"

Cortes was moved by their piteous appeal, and answered, that he desired not their death, but their submission. "Why does your master refuse to treat with me," he said, "when a single hour will suffice for me to crush him and all his people?" He then urged them to request Guatemozin to confer with him, with the assurance that he might do it in safety, as his person should not be molested.

The nobles, after some persuasion, undertook the mission; and it was received by the young monarch in a manner which showed — if the anecdote before related of him be true — that misfortune had, at length, asserted some power over his haughty spirit. He consented to the interview, though not to have it take place on that day, but the following, in the great square of Tlatelolco. Cortes, well satisfied, immediately withdrew from the city, and resumed his position on the causeway.

The next morning he presented himself at the place appointed, having previously stationed Alvarado there with a strong corps of infantry to guard against treachery. The stone platform in the centre of the square was covered with mats and carpets, and a banquet was prepared to refresh the famished monarch and his nobles. Having made these arrangements, he awaited the hour of the interview.

But Guatemozin, instead of appearing himself, sent his nobles, the same who had brought to him the general's invitation, and who now excused their master's absence on the plea of illness. Cortes, though disappointed, gave a courteous reception to the envoys, considering that it might still afford the means of opening a communication with the emperor. He persuaded them without much entreaty to partake of the good cheer spread before them, which they did with a voracity that told how severe had been their abstinence. He then dismissed them with a seasonable supply of provisions for their master, pressing him to consent to an interview, without which it was impossible their differences could be adjusted.

The Indian envoys returned in a short time, bearing with them a present of fine cotton fabrics, of no great value, from Guatemozin, who still declined to meet the Spanish general. Cortes, though deeply chagrined, was unwilling to give up the point. "He will surely come," he said to the envoys, "when he sees that I suffer you to go and come unharmed, you who have been my steady enemies, no less than himself, throughout the war. He has nothing to fear from me." He again parted with them, promising to receive their answer the following day.

On the next morning, the Aztec chiefs, entering the Christian quarters, announced to Cortes that Guatemozin would confer with him at noon in the market-place. The general was punctual at the hour; but without success. Neither monarch nor ministers appeared there. It was plain that the Indian prince did not care to trust the promises of his enemy. A thought of Montezuma may have passed across his mind. After he had waited three hours, the general's patience was exhausted, and, as he learned that the Mexicans were busy in preparations for defence, he made immediate dispositions for the assault.

The confederates had been left without the walls, for he did not care to bring them in sight of the quarry, before he was ready to slip the leash. He now ordered them to join him; and, supported by Alvarado's division, marched at once into the enemy's quarters. He found them prepared to receive him. Their most able-bodied warriors were thrown into the van, covering their feeble and crippled comrades. Women were seen occasionally mingling in the ranks, and, as well as children, thronged the azoteas, where, with famine-stricken visages and haggard eyes, they scowled defiance and hatred on their invaders.

As the Spaniards advanced, the Mexicans set up a fierce war-cry, and sent off clouds of arrows with their accustomed spirit, while the women and boys rained down darts and stones from their elevated position on the terraces. But the missiles were sent by hands too feeble to do much damage; and, when the squadrons closed, the loss of strength became still more sensible in the Aztecs. Their blows fell feebly and with doubtful aim; though some, it is true, of stronger constitution, or gathering strength from despair, maintained to the last a desperate fight.

The arquebusiers now poured in a deadly fire. The brigantines replied by successive volleys in the opposite quarter. The besieged, hemmed in, like deer surrounded by the huntsmen, were brought down on every side. The carnage was horrible. The ground was heaped up with slain, until the maddened combatants were obliged to climb over the human mounds to get at one another. The miry soil was saturated with blood, which ran off like water, and dyed the canals themselves with crimson. All was uproar and terrible confusion. The hideous yells of the barbarians; the oaths and execrations of the Spaniards; the cries of the wounded; the shrieks of women and children; the heavy blows of the Conquerors; the deathstruggle of their victims; the rapid, reverberating echoes of musketry; the hissing of innumerable missiles; the crash and crackling of blazing buildings, crushing hundreds in their ruins; the blinding volumes of dust and sulphurous smoke shrouding all in their gloomy canopy — made a scene appalling even to the soldiers of Cortes, steeled as they were by many a rough passage of war, and by long familiarity with blood and violence. "The piteous cries of the women and children, in particular," says the general, "were enough to break one's heart." He commanded that they should be spared, and that all, who asked it, should receive quarter. He particularly urged this on the confederates, and placed men among them to restrain their violence. But he had set an engine in motion too terrible to be controlled. It were as easy to curb the hurricane in its fury, as the passions of an infuriated horde of savages. "Never did I see so pitiless a race," he exclaims, "or any thing wearing the form of man so destitute of humanity." They made no distinction of sex or age, and in this hour of vengeance seemed to be requiting the hoarded wrongs of a century. At length, sated with slaughter, the Spanish commander sounded a retreat. It was full time, if, according to his own statement — we may hope it is an exaggeration — forty thousand souls had perished! Yet their fate was to be envied, in comparison with that of those who survived.

Through the long night which followed, no movement was perceptible in the Aztec quarter. No light was seen there, no sound was heard, save the low moaning of some wounded or dying wretch, writhing in his agony. All was dark and silent — the darkness of the grave. The last blow seemed to have completely stunned them. They had parted with hope, and sat in sullen despair, like men waiting in silence the stroke of the executioner. Yet, for all this, they showed no disposition to submit. Every new injury had sunk deeper into their souls, and filled them with a deeper hatred of their enemy. Fortune, friends, kindred, home — all were gone. They were content to throw away life itself, now that they had nothing more to live for.

Far different was the scene in the Christian camp, where, elated with their recent successes, all was alive with bustle, and preparation for the morrow. Bonfires were seen blazing along the causeways, lights gleamed from tents and barracks, and the sounds of music and merriment, borne over the waters, proclaimed the joy of the soldiers at the prospect of so soon terminating their wearisome campaign.

On the following morning the Spanish commander again mustered his forces, having decided to follow up the blow of the preceding day before the enemy should have time to rally, and at once to put an end to the war. He had arranged with Alvarado, on the evening previous, to occupy the market-place of Tlatelolco; and the discharge of an arquebuse was to be the signal for a simultaneous assault. Sandoval was to hold the northern causeway, and, with the fleet, to watch the movements of the Indian emperor, and to intercept the flight to the main land, which Cortes knew he meditated. To allow him to effect this, would be to leave a formidable enemy in his own neighbourhood, who might at any time kindle the flame of insurrection throughout the country. He ordered Sandoval, however, to do no harm to the royal person, and not to fire on the enemy at all, except in self-defence.

It was on the memorable 13th of August, 1521, that Cortes led his warlike array for the last time across the black and blasted environs which lay around the Indian capital. On entering the Aztec precincts, he paused, willing to afford its wretched inmates one more chance of escape, before striking the fatal blow. He obtained an interview with some of the principal chiefs, and expostulated with them on the conduct of their prince. "He surely will not," said the general, "see you all perish, when he can so easily save you." He then urged them to prevail on Guatemozin to hold a conference with him, repeating the assurances of his personal safety.

The messengers went on their mission, and soon returned with the cihuacoatl at their head, a magistrate of high authority among the Mexicans. He said, with a melancholy air, in which his own disappointment was visible, that "Guatemozin was ready to die where he was, but would hold no interview with the Spanish commander"; adding in a tone of resignation, "It is for you to work your Pleasure." "Go, then," replied the stern Conqueror, "and prepare your countrymen for death. Their hour is come."

He still postponed the assault for several hours. But the impatience of his troops at this delay was heightened by the rumor that Guatemozin and his nobles were preparing to escape with their effects in the piraguas and canoes which were moored on the margin of the lake. Convinced of the fruitlessness and impolicy of further procrastination, Cortes made his final dispositions for the attack, and took his own station on an azotea, which commanded the theatre of operations.

When the assailants came into presence of the enemy, they found them huddled together in the utmost confusion, all ages and sexes, in masses so dense that they nearly forced one another over the brink of the causeways into the water below. Some had climbed on the terraces, others feebly supported themselves against the wars of the buildings. Their squalid and tattered garments gave a wildness to their appearance, which still further heightened the ferocity of their expressions, as they glared on their enemy with eyes in which hate was mingled with despair. When the Spaniards had approached within bowshot, the Aztecs let off a flight of impotent missiles, showing to the last the resolute spirit, though they had lost the strength, of their better days. The fatal signal was then given by the discharge of an arquebuse — speedily followed by peals of heavy ordnance, the rattle of firearms, and the hellish shouts of the confederates, as they sprang upon their victims. It is unnecessary to stain the page with a repetition of the horrors of the preceding day. Some of the wretched Aztecs threw themselves into the water, and were picked up by the canoes. Others sunk and were suffocated in the canals. The number of these became so great, that a bridge was made of their dead bodies, over which the assailants could climb to the opposite banks. Others again, especially the women, begged for mercy, which, as the chroniclers assure us, was everywhere granted by the Spaniards, and, contrary to the instructions and entreaties of Cortes, everywhere refused by the confederates.

While this work of butchery was going on, numbers were observed pushing off in the barks that lined the shore, and making the best of their way across the lake. They were constantly intercepted by the brigantines, which broke through the flimsy array of boats; sending off their volleys to the right and left, as the crews of the latter hotly assailed them. The battle raged as fiercely on the lake as on the land. Many of the Indian vessels were shattered and overturned. Some few, however, under cover of the smoke, which rolled darkly over the waters, succeeded in clearing themselves of the turmoil, and were fast nearing the opposite shore.

Sandoval had particularly charged his captains to keep an eye on the movements of any vessel in which it was at all probable that Guatemozin might be concealed. At this crisis, three or four of the largest piraguas were seen skimming over the water, and making their way rapidly across the lake. A captain named Garci Holguin, who had command of one of the best sailers in the fleet, instantly gave them chase. The wind was favourable, and every moment he gained on the fugitives, who pulled their oars with a vigour that despair alone could have given. But it was in vain; and, after a short race, Holguin, coming alongside of one of the piraguas, which, whether from its appearance, or from information he had received, he conjectured might bear the Indian emperor, ordered his men to level their crossbows at the boat. But, before they could discharge them, a cry arose from those on it, that their lord was on board. At the same moment, a young warrior, armed with buckler and maquahuitl, rose up, as if to beat off the assailants. But, as the Spanish captain ordered his men not to shoot, he dropped his weapons, and exclaimed, "I am Guatemozin; lead me to Malinche, I am his prisoner; but let no harm come to my wife and my followers."

Holguin assured him that his wishes should be respected, and assisted him to get on board the brigantine, followed by his wife and attendants. These were twenty in number, consisting of Coanaco, the deposed lord of Tezcuco, the lord of Tlacopan, and several other caciques and dignitaries, whose rank, probably, had secured them some exemption from the general calamities of the siege. When the captives were seated on the deck of his vessel, Holguin requested the Aztec prince to put an end to the combat by commanding his people in the other canoes to surrender. But, with a dejected air, he replied, "It is not necessary. They will fight no longer, when they see that their prince is taken." He spoke truth. The news of Guatemozin's capture spread rapidly through the fleet, and on shore, where the Mexicans were still engaged in conflict with their enemies. It ceased, however, at once. They made no further resistance; and those on the water quickly followed the brigantines, which conveyed their captive monarch to land.

Meanwhile Sandoval, on receiving tidings of the capture, brought his own brigantine alongside of Holguin's, and demanded the royal prisoner to be surrendered to him. But his captain claimed him as his prize. A dispute arose between the parties, each anxious to have the glory of the deed, and perhaps the privilege of commemorating it on his escutcheon. The controversy continued so long that it reached the ears of Cortes, who, in his station on the azotea, had learned, with no little satisfaction, the capture of his enemy. He instantly sent orders to his wrangling officers to bring Guatemozin before him, that he might adjust the difference between them. He charged them, at the same time, to treat their prisoner with respect. He then made preparations for the interview; caused the terrace to be carpeted with crimson cloth and matting, and a table to be spread with provisions, of which the unhappy Aztecs stood so much in need. His lovely Indian mistress, Dona Marina, was present to act as interpreter. She had stood by his side through all the troubled scenes of the Conquest, and she was there now to witness its triumphant termination.

Guatemozin, on landing, was escorted by a company of infantry to the presence of the Spanish commander. He mounted the azotea with a calm and steady step, and was easily to be distinguished from his attendant nobles, though his full, dark eye was no longer lighted up with its accustomed fire, and his features wore an expression of passive resignation, that told little of the fierce and fiery spirit that burned within. His head was large, his limbs well proportioned, his complexion fairer than those of his bronze-coloured nation, and his whole deportment singularly mild and engaging.

Cortes came forward with a dignified and studied courtesy to receive him. The Aztec monarch probably knew the person of his conqueror, for he first broke silence by saying, "I have done all that I could, to defend myself and my people. I am now reduced to this state. You will deal with me, Malinche, as you list." Then, laying his hand on the hilt of a poniard, stuck in the general's belt, he added, with vehemence, "Better despatch me with this, and rid me of life at once." Cortes was filled with admiration at the proud bearing of the young barbarian, showing in his reverses a spirit worthy of an ancient Roman. "Fear not," he replied, "you shall be treated with all honour. You have defended your capital like a brave warrior. A Spaniard knows how to respect valour even in an enemy." He then inquired of him, where he had left the princess, his wife; and, being informed that she still remained under protection of a Spanish guard on board the brigantine, the general sent to have her escorted to his presence.

She was the youngest daughter of Montezuma; and was hardly yet on the verge of womanhood. On the accession of her cousin, Guatemozin, to the throne, she had been wedded to him as his lawful wife. She was kindly received by Cortes, who showed her the respectful attentions suited to her rank. Her birth, no doubt, gave her an additional interest in his eyes, and he may have felt some touch of compunction, as he gazed on the daughter of the unfortunate Montezuma. He invited his royal captives to partake of the refreshments which their exhausted condition rendered so necessary. Meanwhile the Spanish commander made his dispositions for the night, ordering Sandoval to escort the prisoners to Cojohuacan, whither he proposed himself immediately to follow. The other captains, and Alvarado, were to draw off their forces to their respective quarters. It was impossible for them to continue in the capital, where the poisonous effluvia from the unburied carcasses loaded the air with infection. A small guard only was stationed to keep order in the wasted suburbs. — It was the hour of vespers when Guatemozin surrendered, and the siege might be considered as then concluded.

Thus, after a siege of nearly three months' duration, unmatched in history for the constancy and courage of the besieged, seldom surpassed for the severity of its sufferings, fell the renowned capital of the Aztecs. Unmatched, it may be truly said, for constancy and courage, when we recollect that the door of capitulation on the most honourable terms was left open to them throughout the whole blockade, and that, sternly rejecting every proposal of their enemy, they, to a man, preferred to die rather than surrender. More than three centuries had elapsed since the Aztecs, a poor and wandering tribe from the far north-west, had come on the plateau. There they built their miserable collection of huts on the spot — as tradition tells us — prescribed by the oracle. Their conquests, at first confined to their immediate neighbourhood, gradually covered the valley, then crossing the mountains, swept over the broad extent of the tableland, descended its precipitous sides, and rolled onwards to the Mexican Gulf, and the distant confines of Central America. Their wretched capital, meanwhile, keeping pace with the enlargement of territory, had grown into a flourishing city, filled with buildings, monuments of art, and a numerous population, that gave it the first rank among the capitals of the Western World. At this crisis, came over another race from the remote East, strangers like themselves, whose coming had also been predicted by the oracle, and, appearing on the plateau, assailed them in the very zenith of their prosperity, and blotted them out from the map of nations for ever! The whole story has the air of fable rather than of history! a legend of romance — a tale of the genii!

Yet we cannot regret the fall of an empire which did so little to promote the happiness of its subjects, or the real interests of humanity. Notwithstanding the lustre thrown over its latter days by the glorious defence of its capital, by the mild munificence of Montezuma, by the dauntless heroism of Guatemozin, the Aztecs were emphatically a fierce and brutal race, little calculated, in their best aspects, to excite our sympathy and regard. Their civilisation, such as it was, was not their own, but reflected, perhaps imperfectly, from a race whom they had succeeded in the land. It was, in respect to the Aztecs, a generous graft on a vicious stock, and could have brought no fruit to perfection. They ruled over their wide domains with a sword, instead of a sceptre. They did nothing to ameliorate the condition, or in any way promote the progress, of their vassals. Their vassals were serfs, used only to minister to their pleasure, held in awe by armed garrisons, ground to the dust by imposts in peace, by military conscriptions in war. They did not, like the Romans, whom they resembled in the nature of their conquests, extend the rights of citizenship to the conquered. They did not amalgamate them into one great nation, with common rights and interests. They held them as aliens — even those who in the valley were gathered round the very walls of the capital. The Aztec metropolis, the heart of the monarchy, had not a sympathy, not a pulsation, in common with the rest of the body politic. It was a stranger in its own land.

The Aztecs not only did not advance the condition of their vassals, but morally speaking, they did much to degrade it. How can a nation, where human sacrifices prevail, and especially when combined with cannibalism, further the march of civilisation? How can the interests of humanity be consulted where man is levelled to the rank of the brutes that perish? The influence of the Aztecs introduced their gloomy superstition into lands before unacquainted with it, or where, at least, it was not established in any great strength. The example of the capital was contagious. As the latter increased in opulence, the religious celebrations were conducted with still more terrible magnificence. In the same manner as the gladiatorial shows of the Romans increased in pomp with the increasing splendour of the capital, men became familiar with scenes of horror and the most loathsome abominations; women and children — the whole nation became familiar with, and assisted at them. The heart was hardened, the manners were made ferocious, the feeble light of civilisation, transmitted from a milder race, was growing fainter and fainter, as thousands and thousands of miserable victims throughout the empire were yearly fattened in its cages, sacrificed on its altars, dressed and served at its banquets! The whole land was converted into a vast human shambles! The empire of the Aztecs did not fall before its time.

Whether these unparalleled outrages furnish a sufficient plea to the Spaniards for their invasion, whether, with the Protestant, we are content to find a warrant for it in the natural rights and demands of civilisation, or, with the Roman Catholic, in the good pleasure of the

Pope — on the one or other of which grounds, the conquests by most Christian nations in the East and the West have been defended — it is unnecessary to discuss, as it has already been considered in a former chapter. It is more material to inquire, whether, assuming the right, the conquest of Mexico was conducted with a proper regard to the claims of humanity. And here we must admit that, with all allowance for the ferocity of the age and the laxity of its principles, there are passages which every Spaniard, who cherishes the fame of his countrymen, would be glad to see expunged from their history; passages not to be vindicated on the score of self-defence, or of necessity of any kind, and which must forever leave a dark spot on the annals of the Conquest. And yet, taken as a whole, the invasion, up to the capture of the capital, was conducted on principles less revolting to humanity than most, perhaps than any, of the other conquests of the Castilian crown in the New World.

It may seem slight praise to say that the followers of Cortes used no blood-hounds to hunt down their wretched victims, as in some other parts of the continent, nor exterminated a peaceful and submissive population in mere wantonness of cruelty, as in the Islands. Yet it is something that they were not so far infected by the spirit of the age, and that their swords were rarely stained with blood unless it was indispensable to the success of their enterprise. Even in the last siege of the capital, the sufferings of the Aztecs, terrible as they were, do not imply any unusual cruelty in the victors; they were not greater than those inflicted on their own countrymen at home, in many a memorable instance, by the most polished nations, not merely of ancient times but of our own. They were the inevitable consequences which follow from war, when, instead of being confined to its legitimate field, it is brought home to the hearthstone, to the peaceful community of the city — its burghers untrained to arms, its women and children yet more defenceless. In the present instance, indeed, the sufferings of the besieged were in a great degree to be charged on themselves — on their patriotic, but desperate, self-devotion. It was not the desire, as certainly it was not the interest, of the Spaniards to destroy the capital, or its inhabitants. When any of these fell into their hands, they were kindly entertained, their wants supplied, and every means taken to infuse into them a spirit of conciliation; and this, too, it should be remembered, in despite of the dreadful doom to which they consigned their Christian captives. The gates of a fair capitulation were kept open, though unavailingly, to the last hour.

The right of conquest necessarily implies that of using whatever force may be necessary for overcoming resistance to the assertion of that right. For the Spaniards to have done otherwise than they did, would have been to abandon the siege, and, with it, the conquest of the country. To have suffered the inhabitants, with their high-spirited monarch, to escape, would but have prolonged the miseries of war by transferring it to another and more inaccessible quarter. They literally, as far as the success of the expedition was concerned, had no choice. If our imagination is struck with the amount of suffering in this, and in similar scenes of the Conquest, it should be borne in mind, that it is a natural result of the great masses of men engaged in the conflict. The amount of suffering does not in itself show the amount of cruelty which caused it; and it is but justice to the Conquerors of Mexico to say that the very brilliancy and importance of their exploits have given a melancholy celebrity to their misdeeds, and thrown them into somewhat bolder relief than strictly belongs to them. It is proper that thus much should be stated, not to excuse their excesses, but that we may be enabled to make a more impartial estimate of their conduct, as compared with that of other nations under similar circumstances, and that we may not visit them with peculiar obloquy for evils which necessarily flow from the condition of war.

Whatever may be thought of the Conquest in a moral view, regarded as a military achievement, it must fill us with astonishment. That a handful of adventurers, indifferently armed and equipped, should have landed on the shores of a powerful empire, inhabited by a fierce and warlike race, and in defiance of the reiterated prohibitions of its sovereign, have forced their way into the interior; — that they should have done this, without knowledge of the language or the land, without chart or compass to guide them, without any idea of the difficulties they were to encounter, totally uncertain whether the next step might bring them on a hostile nation, or on a desert, feeling their way along in the dark, as it were; — that though nearly overwhelmed by their first encounter with the inhabitants, they should have still pressed on to the capital of the empire, and, having reached it, thrown themselves unhesitatingly into the midst of their enemies; — that, so far from being daunted by the extraordinary spectacle there exhibited of power and civilisation, they should have been but the more confirmed in their original design; — that they should have seized the monarch, have executed his ministers before the eyes of his subjects, and, when driven forth with ruin from the gates, have gathered their scattered wreck together, and, after a system of operations pursued with consummate policy and daring, have succeeded in overturning the capital, and establishing their sway over the country; — that all this should have been so effected by a mere handful of indigent adventurers, is in fact little short of the miraculous, too startling for the probabilities demanded by fiction, and without a parallel in the pages of history.

Yet this must not be understood too literally; for it would be unjust to the Aztecs themselves, at least to their military prowess, to regard the Conquest as directly achieved by the Spaniards alone. The Indian empire was in a manner conquered by Indians. The Aztec monarchy fell by the hands of its own subjects, under the direction of European sagacity and science. Had it been united, it might have bidden defiance to the invaders. As it was, the capital was dissevered from the rest of the country; and the bolt, which might have passed off comparatively harmless, had the empire been cemented by a common principle of loyalty and patriotism, now found its way into every crack and crevice of the ill-compacted fabric, and buried it in its own ruins. Its fate may serve as a striking proof, that a government, which does not rest on the sympathies of its subjects, cannot long abide; that human institutions, when not connected with human prosperity and progress, must fall, if not before the increasing light of civilisation, by the hand of violence; by violence from within, if not from without. And who shall lament their fall?

BOOK 7. CONCLUSION. SUBSEQUENT CAREER OF CORTES

THE history of the Conquest of Mexico terminates with the surrender of the capital. But the history of the Conquest is so intimately blended with that of the extraordinary man who achieved it, that there would seem to be an incompleteness in the narrative, if it were not continued to the close of his personal career.

The first ebullition of triumph was succeeded in the army by very different feelings, as they beheld the scanty spoil gleaned from the conquered city, and as they brooded over the inadequate compensation they were to receive for all their toils and sufferings. Some of the soldiers of Narvaez, with feelings of bitter disappointment, absolutely declined to accept their shares. Some murmured audibly against the general, and others against Guatemozin, who, they said, could reveal, if he chose, the place where the treasures were secreted. The white walls of the barracks were covered with epigrams and pasquinades levelled at Cortes, whom they accused of taking "one fifth of the booty as Commander-inchief, and another fifth as King." As Guatemozin refused to make any revelation in respect to the treasure, or rather declared there was none to make, the soldiers loudly insisted on his being put to the torture. But for this act of violence, so contrary to the promise of protection recently made to the Indian prince, Cortes was not prepared; and he resisted the demand, until the men, instigated, it is said, by the royal treasurer, Alderete, accused the general of a secret understanding with Guatemozin, and of a design to defraud the Spanish sovereigns and themselves. These unmerited taunts stung Cortes to the quick, and in an evil hour he delivered the Aztec prince into the hands of his enemies to work their pleasure on him.

But the hero, who had braved death in its most awful forms, was not to be intimidated by bodily suffering. When his companion, the cacique of Tacuba, who was put to the torture with him, testified his anguish by his groans, Guatemozin coldly rebuked him by exclaiming, "And do you think I, then, am taking my pleasure in my bath?" At length Cortes, ashamed of the base part he was led to play, rescued the Aztec prince from his tormentors before it was too late; — not, however, before it was too late for his own honour, which has suffered an indelible stain from this treatment of his royal prisoner.

All that could be wrung from Guatemozin by the extremity of his sufferings was the confession that much gold had been thrown into the water. But, although the best divers were employed, under the eye of Cortes himself, to search the oozy bed of the lake, only a few articles of inconsiderable value were drawn from it. They had better fortune in searching a pond in Guatemozin's gardens, where a sun, as it is called, probably one of the Aztec calendarwheels, made of pure gold, of great size and thickness, was discovered.

The tidings of the fall of Mexico were borne on the wings of the wind over the plateau, and down the broad sides of the Cordilleras. Many an envoy made his appearance from the remote Indian tribes, anxious to learn the truth of the astounding intelligence, and to gaze with their own eyes on the ruins of the detested city. Among these were ambassadors from the kingdom of Mechoacan, a powerful and independent state, inhabited by one of the kindred Nahuatlac races, and lying between the Mexican Valley and the Pacific. His example was followed by ambassadors from the remote regions which had never yet had intercourse with the Spaniards. Cortes, who saw the boundaries of his empire thus rapidly enlarging, availed himself of the favourable dispositions of the natives to ascertain the products and resources of their several countries.

Two small detachments were sent into the friendly state of Mechoacan, through which country they penetrated to the borders of the great Southern Ocean. No European had as yet descended on its shores so far north of the equator. The Spaniards eagerly advanced into its waters, erected a cross on the sandy margin, and took possession of it, with all the usual formalities, in the name of their Most Catholic Majesties. On their return, they visited some of the rich districts towards the north, since celebrated for their mineral treasures, and brought back samples of gold and Californian pearls, with an account of their discovery of the Ocean. The imagination of Cortes was kindled, and his soul swelled with exultation at the splendid prospects which their discoveries unfolded. "Most of all," he writes to the emperor, "do I exult in the tidings brought me of the great Ocean. For in it, as cosmographers, and those learned men who know most about the Indies, inform us, are scattered the rich isles teeming with gold and spices and precious stones." He at once sought a favourable spot for a colony on the shores of the Pacific, and made arrangements for the construction of four vessels to explore the mysteries of these unknown seas. This was the beginning of his noble enterprises for discovery in the Gulf of California.

Although the greater part of Anahuac, overawed by the successes of the Spaniards, had tendered their allegiance, there were some, especially on the southern slopes of the Cordilleras, who showed a less submissive disposition. Cortes instantly sent out strong detachments under Sandoval and Alvarado to reduce the enemy and establish colonies in the conquered provinces. The highly coloured reports which Alvarado, who had a quick scent for gold, gave of the mineral wealth of Oaxaca, no doubt operated with Cortes in determining him to select this region for his own particular domain.

Cortes did not immediately decide in what quarter of the valley to establish the new capital which was to take the place of the ancient Tenochtitlan. The situation of the latter, surrounded by water and exposed to occasional inundations, had some obvious disadvantages. But there was no doubt that in some part of the elevated and central plateau of the valley the new metropolis should be built, to which both European and Indian might look up as to the head of the colonial empire of Spain. At length he decided on retaining the site of the ancient city, moved to it, as he says, "by its past renown, and the memory"— not an enviable one, surely — "in which it was held among the nations"; and he made preparations for the reconstruction of the capital which should, in his own language, "raise her to the rank of Queen of the surrounding provinces, in the same manner as she had been of yore."

The labour was to be performed by the Indian population, drawn from all quarters of the valley, and including the Mexicans themselves, great numbers of whom still lingered in the neighbourhood of their ancient residence. At first they showed reluctance, and even symptoms of hostility, when called to this work of humiliation by their conquerors. But Cortes had the address to secure some of the principal chiefs in his interests, and, under their authority and direction, the labour of their countrymen was conducted. The deep groves of the valley and the forests of the neighbouring hills supplied cedar, cypress, and other durable woods, for the interior of the buildings, and the quarries of tetzontli and the ruins of the ancient edifices furnished abundance of stone. As there were no beasts of draught employed by the Aztecs, an immense number of hands was necessarily required for the work. All within the immediate control of Cortes were pressed into the service. The spot so recently deserted now swarmed with multitudes of Indians of various tribes, and with Europeans, the latter directing, while the others laboured. The prophecy of the Aztecs was accomplished. The work of reconstruction went forward rapidly.

Yet the condition of Cortes, notwithstanding the success of his arms, suggested many causes of anxiety. He had not received a word of encouragement from home — not a word, indeed, of encouragement or censure. In what light his irregular course was regarded by the government or the nation was still matter of painful uncertainty. He now prepared another letter to the emperor, the third in the published series, written in the same simple and energetic style which has entitled his Commentaries, as they may be called, to a comparison with those of Caesar. It was dated at Cojohuacan, 15th of May, 1522; and in it he recapitulated the events of the final siege of the capital, and his subsequent operations, accompanied by many sagacious reflections, as usual, on the character and resources of the country. With this letter he purposed to send the royal fifth of the spoils of Mexico, and a rich collection of fabrics, especially of gold and jewellery wrought into many rare and fanciful forms. One of the jewels was an emerald, cut in a pyramidal shape, of so extraordinary a size, that the base was as broad as the palm of the hand! The collection was still further augmented by specimens of many of the natural products, as well as of animals peculiar to the country.

The army wrote a letter to accompany that of Cortes, in which they expatiated on his manifold services, and besought the emperor to ratify his proceedings and confirm him in his present authority. The important mission was intrusted to two of the general's confidential officers, Quinones and Avila. It proved to be unfortunate. The agents touched at the Azores, where Quinones lost his life in a brawl. Avila, resuming his voyage, was captured by a French privateer, and the rich spoils of the Aztecs went into the treasury of his Most Christian Majesty. Francis the First gazed with pardonable envy on the treasures which his imperial rival drew from his colonial domains; and he intimated his discontent by peevishly expressing a desire "to see the clause in Adam's testament which entitled his brothers of Castile and Portugal to divide the New World between them." Avila found means, through a private hand, of transmitting his letters, the most important part of his charge, to Spain, where they reached the court in safety.

While these events were passing, affairs in Spain had been taking an unfavourable turn for Cortes. It may seem strange, that the brilliant exploits of the Conqueror of Mexico should have attracted so little notice from the government at home. But the country was at that time distracted by the dismal feuds of the comunidades. The sovereign was in Germany, too much engrossed by the cares of the empire to allow leisure for those of his own kingdom. The reins of government were in the hands of Adrian, Charles's preceptor; a man whose ascetic and studious habits better qualified him to preside over a college of monks, than to fill, as he successively did, the most important posts in Christendom — first as Regent of Castile, afterwards as Head of the Church. Yet the slow and hesitating Adrian could not have so long passed over in silence the important services of Cortes, but for the hostile interference of Velasquez, the governor of Cuba, sustained by Fonseca, Bishop of Burgos, the chief person in the Spanish colonial department. This prelate, from his elevated station, possessed paramount authority in all matters relating to the Indies, and he had exerted it from the first, as we have already seen, in a manner most prejudicial to the interests of Cortes. He had now the address to obtain a warrant from the regent which was designed to ruin the Conqueror at the very moment when his great enterprise had been crowned with success. The instrument, after recapitulating the offences of Cortes, in regard to Velasquez, appoints a commisioner with full powers to visit the country, to institute an inquiry into the general's conduct, to suspend him from his functions, and even to seize his person and sequestrate his property, until the pleasure of the Castilian court could be known. The warrant was signed by Adrian, at Burgos, on the 11th of April, 1521, and countersigned by Fonseca.

The individual selected for the delicate task of apprehending Cortes, and bringing him to trial, on the theatre of his own discoveries and in the heart of his own camp, was named Christoval de Tapia, veedor, or inspector of the gold foundries in St. Domingo. He was a feeble, vacillating man, as little competent to cope with Cortes's in civil matters, as Narvaez had shown himself to be in military.

The commissioner, clothed in his brief authority, landed in December, at Villa Rica. But he was coldly received by the magistrates of the city. His credentials were disputed, on the ground of some technical informality. It was objected, moreover, that his commission was founded on obvious misrepresentations to the government; and, notwithstanding a most courteous and complimentary epistle which he received from Cortes, congratulating him, as old friend, on his arrival, the veedor soon found that he was neither to be permitted to penetrate far into the country, nor to exercise any control there. He loved money, and, as Cortes knew the weak side of his "old friend," he proposed to purchase his horses, slaves, and equipage, at a tempting price. The dreams of disappointed ambition were gradually succeeded by those of avarice; and the discomfited commissioner consented to re-embark for Cuba, well freighted with gold if not with glory.

Thus left in undisputed possession of authority, the Spanish commander went forward with vigour in his plans for the settlement of his conquests. The Panuchese, a fierce people, on the borders of the Panuco, on the Atlantic coast, had taken up arms against the Spaniards. Cortes marched at the head of a considerable force into their country, defeated them in two pitched battles, and after a severe campaign, reduced the warlike tribe to subjection.

During this interval, the great question in respect to Cortes and the colony had been brought to a decisive issue. The general must have succumbed under the insidious and implacable attacks of his enemies, but for the sturdy opposition of a few powerful friends zealously devoted to his interests. Among them may be mentioned his own father, Don Martin Cortes, a discreet and efficient person, and the Duke de Bejar, a powerful nobleman, who from an early period had warmly espoused the cause of Cortes. By their representations the timid regent was at length convinced that the measures of Fonseca were prejudicial to the interests of the crown, and an order was issued interdicting him from further interference in any matters in which Cortes was concerned.

While the exasperated prelate was chafing under this affront, both the commissioners Tapia and Narvaez arrived in Castile. The latter had been ordered to Cojohuacan after the surrender of the capital, where his cringing demeanour formed a striking contrast to the swaggering port which he had assumed on first entering the country. When brought into the presence of Cortes, he knelt down and would have kissed his hand, but the latter raised him from the ground, and, during his residence in his quarters, treated him with every mark of respect. The general soon afterwards permitted his unfortunate rival to return to Spain, where he proved, as might have been anticipated, a most bitter and implacable enemy.

These two personages, reinforced by the discontented prelate, brought forward their several charges against Cortes with all the acrimony which mortified vanity and the thirst of vengeance could inspire. Adrian was no longer in Spain, having been called to the chair of St. Peter; but Charles the Fifth, after his long absence, had returned to his dominions, in July, 1522. The royal ear was instantly assailed with accusations of Cortes on the one hand and his vindication on the other, till the young monarch, perplexed, and unable to decide on the merits of the question, referred the whole subject to the decision of a board selected for the purpose. It was drawn partly from the members of his privy council, and partly from the Indian department, with the Grand Chancellor of Naples as its president; and constituted altogether a tribunal of the highest respectability for integrity and wisdom.

By this learned body a patient and temperate hearing was given to the parties. The enemies of Cortes accused him of having seized and finally destroyed the fleet intrusted to him by Velasquez, and fitted out at the governor's expense; of having afterwards usurped powers in contempt of the royal prerogative; of the unjustifiable treatment of Narvaez and Tapia, when they had been lawfully commissioned to supersede him; of cruelty to the natives, and especially to Guatemozin; of embezzling the royal treasures, and remitting but a small part of its dues to the crown; of squandering the revenues of the conquered countries in useless and wasteful schemes, and particularly in rebuilding the capital on a plan of unprecedented extravagance; of pursuing, in short, a system of violence and extortion, without respect to the public interest, or any other end than his own selfish aggrandisement.

In answer to these grave charges, the friends of Cortes adduced evidence to show that he had defrayed with his own funds two-thirds of the cost of the expedition. The powers of Velasquez extended only to traffic, not to establish a colony. Yet the interests of the crown required the latter. The army had therefore necessarily assumed this power to themselves; but, having done so, they had sent intelligence of their proceedings to the emperor and solicited his confirmation of them. The rupture with Narvaez was that commander's own fault, since Cortes would have met him amicably, had not the violent measures of his rival, threatening the ruin of the expedition, compelled him to an opposite course. The treatment of Tapia was vindicated on the grounds alleged to that officer by the municipality at Cempoalla. The violence to Guatemozin was laid at the door of Alderete, the royal treasurer, who had instigated the soldiers to demand it. The remittances to the crown, it was clearly proved, so far from falling short of the legitimate fifth, had considerably exceeded it. If the general had expended the revenues of the country on costly enterprises and public works, it was for the interest of the country that he did so, and he had incurred a heavy debt by straining his own credit to the utmost for the same great objects. Neither did they deny, that, in the same spirit, he was now rebuilding Mexico on a scale which should be suited to the metropolis of a vast and opulent empire.

They enlarged on the opposition he had experienced, throughout his whole career, from the governor of Cuba, and still more from the Bishop of Burgos, which latter functionary, instead of affording him the aid to have been expected, had discouraged recruits, stopped his supplies, sequestered such property as, from time to time, he had sent to Spain, and falsely represented his remittances to the crown, as coming from the governor of Cuba. In short, such and so numerous were the obstacles thrown in his path, that Cortes had been heard to say, "he had found it more difficult to contend against his own countrymen than against the Aztecs." They concluded with expatiating on the brilliant results of his expedition, and asked if the council were prepared to dishonour the man who, in the face of such obstacles, and with scarcely other resources than what he found in himself, had won an empire for Castile, such as was possessed by no European potentate!

This last appeal was irresistible. However irregular had been the manner of proceeding, no one could deny the grandeur of the results. There was not a Spaniard that could be insensible to such services, or that would not have cried out "Shame!" at an ungenerous requital of them. There were three Flemings in the council; but there seems to have been no difference of opinion in the body. It was decided, that neither Velasquez nor Fonseca should interfere further in the concerns of New Spain. The difficulties of the former with Cortes were regarded in the nature of a private suit; and, as such, redress must be sought by the regular course of law. The acts of Cortes were confirmed in their full extent. He was constituted Governor, Captain General, and Chief justice of New Spain, with power to appoint to all offices, civil and military, and to order any person to leave the country whose residence there he might deem prejudicial to the interests of the crown. This judgment of the council was ratified by Charles the Fifth, and the commission investing Cortes with these ample powers was signed by the emperor at Valladolid, 15th of October, 1522. A liberal salary was provided, to enable the governor of New Spain to maintain his office with suitable dignity. The principal officers were recompensed with honours and substantial emoluments; and the troops, together with some privileges, grateful to the vanity of the soldier, received the promise of liberal grants of land. The emperor still further complimented them by a letter written to the army with his own hand, in which he acknowledged its services in the fullest manner.

IN less than four years from the destruction of Mexico, a new city had risen on its ruins, which, if inferior to the ancient capital in extent, surpassed it in magnificence and strength. It occupied so exactly the same site as its predecessor that the plaza mayor, or great square, was the same spot which had been covered by the huge teocalli and the palace of Montezuma; while the principal streets took their departure as before from this central point, and passing through the whole length of the city, terminated at the principal causeways. Great alteration, however, took place in the fashion of the architecture. The streets were widened, many of the canals were filled up, and the edifices were constructed on a plan better accommodated to European taste and the wants of a European population.

On the site of the temple of the Aztec war-god rose the stately cathedral dedicated to St. Francis; and, as if to complete the triumphs of the Cross, the foundations were laid with the broken images of the Aztec gods. In a corner of the square, on the ground once covered by the House of Birds, stood a Franciscan convent, a magnificent pile, erected a few years after the Conquest by a lay brother, Pedro de Gante, a natural son, it is said, of Charles the Fifth. In an opposite quarter of the same square, Cortes caused his own palace to be constructed. It was built of hewn stone, and seven thousand cedar beams are said to have been used for the interior. The government afterwards appropriated it to the residence of the viceroys; and the Conqueror's descendants, the Dukes of Monteleone, were allowed to erect a new mansion in another part of the plaza, on the spot which, by an ominous coincidence, had been covered by the palace of Montezuma.

The general's next care was to provide a population for the capital. He invited the Spaniards thither by grants of lands and houses, while the Indians, with politic liberality, were permitted to live under their own chiefs as before, and to enjoy various immunities. With this encouragement, the Spanish quarter of the city in the neighbourhood of the great square could boast in a few years two thousand families; while the Indian district of Tlatelolco included no less than thirty thousand. The various trades and occupations were resumed; the canals were again covered with barges; two vast markets in the respective quarters of the capital displayed all the different products and manufactures of the surrounding country; and the city swarmed with a busy, industrious population, in which the white man and the Indian, the conqueror and the conquered, mingled together promiscuously in peaceful and picturesque confusion. Not twenty years had elapsed since the Conquest, when a missionary who visited it had the confidence, or the credulity, to assert, that "Europe could not boast a single city so fair and opulent as Mexico."

Cortes stimulated the settlement of his several colonies by liberal grants of land and municipal privileges. The great difficulty was to induce women to reside in the country, and without them he felt that the colonies, like a tree without roots, must soon perish. By a singular provision, he required every settler, if a married man, to bring over his wife within eighteen months, on pain of forfeiting his estate. If he were too poor to do this himself, the government would assist him. Another law imposed the same penalty on all bachelors who did not provide themselves with wives within the same period! The general seems to have considered celibacy as too great a luxury for a young country.

His own wife, Dona Catalina Xuarez, was among those who came over from the Islands to New Spain. According to Bernal Diaz, her coming gave him no particular satisfaction. It is possible; since his marriage with her seems to have been entered into with reluctance, and her lowly condition and connections stood somewhat in the way of his future advancement. Yet they lived happily together for several years, according to the testimony of Las Casas; and whatever he may have felt, he had the generosity, or the prudence not to betray his feelings to the world. On landing, Dona Catalina was escorted by Sandoval to the capital, where she was kindly received by her husband, and all the respect paid to her to which she was entitled by her elevated rank. But the climate of the tableland was not suited to her constitution, and she died in three months after her arrival. An event so auspicious to his worldly prospects did not fail, as we shall see hereafter, to provoke the tongue of scandal to the most malicious, but is scarcely necessary to say, unfounded inferences.

In the distribution of the soil among the Conquerors, Cortes adopted the vicious system of repartimientos, universally practised among his countrymen. In a letter to the emperor, he states, that the superior capacity of the Indians in New Spain had made him regard it as a grievous thing to condemn them to servitude, as had been done in the Islands. But, on further trial, he had found the Spaniards so much harassed and impoverished, that they could not hope to maintain themselves in the land without enforcing the services of the natives, and for this reason he had at length waived his own scruples in compliance with their repeated remonstrances. This was the wretched pretext used on the like occasions by his countrymen to cover up this flagrant act of injustice. The crown, however, in its instructions to the general, disavowed the act and annulled the repartimientos. It was all in vain. The necessities, or rather the cupidity, of the colonists, easily evaded the royal ordinances. The colonial legislation of Spain shows, in the repetition of enactments against slavery, the perpetual struggle that subsisted between the crown and the colonists, and the impotence of the former to enforce measures repugnant to the interests, at all events to the avarice, of the latter.

The Tlascalans, in gratitude for their signal services, were exempted, at the recommendation of Cortes, from the doom of slavery. It should be added, that the general, in granting the repartimientos, made many humane regulations for limiting the power of the master, and for securing as many privileges to the native as were compatible with any degree of compulsory service. These limitations, it is true, were too often disregarded; and in the mining districts in particular the situation of the poor Indian was often deplorable. Yet the Indian population, clustering together in their own villages, and living under their own magistrates, have continued to prove by their numbers, fallen as these have below their primitive amount, how far superior was their condition to that in most other parts of the vast colonial empire of Spain.

Whatever disregard he may have shown to the political rights of the natives, Cortes manifested a commendable solicitude for their spiritual welfare. He requested the emperor to send out holy men to the country; not bishops and pampered prelates, who too often squandered the substance of the Church in riotous living, but godly persons, members of religious fraternities, whose lives might be a fitting commentary on their teaching. Thus only, he adds — and the remark is worthy of note — can they exercise any influence over the natives, who have been accustomed to see the least departure from morals in their own priesthood punished with the utmost rigour of the law. In obedience to these suggestions, twelve Franciscan friars embarked for New Spain, which they reached early in 1524. They were men of unblemished purity of life, nourished with the learning of the cloister, and, like many others whom the Romish Church has sent forth on such apostolic missions, counted all personal sacrifices as little in the cause to which they were devoted.

The conquerors settled in such parts of the country as best suited their inclinations. Many occupied the south-eastern slopes of the Cordilleras towards the rich valley of Oaxaca. Many more spread themselves over the broad surface of the tableland, which, from its elevated position; reminded them of the plateau of their own Castiles. Here, too, they were in the range of those inexhaustible mines which have since poured their silver deluge over Europe. The mineral resources of the land were not, indeed, fully explored, or comprehended till at a much later period; but some few, as the mines of Zacatecas, Guanaxuato, and Tasco — the last of which was also known in Montezuma's time — had begun to be wrought within a generation after the Conquest.

But the best wealth of the first settlers was in the vegetable products of the soil, whether indigenous, or introduced from abroad by the wise economy of Cortes. He had earnestly recommended the crown to require all vessels coming to the country, to bring over a certain quantity of seeds and plants. He made it a condition of the grants of land on the plateau, that the proprietor of every estate should plant a specified number of vines in it. He further stipulated, that no one should get a clear title to his estate until he had occupied it eight years. He knew that permanent residence could alone create that interest in the soil which would lead to its efficient culture; and that the opposite system had caused the impoverishment of the best plantations in the Islands.

While thus occupied with the internal economy of the country, Cortes was still bent on his great schemes of discovery and conquest. In the preceding chapter we have seen him fitting out a little fleet at Zacatula, to explore the shores of the Pacific. It was burnt in the dock-yard, when nearly completed. This was a serious calamity, as most of the materials were to be transported across the country from Villa Rica. Cortes, however, with his usual promptness, took measures to repair the loss. He writes to the emperor, that another squadron will soon be got ready at the same port. A principal object of this squadron was the discovery of a strait which should connect the Atlantic with the Pacific. Another squadron, consisting of five vessels, was fitted out in the Gulf of Mexico, to take the direction of Florida, with the same view of detecting a strait. For Cortes trusted — we, at this day, may smile at the illusion — that one might be found in that direction, which should conduct the navigator to those waters which had been traversed by the keels of Magellan!

The discovery of a strait was the great object to which nautical enterprise in that day was directed, as it had been ever since the time of Columbus. It was in the sixteenth century what the discovery of the North–West passage has been in our own age; the great ignis fatuus of navigators. The vast extent of the American continent had been ascertained by the voyages of Cabot in the North, and of Magellan very recently in the South. The proximity, in certain quarters, of the two great oceans that washed its eastern and western shores had been settled by the discoveries both of Balboa and of Cortes. European scholars could not believe, that Nature had worked on a plan so repugnant to the interests of humanity, as to interpose, through the whole length of the great continent, such a barrier to communication between the adjacent waters.

It was partly with the same view, that the general caused a considerable armament to be equipped and placed under the command of Christoval de Olid, the brave officer who, as the reader will remember, had charge of one of the great divisions of the besieging army. He was to steer for Honduras, and plant a colony on its northern coast. A detachment of Olid's squadron was afterwards to cruise along its southern shore towards Darien in search of the mysterious strait. The country was reported to be full of gold; so full, that "the fishermen used gold weights for their nets." The life of the Spanish discoverers was one long day-dream. Illusion after illusion chased one another like the bubbles which the child throws off from his pipe, as bright, as beautiful, and as empty. They lived in a world of enchantment.

Together with these maritime expeditions Cortes fitted out a powerful expedition by land. It was intrusted to Alvarado, who, with a large force of Spaniards and Indians, was to descend the southern slant of the Cordilleras, and penetrate into the countries that lay beyond the rich valley of Oaxaca. The campaigns of this bold and rapacious chief terminated in the important conquest of Guatemala.

In the prosecution of his great enterprises, Cortes, within three short years after the Conquest, had reduced under the dominion of Castile an extent of country more than four hundred leagues in length, as he affirms, on the Atlantic coast, and more than five hundred on the Pacific; and, with the exception of a few interior provinces of no great importance, had brought them to a condition of entire tranquillity. In accomplishing this, he had freely expended the revenues of the crown, drawn from tributes similar to those which had been anciently paid by the natives to their own sovereigns; and he had, moreover, incurred a large debt on his own account, for which he demanded remuneration from government. The celebrity of his name, and the dazzling reports of the conquered countries, drew crowds of adventurers to New Spain, who furnished the general with recruits for his various enterprises.

Whoever would form a just estimate of this remarkable man, must not confine himself to the history of the Conquest. His military career, indeed, places him on a level with the greatest captains of his age. But the period subsequent to the Conquest affords different, and in some respects nobler, points of view for the study of his character. For we then see him devising a system of government for the motley and antagonist races, so to speak, now first brought under a common dominion; repairing the mischiefs of war; and employing his efforts to detect the latent resources of the country, and to stimulate it to its highest power of production. The narration may seem tame after the recital of exploits as bold and adventurous as those of a paladin of romance. But it is only by the perusal of this narrative that we can form an adequate conception of the acute and comprehensive geinus of Cortes.

IN the last chapter we have seen that Christoval de Olid was sent by Cortes to plant a colony in Honduras. The expedition was attended with consequences which had not been foreseen. Made giddy by the possession of power, Olid, when he had reached his place of destination, determined to assert an independent jurisdiction for himself. His distance from Mexico, he flattered himself, might enable him to do so with impunity. He misunderstood the character of Cortes, when he supposed that any distance would be great enough to shield a rebel from his vengeance.

It was long before the general received tidings of Olid's defection. But no sooner was he satisfied of this, than he despatched to Honduras a trusty captain and kinsman, Francisco de las Casas, with directions to arrest his disobedient officer. Las Casas was wrecked on the coast, and fell into Olid's hands; but eventually succeeded in raising an insurrection in the settlement, seized the person of Olid, and beheaded that unhappy delinquent in the market-place of Naco.

Of these proceedings Cortes learned only what related to the shipwreck of his lieutenant. He saw all the mischievous consequences than must arise from Olid's example, especially if his defection were to go unpunished. He determined to take the affair into his own hands, and to lead an expedition in person to Honduras. He would thus, moreover, be enabled to ascertain from personal inspection the resources of the country, which were reputed great on the score of mineral wealth; and would, perhaps, detect the point of communication between the great oceans, which had so long eluded the efforts of the Spanish discoverers. He was still further urged to this step by the uncomfortable position in which he had found himself of late in the capital. Several functionaries had recently been sent from the mother country for the ostensible purpose of administering the colonial revenues. But they served as spies on the general's conduct, caused him many petty annoyances and sent back to court the most malicious reports of his purposes and proceedings. Cortes, in short, now that he was made Governor General of the country, had less real power than when he held no legal commission at all.

The Spanish force which he took with him did not probably exceed a hundred horse and forty or perhaps fifty foot; to which were added about three thousand Indian auxiliaries. Among them were Guatemozin and the cacique of Tacuba, with a few others of highest rank, whose consideration with their countrymen would make them an obvious nucleus, round which disaffection might gather. The general's personal retinue consisted of several pages, young men of good family, and among them Montejo, the future conqueror of Yucatan; a butler and steward; several musicians, dancers, jugglers, and buffoons, showing, it might seem, more of the effeminacy of the Oriental satrap, than the hardy valour of a Spanish cavalier. Yet the imputation of effeminacy is sufficiently disproved by the terrible march which he accomplished.

On the 12th of October, 1524, Cortes commenced his march. As he descended the sides of the Cordilleras, he was met by many of his old companions in arms, who greeted their commander with a hearty welcome, and some of them left their estates to join the expedition. He halted in the province of Coatzacualco (Huasacualco), until he could receive intelligence respecting his route from the natives of Tabasco. They furnished him with a map, exhibiting the principal places whither the Indian traders, who wandered over these wild regions, were in the habit of resorting. With the aid of this map, a compass, and such guides as from time to time he could pick up on his journey, he proposed to traverse that broad and level tract which forms the base of Yucatan, and spreads from the Coatzacualco river to the head of the Gulf of Honduras. "I shall give your Majesty," he begins his celebrated letter to the emperor, describing this expedition, "an account, as usual, of the most remarkable events of my journey, every one of which might form the subject of a separate narration." Cortes did not exaggerate.

The beginning of the march lay across a low and marshy level, intersected by numerous little streams, which form the head waters of the Rio de Tabasco, and of the other rivers that discharge themselves to the north, into the Mexican Gulf. The smaller streams they forded, or passed in canoes, suffering their horses to swim across as they held them by the bridle. Rivers of more formidable size they crossed on floating bridges. It gives one some idea of the difficulties they had to encounter in this way, when it is stated, that the Spaniards were obliged to construct no less than fifty of these bridges in a distance of less than a hundred miles. One of them was more than nine hundred paces in length. Their troubles were much augmented by the difficulty of obtaining subsistence, as the natives frequently set fire to the villages on their approach, leaving to the wayworn adventurers only a pile of smoking ruins.

The first considerable place which they reached was Iztapan, pleasantly situated in the midst of a fruitful region, on the banks of the tributaries of the Rio de Tabasco. Such was the extremity to which the Spaniards had already, in the course of a few weeks, been reduced by hunger and fatigue, that the sight of a village in these dreary solitudes was welcomed by his followers, says Cortes, "with a shout of joy that was echoed back from all the surrounding woods." The army was now at no great distance from the ancient city of Palenque, the subject of so much speculation in our time. The village of Las Tres Cruzes, indeed, situated between twenty and thirty miles from Palenque, is said still to commemorate the passage of the Conquerors by the existence of three crosses which they left there. Yet no allusion is made to the ancient capital. Was it then the abode of a populous and flourishing community, such as once occupied it, to judge from the extent and magnificence of its remains? Or was it, even then, a heap of mouldering ruins, buried in a wilderness of vegetation, and thus hidden from the knowledge of the surrounding country? If the former, the silence of Cortes is not easy to be explained.

On quitting Iztapan, the Spaniards struck across a country having the same character of a low and marshy soil, chequered by occasional patches of cultivation, and covered with forests of cedar and Brazil-wood, which seemed absolutely interminable. The overhanging foliage threw so deep a shade, that as Cortes says, the soldiers could not see where to set their feet. To add to their perplexity, their guides deserted them; and when they climbed to the summits of the tallest trees, they could see only the same cheerless, interminable line of waving woods. The compass and the map furnished the only clue to extricate them from this gloomy labyrinth; and Cortes and his officers, among whom was the constant Sandoval, spreading out their chart on the ground, anxiously studied the probable direction of their route. Their scanty supplies meanwhile had entirely failed them, and they appeased the cravings of appetite by such roots as they dug out of the earth, or by the nuts and berries that grew wild in the woods. Numbers fell sick, and many of the Indians sank by the way, and died of absolute starvation.

When at length the troops emerged from these dismal forests, their path was crossed by a river of great depth, and far wider than any which they had hitherto traversed. The soldiers, disheartened, broke out into murmurs against their leader, who was plunging them deeper and deeper in a boundless wilderness, where they must lay their bones. It was in vain that Cortes encouraged them to construct a floating bridge, which might take them to the opposite bank of the river. It seemed a work of appalling magnitude, to which their wasted strength was unequal. He was more succesful in his appeal to the Indian auxiliaries, till his own men, put to shame by the ready obedience of the latter, engaged in the work with a hearty good will, which enabled them, although ready to drop from fatigue, to accomplish it at the end of four days. It was, indeed, the only expedient by which they could hope to extricate themselves from their perilous situation. The bridge consisted of one thousand pieces of timber, each of the thickness of a man's body and full sixty feet long. When we consider that the timber was all standing in the forest at the commencement of the labour, it must be admitted to have been an achievement worthy of the Spaniards.

The arrival of the army on the opposite bank of the river involved them in new difficulties. The ground was so soft and saturated with water, that the horses floundered up to their girths, and, sometimes plunging into quagmires, were nearly buried in the mud. It was with the greatest difficulty that they could be extricated by covering the wet soil with the foliage and the boughs of trees, when a stream of water, which forced its way through the heart of the morass, furnished the jaded animals with the means of effecting their escape by swimming. As the Spaniards emerged from these slimy depths, they came on a broad and rising ground, which by its cultivated fields teeming with maize, agi, or pepper of the country, and the yuca plant, intimated their approach to the capital of the fruitful province of Aculan. It was the beginning of Lent, 1525, a period memorable for an event of which I shall give the particulars from the narrative of Cortes.

The general at this place was informed by one of the Indian converts in his train, that a conspiracy had been set on foot by Guatemozin, with the cacique of Tacuba, and some other of the principal Indian nobles, to massacre the Spaniards. They would seize the moment when the army should be entangled in the passage of some defile, or some frightful morass like that from which it had just escaped, where, taken at disadvantage, it could be easily overpowered by the superior number of the Mexicans. After the slaughter of the troops, the Indians would continue their march to Honduras, and cut off the Spanish settlements there. Their success would lead to a rising in the capital, and throughout the land, until every Spaniard should be exterminated, and vessels in the ports be seized, and secured from carrying the tidings across the waters.

No sooner had Cortes learned the particulars of this formidable plot, than he arrested Guatemozin, and the principal Aztec lords in his train. The latter admitted the fact of the conspiracy, but alleged, that it had been planned by Guatemozin, and that they had refused to come into it. Guatemozin and the chief of Tacuba neither admitted nor denied the truth of the accusation, but maintained a dogged silence. — Such is the statement of Cortes. Bernal Diaz, however, who was present at the expedition, assures us, that both Guatemozin and the cacique of Tacuba avowed their innocence. They had, indeed, they said, talked more than once together of the sufferings they were then enduring, and had said that death was preferable to seeing so many of their poor followers dying daily around them. They admitted, also, that a project for rising on the Spaniards had been discussed by some of the Aztecs; but Guatemozin had discouraged it from the first, and no scheme of the kind could have been put into execution without his knowledge and consent. These protestations did not avail the unfortunate princes; and Cortes, having satisfied, or affected to satisfy, himself of their guilt, ordered them to immediate execution.

When brought to the fatal tree, Guatemozin displayed the intrepid spirit worthy of his better days. "I knew what it was," said he, "to trust to your false promises, Malinche; I knew that you had destined me to this fate, since I did not fall by my own hand when you entered my city of Tenochtitlan. Why do you slay me so unjustly? God will demand it of you!" The cacique of Tacuba, protesting his innocence, declared that he desired no better lot than to die by the side of his lord. The unfortunate princes, with one or more inferior nobles (for the number is uncertain), were then executed by being hung from the huge branches of a ceiba tree, which overshadowed the road.

In reviewing the circumstances of Guatemozin's death, one cannot attach much weight to the charge of conspiracy brought against him. That the Indians, brooding over their wrongs and present sufferings, should have sometimes talked of revenge, would not be surprising. But that any chimerical scheme of an insurrection, like that above mentioned, should have been set on foot, or even sanctioned by Guatemozin, is altogether improbable. That prince's explanation of the affair, as given by Diaz, is, to say the least, quite as deserving of credit as the accusation of the Indian informer. The defect of testimony and the distance of time make it difficult for us, at the present day, to decide the question. We have a surer criterion of the truth in the opinion of those who were eyewitnesses of the transaction. It is given in the words of the old chronicler, so often quoted. "The execution of Guatemozin," says Diaz, "was most unjust; and was thought wrong by all of us."

The most probable explanation of the affair seems to be, that Guatemozin was a troublesome, and, indeed, formidable captive. Thus much is intimated by Cortes himself in his letter to the emperor. The Spaniards, during the first years after the Conquest, lived in constant apprehension of a rising of the Aztecs. This is evident from numerous passages in the writings of the time. It was under the same apprehension that Cortes consented to embarrass himself with his royal captive on this dreary expedition. The forlorn condition of the Spaniards on the present march, which exposed them to any sudden assault from their wily Indian vassals, increased the suspicions of Cortes. Thus predisposed to think ill of Guatemozin, the general lent a ready ear to the first accusation against him. Charges were converted into proofs, and condemnation followed close upon the charges. By a single blow he proposed to rid himself and the state for ever of a dangerous enemy. Had he but consulted his own honour and his good name, Guatemozin's head should have been the last on which he should have suffered an injury to fall.

It was not long after the sad scene of Guatemozin's execution, that the wearied troops entered the head town of the great province of Aculan; a thriving community of traders, who carried on a profitable traffic with the furthest quarters of Central America. Cortes notices in general terms the excellence and beauty of the buildings, and the hospitable reception which he experienced from the inhabitants.

After renewing their strength in these comfortable quarters, the Spaniards left the capital of Aculan, the name of which is to be found on no map, and held on their toilsome way in the direction of what is now called the lake of Peten. It was then the property of an emigrant tribe of the hardy Maya family, and their capital stood on an island in the lake, "with its houses and lofty teocallis glistening in the sun," says Bernal Diaz, "so that it might be seen for the distance of two leagues." These edifices, built by one of the races of Yucatan. displayed, doubtless, the same peculiarities of construction as the remains still to be seen in that remarkable peninsula. But, whatever may have been their architectural merits, they are disposed of in a brief sentence by the Conquerors.

The inhabitants of the island showed a friendly spirit, and a docility unlike the warlike temper of their countrymen of Yucatan. They willingly listened to the Spanish missionaries who accompanied the expedition, as they expounded the Christian doctrines through the intervention of Marina. The Indian interpreter was present throughout this long march, the last in which she remained at the side of Cortes. As this, too, is the last occasion on which she will appear in these pages, I will mention, before parting with her, an interesting circumstance that occurred when the army was traversing the province of Coatzacualco. This, it may be remembered, was the native country of Marina, where her infamous mother sold her, when a child, to some foreign traders, in order to secure her inheritance to a younger brother. Cortes halted for some days at this place, to hold a conference with the surrounding caciques on matters of government and religion. Among those summoned to this meeting was Marina's mother, who came attended by her son. No sooner did they make their appearance than all were struck with the great resemblance of the cacique to her daughter. The two parties recognised each other, though they had not met since their separation. The mother, greatly terrified, fancied that she had been decoyed into a snare, in order to punish her inhuman conduct. But Marina instantly ran up to her, and endeavoured to allay her fears, assuring her that she should receive no harm, and, addressing the bystanders, said, "that she was sure her mother knew not what she did, when she sold her to the traders, and that she forgave her." Then tenderly embracing her unnatural parent, she gave her such jewels and other little ornaments as she wore about her own person, to win back, as it would seem, her lost affection. Marina added, that "she felt much happier than before, now that she had been instructed in the Christian faith, and given up the bloody worship of the Aztecs."

In the course of the expedition to Honduras, Cortes gave Marina away to a Castilian knight, Don Juan Xamarillo, to whom she was wedded as his lawful wife. She had estates assigned to her in her native province, where she probably passed the remainder of her days. From this time the name of Marina disappears from the page of history. But it has been always held in grateful remembrance by the Spaniards, for the important aid which she gave them in effecting the Conquest, and by the natives, for the kindness and sympathy which she showed them in their misfortunes.

By the Conqueror, Marina left one son, Don Martin Cortes. He rose to high consideration, and was made a comendador of the order of St. Jago. He was subsequently suspected of treasonable designs against the government; and neither his parents' extraordinary services, nor his own deserts, could protect him from a cruel persecution; and in 1568, the son of Hernando Cortes was shamefully subjected to the torture in the very capital which his father had acquired for the Castilian crown!

At length the shattered train drew near the Golfo Dolce, at the head of the Bay of Honduras. Their route could not have been far from the site of Copan, the celebrated city whose architectural ruins have furnished such noble illustrations for the pencil of Catherwood. But the Spaniards passed on in silence. Nor, indeed, can we wonder that, at this stage of the enterprise, they should have passed on without heeding the vicinity of a city in the wilderness, though it were as glorious as the capital of Zenobia; for they were arrived almost within view of the Spanish settlements, the object of their long and wearisome pilgrimage.

The place which they were now approaching was Naco, or San Gil de Buena Vista, a Spanish settlement on the Golfo Dolce. Cortes advanced cautiously, prepared to fall on the town by surprise. He had held on his way with the undeviating step of the North American Indian, who, traversing morass and mountain and the most intricate forests, guided by the instinct of revenge, presses straight towards the mark, and, when he has reached it, springs at once on his unsuspecting victim. Before Cortes made his assault, his scouts fortunately fell in with some of the inhabitants of the place, from whom they received tidings of the death of Olid, and of the reestablishment of his own authority. Cortes, therefore, entered the place like a friend, and was cordially welcomed by his countrymen, greatly astonished, says Diaz, "by the presence among them of the general so renowned throughout these countries."

The colony was at this time sorely suffering from famine; and to such extremity was it soon reduced, that the troops would probably have found a grave in the very spot to which they had looked forward as the goal of their labours, but for the seasonable arrival of a vessel with supplies from Cuba.

After he had restored the strength and spirits of his men, the indefatigable commander prepared for a new expedition, the object of which was to explore and to reduce the extensive province of Nicaragua. One may well feel astonished at the adventurous spirit of the man, who, unsubdued by the terrible sufferings of his recent march, should so soon be prepared for another enterprise equally appalling. It is difficult, in this age of sober sense, to conceive the character of a Castilian cavalier of the sixteenth century, a true counterpart of which it would not have been easy to find in any other nation, even at that time — or anywhere, indeed, save in those tales of chivalry, which, however wild and extravagant they may seem, were much more true to character than to situation. The mere excitement of exploring the strange and unknown was a sufficient compensation to the Spanish adventurer for all his toils and trials. Yet Cortes, though filled with this spirit, proposed nobler ends to himself than those of the mere vulgar adventurer. In the expedition to Nicaragua, he designed, as he had done in that to Honduras, to ascertain the resources of the country in general, and, above all, the existence of any means of communication between the great oceans on its borders. If none such existed, it would at least establish this fact, the knowledge of which, to borrow his own language, was scarcely less important.

The general proposed to himself the further object of enlarging the colonial empire of Castile. The conquest of Mexico was but the commencement of a series of conquests. To the warrior who had achieved this, nothing seemed impracticable; and scarcely would anything have been so, had he been properly sustained. But from these dreams of ambition Cortes was suddenly aroused by such tidings as convinced him, that his absence from Mexico was already too far prolonged, and that he must return without delay, if he would save the capital or the country.

THE intelligence alluded to in the preceding chapter was conveyed in a letter to Cortes from the licentiate Zuazo, one of the functionaries to whom the general had committed the administration of the country during his absence. It contained full particulars of the tumultuous proceedings in the capital. No sooner had Cortes quitted it, than dissensions broke out among the different members of the provisional government. The misrule increased as his absence was prolonged. At length tidings were received, that Cortes with his whole army had perished in the morasses of Chiapa. The members of the government showed no reluctance to credit this story. They now openly paraded their own authority; proclaimed the general's death; caused funeral ceremonies to be performed in his honour; took possession of his property wherever they could meet with it, piously devoting a small part of the proceeds to purchasing masses for his soul, while the remainder was appropriated to pay off what was called his debt to the state. They seized, in like manner, the property of other individuals engaged in the expedition. From these outrages they proceeded to others against the Spanish residents in the city, until the Franciscan missionaries left the capital in disgust, while the Indian population were so sorely oppressed, that great apprehensions were entertained of a general rising. Zuazo, who communicated these tidings, implored Cortes to quicken his return. He was a temperate man, and the opposition which he had made to the tyrannical measures of his comrades had been rewarded with exile.

The general, greatly alarmed by this account, saw that no alternative was left but to abandon all further schemes of conquest, and to return at once, if he would secure the preservation of the empire which he had won. He accordingly made the necessary arrangements for settling the administration of the colonies at Honduras, and embarked with a small number of followers for Mexico.

He had not been long at sea, when he encountered such a terrible tempest as seriously damaged his vessel, and compelled him to return to port and refit. A second attempt proved equally unsuccessful; and Cortes, feeling that his good star had deserted him, saw, in this repeated disaster, an intimation from Heaven that he was not to return. He contented himself, therefore, with sending a trusty messenger to advise his friends of his personal safety in Honduras. He then instituted processions and public prayers to ascertain the will of Heaven, and to deprecate its anger. His health now showed the effects of his recent sufferings, and declined under a wasting fever. His spirits sank with it, and he fell into a state of gloomy despondency. Bernal Diaz, speaking of him at this time, says, that nothing could be more wan and emaciated than his person, and that so strongly was he possessed with the idea of his approaching end, that he procured a Franciscan habit — for it was common to be laid out in the habit of some one or other of the monastic orders — in which to be carried to the grave.

From this deplorable apathy Cortes was roused by fresh advices urging his presence in Mexico, and by the judicious efforts of his good friend Sandoval, who had lately returned, himself, from an excursion into the interior. By his persuasion, the general again consented to try his fortunes on the seas. He embarked on board of a brigantine, with a few followers, and bade adieu to the disastrous shores of Honduras, 25th of April, 1526. He had nearly made the coast of New Spain, when a heavy gale threw him off his course, and drove him to the island of Cuba. After staying there some time to recruit his exhausted strength, he again put to sea on the 16th of May, and in eight days landed near San Juan de Ulua, whence he proceeded about five leagues on foot to Medellin.

Cortes was so much changed by disease, that his person was not easily recognised. But no sooner was it known that the general had returned, than crowds of people, white men and natives, thronged from all the neighbouring country to welcome him. The tidings spread on the wings of the wind and his progress was a triumphal procession. At all the great towns where he halted he was sumptuously entertained. Triumphal arches were thrown across the road, and the streets were strewed with flowers as he passed. After a night's repose at Tezcuco, he made his entrance in great state into the capital. The municipality came out to welcome him, and a brilliant cavalcade of armed citizens formed his escort; while the lake was covered with barges of the Indians, all fancifully decorated with their gala dresses, as on the day of his first arrival among them. The streets echoed to music, and dancing, and sounds of jubilee, as the procession held on its way to the great convent of St. Francis, where thanksgivings were offered up for the safe return of the general, who then proceeded to take up his quarters once more in his own princely residence. — It was in June, 1526, when Cortes re-entered Mexico; nearly two years had elapsed since he had left it, on his difficult march to Honduras, a march which led to no important results, but which consumed nearly as much time, and was attended with sufferings as severe, as the conquest of Mexico itself. Cortes did not abuse his present advantage. He, indeed, instituted proceedings against his enemies; but he followed them up so languidly as to incur the imputation of weakness, the only instance in which he has been so accused.

He was not permitted long to enjoy the sweets of triumph. In the month of July, he received advices of the arrival of a juez de residencia on the coast, sent by the court of Madrid to supersede him temporarily in the government. The crown of Castile, as its colonial empire extended, became less and less capable of watching over its administration. It was therefore obliged to place vast powers in the hands of its viceroys; and, as suspicion naturally accompanies weakness, it was ever prompt to listen to accusations against these powerful vassals. In such cases the government adopted the expedient of sending out a commissioner, or juez de residencia, with authority to investigate the conduct of the accused, to suspend him in the meanwhile from his office, and, after a judicial examination, to reinstate him in it, or to remove him altogether, according to the issue of the trial. The enemies of Cortes had been, for a long time, busy in undermining his influence at court, and in infusing suspicions of his loyalty in the bosom of the emperor. Since his elevation to the government of the country, they had redoubled their mischievous activity, and they assailed his character with the foulest imputations. They charged him with appropriating to his own use the gold which belonged to the crown, and especially with secreting the treasures of Montezuma. He was said to have made false reports of the provinces he had conquered, that he might defraud the exchequer of its lawful revenues. He had distributed the principal offices among his own creatures; and had acquired an unbounded influence, not only over the Spaniards, but the natives, who were all ready to do his bidding. He had expended large sums in fortifying both the capital and his own palace; and it was evident from the magnitude of his schemes and his preparations, that he designed to shake off his allegiance, and to establish an independent sovereignty in New Spain.

The government, greatly alarmed by these formidable charges, the probability of which they could not estimate, appointed a commissioner with full powers to investigate the matter. The person selected for this delicate office was Luis Ponce de Leon, a man of high family, young for such a post, but of a mature judgment, and distinguished for his moderation and equity. The nomination of such a minister gave assurance that the crown meant to do justly by Cortes.

The emperor wrote at the same time with his own hand to the general, advising him of this step, and assuring him that it was taken, not from distrust of his integrity, but to afford him the opportunity of placing that integrity in a clear light before the world.

Ponce de Leon reached Mexico in July, 1526. He was received with all respect by Cortes and the municipality of the capital; and the two parties interchanged those courtesies with each other, which gave augury that the future proceedings would be conducted in a spirit of harmony. Unfortunately, this fair beginning was blasted by the death of the commissioner in a few weeks after his arrival, a circumstance which did not fail to afford another item in the loathsome mass of accusation heaped upon Cortes. The commissioner fell the victim of a malignant fever, which carried off a number of those who had come over in the vessel with him.

On his death-bed, Ponce de Leon delegated his authority to an infirm old man, who survived but a few months, and transmitted the reins of government to a person named Estrada or Strada, the royal treasurer, one of the officers sent from Spain to take charge of the finances, and who was personally hostile to Cortes. The Spanish residents would have persuaded Cortes to assert for himself at least an equal share of the authority, to which they considered Estrada as having no sufficient title. But the general, with singular moderation, declined a competition in this matter, and determined to abide a more decided expression of his sovereign's will. To his mortification, the nomination of Estrada was confirmed, and this dignitary soon contrived to inflict on his rival all those annoyances by which a little mind, in possession of unexpected power, endeavours to make his superiority felt over a great one. The recommendations of Cortes were disregarded; his friends mortified and insulted; his attendants outraged by injuries. One of the domestics of his friend Sandoval, for some slight offence, was sentenced to lose his hand; and when the general remonstrated against these acts of violence, he was peremptorily commanded to leave the city! The Spaniards, indignant at this outrage, would have taken up arms in his defence; but Cortes would allow no resistance, and, simply remarking, "that it was well, that those, who at the price of their blood, had won the capital, should not be allowed a footing in it," withdrew to his favourite villa of Cojohuacan, a few miles distant, to wait there the result of these strange proceedings.

The suspicions of the court of Madrid, meanwhile, fanned by the breath of calumny, had reached the most preposterous height. One might have supposed, that it fancied the general was organising a revolt throughout the colonies, and meditated nothing less than an invasion of the mother country. Intelligence having been received, that a vessel might speedily be expected from New Spain, orders were sent to the different ports of the kingdom, and even to Portugal, to sequestrate the cargo, under the expectation that it contained remittances to the general's family, which belonged to the crown; while his letters, affording the most luminous account of all his proceedings and discoveries, were forbidden to be printed. Fortunately, three letters, forming the most important part of the Conqueror's correspondence, had already been given to the world by the indefatigable press of Seville.

The court, moreover, made aware of the incompetency of the treasurer, Estrada, to the present delicate conjuncture, now intrusted the whole affair of the inquiry to a commission dignified with the title of the Royal Audience of New Spain. This body was clothed with full powers to examine into the charges against Cortes, with instructions to send him back, as a preliminary measure, to Castile — peacefully if they could, but forcibly if necessary. Still afraid that its belligerent vassal might defy the authority of this tribunal, the government resorted to artifice to effect his return. The president of the Indian Council was commanded to write to him, urging his presence in Spain to vindicate himself from the charges of his enemies, and offering his personal co-operation in his defence. The emperor further wrote a letter to the Audience, containing his commands for Cortes to return, as the government wished to consult him on matters relating to the Indies, and to bestow on him a recompense suited to his high deserts. This letter was intended to be shown to Cortes.

But it was superfluous to put in motion all this complicated machinery to effect a measure on which Cortes was himself resolved. Proudly conscious of his own unswerving loyalty, and of the benefits he had rendered to his country, he felt deeply sensible to this unworthy requital of them, especially on the very theatre of his achievements. He determined to abide no longer where he was exposed to such indignities; but to proceed at once to Spain, present himself before his sovereign, boldly assert his innocence, and claim redress for his wrongs, and a just reward for his services. In the close of his letter to the emperor, detailing the painful expedition to Honduras, after enlarging on the magnificent schemes he had entertained of discovery in the South Sea, and vindicating himself from the charge of a too lavish expenditure, he concludes with the lofty, yet touching, declaration, "that he trusts his Majesty will in time acknowledge his deserts; but, if that unhappily shall not be, the world at least will be assured of his loyalty, and he himself shall have the conviction of having done his duty; and no better inheritance than this shall he ask for his children."

No sooner was the intention of Cortes made known, than it excited a general sensation through the country. Even Estrada relented; he felt that he had gone too far, and that it was not his policy to drive his noble enemy to take refuge in his own land. Negotiations were opened, and an attempt at a reconciliation was made through the Bishop of Tlascala. Cortes received these overtures in a courteous spirit, but his resolution was unshaken. Having made the necessary arrangements, therefore, in Mexico, he left the valley, and proceeded at once to the coast. Had he entertained the criminal ambition imputed to him by his enemies, he might have been sorely tempted by the repeated offers of support which were made to him, whether in good or in bad faith, on the journey, if he would but re-assume the government, and assert his independence of Castile.

On his arrival at Villa Rica, he received the painful tidings of the death of his father, Don Martin Cortes, whom he had hoped so soon to embrace, after his long and eventful absence. Having celebrated his obsequies with every mark of filial respect, he made preparations for his speedy departure. Two of the best vessels in the port were got ready and provided with everything requisite for a long voyage. He was attended by his friend, the faithful Sandoval, by Tapia, and some other cavaliers, most attached to his person. He also took with him several Aztec and Tlascalan chiefs, and among them a son of Montezuma, and another of Maxixca, the friendly old Tlascalan lord, both of whom were desirous to accompany the general to Castile. He carried home a large collection of plants and minerals, as specimens of the natural resources of the country; several wild animals and birds of gaudy plumage; various fabrics of delicate workmanship, especially the gorgeous feather-work; and a number of jugglers, dancers, and buffoons, who greatly astonished the Europeans by the marvellous facility of their performances, and were thought a suitable present for his Holiness, the Pope. Lastly, Cortes displayed his magnificence in a rich treasure of jewels, among which were emeralds of extraordinary size and lustre, gold to the amount of two hundred thousand pesos de oro, and fifteen hundred marks of silver.

After a brief and prosperous voyage, Cortes came in sight once more of his native shores, and crossing the bar of Saltes, entered the little port of Palos in May, 1528 — the same spot where Columbus had landed five and thirty years before on his return from the discovery of the Western World. Cortes was not greeted with the enthusiasm and public rejoicings which welcomed the great navigator; and, indeed, the inhabitants were not prepared for his arrival. From Palos he soon proceeded to the convent of La Rabida, the same place, also, within the hospitable walls of which Columbus had found a shelter. An interesting circumstance is mentioned by historians, connected with his short stay at Palos. Francisco Pizarro, the Conqueror of Peru, had arrived there, having come to Spain to solicit aid for his great enterprise. He was then in the commencement of his brilliant career, as Cortes might be said to be at the close of his. He was an old acquaintance, and a kinsman, as is affirmed, of the general, whose mother was a Pizarro. The meeting of these two extraordinary men, the Conquerors of the North and of the South, in the New World, as they set foot, after their eventful absence, on the shores of their native land, and that, too, on the spot consecrated by the presence of Columbus, has something in it striking to the imagination.

While reposing from the fatigues of his voyage at La Rabida, an event occurred which afflicted Cortes deeply, and which threw a dark cloud over his return. This was the death of Gonzalo de Sandoval, his trusty friend, and so long the companion of his fortunes. He was taken ill in a wretched inn at Palos, soon after landing; and his malady gained ground so rapidly, that it was evident his constitution, impaired, probably, by the extraordinary fatigues he had of late years undergone, would be unable to resist it. Cortes was instantly sent for, and arrived in time to administer the last consolations of friendship to the dying cavalier. Sandoval met his approaching end with composure, and, having given the attention, which the short interval allowed, to the settlement of both his temporal and spiritual concerns, he breathed his last in the arms of his commander.

Before departing from La Rabida, Cortes had written to the court, informing it of his arrival in the country. Great was the sensation caused there by the intelligence; the greater, that the late reports of his treasonable practices had made it wholly unexpected. His arrival produced an immediate change of feeling. All cause of jealousy was now removed; and, as the clouds which had so long settled over the royal mind were dispelled, the emperor seemed only anxious to show his sense of the distinguished services of his so dreaded vassal. Orders were sent to different places on the route to provide him with suitable accommodations, and preparations were made to give him a brilliant reception in the capital.

The tidings of his arrival had by this time spread far and wide throughout the country; and, as he resumed his journey, the roads presented a spectacle such as had not been seen since the return of Columbus. Cortes did not usually effect an ostentation of dress, though he loved to display the pomp of a great lord in the number and magnificence of his retainers. His train was now swelled by the Indian chieftains, who, by the splendours of their barbaric finery, gave additional brilliancy, as well as novelty, to the pageant. But his own person was the object of general curiosity. The houses and the streets of the great towns and villages were thronged with spectators, eager to look on the hero, who, with his single arm, as it were, had won an empire for Castile, and who, to borrow the language of an old historian, "came in the pomp and glory, not so much of a great vassal, as of an independent monarch."

As he approached Toledo, then the rival of Madrid, the press of the multitude increased, till he was met by the Duke de Bejar, the Count de Aguilar, and others of his steady friends, who, at the head of a large body of the principal nobility and cavaliers of the city, came out to receive him, and attended him to the quarters prepared for his residence. It was a proud moment for Cortes; and distrusting, as he well might, his reception by his countrymen, it afforded him a greater satisfaction than the brilliant entrance, which, a few years previous, he had made into the capital of Mexico.

The following day he was admitted to an audience by the emperor; and Cortes, gracefully kneeling to kiss the hand of his sovereign, presented to him a memorial which succinctly recounted his services and the requital he had received for them. The emperor graciously raised him, and put many questions to him respecting the countries he had conquered. Charles was pleased with the general's answers, and his intelligent mind took great satisfaction in inspecting the curious specimens of Indian ingenuity which his vassal had brought with him from New Spain. In subsequent conversations the emperor repeatedly consulted Cortes on the best mode of administering the government of the colonies; and by his advice introduced some important regulations, especially for ameliorating the condition of the natives, and for encouraging domestic industry.

The monarch took frequent opportunity to show the confidence which he now reposed in Cortes. On all public occasions he appeared with him by his side; and once, when the general lay ill of a fever, Charles paid him a visit in person, and remained some time in the apartment of the invalid. This was an extraordinary mark of condescension in the haughty court of Castile; and it is dwelt upon with becoming emphasis by the historians of the time, who seem to regard it as an ample compensation for all the sufferings and services of Cortes.

The latter had now fairly triumphed over opposition. The courtiers, with that ready instinct which belongs to the tribe, imitated the example of their master; and even envy was silent, amidst the general homage that was paid to the man who had so lately been a mark for the most envenomed calumny. Cortes, without a title, without a name but what he had created for himself, was, at once, as it were, raised to a level with the proudest nobles in the land.

He was so still more effectually by the substantial honours which were accorded to him by his sovereign in the course of the following year. By an instrument, dated 6th July, 1529, the emperor raised him to the dignity of the Marquess of the Valley of Oaxaca. Two other instruments, dated in the same month of July, assigned to Cortes a vast tract of land in the rich province of Oaxaca, together with large estates in the city of Mexico and other places in the valley. The princely domain thus granted comprehended more than twenty large towns and villages, and twenty-three thousand vassals. The language in which the gift was made greatly enhanced its value. The unequivocal testimony thus borne by his sovereign to his unwavering loyalty was most gratifying to Cortes; — how gratifying, every generous soul, who has been the subject of suspicion undeserved, will readily estimate.

Yet there was one degree in the scale, above which the royal gratitude would not rise. Neither the solicitations of Cortes, nor those of the Duke de Bejar, and his other powerful friends, could prevail on the emperor to reinstate him in the government of Mexico. The country reduced to tranquillity had no longer need of his commanding genius to control it; and Charles did not care to place again his formidable vassal in a situation which might revive the dormant spark of jealousy and distrust. It was the policy of the crown to employ one class of its subjects to effect its conquests, and another class to rule over them. For the latter it selected men in whom the fire of ambition was tempered by a cooler judgment naturally, or by the sober influence of age. Even Columbus, notwithstanding the terms of his original "capitulation" with the crown, had not been permitted to preside over the colonies; and still less likely would it be concede this power to one possessed of the aspiring temper of Cortes.

But although the emperor refused to commit the civil government of the colony into his hands, he reinstated him in his military command. By a royal ordinance, dated also in July, 1529, the Marquess of the Valley was named Captain–General of New Spain, and of the coasts of the South Sea. He was empowered to make discoveries in the Southern Ocean, with the right to rule over such lands as he should colonise, and by a subsequent grant he was to become proprietor of one-twelfth of all his discoveries. The government had no design to relinquish the services of so able a commander. But it warily endeavoured to withdraw him from the scene of his former triumphs, and to throw open a new career of ambition, that might stimulate him still further to enlarge the dominions of the crown.

Thus gilded by the sunshine of royal favour, with brilliant manners, and a person, which, although it showed the effects of hard service, had not yet lost all the attractions of youth, Cortes might now be regarded as offering an enviable alliance for the best houses in Castile. It was not long before he paid his addresses, which were favourably received, to a member of that noble house which had so steadily supported him in the dark hour of his fortunes. The lady's name was Dona Juana de Zuniga, daughter of the second Count de Aguilar, and niece of the Duke de Bejar. She was much younger than himself, beautiful, and, as event showed, not without spirit. One of his presents to his youthful bride excited the admiration and envy of the fairer part of the court. This was five emeralds, of wonderful size and brilliancy. These jewels had been cut by the Aztecs into the shapes of flowers, fishes, and into other fanciful forms, with an exquisite style of workmanship which enhanced their original value. They were, not improbably, part of the treasure of the unfortunate Montezuma, and, being easily portable, may have escaped the general wreck of the noche triste. The queen of Charles the Fifth, it is said — it may be the idle gossip of a court — had intimated a willingness to become proprietor of some of these magnificent baubles; and the preference which Cortes gave to his fair bride caused some feelings of estrangement in the royal bosom, which had an unfavourable influence on the future fortunes of the marquess.

Late in the summer of 1529, Charles the Fifth left his Spanish dominions for Italy. Cortes accompanied him on his way, probably to the place of embarkation: and in the capital of Aragon we find him, according to the national historian, exciting the same general interest and admiration among the people as he had done in Castile. On his return, there seemed no occasion for him to protract his stay longer in the country. He was weary of the life of idle luxury which he had been leading for the last year, and which was so foreign to his active habits and the stirring scenes to which he had been accustomed. He determined, therefore, to return to Mexico, where his extensive property required his presence, and where a new field was now opened to him for honourable enterprise.

EARLY in the spring of 1530, Cortes embarked for New Spain. He was accompanied by the marchioness, his wife, together with his aged mother (who had the good fortune to live to see her son's elevation), and by a magnificent retinue of pages and attendants, such as belonged to the household of a powerful noble. How different from the forlorn condition in which, twenty-six years before, he had been cast loose, as a wild adventurer, to seek his bread upon the waters!

The first point of his destination was Hispaniola, where he was to remain until he received tidings of the organisation of the new government that was to take charge of Mexico. In the preceding chapter it was stated that the administration of the country had been intrusted to a body called the Royal Audience; one of whose first duties it was to investigate the charges brought against Cortes. Nunez de Guzman, his avowed enemy, was placed at the head of this board; and the investigation was conducted with all the rancour of personal hostility. A remarkable document still exists, called the Pesquisa Secreta, or "Secret Inquiry," which contains a record of the proceedings against Cortes.

The charges are eight in number; involving, among other crimes, that of a deliberate design to cast off his allegiance to the crown; that of the murder of two of the commissioners who had been sent out to supersede him; of the murder of his own wife, Catalina Xuarez; of extortion, and of licentious practices — of offences, in short, which, from their private nature, would seem to have little to do with his conduct as a public man. The testimony is vague and often contradictory; the witnesses are, for the most part, obscure individuals, and the few persons of consideration among them appear to have been taken from the ranks of his decided enemies. When it is considered that the inquiry was conducted in the absence of Cortes, before a court, the members of which were personally unfriendly to him, and that he was furnished with no specification of the charges and had no opportunity of disproving them, it is impossible, at this distance of time, to attach any importance to this paper as a legal document. When it is added, that no action was taken on it by the government to whom it was sent, we may be disposed to regard it as a monument of the malice of his enemies.

The high-handed measures of the Audience and the oppressive conduct of Guzman, especially towards the Indians, excited general indignation in the colony, and led to serious apprehensions of an insurrection. It became necessary to supersede an administration so reckless and unprincipled. But Cortes was detained two months at the island, by the slow movements of the Castilian court, before tidings reached him of the appointment of a new Audience for the government of the country. The person selected to preside over it was the Bishop of St. Domingo, a prelate whose acknowledged wisdom and virtue gave favourable augury for the conduct of his administration. After this, Cortes resumed his voyage, and landed at Villa Rica on the 15th of July, 1530. An edict, issued by the empress during her husband's absence, had interdicted Cortes from approaching within ten leagues of the Mexican capital, while the present authorities were there. The empress was afraid of a collision between the parties. Cortes, however, took up his residence on the opposite side of the lake, at Tezcuco.

No sooner was his arrival there known in the metropolis, than multitudes, both of Spaniards and natives, crossed the lake to pay their respects to their old commander, to offer him their services, and to complain of their manifold grievances. It seemed as if the whole population of the capital was pouring into the neighbouring city, where the marquess maintained the state of an independent potentate. The members of the Audience, indignant at the mortifying contrast which their own diminished court presented, imposed heavy penalties on such of the natives as should be found in Tezcuco; and, affecting to consider themselves in danger, made preparations for the defence of the city. But these belligerent movements were terminated by the arrival of the new Audience; though Guzman had the address to maintain his hold on a northern province, where he earned a reputation for cruelty and extortion unrivalled even in the annals of the New World.

Everything seemed now to assure a tranquil residence to Cortes. The new magistrates treated him with marked respect, and took his advice on the most important measures of government. Unhappily, this state of things did not long continue; and a misunderstanding arose between the parties, in respect to the enumeration of the vassals assigned by the crown to Cortes, which the marquess thought was made on principles prejudicial to his interests, and repugnant to the intentions of the grant. He was still further displeased by finding that the Audience were intrusted, by their commission, with a concurrent jurisdiction with himself in military affairs. This led, occasionally, to an interference, which the proud spirit of Cortes, so long accustomed to independent rule, could ill brook. After submitting to it for a time, he left the capital in disgust, no more to return there, and took up his residence in his city of Cuernavaca.

It was the place won by his own sword from the Aztecs, previous to the siege of Mexico. It stood on the southern slope of the Cordilleras, and overlooked a wide expanse of country, the fairest and most flourishing portion of his own domain. He had erected a stately palace on the spot, and henceforth made this city his favourite residence. It was well situated for superintending his vast estates, and he now devoted himself to bringing them into proper cultivation. He introduced the sugar cane from Cuba, and it grew luxuriantly in the rich soil of the neighbouring lowlands. He imported large numbers of merino sheep and other cattle, which found abundant pastures in the country around Tehuantepec. His lands were thickly sprinkled with groves of mulberry trees, which furnished nourishment for the silk-worm. He encouraged the cultivation of hemp and flax, and, by his judicious and enterprising husbandry, showed the capacity of the soil for the culture of valuable products before unknown in the land; and he turned these products to the best account, by the erection of sugar-mills, and other works for the manufacture of the raw material. He thus laid the foundation of an opulence for his family, as substantial, if not as speedy, as that derived from the mines. Yet this latter source of wealth was not neglected by him; and he drew gold from the region of Tehuantepec, and silver from that of Zacatecas. The amount derived from these mines was not so abundant as at a later day. But the expense of working them was much less in the earlier stages of the operation, when the metal lay so much nearer the surface.

But this tranquil way of life did not long content his restless and adventurous spirit; and it sought a vent by availing itself of his new charter of discovery to explore the mysteries of the Great Southern Ocean. In 1527, two years before his return to Spain, he had sent a little squadron to the Moluccas. Cortes was preparing to send another squadron of four vessels in the same direction, when his plans were interrupted by his visit to Spain; and his unfinished little navy, owing to the malice of the Royal Audience, who drew off the hands employed in building it, went to pieces on the stocks. Two other squadrons were now fitted out by Cortes, in the years 1532 and 1533, and sent on a voyage of discovery to the North-west. They were unfortunate, though, in the latter expedition, the Californian peninsula was reached, and a landing effected on its southern extremity at Santa Cruz, probably the modern port La Paz. One of the vessels, thrown on the coast of New Galicia, was seized by Guzman, the old enemy of Cortes, who ruled over that territory, the crew were plundered, and the ship was detained as a lawful prize. Cortes, indignant at the outrage, demanded justice from the Royal Audience; and, as that body was too feeble to enforce its own decrees in his favour, he took redress into his own hands.

He made a rapid but difficult march on Chiametla, the scene of Guzman's spoliation; and as the latter did not care to face his incensed antagonist, Cortes recovered his vessel, though not the cargo. He was then joined by the little squadron which he had fitted out from his own port of Tehuantepec — a port which, in the sixteenth century, promised to hold the place since occupied by that of Acapulco. The vessels were provided with everything requisite for planting a colony in the newly discovered region, and transported four hundred Spaniards and three hundred Negro slaves, which Cortes had assembled for that purpose. With this intention he crossed the Gulf, the Adriatic — to which an old writer compares it — of the Western World.

Our limits will not allow us to go into the details of this disastrous expedition, which was attended with no important results either to its projector or to science. It may suffice to say, that, in the prosecution of it, Cortes and his followers were driven to the last extremity by famine; that he again crossed the Gulf, was tossed about by terrible tempests, without a pilot to guide him, was thrown upon the rocks, where his shattered vessel nearly went to pieces, and, after a succession of dangers and disasters as formidable as any which he had ever encountered on land, succeeded, by means of his indomitable energy, in bringing his crazy bark safe into the same port of Santa Cruz from which he had started.

While these occurrences were passing, the new Royal Audience, after a faithful discharge of its commission, had been superseded by the arrival of a viceroy, the first ever sent to New Spain. Cortes, though invested with similar powers, had the title only of governor. This was the commencement of the system afterwards pursued by the crown, of intrusting the colonial administration to some individual, whose high rank and personal consideration might make him the fitting representative of majesty. The jealousy of the court did not allow the subject clothed with such ample authority to remain long enough in the same station to form dangerous schemes of ambition, but at the expiration of a few years he was usually recalled, or transferred to some other province of the vast colonial empire. The person now sent to Mexico was Don Antonio de Mendoza, a man of moderation and practical good sense, and one of that illustrious family who in the preceding reign furnished so many distinguished ornaments to the church, to the camp, and to letters.

The long absence of Cortes had caused the deepest anxiety in the mind of his wife, the Marchioness of the Valley. She wrote to the viceroy immediately on his arrival, beseeching him to ascertain, if possible, the fate of her husband, and, if he could be found, to urge his return. The viceroy, in consequence, despatched two ships in search of Cortes, but whether they reached him before his departure from Santa Cruz is doubtful. It is certain that he returned safe, after his long absence, to Acapulco, and was soon followed by the survivors of his wretched colony.

Undismayed by these repeated reverses, Cortes, still bent on some discovery worthy of his reputation, fitted out three more vessels, and placed them under the command of an officer named Ulloa. This expedition, which took its departure in July, 1539, was attended with more important results. Ulloa penetrated to the head of the Gulf; then, returning and winding round the coast of the peninsula, doubled its southern point, and ascended as high as the twenty-eighth or twenty-ninth degree of north latitude on its western borders. After this, sending home one of the squadron, the bold navigator held on his course to the north, but was never more heard of.

Thus ended the maritime enterprises of Cortes; sufficiently disastrous in a pecuniary point of view, since they cost him three hundred thousand castellanos of gold, without the return of a ducat. He was even obliged to borrow money, and to pawn his wife's jewels, to procure funds for the last enterprise; thus incurring a debt which, increased by the great charges of his princely establishment, hung about him during the remainder of his life. But, though disastrous in an economical view, his generous efforts added important contributions to science. In the course of these expeditions, and those undertaken by Cortes previous to his visit to Spain, the Pacific had been coasted from the Bay of Panama to the Rio Colorado. The great peninsula of California had been circumnavigated as far as to the isle of Cedros or Cerros, into which the name has since been corrupted. This vast tract, which had been supposed to be an archipelago of islands, was now discovered to be a part of the continent; and its general outline, as appears from the maps of the time, was nearly as well understood as at the present day. Lastly, the navigator had explored the recesses of the Californian Gulf, or Sea of Cortes, as, in honour, of the great discoverer, it is with more propriety named by the Spaniards; and he had ascertained that, instead of the outlet before supposed to exist towards the north, this unknown ocean was locked up within the arms of the mighty continent. These were results that might have made the glory and satisfied the ambition of a common man; but they are lost in the brilliant renown of the former achievements of Cortes.

Notwithstanding the embarrassments of the Marquess of the Valley, he still made new efforts to enlarge the limits of discovery, and prepared to fit out another squadron of five vessels, which he proposed to place under the command of a natural son, Don Luis. But the viceroy Mendoza, whose imagination had been inflamed by the reports of an itinerant monk respecting an El Dorado in the north, claimed the right of discovery in that direction. Cortes protested against this, as an unwarrantable interference with his own powers. Other subjects of collision arose between them; till the marquess, disgusted with this perpetual check on his authority and his enterprises, applied for redress to Castile. He finally determined to go there to support his claims in person, and to obtain, if possible, renumeration for the heavy charges he had incurred by his maritime expeditions, as well as for the spoliation of his property by the Royal Audience, during his absence from the country; and, lastly, to procure an assignment of his vassals on principles more comfortable to the original intentions of the grant. With these objects in view, he bade adieu to his family, and, taking with him his eldest son and heir, Don Martin, then only eight years of age, he embarked from Mexico, in 1540, and, after a favourable voyage, again set foot on the shores of his native land.

The emperor was absent from the country. But Cortes was honourably received in the capital, where ample accommodations were provided for him and his retinue. When he attended the Royal Council of the Indies to urge his suit, he was distinguished by uncommon marks of respect. The president went to the door of the hall to receive him, and a seat was provided for him among the members of the Council. But all evaporated in this barren show of courtesy. justice, proverbially slow in Spain, did not mend her gait for Cortes; and at the expiration of a year, he found himself no nearer the attainment of his object than on the first week after his arrival in the capital.

In the following year, 1541, we find the Marquess of the Valley embarked as a volunteer in the memorable expedition against Algiers. Charles the Fifth, on his return to his dominions, laid siege to that stronghold of the Mediterranean corsairs. Cortes accompanied the forces destined to meet the emperor, and embarked on board the vessel of the Admiral of Castile. But a furious tempest scattered the navy, and the admiral's ship was driven a wreck upon the coast. Cortes and his son escaped by swimming; but the former, in the confusion of the scene, lost the inestimable set of jewels noticed in the preceding chapter.

On arriving in Castile, Cortes lost no time in laying his suit before the emperor. His applications were received by the monarch with civility — a cold civility, which carried no conviction of its sincerity. His position was materially changed since his former visit to the country. More than ten years had elapsed, and he was now too well advanced in years to give promise of serviceable enterprise in future. Indeed his undertakings of late had been singularly unfortunate. Even his former successes suffered the disparagement natural to a man of declining fortunes. They were already eclipsed by the magnificent achievements in Peru, which had poured a golden tide into the country, that formed a striking contrast to the streams of wealth that, as yet, had flowed in but scantily from the silver mines of Mexico. Cortes had to learn that the gratitude of a court has reference to the future much more than to the past. He stood in the position of an importunate suitor, whose claims, however just, are too large to be readily allowed. He found, like Columbus, that it was possible to deserve too greatly.

In the month of February, 1544, he addressed a letter to the emperor — it was the last he ever wrote him — soliciting his attention to his suit. He begins by proudly alluding to his past services to the crown and beseeching his sovereign to "order the Council of the Indies, with the other tribunals which had cognisance of his suits, to come to a decision; since he was too old to wander about like a vagrant, but ought rather, during the brief remainder of his life, to stay at home and settle his account with Heaven, occupied with the concerns of his soul, rather than with his substance."

This appeal to his sovereign, which has something in it touching from a man of the haughty spirit of Cortes, had not the effect to quicken the determination of his suit. He still lingered at the court from week to week, and from month to month, beguiled by the deceitful hopes of the litigant, tasting all that bitterness of the soul which arises from hope deferred. After three years more, passed in this unprofitable and humiliating occupation, he resolved to leave his ungrateful country and return to Mexico.

He had proceeded as far as Seville, accompanied by his son, when he fell ill of an indigestion, caused, probably, by irritation and trouble of mind. This terminated in dysentery, and his strength sank so rapidly under the disease, that it was apparent his mortal career was drawing towards its close. He prepared for it by making the necessary arrangements for the settlement of his affairs. He had made his will some time before; and he now executed it. It is a very long document, and in some respects a remarkable one.

The bulk of his property was entailed to his son, Don Martin, then fifteen years of age. In the testament he fixes his majority at twenty-five; but at twenty his guardians were to allow him his full income, to maintain the state becoming his rank. In a paper accompanying the will, Cortes specified the names of the agents to whom he had committed the management of his vast estates scattered over many different provinces; and he requests his executors to confirm the nomination, as these agents have been selected by him from a knowledge of their peculiar qualifications. Nothing can better show the thorough supervision which, in the midst of pressing public concerns, he had given to the details of his widely extended property.

He makes a liberal provision for his other children, and a generous allowance to several old domesties and retainers in his household. By another clause he gives away considerable sums in charity, and he applies the revenues of his estates in the city of Mexico to establish and permanently endow three public institutions — a hospital in the capital, which was to be dedicated to Our Lady of the Conception, a college in Cojohuacan for the education of missionaries to preach the gospel among the natives, and a convent, in the same place, for nuns. To the chapel of this convent, situated in his favourite town, he orders that his own body shall be transported for burial, in whatever quarter of the world he may happen to die.

After declaring that he has taken all possible care to ascertain the amount of tributes formerly paid by his Indian vassals to their native sovereigns, he enjoins on his heir, that, in case those which they have hitherto paid shall be found to exceed the right valuation, he shall restore them a full equivalent. In another clause, he expresses a doubt whether it is right to exact personal service from the natives; and commands that strict inquiry shall be made into the nature and value of such services as he had received, and, that, in all cases, a fair compensation shall be allowed for them. Lastly, he makes this remarkable declaration: "It has long been a question, whether one can conscientiously hold property in Indian slaves. Since this point has not yet been determined, I enjoin it on my son Martin and his heirs, that they spare no pains to come to an exact knowledge of the truth; as a matter which deeply concerns the conscience of each of them, no less than mine."

Cortes names, as his executors, and as guardians of his children, the Duke of Medina Sidonia, the Marquess of Astorga, and the Count of Aguilar. For his executors in Mexico, he appoints his wife, the marchioness, the Archbishop of Toledo, and two other prelates. The will was executed at Seville, 11th of October, 1547.

Finding himself much incommoded, as he grew weaker, by the presence of visitors, to which he was necessarily exposed at Seville, he withdrew to the neighbouring village of Castilleja de la Cuesta, attended by his son, who watched over his dying parent with filial solicitude. Cortes seems to have contemplated his approaching end with the composure not always to be found in those who have faced death with indifference on the field of battle. At length, having devoutly confessed his sins and received the sacrament, he expired on the 2nd of December, 1547, in the sixty-third year of his age.

The inhabitants of the neighbouring country were desirous to show every mark of respect to the memory of Cortes. His funeral obsequies were celebrated with due solemnity by a long train of Andalusian nobles and of the citizens of Seville, and his body was transported to the chapel of the monastery, San Isidro, in that city, where it was laid in the family vault of the Duke of Medina Sidonia. In the year 1562, it was removed, by order of his son, Don Martin, to New Spain, not as directed by his will, to Cojohuacan, but to the monastery of St. Francis, in Tezcuco, where it was laid by the side of a daughter, and of his mother, Dona Catalina Pizarro. In 1629, the remains of Cortes were again removed; and on the death of Don Pedro, fourth Marquess of the Valley, it was decided by the authorities of Mexico to transfer them to the church of St. Francis, in that capital.

Yet his bones were not permitted to rest here undisturbed; and in 1794, they were removed to the Hospital of Jesus of Nazareth. It was a more fitting place, since it was the same institution which, under the name of "Our Lady of the Conception," had been founded and endowed by Cortes, and which, with a fate not too frequent in similar charities, has been administered to this day on the noble principles of its foundation. The mouldering relics of the warrior, now deposited in a crystal coffin secured by bars and plates of silver, were laid in the chapel, and over them was raised a simple monument, displaying the arms of the family, and surmounted by a bust of the Conqueror, executed in bronze, by Tolsa, a sculptor worthy of the best period of the arts.

Unfortunately for Mexico, the tale does not stop here. In 1823, the patriot mob of the capital, in their zeal to commemorate the era of the national independence, and their detestation of the "old Spaniards," prepared to break open the tomb which held the ashes of Cortes, and to scatter them to the winds! The authorities declined to interfere on the occasion; but the friends of the family, as is commonly reported, entered the vault by night, and secretly removing the relics, prevented the commission of a sacrilege which must have left a stain, not easy to be effaced, on the scutcheon of the fair city of Mexico.

Cortes had no children by his first marriage. By his second he left four; a son, Don Martin — the heir of his honours — and three daughters, who formed splendid alliances. He left, also, several natural children, whom he particularly mentions in his testament and honourably provides for. Two of these, Don Martin, the son of Marina, and Don Luis Cortes, attained considerable distinction, and were created comendadores of the Order of St. Jago.

The male line of the Marquess of the Valley became extinct in the fourth generation. The title and estates descended to a female, and by her marriage were united with those of the house of Terranova, descendants of the "Great Captain" Gonsalvo de Cordova. By a subsequent marriage they were carried into the family of the Duke of Monteleone, a Neapolitan noble. The present proprietor of these princely honours and of vast domains, both in the Old and the New World, dwells in Sicily, and boasts a descent — such as few princes can boast — from two of the most illustrious commanders of the sixteenth century, the "Great Captain," and the Conqueror of Mexico.

The personal history of Cortes has been so minutely detailed in the preceding narrative, that it will be only necessary to touch on the more prominent features of his character. Indeed, the history of the Conquest, as I have already had occasion to remark, is necessarily that of Cortes, who is, if I may so say, not merely the soul, but the body, of the enterprise, present everywhere in person, in the thick of the fight, or in the building of the works, with his sword or with his musket, sometimes leading his soldiers, and sometimes directing his little navy. The negotiations, intrigues, correspondence, are all conducted by him; and, like Caesar, he wrote his own Commentaries in the heat of the stirring scenes which form the subject of them. His character is marked with the most opposite traits, embracing qualities apparently the most incompatible. He was avaricious, yet liberal; bold to desperation, yet cautious and calculating in his plans; magnanimous, yet very cunning; courteous and affable in his deportment, yet inexorably stern; lax in his notions of morality, yet (not uncommon) a sad bigot. The great feature in his character was constancy of purpose; a constancy not to be daunted by danger, nor baffled by disappointment, nor wearied out by impediments and delays.

He was a knight-errant, in the literal sense of the word. Of all the band of adventurous cavaliers whom Spain, in the sixteenth century, sent forth on the career of discovery and conquest, there was none more deeply filled with the spirit of romantic enterprise than Hernando Cortes. Dangers and difficulties, instead of deterring, seemed to have a charm in his eyes. They were necessary to rouse him to a full consciousness of his powers. He grappled with them at the outset, and, if I may so express myself, seemed to prefer to take his enterprises by the most difficult side. He conceived, at the first moment of his landing in Mexico, the design of its conquest. When he saw the strength of its civilisation, he was not turned from his purpose. When he was assailed by the superior force of Narvaez, he still persisted in it; and, when he was driven in ruin from the capital, he still cherished his original idea. How successfully he carried it into execution, we have seen. After the few years of repose which succeeded the Conquest, his adventurous spirit impelled him to that dreary march across the marshes of Chiapa; and, after another interval, to seek his fortunes on the stormy Californian Gulf. When he found that no other continent remained for him to conquer, he made serious proposals to the emperor to equip a fleet at his own expense, with which he would sail to the Moluccas, and subdue the Spice Islands for the crown of Castile!

This spirit of knight-errantry might lead us to undervalue his talents as a general, and to regard him merely in the light of a lucky adventurer. But this would be doing him injustice; for Cortes was certainly a great general, if that man be one, who performs great achievements with the resources which his own genius has created. There is probably no instance in history where so vast an enterprise has been achieved by means apparently so inadequate. He may be truly said to have effected the conquest by his own resources. If he was indebted for his success to the co-operation of the Indian tribes, it was the force of his genius that obtained command of such materials. He arrested the arm that was lifted to smite him, and made it do battle in his behalf. He beat the Tlascalans, and made them his staunch allies. He beat the soldiers of Narvaez, and doubled his effective force by it. When his own men deserted him, he did not desert himself. He drew them back by degrees, and compelled them to act by his will, till they were all as one man. He brought together the most miscellaneous collection of mercenaries who ever fought under one standard; adventurers from Cuba and the Isles, craving for gold; hidalgos, who came from the old country to win laurels; broken-down cavaliers, who hoped to mend their fortunes in the New World; vagabonds flying from justice; the grasping followers of Narvaez, and his own reckless veterans — men with hardly a common tie, and burning with the spirit of jealousy and faction; wild tribes of the natives from all parts of the country, who had been sworn enemies from their cradles, and who had met only to cut one another's throats, and to procure victims for sacrifice; men, in short, differing in race, in language, and in interests, with scarcely anything in common among them. Yet this motley congregation was assembled in one camp, compelled to bend to the will of one man, to consort together in harmony, to breathe, as it were, one spirit, and to move on a common principle of action! It is in this wonderful power over the discordant masses thus gathered under his banner, that we recognise the genius of the great commander, no less than in the skill of his military operations.

Cortes was not a vulgar conqueror. He did not conquer from the mere ambition of conquest. If he destroyed the ancient capital of the Aztecs, it was to build up a more magnificent capital on its ruins. If he desolated the land and broke up its existing institutions, he employed the short period of his administration in digesting schemes for introducing there a more improved culture and a higher civilisation. In all his expeditions he was careful to study the resources of the country, its social organisation, and its physical capacities. He enjoined it on his captains to attend particularly to these objects. If he was greedy of gold, like most of the Spanish cavaliers in the New World, it was not to hoard it, nor merely to lavish it in the support of a princely establishment, but to secure funds for prosecuting his glorious discoveries. Witness his costly expeditions to the Gulf of California. His enterprises were not undertaken solely for mercenary objects; as is shown by the various expeditions he set on foot for the discovery of a communication between the Atlantic and the Pacific. In his schemes of ambition he showed a respect for the interests of science, to be referred partly to the natural superiority of his mind, but partly, no doubt, to the influence of early education. It is, indeed, hardly possible that a person of his wayward and mercurial temper should have improved his advantages at the university, but he brought away from it a tincture of scholarship, seldom found among the cavaliers of the period, and which had its influence in enlarging his own conceptions. His celebrated Letters are written with a simple elegance, that, as I have already had occasion to remark, have caused them to be compared to the military narrative of Caesar. It will not be easy to find in the chronicles of the period a more concise, yet comprehensive, statement, not only of the events of his campaigns, but of the circumstances most worthy of notice in the character of the conquered countries.

In private life he seems to have had the power of attaching to himself, warmly, those who were near his person. The influence of this attachment is shown in every page of Bernal Diaz, though his work was written to vindicate the claims of the soldiers, in opposition to those of the general. He seems to have led a happy life with his first wife, in their humble retirement in Cuba; and regarded the second, to judge from the expressions in his testament, with confidence and love. Yet he cannot be acquitted of the charge of those licentious gallantries which entered too generally into the character of the military adventurer of that day. He would seem, also, by the frequent suits in which he was involved, to have been of an irritable and contentious spirit. But much allowance must be made for the irritability of a man who had been too long accustomed to independent sway, patiently to endure the checks and control of the petty spirits who were incapable of comprehending the noble character of his enterprises. "He thought," says an eminent writer, "to silence his enemies by the brilliancy of the new career on which he had entered. He did not reflect, that these enemies had been raised by the very grandeur and rapidity of his success." He was rewarded for his efforts by the misinterpretation of his motives; by the calumnious charges of squandering the public revenues, and of aspiring to independent sovereignty. But, although we may admit the foundation of many of the grievances alleged by Cortes, yet, when we consider the querulous tone of his correspondence and the frequency of his litigation, we may feel a natural suspicion that his proud spirit was too sensitive to petty slights, and too jealous of imaginary wrongs.

In the earlier part of the History, I have given a description of the person of Cortes. It may be well to close this review of his character by the account of his manners and personal habits left us by Bernal Diaz, the old chronicler, who has accompanied us through the whole course of our narrative, and who may now fitly furnish the conclusion of it. No man knew his commander better; and, if the avowed object of his work might naturally lead to a disparagement of Cortes, this is more than counterbalanced by the warmth of his personal attachment, and by that esprit de corps which leads him to take a pride in the renown of his general.

"In his whole appearance and presence," says Diaz, "in his discourse, his table, his dress, in everything, in short, he had the air of a great lord. His clothes were in the fashion of the time; he set little value on silk, damask, or velvet, but dressed plainly and exceedingly neat; nor did he wear massy chains of gold, but simply a fine one of exquisite workmanship, from which was suspended a jewel having the figure of our Lady the Virgin and her precious Son, with a Latin motto cut upon it. On his finger he wore a splendid diamond ring; and from his cap, which, according to the fashion of that day, was of velvet, hung a medal, the device of which I do not remember. He was magnificently attended, as became a man of his rank, with chamberlains and major-domos and many pages; and the service of his table was splendid, with a quantity of both gold and silver plate. At noon he dined heartily, drinking about a pint of wine mixed with water. He supped well, though he was not dainty in regard to his food, caring little for the delicacies of the table, unless, indeed, on such occasions as made attention to these matters of some consequence.

"He was acquainted with Latin, and, as I have understood, was made Bachelor of Laws; and, when he conversed with learned men who addressed him in Latin, he answered them in the same language. He was also something of a poet; his conversation was agreeable, and he had a pleasant elocution. In his attendance on the services of the Church he was most punctual, devout in his manner, and charitable to the poor.

"When he swore, he used to say, 'On my conscience'; and when he was vexed with any one, 'Evil betide you.' With his men he was very patient; and they were sometimes impertinent, and even insolent. When very angry, the veins in his throat and forehead would swell, but he uttered no reproaches against either officer or soldier.

"He was fond of cards and dice, and, when he played, was always in good humour, indulging freely in jests and repartees. He was affable with his followers, especially with those who came over with him from Cuba. In his campaigns he paid strict attention to discipline, frequently going the rounds himself during the night, and seeing that the sentinels did their duty. He entered the quarters of his soldiers without ceremony, and chided those whom he found without their arms and accoutrements, saying, 'it was a bad sheep that could not carry its own wool.' On the expedition to Honduras, he acquired the habit of sleeping after his meals, feeling unwell if he omitted it; and, however sultry or stormy the weather, he caused a carpet or his cloak to be thrown under a tree, and slept soundly for some time. He was frank and exceedingly liberal in his disposition, until the last few years of his life, when he was accused of parsimony. But we should consider, that his funds were employed on great and costly enterprises; and that none of these, after the Conquest, neither his expedition to

Honduras, nor his voyages to California, were crowned with success. It was perhaps intended that he should receive his recompense in a better world; and I fully believe it; for he was a good cavalier, most true in his devotions to the Virgin, to the Apostle St. Peter, and to all the other Saints."

Such is the portrait, which has been left to us by the faithful hand most competent to trace it, of Hernando Cortes, the Conqueror of Mexico.

Printed in Great Britain
by Amazon